THE GREENBACK ERA

THE GREENBACK ERA

A SOCIAL AND POLITICAL HISTORY OF AMERICAN FINANCE, 1865-1879

BY IRWIN UNGER

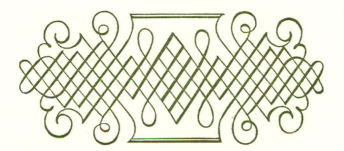

PRINCETON, NEW JERSEY

PRINCETON UNIVERSITY PRESS

1964

To Bernate

CONTENTS

ABBREVIATIONS

AHR	*American Historical Review.*
AM	(St. Paul) *Anti-Monopolist.*
CDT	*Chicago Daily Tribune.*
CFC	*Commercial and Financial Chronicle.*
IA	*Industrial Age.*
LC	Library of Congress.
MVHR	*Mississippi Valley Historical Review.*
NYDT	*New York Daily Tribune.*
NYT	*New York Times.*
NYW	*New York World.*
WA	(Chicago) *Workingman's Advocate.*

THE GREENBACK ERA

INTRODUCTION

SINCE the seventeenth century, financial questions have often been the distinctive form social conflict has taken in America. Periodically, from the earliest colonial difficulties in finding a sufficient circulating medium to the most recent dispute over a balanced budget, differences over currency and the related subject of banking have expressed basic American social and political antagonisms.[1] It is not surprising, then, that the Civil War, initiating sweeping financial change, made the problems of money and banking of extraordinary national concern. In the decade and a half following Appomattox, national finance absorbed more of the country's intellectual and political energy than any other public question except Reconstruction. The debate over paper money, debt repayment, the national banks, and silver remonetization reflected the ambitions, aspirations, and frustrations of the most active and vigorous men of the republic and set the terms of American political conflict for the remainder of the century.[2]

The passion and drama surrounding the post-Civil War money debate are enough to justify its description. Yet more important is the light the conflict sheds on the question of national political power in the momentous postwar era. The pushes and pulls of competing groups, local and national, in the unfolding of federal financial legislation, identify the locus of control in emerging modern America.

The interest in American *Realpolitik* is, of course, not new. For the last half-century, scholars have sought to peel away the opaque surface of post-Civil War political life to reveal its inner workings. In particular, Charles A. Beard, J. Allen Smith, and their disciples, have been concerned with the question: who ran the United States? And their conclusions have long since become part of the accepted historical canon. To the Beardians,

[1] This theme is developed on a massive scale in the five volumes of Joseph Dorfman's *The Economic Mind in American Civilization* (New York: The Viking Press, 1946-1959).

[2] And even beyond, in a minor way. As late as 1944 there was a Greenback candidate for President!

the formal politics of the late nineteenth century were an elaborate ritual designed to disguise the blunt truths of domestic power politics. Beneath the day-to-day intrigues for place and perquisite, they argued, one could discern a raw struggle between the older agrarian America and the emerging, assertive, industrial America.

The key to our nineteenth-century history, the Beardians claimed, was the confrontation of farmer and capitalist along a broad front of vital public issues. The Civil War itself was the culmination of eighty years of economic rivalry between the plantation South and the business-dominated Northeast, allied at the end with the grain-producing West. But while the nation's agricultural heartland poured out its blood and its wealth in the common cause, Union victory in the "Second American Revolution" was a triumph of the "investing section" alone. Acting through their servile instrument, the Republican Party, eastern businessmen crammed through Congress a legislative program which subordinated public interest to private profit and ushered in a reign of predatory capitalism. Tariff protection, federal subsidies for railroads, government-sponsored rivers and harbors improvements, and, finally, "sound money," the story goes, all testified to the postwar capture of the national government by the "business interests." Although bemused for a while by appeals to northern solidarity against a resurgent South, the western farmer finally rose against the dominant Northeast. The Granger movement, Greenbackism, the free silver and Populist crusades, were in turn all manifestations of agrarian resistance to capitalist control and exploitation.[3]

[3] The most complete expression of Beard's thesis is to be found in his two-volume work, written in collaboration with Mary R. Beard, *The Rise of American Civilization* (New Revised and Enlarged Edition, New York: The Macmillan Company, 1944). For the period and issues under discussion see especially chs. XVII, XVIII, XX, XXIII. The literature on Beard is voluminous and growing, but much of the best, and certainly the most sympathetic, can be found in Howard K. Beale (ed.), *Charles A. Beard, An Appraisal* (Lexington, Kentucky: University of Kentucky Press, 1954). See particularly Beale's own article "Charles Beard: Historian." A perceptive appraisal of Beard's contribution to the historiography of the Civil War era will be found in Thomas J. Pressly, *Americans Interpret Their Civil War* (Princeton: Princeton University Press, 1954), pp. 204-214.

The Beardian story is so familiar that we tend to overlook the assumptions that underlie it. As a picture of American history it is fundamentally dualistic. Capitalist versus farmer, debtor versus creditor, East versus West, conservative versus radical, hard money versus soft money—these appear as successive guises of the same inherent division. The nation's story is a battle of two great antagonists who, although their names may vary, always remain essentially the same.[4] As two disciples of Beard have recently written, "a single basic cleavage can be distinguished as running through most of our history." ". . . the 'two major complexes of interest' which have been arrayed against one another time and again are the agricultural interest on the one hand and the mercantile and financial interests, together with the industrial interest which grows out of them, on the other. Primarily this dualism may be defined as a contest between wealth in the form of land and wealth seeking outlets in commerce and industry."[5]

As the quotation implies, along with the dualism the Beardians also accepted the central role of economic drives in our history. Both contenders in the power struggle are interest groups propelled by the acquisitive instincts appropriate to their role in the economy. It is true that the disciples of Beard and Smith, political liberals to a man, displayed far greater tender-

[4] On the frontispiece of his work, *The Economic Origins of Jeffersonian Democracy*, as several of Beard's critics have noted, he quotes Frederick Jackson Turner's remark: "We may trace the contest between the capitalist and the democratic pioneer from the earliest colonial days." See Harvey Wish, *The American Historian* (New York: Oxford University Press, 1960), p. 275. Beard told Amherst students in 1916 that "a landed interest, a transport interest, a railway interest, a shipping interest, an engineering interest, a manufacturing interest, a public official interest, with many lesser interests, group up of necessity in all great societies and divide them into different classes activated by different sentiments and views." Unfortunately, however, he rejected this valuable insight into the complexity of interest politics and tended to fuse these elements, as in his *An Economic Interpretation of the Constitution*, into "consolidated" groups identified respectively with "capitalist and agrarian interests." See Beale, "Charles Beard: Historian," Beale, *op.cit.*, p. 117. See also Lee Benson, *Turner and Beard: American Historical Writing Reconsidered* (Glencoe, Illinois: The Free Press, 1960), Part III, ch. I.

[5] This quotation is from the introduction to *Party Politics and Public Action, 1877-1917* (New York: Henry Holt, 1960), edited by David Potter, revised by Howard R. Lamar, p. 16.

ness for the agrarian than for the capitalist,[6] but if they were partial to the farmer or the "little man," they had no illusions about his altruism. Like the capitalist, his primary concern was for his livelihood.[7]

This economic emphasis, of course, parallels that of Marx, and it is clear that Beard was aware of the most ambitious and challenging analysis of historical forces that the nineteenth century produced.[8] Nevertheless, Beard was not a Marxist. He owed far more to the very agrarian tradition he so sympathetically described. Beard was a neo-Populist, and his version of post-Civil War America leaned heavily on the interpretation accepted by the contemporary leaders of agrarian dissent. There is little in Beard's "Second American Revolution" thesis that cannot be found in the reform polemics of the Granger era, the Populist revolt, and most immediately, the Progressive movement. The Manichaean view of the basic struggle, the belief in conspiracy, even the economic determinism, all belong to the Jacksonian antimonopoly thread connecting all three movements. It is this native neo-Populism, rather than an exotic European Socialism, that is responsible for both the dualism and the determinism of the Beardian philosophy.[9]

[6] Max Lerner notes that Beard "was never to cast himself loose from Jefferson, whether in his agrarian sympathies, his attitudes toward capitalism, his conception of a gracious life, his cultural values, or his outlook on Europe's entanglements and their relation to American foreign policy." Lerner, "Charles Beard's Political Theory," Beale, *op. cit.*, p. 36.

[7] William Appleman Williams in his sympathetic essay, "A Note on Charles Austin Beard's Search for a General Theory of Causation," *AHR*, LXII, No. 1 (October 1956), notes that in his *Jeffersonian Democracy* Beard "concluded that the [Jeffersonian] Republicans, too, went into politics on the basis of their economics." See p. 72.

[8] Beard himself belittled his debt to Marx, but he apparently borrowed from E. R. A. Seligman's *The Economic Interpretation of History*, a work which did much to introduce Marxist historical ideas to American readers. See Louis Hartz, *The Liberal Tradition in America* (New York: Harcourt Brace and Co., 1955), p. 248; Cushing Strout, *The Pragmatic Revolt in American History: Carl Becker and Charles Beard* (New Haven: Yale University Press, 1958), pp. 90, 95; Bernard C. Borning, *The Political and Social Thought of Charles A. Beard* (Seattle: University of Washington Press, 1962), pp. 47ff.

[9] Richard Hofstadter describes the Progressives, among whom he numbers Beard, as seeing "reality" as "rough and sordid; it was hidden and neglected, and so to speak off-stage, and it was essentially a stream of external and material events of which psychic events were a kind of pale reflex." See Hofstadter, "Charles Beard and the Constitution," in Beale, *op. cit.*, p. 87. Wil-

In what follows it is this neo-Populist picture of post-bellum America that I am seeking to evaluate. This is primarily a political, not a financial history. Although fixed to a skeleton of financial events, my story is largely concerned with the decision-making process in American society. I do not wish to compete with the existing excellent surveys of financial history. I shall examine the politics of money between the end of the Civil War and the resumption of specie payments in 1879, but I shall emphasize the events of the 1870's. A recent study of the immediate postwar half-decade by Dr. Robert Sharkey of Johns Hopkins University[10] enables me to limit my work. It has also made my task more challenging. Though we share similar conclusions,[11] we do disagree on several important points. Briefly, Dr. Sharkey remains convinced that the governing forces in America after 1865 were economic; he disputes Beard's implied "monolithic" business, labor, and agricultural interests, but adopts an economic determinism even more complete.[12] I cannot accept this conclusion. The events of our lifetime seemingly have revealed how weak in crisis are social and ethical restraints. Yet we must not in our despair read our own attitudes and experiences into the past. Implanted values and controls were, I believe, tougher then than now. In the matter of post-Civil War finance men indeed marshaled principle to rational-

---

liam Appleman Williams, on the other hand, rejects this view. In analyzing the ingredients that entered into Beard's historical philosophy, he accepts the influence of Marx although he denies that Beard was a Socialist. He also rejects, however, the Populist—or Progressive—origin of Beard's views, deriving them from James Madison's Federalist 10. In addition, he ascribes to Beard, though not to *The Rise of American Civilization*, a more sophisticated theory of causation than I do. He and Lee Benson refer to this theory as "economic interpretation" as distinguished from "economic determinism." On the other hand, if I disagree with Professor Williams on this point I recognize that he per-

ceives the crude, inadequate dualism of Beard's "Second American Revolution" thesis. See Williams, *op. cit.,* p. 74; Benson, *op. cit.,* pp. 96-101.

[10] Sharkey, *Money, Class, and Party: An Economic Study of Civil War and Reconstruction* (Baltimore: The Johns Hopkins Press, 1959).

[11] Particularly on the subject of business attitudes see my "Business Men and Specie Resumption," *Political Science Quarterly,* LXXIV, No. 1 (March 1959), 46-70. I have also covered the ground more thoroughly in "Men, Money and Politics: The Specie Resumption Issue, 1865-1879" (unpublished Ph.D. dissertation, Columbia University, 1958), particularly chs. I-III.

[12] Sharkey, *op. cit.,* ch. VII, particularly pp. 290ff.

ize expediency, but they also rejected perceived interest for conscience' sake. In general, most men tried to strike a balance between their pocket books and their duty. This mixture of ethics and interest, this very human attempt to serve both God and Mammon, must be recognized if we hope to understand the events of these years.

Unfortunately, adding ethics to interest greatly complicates any attempt to analyze the postwar money question. When economic self-interest is made the prime mover of human events, profit or loss will explain any historical happening. This simplification is all the more appealing since it becomes possible to deal with measurable quantities which may be summarized on a balance sheet. We record changing price per bushel, the rise and fall of interest rates, miles of track built, tons of iron produced, annual bankruptcy rates, and perform the appropriate additions and subtractions; history loses its human complexities and becomes a form of social accountancy. Moral and ideological considerations not only defy quantifying—how does one count or weigh a man's religious convictions?—but they also raise special new problems. With several determinants instead of a single one, every historical effect becomes a conundrum. It is certain to be the resultant of several forces; but which— and even more puzzling, in what proportions? It is not surprising, therefore, that such a method is unsatisfactory to many social analysts. Nevertheless, it is probably the inevitable limitation of our discipline. Paring down human events for the sake of simple answers not only distorts reality but in the end denies the special quality of historical knowledge itself.

At the outset it would be well to settle certain problems of definition. American historians conventionally use the tags "hard money" and "soft money" to describe post-Civil War financial opinion. The Reconstruction money question, however, was a cluster of loosely related problems rather than a single issue, and it is difficult to see how they can be measured by a single scale. A "hard money" attitude toward paper money is easy to grasp, but what is a hard money view of banks, or resumption, or bond repayment? Was it possible to be simultaneously "hard" on bonds and "soft" on greenbacks? Were there middle positions that were neither "hard" nor "soft"?

There are no simple answers to these questions, and it is tempting to throw out all labels in the interest of strict accuracy. But such extreme nominalism would be cumbersome if not unintelligible. The problem is a practical one and must be solved practically; there must be a yardstick of hard and soft money, however imperfect, to permit a logical grouping of the facts. Fortunately there is no need to be arbitrary. The specie payment question was the central financial issue of this period and is the most valid gauge of opinion before 1880. As used in the following chapters, the term "soft money" describes those men who resisted resumption and the deflation it implied. It is not synonymous with "inflation." All inflationists were anti-resumptionists, but not all the enemies of resumption favored inflation. The term "soft money" describes men with often violently differing attitudes toward banks, bond holders, and paper money—all united by a distaste for returning to a gold-redeemable circulation. "Hard money" embraced a range of partisans from intransigent contractionists, to gradualists, to eventualists, all intent on reaching gold payments painlessly, or quickly, or cheaply—or, preferably, all three.

One final word. I should like to make clear at the outset my profound respect and admiration for Charles A. Beard and his work. Beard's writing on the interactions of politics and economics is currently being subjected to a searching reappraisal which has revealed serious weaknesses in both his methods and conclusions.[13] But we must remember that he was a courageous pioneer who destroyed in a succession of powerful blows the stifling pieties of nineteenth-century historiography. Our debt to him is profound. If we are able to see farther it is only because, like the Moderns of the old quarrel of Ancients and Moderns, we stand on the shoulders of giants.

[13] See particularly Robert E. Brown, *Charles Beard and the Constitution* (Princeton: Princeton University Press, 1956); and Forrest McDonald, *We the People: The Economic Origins of the Constitution* (Chicago: University of Chicago Press, 1958). Beard's critics are in turn criticized in Benson, *op. cit.*, and John Higham, "The Cult of 'American Consensus,'" *Commentary*, xxvii, No. 2 (February 1959), 93-100.

Any scholarly enterprise which, like this one, has taken almost a decade to complete, necessarily involves its author in obligations to an immense number of individuals and institutions. Among institutions I wish particularly to thank the Social Science Research Council and the American Philosophical Society for grants-in-aid which enabled me to use the resources of several Mid-western libraries and to devote two duty-free summers to writing. My colleagues and associates at Columbia University, Long Beach State College, and the University of California at Davis, all have my gratitude for the aid and comfort they have given me and my endeavors. Beyond this I should like to single out for special thanks the Library of Congress and the Hayes Memorial Library at Fremont, Ohio. The staff of the first catered with unfailing good humor to the wants of what must have appeared at times to be a very eccentric research program. The latter, in the person of Mr. Watt Marchman, extended courtesies far greater than those usual for research libraries. I have, of course, never failed to receive prompt and cheerful help from any of the librarians whom I have consulted. For all these favors I am truly grateful. But perhaps I may be forgiven if I allow my citations to suggest where, specifically, my gratitude lies.

Among individuals I am most profoundly indebted to Professor David Donald of Johns Hopkins University. From the very inception of this work Professor Donald has extended sympathy, interest, and a helping hand far beyond the common obligations of mentor, colleague, or even friend. He has read my manuscript in drafts so numerous as to interfere, I am certain, with his own important work. I have, indeed, been the beneficiary of a selflessness in encouraging the work of young historians that has become a by-word among those who know the historical profession. I am also deeply grateful to Mr. Bray Hammond, a mature and wise scholar, who never forgot the needs and hopes of a younger colleague. Professor Richard Hofstadter of Columbia University read a late draft of my work with welcome celerity and great perception. Professor Jeannette Nichols of the University of Pennsylvania read several of my later chapters with the understanding that only her special knowledge of John Sherman could provide. Mrs. Eve Hanle of the Princeton University Press, by combining firmness with good humor, expedited immeasurably the processing of the manuscript. Other friends, colleagues, and fellow workers who have read and criticized portions of this study include: Professor Joseph Dorfman of Columbia University, Professor Ari Hoogenboom of Pennsylvania State University, Professors Alan Brownsword and Irving F. Ahlquist of Long Beach State College, Professor H. Grady McWhiney of Northwestern University, and Professor P. J. Staudenraus of the University of California at Davis. I have not always accepted their judicious and informed advice, preferring sometimes to follow my own bent even when that entailed risks. Needless to say, they cannot be held responsible for the failings of the completed work.

Finally I wish to thank Mrs. Lee Barker, Mrs. Nancy Berg, Mrs. Marlene Frady, and Mrs. Geraldine Hassl for converting my disheveled copy into neat and readable typescript.

Several of my chapters have, in somewhat different versions, appeared in professional journals. Parts of chapter eight appeared in *The Business History Review*, Vol. xxxv (Summer 1961); another part of the same chapter in *Mid-America: An Historical Review*, Vol. xli (January 1959). The material of several other chapters was published in the *Political Science Quarterly*, Vol. lxxiv (March 1959), and in the *Journal of Presbyterian History*, Vol. xl (March 1962). I am grateful to the editors of all four journals for permission to reprint this material.

THE ROOTS OF CONFLICT

I

THE problems of Reconstruction finance were sown in the thirteen feverish months following Lincoln's election. The acute political crisis, the unprecedented drain on the country's human and economic resources, the releasing of restraints as the political and military shock jarred men loose from customary practices—all combined to raise up a host of new financial problems that would trouble America for a generation.

Secession not only rocked the country to its political foundations; it also set off a short but acute business slump which, joined with the loss of the South, cut deep into federal revenues. Still shaky from the effects of the 1857 panic, the Treasury was soon in desperate straits, unable to meet its current demands and forced to pay as much as 12 per cent to keep the government in funds.[1]

This was the critical situation when the new Secretary of the Treasury, Salmon P. Chase, took up his duties in March 1861. In August the Treasury negotiated the first war loan with an association of New York, Philadelphia, and Boston banks and set in motion the forces of postwar financial strife. Under the agreement concluded, the banks were to take $50 million of 7.3 per cent Treasury notes, to be followed, at the bankers' option, by two additional $50 million lots later in the year.[2] Contrary

[1] Robert T. Patterson, *Federal Debt-Management Policies, 1865-1879* (Durham: Duke University Press, 1954), ch. i.

[2] Actually, the bankers advanced $50 million to the Treasury on Chase's warrants to be redeemed as soon as the Secretary's fiscal agents could sell sufficient 7.30 treasury notes to the public. If Chase proved unable to sell these notes fast enough, he could deliver them to the banks which could, in turn, either attempt themselves to sell to the public, hold the notes for later redemption by the Treasury, or, finally convert them into 6 per cent government bonds. Ellis Paxson Oberholtzer, *Jay Cooke, Financier of the Civil War* (Philadelphia: George W. Jacobs and Co., 1907), i, 150-151.

to the bankers' advice, Chase, a rather primitive bullionist Democrat, expected an immediate payment in gold delivered to the Sub-treasury door. Complying with his terms was a serious drain on the banks' reserves, offset only by resales of securities to the public and rapid government spending, which soon returned the gold to the banks' vaults. Although still uneasy, the banks took their second installment in October and the third in mid-November. Then disaster. The Trent Affair and the threat of war with England, the controversial removal of Fremont from command of the Western Department, Grant's failure before Belmont, and, finally, Chase's *Annual Report* which revealed the probability of a large Treasury deficit, shook public confidence, stopping resales and sending gold into hiding. Specie reserves quickly fell to dangerous levels. Between December 7 and 28 the New York banks alone lost almost $13 million of their gold. Two days later banks all over the country, immediately followed by the Treasury, ceased paying coin for their obligations. The nation had left the gold standard.[3]

Specie suspension was to create one of the most urgent financial questions of the postwar years, but three areas of wartime financial legislation gave rise to equally troublesome problems. The most important of these was the emission of legal tender paper money early in 1862 to help pay for what was fast

---

[3] Another factor depleting the banks' gold supply was the Treasury's issue of demand notes. These were a means by which the public drained specie out of the banks, since the latter paid out gold for them. It should be noted that it is quite likely that whatever Chase's policies might have been, suspension would have occurred. See Paul Studenski and Herman Krooss, *Financial History of the United States* (New York: McGraw-Hill Book Co., Inc., 1952), p. 143. My account of suspension has been drawn from the following standard works: Wesley Clair Mitchell, *A History of the Greeenbacks, With Special Reference to the Economic Consequences of Their Issue, 1862-1865* (Chicago: University of Chicago Press, 1903), ch. II; Albert S. Bolles, *The Financial History of the United States from 1861 to 1885* (2nd ed., New York: D. Appleton and Co., 1894), ch. III; Fritz Redlich, *The Molding of American Banking: Men and Ideas,* part II (New York: Hafner Publishing Co., 1951), pp. 88-95; Davis Rich Dewey, *Financial History of the United States* (New York: Longmans, Green and Co., 1939), pp. 281-284; Don C. Barrett, *The Greenbacks and Resumption of Specie Payments, 1862-1879* (Cambridge: Harvard University Press, 1931), ch. I; Horace White, *Money and Banking Illustrated by American History* (Boston: Ginn and Company, 1911), pp. 107-109.

becoming the most costly war in the nation's history. Against its better judgment, but under the relentless pressure of military needs and the strong urging of many eastern bankers,[4] Congress authorized the first of three issues of legal tender treasury notes in February 1862. In June, Chase, who had still not formulated a comprehensive tax plan, requested an additional issue. Finally, in January 1863, a further issue was approved. All told, by the end of the War, some $450 million of these United States notes, soon called "greenbacks" by the public, had been authorized.[5]

The greenbacks were actually to be the source of two vexatious difficulties. One arose from their rapid decline in terms of both commodities and gold. Conservatives of both parties had warned when the first greenback issue was debated that the new notes would quickly depreciate.[6] And the seers proved right. The very first notes, when they appeared in April 1862, passed at a discount in gold. Thereafter the rapidly rising gold premium, reaching 185 in 1864,[7] registered every additional issue and every military setback.[8] More significant was the greenbacks' decline in terms of rents, commodities, and services. The wartime paper money contributed to the most

---

[4] Bray Hammond, "The North's Empty Purse, 1861-1862," *AHR*, LXVII, No. 1 (October 1961). See also Bolles, *op. cit.*, p. 47

[5] Fifty million of this amount, however, represented security for temporary loan deposits with the Treasury and was retired by 1867 with repayment of these loans. But to complicate the matter further, actually only a little over $33 million of this $50 million was ever issued. This additional $33 million was usually ignored, and it was generally assumed that there were only $400 million of greenbacks circulating. The Treasury also authorized $50 million of fractional paper money to replace silver coin that had disappeared into hoards after suspension, of which only about $30 million were circulated. Patterson, *op. cit.*, p. 179; and Bolles, *op. cit.*, p. 84.

[6] Mitchell, *op. cit.*, pp. 51ff.; Elbridge Gerry Spaulding, *History of the Legal Tender Paper Money Issued During the Great Rebellion* . . . (Buffalo: Express Printing Co., 1869), pp. 18-19; *Congressional Globe*, 37 Cong., 2 sess., pp. 551, 630.

[7] That is, 184 per cent greater than in 1861, before suspension, when, of course, the premium was zero. Sometimes the price of gold, rather than the premium was used to measure the divergence of gold and paper. In this case a "premium" of 184 would become a "price" of 284, indicating that $2.84 had to be paid for the same amount of gold that had formerly cost $1.00. Par in this latter form of quotation meant 100; in the premium form par was 0.

[8] Mitchell, *op. cit.*, ch. III.

severe inflation the country had experienced since the Revolution. By January 1865 wholesale prices of some 135 key commodities had risen to an average level more than 2½ times that of 1860; the general cost of living had almost doubled.[9]

The second greenback problem was the question of their redemption. Although soon after the fighting had ceased the attempt to tie the legal tenders to specie would become controversial, the greenback issue at first was generally considered a loan without interest. But in what sense was it redeemable? Returning to gold payments presumably would make the legal tenders convertible on demand into coin, but given the inflated price level, could such conversion be achieved without a drastic contraction of their volume? Little had been said on the subject of redemption when Congress debated the legal tender emissions, but the problem of making almost half a billion dollars in greenbacks as good as gold was to become the largest single financial problem facing the United States after 1865.

Two further aspects of wartime financial legislation were to trouble the country following Appomattox. The first of these was the immense debt laid by Congress on the nation's back. All told, the Lincoln government spent well over $3 billion for all purposes during the four years of conflict. Less than a fifth of this was paid for by taxes, leaving the federal debt at over $2.8 billion at its highest point in August 1865,[10] when it equalled about one-half the annual gross national product. This was by far the largest debt the nation had ever experienced, and the interest on it alone far exceeded the total federal debt before 1861.[11] To compound postwar repayment difficulties, this debt was not of uniform character. Besides the three initial 7-30 loans and the greenbacks, an incredible profusion of other credit instruments were used to finance the war, from short-term treasury notes and certificates of indebtedness, many

[9] *Ibid.*, p. 248, Table x; and Wesley Clair Mitchell, *Gold, Prices and Wages Under the Greenback Standard* (Berkeley: The University [of California] Press, 1908), p. 279, Table 74.

[10] Patterson, *op. cit.*, pp. 50-51.

[11] For the federal debt in the nineteenth century, see United States Bureau of the Census, *Historical Statistics of the United States, Colonial Times to 1957* (Washington: Government Printing Office, 1960), series Y-368 and Y-373, pp. 720 and 721.

of which had quasi-monetary qualities, to securities running as long as forty years.[12] The most important, and ultimately the most controversial, of these issues were the so-called 5-20's, tax-exempt securities bearing 6 per cent interest in gold which the government could "pay" in five years, if it chose, and which it must "redeem" in twenty.[13] Purchasable with the new legal tenders, these bonds were sold to the public through the aggressive agents of Jay Cooke and Company, a Philadelphia banking firm led by an old Ohio friend of Secretary Chase. By the end of the war over $800 million had been issued, and by 1869—after large postwar issues for refunding purposes—some $1.6 billion. Unfortunately for the nation's later serenity, although interest on the 5-20's was specifically payable in gold, under the law nothing had been said about the mode of repaying the principle, and the omission would help fan a decade of intense and exasperating conflict.

As the third and final element of controversial financial legislation, the War produced a revolution in the country's banking structure. In the two decades preceding Sumter, American banking had been chaotic. Ever since the destruction of the Second Bank of the United States by the combined assault of naïve bullionists, impatient driving enterprisers, radical democrats, jealous state bankers, and Andrew Jackson, the American banking system had been without central direction. Organized under at least as many distinct laws as there were states,[14] the hundreds of commercial banks that spotted the nation varied from the strong, solvent institutions of the major commercial centers, to firms, particularly in the newer areas of the West and South, that were little more than legal counterfeiting shops. In New England, New York, South Carolina, and Louisiana

---

[12] A complete description of the varieties of Civil War obligations will be found in Patterson, *op. cit.*, ch. IV.

[13] That is, the government had the option of paying the bonds at any time after five years from the date of purchase. After no more than twenty years, the bonds were to be redeemed and canceled. On the quantity of 5-20's see Studenski and Krooss, *op. cit.*, p. 156, Table 20; Patterson, *op. cit.*, p. 80.

[14] Indeed, until the late '30's, when a number of states, most notably New York and Michigan, adopted general incorporation, or "free banking" laws, there were almost as many laws under which banks were organized as there were separate institutions.

strict limits were placed either by law or self-regulation on reserves against note issue and loans. In many other places a good-
humored laxity, leading to credit overexpansion—often followed
by abrupt collapse and a painful period of readjustment—was
common. Although the easy money policies of "wildcat" banks
perhaps performed a useful function in the capital-poor American economy of the early nineteenth century, it was only at the
considerable price of chronic instability for the economy as a
whole and severe private suffering among men unfortunate
enough to be caught holding the assets of "broken banks."

Aside from the controversy that swirled around the economic
impact of liberal banking policies, the banking system had, for
over half a century, been embroiled in the political and ideological struggles of the early Republic. To summarize briefly here,
to many followers of Jefferson and Jackson, all banks, but particularly the First and Second Banks of the United States,
smacked of plutocracy if not autocracy and seemed to threaten
the free government of small producers, which both groups
cherished as the ideal for America. To Federalists like Hamilton and Whigs like Henry Clay and Nicholas Biddle, on the
other hand, a strong, federally chartered central bank, aggressive enough to act as a balance wheel in the economy, seemed
essential to the strength and well-being of the new Republic.

It was this latter Federalist-Whig tradition, strongly en-
trenched in the new Republican party, which triumphed with
the passage of the National Banking Act in 1863. Yet the fiscal
needs of the Treasury were probably the most powerful propul-
sive force behind the new system. In his first Treasury *Report*,
Secretary Chase, although an erstwhile Democrat, had recommended a new system of banks under federal charter to provide,
along with a new safety to note-holders and depositors, a large
market for government bonds. The Act of January 1863, sup-
plemented the following year, provided that any group of five
persons possessing a specified amount of capital could organize
themselves into a banking corporation to do all business normal
to banking firms in the more strictly regulated states. These
"associations," upon the deposit of federal bonds with the Comptroller of the Currency as security, would be issued new national

bank notes equal in amount to 90 per cent of either market or par value of the bonds, whichever was lower. These new notes were to be receivable for all public debts except customs and payable for all government obligations except interest on the national debt. Although not legal tender like the greenbacks, in the absence of gold payments, national bank notes were redeemable in greenbacks and hence virtually their equivalent. Unfortunately, rather than truly freeing banking from all quantitative restraints, the law placed an effective ceiling on the extent of the system by restricting total note issue to $300 million. Finally, the law provided that the national banks, like the old Bank of the United States, should perform various services as depositories and agents for the federal government.[15]

The new law, although conceived with an eye to strengthening the weak and disorganized banking structure of the country, at first met stiff resistance from the banking fraternity. State bankers, preferring the accustomed and generally looser rein of state law, helped delay passage of the 1863 measure.[16] When it finally was enacted, they resisted conversion to the new system and had to be prodded to join by a prohibitive 10 per cent tax on their notes. Nevertheless, by the end of 1865 there were over 1,600 national banks in existence, largely eastern, most of them former state institutions.

II

These were the basic ingredients for a generation of financial argument. The national banking system, the federal debt, the 5-20 bonds, the redemption of greenbacks—all provoked excited debate after 1865. But coloring the whole noisy quarrel was the memory of the home-front economy in wartime.

It is now clear that inflation would have occurred even

[15] Andrew McFarland Davis, *The Origins of the National Banking System* (Washington: Government Printing Office, 1910), especially pp. 155-197; Bolles, *op. cit.*, ch. xi; Oberholtzer, *op. cit.*, i, ch. vi. The text of the two major wartime measures establishing the system will be found in Charles F. Dunbar, *Laws of the United States Relating to Currency, Finance, and Banking. . .* (Boston: Ginn and Company, 1897) pp. 171-173, 178-191.

[16] Robert P. Sharkey, *Money, Class, and Party: An Economic Study of Civil War and Reconstruction* (Baltimore: The Johns Hopkins Press, 1959), p. 226.

without the greenback issue. Only a fifth of the War's costs
were paid for by taxation as we have seen; the rest were financed by loans. This system grossly inflated the money supply.[17]
All together, according to one recent estimate, the country's
total money stock expanded 2.32 times between the outbreak
of war and the wartime price peaks in 1865.[18] Add to this the
massive government spending, the consumer and investor optimism, and the prevailing full employment, and it is easy to see
how prices had to rise after 1861, even if not a single dollar of
paper money had been printed.

Prosperity was the other important economic consequence
of the War. Government spending and inflation set off a business
boom that cast a golden glow over the war years.[19] An historian
of American industry remarks that the only manufacturers
who lost money during the War were those who gambled on
an early peace. Luxury industries—cut glass manufacture,
decorated porcelains, silks, and expensive dress goods—"throve
beyond example." Profits in woolen manufacturing "were enormous, thanks to the high prices of government contracts and

[17] Some government borrowing no
doubt absorbed disposable consumer income; much of it was inflationary. About 20 per cent of the
amount borrowed was monetized
directly as the greenback issue, but
a large part of the remaining $2
billion also contributed to the money
supply. The 5-20 bonds, of course,
served as security for $300 million
of national bank notes, which more
than balanced the state bank notes
they replaced. The disappearance of
gold as domestic money withdrew
about $250 million of coin from
circulation, but this was at least
partly offset by short-term securities totalling about $1 billion, some
of them legal tenders, which served
as bank reserves and also, as suggested above, to some extent as
hand-to-hand currency. In addition
there was a great expansion of demand deposits as a result of increased business activity. In 1860
bank deposits, which already were

a major portion of the money stock,
totalled almost $310 million. By
1865 this figure had risen to $689
million. See the following: *Historical Statistics*, pp. 625 and 629,
series X-34 and X-83; Mitchell,
History of the Greenbacks, pp.
174-178.

[18] Milton Friedman, "Price, Income and Monetary Changes in
Three Wartime Periods," *Papers
and Proceedings of the Sixty-
Fourth Annual Meeting of the
American Economic Association*
(1951), p. 624.

[19] Recently, economic historians
have begun to doubt the older view
of the Civil War as a great industrial accelerator. My point here,
however, is not that the War marked
the shift from commercial to industrial capitalism, or even that it
reinforced the industrialization process. I am simply suggesting that
the War made the nation prosperous and many men rich.

the scarcity of cotton."[20] Commercial profits followed closely behind those of industry. Dun's Mercantile Agency reported in 1864 that net returns from trade in that year had averaged from 12 to 15 per cent. As one "old merchant" wrote to William Pitt Fessenden, Chase's successor at the Treasury, "the importers, jobbers, shopkeepers and all others engaged in the vending of merchandise [were] . . . making much larger profits than they did before the breaking out of the rebellion."[21]

Banks profits are difficult to estimate for the period, since the few figures that are available are confused by the banking revolution of the war years. It seems clear, however, that the banks were prosperous by the end of the War. While creditors lost by inflation, this did not disturb the banks seriously. A doubling of price levels in four years hurt savings banks, land mortgage companies, and similar long-term lenders, perhaps, but most commercial institutions lent on 90-day or other short-term paper, besides being themselves indebted to their depositors, and so had little cause for distress.[22] In general, the nation's banks seem to have profited from the great expansion of loans and discounts that accompanied the general business prosperity. One schedule of profits of eight Boston banks between 1859 and 1866 indicates a sharp upturn in the last two years of the War which, after several bad years, pushed dividends over the 1859 level.[23] Bank clearings at New York, which totalled a little over $7 billion in 1860, reached $26 billion in 1865.[24]

[20] Victor S. Clark, *History of Manufactures in the United States* (New York: Peter Smith, 1949), II, 36; Emerson David Fite, *Social and Industrial Conditions in the North During the Civil War* (New York: Peter Smith, 1930), p. 84.

[21] For Dun's: Mitchell, *History of the Greenbacks*, p. 389; for "old merchant," Nash P. Hood to Fessenden, Philadelphia, Dec. 14, 1864, Fessenden MSS, LC.

[22] Bray Hammond, *Banks and Politics in America from the Revolution to the Civil War* (Princeton: Princeton University Press, 1957), pp. 671-688. Although, as explained below, there was a strong mercan-tilist tradition in America of long-term loans for capital growth purposes.

[23] N. S. B. Gras and Henrietta M. Larson, *Casebook in American Business History* (New York: Appleton-Century-Crofts, Inc., 1939), p. 704. Emerson D. Fite says that the profits of the Associated Banks of the City of New York rose from $8 million to close to $21 million during the War. See Fite, *op. cit.*, p. 123.

[24] *Historical Statistics*, p. 640, series X-227. The 1865 figure must, of course, be discounted for the price rise. Nevertheless, it represents a substantial real gain.

The farmers of the North had good reason to bless the South. The War produced labor shortages which were made up only by large outlays of capital for machinery or high wages for agricultural labor. Nevertheless, farm income rose sharply after the first two years in response to skyrocketing prices for wheat, corn, beans, pork, beef, eggs, butter, lard, potatoes, cheese, which more than offset both rising costs of production and higher living costs on the farm. Certainly, from the vantage of the '70's, farmers would regret the war years.[25]

The effects of prosperity and inflation on labor, by contrast, were ambiguous. Real wages declined between a fifth and a sixth,[26] but jobs became plentiful once the initial shock of secession had passed. As business boomed and men were drawn off into the army, unemployment, a problem since the 1857 panic, disappeared. At the same time, labor organizations burgeoned. After the early business uncertainty following Sumter, local trades assemblies once more appeared in the major cities. This growth suggests discontent. But actually, labor organization in America has traditionally advanced in good times rather than bad. Full employment gave skilled labor the freedom to organize and deprived employers of a ready weapon to retaliate. Strikes were not frequent in those turbulent years, largely because employers generally submitted to labor demands without a struggle.[27]

Despite this very real progress, however, it is difficult to cast

[25] For farmers' added wartime outlays for labor and machinery see Fred A. Shannon, *The Farmer's Last Frontier: Agriculture, 1860-1897* (New York: Rinehart and Company, 1945), p. 126; for rising farm commodity prices in detail, Mitchell, *Gold, Prices and Wages*, pp. 56-57, table 17; pp. 72-75, table 22; for greater increase in farmers' costs see *ibid.*, pp. 49-50, table 16. Mitchell's conclusion regarding the farmers' wartime fate, which I think is based on a strong sound money bias rather than the logic of his facts, is that farmers probably lost more than they gained by the wartime price increases. See Mitchell, *History of the Greenbacks*, p. 388. Actually there is evidence that farm prices rose more rapidly than non-farm prices following 1861. See John D. Black, "Agriculture," in Seymour E. Harris (ed.), *American Economic History* (New York: McGraw-Hill Book Co., 1961), p. 509, chart 6.

[26] For real wages: Mitchell, *Gold, Prices and Wages*, p. 279, table 74; and Mitchell, *History of the Greenbacks*, pp. 347-351.

[27] John R. Commons and associates, *The History of Labour in the United States* (New York: The Macmillan Co., 1946), II, 14, 17-26.

an account for labor as a whole during the war period. For the factory worker or skilled craftsman who had been employed full-time in 1860, the decline in real income hurt. To others, out of work or working part-time, it was a boon. But whatever happened to individual workingmen between 1861 and 1865, these years did not fundamentally change labor's condition. Incomes remained low for the mass of American wage earners by the standards of more recent times or of the contemporary business and professional classes. Although he enjoyed advantages and comforts denied the European worker and his hope of rising from the laboring class was somewhat more real,[28] the American worker nonetheless confronted a society which promised more than it fulfilled. Job insecurity, the uncertainties of an unregulated market economy, and the universal hazards of injury and illness produced the anxieties that a poorer but more organic society cushioned. Courted by the politicians, possessing the political rights enjoyed by almost none of his fellows elsewhere, he found himself denied the economic benefits of a wealthy, growing country. These frustrations, as much perhaps as the economic experience of the war years, would help determine labor's role in the postwar financial dispute.

One large class of citizens who clearly lost ground during the War were those living on fixed incomes. At one end it included affluent lenders of capital, men of "independent means" living on funds safely invested in land and gilt edge securities. Landlords lost as rents fell behind general commodity price rises.[29] Holders of fixed-yield bonds of course were also injured by price inflation. A "rentier" like Charles Francis Adams, Sr., returning in 1868 from seven years in England, found it hard, though living quietly at Quincy, to make ends meet.[30] At the other social

---

[28] In 1875 Edward Young, Chief of the United States Bureau of Statistics, concluded, after a comprehensive examination of foreign and domestic wages and living costs, that the United States enjoyed a "degree of prosperity rarely if ever" experienced elsewhere, and that this prosperity had "rarely, if ever, in the history of the world... been so largely shared by those usually denominated the working classes." Young, *Labor in Europe and America...* (Philadelphia: S. A. George and Company, 1875), p. 820.

[29] Mitchell, *History of the Greenbacks*, ch. vi, especially, p. 355, table 54.

[30] Charles Francis Adams, Sr., MS Diary, Sept. 29, 1868, Adams MSS, Massachusetts Historical Soci-

extreme were the widows, the pensioners, the college professors, the clergy, and the other genteel poor, who always make a special claim on the sympathies of the community during inflationary periods.[31]

III

Scarcely anyone who was enmeshed in the market economy escaped the impact of the financial innovations and altered economic conditions that flowed from the great civil conflict. Some men rode the boom triumphantly; others found themselves on an economic treadmill, running hard to stay where they were; still others fell behind and were submerged by rising prices or monetary shortages. It is tempting to extrapolate the alignments of postwar currency opinion directly from these wartime effects. In simplest terms, hard money sentiment would derive from the debit side, soft money from the credit side of the wartime experience. Aside from the difficulties of determining debits and credits in the case of some groups—labor, for example—such a convenient shortcut would be valid only if we could make two assumptions: first, that manufacturers, farmers, wage earners, merchants, rentiers, and the various subgroups which composed these, both understood the personal effects of price changes and deliberately followed the logic of their positions; second, that the postwar financial controversy was purely an economic struggle. Neither of these assumptions is true. Neither the degree of public awareness nor of public calculation required by the hypothesis actually existed. Nor is it always true that "men's judgments are a parcel of their fortunes." In the great postwar debate over the currency, ideas and values were often as important as acquisitiveness, and "interests" came to include men united by more than economic ambitions.

Ultimately the postwar struggle over finance was shaped by a small number of elements. The most visible, but not always the

---

ety. I have used the Adams manuscripts in a microfilm copy at Columbia University.

[31] See the following: J. M. Forbes to Hugh McCulloch, Boston, Dec. 10, 1865, McCulloch MSS, LC; Francis Bowen to Charles Sumner, Harvard College, March 27, 1866, Sumner MSS, Harvard University Library; *The Christian Mirror*, XLIV (Nov. 21, 1865), p. 70; *Congregational Review*, VIII (January 1868).

most formidable element was, of course, the acquisitiveness normal to men in our society; another was the adventitious—accident, coincidence, personal idiosyncrasy; a third was in a sense purely political. Political man often subdued economic man in the struggle over money. There were periods between 1865 and 1879 when party considerations acted autonomously to mold important financial decisions. Prestige drives, social anxieties, and class frustration represent another category of motives that demand attention. Finally, accepted values—religion, the prevailing intellectual milieu, and even folk belief and social mythology—played a vital part in fixing the pattern of events.

Of the five elements suggested above as most pertinent to the Reconstruction money question, the last in particular requires some probing beyond our period. Men brought to the financial question, as to all complex public issues, a wide range of attitudes, moral postures, and preconceptions deeply rooted in the past. These not only shaped responses through direct confrontation; they often determined what was perceived.[32]

To contemporaries, the money issue was as much a moral as a political or economic problem. Economic concerns, at least until our own day, have always been considered at heart ethical. It is no accident that modern economic science was the creation of a Scottish Professor of Moral Philosophy. Still more clearly has moral significance been attributed to questions of money, price, and interest. The social ethic of the medieval Catholic Church condemned usury and profiteering,[33] and its precepts became

[32] What follows at points overlaps the "four American traditions" of the "Trustees," the "Squires," the "Artisans," and the "Yeoman," described by Professor William B. Hesseltine as the basic ordering systems of American values. Where Professor Hesseltine and I differ is in, first, his view that these traditions were largely unifying forces; and, second, in the more important matter of the precise nature of these systems. Briefly, my "Calvinist" category closely resembles his Trustee or Stewardship one, but my "Agrarian" ethic combines parts of all three of his other categories. In addition my analysis seeks to distinguish competing schools of economic thought. The differences between us may well be explained by the differing scope of our concerns. Professor Hesseltine is seeking to encompass all of American history; I am concerned with the far narrower area of Reconstruction finance. See Hesseltine, "Four American Traditions," *Journal of Southern History*, xxvii, No. 1 (February 1961), 3-32.

[33] R. H. Tawney, *Religion and the Rise of Capitalism: A Historical Study* (New York: Harcourt, Brace and Company, 1926), ch. i.

deeply imbedded in European secular values. More accessible to nineteenth-century America, however, was the influence of sixteenth- and seventeenth-century Calvinism.[34] While it is true that Calvinism rejected the Catholic blanket indictment of interest, and in general produced a freer atmosphere for the pursuit of private gain, the Reformed churches never relinquished the view that economic activities must meet the same stern moral test as other human striving. There was, to be sure, no sin in money-making per se, but the pursuit of riches must be circumscribed by the same religious and moral safeguards that hedged about the other endeavors of men. Riches were unexceptionable if they reflected hard work and attention to duty; profits were not sinful if they resulted from fair dealing and an honest exchange of values. But gains arising from gambling, deceit, and sharp practice were abhorrent, and even windfalls representing mere good fortune, for which the beneficiary was not himself responsible, were tainted.

In short, Calvinism did not destroy the moral barriers that checked unbridled greed. It created instead a new urban-commercial ethic to suit a changed world. True, to the Calvinist commerce is no longer discreditable; the businessman is no longer a pariah. But an attempt is still made to tame the acquisitive drives, both by moral stewardship and by implanting the ideal of the Christian Tradesman—abstemious, diligent, morally fastidious, and above all, trustworthy. This change does represent adjustment to economic reality—neither Calvin nor the Geneva citizenry could accept a code that had sprung from a rural-hierarchical society—but it was not a simple surrender to expediency. Perhaps it is a mistake to assume that businessmen at this time expected complete economic freedom, but it is even

[34] The economic fastidiousness of Calvinism has not always been acknowledged in recent years. The work of Max Weber, Ernst Troeltsch, and R. H. Tawney and their disciples has left the impression that Calvinism rejected the church's moral oversight of economic affairs and encouraged laxity in business and financial dealings. Yet there is good evidence that the contrary was really the case. The most convenient source for the pros and cons of the Weber Thesis is Robert W. Green (ed.), *Protestantism and Capitalism: The Weber Thesis and Its Critics* (Boston: D. C. Heath and Company, 1959).

more of an error to assume that Calvin and his successors were merely accommodating the moral code to business needs.

While the precise influence of the Calvinist ethic on the course of capitalist apologetics is admittedly controversial, it is clear that the Geneva Reform at the very least encouraged a tendency to view the world of affairs in moral terms. Such a tendency was to embroil the "ascetic" Protestant churches of America in public issues from vaccination in colonial Boston, to the later struggle against the British tyrant, to the abolitionist crusade, to the Social Gospel Movement of the early twentieth century.[35]

It also left its mark on American financial controversy. From the late years of the seventeenth century on, the puritan clergy and laity took an extraordinary interest in financial matters.[36] The nagging colonial money problem produced a public fracas of major proportions, in which puritan divines generally saw the devil's hand in soft money schemes. At an early date the Congregational ministry denounced the depreciated bills of Connecticut and Massachusetts as the means of perpetrating a fraud on the public.[37] In 1724 the Reverend Joseph Sewall of Boston appealed to the Saints of the Bay Colony, in words that foreshadowed his successors of a century and a half later, to preserve the "Public Faith and Justice . . . relating to our Bills of Credit."[38] In a later generation the New England ministry referred to the Continental notes of the Revolutionary War as that "faithless, depre-

[35] See, for example: Perry Miller, *The New England Mind: From Colony to Province* (Cambridge: Harvard University Press, 1953), especially chs. xxi and xxiv; John R. Bodo, *The Protestant Clergy and Public Issues, 1812-1848* (Princeton: Princeton University Press, 1954), *passim;* Charles C. Cole, *The Social Ideas of the Northern Evangelists, 1826-1860* (New York: Columbia University Press, 1954), *passim;* Henry F. May, *Protestant Churches and Industrial America* (New York: Harper and Brothers, 1949), *passim.*

[36] E. A. J. Johnson, *American Economic Thought in the Seventeenth Century* (London: P. S. King and Son, Ltd., 1932), pp.

159ff.

[37] Joseph Dorfman, *The Economic Mind in American Civilization, 1606-1865* (New York: The Viking Press, 1946), i, 159.

[38] Miller, *op. cit.,* p. 314. Chapter xix of this work contains an extended discussion of the clerical attitude toward early Massachusetts money questions. Both Miller and Dorfman point out, it should be noted, that there were important exceptions to the prevailing hard money attitudes of the Bay Colony ministry. John Wise, for example, on this question as on so many others, was a dissenter, as was— more surprisingly—Cotton Mather, at least for a time. See *ibid.,* and Dorfman, *op. cit.,* i, 141, 147.

ciating currency."[39] In the Jacksonian period, with its complicating bank question, the Whiggish New England clergy did accept paper money, but only in the form of a conservative bank-note issue based on a large gold reserve.[40]

Given the heritage of Geneva and the conservative financial tradition of the American puritan clergy, the post-Civil War role of the Protestant churches, particularly those of Reformed affiliation, was almost preordained. In an era when a popular pulpit orator like Henry Ward Beecher could earn $20,000 a year by his writing and lectures alone, and a religious weekly like the New York *Independent* enjoyed a circulation of over 100,000—in such a pious age, the financial views of the clergy would be a powerful force for hard money.

Another ethical tradition—one still more venerable—competed with Calvinism for a hearing on financial matters. This credo was not primarily religious, however—or at least not primarily Protestant. It drew part of its ethical inspiration from the New Testament, much of its vocabulary from the Old. It perhaps owed something to evangelical, Arminian Protestantism as well.[41] It is, however, in the "Agrarian Myth,"[42] possibly as much pagan as Christian, that the opponents of specie payment found inspiration and emotional support.

[39] This was the phrase of the Reverend Joseph Huntington of Connecticut, *ibid.*, I, 214. Also, during the Critical Period, the Massachusetts General Court assailed the current paper issues on the familiar Calvinist grounds that they would corrupt morals. *Ibid.*, I, 268.

[40] These were the views, for example, of the Reverend John Bascom of Congregational Williams College and Francis Wayland of Baptist Brown. *Ibid.*, II, 753-754, 762-763, 765-766.

[41] The divergent political emphases of Arminian and predestinarian Protestantism in America are suggestive here. The Baptists and Methodists have been seen as Jeffersonians and Jacksonians; the Calvinists as Federalists and Whigs. See Russel Blaine Nye, *The Cultural Life of the New Nation, 1776-1830, The New American Nation Series* (New York: Harper and Brothers, Publishers, 1960), pp. 220-221. See also Daniel Bell, *The End of Ideology* (Glencoe, Illinois: The Free Press, 1960), pp. 103-104.

[42] I am borrowing this term—while recognizing a more fundamental debt as well—from Professor Richard Hofstadter. See his stimulating discussion of Agrarian values in *The Age of Reform: From Bryan to F. D. R.* (New York: Alfred A. Knopf, 1956), pp. 23-59. Hereafter when using "Agrarian" in the special sense of an ethic, I shall capitalize it to distinguish it from "agrarian" meaning pertaining to agriculture.

Perfected in its American version by Thomas Jefferson and John Taylor of Caroline,[43] the myth derived from an ancient tradition of the western world. From the first it had reference to a different social environment from Calvinism. The morality of Calvin was that of the urban, quasi-capitalist world of sixteenth-century Geneva; the Agrarian frame of reference was of course rustic, at least originally. Calvinist morality was the morality of the Christian businessman and emphasized sanctity of contract and the virtues of law, honor, and mutual trust. The Agrarian morality was that of the husbandman and laborer as well as the patrician romanticist and emphasized mercy and compassion.

While in its oldest version the myth was aristocratic and exalted the life of the landed gentleman, in America the yeoman was cast as the Agrarian hero. Independent and incorruptible, the small farmer was the repository of republican virtue and the hope of free government. In Jefferson's familiar words, "Cultivators of the earth are the most valuable citizens. They are the most vigorous, the most independent [*sic*], the most virtuous, and they are tied to their country and wedded to its liberty and interests by the most lasting bands."[44] The small freeholder also made a unique contribution to economic life. On his broad back rested the well-being of the nation, and his toil, wrote John Taylor, was the source "from which all classes . . . must derive their sustenance and prosperity."[45]

Though leadership passed from the Sage of Monticello and his epigoni to the rougher hands of the Tennessee border captain, Andrew Jackson, the Agrarian credo underwent little basic change. Jackson was an orthodox Jeffersonian, and the influence of Agrarian ideas in the administration that came to Washington in 1829 was profound.[46] Though the Jacksonian leaders were no

[43] Although Jefferson and Taylor were preceded in America by Benjamin Franklin and Jared Eliot in proclaiming the glories of the bucolic life. See Max Savelle, *Seeds of Liberty: The Genesis of the American Mind* (New York: Alfred A. Knopf, 1948), pp. 196-199.

[44] Jefferson to John Jay, Paris, Aug. 23, 1785, Julian P. Boyd (ed.), *The Papers of Thomas Jefferson* (Princeton: Princeton University Press, 1953), VIII, 426.

[45] Eugene Tenbroeck Mudge, *The Social Philosophy of John Taylor of Caroline* (New York: Columbia University Press, 1939), p. 156.

[46] For the Jeffersonian origin of most of Jackson's social and economic views see the following:

more simple farm folk than the Jeffersonians, they, too, talked of the special virtue of the yeomen and their role in preserving the Republic.[47] Like their forebears, they saw society resting on the broad base of agriculture, "the first and most important occupation of man."[48]

But the Jacksonians broadened the list of virtuous classes to embrace groups outside the charmed Jeffersonian circle—and in the process redefined Agrarianism. At the very least, they added the "mechanic." In men like Thomas Skidmore, George Henry Evans, Ely Moore, and William Leggett, leaders of the "Locofocos" or Anti-Monopoly Party of New York, the Jacksonians established links with the urban working class,[49] links which were to strengthen immeasurably the Jacksonian coalition. Jacksonians came to speak of the mechanic and artisan, and even the factory worker, in the same breath with farmer, and Jacksonians in New York, Massachusetts, and elsewhere came to defend the shorter work day and emerging trade-unionism.[50]

In time the Jacksonians created an Agrarian social ethic which exalted the "producing classes"—the yeomen, the wage earners, and, marginally, even the small businessmen.[51] Outside the fold,

---

Redlich, op. cit., part I, pp. 162ff.; Arthur M. Schlesinger, Jr., The Age of Jackson (Boston: Little, Brown & Co., 1946), ch. III and pp. 306-311; Charles Grier Sellers, "Banking and Politics in Jackson's Tennessee, 1817-1827," MVHR, XLI (June 1954), pp. 76ff.

[47] See Jackson's Fourth Annual Message, December 1832, in James D. Richardson (ed.), A Compilation of the Messages and Papers of the Presidents, 1789-1902 (n.p.: Bureau of National Literature and Art, 1903), II, 600. "The wealth and strength of a country are its population and the best part of that population are the cultivators of the soil."

[48] Ibid., II, 545. For a general discussion of the Agrarian philosophy of the Jacksonians see Marvin Meyers, The Jacksonian Persuasion, Politics and Belief (New York: Vintage Books, 1960), passim, but especially pp. 18-24.

[49] The most recent study of the New York "Workingmen" makes it clear, however, that the Locofoco leaders, as well as the rank and file were recruited largely from among skilled artisans and small tradesmen. Walter Hugins, Jacksonian Democracy and the Working Class, A Study of the New York Workingmen's Movement, 1829-1837 (Stanford, California: Stanford University Press, 1960), ch. v.

[50] Schlesinger, op. cit., ch. XXVI. I am not here claiming that labor necessarily supported Jackson, but that Jacksonians frequently supported labor.

[51] Hugins, op. cit., pp. 52-53, makes the point that the Jacksonian term "mechanic" meant small producers of all sorts, including small businessmen. See also Meyers, op. cit., p. 21.

generally, was the lawyer, sometimes the merchant, often the speculator and promoter, and always the money lender—the "capitalist," in the restricted usage of the day. The financier, who dealt in the pure manipulation of abstractions, was by far the greatest offender against the Agrarian order of virtue. Taylor and Jefferson had attacked the "Paper System" and the "stock jobbers," and had fought the Federalist attempt, as they saw it, to raise up a powerful financial interest—a "paper aristocracy." To the Jacksonians, the banks, and particularly the Second Bank of the United States, came to represent the whole power of evil in the Republic.

There was much rational self-interest in the Jacksonian polemic against banks. Western farmers, urban artisans, and those eager enterprisers and businessmen who made the Democratic party their home despite the unfriendly Jacksonian ideology, all correctly viewed the Bank as a real danger to their interests.[52] There was even something to be said for the charge that the institution was a threat to the Republic. President Nicholas Biddle, perhaps, was a public-spirited man, but the Bank's earlier mismanagement and its great wealth gave valid grounds for distrust.[53] With a large group of Jacksonians, however, hatred of the Bank—and often by extension the whole system of banks— was remarkably abstract. As one supporter of the General contemptuously remarked of the Second Bank, it had "never raised a single bushel of wheat, nor even a single head of cabbage nor a single pumpkin, potato or turnip during its whole existence, nor never will."[54] Banks, moreover, violated the often naïve economic prejudices of yeomen, mechanics, and untutored politicians alike: gold and silver—hard coin—alone were money.

---

[52] Bray Hammond, *Banks and Politics*, ch. XII.

[53] This conclusion seems to emerge clearly from a reading of even so strongly pro-Biddle a work as Thomas Payne Govan's *Nicholas Biddle: Nationalist and Public Banker, 1786-1844* (Chicago: University of Chicago Press, 1959). In the end Mr. Govan does not present a convincing case for Biddle's restraint after Jackson had removed the government's deposits

from the Bank. Moreover, as a state banker, following 1836, Biddle exhibited the sort of imprudence that underscores the frailty of the protection that the law actually gave the public against the Bank's abuse of power.

[54] Quoted in Harry E. Miller, *Banking Theories in the United States Before 1860* (Cambridge: Harvard University Press, 1927), p. 19.

Even men as knowing as William Gouge and Amos Kendall, Jackson's shrewd Kitchen Cabinet advisor, demanded an exclusive coin circulation.[55] Simpler minds, like Thomas Hart ("Bullion") Benton's, gave the precious metals a quality that was almost fetishistic.[56] Banks seemed to violate natural economic law by attempting to supersede the money that God had provided. They were economic engines with the sinister and even blasphemous power of creating money out of nothing.[57]

The Second Bank, "a monster," roared Benton, "vast, foul, and hideous to behold,"[58] eventually became the focus of many irrelevant fears. It was the most conspicuous national example of exclusive monopoly privilege. As such it incited the particular ire of groups like the New York Locofocos, to whom "Anti-Monopoly" was itself a symbolic assault on a generalized social evil.[59] Xenophobia also powered the anti-Bank movement. Jackson's Bank Veto message referred to foreign control of the economy as one of the more serious dangers growing out of the Bank's monopoly.[60] The xenophobia was only a special case of a more general imbalance that suffused the attack on the Bank. To men like Benton, Biddle became the personification of evil— "Old Nick" himself—who had marshalled the Rebel Angels to raise impious war in yeoman heaven. He, too, must be cast down to bottomless perdition before he destroyed the young Republic.[61] Ultimately, to Gouge, the banking system as a whole became "the *principal* cause of social evil in the United States."[62] Whatever the valid core of anxiety regarding bank power, it

[55] For Kendall see Walter B. Smith, *The Economic Aspects of the Second Bank of the United States* (Cambridge: Harvard University Press, 1953), pp. 6-8; on Gouge see his *A Short History of Paper Money and Banking in the United States . . .* (Philadelphia, 1833), p. 86, and Schlesinger, *op. cit.*, pp. 117-118.

[56] On Benton see Elbert B. Smith, *Magnificent Missourian: The Life of Thomas Hart Benton* (Philadelphia: J. B. Lippincott Co., 1958), pp. 119-120; William Nesbit Chambers, *Old Bullion Benton, Senator from the New West* (Boston: Little, Brown & Co., 1956), chs. ix and x.

[57] Meyers, *op. cit.*, p. 27.

[58] Elbert Smith, *op. cit.*, p. 177.

[59] Hugins, *op. cit.*, ch. viii. See also Jackson's Veto Message, Richardson, *op. cit.*, ii, 577.

[60] *Ibid.*, ii, 580-581.

[61] See Meyers, *op. cit.*, pp. 10-13, for the transcendent significance of the bank symbol for the Jacksonians.

[62] Gouge, *op. cit.*, p. 133.

tipped over into exaggerated, nameless fear that finally exhibited elements of paranoia.

Not all who called themselves Jacksonians accepted the whole package of Jacksonian dogma. As several writers have recently noted, many of Jackson's supporters were closer to the new aggressive thrust of business enterprise than to the bucolic past. These enterpriser-Democrats were not repelled by banks, although as state bankers, land speculators, and internal improvements promoters, they often disliked Biddle's conservative credit policies. They favored easy money, which at this time meant "free banking"—an expansible state banking system—and had little sympathy for Jackson's and Benton's simple-minded bullionism.[63] But they sometimes accepted the Jacksonian "producer," and particularly the anti-monopoly rhetoric, talking, as Bray Hammond remarks, "as if they were all back on the farm."[64]

But enterprisers in these years were not all Democrats. Indeed, more of them were Whigs, although not necessarily pro-Biddle Whigs. While there were important philosophical differences between the political parties, there was also a significant overlap on financial matters and social philosophy. Undoubtedly more Whigs supported the Bank of the United States than did Democrats, but there were a few Whigs who detested all banks and very many who wanted free banking rather than the more tightly controlled central bank favored by the national party leaders. In New York the Whigs were more enthusiastic about a general bank incorporation law than the Jackson men and were largely responsible for passing the famous Free Banking Act of 1838.[65] Henry C. Carey, the Whig economist of Philadelphia who was to play an imposing role in postwar monetary affairs, as early as 1838 advocated free banking under general incorporation laws to prevent the evils of money monopoly.[66]

[63] See Bray Hammond, *Banks and Politics*, ch. xii; Richard Hofstadter, *The American Political Tradition* (New York: Alfred A. Knopf, 1949), pp. 55ff.; Redlich, *op. cit.*, part i, pp. 171ff.

[64] Hammond, *Banks and Politics*, p. 329.

[65] Glyndon G. Van Deusen, "Some Aspects of Whig Thought and Theory in the Jacksonian Period," *AHR*, lxiii, No. 2 (January 1958), 314-315. See also Van Deusen, *The Jacksonian Era, 1828-1848, The New American Nation Series* (New York: Harper & Bros., Publishers, 1959), pp. 96-97.

[66] Henry Charles Carey, *Principles*

Nor was the glorifying of the "producer" purely Jacksonian. It must not be forgotten that Whigs and Democrats shared a Jeffersonian ancestry. Clay, John Quincy Adams, even Biddle himself, started as National Republicans, and the Whig "American System" had to appeal to the yeoman and the laborer as well as the manufacturer. Whigs like Carey condemned the money lenders and capitalists—the "middlemen" who "produce nothing and grow rich by standing between the producer and consumer." Carey even complained at times about great financial organizations capable of exerting "almost irresistible" influence on legislation.[67] Still, the Whig version of the producer ethic did differ from the Jacksonian enterpriser version. Whigs did not often fear bigness as such, and consistently included even the great manufacturers in the producer pantheon. There is no hint in Carey, for example, that there was any serious danger in corporate concentration—the "monopoly" that the Jacksonians so feared.[68]

Not only was the Whig social philosophy more inclusive, it was also more consistently business oriented. Although Whigs proved adept at manipulating for political ends the popular symbols of rural America,[69] with their profound respect for breeding and birth they never truly absorbed the popular spirit which remained the heart of Agrarianism. All told, the wellbeing of the producer was a marginal concern of the enterpriser element, whether Whig or Jacksonian—a clever, sometimes sincere, adaptation of powerful ideas for purposes very distant from those originally intended. Nor was the producer ethic the whole of Agrarianism, which contained at its heart an intense concern with saving free government and the small man from the concentrated and massive economic power of the "banks," the "money power," and the "bondholders."

Calvinism and Agrarianism between them framed the moral

of *Political Economy* (Philadelphia: Carey, Lea and Blanchard, 1837-1840), I, pp. 255ff.

[67] Quoted in George Winston Smith, *Henry C. Carey and American Sectional Conflict* (Albuquerque University of New Mexico Press, 1951), pp. 17-18.

[68] The fear of banking concentration seems to be a special case prompted by Carey's interest in cheap credit for the industrial interests whose spokesman he was.

[69] Most notably in the "Log Cabin-Hard Cider" Presidential campaign of 1840.

and emotional limits of the post-Civil War currency debate. But another set of ideas helped define the intellectual bounds of the discussion. These were the concepts that made up the body of economic doctrine.

It is easy to dismiss economic theory as learned rationalization, but in the context of the post-Civil War financial debate such contempt would be a mistake. Lord Keynes's famous dictum that "the ideas of economists and political philosophers, both when they are right and when they are wrong, are more powerful than is commonly understood," emphatically applies to the events of 1865-1879. The money question was an intellectual labyrinth that easily confused the untrained and the ill-informed. The man who attempted to thread its twists and turns without special knowledge risked finding himself hopelessly befuddled. "In the great diversity of opinion existing amongst minds equally educated," one private citizen complained, it was "difficult to know where the *right* is."[70] Ordinary folk might well lose their way in the tortuous problems of money, but even businessmen found themselves perplexed by the mysteries of gold premiums, refunding, hedging, and—eventually—mint ratios, seignorage charges, bimetallism, and remonetization. Under the circumstances the interested public—a remarkably large group for so abstruse a subject—turned to the "experts" for guidance. "We dabble in theories of our own," wrote one businessman, "and clutch convulsively at the doctrines of others; we discuss newspaper essays on the question and dissect the money articles of the day; and all to no purpose. From the vast tract of mire, by which the subject is surrounded, overlaid and besmeared, it is almost impossible to arrive at anything like a fair estimate of its real nature."[71]

As this man's plaint suggests, however, the public did not find in the writings of contemporary authorities—academic economists, professional financial writers, and self-trained amateurs— the clear formulas they sought. On the simplest matters the

[70] Crofts J. Wright to John Sherman, Chicago, Jan. 19, 1878, Sherman MSS, LC.

[71] This is from a column in the *Philadelphia Sunday Morning Times,* written by George W. Hewes and included in Hewes to Benjamin F. Butler, Philadelphia, April 11, 1868, Butler MSS, LC.

experts disagreed; even in defining "money" there was no consensus. Some writers held that only gold and silver coin, bank notes, and government paper that performed exchanges and passed from hand to hand functioned as money;[72] others said bank credit and deposits also qualified.[73] They disagreed, too, over the significance of the interest bearing debt, much of which circulated as money between interest paying periods.[74] From the point of view of a modern economist the whole financial discussion has an air of unreality, since it rested on a faulty understanding of what constituted money and how money affected prices. According to present figures, the actual per capita money stock, defined to include bank deposits, grew from $45 to $72 between 1869 and 1879.[75] Yet even the hard money men, whose case against further expansion would have been strengthened by the broadest definition of money, almost always failed to perceive this trend, or at least failed to use it against their opponents.[76] As far as the laity—the newspaper editors, the

[72] See Arthur Latham Perry to James A. Garfield [Williamstown, Mass.], May 30, 1868, Garfield MSS, LC; Robert W. Hughes, A Popular Treatise on the Currency Question, . . . from a Southern Point of View (New York, 1879), pp. 16-17.

[73] Lloyd W. Mints, A History of Banking Theory in Great Britain and the United States (Chicago: University of Chicago Press, 1945), p. 68; Harry Miller, op. cit., pp. 109-110, 120; Amasa Walker to James A. Garfield, North Brookfield, Mass., June 6, 1868, Garfield MSS; Nation, vi (Feb. 13, 1868), 125-126; Iron Age, v (Nov. 28, 1867); Charles H. Carroll to Benjamin F. Butler, West Newton, Mass., Nov. 22, 1867, Butler MSS. Mr. Bray Hammond has, I think, somewhat exaggerated the novelty of Charles Dunbar's sophisticated concept of money in the 1880's, though he is clearly right on his main point that not before the end of the century was the monetary character of bank deposits generally acknowledged. See Hammond, Banks and Politics, pp. 80, 189-190.

[74] Some of these short-term notes had attached interest coupons which were paid periodically. As the time for payment approached, they were withdrawn from circulation. After the interest had been collected they were once more used as money. See White, op. cit., pp. 115-116. Generally speaking, it was the soft money men, who in later years wished to emphasize the remorseless monetary contraction the nation had undergone in the immediate postwar period, who insisted that these notes had been part of the nation's money stock.

[75] See J. G. Gurley and E. S. Shaw, "Money," in Harris, op. cit., ch. i, p. 105, Table 1. A similar conclusion is reached by James K. Kindahl in his "The Economics of Resumption: The United States, 1865-1879" (unpublished doctoral dissertation, University of Chicago, 1958), Table v, p. 30.

[76] One reason for this was the "real bills" doctrine, which held that bank credit, unlike currency,

politicians, the businessmen, the ordinary middle-class citizen—were concerned, money was cash, and it was at this level that most of the debate was conducted.

The dispute over the definition of money divided the informed from the ignorant rather than the softs from the hards. But one difference over a theoretical point helped distinguish the two extreme currency views. From the outset, one group of soft money men accepted a financial doctrine which was, at its core, mercantilist. Money had been regarded by the sixteenth- and seventeenth-century mercantilists, as one modern student writes, as "not only the sinews of war and State, but of trade and commerce; it was the indispensible agency that stirred, quickened and moved merchandise, the *vena porta*, the chief vein of the body politic."[77] A plentiful supply of the precious metals, it was held, would not only stimulate spending, but also lower interest rates in the same way that increasing the supply of any commodity would reduce its price. What followed would be the economic flowering that early seventeenth-century political economists craved almost as much as modern rulers of "underdeveloped" lands.[78]

---

represented "instruments rising out of production and trade" which were liquidated when the loan was repaid. See, e.g., Henry Varnum Poor, *Resumption and the Silver Question...*(New York, 1878), pp. iii-iv. On the other hand, what are we to make of such illogic as represented in the views of A. A. Low, an aggressive hard money man, who acknowledged that "bank bills, credit and checks" exerted the same influence on prices as gold, and who then failed to see that the rapid growth of such "bank money" was far more inflationary than a few million extra of silver or greenbacks? Perhaps the answer is that the argument cut two ways. While the growth of bank money could be used to deny the need for greenback expansion, it could also be cited to demonstrate that fear of additional money was unwarranted, since at the very time bank credit was growing, prices

were in fact falling. In the end the whole discussion reveals how frequently the post-Civil War financial issue retreated from rational discourse into the area of emotion and even myth and symbol. For Low's views see United States Senate, 44 Congress, 2 session, *Report No. 703*, part 2, p. 178.

[77] M. Beer, *Early British Economics from the XIIIth to the Middle of the XVIIIth Century* (London: George Allen and Unwin, Ltd., 1938), p. 66. See also E. A. J. Johnson, *Predecessors of Adam Smith: The Growth of British Economic Thought* (New York: Prentice-Hall, 1937), p. 62.

[78] Douglas Vickers, *Studies in the Theory of Money, 1690-1776* (Philadelphia: Chilton Co., 1959), p. 168; Eli F. Heckscher, *Mercantilism* (Revised Edition; London: George Allen and Unwin, 1955), pp. 199ff.

One obvious way of increasing the money stock was to enlarge the supply of precious metals. From this flowed both the familiar mercantilist concern for a favorable trade balance and the quest for colonies. But the early experience of Italian, Dutch, and North German merchants and bankers suggested that banks could also augment the money supply,[79] and efforts were made to establish banks based on land or some sort of property. These mercantilist banks were seen as a source primarily of growth capital, not of credit for financing trade. Their *raison d'être* was long-term loans to enterprisers, developers, and the state, rather than short-term credit to merchants.[80]

This early soft money policy came under attack by the precursors of the Classical Economists, who shifted attention from the money stock, which they held to be only a lubricant of exchanges, to "real capital"—that is, capital goods. It was only by the painful accumulation of such real capital through saving that wealth and productive growth could be attained.[81] The idea that an increase in the money supply might lower interest rates and encourage the use of unemployed resources was dismissed as ignorant confusion.[82] All it would do, declared David Hume, the leading early exponent of the quantity theory of money, was to raise price levels and leave the economy where it had been before.[83]

Following the collapse of John Law's grandiose monetary schemes in the early eighteenth century, "real" capital doctrines were virtually unopposed in Europe. Then in the quarter century following the 1797 Bank of England suspension the dialogue revived.[84] It was during this exchange that David Ricardo gave final form to what was to be the "bullionist" approach to paper money. In his famous pamphlet of 1810, *The High Price of Bullion,* he argued that the gold premium on the paper pound, the existing inflated price levels, and the unfavorable exchange rate

[79] *Ibid.*, pp. 231-233.
[80] *Ibid.*, pp. 233ff.
[81] Vickers, *op. cit.*, pp. 91ff.
[82] Karl H. Niebyl, *Studies in the Classical Theories of Money* (New York: Columbia University Press, 1946), pp. 70-71.
[83] Johnson, *Predecessors of Adam Smith*, pp. 170ff.

[84] For the extensive literature generated by the suspension see Jacob Viner, *Studies in the Theory of International Trade* (New York: Harper and Bros., 1937), chs. III and IV.

that oppressed England were all produced by an excess of paper circulation. Only a contraction of the bank-note issue and a rapid return to cash payments could end these evils.[85] In a later work he reiterated Hume's view that "the rate of interest for money is totally independent of the nominal amount of the circulating medium" and was "regulated solely by the competition of capital, not consisting of money."[86]

Ricardo's views were the immediate source of orthodox nineteenth-century monetary and interest theory. His disciples, founders of the "Classical School"—above all John Stuart Mill—attacked the monetary doctrines of the mercantilists as they attacked their economic paternalism. They denied to money any significant role in economic growth. Money was a mere counter; it was not "capital." Increasing its quantity would only raise prices, leaving all other relationships, including interest, unaffected in the end.[87] On this side of the Atlantic the monetary teachings of the Classical Economists were carried, along with their laissez-faire, free trade doctrines, into the mainstream of orthodox academic economics.

Nevertheless, although repudiated in England by the middle of the century, mercantilist doctrines survived in America, which in its urgent need for growth capital so closely resembled sixteenth- and seventeenth-century Europe. The inspiration of much of the mercantilist banking theory of colonial and early national America was apparently the work of Sir James Steuart, whose *Inquiry into the Principles of Political Economy* appeared in 1767. Steuart's ideas regarding the nature and functions of banks were already old-fashioned in his day, but they suited American conditions and were widely disseminated during the early nineteenth century. Fritz Redlich, who ascribes great signif-

[85] Ricardo had little doubt that inflation was an unqualified evil and quoted Adam Smith extensively to that effect. See Piero Sraffa (ed.), *The Works and Correspondence of David Ricardo* (Cambridge [England] at the University Press, 1951), III, 95-99; Viner, *op. cit.*, pp. 119-136.

[86] Quoted by R. S. Sayers, "Ri-

cardo's Views on Monetary Questions," in T. S. Ashton and R. S. Sayers (eds.), *Papers in English Monetary History* (Oxford: at the Clarendon Press, 1953), p. 93.

[87] John Stuart Mill, *Principles of Political Economy* (London: Longmans, Green and Co., 1929), pp. 54ff. and 644ff.

icance to mercantilist thought in early American banking, writes that "in the minds of average citizens anywhere in Kentucky in 1810 or Illinois in 1825 or Michigan in 1835, the functions of banks were to overcome the scarcity of money. They were also supposed to finance capital formation, just as Steuart had expressed it: They melt down property for the encouragement of industry and for improvements of all sorts."[88] Redlich may be exaggerating the impact of these ideas, but among businessmen of the young nation mercantilist doctrines were to win wide and influential acceptance.

Calvinism and Agrarianism, Mercantilism and the Classical Economics—as well as the events of the War—were to be woven into the debate over Reconstruction finance. Men not only mouthed the rhetoric of these systems, they believed it. No doubt they often selected from the existing ideological stock only what they thought valuable, but generally their creed long antedated 1865 and supplied the ready-made means by which they ordered and interpreted their new situation. When it did not simply tell them what to believe, ideology often served the essential function of reassuring men united by prior interests. The men who listened were, often, not the uncommitted, but those desiring conviction. The relationships of received ideas and interest were frequently complex. In the remaining chapters these elaborate interconnections will be one of my major concerns.

[88] Fritz Redlich, "Mercantilist Thought and Early American Banking," *Essays in American Economic History* (n.p., 1944), *passim*, especially p. 117.

THE SOFT MONEY INTEREST

(1865-1870), PART I

FIVE days after his appointment as Secretary of the Treasury, in March 1865, Hugh McCulloch unobtrusively opened the Reconstruction financial battle. "My chief aim," he told his subordinates, who had gathered at the Treasury Building to meet their new chief, "will ... be to provide the means to discharge the claims upon the Treasury at the earliest date practicable, and to institute measures to bring the business of the country gradually back to the specie basis, a departure from which ... is no less damaging and demoralizing to the people than expensive to the government."[1] McCulloch followed this declaration by quietly funding a large block of interest bearing legal tenders, as well as other quasi-monetary notes.[2] But the Secretary felt his power under the existing laws too limited,[3] and at the earliest opportunity—his first *Annual Report* in December—he asked Congress for authority to retire the greenback issue as a first step toward resumption.[4]

Congress moved promptly. On December 18, by a vote of 144 to 6, the House passed a resolution by Representative John Alley of Massachusetts, pledging "cooperative action" with the Treasury in a "contraction of the currency with a view to as early a resumption of specie payments as the business interests of the country will permit."[5] After the Christmas recess, the Ways and Means Committee began to consider actual enabling

[1] *Banker's Magazine*, XIX (April 1865), 783.

[2] Robert T. Patterson, *Federal Debt-Management Policies, 1865-1879* (Durham: Duke University Press, 1954), p. 62.

[3] McCulloch to Manton Marble, Washington, Sept. 16, 1865, Marble MSS, LC.

[4] U.S. Treasury, *Annual Report of the Secretary of the Treasury on the State of the Finances for the Year 1865*, pp. 9-14.

[5] *Congressional Globe*, 39 Cong., 1 sess., p. 75.

legislation. Finally in April, although the mood of the nation had changed since the Alley Resolution and members now knew that deflation would be resisted, Congress passed the Contraction Act.[6]

The new law disappointed McCulloch,[7] who had hoped for a completely free hand in withdrawing greenback circulation.[8] While authorizing unlimited refunding of the interest bearing debt, the measure restricted the Secretary's power to withdraw United States notes to $10 million in the first six months following passage and not more than $4 million a month thereafter.[9] Nevertheless, McCulloch actively wielded his new authority, and through the remaining months of 1866 reduced greenbacks from their August 1865 maximum of slightly over $433 million to $399 million by October 1866.[10] He also continued to fund the quasi-monetary, interest bearing securities, and by October 31, 1866, $290 million of these—almost a third of the total—had been converted into long-term bonds.[11] All told, it is probable that even taking into account the large increase in bank deposits, the Treasury succeeded in contracting the country's money supply substantially during these months.[12]

[6] The story of the evolution of this bill—sometimes called the *Loan Act*, since it also authorized a new funding loan—is told in Robert P. Sharkey, *Money, Class, and Party: An Economic Study of Civil War and Reconstruction* (Baltimore: The Johns Hopkins Press, 1959), ch. II; and my "Men, Money, and Politics: The Specie Resumption Issue, 1865-1879" (unpublished Ph.D. dissertation, Columbia University, 1958), pp. 13-40.

[7] *NYT*, March 24, 1866.

[8] This power was actually granted the Secretary under the bill originally reported by the House Ways and Means Committee on Feb. 21, but owing to resistance it was withdrawn. See Unger, "Men, Money, and Politics," p. 33.

[9] For the text of the bill as finally enacted, see Charles Francis Dunbar, *Laws of the United States Relating to Currency, Finance and Banking from 1789 to 1896* (Boston: Ginn & Co., 1897), pp. 199-200.

[10] *CFC*, IV (Feb. 9, 1867), 64. Actually these figures are somewhat misleading, since a substantial part of this reduction included withdrawals from the $50 million of legal tenders held by the Treasury against temporary loan deposits. It is impossible to tell what proportion of these withdrawals actually came from the $400 million generally considered "authorized."

[11] U.S. Treasury, *Annual Report of the Secretary . . . for the Year 1866*, pp. 6-7.

[12] This is the informed conclusion of Professor Milton Friedman of the University of Chicago. Friedman, "Price, Income and Monetary Changes in Three Wartime Periods," *Papers and Proceedings of the Sixty-Fourth Annual Meeting of the American Economic Association* (1951), pp. 612-625.

Unfortunately for McCulloch these reductions coincided with a business recession set off by the Overend, Gurney failure in London, and through 1866 direct contraction met ever-stiffening resistance from businessmen, Agrarians, and the Administration's political opponents.[13] A number of times in 1867 the Secretary abstained from his permitted $4 million monthly withdrawal. Yet resistance to contraction, both in Congress and among important sectors of the public, grew rapidly, culminating in February 1868 in the repeal of the 1866 Act. By this time some $44 million of greenbacks had been retired.[14]

This victory of the soft money forces was followed, in a little over a year, by their defeat on the related issue of bond repayment. Even before the War ended, Copperhead Democrats had begun to grumble about the federal debt. After Appomattox, western Democrats, with Ohioans in the lead, began to demand that the 5-20 bonds be redeemed in greenbacks. In 1868 the national Democracy endorsed this "Ohio Idea," and in the Presidential campaign of that year made political capital of the bond repayment issue, particularly in the trans-Appalachian West. For a while, western Republicans retreated before the attack, temporizing or equivocating or simply surrendering outright to the "rag baby." Democratic defeat restored the confidence of the hard money men, and in March 1869 Congress passed the Public Credit Act, pledging the Treasury to redeem the 5-20's, principal and interest, in gold. Although this move did not end the agitation for greenback repayment, it made the greenbackers' task more difficult. Hereafter, the bondholders would have the positive support of law, and a Presidential veto would stand between the nation and "repudiation."

Very briefly, these are the political events that opened the postwar financial battle. The legislative thread stretching from the Contraction Act to the Public Credit Act has already been described elsewhere,[15] and there is little point in covering the ground again. The play of forces underlying these events does,

---

[13] On the Radical opposition to McCulloch's contraction see Unger, *op. cit.*, pp. 35-36, 54-56, 70-71, 371; Sharkey, *op. cit.*, pp. 77-78, 109-110, 279ff.

[14] Unger, *op. cit.*, chs. i and ii; Sharkey, *op. cit.*, chs. ii and iii.

[15] Most notably Sharkey, *op. cit.*, and my "Men, Money and Politics."

however, deserve a closer look, for it is at this point that the basic pattern of later financial conflict was set. The alignments of 1865-1870, in effect, form the base line from which to measure the whole succeeding struggle over the nation's financial future.

Pulling in the direction of soft money in these years was a heterogeneous group of businessmen, politicians, labor leaders, and Agrarians whose combined efforts ultimately thwarted the Treasury's contraction policy. Leading the anti-contractionist drive was a surprisingly large section of the business community. The worsening commercial picture soon after passage of the Contraction Act drove into the anti-resumption camp many businessmen who might not otherwise have resisted McCulloch's policy. Boot and shoe manufacturers, farm machinery producers, carriage makers, brokers, even merchants and bankers, joined the attack on the Contraction Act after April 1866,[16] and tipped the balance of forces that in these years normally immobilized Congress. It is obvious from the Congressional debates preceding repeal that leaders of the Republican majority, many of them influential Radicals, gave serious attention to the businessmen's cries of distress. George S. Boutwell, Thaddeus Stevens, John Sherman, William D. Kelly, Benjamin F. Butler, William Sprague, Oliver P. Morton, and others, from June 1866 to actual repeal in 1868 kept up a steady fire against contraction on the grounds that it would damage the nation's industrial interests.[17] With the exception of Boutwell and Morton, each of these men had close industrial contacts[18] and was highly sensi-

[16] See respectively, *Shoe and Leather Reporter*, xi (Dec. 26, 1867), 4; Whitely, Fassler, and Kelley to John Sherman, Springfield [Ohio?], Dec. 27, 1867, Sherman MSS, LC; N. G. Olds to John Sherman, Fort Wayne, Ind., Dec. 11, 1866, *ibid.*; G. S. Hubbard to James A. Garfield, Chicago, Jan. 10, 1867, Garfield MSS, LC; Unger, *op. cit.*, pp. 45-48.

[17] *Ibid.*, pp. 33ff., 67ff., 160ff.; Sharkey, *op. cit.*, ch. III.

[18] Boutwell was a professional politician but represented the textile city of Lowell and was apparently concerned about the possibility of unemployment among his constituents. Morton, although seemingly without close business affiliations, was highly sensitive to businessmen's fears. Sprague of Rhode Island was one of the largest cotton manufacturers of New England, and unlike most other Yankee cotton magnates, was also a speculator. Sherman of Ohio was a large investor in real estate and bank and railroad shares. Finally, Butler was a woolen manufacturer and was also involved for a while in bullish gold speculations.

tive to the fortunes and moods of manufacturers and business-men in general.

But this assault on McCulloch's policies, a product of the economic crisis, was not at the heart of business oriented soft money. Transcending day-to-day factors was a deep entrepreneurial concern for easy credit, reminiscent of Jackson's day. Growth and flux dominated American business in these post-Civil War years. The country was throbbing with energy and activity as it began the swift "drive to maturity." This was to be an era of magnificent economic fulfillment. In every productive index the nation would outstrip its past achievements. Before 1900 a third of a continent would be wrested from primeval wilderness and brought into the modern world economy. From the plains would spring great cities, with their bustle, dirt, and clatter. Giant factories would soon spew forth smoke and grime and endless streams of goods. By the new century modern industrial America would be born.

Much of this burgeoning occurred before 1880 and left its mark on the postwar money debate. Wherever zealous, enterprising, and aggressive men sought to ride the crest of the economic wave easy money sentiment flourished. Leading the rest were the "promoters"—men engaged in bold, chancy schemes for building railroads, platting cities and towns, and developing the nation's timber lands, its fertile prairies, and its mining resources. Often identified with western expansion, these men were betting on America's future economic greatness, and as they saw it, they had good reason to oppose a timid and conservative financial policy.

At the far edge of this group were men of reckless temperament whose expansionist views went beyond anything that even the most extreme Agrarians could endorse. Mark Twain caricatured such men in Beriah Sellers, the flamboyant promoter of the *Gilded Age*, who wanted the currency based on "everything," including pork, to encourage western "improvements." But for all his extravagance the Colonel had a real life counterpart in George Francis Train, a notorious economic adventurer, railroad speculator, crank, gadfly, and general disturber of the peace,[19] who at various times in the postwar decades demanded an immense new issue of greenbacks to help speed along the boom. "Give us greenbacks we say," he declared in 1867, "and build cities, plant corn, open coal mines, control railways, launch ships, grow cotton, establish factories, open gold and silver mines, erect rolling mills. . . . Carry my resolution and there is sunshine in the sky."[20]

Train's personal eccentricity—he would be giving public boxing exhibitions when he was in his seventies—makes it easy to dismiss his financial views. But the more stable men among the promoters and speculators—men like Jay Cooke and Richard Schell—spoke the same language. Cooke, of course, had been the Treasury's chief bond agent during the War and deplored anything that smacked of "repudiation." He feared, moreover, that an uncontrolled inflation would destroy federal credit[21] and in 1866 had helped lobby the Contraction Act through Congress.[22] By the late '60's, however, Cooke was caught up in a multitude of risky new ventures, ranging from life insurance to speculations in coal, iron, and timber lands, and was also involved in the western railroads that were finally to prove his undoing. "Regardless of what the immediate future held," remarks his biographer, "Jay Cooke was a bull on the longrun prospects of American business."[23] By 1869 he was proclaiming

[19] For Train's amazing career on three continents see Thornton Willis, *The Nine Lives of Citizen Train* (New York: Greenberg, 1948); and Clive Turnbull, *Bonanza: The Story of George Francis Train* (Melbourne, Australia: The Hawthorn Press, 1946).

[20] *Cincinnati Enquirer*, Aug. 17, 1867. See also *Iron Age*, v (June 24, 1868); vi (Oct. 8, 1868).

[21] Henrietta M. Larson, *Jay Cooke, Private Banker* (Cambridge: Harvard University Press, 1936), pp. 207-208; Herbert S. Schell, "Hugh McCulloch and the Treasury Department, 1865-1869," *MVHR*, xvii, No. 3 (December 1930), 411.

[22] The actual lobbying was done by his brother, Henry D. Cooke, who handled the Washington business of Jay Cooke and Company.

Henry was not primarily concerned with the greenback contraction feature of the measure, however. At this point the Cookes were refunding the short-term debt for the Treasury and regarded the bill as a necessary adjunct to their operations. See Henry Cooke to Jay Cooke, Washington, Dec. 6, 1865; Jan. 29, 1866; March 17, 1866; H. Fahnestock to J. Cooke, Washington, Jan. 25, 1866, Cooke MSS, Historical Society of Pennsylvania.

[23] N. S. B. Gras and Henrietta M. Larson, *Casebook in American Business History* (New York: Appleton-Century-Crofts, Inc., 1939), p. 302. For a general description of Cooke's expanding business promotions see Larson, *op. cit.*, pp. 238-253.

the virtues of a "currency expansion *moderate* but keeping pace with the new habits and enlarged area of Country." "Why," he asked, "should this Grand and Glorious Country be stunted and dwarfed—its activities chilled and its very life blood curdled by these miserable 'hard coin' theories—the musty theories of a by gone age—These men who are urging on premature resumption know nothing of the great & growing west which would grow twice as fast if it was not cramped for the means necessary to build RailRoads and improve farms and convey the produce to market."[24]

Richard Schell was more typical of the outright "speculators" whom monetary conservatives often blamed for the soft money agitation. Brother of August Schell, a prominent New York Democrat, Richard had entered Wall Street in the '40's, where he quickly made a fortune by stock manipulation. After the War, Schell, who was by now an "investor" in the nation's future as well as a stock gambler, aligned himself with the soft money group. In the '60's we find him writing Benjamin F. Butler that more currency was needed to bolster the enterprise of the country.[25] In 1874, following the collapse of the railroad boom, Schell was sent to Congress[26] and distinguished himself by advocating what seemed to his conservative associates an outrageous inflationist scheme. Essentially he favored a Keynesian spending program, financed by a huge issue of greenbacks, to stimulate economic recovery. If necessary, he told his astounded colleagues, he would have the government dig a canal from New York to San Francisco, financed by paper money.[27] Four years later, when he was in his seventieth year, he was still hitting at the

[24] Quoted in *ibid.*, pp. 205-206. I have used Miss Larson's version, slightly amended by one contained in the Treasury papers at the National Archives. For the latter see Jay Cooke to Henry D. Cooke, Philadelphia, Nov. 23, 1869, Treasury Dept., Misc. Letters Received by the Secretary (1869), No. 292, National Archives.

[25] Schell to Butler, New York, Nov. 18, 1867; Nov. 21, 1867; Dec. 18, 1869, Butler MSS, LC.

[26] This was to complete an un-finished term. Schell was not present during the financially important first session of the Forty-third Congress.

[27] *Congressional Record*, 45 Cong., 1 sess., pp. 625-626. This contains the remarks of merchant Simeon Chittenden of New York, reporting Schell's words of the previous session. Schell's observations must have been made in private to his fellow members, since there is no account of them in the *Record*.

gold standard. "I cannot get it through my head," he told a reporter, "that a great country like this should take for the basis of her wealth a commodity of which there are only eleven hundred millions worth in the world." Let the federal government pay off all state and local debts with greenbacks and spend several hundred millions on internal improvements in the South, and the country would blossom.[28]

Stock speculation and the railroad boom were only the most flamboyant examples of the postwar business explosion. The windfalls of a growing economy were shared by heavy industry, particularly by iron and steel. The mills, furnaces, and converters of Pennsylvania, Ohio, and Illinois measured the pace of the nation's spectacular economic burgeoning. Between 1860 and 1870 pig iron production doubled; in the following decade it doubled again.[29] In iron, change was superimposed on growth. Technologically, bituminous coke succeeded anthracite coal as the major ore reducing agent; geographically the industry's center moved from the Atlantic Coast to the trans-Appalachian West.[30] Still more remarkable was the booming steel industry. The first American Bessemer steel was produced in 1864;[31] by 1880 the United States produced as much as Britain.[32]

Westward migration and the replacement of old plant and equipment were enormously expensive and placed great burdens on the industry's resources. Between the censuses of 1860 and 1880 capital investment in iron and steel grew from $76 million to $231 million.[33] Unfortunately for the iron manufacturers these were also years of falling prices: the industry moved forward only against a strong deflationary current.[34] In April 1865 median

[28] AM, May 9, 1878.

[29] Compiled from U.S. Bureau of the Census, Eighth Census (1860), p. clxxviii; Compendium of the Ninth Census, p. 909; and Tenth Census (1880), "Statistics of the Iron and Steel Production of the United States," p. 7.

[30] James M. Swank, History of the Manufacture of Iron in All Ages . . . (Philadelphia: American Iron & Steel Association, 1892), p. 376; Frank W. Taussig, "The Iron Industry in the United States,"

Quarterly Journal of Economics, XIV (February 1900), 145-148.

[31] Swank, op. cit., p. 409.

[32] Ibid., p. 414. By 1880, 112 thousand tons of open hearth ingots were also being produced. Ibid., pp. 422ff.

[33] Compiled from U.S. Bureau of Census, Eighth Census (1860), pp. clxxviii-clxxxvii, cxcii (1880), "Statistics of the Iron and Steel Production of the United States," p. 2.

[34] It is interesting, however, that in recent years several economic

wholesale prices of 92 key commodities stood at 190 per cent of the 1860 figure. By April 1870 they were down to 140 per cent, and by April 1878 to 96 per cent. Iron prices declined still faster. Rolled bar averaged 181 per cent of 1860 prices in 1865. By 1876 it, too, had fallen below 1860 levels and touched 78 in 1878. Wages, however, remained relatively high in the metal trades,[35] making price declines particularly painful. Despite these trends, the iron industry was prosperous until 1873, but it was only by running very hard that the iron manufacturers kept up with falling prices and the huge capital outlays for new technology.

These difficulties may well have made the iron men receptive to economic panaceas, but they do not explain why they became noisy crusaders for soft money. Actually, falling commodity prices in the years between the War and 1880 were not the result of monetary contraction. The money supply, as we have seen, actually expanded from at least 1870 on. The long secular price decline that began in the 1860's probably resulted from the nineteenth-century production revolution, joined with the intense competition that relentlessly forced prices to follow declining costs.[36] As for the high interest rates that manufacturers allegedly paid, although there were doubtless special problems in the trans-Allegheny region, the overall trend in the period was steadily downward. By 1880 short-term commercial paper and call money rates, as well as long-term security yields, were considerably below those of 1860.[37] With the actual money

---

historians, under the influence of the Keynesian version of neo-mercantilism, have seen a moderate inflation as the best environment for capital growth. See, for example, E. J. Hamilton, "Prices as a Factor in Business Growth," *Journal of Economic History*, XII, No. 4 (Fall 1952), *passim*. For a modern dissent see David Felix, "Profit, Inflation and Industrial Growth," *Quarterly Journal of Economics*, LXX (August 1956), *passim*.

[35] These figures are derived from Wesley Clair Mitchell, *Gold, Prices, and Wages Under the Greenback Standard* (Berkeley: The University [of California] Press, 1908), pp. 23-24, Table 4, 374-375; 477-497, Appendix, Table 5.

[36] Like most questions concerning business cycles the reasons for the "Great Depression" are controversial. But see A. E. Musson, "The Great Depression in Britain, 1873-1896: A Reappraisal," *Journal of Economic History*, XIX, No. 2 (June 1959), 202-205.

[37] Peter B. Kenen, "A Statistical Survey of Basic Trends," in Seymour E. Harris (ed.), *American Economic History* (New York: McGraw-Hill Book Co., 1961), p. 83, Table 13.

supply constantly growing and interest rates falling, business consolidation, to end competition and maintain prices, would seem to have been a more promising avenue of relief for the industrialists than easy money. By 1900 they had indeed taken this road. That soft money seemed the answer before 1875 was not the result of obvious self-interest but largely the work of one of Keynes's "economic scribblers"—Henry C. Carey of Philadelphia.

We have already seen Carey as a social thinker who had bent the Jacksonian producer ethic to Whiggish ends. Son of an Irish-born social philosopher, he actually began his mature professional career as an economist in the free trade tradition of the Jeffersonians. By the 1840's, however, he had rejected the economic dogmas of free trade Democracy and had begun the quest for a system that would adapt economic wisdom to the circumstances of a "new" country.[38]

The essence of the "American School" of political economy that Carey created by 1850 was the harmony of all "producing" economic groups in America—agricultural, wage earning, and industrial. He denied the "wages fund" theory of the Classical Economists which pitted laborer against employer, and also questioned the relevance to America of Ricardian rent theory, which made a grasping villain of the landlord. In America, with its abundant land and untapped resources, there was a community of interest among all the producing classes,[39] and it followed that domestic industrial growth—which the patriotic Philadelphian saw as the country's most pressing need—was not in the

[38] The best brief description of Carey's pre-Civil War career and of his early economic thought is contained in Joseph Dorfman, *The Economic Mind in American Civilization, 1606-1865* (New York: The Viking Press, 1946), II, 789-805. More extended treatments can be found in Arnold W. Green, *Henry Charles Carey, Nineteenth Century Sociologist* (Philadelphia: University of Pennsylvania Press, 1951); Abraham D. Kaplan, *Henry Charles Carey: A Study in American Economic Thought* (Baltimore: Johns Hopkins University Press, 1931); and George Winston Smith, *Henry C. Carey and American Sectional Conflict* (Albuquerque: University of New Mexico Press, 1951).

[39] Henry Charles Carey, *The Harmony of Interests, Agricultural, Manufacturing and Commercial* (Philadelphia: H. C. Baird, 1890), pp. iii-iv. This is a reprint of the 1852 edition. William Elder, *A Memoir of Henry C. Carey* (Philadelphia: The American Iron & Steel Association, 1880), pp. 14-15.

interests of manufacturers alone. Like Hamilton before him, Carey argued that a protective tariff would benefit farmers and laborers as well as manufacturers, and confer a general boon on the nation.[40]

Carey's "harmony of interests" was a socially conservative doctrine, as befitted a major Whig thinker. It contained none of the Jacksonian passion for the economic underdog. It was business oriented at its center, not merely at its margins, elevating the manufacturers to the position of great national benefactors. But the Careyite philosophy paradoxically retained socially divisive overtones. There was still a social enemy. It was not the landlord, as in the Classical Economics, for in America sparse population and the empty West made rents low and spared the landowner from attack. The scarcity of capital, on the other hand, made interest high and directed Carey's fire against the "money lenders." This assault had a Jacksonian ring, but it was not Agrarian. The money lenders were primarily enemies not of the poor but of "productive" capital. The high cost of borrowing money, Carey wrote before the War, "causes a deduction from the profits of the trader, from the rents of houses, from the freight of ships. The owner of money, then, profits at the expense of all other capitalists."[41] In America, where land was plentiful and financial institutions rudimentary, the money lender was the chief danger to productive endeavor.

This attack on the money lender contains the germ of Carey's specific financial doctrines. Having rejected the Classical Economists' free trade dogmas, he also rejected their monetary and capital theories. In words that echo the doctrines of his seventeenth- and eighteenth-century mercantilist predecessors,[42] Carey

[40] Kaplan, *op. cit.*, pp. 44-45, 59.

[41] Henry C. Carey, *Principles of Social Science* (Philadelphia: J. B. Lippincott Co., 1888), II, 337. This is a reprint of the 1858 edition.

[42] So far as I can discover, Carey himself never acknowledged his debt to the mercantilist theoreticians, but this is understandable in light of their bad reputation in his day. The economist-statistician, Alexander Del Mar, however, who knew Carey in the '60's, ascribed the Philadelphian's monetary views to the Scottish historian-economist Archibald Alison, who, in his multi-volume *History of Europe from the French Revolution to 1815*, published in 1840, upheld the dissenting neo-mercantilist doctrine of interest and prices. See Del Mar, *Social Economist (Gunton's Magazine)*, IX (November 1895), 256-263. More conclusive, perhaps, Carey's nephew and disciple, Henry Carey Baird, was aware of his uncle's debt

declared money to be a part of "capital" and its scarcity the cause of high interest rates. In the American West, he noted, interest charges were prohibitive "because money—the thing for which alone interest is paid—is scarce."[43]

From this rejection of the Ricardian interest theory flowed Carey's faith in an abundant money stock as a stimulus to the economy. The very essence of prosperity, he believed, was the increase in "societary circulation." In the late 1850's, Carey described the quickening effects of enlarging the coin supply: "The larger the quantity of gold sent to the chief manufacturing centers of the earth the lower will be the rate of interest there— the greater will be the facilities for constructing new roads and mills—and the more rapid those exchanges from hand to hand which constitute commerce and for the making of which money is so absolutely indispensable."[44]

But as early as the 1840's he also recognized the identical effects of a highly developed banking system. Implicitly he accepted the mercantilist concept of banks as long-term lenders to industry, as well as short-term lenders to trade. As the wealth of a country grows, coin becomes increasingly less important, and banks and their note deposits take on the function of adding to the circulation. In New England, where banks were plentiful, money was abundant, interest rates low, and general prosperity prevailed.[45] As a good Whig, Carey supported the Bank of the United States against Jacksonian attacks,[46] but he was primarily

to the mercantilists. See Baird, *Political Economy* (Philadelphia: H. C. Baird & Co., 1888), *passim;* Baird, *Letters on the Crisis, the Currency and the Credit System* (Philadelphia, 1873), pp. 8ff.; Baird, *The Results of the Resumption of Specie Payments in England, 1819-1833* . . . (Philadelphia, 1874), *passim.* A more recent writer, Charles F. Dunbar, has observed that in his "theorizing as to money," Carey's "priority might be disputed by a series of writers from John Law down." See O. M. W. Sprague (ed.), *Economic Essays by Charles Franklin Dunbar* (New York: The Macmillan Co., 1904), p. 139. An immediate American predecessor of

Carey who may well have influenced his thinking was Alexander Hamilton, who held capital theories of the most unorthodox, mercantilist sort. See Broadus Mitchell, *Alexander Hamilton: The National Adventure, 1788-1804* (New York: The Macmillan Company, 1962), pp. 139ff.

[43] Carey, *Principles of Social Science,* II, 337-338.

[44] *Ibid.,* II, 325.

[45] Carey, *The Past, the Present, and the Future* (Philadelphia: Carey & Hart, 1848), pp. 158ff.

[46] Dorfman, *op. cit.,* II, 791. On Carey's Whig activities see George Winston Smith, *op. cit.,* ch. IV.

a free banker and was actually rather suspicious of money monopolies which could restrict circulation.[47] New England, with its virtually free banking, was a model of adequate societary circulation without excess.[48]

Carey gathered around him a distinguished band of followers, who helped disseminate his neo-mercantilist views. Several of these men—E. Peshine Smith, William Elder, and Stephen Colwell—were trained economists in their own right and before the War helped elaborate the monetary doctrines of the American School.[49] Colwell and Elder, along with Henry Carey Baird, Carey's nephew and intellectual heir,[50] became deeply involved in the postwar financial controversy. But Carey himself was to take the leading role in the postwar years in creating an intellectually respectable soft money philosophy. In February 1865 he began an assault on the doctrines of the bullionists that ended only with his death in 1879 at the age of 86. In the course of these fourteen years he wrote over twenty pamphlets—close to a thousand pages—devoted to the currency question, all reiterating with stubborn insistence the financial ideas which he had developed in his earlier works.[51]

Carey has recently been called one of America's most original economic thinkers,[52] but his contemporary influence was limited. His was always a dissenting voice, and he never won the regard of the academic community or the orthodox economic writers of his own day.[53] But if his appeal was restricted, it was nonethe-

[47] Carey, *Principles of Political Economy* (Philadelphia: Carey, Lea & Blanchard, 1837-1840), II, 254ff. See also Carey's attack on the Bank of England as a monopoly, *The Past, the Present, and the Future,* pp. 170-172.

[48] *Ibid.,* p. 163; *Principles of Political Economy,* II, 257ff. It is strange that in the late '30's Carey should choose New England rather than New York, where, in 1838, "free banking" was established by legislative enactment.

[49] On the "Carey-Colwell" school before the War see Dorfman, *op. cit.,* II, 805-826.

[50] The only source for Baird's

part in the postwar financial controversy is his own voluminous currency writings listed in the Bibliography. His later role is discussed below.

[51] A complete listing of Carey's works can be found in William Elder, *op. cit.,* pp. 37ff.

[52] See R. L. Bruckberger, *Image of America* (London: Longmans, Green and Co., 1959), ch. XVII.

[53] Green sees Carey's academic influence as reaching even to Harvard and Yale. But according to Kaplan, Carey's friend Rufus Griswold complained that the Philadelphian's works were "text books in the colleges even of Sweden and

less intense. By 1865 he had become the chief apologist and unchallenged intellectual spokesman for American heavy industry. His influence was particularly potent among the ironmasters, whose long fight for protection he had come to champion. Carey and Colwell were themselves iron manufacturers,[54] and at the Carey "Vespers"—evenings of talk on economics and politics washed down by good hock—men like ironmaster Joseph Wharton, railroad promoter Thomas A. Scott, manufacturers Robert Patterson and William Sellers, and publisher Henry C. Lea, absorbed the Carey financial philosophy.[55] From Wharton and other Philadelphia iron manufacturers neo-mercantilism spread to iron men throughout the country. Daniel Morrell of the Cambria Iron Works and Eber B. Ward, a pioneer western ironmaster, were in close touch with Carey. Morrell, whose iron works at Johnstown were the largest in the country, served two terms in Congress between 1867 and 1871, where he regaled his colleagues with the Carey philosophy.[56] Ward, president of the Iron and Steel Association in the late '60's,[57] was also a disciple and used his great wealth to finance distribution of the Master's monetary writings.[58]

Norway, while at the University, on the street next door to that which the author has his residence [i.e., the University of Pennsylvania], books are adopted, composed of ideas from imperial and nearly dissolute systems [i.e., The works of the Classical Economists]." See Green, *op. cit.*, p. 177; and Kaplan, pp. 52 and 59. The Careyites in turn were quite openly contemptuous of their orthodox opponents. See Elder, *op. cit.*, pp. 5-6; Baird, *Political Economy, passim.*

[54] For Colwell, see Dorfman, *op. cit.*, ii, 812; Herbert Ronald Ferleger, *David A. Wells and the American Revenue System, 1865-1870* (New York: n.p., 1942), pp. 27-28. In 1864 Carey's business interests included investments in coal lands in Schuylkill County, in a coal and iron company, and in Philadelphia real estate. See Smith, *op. cit.*, p. 14.

[55] For the Carey Vespers see

ibid., pp. 114-115; Alexander Del Mar, "Henry C. Carey's Round Table," *Gunton's Magazine*, xiii (August 1897), 99ff.

[56] For Morrell's soft money views in Congress see below, this chapter. For Carey's influence on Morrell's financial views see Morrell to Carey, Johnstown, Pa., Sept. 21, 1869; Washington, Feb. 18, 1871, Carey MSS, Historical Society of Pennsylvania.

[57] For a brief account of Ward's career see the obituary in the *CDT*, Jan. 6, 1875; and Fritz Redlich, *History of American Business Leaders, A Series of Studies* (Ann Arbor, Michigan: Edwards Bros., 1940), i, 95-96.

[58] See G. B. Stebbins to H. C. Carey, Rochester, N. Y., June 24, 1867; E. B. Ward to Carey, Detroit, Dec. 22, 1868, Carey MSS. There are many other Ward letters in the Carey papers.

Serving as sounding boards for the Carey coterie were several manufacturers' trade associations. The American Industrial League, launched in 1867, was one of these. The League ostensibly represented all sectors of industry and all sections of the country. Its first president was Peter Cooper, the New York ironmaster and railroad promoter; Ward, a westerner, was a prominent early sponsor. At the outset it included state leagues in New York, Ohio, and Michigan, as well as Pennsylvania.[59] But it is evident that it was inspired by a small group of Carey's Philadelphia disciples,[60] and from the beginning, Carey's influence was dominant. The first issue of the League's paper, the *National American*, contained several articles by William Elder,[61] and in 1867 and 1868 the League, too, aided in the national distribution of Carey's currency pamphlets.[62] By 1868 the national body was moribund, and the role of spokesman for the manufacturers had been assumed by a vigorous Pennsylvania League[63]—an organization that was even more clearly a vehicle for Carey's views. In 1870 Morrell was president of the body, Wharton, Lea, and Sellers composed the executive subcommittee, while Colwell was a prominent member of the Representative Council.[64] Through the '70's the Pennsylvania Industrial League, claiming to speak for the manufacturers of the nation, disseminated the money philosophy of the American School among an influential section of the business public.[65]

The Iron and Steel Association,[66] with its semi-official publi-

[59] For the early history of the League see Ida M. Tarbell, *The Tariff in Our Times* (New York: The Macmillan Co., 1911), p. 86; *Iron Age*, iv (May 23, 1867); v (Sept. 26, 1867); v (Nov. 21, 1867); *The League*, No. 1 (June 1867), p. 1; No. 3 (August 1867), p. 25.

[60] Joanna Wharton Lippincott, *Biographical Memoranda Concerning Joseph Wharton, 1826-1909* (Philadelphia: Printed for Private Circulation by J. B. Lippincott Company, 1909), pp. 44-45.

[61] *Iron Age*, v (Oct. 10, 1867). Unfortunately there does not seem to be a surviving run of the *National American* itself.

[62] G. B. Stebbins to Carey, Rochester, N. Y., June 24, 1867; E. B. Ward to Carey, Detroit, Dec. 22, 1868, Carey MSS; and *Iron Age*, v (April 16, 1868).

[63] A. T. Volwiler, "Tariff Strategy and Propaganda in the United States, 1887-1888," *AHR*, xxxvi, No. 2 (Jan. 1931), 76, n. 2.

[64] *Industrial Bulletin*, i (August 1, 1870).

[65] Primarily through its publication, the *Industrial Bulletin*.

[66] Founded in 1864, the Association, until 1874, shared the role of representing the ironmasters with the National Association of Iron

cation, *Iron Age,* was yet another Carey forum. Carey was a frequent guest at Association meetings.[67] Along with Elder, Colwell, and Smith, he was a "special contributor" to the *Age* in the 1860's, and although with time his direct contribution declined, his influence on the paper's editorial policy continued well into the following decade.[68] John Williams, editor of *Iron Age,* was a Carey disciple[69] and treated his mentor's writings as the Bible of the trade and an absolute guide to economic wisdom.

But the chief instrument for transmitting Carey's ideas to the iron men, the politicians, and the general public in the postwar years was his and his disciples' voluminous output of broadsides, pamphlets, and public letters. The theme running through all these publications, as through the prewar writings of the American School, was the vitalizing effect of easy money on an economy suffering from stagnation. In his postwar works Carey simply adapted neo-mercantilist principles to the country's experiences since 1861. The War was cited as proof that abundant money was the great engine of economic progress. On the day of Lincoln's inauguration the country was paralyzed, Carey explained. Millions were unemployed, factories were silent, business stagnant, the Treasury empty. Men wanted to pay their debts, to work, and to employ labor, yet all economic activities shrank "as the societary circulation became more and more impeded." With the appearance of the greenbacks all this changed. Factories started up, trade became brisk, agriculture prospered, men were soon busy working and earning good wages.[70] Perhaps paper money did produce "speculation," Carey admitted, but what was speculation? Every useful man in the country was a speculator in some sense. Every employer of capital was spec-

---

Manufacturers and the American Pig Iron Manufacturers Association. See *Iron Age,* xiii (Feb. 12, 1874).

[67] Robert Lamborn to H. C. Carey, Philadelphia, May 13, 1865; James M. Cooper to Carey, Pittsburgh, Dec. 11, 1865, Carey MSS.

[68] *Iron Age,* v (June 25, 1868). Specifically a soft money article by Carey will be found in *ibid.,* v (Nov. 7, 1867).

[69] Williams, editor of the *Hard-*

ware Reporter during the War, had been a force behind the American Emigrant Company scheme to import contract labor for northern factories. He had, as a result, been thrown into contact with Carey, whose aid he solicited. See Smith, *op. cit.,* p. 105.

[70] Carey, *The Currency Question: Letters to the Hon. Schuyler Colfax* (Chicago, 1865), pp. 1-5.

ulating for a rise—"farmers, laborers, mechanics, manufacturers, road makers and others." Indeed, we owed to these speculators the country's extraordinary increase in wealth and the great expansion of its railroads, mills, oil wells, and mines.[71]

The Careyites welcomed the wartime greenbacks, but at least until the 1870's they held banks and their issues in greater esteem as sources of societary circulation. Elder scolded greenbackers for working to destroy the national banking system.[72] Colwell was an early supporter of the national banks.[73] Carey, too, regarded banks as necessary institutions,[74] though he complained bitterly of their concentration in New England and New York.[75] This grievance was widespread and would become the basis of later efforts to extend the system by "free banking."

Needless to say, the Carey group fought contraction and resumption from the beginning. Even before McCulloch took office, Carey warned that any contraction would prove disastrous.[76] McCulloch's address to the Treasury employees produced an immediate retort from the Philadelphian, who charged that the Treasury's policy would destroy the country's manufacturers. Despite reassurances from the Secretary that his "apprehensions" were "without reasonable foundation,"[77] Carey persisted. In 1866 he published another warning against the contraction folly[78] and before 1870 had written at least five other polemical works against resumption.[79] Colwell, too, as a dissent-

---

[71] Carey, *Contraction or Expansion? Repudiation or Resumption? Letters to the Honorable Hugh McCulloch, Secretary of the Treasury* (Philadelphia, 1866), pp. 23-24. Elder, too, defended monetary abundance. "The evils of a depreciated currency," he wrote in 1871, "when admitted to the full, are as nothing to the lack of a money supply that keeps productive industry active." See Elder, *Questions of the Day, Economic and Social* (Philadelphia: Henry Carey Baird, 1871), pp. 137, 153-156.

[72] *Ibid.*, pp. 153-154.

[73] Stephen Colwell, *Remarks on Gold, Banks and Taxation* (Philadelphia, 1864), pp. 16-17. As a member, along with David Wells, of President Andrew Johnson's Revenue Commission, Colwell used his official position to propagate soft money ideas. See Ferleger, *op. cit.*, pp. 93-94.

[74] Carey, *The Finance Minister, the Currency, and the Public Debt* (Washington, 1868), pp. 13-14.

[75] *Ibid.*, pp. 5-10.

[76] Carey, *The Currency Question*, p. 38.

[77] *Banker's Magazine*, XIX (May 1865), 916-918. See also Hugh McCulloch to Manton Marble, Washington, May 4, 1865, Marble MSS.

[78] Carey, *Contraction or Expansion?, passim.*

[79] *Reconstruction: Industrial, Financial and Political. Letters to the Hon. Henry Wilson* (Philadelphia,

ing member of Johnson's Revenue Commission, attacked contraction, a "remedy . . . vastly worse than the disease," which if continued would "inflict upon individuals . . . a loss of thousands of millions, besides crippling trade and industry and seriously lessening the national revenue for many years."[80] Other members of the Carey circle, Elder, E. Peshine Smith, and Henry Carey Baird also opposed specie payments.[81] All told, Carey and his disciples succeeded in these years in producing a coherent alternative to the hard money orthodoxy, one that was to prove indispensable to the anti-resumptionist forces.

While it is always difficult to establish the connections between ideas and action, the line between Carey's doctrines and the beliefs of much of the industrial community is unusually clear. Iron men wrote Carey that his writings had ended their blind gropings and brought "consoling" certitude.[82] Their complaints against hard money monotonously echoed Carey's neo-mercantilist teachings. Interest rates were high because currency was "not equal to a healthy demand," declared one Pennsylvanian.[83] Eber Ward maintained that western ironmasters paid 12 per cent because "the steady increase of business of various kinds has largely outgrown the amount of currency that the government has furnished us."[84] John Williams of *Iron Age* lifted whole pages from Carey's work to prove that currency abundance "stimulates, promotes and assists the *production* that meets . . . ever enlarged wants, and is thus far from being mere

---

1867); *The Finance Minister; Resumption! How it May Profitably Be Brought About* (Philadelphia, 1869); *Shall We Have Peace? Peace Financial and Peace Political. Letters to the President Elect of the United States* (Philadelphia, 1869); *Review . . . of the Report of the Honorable David A. Wells* (Philadelphia, 1870).

[80] *Washington Daily Morning Chronicle,* Feb. 18, 1867.

[81] For Elder see *Questions of the Day,* especially p. 146; for Smith see Smith to Carey, Washington, Nov. 24, 1865 and Feb. 4, 1866, Carey MSS; for Baird, during this early period, see Baird to James A.

Garfield, Philadelphia, April 13, 1870, Garfield MSS.

[82] See Seyfert, McManus & Co., "Reading Iron Works, Scott Foundry and Steel Forge," to Carey, Reading, Pa., Feb. 15, 1866, Carey MSS.

[83] Alfred Gilman to Benjamin F. Butler, Philadelphia, Dec. 13, 1867, Butler MSS. See also John McManus to Thaddeus Stevens, Reading, Pa., January 2, 1866, Stevens MSS, LC. McManus was a proprietor of the Seyfert, McManus & Co. mentioned in the preceding note.

[84] U.S. House of Representatives, *Report No. 328,* 43 Cong., 2 sess., pp. 124-126.

dead capital, . . . a counter . . . of the value of other things."
A short supply raised interest rates and depressed business and
enterprise. Those who failed to see this relationship were enslaved by the foreign dogmas of John Stuart Mill.[85]

It has been argued recently that the tariff was the key to the
industrialists' fear of resumption.[86] In this view Carey is reduced
to a spokesman for the immediate economic anxieties of the
business community. It is true that a falling gold premium hurt
domestic manufacturers. Foreign goods were bought with gold
or its equivalent in exchange on gold standard nations. A drop
in the gold premium, accordingly, made foreign wares cheaper
in greenbacks and improved the competitive position of imported
goods on the American market. Carey himself pointed out that
the gold premium acted as a duty.[87] Ironmasters, moreover, were
obviously disturbed after 1865 by the influx of English plates,
rails, and castings that accompanied the fall in gold.[88] It is also
true that many advocates of protection were soft money men,
while many free traders were hard.[89] But none of this warrants
viewing the tariff effect of a high gold premium as the chief
lure which drew manufacturers into the soft money camp.
Among the ironmasters, at least, the concern with the tariff-
lowering effect of falling gold was marginal. If they talked about
it, it was often only as another argument for compensatory new
iron duties.[90] While many favored an expanded banking system,
it should be noted that few industrialists, at least before 1873,
advocated the greenback expansion which alone could have
restored the gold premium and its incidental tariff effect. Ultimately, the tariff effect argument loses sight of the larger issue
of growth and expansion in the pulsing, vital years of post-
bellum America. Soft money became the hallmark of industrialists, promoters, and speculators because they believed it would
encourage continued economic buoyancy and meet the needs of
a capital-scarce nation.

[85] *Iron Age,* VII (March 17, 1870).

[86] See Sharkey, *op. cit.,* ch. IV,
especially p. 165.

[87] Carey, *The Currency Question,*
p. 33; *Reconstruction: Industrial,
Financial, and Political,* p. 23.

[88] Unger, *op. cit.,* pp. 49-50.

[89] *Ibid.,* pp. 51-52.

[90] See National Commercial Convention, *Proceedings of the ... Convention Held in Boston* (1868), p.
46. E. Peshine Smith to H. C.
Carey, Washington, Nov. 24, 1865,
Carey MSS.

This conclusion seems once more to make enlightened self-interest the essence of the business version of soft money. But such an assumption is at best a misleading half-truth, for rising prices and easy money are not essential to industrial growth. That manufacturers, promoters, and speculators in this period often thought they were, was not the result of simple observation but must be credited to the teachings of neo-mercantilism and, particularly, to the efforts of the Philadelphia sage.

II

A few businessmen—Schell and Train, for example—were greenback expansionists. But most soft money businessmen, as I have suggested, placed their trust in a system of banking that could be expanded to meet business needs. These men were suspicious of the "Ohio Idea," with its alleged endorsement of unlimited federal printing press money, and called its supporters "repudiators"—a harsh epithet in those years.[91] They also had little of the Agrarian distaste for bankers and found the national banking system a perfectly acceptable instrument for achieving their ends. This disagreement over the banking system, until time homogenized the soft money interest in the late '70's, was an important point of distinction between Agrarian and business versions of financial dissent.

Not that the national banking system as originally established was particularly well suited to the needs of soft money businessmen. For the promoters and the ironmasters associated with trans-Allegheny enterprise, a total note issue limited to $300 million—disproportionately allotted to New York and New England[92]—clearly was inadequate. To businessmen west of the Hudson, the safe and sensible approach to easy money, free of repudiationist taint, was to modify and liberalize the system,

[91] Jay Cooke to Henry Cooke, Philadelphia, July 17, 1868, telegram in the William E. Chandler MSS, LC; *Iron Age*, v (Sept. 26, 1867); and v (Oct. 10, 1867).

[92] In April 1866, per capita banknote circulation in Massachusetts was $52, in Rhode Island $77, in Connecticut $42, and in New York almost $20. By contrast, Ohio had $8.15, Indiana $8.32, and Illinois $5.87. Even Pennsylvania had only $14, and the far West and South had far less than any other part of the country. U.S. Senate, *Miscellaneous Document No. 100*, 39 Cong., 1 sess., p. 10.

rather than abolish it. Even businessmen who urged revision of the federal banking laws were not entirely agreed, however, on the amount of patching and mending that would be necessary. The most conservative elements held that a circulation shift from the Northeast to the South and West within the existing note limit, or alternatively, a bank-note increase tied to some proportional greenback withdrawal, would be sufficient. Radicals, although willing to support simple redistribution, preferred what was, by analogy with the 1838 New York measure, often called "free banking"—and free banking commenced before resumption. This meant ending all bank-note limitation, making note expansion as free as deposit expansion, and, in effect, permitting free entry of new capital into the banking business, either through new institutions or through expanded old ones. Even this "radical" position, while expansionist, was not necessarily inflationary in the eyes of its proponents. The banking system, many believed, could not expand beyond the wants of trade, since an excessive note issue would be unprofitable for the banks.[93] There were free banking men who really wanted price inflation without the stigma, but many of the free bankers sincerely opposed a large increase in the total note issue. Even many sound money men were willing to accept unlimited bank-note circulation *after* resumption, believing that when notes were tied to gold[94] there could be no overissue.

As in so much else concerning post-Civil War finance, there is a fanciful quality to the free banking discussion. At the very time that businessmen were shouting the loudest for more bank-notes, "check money" was becoming the common instrument of commerce.[95] Later, when free banking was enacted, it had very little effect in expanding note issue. Few contemporaries, as we have noted, observed or understood the new importance of deposits, however, and important sectors of the business community took the shortage of bank-notes seriously.

[93] See the remarks of Senator Cornelius Cole of California, *Congressional Globe*, 40 Cong., 2 sess., p. 3151.

[94] Bank-notes were payable on demand in legal tenders and thus, after resumption, would also be in-directly redeemable in gold.

[95] See Staff, Board of Governors of the Federal Reserve System, *Banking Studies*, p. 417, for the more rapid growth of bank deposits than notes.

The manufacturers were particularly concerned with the problem. Carey had been among the first to point to the over-concentration of banks and their notes in the region east of the Hudson, and his business disciples soon picked up the lead. *Iron Age* applauded bank expansion, especially for the South and West;[96] *American Manufacturer*, spokesman for the trans-Allegheny industrial interests, similarly endorsed free banking, claiming it would provide the elasticity needed for the growth of trade and manufacturing.[97] Daniel Morrell in 1869 and again in 1870 introduced a free banking measure in Congress, for the purpose of making "money cheap and plentiful."[98]

There was also support for unlimited note issue among industrialists outside the Carey orbit. The first meeting of the National Manufacturers' Association in May 1867 demanded that the "privileges and benefits" of the National Banking Acts be extended "to the end that banking facilities and bank circulation may be equalized in all States and Territories to meet the business necessities indicated by the natural and unerring law of supply and demand."[99] A similar resolution was adopted in 1868,[100] while the following December a committee of the Detroit Manufacturers' Association recommended an additional $200 million of bank capital to be offset by a corresponding contraction of greenbacks.[101]

The support of the Pennsylvania industrial interests suggests an intersectional following for free banking. But Pittsburgh was really "western" in its outlook, sharing the western sense of monetary deprivation, and Pennsylvania as a whole generally responded like Ohio and Indiana on financial matters. Even more than the industrialists, the commercial interests divided along sectional lines on the bank question. At the 1868 National

[96] *Iron Age*, v (Sept. 27, 1867).
[97] *American Manufacturer*, XIII (Sept. 18, 1873), 11.
[98] *Congressional Globe*, 41 Cong., 2 sess., Appendix, pp. 142-144. For the 1869 instance see *Iron Age*, VII (Dec. 16, 1869).
[99] See the printed brochure in the Thomas Jenckes MSS, LC, enclosed in G. B. Stephens to the manufacturers and businessmen of Rhode Island, Detroit, Nov. 13, 1868. This item was called to my attention by Professor Ari Hoogenboom of Pennsylvania State University.
[100] *NYDT*, June 4, 1868.
[101] Quoted in D. M. Richardson, *Policy of Finance: A Plan for Returning to Specie Payments, without Financial Revulsion* (Detroit, 1869), pp. 3-6.

Commercial Convention when delegates from Detroit and Chicago—including Moses Field, a future greenback leader—tried to win endorsement for free banking, they were assailed by William Endicott and Edward Atkinson of the Boston Board of Trade, who rejected free banking without a one-for-one greenback contraction.[102] In the end the motion was voted down by a large majority.[103]

The sectional split also extended to the country's bankers. With the nature of check money little understood, particularly in the West,[104] bank loans and, consequently, bank profits seemed to be limited by the available note issue. After 1866 the circulation apparently needed to increase the loan facilities of established banks or, of course, to found new institutions, had all been distributed. There were always a few unclaimed notes, the result of bank failures or voluntary surrenders, and a ready market existed for this circulation.[105] But buying bank notes at a premium was indeed paying "blood money," as one Kansas banker described it,[106] and western bankers agitated for Congressional action to end the note famine.[107]

[102] Among the Easterners present, only George Buzby of the Philadelphia Board of Trade can be identified as supporting the resolution. It is significant that Buzby, although a grain and flour merchant, was among the small circle of Philadelphians who were present at the Pennsylvania Historical Society meeting in the late '70's at which William Elder eulogized the recently deceased Carey. See Elder, *A Memoir of Henry C. Carey*, p. 3.

[103] National Commercial Convention, *Proceedings*, pp. 144-145, 170, 184-185, 189-191. Actually neither Atkinson nor Endicott was as friendly toward free banking as his position at the convention suggested. Endicott was willing to accept redistribution of bank notes from the East, but he opposed "any further increase of currency." Atkinson thought free banking under any conditions would overburden the Treasury, which was the ultimate guarantor for the bank notes. See

W. Endicott, Jr., to James A. Garfield, Boston, March 31, 1869; Edward Atkinson to Garfield, Boston, Jan. 23, 1869, Garfield MSS. For a full description of this convention see ch. IV.

[104] As a means of payment, even as late as 1881, checks were less widely used than cash in the newer states; while in the territories and California, cash—coin at this time—completely dominated the picture. See *Annual Report of the Comptroller of the Currency to the First Session of the Forty-Seventh Congress*, pp. xvi-xvii.

[105] George LaVerne Anderson, "The National Banking System: A Sectional Institution" (unpublished Ph.D. dissertation, University of Illinois, 1933), pp. 131-133. Professor Anderson's fine study still stands as the definitive work in its field.

[106] *Ibid.*, p. 131.

[107] See James M. Clymonds to James A. Garfield, Cleveland, March 13, 1869 and May 14, 1870; I. Irv-

Again Pennsylvania upheld the western position[108] but it was generally opposed, at least before resumption, by the financial men of New York and New England. In the metropolis it was believed that a free banking law would "authorize the creation of machines for grinding out circulating notes, for the use of Wall Street operations, and not for the benefit of the trading community, or the promotion of any legitimate business interest."[109] If anything, State Street was even more hostile to an expanded bank-note issue than Wall Street. In March 1869 a group of Boston bank officials, hoping to protect their own circulation, endorsed additional issues for the South and West. This was not an endorsement of inflationist principles. Nevertheless, it provoked a quick reaction among the rest of the Boston banking fraternity who immediately repudiated the statement. As Atkinson explained, it expressed the views of only a few bankers who had more than their just share of circulation and knew they would be compelled to disgorge notes under any redistribution scheme.[110]

Still, even conservative eastern financiers were willing to concede free banking after resumption. Elbridge Gerry Spaulding, the Buffalo banker-Congressman who had formally sponsored the Legal Tender Act, agreed that "as soon as specie payments

---

ing Brooks to Garfield, Salem, Ohio, Jan. 26, 1870, Garfield MSS; Henry Kuhn to Senator Samuel Pomeroy, and F. W. Waller to Lyman Trumbull, both quoted in Anderson, *op. cit.*, pp. 327-328, and p. 192, n. 17, respectively.

[108] See George A. Berry, President of the Citizen's National Bank of Pittsburgh, to Garfield, Pittsburgh, Jan. 13, 1870; J. T. Phillips, President of the First National Bank of New Castle to Garfield, New Castle, Pa., Nov. 25, 1873, Garfield MSS. In New York Henry Clews, a soft money private banker, also favored free banking. See Clews, *Our Monetary Evils: Some Suggestions for Their Remedy* (New York, 1872), *passim*.

[109] John Earl Williams, *A New York View of Finance and Banking* (n.p., n.d.), p. 4. (This originally appeared in *Old and New,* November 1873.) Actually Williams was a *rara avis* among businessmen—a banker-greenbacker—and he was criticizing expanded bank-note issue from the greenback rather than the hard money side. His hostility to free banking, if not his reasons for it, were nonetheless common in New York banking circles. See, e.g., R. B. Minturn to William Allison, New York, April 27, 1874, William Allison MSS, Iowa State Department of History and Archives.

[110] The incident is described at length in Atkinson to Garfield, Boston, March 26, 1869, and the enclosed clipping from the *Boston Daily Advertiser,* Garfield MSS.

are resumed it would no doubt be safe and better for the country to throw open the bank law and make it free to all."[111] S. H. Walley of Boston's National Reserve Bank, one of the institutions that had opposed the March resolutions, told Congressman James A. Garfield that while he had "always favored *free banking* as the only fair thing for *all*," he "desired to wait for a return to *specie payment* before adopting it."[112]

This willingness to accept free banking in principle brought eastern and western businessmen closer together on this aspect of postwar finance than on most others. Even A. A. Low, the doughtiest champion of sound finance in the New York commercial fraternity, conceded that outright bank-note inflation was preferable to more greenbacks.[113] But the sectional differences remained, if only over timing; and with resumption becoming increasingly remote after 1868, tying free banking to specie payments became tantamount to rejecting it outright.

The echo of this East-West conflict could be heard in the Capitol when Congress came to debate banking reform. Western Republicans and Pennsylvanians, loyal to their party's own financial creation but responsive to expansionist pressures, led the fight to liberalize the national banking law. In both sessions of the Thirty-ninth Congress they tried unsuccessfully to redistribute note circulation.[114] In the next Congress a measure introduced by John Sherman made considerable progress. This bill proposed a $20 million note increase to be distributed to states having less than a $5 per capita circulation.[115] The discussion that followed became a bitter and undignified sectional dogfight among Republican Senators. Pomeroy of Kansas, Cornelius Cole of California, Henderson and Drake of Missouri, and Morton of

---

[111] National Bank Convention, *Proceedings of the Convention Held in New York City, June 23, 1869* (Syracuse, 1869), p. 8.

[112] Walley to James A. Garfield, Boston, Nov. 24, 1869, Garfield MSS.

[113] New York State Chamber of Commerce, *Proceedings of the Centennial Celebration, 1868* (New York, 1868), p. 24.

[114] Two Senate redistribution measures were introduced early in 1866, during the first session, but they never got out of Committee. U.S. Senate, *Miscellaneous Document No. 100*, pp. 1-9. Anderson also mentions a House proposal of the same period, *op. cit.*, p. 225. For the second session bill see *Congressional Globe*, 39 Cong., 2 sess., p. 161.

[115] Anderson, *op. cit.*, pp. 195-201, 232-237.

Indiana demanded free banking or redistribution as the right of the West. Justin Morrill of Vermont, Henry Wilson of Massachusetts, and Roscoe Conkling of New York retorted that the westerners wanted inflation even if it "confiscate[d] the property of the widows and orphans of the East."[116]

The Sherman proposal for a straight increase failed, but a substitute measure, shifting to the West and South some of the originally authorized $300 million passed the Senate.[117] This bill reached the House in February 1869 but was defeated, and the banking system remained undisturbed until the next Congress.[118]

During the winter of 1868-1869, the South, by now recovering rapidly from its economic paralysis, began absorbing large amounts of the greenback circulation which had previously returned to the Northeast during the spring and summer. As a result an extraordinary mid-year money stringency developed in 1869, and by crop moving time the situation in the financial centers was perilous.[119] When the second session of the Forty-first Congress opened in December 1869 the bank reform interests could make a strong case for lifting the note ceiling. On January 11, 1870, Sherman introduced a redistribution bill from the Finance Committee to increase the authorized bank issue by $45 million. To offset any inflationary effect, the $45 million of outstanding 3 per cent certificates were simultaneously to be redeemed and withdrawn.[120] An amended version of this measure was roughly treated in the House. Western Democrats, representing greenback districts, wanted nothing to do with the national bank "money monopolies."[121] But the House Republicans were firmly in control and not only defended free banking but substituted their more radical measure, providing for a direct $95 million note increase.[122] Finally, on July 7, after the calling

116 *Congressional Globe*, 40 Cong., 2 sess., pp. 3088, 3151-3152.
117 *Ibid.*, p. 3223.
118 Anderson, *op. cit.*, p. 231.
119 *Ibid.*, pp. 165-169.
120 These certificates could be used as bank reserves and so released greenbacks, the normal reserve, for circulation. As they were retired, the banks would be forced to replace them with greenbacks withdrawn from circulation, thus offsetting the additional bank note issue. *Congressional Globe*, 41 Cong., 2 sess., pp. 697-698.
121 Anderson, *op. cit.*, pp. 253-254.
122 *Congressional Globe*, 40 Cong., 2 sess., pp. 4264ff., 4433-4478.

of two conference committees,[123] Congress, by a coalition of Republicans from Pennsylvania and the South and West, passed a measure authorizing $54 million of new notes and a $25 million shift to the South and West, which became law on July 12.[124]

An additional $54 million of circulation was indeed a victory for soft money. It was won over the ever-present inertia of government and over the determined and well-organized opposition of anti-bank greenbackers on the one hand, and hard money ideologues, Northeastern commercial and financial interests, and the conservative financial groups in the nation on the other. Although modest, it was a tribute to the vigor of the enterpriser group. But the whole struggle disposes of the cliché that these men were in the saddle and riding the country hard. It is clear that many—though by no means all—of the men usually recognized as the triumphant postwar business generation were in fact advocates of easy money. Yet up to 1870, at least, their achievements were limited. Defeat of the contraction policy and $54 million of new bank notes were paltry results for a new national elite after five years of striving. In strictly economic terms, perhaps, the War had elevated a new generation of businessmen to prominence, but it had not destroyed the prestige and power of older business groups. Nor, as we shall presently see, had it entirely enfeebled the older agrarian America.

[123] *Ibid.*, pp. 4881, 4950, 4962ff., 5050.

[124] *Ibid.*, p. 5302. A more complete discussion of the 1872 Redistribution Act will be found in Anderson, *op. cit.*, pp. 242-260. The House vote adopting the conference report clearly reveals the party and sectional support of free banking. Only 1 western Democrat voted affirmatively; 12 others opposed. Southern Democrats opposed 6 to 3. Thirty-eight western Republicans voted for the bill, 14 against it. Southern Republicans favored it 22 to 3. The Republican vote in the Middle-Atlantic States, especially Pennsylvania, was overwhelmingly favorable: all 29 affirmative votes from that section were Republican. By sections, New England opposed redistribution 13 to 7; the middle states approved it 29 to 25, as did the West and South by votes of 34 to 26 and 25 to 9 respectively.

THE SOFT MONEY INTEREST

(1865-1870), PART II

I

THERE was a distinct dialectic rhythm in the financial events which occurred between 1865 and 1870. First the contraction measure and McCulloch's withdrawals; then resistance and repeal; and, finally, equilibrium in the Public Credit Act. Behind these shifts in direction was the ebb and flow of soft money strength. When united, the soft money forces swept all before them; when divided, they went down to defeat. Free banking, supported by business groups alone, failed. The attack on contraction by allied Agrarians and soft money businessmen triumphed. The promoters, the aggressive new enterprisers, and the ironmasters led the fight against McCulloch, but without the added thrust of the Agrarian greenback impulse that appeared soon after Appomattox they could not have succeeded.

"Greenbackism" was a complex phenomenon. Like neo-mercantilism it was hostile to contraction, but in most other respects it differed from business oriented soft money. Above all, the greenbackers detested the banks, which the Careyites valued as the source of easy money, and were determined to replace their issues with federal legal tenders. With notable exceptions,[1] the greenbackers were not businessmen. They were Agrarian intellectuals and politicians who, with their working-class and rural following, drew their inspiration from the anti-monopoly and—paradoxically—hard money tradition of Jeffersonian and Jacksonian Democracy. Beyond this fundamental accord, however, they agreed on little else. A few were outright inflationists. Al-

---

[1] Train and Schell and banker John Earl Williams, for example. See above, ch. II. A temporary interest in greenback doctrines did occur among the ironmasters after the 1873 panic, however. See below, ch. VII.

most all were anxious to avoid the stigma of inflation and at most, considered inflation an unimportant by-product of their proposals. On the bond repayment question they ranged from intemperate repudiationists to cautious dissenters from the gold shibboleth. Some were hard-headed, practical men, others were visionaries, full of schemes, nostrums, and programs designed to remake the world. Practical or utopian, they frequently attacked one another as vigorously as they did the common foe.

The political strain of postwar greenbackism was Democratic in origin. The War, rather than destroying the Jacksonian money philosophy, merely changed its terms. During the conflict itself there was little change. Agrarian bullionists in Congress generally denounced the greenback issues as contrary to sound principles of finance and foresaw "private ruin and public bankruptcy" following their emission.[2] Consistently, in the 1864 Presidential campaign the Democrats attacked the Republicans for the high prices paper money had produced.[3]

This was largely political expediency. The greenback, however reluctantly accepted by conservative Republicans, was a party war measure and thus fair game for Copperhead Democrats. As the legal tenders became for many Republicans the "patriotic" greenback, identified with the righteous war,[4] so they became for anti-war Democrats another infernal instrument of unjust aggression. But equally important was the antipathy of old Agrarian bullionism; for whatever their own biases, Democratic leaders were directing their appeal to the large electorate conditioned to the old Bentonian-Locofoco gold faith.

Not that the postwar Democracy was, any more than the prewar party, composed exclusively of old-line bullionists. Both parties after 1865 carried a mixed load of ideological baggage from the past which helped condition their postwar financial behavior. The anti-bank, bullionist group had predominated in

[2] These are George Pendleton's words in 1862. Quoted in Charles H. Coleman, *The Election of 1868: The Democratic Effort to Regain Control* (New York: Columbia University Press, 1933), p. 31.

[3] William F. Zornow, *Lincoln and the Party Divided* (Norman, Okla.: University of Oklahoma Press, 1954), p. 170.

[4] It was this sentiment that was responsible in part for Republican dismay at the first Legal Tender decision. See below, ch. v.

the prewar Democracy, but we must not forget that the party had sheltered at least two other groups with radically different attitudes toward banks and currency. One was the "Jackson men with feet of Clay," to use Professor Charles G. Sellers' witty tag,[5] who yielded nothing to Nicholas Biddle or the Great Compromiser himself in advocating a strong federal bank and a conservatively managed, gold redeemable bank currency. The other faction was composed of speculative business elements, who wanted easy money based upon a loosely reined state bank system. Judging by later events, this group had been reduced to a minor factor by defections to the Republicans. But each of these three elements was to be found in varying proportions in the postwar Democracy, and their presence helps explain the emergence of hard and soft money wings within the party. The Republicans, on the other hand, inherited much from prewar Whiggery. In the new party, in addition to Whig state bank men like Carey, there was a conservative Whig element which supported a strong, well-managed central bank. It must be remembered, however, that slavery extension, not money or banks, was the issue that shattered prewar political alignments and produced the Republican party. Substantial numbers of free-soil Democrats, holding a wide range of financial views, also drifted into the new party and gave the Republicans almost as great a diversity of financial heritage as their Democratic opponents. Nevertheless, ideologically the two parties were to have different centers of gravity. Among the Democrats, the old Jacksonians, opposed to banks and their note issues, continued to dominate party opinion. Postwar Republicanism contained more of the pro-bank attitudes of the Whig core around which the early free-soil groups had coalesced.

Besides these doctrinal divergences, ethnic, social, and, to some extent, class and religious differences distinguished the two parties after the War. Both exhibited much of the diversity and structural complexity of their modern successors. Each was composed of a loose federation of local and state organizations; each was a coalition of many elements, often discordant and conten-

[5] Charles G. Sellers, Jr., "Jackson Men with Feet of Clay," *AHR*, LXII, No. 3 (April 1957).

tious. In New England and the Middle States, Democratic strength centered in the urban areas and among recent immigrants, often of Catholic, and particularly Irish, origin.[6] In the West, in addition to the Irish population of the large cities, farmers of southern antecedents and those from the poorer agricultural areas were Democrats. South of Pennsylvania and the Ohio River, loyalty to the party of Jefferson and Calhoun was expected of virtually all white men.[7]

With the exception of the South, then, the postwar Democracy represented largely the socially marginal, less "respectable," elements of the nation. But the Democracy was not, as its rhetoric of those years often asserted, the "party of the people." The old radical Locofoco tradition did linger on after the War, and occasionally the Democracy became the political vehicle of disaffected groups. But in both East and West, Democratic machinery was often controlled by men of conservative temper. In New York, an uneasy alliance gave Tammany control of the city, while a group affiliated with banking, railroad, and commercial interests—heirs of the old "Hunker" element—generally dominated state affairs.[8] In the Northwest, the "Bourbon Democracy," allied with local business interests, fought for control with leaders closer to the Jacksonian rank and file.[9]

[6] According to one West Virginia Republican, in his state, "as is the almost universal case, the Irish, are on [the] 'Dimmocrat' side, whilst we 'gobble all the Germans, save about so,' and we might get all them save the German Jews." W. H. McKinney to William Henry Smith, Smith MSS, Ohio Historical Society.

[7] Without a doubt the most acute observer of the American political scene in these years was the Englishman James Bryce, whose *American Commonwealth*, though written a few years after the period under discussion is generally valid for the 1860's and 1870's. I have drawn largely on Bryce, *The American Commonwealth* (second edition; London: Macmillan and Company, 1891) for this paragraph, and also on the pertinent sections of Wilfred E. Binkley, *American Political Parties, Their Natural History* (New York: Alfred A. Knopf, 1945). Also see Frank L. Klement, *The Copperheads in the Middle West* (Chicago: University of Chicago Press, 1960), pp. 31ff., for some interesting remarks about the Democracy of the Northwest.

[8] Binkley, *op. cit.*, pp. 271, 305. This group was sometimes referred to, following the War, as the "swallowtail" element and was affiliated with the Manhattan Club, an organization distinct from the more plebeian Tammany Society. See the interesting description of these two organizations in the *CDT*, June 17, 1877.

[9] Horace Samuel Merrill, *Bourbon Democracy of the Middle West,*

Middle-class status and Yankee blood were the mainstays of Republican strength. Lord Bryce remarks of a slightly later period that in almost any northern city, when dining out with "the best people," one's neighbor was almost certain to be a Republican.[10] Indeed, Democrats themselves grudgingly recognized their opponents' social superiority, sneering at them as the "God and Morality Party."[11] In New England the backbone of the party was composed of the prosperous Yankee yeomanry, the small businessmen, and the Congregational-Unitarian merchants and manufacturers of the towns and cities. In the Middle States and the West the solid business and professional classes and the more prosperous farmers, often of New England Congregational background, were Republicans; while in a tier of counties in northern Ohio, Illinois, and southern Michigan, settled by Yankees early in the century, Democrats were an embattled minority.[12]

These differences of ideology and sociology encouraged different party attitudes toward the postwar money question: in simplest terms they made the Republicans far less susceptible than the Democrats to the greenback version of soft money. But beyond this, the two parties found themselves in very different circumstances after 1865. The Republican party emerged from the War tempered in the furnace of battle, its prestige inflated by Union victory, endowed with a national saint in the martyred President. The Democrats found their very existence precarious. Even before secession, the Democracy—torn between its proslavery and popular sovereignty wings—was in serious trouble. The War threatened to complete its destruction. Like the Federalists half a century before, many northern Democrats had supported a peace policy, and a few had flirted with treason. Unfortunately for these "Copperheads," as for their predecessors, the war they opposed had been won, and for a while it appeared that with shattered prestige and morale the Democracy, like the

1865-1896 (Baton Rouge, Louisiana: Louisiana State University Press, 1953), *passim*, but especially pp. 1-6.

[10] Bryce, *op. cit.*, II, 30.

[11] *Pomeroy's Democrat*, Jan. 19, 1870.

[12] Bryce, *op. cit.*, II, 30; Binkley, *op. cit.*, pp. 208-209, 221, 279, 283.

Federalists, would pass into oblivion.[13] Its only hope for survival seemed to lie in reviving the old Democratic coalition of "producers" that had dominated American politics from Jackson through Buchanan. Northern Democrats in the postwar years played on a number of themes to attract voters. In areas of strong Copperhead or southern sympathies, particularly in the old Northwest, the Democrats waved their own reverse "bloody shirt," reminding the electorate of the unpopular draft, the suspension of civil liberties, and other arbitrary acts of the Republican wartime administration. Wherever useful, they played on anti-Negro sentiment and the traditional states' rights and free trade doctrines that had long served as texts for Democratic sermons. But the issues growing out of wartime finance were to become especially important to an aspiring postwar Democracy.

Above all, the wartime federal debt proved a congenial target for the Democrats. Its size alone, implying an extended period of high taxes, made it abhorrent to Jeffersonian advocates of frugal government. To the peace wing of the party, the war debt was an object of special hatred. A vast burden, incurred in an unjust war, it offered a way for the frustrated Democrat to avenge himself on the Black Republicans, and it was an opportunity eagerly seized. To pay the debt would be to condone the injustice of the recent conflict, declared Henry Clay Dean, an Iowa Copperhead. It would give public sanction to a vicious war against the ancient liberties of the people and the rights of the sovereign, equal states.[14]

But there was more to the Copperhead assault on the debt than belated vengefulness. To men of Agrarian sympathies, the bondholders' position was legally and morally, as well as politically vulnerable. Both principal and interest of several wartime loans were legally payable in coin, but the law only specified coin payment for the *interest* of the 5-20's. Jay Cooke, in his high-pressure sales campaign, had told the public that the prin-

---

[13] See George B. McClellan to S. L. M. Barlow, June 3, 1866, quoted in Howard K. Beale, *The Critical Year: A Study of Andrew Johnson and Reconstruction* (New York: Harcourt, Brace & Co., 1930),
p. 29, n. 41.

[14] Henry Clay Dean, *Crimes of the Civil War and Curse of the Funding System* (Baltimore, 1868), pp. 200ff.

cipal, too, would be redeemed in gold,[15] but this was not a legal commitment. The bonds were sold at par for greenbacks and moved quickly only after paper money had depreciated. In effect, then, the bondholder had bought with depreciated paper a security paying 6 per cent interest in gold—and perhaps twice as much in greenbacks—and expected to be repaid in coin which was never legally promised. It can be argued that such exceptionally adverse terms for the Treasury were necessary to entice timid wartime lenders into the capital market. But such a contention was too abstract to carry much political weight. The generous terms given the bond buyers, combined with the seemingly gratuitous additional gift of complete tax exemption, lent great weight to Copperhead charges of favoritism.[16] Old Jeffersonian Agrarians,[17] the erstwhile peace Democrats, identified the new federal debt with Hamilton's funded debt and Hamiltonian centralization and pictured it as the precursor of a train of evils that would destroy Jeffersonian pluralism, private freedom, and ultimately the virtuous Republic itself. "The whole money of the funding system," wrote Dean, was "at the service of the monopolists" and would be used to corrupt courts, officials, and legislatures. "Constitutional laws, or long established judicial decisions, are as dust in the balances when weighed with the moneys at the command of the funding system."[18]

The new national banking structure erected on the federal debt only confirmed the parallel with the past. Dean quoted Jefferson on the dangers of banking monopolies and demanded the instant abolition of the new system.[19] Marcus Mills "Brick" Pomeroy, the vituperative Copperhead editor of *The La Crosse Democrat*, insisted on the equivalence of the national banks and

[15] Ellis Paxson Oberholtzer, *Jay Cooke: Financier of the Civil War* (Philadelphia: George W. Jacobs and Co., 1907), i, 235, 239-240; ii, 41.

[16] Two modern studies endorse both the legal and moral position of the Pendleton Plan. See Max L. Shipley, "The Background and Legal Aspects of the Pendleton Plan," *MVHR*, xxiv, No. 3 (December 1937); Chester M. Destler, "Legal and Sectional Aspects of the Pendleton Plan," in *American Radicalism, 1865-1901: Essays and Documents* (New London, Conn.: Connecticut College Monograph No. 3, 1946), pp. 44-48.

[17] Klement, *op. cit.*, pp. viii, 1, 37.

[18] Dean, *op. cit.*, pp. 321ff. See also *Pomeroy's Democrat*, Jan. 5, 1870.

[19] Dean, *op. cit.*, pp. 241-259, 366, 374ff.

Nicholas Biddle's "Monster." "Parties then as now tried to force upon the people a vitiated system of banking and a worthless paper currency," he wrote. "Andrew Jackson roused the people against the monstrous injustice. He showed the farmers, mechanics, and producers of all classes that the inevitable tendency of the rotten bonding system was to pauperize them and reduce them to commercial dependence and finally political slavery."[20]

In their attitudes toward monopoly, banks, the debt, and the bondholders, Agrarian Democrats could appeal to the pure Jefferson-Jackson tradition. But there were some serious difficulties in reconciling past and present when it came to the greenback. The federal issue was, after all, paper money, the *bête noir* of Agrarian ideologues. Many old Jacksonians deplored the new federal money and were to be found in the bullionist camp after 1865 as before.[21] At the other extreme, some surrendered hard money principles without a qualm and frankly announced for inflation.[22] Most greenback Democrats managed to find a formula to accommodate their Agrarianism to the new circumstances. Dean, for instance, always remained a hard money man at heart. In 1868 he fumed at the wartime inflation which had raised the cost of living of the poor,[23] and hoped to "restore in full force the specie basis of our currency" for all debts contracted after 1867, although he would permit debtors to repay wartime debts in paper.[24] Pomeroy quoted Jackson's admonitions against a federal paper money in the same column with his attack on banking, but blithely ignored the conflict with greenbackism.[25] On a later occasion he acknowledged the clash between bullionist orthodoxy and his own crusade for legal tender

[20] *Pomeroy's Democrat*, March 30, 1870.

[21] For example, see Peter T. Homer to James A. Garfield, Boston, May 25, 1868, Garfield MSS, LC; Burton Phillips to Thaddeus Stevens, New York, Dec. 3, 1867, Stevens MSS, LC; James Porter to Benjamin F. Butler, St. Louis, Dec. 6, 1867, Butler MSS, LC; S. W. Fuller to Samuel J. Tilden, Chicago, June 10, 1868, Tilden MSS, NYPL; W. S. Groesbeck to William H. English.

Groesbeck to William H. English, MSS, Indiana Historical Society.

[22] This was sometimes the rankest sort of opportunism. See the exceedingly frank letter of Wilbur Storey, editor of the Democratic *Chicago Times*, to Manton Marble, Chicago, Feb. 12, 1868, Marble MSS, LC.

[23] Dean, *op. cit.*, pp. 7, 198ff.

[24] *Ibid.*, p. 238.

[25] *Pomeroy's Democrat*, March 16, 1870.

paper, but reluctantly concluded that "a 'hard money' or specie currency probably belongs to a bygone age and is incompatible with modern progress and activity."[26]

But the difficulty was never fully resolved. Particularly in the first postwar years the greenback clearly disturbed even western Democrats. In the end, political expediency overwhelmed scruples. Paper money was too tempting a political tool to be put aside lightly. Above all, it supplied the means for rebuilding the old producer coalition. The legal tenders promised simultaneously to deflate federal power by scaling down the national debt, to strike a blow for the "people" against the federal creditors, and to save the Republic from the plutocratic bankers. At heart it was always this Jacksonian program, emphasizing the danger and injustice of the debt and the banking system, that took precedence over inflation in the Democrats' financial philosophy.

Copperhead vindictiveness, the old Agrarianism of Jackson and Benton, and immediate political opportunities were the forces that engendered Democratic greenbackism. All were in solution by the end of the War, and even before Appomattox they had begun to produce a political reaction. In March 1865, one of Cooke's bond agents, Samuel Wilkeson, reported that leading Massachusetts Democrats had told him *"plainly* that the Democratic Party, deprived of its anti-negro, and pro-slavery and Slave State alliance to stand on, is going to get upon an anti National Bank—and a quasi *Repudiation Platform.* This war on the National Banking system will commence in the New Hampshire election struggle next week.

"This war will have for its object the issue of paper money directly by the Government, instead of by the agency of a thousand Banks. It will be supported by the plea of economy, and the plea of safety and the old cant about 'the rich richer and the poor poorer.' "[27]

Allowing for Wilkeson's partisanship, this is a remarkable foreshadowing of the general course of events. Wilkeson's friends

[26] *Ibid.*, Nov. 30, 1870.
[27] Wilkeson to Jay Cooke, Boston, March 8, 1865, Cooke MSS, Historical Society of Pennsylvania.

were mistaken about the New Hampshire Democrats,[28] but there were numerous intimations that fall that the Democrats were drifting in the predicted direction. By the end of the year, Dean was touring the East and Midwest urging a scheme to pay off the bonds in greenbacks.[29] In their 1865 platform the Massachusetts Democrats themselves, while acknowledging the legality of the debt, protested against putting the entire burden of repayment on the producing classes.[30] Soon the West began to show signs of financial revolt. In the 1865 Ohio gubernatorial campaign, the Democrats attacked the exorbitant interest rates that wartime creditors had extracted from the desperate government.[31] Again, in January, the defeated candidate George W. Morgan chided the Republicans for subservience to the "money lenders of Boston and New York." Republican finance had flaunted the interests of the soldier and the general public in order to shower benefits on a tax exempt paper aristocracy.[32]

Soon after, Pomeroy struck his first blow against the "bondocracy." In an 1866 pamphlet he pungently developed the emerging Democratic line and in the process introduced an element of sectional malice[33] which was to mark western soft money polemics for the next forty years. In a series of artfully disingenuous vignettes, he played on the prejudices of his western rural readers against the East and the "Bondholder." We see in these the sybaritic "Mr. Bond" sitting in his "parlor" smoking imported cigars and drinking French champagne, gloating over his tax-free bonds which paid him 11 per cent a year. We see his poor neighbor, a disabled Union veteran, crushed by the taxes to pay Mr. Bond's 11 per cent.[34] The contrast between bondholder and

---

[28] At least an examination of several New Hampshire newspapers failed to uncover any such Democratic attempt.

[29] Dean, *op. cit.*, pp. 242-243; *Cincinnati Enquirer*, Jan. 4, 1866.

[30] See the Massachusetts state platform adopted at Worcester, September 28, 1865, *NYDT*, Sept. 29, 1865.

[31] *Ibid.*, Oct. 9, 1865.

[32] Speech of Morgan to the "Democratic Festival" at Columbus, Jan. 4, 1866, *Cincinnati Enquirer*,

Jan. 7, 1866.

[33] Actually there had been an element of sectional resentment in the Jacksonian bank controversy, with westerners, like Benton, attacking the Bank of the United States as an agent of eastern domination. See Elbert B. Smith, *Magnificent Missourian: The Life and Times of Thomas Hart Benton* (Philadelphia: J. B. Lippincott Co., 1958), pp. 122-123.

[34] Pomeroy, *Soliloquies of the Bondholder, the Poor Farmer, the*

veteran is soon translated into political and sectional terms. Pomeroy's "Radical member of Congress" readily confesses that he is controlled by the "New England bondholders" who "own the government." Yankee "nabobs" are seen "rid[ing] . . . in their easy carriages" and "revel[ing] in wine dinners," their bonds secured against taxation by Northeastern control of Congress. "We piled up a mountain of debt," Pomeroy declared, "astride of which sit thousands of New England bondholders, and we have got to bend our backs to the load while they crack the whip over us, the poor white trash of the West."[35]

At this point, Pomeroy's answer to the bond problem was the cryptic but ominous formula, "equal taxation or repudiation."[36] But sometime during the year *The La Crosse Democrat* came out for paying the bondholders in greenbacks.[37] By early 1866, "repudiation" demands were circulating so widely in the West that Massachusetts Senator Charles Sumner suggested a constitutional amendment upholding the sanctity of the federal debt.[38]

Up until this point the Democratic response had been little more than a Jacksonian reflex rejection of the whole apparatus of modern finance. The crucial 1866 Congressional election was to help refashion this reaction into a useful political weapon. On October 31, the financial editor of the Democratic *Chicago Times* published a vehement denunciation of the public creditors and the national banks for "corrupting politics and commerce" by their "influence and power." Going beyond this conventional rhetoric, however, the editor suggested a scheme to dispose of both the debt and the banks simultaneously that closely foreshadowed the Pendleton Plan. The banks, he noted, received $9 million in interest annually from the bonds they held. If these were paid off immediately, and the interest progressively saved

---

Soldier's Widow . . . and Other Political Articles (New York, 1866), pp. 3-7.

[35] *Ibid.*, pp. 16, 21-23.

[36] *Ibid.*, pp. 8, 27ff.

[37] Marcus Mills Pomeroy, *A Journey of Life: Reminiscences and Recollections of Brick Pomeroy* (New York, 1890), I, 211; *The Great Campaign*, Oct. 3, 1876. I

have not discovered this editorial but have uncovered several others advocating taxing the bonds and/or repudiating them. *La Crosse Democrat*, August 7 and 15, 1866.

[38] See Max L. Shipley, "The Greenback Issue in the Old Northwest, 1865-1880" (unpublished Ph.D. dissertation, University of Illinois, 1929), pp. 38-39.

by this move and by subsequent redemptions, were to be applied to retiring the debt, in 38 years the nation would be free of both its chief burdens without a single penny of additional taxes.[39]

This scheme presupposed continuing the heavy wartime taxes, a feature which inevitably reduced its political appeal. For this reason, perhaps, the Democrats paid more attention to Radical "usurpations" and Negro suffrage during the campaign than to finance.[40] Their crushing defeat produced a self-appraising mood, however. On November 12, Wilbur Storey of the *Times*, in a sober editorial headed "Shall the Democratic Party Die or Live," declared the Democracy could only survive by becoming "what it was in its palmy days, a progressive and aggressive party." It must abandon the Johnson regime, he concluded, and bury the Negro question by accepting Negro suffrage as inevitable. Let the Democracy "once more turn to those material questions of public policy, the right disposition of which is so essential to public prosperity. It will be upon these questions that the democratic party will triumph."[41] In the next few weeks the *Times* hinted that the tariff, and particularly the financial issue, might be among those invigorating "material questions."[42] On December 10, a *Times* columnist declared for paying the federal debt in greenbacks, and the next day he was seconded by Storey himself.[43]

By 1867, then, most of the "Ohio Idea" was already in being. It only remained to elaborate, publicize, and rationalize this scheme to make it a formidable Democratic weapon. This treatment it soon received in Ohio in response to the plight of the local Democracy.

Factionalism and ideological conflict had plagued the Ohio Democrats in the years immediately preceding the War. Defections to the Republicans and the stigma of treason further weakened the party during the War and resulted in a series of damaging setbacks at the polls before 1865. In the gubernatorial can-

---

[39] *Chicago Times*, Oct. 31, 1866.
[40] But see the *Times* editorial of Oct. 17, 1866.
[41] *Ibid.*, Nov. 12, 1866.
[42] *Ibid.*, Nov. 15, 1866; Nov. 23, 1866.

[43] *Ibid.*, Dec. 10, 1866; Dec. 11, 1866. See also the 3½ columns of "Democrat" in the *Times* of Dec. 21 advocating replacing the national bank issue with greenbacks.

vass of that year the Democrats attempted to win votes on the issue of Negro suffrage, but were once again defeated; and by 1866 they were ready to try coalition with the moderate Johnson Republicans. This, too, proved disastrous, the Radicals carrying 16 of 19 Ohio Congressional districts.[44]

The nation's Democrats generally were plagued by bad luck in these years, but in Ohio the party leaders were men of exceptional ability and drive, ready to invest money and energy to restore the party's decayed fortunes. The architect of the revival was to be Washington McLean, a rich manufacturer and editor of the influential Copperhead daily, the *Cincinnati Enquirer*. As Professor Chester M. Destler has shown, McLean had ambitions as a Kingmaker and hoped by rehabilitating the Democracy under Ohio auspices to make himself a power in national politics.[45] This plan required a relevant contemporary issue which could also appeal to deeply felt traditional values and thereby draw attention from recent Democratic errors and failures. In effect, McLean was seeking the new base for his party that Storey had called for; but he was to feel his way slowly. He, like other Democrats, was disturbed by the greenback and the inflation it implied. As late as December 1865, in an editorial occasioned by McCulloch's first Report, the *Enquirer* had endorsed contraction as "the easiest way for the public at large to get quit of the legal tenders."[46] Between this time and early spring of 1867, the conflict between politics and ideology was fought out in McLean's mind. During the opening months of 1867, the *Enquirer* attacked national banks and, as business conditions worsened, began to have doubts about contraction. But the paper did not endorse a new issue of greenbacks to redeem the federal debt

[44] For the Ohio Democracy during the War and immediately after, see Eugene H. Roseboom, *The Civil War Era, 1850-1873*, Vol. IV of *The History of the State of Ohio* (Columbus: Ohio State Archeological and Historical Society, 1944), chs. IX-XI, XIII-XIV; George H. Porter, *Ohio Politics During the Civil War Period* (New York, 1911), pp. 183-199, 200-219.

[45] Destler, "Origin and Character of the Pendleton Plan," p. 33. See also McLean's interesting letter to S. L. M. Barlow in which he boasts that with Pendleton as the nominee "and the payment of the public debt in greenbacks as our platform," the Democracy would sweep back into national office. Washington McLean to S. L. M. Barlow, Cincinnati, Oct. 11, 1867, Barlow MSS, Henry E. Huntington Library.

[46] *Cincinnati Enquirer*, Dec. 9, 1865.

until April 24. In an editorial entitled "A Popular Plan to Pay Off the National Debt," McLean expressed sympathy with recent suggestions to cancel the principal of the debt with a new legal tender issue. He admitted that the greenback was depreciated, but so were the notes lent the government by the creditors.[47]

As elaborated in the next few months, the *Enquirer* scheme was an untidy patchwork, full of ambiguities, which attempted to appeal to both the Agrarian and the remaining business elements of the party. The *Enquirer* attacked the iniquitous bondholder and "the moneyed aristocracy," and by now unequivocally condemned McCulloch's contraction;[48] but McLean also touted the invigorating effects of a "few hundred millions of legal tenders" "poured into the channels of trade."[49] These last phrases obviously condoned expansion; but inflation, the paper declared, was not central to its proposals. It was true that there was too much money already in circulation, "but let it be remembered," McLean rationalized, "that we are not proposing the payment of the bonded debt in currency for the purpose of increasing the amount of paper. Such a result would be unavoidable for the adoption of the plan; but it is only incidental to it, not the object for which it is suggested."[50]

McLean's murky logic reflected his discomfort with this inflation scheme, and he seized eagerly on the plan which, by the summer of 1867, was becoming identified with George Hunt Pendleton, one of the most popular and talented of Ohio Democratic politicians. Handsome and gracious, of prominent Virginia stock, "Gentleman George" had represented Ohio's first district in Congress between 1859 and 1865. In 1864 he had been the Democratic Vice-Presidential candidate on the ticket with McClellan. Like most western Democrats, he had been a hard money man and as a wartime Congressman had spoken and voted against the greenback emission. With the War won and Radicalism in the saddle, he found himself facing the same bleak political prospects as other Democratic leaders.[51]

---

[47] *Ibid.*, April 24, 1867.
[48] *Ibid.*, June 13, 1867.
[49] *Ibid.*, May 27, 1867; June 13, 1867.

[50] *Ibid.*, June 3, 1867.
[51] *Biographical Directory of the American Congress, 1774-1949* (Washington: U.S. Government

As late as April 1867 Pendleton still endorsed hard money,[52] but by the summer, partly through the influence of the *Enquirer*, he began to toy with greenback ideas. With an uncompromising and very public record of hard money, however, Pendleton found it even more difficult than most Democrats to embrace outright greenback expansion. Thus an idea of Hugh J. Jewett which offered an escape from the impasse greatly appealed to him. Jewett, an Ohio Democrat, had devised a scheme, based on familiar elements, to pay off part of the debt with just enough new greenbacks to offset and replace the national bank-note issue. The remainder would come from the federal surplus and tax money saved by *not* funding the non-interest legal tenders into interest paying bonds.[53]

By the opening of the 1867 state campaigns, Pendleton was ready to place a version of the Jewett scheme before the people as the new Democratic solution to the financial problem. In a series of addresses commencing at St. Paul, Minnesota, in mid-July and culminating at Milwaukee on November 2, Pendleton outlined the plan that has ever since been associated with his name. He denied at the outset that he wanted or intended inflation. The banks held some $338 million of 5-20's as security against note issue; let these be redeemed in greenbacks and the bank issues withdrawn. Ignoring the $38 million difference between the par value of the bonds and the $300 million of bank notes, he asserted that this would not expand the money supply. The 5-20's remaining would still total some $1.4 billion. But take the $18 million in gold interest annually saved by liquidating the bank holdings, add the $48 million in gold received by the Treasury from customs, convert this $66 million into $92 million of greenbacks at the current market rate, and use it as a sinking fund to discharge the rest of the debt. In 13 years, without a penny of additional taxes or a new paper dollar, the remaining 5-20's would be canceled. If in addition federal expenses were

---

Printing Office, 1950), p. 1666; Destler, "Origin and Character of the Pendleton Plan," p. 38.

[52] *Ibid.*

[53] Destler ascribes Jewett's idea to a suggestion appearing in the *Cincinnati Gazette* in 1865. But as has been shown much of the plan was foreshadowed in the *Chicago Times. Ibid.*, pp. 37-38; *Cincinnati Enquirer*, July 6, 1867.

cut to their proper level, the debt could be liquidated in five years. The bondholders must not be greedy, Pendleton concluded; they were already the beneficiaries of tax exemptions denied labor, the farmer, and other classes of the community. If they demanded gold repayment also, they might well find themselves faced with total repudiation.[54]

Toward the end of his Milwaukee address, Pendleton could not help casting his net for inflationist businessmen by remarking that commercial interest rates were high and the country could "well bear more currency."[55] But this was clearly an afterthought. The whole tenor of the Pendleton Plan was Agrarian, and if Pendleton and McLean had some hope of winning over the soft money business groups they were alone among Democratic campaigners in 1867. In Ohio the Democrats revived all the old Jacksonian-Agrarian dogmas and gave very little comfort to the enterprisers. Judge Rufus P. Ranney called on "Old Democrats who used to think something of general Jackson" to consider how much greater danger there was in the system that had replaced the Bank of the United States. If with its $35 million in capital the old Bank had suborned the press and Congress, "what are we to think of the numerous banks with their hundreds of millions of capital?"[56] Daniel Voorhees, a visiting Indiana Democrat who was to remain a leading greenbacker for over a decade, took positive delight in abusing the party's potential business allies. The federal debt, he thundered, was a rich man's speculation. The poor could not buy the bonds during the War, while of course the "banker, the broker, the moneychanger" could. These were the Agrarian's traditional enemies, and calling them names was part of the Jacksonian ritual. But Voorhees also placed the "wealthy merchant . . . the bloated plethoric manufacturers of the East, who have stolen by way of the tariff, . . . the ship owners" among the "leeches, the cormorants, the money vultures that preyed upon the Government during the war."[57]

The results of the 1867 Ohio campaign brilliantly vindicated

---

[54] Pendleton, *Payment of the Public Debt in Legal Tender Notes!! Speech [in] . . . Milwaukee, Nov. 2, 1867* (n.p., n.d.), *passim.*

[55] *Ibid.*, p. 11.

[56] *Cincinnati Commercial*, Aug. 8, 1867.

[57] *Ibid.*, Oct. 1, 1867.

the new Democratic course. Bourbon Democrat Allen Thurman —who himself was unenthusiastic about the greenback[58]—was defeated by Rutherford B. Hayes, but by the narrow margin of under 3000 votes in a total of nearly half a million.[59] The Republicans, it is true, had also been saddled with an unpopular Negro suffrage amendment, but most observers—Democratic and Republican alike—agreed that the currency question had produced the sudden change in Democratic prospects.[60]

The election made the Ohio Idea a formidable political force, and for a while it threatened to sweep the national Democracy. But novel ideologies have a way of creating antibodies; opposition within the party itself quickly crystallized. Despite Pendleton's earnest protests, he was roundly abused by fellow Democrats as both a repudiator and an inflationist,[61] charges unfair to Pendleton himself and perhaps to McLean, who soon adopted Gentleman George and his platform.[62] Wherever the party was a going concern in the '60's, conservative Democrats were frightened by the attack on the "public credit" and the banks, and fought to keep their local organizations out of the hands of the greenbackers.[63] In the West the Bourbon Democracy, representing established wealth and social conservatism, resisted the Pendletonians.[64] More dangerous, however, was the conservative eastern Democracy. In New York, men like Sanford E. Church, S. L. M. Barlow, Horatio Seymour, Samuel J. Tilden, and National Chairman August Belmont—heirs of the old Hunker element of the Albany Regency—would join with Tammany leaders

[58] Thurman always remained at heart opposed to the Pendleton-McLean wing, although in this campaign he was willing to bait the bondholders. See *ibid.*, Aug. 10, 1867.

[59] Charles R. Williams, *The Life of Rutherford Birchard Hayes, Nineteenth President of the United States* (Columbus: Ohio State Archeological and Historical Society, 1918), I, 328.

[60] See the following: Schuyler Colfax to John Sherman, South Bend, Indiana, Oct. 12, 1867, Sherman MSS, LC; M. Sutliff to Butler, Warren, Ohio, Oct. 8, 1867, Butler MSS; Washington McLean to S. L. M. Barlow, Cincinnati, Oct. 11, 1867, Barlow MSS.

[61] See, for example, Pendleton's complaint of misrepresentation. Pendleton to Manton Marble, Cincinnati, Nov. 13, 1867, Marble MSS.

[62] Destler, "Origin and Character of the Pendleton Plan," pp. 41-42.

[63] For the fears of conservative Democrats see W[illiam] H B[ryant] to Manton Marble, Albany, Jan. 16, 1868, Marble MSS; William Bigler to Samuel J. Tilden, Clearfield, Pa., Feb. 3, 1868, Tilden MSS.

[64] Merrill, *op. cit., passim*, but especially pp. 1-6.

from the city to drive financial heresy from the party. At the 1867 State Democratic Convention, Sanford Church and Tammany stalwart Mayor John T. Hoffman, prompted by Samuel S. "Sunset" Cox, a transplanted Ohioan, defeated an attempt to commit the party to a bond taxation, anti-bank program.[65] Elsewhere in the East, leaders like Thomas Bayard of Delaware, William Bigler of Pennsylvania, and Montgomery Blair of Maryland helped quash incipient greenbackism in their states.[66] In Manton Marble's *New York World* the eastern conservatives had a powerful propaganda weapon, while August Belmont's Rothschild millions[67] would provide unlimited resources for effective political action.

The Republicans did not entirely escape greenbackism, despite the natural resistance of the Yankee, Protestant, middle-class Republican voter. In mid-1866—a year before Pendleton's conversion to soft money—Ben Butler, who had started political life as a Jacksonian, first began to question the claims of the bondholders.[68] The following year he publicly announced his plan "to borrow money on a new loan to pay an indebtedness of the United States according to its terms."[69] Despite explicit denials, Butler's bond repayment views and his attitude toward the national banking system were almost identical with Pendleton's. As a good Republican he praised the banks for performing a useful function in raising war loans. But they provided an expensive currency, and it would be better to replace their issue with

[65] *NYDT*, Oct. 3, 1867; Oct. 5, 1867; Oct. 6, 1867; Oct. 7, 1867; S. S. Cox to William E. Chandler, Putnam, Ohio, Oct. 12, 1867, Chandler MSS, LC.

[66] See Charles C. Tansill, *The Congressional Career of Thomas Francis Bayard, 1868-1885* (Washington: Georgetown University Press, 1946), pp. 205-207, 215-216; Montgomery Blair to S. L. M. Barlow, Washington, April 19, 1868, Barlow MSS.

[67] There is no adequate biography of Belmont, but see Perry Belmont, *An American Democrat: The Recollections of Perry Belmont* (New York: Columbia University Press, 1941); and Allen Johnson and Dumas Malone (eds.), *Dictionary of American Biography*, ii, 169-170.

[68] William E. Chandler to Butler, Washington, June 4, 1866, Butler MSS.

[69] Butler, *The Currency Question . . . Letter to the . . . Boston Daily Advertiser, Oct. 12, 1867* (n.p., n.d.), *passim; NYDT*, Sept. 14, 1867; Oct. 2, 1867; *NYW*, Sept. 6, 1867.

greenbacks.[70] Thaddeus Stevens, the leading Republican "vindictive," was a later and more reserved convert to greenbackism. He never assailed the national banking system, although he had not supported it when first proposed; but, in almost his final public act, he directed his withering scorn and sarcasm at gold repayment.[71]

Both Butler and Stevens must be judged greenbackers by conviction. Butler's views were politically inexpedient in Yankee Massachusetts, and he probably suffered more than he gained by attacking the bondholders.[72] Stevens—a man of often brutal honesty, with a sincere concern for the underdog—rejected the bondholders claims as unjust, although he must have realized that his position might seriously weaken his party leadership.[73] But there were other Republicans whose feelings about banks, paper money, and the debt fluctuated with the supposed mood of their constituents. During the 1867 Ohio campaign, while John Sherman and candidate Hayes himself stood firm on the bond question,[74] many Republicans bowed low before the people's putative new idol.[75]

As the 1868 national election approached, many more panicked. The chief defector from the conservative ranks was Sherman, who after 1867 found himself in an increasingly awkward

[70] *Ibid.;* and Butler to Jay Cooke, on back of Cooke to Butler, Philadelphia, Nov. 6, 1867, Butler MSS.

[71] James Albert Woodburn, *The Life of Thaddeus Stevens* (Indianapolis: The Bobbs-Merrill Company, 1913), pp. 561-583.

[72] Butler, as a good Radical, would have retained the good will of the Brahmin element if not for his heterodox financial ideas. Instead, by his financial policy, he incurred their wrath and for the remainder of his political career found them among his most implacable foes. See Butler to S. W. Hopkinson, Lowell, Sept. 3, 1876; Butler to Reverend F. P. Wood, Washington, Feb. 25, 1878, Butler MSS. See also Hans Louis Trefousse, *Ben Butler: The South Called Him BEAST!* (New York: Twayne Publishers, 1957), pp. 193-194.

[73] Stevens came under severe attack during the 1868 Presidential campaign for remarks he made apparently endorsing the Democratic financial plank. See D. M. Muntril to Stevens, Huntingdon, Pa., July 22, 1868; Jeremiah Black to Stevens, Columbia, Pa., July 23, 1868, Stevens MSS. Stevens's death shortly after this address makes it impossible to say how much he would have damaged his leadership by continuing this course.

[74] Henry D. Cooke to John Sherman, Washington, Sept. 9, 1867, Sherman MSS; *New York Herald,* Sept. 24, 1867; *Cincinnati Commercial,* Aug. 2, 1867; Sept. 6, 1867.

[75] *Ibid.,* Aug. 27, 1867; Aug. 30, 1867.

political position. The Ohio politician's lot in general was not a happy one, and his situation became more uncomfortable after the advent of the financial question. Any man who attempted to speak for the whole state on the currency issue had an impossible task. Settled in layers from north to south by Yankees, Middle Staters, and Southerners, with large foreign-born groups in the cities; with prosperous agricultural counties through the central portion and the lake plain, great commercial cities in Cleveland and Cincinnati, rich coal fields and a major iron industry in the south and east—the state was as variegated as the nation itself. This ethnic and economic diversity engendered a vigorous political life and—a rare thing in these years—a working two-party system. But however healthy for the commonwealth, this situation was hazardous for the politicians and encouraged trimming and accommodation. On the money issue, James A. Garfield, representing the Yankee Western Reserve, could generally be orthodox;[76] but a United States Senator, who perforce represented the whole state, could not afford to be rigid. Pendletonism and the general money question caused a prolonged political headache for Sherman, particularly since as Chairman of the Finance Committee after 1866, he could not easily evade the issue. He was fundamentally a sound money man,[77] but like all successful politicians he felt a primary obligation to stay in office. The near victory of the Ohio Democrats in 1867 had disturbed Sherman as it had other Republicans, and with the 1868 election just ahead, he tried cautiously to identify himself with the upsurge of greenback feeling in his state.

The occasion for Sherman's temporary defection was the 1868 funding bill, which authorized the issue of a tax exempt 5 per cent bond, payable principal and interest in gold, into which all other federal obligations except other 5 per cent securities might

[76] He liked to picture himself, however, as an heroic fighter for the right in his own district. See Garfield to Edward Atkinson, Washington, May 17, 1868, Atkinson MSS, Massachusetts Historical Society.

[77] For Sherman's private financial views in the 1860's, see Sherman to William Tecumseh Sherman, Washington, Dec. 24, 1868, in Rachel Sherman Thorndike (ed.), *The Sherman Letters: Correspondence Between General and Senator Sherman from 1837 to 1891* (New York: Charles Scribner's Sons, 1894), p. 325; Jeannette Nichols, "John Sherman: A Study in Inflation," *MVHR*, xxi, No. 2 (Sept. 1934), pp. 185-186.

be converted. It permitted any holder of legal tenders, or of any interest-bearing obligations but other 5 per cents, to convert his securities into new federal bonds which could be "reconverted" into greenbacks, provided that the total greenback issue never exceeded $400 million.[78] This was a complicated bill, and made strange bedfellows. Though it was generally acknowledged that it was time to take advantage of improved federal credit and refund the 5-20's at a lower rate, many of the measure's specific provisions were controversial. The reconvertible or "interconvertible" bond feature, as we shall see, was fast becoming popular among a group of labor greenbackers associated with the National Labor Union,[79] and could be expected to win labor support. But it was also beginning to come under a conservative attack. In the Senate Justin Morrill of Vermont and New Yorker Roscoe Conkling ridiculed it.[80] But the rigidly orthodox Charles Sumner of Massachusetts, and a group of Sumner's Boston advisers, thought they saw the possibility through the convertible provision of almost surreptitiously funding the whole greenback issue into a long-term bond, and thus the Massachusetts Senator unexpectedly defended it.[81]

The convertible feature was all but forgotten, however, when Sherman in his introductory speech suggested that if holders of 5-20's did not voluntarily convert them into the new issue they could legally be compelled to take greenbacks instead. There need not be any new greenback issue, he added; it would be possible to pay off the debt out of the government's annual surplus. We could ascribe Sherman's new view to conviction if he had not been so acutely conscious of the Democratic threat.

[78] Sherman brought the measure to the Senate for a first reading in December 1867. It was reintroduced on Feb. 27, 1868, with changes. It is this later version which is described. See *Congressional Globe*, 40 Cong., 2 sess., p. 1464.

[79] See below, this chapter, part II.

[80] For Morrill, *Congressional Globe*, 40 Cong., 2 sess., pp. 1626ff.; for Conkling, *ibid.*, pp. 4047-4048.

[81] Sumner's advisers, Joseph Ropes and Edward Atkinson, held that the "convertible" feature would be a one-way street: greenbacks funded into bonds would never return to circulation, and the problem of contraction and resumption would be solved. See Ropes to William P. Fessenden, Boston, July 9, 1868, Fessenden MSS, LC; Atkinson to Garfield, Brookline, Mass., July 4, 1868, and Boston, July 14, 1868, Garfield MSS. For Sherman's defense of the measure see *Congressional Globe*, 40 Cong., 2 sess., p. 4046.

The Democrats had raised the debt repayment question, Sherman reminded his fellow Senators, and it would "be made the basis of every election next fall in nearly all the Northwestern States." No man would be elected to Congress who did not take the right stand on the bond question.[82]

Sherman's apparent defection to the Pendletonians shocked the soft money business elements and the "conscience" honest money men alike. "Your last speech," Jay Cooke wrote the Ohio Senator, "created in the minds of our business citizens an universal feeling of sorrow that one standing so high, of whom they expected so much . . . has seemingly joined hands with the Pendletonians."[83] Even the Wall Street operators, it was reported, were in a dither over Sherman's remarks.[84] New England honest money men labeled the speech a "national perfidy," and Sumner was asked to deliver "one ringing speech . . . urging the practice of *simple honesty.*"[85] In the end, despite Sumner's qualified support, conservative Republicans stripped the bill of its offending interconvertible bond feature and it passed as a simple refunding measure.[86] Sherman may have pleased some of his constituents, but it was a long time before he was forgiven by the more doctrinaire conservatives.

As Sherman had predicted, the Pendleton Plan became a major issue of the 1868 Presidential campaign, and in the end it suffered a major setback. After some hesitation, the Republicans at their May convention took a firm and united stand against "all forms of repudiation."[87] No one expected such harmony from the Democrats at New York; but when it came to a showdown, the natural leaders of the anti-Pendleton forces showed surprising flexibility. Tammany stalwart Henry C. Murphy drew up a

[82] *Ibid.*, Appendix, pp. 181ff.
[83] Jay Cooke to Sherman, Philadelphia, March 21, 1868, Sherman MSS.
[84] *NYDT*, Dec. 23, 1867.
[85] William Endicott, Jr., to Charles Sumner, Boston, Feb. 29, 1868; E. L. Pierce to Sumner, Boston, Feb. 29, 1868, Sumner MSS, Houghton Library, Harvard University.
[86] *Congressional Globe*, 40 Cong.,
2 sess., pp. 4041-4050. The measure passed both houses but did not become law because of Johnson's pocket veto. Two years later, however, essentially the same measure was repassed. See below, ch. v.
[87] The plank adopted was almost identical with that of the Illinois Republicans'. See *New York Herald*, May 20, 1868; May 21, 1868; May 22, 1868; *NYDT*, May 19, 1868.

financial plank that conceded almost every issue to the Pendleton men. The plank recommended repayment of federal obligations in "strict accordance with their terms," taxation of government bonds, and "one currency for the Government and the
people, the laborer and the office holder, the pensioner and the
soldier, the producer and the bondholder." This program was
accepted by the Resolutions Committee,[88] and it was adopted by
the convention without debate.[89]

The soft money men were not so fortunate in the nominations.
The candidate of the party's eastern financial-commercial element was Chief Justice Salmon Chase. Despite his earlier spon-
sorship of the Legal Tender Acts, he had never felt happy with
paper money and was expected to resist the greenback faction.[90]
Pendleton, of course, was the candidate of the western soft money men, although not all the western delegates were as enthusiastic for the man as the Plan.[91] In the balloting Pendleton proved
unable to win a majority, much less the two-thirds required by
Democratic rules, and had to be abandoned by the westerners.
The Chief Justice was no more successful. His erratic political
wanderings, from Whiggery to anti-slavery Democracy, to Radical Republicanism, and back to a strongly anti-Negro Democracy
—in addition to his haughty self-righteousness—offended many
delegates. But there is reason to believe that the money issue
also helped defeat him. Had the Ohio delegation swung to
Chase after Pendleton's candidacy became hopeless, a stampede
might well have begun. At one point such a move appeared im-

[88] But only after removing the
ambiguities in the first clause. "In
strict accordance with their terms"
could have meant in gold as well as
in paper, since greenbackers and
anti-greenbackers interpreted the
actual "terms" in opposite ways. To
end the confusion, the Committee
revised the clause to commit the
party to payment of the debt "in
lawful money of the United States"
—i.e., greenbacks or gold—where
there was no express provision to
the contrary. See *Official Proceedings of the National Democratic
Convention Held at New York,
July 4-9, 1868* (Boston: Rockwell

and Rollins, 1868), p. 58.
[89] *Ibid., passim;* NYW, July 6,
1868; Charles H. Coleman, *op. cit.,*
pp. 198, 207.
[90] The young Thomas F. Bayard,
wrote his father, after reading a
note from S. L. M. Barlow endorsing Chase, that he supposed "Barlow's friends are scared on the financial question." Not yet set in his
later hard money mold he concluded
that "if the plutocrats want Chase
let them run him on a Third Ticket." See T. F. Bayard to James
Bayard, Wilmington, Del., May
31, 1868, Bayard MSS, LC.
[91] NYW, July 2, 1868.

minent until Henry Clay Dean, who had come to New York to fight for Pendleton and greenbacks, denounced Chase to the Ohio delegation. According to one report, Dean's attack, coming at just the right moment, was enough to check the impending switch, and the Chase boom collapsed. The Ohioans, satisfied with having won their platform, then turned to Horatio Seymour, New York's wartime Governor, who took the nomination on the twenty-second ballot.[92]

In the campaign that followed, the public was treated to a rare performance of political legerdemain. Seymour was an avowed hard money man running on a "repudiation" platform, yet both Democratic factions were able to assure their adherents that all was well. Despite appearances, wrote Marble in the *New York World*, the financial plank was sound. The single currency for government, pensioner, and bondholder meant nothing less than a uniform gold standard![93] At the opposite end of the spectrum, McLean, ignoring Seymour's past record, convinced himself that in accepting the platform the candidate had undergone a sincere conversion.[94]

Wherever soft money was reputedly strong, the Democrats emphasized finance; where it was weak, Reconstruction or Negro suffrage was stressed. In the West and upper South Pendleton rode the greenback hobby.[95] In the East, if we except the curious invasion of New York by Pomeroy,[96] the Democrats spoke much of Radical "usurpation of power" and the tyrannical Fourteenth Amendment.[97]

Republican strategy followed the same pattern, in reverse. Joseph Medill of the *Chicago Tribune* and A. H. Connor of the

[92] Coleman, *op. cit.*, ch. IX; and Stewart Mitchell, *Horatio Seymour of New York* (Cambridge: Harvard University Press, 1938), ch. XVII.

[93] *NYW*, July 8, 1868.

[94] Coleman, *op. cit.*, p. 246.

[95] *NYDT*, July 18, 1868; July 27, 1868.

[96] *Pomeroy's Democrat*, Jan. 6, 1869. Pomeroy established two papers, a daily—*The New York Democrat*—and a weekly—*Pomeroy's Democrat*—in competition with Marble's hard money *World*. Both

papers, for a while, enjoyed considerable success but were later sold when Pomeroy moved to Chicago. See Pomeroy, *A Journey of Life*, I, 216ff.; Frank Klement, "'Brick' Pomeroy: Copperhead and Curmudgeon," *Wisconsin Magazine of History*, XXXV, No. 2 (Winter 1951), p. 156.

[97] Coleman, *op. cit.*, pp. 287-288; *NYW*, July 28, 1868; Aug. 6, 1868; and other *World* editorials during the campaign.

Indiana Republican State Committee warned that the party would have to take western soft money into account or come to grief, and advised soft-pedaling the financial question.[98] Eastern Republicans pictured a Seymour victory as an invitation to repudiation. If the Democrats won, American "honor" and credit would be dragged to the level "which prevails among the Barbary Pirates and the Princes of Abyssinia."[99]

The October elections went badly for the Democrats. Republicans carried Iowa, Ohio, Indiana, and Pennsylvania by increased majorities over previous state contests, and for a time there was serious talk of replacing Seymour and Vice-Presidential nominee Frank Blair with stronger candidates.[100] In a last-minute attempt to save the campaign, Seymour, who had retired to his Utica farm shortly after the nomination, was induced to stump for soft money in the western and middle states. At Buffalo, Cleveland, Chicago, Indianapolis, Pittsburgh, and other cities, he played on the money issue in an attempt to arouse enthusiasm for the Democratic ticket. He condemned the Republicans for granting a banking monopoly to a few first-comers and endorsed the party's bond repayment plank.[101] This move, by the man who represented the conservative New York Democracy, was the measure of Democratic desperation. But the frantic salvage effort proved futile, and the Democrats were decisively beaten on election day.

Though Seymour's efforts to recover the West were unavailing, he did succeed in turning the Ohio Idea into a major campaign issue.[102] For a while the Ohio Idea unsettled western Republicans, many of whom ran to embrace Pendletonism. Few of the conversions survived the election. Democratic defeat was followed in the third session of Congress by a rush of contrite western Republicans and determined easterners to settle the

[98] Medill to John Sherman, Chicago, June 25, 1868, Sherman MSS; A. H. Conner to William E. Chandler, Indianapolis, June 20, 1868, Chandler MSS.

[99] *NYDT*, Aug. 11, 1868; July 16, 1868; Aug. 4, 1868.

[100] Coleman, *op. cit.*, pp. 340, 344ff.

[101] *Cincinnati Commercial*, Oct. 23, 1868; Oct. 25, 1868; *CDT*, Oct. 24, 1868.

[102] Seymour believed that the financial plank lost the Democrats the election. See Horatio Seymour to George L. Miller, Utica, New York, Dec. 20, 1869, Seymour MSS, New York Historical Society.

bond question as a political issue. On January 20, 1869, Chairman Robert Schenck of the House Ways and Means Committee introduced a bill entitled "An Act to Strengthen the Public Credit." To "remove any doubt as to the purpose of the Government to discharge all just obligations to the public creditors, and to settle conflicting questions and interpretations of the laws by virtue of which such obligations have been contracted," the measure read, the "faith of the United States is solemnly pledged to the payment in coin or its equivalent" of all federal obligations except where specifically exempted.[103]

Republican members debating the measure professed to see in the Presidential campaign a mandate for "honest" debt repayment. John Logan of Illinois frankly admitted that he had adopted Pendletonian views during the campaign. He had returned to sound money after November, convinced that "the decision of the people of my state on this campaign was given in such a manner as should satisfy their representatives that the decision must be sustained."[104]

Despite western Democratic opposition, the resolution passed the House by a large majority.[105] Slightly altered by a clause pledging the United States to "make provision at the earliest practicable period" for a return to specie, this basic bill passed both Houses on the last day of the Fortieth Congress.[106]

President Johnson, who had reverted to the old Jacksonian faith in his last State of the Union message and had blasted the bondholders,[107] could not be expected to approve the measure. Nevertheless, the Radical Congress sent it to him in the Administration's last hours. Johnson refused to sign.[108] An identical bill became the first important business of the new Forty-first

---

[103] *Congressional Globe*, 40 Cong., 3 sess., p. 476. As introduced, the measure also legalized gold contracts voluntarily entered into by private persons.

[104] *Ibid.*, p. 536. For a similar expression see the remarks of Representative George Miller of Pennsylvania, *ibid.*, p. 228.

[105] *Ibid.*, p. 1538.

[106] *Ibid.*, pp. 1829, 1835, 1841.

The measure went through a tortuous course before final passage, which it is neither necessary nor profitable to describe.

[107] James D. Richardson (ed.), *A Compilation of the Messages and Papers of the Presidents, 1789-1902* (n.p.: Bureau of National Literature and Art, 1903), vi, 572-573.

[108] *NYDT*, March 10, 1869.

Congress and was passed by large majorities,[109] in time to become the first measure approved by Grant after inauguration.

The Public Credit Act of March 1869 and contraction repeal in January of the previous year seem to represent opposite ends of the currency scale. The new measure was, of course, a setback to the Pendletonians. Yet a majority of Congressmen who voted to take away McCulloch's deflation powers in the second session of the Fortieth Congress voted to protect the federal debt against the "repudiators" in the third session. Of the four possible combinations of positions on the two measures, the first and by far the largest was composed of moderates—mainly western Republicans—whose currency position, simply stated, was "no contraction, no repudiation."[110] And this was the view that the bill at heart expressed. In effect, then, these two measures of the Fortieth Congress together set the terms of a general Republican currency settlement. Not by conscious direction, perhaps, but by the erosions and compromises of American politics, the Republican majority in Congress had arrived at a *modus vivendi* that was to last for five years. By repealing contraction, Congress gave notice that the country need no longer fear a forced deflation of prices and profits. By the Public Credit Act, the "national faith and credit"—and the bondholders' profits—were to be placed beyond the reach of the "demagogues" and "repudiators."

II

The Democratic greenback movement was the offspring of

[109] The vote in the House was 98 to 47; in the Senate, 42 to 13. *Congressional Globe*, 41 Cong., 1 sess., pp. 60, 70.

[110] The second largest group were greenbackers, and included Butler and Kelley and the greenback Democrats who opposed both contraction and the bondholders. A third group of 19 were conservative eastern Republicans—hard-core resumptionists. The last group was composed of men who were confused or who had changed their minds. In detail, the first group totalled 64, 61 of whom were Re-publicans; the second group—the greenbackers—numbered 39, 12 Democrats and 27 Republicans; the third group, representing uncompromising hard money, included 19 Representatives, 14 of them Republicans; while the last group numbered only 5. The surprisingly small number of Democrats included in group two, the greenbackers, can be explained by the small number of Democrats in the whole sample (24), which in turn reflects the decided minority status of the party in Congress. For these results in tabular form see Appendix A.

political necessity and the American Agrarian tradition. Simultaneously, the postwar social and economic confusion and the frustration of the "producing classes" sired another version of greenbackism out of the Jeffersonian social ethic. The intellectual father of wage-earner greenbackism was an obscure New York dry goods merchant named Edward Kellogg, who failed following the panic of 1837 and spent his remaining years examining the financial problem.[111] In 1841 he published pseudonymously a pamphlet entitled *Remarks Upon Usury and its Effects: A National Bank a Remedy,* which contained the germ of all his later writing. Kellogg was not an original thinker, and his work is a pastiche of slogans, bits of ideas, and whole concepts borrowed from the works of contemporaries and predecessors. "Usury" was the cause of the nation's past and present distress, Kellogg believed. Money was everywhere scarce in relation to the work it had to perform and was readily monopolized by "money lenders," who in times of crisis could exact an enormous toll for its use from perfectly solvent businessmen. The usurers were abetted by the state banks, which in periods of stringency were more willing to lend to loan sharks and "note shavers" than to legitimate businessmen. Moreover, with their alternate tightening and easing of credit, the banks produced the booms and busts that afflicted the economy, while their counterfeit and depreciated notes defrauded the public.

At this point it is tempting to label Kellogg a Locofoco and call his disciples primitive Jeffersonians. But on the contrary, in 1841 at least, Kellogg was an upholder of a central bank modeled after the recently defunct Bank of the United States! All his complaints against the existing banking system were as much Whig as Democrat, and his ideas drew on Carey as much as on Gouge. Unlike the Locofocos, Kellogg was not a bullionist, opposed to banks of issue. "Notwithstanding the attacks constantly made in some political contests upon banks and banking," he wrote, "the importance of such institutions, properly

---

[111] For the definitive description of Kellogg's career see Destler, "The Influence of Edward Kellogg Upon American Radicalism, 1865-1896," in *op. cit., passim.* See also Joseph Dorfman, *The Economic Mind in American Civilization, 1606-1865* (New York: The Viking Press, 1946), II, 678-681.

regulated, and the convenience of a paper currency always redeemable in specie . . . is . . . fully recognized."[112] Gold represented a minute part of the already insufficient circulation, and confining the nation to government issued coin was not a part of
Kellogg's plan. Borrowing from the neo-mercantilist ideas afloat
in his day, he saw the scarcity of money not only as an advantage to usurers in times of crisis, but as a deterrent to the
country's growth. Abundance of money encouraged enterprise
and fostered industry; scarcity raised interest rates beyond the
point where productive enterprise was possible. If interest exceeded net returns on invested capital, the money lenders
would eventually gather to themselves the whole wealth of the
nation.

The issue for America was how to avoid the alternate problems of the tribute exacted by the money lenders and "a narrow,
inconvenient, and unprofitable cash system." The answer, broadly stated, was to establish a "central bank" so regulated as to
end money monopoly. Let the bank, which was to be private—
although Kellogg sidestepped the details of its capitalization[113]—
lend money to anyone on good security and at uniform rates.
Establish a fixed 5 per cent maximum return on capital and keep
interest rates low enough at all times so that the bank could
never earn more than this amount. With little opportunity for
higher profit, he reasoned, the last incentive to dangerous expansion or contraction would disappear. The bank's rates in
effect would set a ceiling on all interest charges. Its notes would
circulate without discount all over the country. All state banks
would be forced to keep their notes at par, and, in general, the
country would be given a safe, abundant, uniform paper circulation, at low rates of interest, that would be free from the control
of gamblers and state bankers.[114]

In essence, what Kellogg wanted in 1841 was a reformed Bank
of the United States,[115] but he soon abandoned the idea of a

[112] Whitehook [Edward Kellogg],
*Remarks Upon Usury and Its Ef-
fects: A National Bank a Remedy*
(New York: Harper & Bros., 1841),
p. 5.
[113] *Ibid.*, p. 64.

[114] *Ibid., passim.*
[115] At one point he said of Biddle's "Monster" that "when the
later United States Bank was in
full operation usury was *compara-
tively* but little known; and if

private bank; by 1843 he had conceived the notion of a federal "Safety Fund" which would issue government notes at 3 per cent on mortgages and commercial paper. This would establish a limit on all interest charges, making it possible for productive labor to enjoy the fruits of its exertion. Loosely joined with this Safety Fund was a scheme for a "Treasury note," paying 2 per cent interest in gold or silver, which was to serve largely as a convenient investment for people with idle funds.[116] In 1849 Kellogg elaborated these ideas still further in *Labor and Other Capital*, a 300-page volume, which, under a different title,[117] had passed through five editions by 1883.

Despite the beliefs of Professor Chester M. Destler and others,[118] there is no provision in any of Kellogg's writings for a system which would automatically and simultaneously regulate interest rates and the volume of circulation.[119] This important mechanism is not evident until the work of Alexander Campbell which appeared at the end of the War. Like Kellogg, Campbell was a businessman, but significantly, a manufacturer and promoter rather than a merchant. Born in Pennsylvania in 1814, he entered the iron business in 1834 and soon rose to become manager of a number of forges in central Pennsylvania, and later in Virginia and Missouri. In the late '40's he moved to La Salle, Illinois, to look after some lands he had acquired through the Bank of the United States and stayed when he became interested in the coal of the area. Like many western

---

that United States Bank had been under suitable restriction, it would have ceased instantly." *Ibid.*, p. 62.

[116] [Edward Kellogg], *Currency: The Evil and the Remedy* (4th ed.; New York, 1843?), p. 17.

[117] The full original title was *Labor and Other Capital: The Rights of Each Secured and the Wrongs of Both Eradicated* (New York, 1849). The later title was *A New Monetary System: The Only Means of Securing the Respective Rights of Labor and Property and Protecting the Public from Financial Revulsions* (New York, 1868).

[118] Destler, "Influence of Edward Kellogg," p. 55; Robert P. Sharkey, *Money, Class, and Party: An Economic Study of Civil War and Reconstruction* (Baltimore: The Johns Hopkins Press, 1959), pp. 190-191.

[119] The above writers have assumed that the 2 per cent "Treasury note" associated with the original Safety Fund scheme was viewed as similar in function to the later 3.65 per cent interconvertible bond. The Treasury notes could indeed be cashed after a year, but Kellogg never intended to provide an "automatic regulator" of interest rates and currency volume. His notes were conceived of primarily as a convenient savings bond.

businessmen, he engaged in "general land business"—a euphemism for speculation—and soon was caught up in Whig politics. In 1862, as a Whig, he was elected Mayor of La Salle, but by the late '50's he had joined the new Republican party.[120]

Early in the War, Campbell began to brood on the financial question and the problem of raising money for the Union cause.[121] In June 1861 we find him writing to Secretary Chase to urge a government paper money to replace the worthless bank notes in circulation.[122] By 1862 he had apparently stumbled on Kellogg's work and by 1864 had hammered out a financial program combining Kellogg's doctrines with important new ideas of his own.

Campbell borrowed Kellogg's concept of the central role of the interest rate and shared his fear that high interest charges would concentrate all wealth in the hands of the money monopolists. He calculated the rate of national growth from 1790 to 1860 and found it much below the interest rates prevailing through the period. This fact accounted "fully for the many monetary crises we have had during that period and for the rapid centralization of the property of the nation in the hands of a few capitalists who produce no part of the national wealth, and for the impoverishing of the wealth producing classes."[123]

There is nothing in this that conflicts with the Whiggish variant of Agrarianism, but beyond this point Campbell diverges from the Whig tradition in a disconcerting way. He drops Kellogg's central bank proposal, and indeed, launches a vigorous attack on the new national banking system. The wants and interests of producers would not, he charged, be promoted by the recently established banking system or any other system. The new struc-

---

[120] This biographical data on Campbell comes from one of a series of "American Labor Portraits" appearing in *Workingman's Advocate*. See *WA*, Aug. 8 and Aug. 15, 1874.

[121] *Ibid.* The author of this biographical sketch, however, was certainly exaggerating the clarity of Campbell's early views. He has Campbell, for example, attacking the national banking system in September 1862, before it was

established, although not before such a scheme was discussed.

[122] Andrew McFarland Davis, *The Origins of the National Banking System* (Washington: Government Printing Office, 1910), p. 44.

[123] A[lexander] Campbell, *The True American System of Finance: The Rights of Labor and Capital. . . . No Banks: Greenbacks the Exclusive Currency* (Chicago, 1864), pp. 9ff.

ture would give the Secretary of the Treasury too much power and lodge monetary control in the eastern urban centers. "These banks will have the entire control of the currency of the whole nation, with power to expand and contract it at pleasure, to suit their own selfish views and ends without regard to the interests of the Government and wealth producing classes."[124]

If he detested the new banks, Campbell admired the new greenback, which, he believed, "the people . . . infinitely prefer . . . to the guilded [*sic*] frauds of our shoddy banking system." Therefore, let Congress repeal the National Bank Act and replace the bank notes with legal tenders as the exclusive circulation of the country.[125]

Campbell had thus managed first to single out and then to merge two related elements of Careyite and Agrarian philosophy. From the Careyite element of Kellogg he had taken over the concern with the interest rate and the unity of all producing classes. From the Jeffersonian tradition he had adopted the animus toward what he called "the fudal [*sic*] or aristocratic idea of money."[126] The praise of government notes seems to be a logical outgrowth of Kellogg's Safety Fund notes, with the important difference that a federal bank has been eliminated from the picture.

Campbell succeeded in transposing Kellogg into postwar terms while at the same time giving his ideas a Jacksonian twist that added to their potential appeal. Equally important, he took Kellogg's vague Safety Fund scheme—almost an afterthought in the original—modified it, and moved it to a central position. Dropped from Kellogg is the Safety Fund bank, with its overtones of the Bank of the United States. Campbell apparently did not conceive of the federal government substituting as a direct lending agent to the general public. His scheme is the ingenious and highly plausible one of a government bond paying 3 per cent interest and "interchangeable" or "interconvertible" with federal greenbacks. He accepted the mercantilist idea that interest rates were responsive to the changing volume of cash and believed that the new bonds would serve to prevent both inflation and contraction. If greenbacks were issued to

[124] *Ibid.*, p. 22.   [125] *Ibid.*, pp. 25-26.   [126] *Ibid.*, p. 25.

excess, commercial interest rates would fall below the bond rate and the legal tenders would be withdrawn from circulation by bond purchases. Were interest rates to exceed 3 per cent because of an increased demand for money, the bonds would be cashed and money would become available for loans. Thus the interconvertible bond would effectively put a roof over—and also a floor under—interest rates, at a figure that would end the exactions that money lenders and bankers could impose. At a stroke, a cheap, secure, and flexible medium of circulation would be provided.[127]

It is important to note that this scheme is inherently neither inflationist nor repudiationist. Inflation need not be feared, because under the interconvertible feature excess money would be soaked up by the bonds. Nor is anything said about paying the holders of the 5-20's in paper. Campbell did vaguely mention additional greenbacks to redeem the debt,[128] but he was still, at this point, an ardent Republican who hoped to see soldiers' pay and allotments increased, and he was not inclined to undermine the war effort by serious talk of squeezing the public creditor.[129] Campbell's interconvertible bond was to have a curious magnetic power, however. Around it were eventually to coalesce inflationists, repudiationists, and resumptionists, and at various times it was to make uneasy allies of western farmers, urban mechanics, eastern manufacturers, and middle-class reformers.

Campbellism came to dominate the "labor reform" movement of the '60's by a process that demonstrates as do few other events of these years the amazing power of both personality and ideology. The War had been a mixed blessing for labor. As we have seen, jobs became plentiful after Sumter, but real wages fell sharply. In 1863 Jonathan Fincher, editor of a widely read labor paper, noted that although he "had flattering accounts of the demand for men, an abundance of work and increased wages," these were "sadly neutralized by the unprecedented high price of all the necessaries of life."[130] The following year *Fincher's Trades' Review*, after reiterating the

[127] *Ibid.*, pp. 27ff.
[128] *Ibid.*, pp. 29-30.
[129] *Ibid.*, pp. 35ff.
[130] *Fincher's Trades' Review*, June 6, 1863.

complaint against high prices for "rents, groceries, provisions, cotton goods, clothing and every article essential to family comfort," concluded that only gold, or gold redeemable paper money, could be considered "the legitimate currency of the country."[131]

Labor spokesmen recognized, then, the disadvantages of paper money for the wage earner, and labor as a whole had little clear economic reason to support the greenback. Nor is there a tradition of paper money in the prewar labor movement on which labor greenbackism might draw. On the contrary, prewar labor had accepted Locofocoism and had been strongly bullionist. Thus, tradition and interest together should have propelled postwar labor into the hard money camp. But instead, organized labor absorbed the Campbellite defense of the wartime paper issue and soon made greenbackism its central dogma.

At least in its rejection of tradition, this startling result resembles the shift of Democratic viewpoint during the same period; and there are obvious analogies between the two events. At the outset it should be recognized that neither Pendleton nor Campbell desired unlimited expansion, and indeed, the Campbellite scheme had a built-in safeguard against inflation that labor leaders were generally careful to emphasize.[132] Moreover, labor greenbackism, like Democratic greenbackism, represented a revival of the anti-bank and anti-monopoly sentiment that had permeated prewar America. Nevertheless, as in the parallel Democratic conversion, only a powerful jolt forced the change from bullionism to paper money. This was supplied by a postwar crisis that drove the labor intelligentsia from the hard realities of the economic world to the plausible and congenial utopianism of the Campbellite system.

More specifically, this utopianism, which had also characterized discouraging periods of the prewar labor movement,[133] was

[131] *Ibid.*, April 23, 1864.

[132] *Coopers' Monthly Journal*, VI (June 1875), 156; *WA*, Nov. 27, 1875.

[133] John R. Commons and his associates and disciples have made the largely valid point that utopianism was the common response of labor to depression and trade-union failure. See Commons and associates, *History of Labour in the United States* (New York: The Macmillan Co., 1946), I, Introduction, especially pp. 12-21, and pp. 493ff. and 575ff.; Mark Perlman, *Labor Union Theories in America*:

a response to serious setbacks to "pure and simple trade-unionism." Taking advantage of full employment and high profits, trade-unionism had won unprecedented victories during the War. Higher wages, shorter hours, and recognition of collective bargaining had been readily won from employers unable to hire scabs and determined to avoid even a temporary stoppage of lucrative production. Easy victories had enhanced union prestige and union methods, and membership rolls had boomed. Appomattox was a dash of cold water to organized labor. The demobilization of hundreds of thousands of men, the end of war orders, falling prices, and the recession of 1866-1868 stiffened employer resistance. Continued labor militancy produced a wave of strikes that ended disastrously. Trade-unionism entered on dark days.[134] By 1870 the union efflorescence of the war years had been cut back to the roots, and these alone survived to regenerate labor organization when the economic climate once again improved.

These events had traumatic effects on a small group of labor leaders associated with the Chicago *Workingman's Advocate*. The most influential of these men was Andrew C. Cameron, a former printer—like so many working-class intellectuals from Ben Franklin to Horace Greeley—who in July 1864 founded the *Advocate* as the official organ of the Chicago Trades Assembly.[135] The first issue of the new paper appeared in the middle of a typographers lockout—by, ironically, the greenback *Chicago Times*—that ended disastrously for the union.[136] Conceived in trade-union adversity, the *Workingman's Advocate* was from the beginning reformist in its orientation. In March 1865 Cameron wrote an editorial which pointed out the basic weakness of accepting capitalism and attempting to soften it by trade-union activities. Free land in America had kept wages high, he admitted, but free land would soon give out and labor would be pauperized. Only two ways of escaping from this gloomy fate seemed possible to Cameron at this time. The first was through consumers' and producers' cooperatives; the second

Background and Development (Evanston, Ill.: Row, Peterson and Company, 1958), pp. 190ff.

[134] Commons, *op. cit.*, II, 94.
[135] *Ibid.*, 16.
[136] *WA*, Sept. 17, 1864.

by political organization to force both government and capital to recognize labor's rights to protection, and particularly to shorter hours.[137]

For the next year Cameron's attention was focused on the political Eight Hours Movement, the lineal descendant of the Jacksonian Ten Hours Movement. The defeat by the Ohio legislature of an eight hours bill early in 1866 drove Cameron to pledge that "from this day henceforth, the policy of the *Advocate* will be to aid in the formation of a *Workingman's* Party, independent of either political faction."[138] Added to the long string of similar defeats which followed in Massachusetts, New York, Pennsylvania, and Wisconsin,[139] it drove home to Cameron the necessity for political agitation. In April and May 1866 he was active in organizing the Illinois Grand Eight Hour League —a body which endorsed political action not only for a shorter work day but also for a long list of general reformist measures.[140]

Cameron had not, like Ira Steward in Massachusetts,[141] completely committed himself to the eight-hour panacea. A series of crushing labor defeats in early 1866—part of the damaging series of postwar strikes—reinforced Cameron's convictions regarding the futility of unions, which could not cope with the "wealth, the tremendous influence and the unity of our incorporated monopolies."[142] As the very language of this statement implies, these disasters brought him face to face with the main anti-monopoly element of the Jacksonian critique. On June 9 the *Advocate* carried on its first page a five-column article entitled "Our National Debt. The People's Plan of Paying it and Emancipating Labor. The True American Monetary System," signed "A. Campbell." On page two was a pro-greenback editorial, also signed by Campbell. Editor Cameron had become a convert to the interconvertible bond.[143]

A similar hegira characterized the career of William Sylvis, the talented leader of the Iron Molders' International Union, who in 1868 joined Cameron as joint editor of the *Advocate*.

[137] *Ibid.*, March 25, 1865.
[138] *Ibid.*, April 21, 1866.
[139] *Ibid.*, April 28, 1866.
[140] *Ibid.*, May 5, 1866.

[141] On Steward see Commons, *op. cit.*, II, 86-96.
[142] *WA*, May 19, 1866.
[143] *Ibid.*, June 9, 1866.

Born in southwestern Pennsylvania, not far from Campbell's birthplace, Sylvis had known bone poverty as a boy. He had gone to work at eleven with virtually no formal schooling and in the 1840's drifted into the iron industry as a molder. In 1857 he joined the iron molders' union, and natural eloquence, energy, and imagination rapidly carried him to a position of leadership.[144] During the War the Iron Molders' International under Sylvis' presidency, like organized labor as a whole, profited enormously from the bargaining power of full employment.[145] Prosperity continued until 1867, when the business downturn following the Overend, Gurney panic closed foundries and machine shops and stiffened the backs of employers. The next two years brought to the Molders, as to other groups, bitter defeat. Wages were cut, and then cut again; strikes were smashed one after the other; locals disbanded. Exhausted and demoralized, the Molders appeared about to disintegrate. Sylvis fought back and saved the Union, but it never entirely recovered.[146]

Even during the Molders' palmy days, Sylvis had never fully accepted trade-unionism as labor's salvation. Labor's powerlessness, ignorance, and poverty in a free republic, he felt, came from causes more fundamental than disunity; and its salvation must lie beyond mere collective bargaining. Like Cameron, another anxious seeker, Sylvis tried out a number of answers before discovering Campbell's doctrines. For a while he considered cooperation labor's "first object."[147] Later he called for political action and a labor party.[148] But by 1868 Sylvis, too, had embraced the interconvertible bond as the answer to the "labor question."[149]

The appeal of the Campbellite scheme to labor is not at first

[144] Sylvis' career is definitively treated in Jonathan Grossman, *William Sylvis, Pioneer of American Labor: A Study of the Labor Movement During the Era of the Civil War* (New York, 1945). For his early career see chs. I and II.

[145] *Ibid.*, ch. IV.

[146] *Ibid.*, ch. VIII.

[147] James C. Sylvis, *The Life,*

Speeches, Labors and Essays of William H. Sylvis, Late President of the Iron Molders International Union.... (Philadelphia, 1872), pp. 97ff.

[148] *Ibid.*, pp. 182ff.

[149] *Ibid.*, pp. 222ff., and especially the speech of Sept. 16, 1868, at Sunbury, Pennsylvania, pp. 231ff.

easy to understand. It did not lie, as is generally claimed,[150] in a desire to ease credit for producers' cooperatives or small enterprise. There was a parallel scheme advanced by Proudhon in France at this time that indeed envisaged government loans to workers enterprises,[151] but Campbell was explicit "that government has no constitutional right to become a money lender under any circumstances."[152] Moreover, labor greenbackism was not primarily concerned with elevating labor to the employer class, which is what Proudhon's scheme implied. In adopting Campbellite ideas, labor leaders largely abandoned producers' cooperatives. *Workingman's Advocate* in September 1866 denied that the laborer any longer expected to enter "the charmed circle of monopoly." "The great object and aim of the whole labor reform is *not* to make the workingman a capitalist," Cameron remarked emphatically, *"but to secure to him in his present condition those rights which are essential to his*

---

[150] See the following for this point of view: Commons, *op. cit.*, II, 112; Philip Foner, *History of the Labor Movement in the United States* (New York: International Publishers, 1947), I, 420-421; Thomas H. Greer, *American Social Reform Movements: Their Pattern Since 1865* (New York: Prentice-Hall, Inc., 1949), p. 17; Gerald N. Grob, "Trade vs. Reform Unionism: The Emergence of the Modern American Labor Movement, 1865-1896" (unpublished Ph.D. dissertation, Northwestern University, 1958), pp. 127-128. These writers have been misled, I believe, by their reasonable desire to establish a connection between the Kellogg-Campbell scheme and labor's rational self-interest. They have failed to notice sufficiently, however, the utopian element in the labor-greenback platform and have forced the facts further than they will legitimately go. An example of such forcing will be found in the introduction by John R. Commons and John B. Andrews to Vol. IX of Commons and Andrews, *A Documentary History of American Industrial Society* (Cleveland: The Arthur H. Clarke Co., 1910), p. 40, at which point the authors imply that the 1867 National Labor Union Convention specifically linked the interconvertible bond and producers' cooperatives as means to ends. The actual resolution, however, makes it clear that the interconvertible bond was seen as ushering in the millennium which would in turn produce a cooperative society. See *ibid.*, pp. 179-180. Professor Grob, in a published revision of his dissertation, has since relegated the producers' cooperative aspect of labor greenbackism to a secondary place. See Grob, *Workers and Utopia: A Study of Ideological Conflict in the American Labor Movement, 1865-1900* ([Evanston]: Northwestern University Press, 1961), p. 20, n.32.

[151] Grossman, *op. cit.*, p. 248, n. 31. Moreover, through the prewar Fourierist, Albert Brisbane, Proudhonist ideas did merge with the Campbell scheme. See below, this chapter.

[152] *WA*, Sept. 1, 1866.

well being, and to which he is entitled as a human being."[153]
Nor did the attraction of the Kellogg-Campbell bond scheme lie,
as a recent scholar has suggested, in labor's desire to restore
good times by lowering interest rates,[154] which would have made
it primarily a depression remedy. The hard times after 1873 did
substantially swell the greenback following among labor, yet
labor greenbackism was born in the largely prosperous years
of the '60's and flourished in the early '70's, as well as during
the difficult years after 1873.

The greenback appeal was more abstract than has been
recognized. The second half of the nineteenth century was a
period in America of deep anxiety about the relations of capital
and labor. "The greatest thinkers and critics of our time,"
Railroad Gazette noted in 1873, are "engaged in attempting to
solve the problem which it presents and formulate the social
phenomena which are being evolved."[155] To the labor intellectuals whose views ultimately prescribed organized labor's credo,
the Carey-Campbell concept that high interest meant low
wages was a revelation—a liberating insight. With trade-unionism seemingly discredited by events, many labor leaders saw
Campbell's claim that usury steadily concentrated the national
wealth in the hands of money lenders as the key to the great
labor puzzle.

Unlike the Eight Hour Movement and cooperation—competing home-grown ideologies—Campbellism was not only a
remedy but a diagnosis. It seemed to cut through the mystery
that surrounded labor's impotence and anguish in a democratic
society. "For twenty years," declared Sylvis in a revealing

---

[153] *Ibid.*, July 28, 1877. See also
ibid., March 7, 1874. By this
later period there are indeed a few
suggestions that the government
lend greenbacks to cooperatives,
but these are rare and seem to be
the work of one man, J. F. Bray
of Pontiac, Michigan, a transplanted English Chartist. See
National Labor Tribune, April 24,
1875; July 10, 1875.

[154] Edward Topping James,
"American Labor and Political
Action, 1865-1896: The Knights of

Labor and Its Predecessors" (unpublished Ph.D. dissertation, Harvard University, 1954), pp. 26ff.
It should be noted that Dr. James
also denies the cooperative motive
in labor greenbackism.

[155] *Railroad Gazette*, April 5,
1873. I have taken this quotation
from a version laboriously copied
out in longhand by a Wisconsin
Agrarian greenbacker, J. K. Osborn, Osborn MSS, State Historical
Society of Wisconsin.

apologia for his greenback faith, "I have been trying to discover some remedy for the great wrongs imposed upon labor—to find the reasons why a small portion of the population enjoyed ninety percent of the wealth of the nation, while the many whose labor produced everything, lived in poverty and want." The riddle was solved. Interest kept labor enslaved. "Interest acts like a tax-gatherer; it enters into all things and eats up the price of labor. . . . It produces nothing; all it does is to transfer the products of labor to the pockets of the money lenders, bankers and bondholders."[156]

Campbell's ideas had the same emotional impact on Sylvis, Cameron, Richard Trevellick of Detroit, John Magwire of St. Louis, John Hinchcliffe of the Illinois Miners, Alexander Troup, Robert Schilling of the Coopers, and other labor leaders as the Marxist revelation had had on European labor reformers and disaffected intellectuals. Lacking the power and rigor of Marx, without the vast philosophical and scholarly apparatus that gave the Marxist canon its persistent academic appeal, the Campbellite analysis and the interconvertible bond nonetheless filled the same function of interpreting the world for a strategic group of sensitive men. At the same time, it promised a conservative—and easy—solution to the labor problem. In later years, following the organization of the First International in America, when Marxist and Greenbacker bitterly opposed one another within the American labor movement,[157] the soft money men emphasized their moderation as against the extremist—and demanding—doctrines of their opponents. Speaking of the tangled and delicate questions of wealth inequalities and property relations following the 1877 railroad strikes, Robert Schilling noted that "sensible monetary laws" would "cause all these things to regulate themselves without government interference."[158] In a word,

---

[156] J. Sylvis, *op. cit.*, pp. 231-232, 247. Cf. the *National Labor Tribune's* strictures on interest: "It eats like a cancer; it drags the strongest down; it makes the rich poor; it makes the beggar wealthy, if he can get it; it drives millions into starvation; it ruins nations; it holds the struggling worker in dependence to those who have a little money; it makes children pale and haggard; it makes men sunken eyed and dejected; it makes mothers sad; it drives men from their homes and sends them down to Ruin." *National Labor ..Tribune*, Dec. 21, 1876.

[157] See below, ch. ix.

[158] *Labor Advocate*, Aug. 11, 1877.

the charm of Campbellism was that it came close to being the perfect cure-all, offering relief from distress quickly, painlessly, and cheaply.

But while Campbell's financial system could inspire part of the labor intelligentsia and the more speculative among the rank-and-file, it was incompatible with the old bullionist convictions of other sectors of labor. Fincher of the *Trades' Review*, although he did not like national banks and tax exempt bonds, feared that the interconvertible bond would create a field day for speculators and money market manipulators. Lewis A. Hine, an Ohio labor leader, continued to believe coin was "the workingman's currency, and the only honest currency." The interconvertible bond would produce inflation, and "inflation puts up prices, which the toiler must pay long before his wages climb up to the same level."[159] The Campbell scheme was also uncongenial to the strong pragmatic current that flowed through the American labor movement. Workingmen, asking Sylvis why interest rates were any concern of theirs since they were not borrowers, were not always satisfied with the Campbellite theorizing about the relation of interest to growth and prosperity.[160]

The most persuasive bread-and-butter argument of the labor greenbackers was that as long as employers had to pay high interest rates their profits must be low and labor consequently ill-paid.[161] But this tender concern for business profits was so out of character[162] that it was clearly a *post hoc* rationalization. It probably convinced no one when first expressed and is not convincing today. In the end the greenbackers had to rely on the same emotional appeal to a deeply embedded Agrarian distaste for privilege and concentrated wealth as did the Democracy. Sylvis told labor audiences that their "dearest rights" were "being stolen . . . by the power of gold"; that "bonds and banks" were "the Alpha and Omega of the devil's

---

[159] These remarks were made by Fincher and Hine at the National Labor Union Convention in New York in September 1868. *WA*, Oct. 10, 1868.

[160] J. Sylvis, *op. cit.*, p. 247.

[161] *WA*, Oct. 10, 1868.

[162] In 1863, for example, Sylvis had attacked employers who pleaded poverty in order to force lower wages on their employees. Now the labor leaders were making the plea for the employers! Commons, *op. cit.*, II, 6-7.

alphabet."[163] Labor greenbackers talked of the injustice of "unproductive capital" exploiting the "producing classes," and of the power of "irresponsible banking associations."[164] John M. Davis of the Knights of Labor traced the national banking system to Hamilton's bank scheme, "which from that day to this has cursed the people."[165] In the '70's the traditional Agrarian epithets "money power," "monster of the Age," "aristocracy of untaxed wealth," were still being hurled at the banking system by labor leaders.[166] This Jacksonian content was a major source of whatever following the Campbell scheme enjoyed among the lower echelons of labor. But it really did not answer the working-class skeptics who saw little connection between paper money and their pay envelopes.

Labor greenbackism rested ultimately as much on faith as on reason. To the self-made intellectuals who led the labor movement, Campbellite doctrines had a profound emotional, and indeed, almost spiritual significance. As at least one of its enemies noted, it was a secular religion which explained man's fall and promised his eventual redemption.[167] It is noteworthy that labor greenbackers were generally very fuzzy about the legislative details of the interchangeable bond; when confronted by opponents with the practical difficulties of launching their scheme, they replied with polemics rather than programs.[168] The closest approach to bringing the interconvertible bond down to earth and giving it some immediate relevance to the wage earner's life was the "interchangeable postal savings plan" suggested in the 1870's. This scheme emphasized the value of small denomination convertible bonds as safe investments for working-class savings.[169] It was clearly an afterthought, however,

[163] J. Sylvis, *op. cit.*, p. 247.
[164] *WA*, Oct. 10, 1868; *National Labor Tribune*, June 6, 1875; April 8, 1876; April 22, 1876.
[165] *Ibid.*, Nov. 28, 1876. For other attempts to link the Reconstruction money issue with the Jefferson-Jackson battles see the anonymous pamphlet *Opinions of John C. Calhoun and Thomas Jefferson on the Subject of Paper Currency* (n.p., n.d.); and *WA*, Oct. 10, 1867.
[166] *Labor Advance*, Jan. 19, 1878.
[167] George Wilson, Jr., *The Greenbackers and Their Doctrines* (Lexington, Missouri, 1878), p. 71.
[168] For example, *WA*, April 27, 1875.
[169] *IA*, June 3, 1876, article by S. J. Davis.

although it was probably the ancestor of the Populist and Progressive postal savings banks.

Such a strongly chiliastic movement proved irresistible to the more eccentric prewar humanitarians and social reformers—the congenital mavericks, nay-sayers, and professional outsiders seeking a cause in the postwar world. Wendell Phillips[170] and Edward M. Davis,[171] both well-known abolitionists, were drawn into the labor reform movement after 1865 and became prominent champions of the interconvertible bond. A number of prewar communitarians were caught up by the new social panacea: Albert Brisbane, the chief propagandist for Fourierist ideas before the War;[172] Charles Lewis Sears, a leader of the highly successful North American Phalanx; and John Drew, a youthful member of Brook Farm, who later joined Sears at the New Jersey Phalanx.[173] Short-haired women—Susan B. Anthony, Elizabeth Cady Stanton, Abby Hopper Gibbons—as well as long-haired men, became interconvertible bond greenbackers. In 1868 the Central Committee of the National Woman's Suffrage Association petitioned for a 3 per cent "convertible" bond.[174] In the early '70's Victoria Woodhull, a flamboyant feminist who managed to combine successful stock speculation, with yellow journalism and free love, added the interconvertible bond to her long list of indecorous causes.[175]

The actual circumstances of Andrew Cameron's encounter with Campbell's ideas are not hard to reconstruct. Campbell was an enormously energetic man with a zealot's need for disciples. The version of his scheme which the *Workingman's Advocate* published was a revision of his 1864 work, obviously written with an eye to attracting wage earners.[176] Campbell probably made the necessary contacts with Cameron himself. The

---

[170] Oscar Sherwin, *Prophet of Liberty: The Life and Times of Wendell Phillips* (New York: Bookman Associates, 1958), pp. 627-630; Sharkey, *op. cit.*, pp. 201-206, 281-282; *AM*, May 23, 1878; *IA*, Feb. 21, 1874, April 25, 1875.

[171] E. M. Davis to Benjamin F. Butler, Philadelphia, Sept. 6, 1867; Oct. 3, 1867, Butler MSS.

[172] *WA*, July 7, 1868.

[173] *Ibid.*, Sept. 4, 1874.

[174] *NYW*, July 1, 1868. For later greenback activities by suffragettes see *NYDT*, May 8, 1871.

[175] Victoria Woodhull, *A Speech on the Principles of Finance...Delivered at Cooper Institute* (New York, 1871), *passim*, especially p. 23.

[176] *WA*, June 9, 1866.

"father of the Greenback Movement"[177] was happy to advertise his ideas wherever he could[178] and willing to adapt them to diverse circumstances. Shortly after the "True American Monetary System" appeared in the *Advocate* in June 1866, we find Campbell at downstate Bloomington, making an important contact with the embryonic Illinois farmers' movement. On June 30 the *Advocate* noted that Campbell had lectured at the Bloomington Court House and had succeeded in getting his interconvertible bond endorsed by "a mass meeting of Farmers and others opposed to the money monopoly."[179] Three months later Campbell was presiding at a meeting of a state Anti-Monopoly Association at LaSalle.[180]

But Campbell's chief successes before the 1870's were with labor, through the National Labor Union, which until 1871 was to be the chief repository of postwar labor aspirations. Organized in August 1866, the N.L.U. was composed originally of national trade-unions, local trades assemblies, and Eight Hour Leagues. At its peak in the late '60's it had half a million members,[181] including groups of middle-class reformers and labor intellectuals, as well as horny-handed wage-earners.[182] At the first N.L.U. convention at Baltimore, despite Cameron's presence, not a word was said about finance.[183] Campbell himself attended the 1867 Chicago meeting, however, being admitted on special motion as representative of the Illinois State Anti-Monopoly Association. He was made chairman of the Committee on United States Bonds, possibly at Cameron's behest, and exerted immense influence on the convention. Campbell's own committee, which included Trevellick and Andrew J. Kuykendall, an Illinois Congressman who had recently sponsored an interconvertible bond bill,[184] brought

[177] This was the misleading title that Campbell acquired in the 1870's.

[178] Dr. Edward Topping James also sees Campbell as an active promoter of his own scheme. See James, *op. cit.*, p. 23.

[179] *WA*, June 30, 1866. As to the authenticity of this group's "farmer" credentials, see below, ch. VI.

[180] *WA*, Sept. 1, 1866.

[181] Gerald Grob, "Reform Unionism: The National Labor Union," *Journal of Economic History*, XIV, No. 2, (Spring 1954), 126.

[182] Commons, *op. cit.*, II, 94-102.

[183] The most convenient source of the proceedings of the first convention of the Union is Commons and Andrews, *op. cit.*, IX, 127-141. A more complete account will be found in *WA*, Sept. 1, 1866.

[184] *Congressional Globe*, 39 Cong., 2 sess., pp. 576-583.

in a limited recommendation for taxing the 5-20 bonds; but Cameron's committee on Political Organization submitted a platform outlining the entire Campbell money scheme and repeating almost verbatim sections of the Bloomington resolutions of the previous year. This was adopted without opposition, and Campbell's "True American System" in effect became the official financial creed of the Union.[185]

Thereafter the new doctrine diffused rapidly through the whole of organized labor. At the 1868 N.L.U. convention in New York, where Campbell again appeared, along with Sylvis, Cameron, Trevellick, and Mary Kellogg Putnam, daughter of the founder himself, the interconvertible bond, although attacked by Fincher, was again adopted as the official Union policy, with only two dissenting votes. The election of Sylvis as president ensured the active propagation of labor greenbackism.[186] By the 1869 meeting Sylvis was dead, but again the N.L.U. endorsed the interconvertible bond,[187] and it did so once more in 1870.[188] All through the '60's and into the '70's the *Workingman's Advocate* continued to propagandize for the Campbell scheme[189] and for over a year in 1869 and 1870 serialized Kellogg's *A New Monetary System*. Only in Massachusetts did Campbellism encounter opposition from organized labor, and even this was eventually overcome.[190]

The interconvertible bond was to be the identifying mark of "labor-reform" greenbackism until shortly before resumption. Along with the Campbellite analysis of the capitalists' exploitation of the producer, it differentiated labor soft money from Democratic soft money, particularly before 1870. Cameron denied the charge that "the Pendleton scheme and the Labor Platform" were "one and the same thing," seeing the "anxiety to saddle Pendleton, at all hazards, on the working class," as "very bad taste."[191] Yet there was a considerable overlap, even during the '60's. The labor reformers shared the antipathy to banks and

---

[185] *WA*, Aug. 24, 1867.
[186] *NYW*, Sept. 26, 1868; *WA*, Oct. 10, 1868.
[187] Commons and Andrews, *op. cit.*, IX, 235-236.
[188] *Ibid.*, p. 265.

[189] *WA*, April 11, 1868; July 9, 1870; Nov. 8, 1870; April 22, 1871.
[190] Sharkey, *op. cit.*, pp. 199-206; *Pomeroy's Democrat*, Feb. 2, 1870.
[191] *WA*, June 6, 1868.

bondholders of the soft money Democracy. Like the latter, they, too, wished to tax the bonds and to abolish the national banks, substituting greenbacks for bank notes.[192] They were also, of course, anti-resumptionists. Sylvis, Cameron, and other labor leaders ridiculed McCulloch's contraction and called resumption unworkable.[193] Nonetheless, a practical political neutrality, intended to avoid unnecessary conflicts of allegiance, and a rather weak commitment to a separate labor party, until 1869 kept the National Labor Union from accepting the Democratic paper repayment plank. On the other hand, it was only in the following decade that the interconvertible bond became an important factor in Democratic politics.

Labor greenbackism was also distinguishable from the enterpriser version of soft money. The two creeds shared certain ideological elements—primarily a similar analysis of the role of interest rates—but here the affinity ended.[194] The greenback and the interconvertible bond were not endorsed by the ironmasters until after the panic of 1873, and then only momentarily.[195] Organized labor in turn had serious doubts of protection,[196] and I have not uncovered a single instance of a labor spokesman defending paper money on the ground that it would protect either American industry or the wage earner. Indeed, the labor reformers carried on a feud with many of the leading Careyites. *Iron Age* and E. B. Ward were attacked for anti-labor views;[197] Daniel Morrell was accused of paying his Cambria employees starvation wages at Johnstown.[198] Carey himself was treated contemptuously by Sylvis as an economist of the "higher orders," who, like the Classical Economists, pontificated about labor without himself having done an ounce of honest work.[199] In later years, when out of the distinct strands of the 1860's a syncretic greenbackism

---

[192] Resolutions to this effect were passed at the National Labor Union Conventions of both 1867 and 1869.

[193] J. Sylvis, *op. cit.*, pp. 298ff.; WA, July 24, 1869; Dec. 18, 1869.

[194] I believe Dr. Sharkey exaggerates the "congruity" of the labor and Careyite approaches. See Sharkey, *op. cit.*, pp. 206-210.

[195] See below, ch. VII.

[196] Even Sharkey, who sees the protectionist element as central to soft money, paints an equivocal picture of labor's attitude toward the tariff. Sharkey, *op. cit.*, pp. 206-210. See also WA, April 8, 1871, and March 30, 1872, for strong attacks on protection.

[197] *Ibid.*, Aug. 29, 1868.

[198] *Ibid.*, May 14, 1870.

[199] Grossman, *op. cit.*, p. 120.

took shape, these hard words would be forgotten; but we must avoid reading later events into this period.

The labor reform variant of the interconvertible bond was clearly a soft money doctrine. But there was another version, one that was financially ambiguous, that won a following among New York businessmen. This variety can perhaps be traced back to early nineteenth-century England.[200] In America it appeared, independently of Kellogg, as the creation of Pliny Freeman, President of the Globe Life Insurance Company of New York, who in 1862 concocted a 6 per cent "reconvertible" bond, for stabilizing both interest rates and the total money stock.[201] Although five years later Freeman changed the prescribed rate of interest to 4 per cent,[202] his publicly professed purpose was not, like the labor reformers', to keep interest rates low, but to keep both cost of borrowing and price levels *constant*, and to provide an interest-earning outlet for idle funds.[203]

Freeman actually did not conduct a bona fide insurance business. This was an era of shocking laxity in insurance underwriting, and the New Yorker seems to have been among the less reputable men in the field. When the Globe Company failed in 1878, the public learned of the scandalous misappropriation of funds by Freeman and his family for their railroad and real estate speculations.[204] Despite his professions, Freeman, as a promoter and speculator, was a soft money man who wanted an "increase" of currency "instead of a curtailment."[205] Nevertheless, it was entirely appropriate for a conservative life insurance

[200] Fritz Redlich, *The Molding of American Banking* (New York: Hafner Publishing Co., 1951), II, part II, 124.

[201] Pliny Freeman, *Correspondence on National Finance from 1862 to 1875* (New York, 1876), pp. 3-4.

[202] *Ibid.*, p. 5.

[203] Pliny Freeman, *The National Standard Rate of Interest as a Regulator* . . . (New York, 1872), pp. 3-4. In this pamphlet, containing writings of 1865, Freeman attacked contraction but did not endorse expansion. Freeman's company had, during the War, often

invested sizeable amounts of its funds in federal temporary loan certificates, and he regarded an interconvertible bond as a substitute for these earlier securities as a temporary investment. Congressman William D. Kelley later referred to Freeman's and other insurance men's practices in his pamphlet, *Judge Kelley on the Crisis* (Philadelphia, 1874), p. 6.

[204] *The Public*, XIII (June 27, 1878), 208.

[205] Pliny Freeman to John Sherman, New York, March 26, 1866, Sherman MSS.

executive, whose actuarial and profit calculations required price stability, to support the interconvertible bond; and Freeman's scheme received an enthusiastic response among other New York insurance writers, whose business practices were more legitimate.[206]

Freeman's idea also won a business following in other fields. The interconvertible bond seemed likely to solve the major problem of "flexibility" that beset the American banking system after 1865. Besides the $300-million ceiling on national bank circulation that placed an overall total limit on the system, there was a short-run rigidity that deeply concerned the business advocates of interconvertibility. Whatever current commercial needs, the note issue remained at $300 million, neither expanding to meet enlarged seasonal demand nor contracting in time of slack. Indeed, in operation the system was not only unresponsive, it actually developed a dangerous negative elasticity. Through late spring and summer, in particular, when only the corn was stirring in the great farm areas, unused assets piled up on the books of the country banks. These were often transferred to New York, where they found on interest-paying outlet. Unfortunately, they did not serve the general New York business community well, since they had to be kept liquid for instant return if needed by the western banks. This restricted their use to call loans, which could be employed only by brokers and stock market speculators. During the summer, then, with call loan funds available, the stock market and the speculative exchanges boomed. In the fall, when rural banks withdrew their funds to help finance crop movements, an annual stringency occurred in New York which often approached panic proportions.[207]

---

[206] At least three other presidents of New York life insurance companies besides Freeman signed a petition in 1869 recommending an interconvertible bond. These were Fred S. Winston of the Mutual Insurance Company, Morris Franklin of New York Life, and John Eadie of the United States Life Insurance Company. See Wallace Groom, *Currency Needs of Commerce* (New York, 1873), p. 6. For an explanation of the stake of the insurance men in a stable monetary unit see the broadside by Elizur Wright, the prominent insurance actuary and former abolitionist, in the folder for Jan. 11, 1878, Rutherford B. Hayes MSS, Hayes Memorial Library, Fremont, Ohio.

[207] On the inelasticity of the monetary system during the national bank era see Albert Bolles, *The Financial History of the United*

The rigidity and the alternation of boom and bust that appeared to be built into the system disturbed even conservative business groups. The contractionist *Commercial and Financial Chronicle,* speaking for an important element of hard money opinion, believed that establishing a redemption system for national bank notes in New York would solve the elasticity problem.[208] But one group of New York businessmen, led by Wallace Groom, looked to interchangeability for a solution. Groom was editor of the *New York Mercantile Journal,* a paper catering to the trading interests of New York, and might have been expected to accept the resumptionist views of a majority of the New York commercial community.[209] But he belonged to a group of dissenters, which included George Opdyke, Horace B. Claflin, and F. B. Thurber, which would eventually break openly with the conservative majority of the New York Chamber of Commerce. Groom turned the *Mercantile Journal* into a forum for various unorthodox monetary views and eventually allied himself with the outright greenbackers.[210] In the '60's, however, he was still a moderate, chiefly interested in flexibility. In 1869 he circulated a petition for an interconvertible bond paying the convenient sum of 3.65 per cent interest a year—or one cent a day per hundred dollars.[211] The new bond issue would not inflate the economy, Groom held, but would end the monetary feast and famine, provide a valuable investment for unemployed cash, and serve as reserves for the banks in place of greenbacks.[212] This last pro-

---

States from 1861 to 1885 (2nd ed.; New York: D. Appleton & Co., 1894), pp. 347ff.; Redlich, *op. cit.,* pp. 119-120; Margaret G. Myers, *The New York Money Market* (New York: Columbia University Press, 1931), pp. 399ff.

[208] *CFC,* v (July 20, 1867), 69; IX (Oct. 2, 1869), 423. On the redemption problem see John Jay Knox, *A History of Banking in the United States* (New York: Bradford Rhodes & Co., 1900), pp. 101-105.

[209] For the New York mercantile community see below, ch. IV.

[210] See below, ch. VIII.

[211] It is not clear whether Groom or someone else was responsible for the change from the old three per cent figure to the enticing 3.65 per cent. At all events, the change was made at about this time. Note the fact that no provision was made for leap years.

[212] Groom, *op. cit.,* pp. 4-6. The interest shared by both Freeman and Groom in a short-term security as a convenient earning asset for idle funds has persisted among businessmen. In our day the need has been met by short-term Treasury notes, which function in much the same way as the interconvertible bond.

vision promised to increase bank profits by providing an interest earning asset to replace the non-interest bearing greenback reserve required by law. Groom succeeded in getting the endorsement of a large number of New York national bankers, along with some insurance executives,[213] merchants, and even a few manufacturers.[214]

Groom and Freeman were at least incipient soft money men, whatever their pose, but their supporters represented a wide range of opinion. A. A. Low, one of the most consistent hard money men among the New York merchants, was a signer of Groom's petition. Another supporter was the editor of the *New York Tribune*, Horace Greeley, a man whose monetary views have generally been misunderstood. On the strength of his support for the interconvertible bond he has been described as a soft money man,[215] but nothing could be further from the truth. Greeley's intransigent prescription, "the way to resume is to resume," startled even conservatives.[216] The *Tribune's* demand for remorseless contraction even if it should "shut down the gates of half our mills, close some of our stores," and drive "a half million or so workers" to the West to grow corn,[217] outraged both enterpriser and Agrarian soft money elements.[218] Greeley accepted the interconvertible bond because he believed it would help fund the maturing debt without recourse to foreign bankers and investors and would help rather than hinder resumption. He wanted the Treasury to offer the American public a new 3.65

[213] This latter group included Freeman, and it is probable that Freeman and Groom collaborated in drawing up the petition.

[214] Groom, *op. cit.*, p. 6.

[215] Sharkey, *op. cit.*, p. 168; Destler, "The Influence of Edward Kellogg," p. 62.

[216] Greeley borrowed this catch phrase from former Treasury Secretary, now Chief Justice, Salmon Chase. See Chase to Greeley, Washington, June 5, 1866, Chase MSS, LC. On the negative response to Greeley's draconian formula see the anonymous article, "Greeley and Carey," *Social Economist* (*Gunton's Magazine*), VII,

(September 1894), 142.

[217] *NYDT*, March 19, 1866; March 24, 1866.

[218] For the enterprisers see E. P. Smith to Henry Carey, Washington, March 26, 1866, Carey MSS, Historical Society of Pennsylvania. As late as 1869 Carey, who before the War had been a friend of Greeley and a contributor of protectionist articles to the *Tribune*, was still angry at the *Tribune* editor for his contractionist sentiments. See Carey, *Resumption! How It May Profitably Be Brought About* . . . (Philadelphia, 1869), p. 3. For the Agrarian criticism see *WA*, April 10, 1869.

bond, paying interest in gold, and with the proceeds redeem the 5-20's. Not only would this save the nation from paying 5 per cent interest to foreigners and commissions to foreign bankers, but it was expected, by some unexplained sleight of hand, to bring the greenbacks up to gold.[219]

There were, then, at least three well-defined soft money currents in the early postwar years. One of these, identified politically with western and Pennsylvania Republicans, drew its support from promotional business elements. This was the very group which recent historiography has pictured as the controlling postwar elite. Yet through 1870 their program of free banking had been frustrated by the resistance of Agrarians and more conservative business elements. A second soft money force was compounded largely of political elements—Jeffersonian Agrarianism, Democratic opportunism, and Copperhead thirst for revenge. It was greenback in orientation and largely Democratic— though there was a minor Republican variant—and flourished particularly in the West where rural Agrarian traditions were strongest. Suffering from the early postwar feebleness of the Democracy, political greenbackism could nonetheless claim a modest victory in helping to stop McCulloch's contraction. A third current, which drew from the same ideological reservoir as the postwar greenback Democracy, was utopian and reformist in nature and expressed the frustrations and aspirations of labor and the extremist humanitarian reformers in the uncongenial postwar era. In the 1860's it was not politically affiliated; in later years it was strongly drawn to third-party politics, although it also succeeded in infiltrating the western Democracy, particularly in Ohio. Its early political impotence hindered any progress toward advancing its goal of an automatically adjusting currency system based on the interconvertible bond.

It would be stretching the truth for the sake of specious clarity to insist that these three streams flowed side by side, self-contained and unmingled. To some extent the distinctions made here are artificial. Seldom were these three varieties of soft

---

[219] Greeley's reasons for supporting the interconvertible bond are quoted in Henry Carey, *Currency Inflation, How It Has Been Pro-* *duced and How It May Profitably Be Reduced . . .* (Philadelphia, 1874), pp. 15-16.

money found in their pure form. Even in the '60's soft money men borrowed generously from all available sources for ideological weapons. One such eclectic was Butler—a displaced Jacksonian, a textile manufacturer, a friend of labor—who not only took up the Democratic attack on the bondholders but also adopted the interconvertible bond, which—to make his affiliations the more remarkably inclusive—he apparently derived not from Campbell but from Pliny Freeman.[220] More typical, however, would be the attempt to ally labor reform and Democratic greenbackism, and by the mid-'70's distinctions among greenbackers would become increasingly blurred. But before the new decade, soft money was a triune entity, enfeebled by disagreement in the face of a composite but essentially united and implacable hard money foe.

[220] See Pliny Freeman to Butler,   28, 1867, Butler MSS.
New York, Oct. 12, 1867 and Oct.

THE HARD MONEY INTEREST

(1865-1870)

I

A SINGLE-MINDED devotion to specie payments gave a unity to the hard money cause that the anti-resumptionists, distracted and divided by bonds and banks, could not match. Financial conservatives often argued over means and bickered over details. Some were intransigent contractionists who expected quick and total withdrawal of all greenbacks; others, advocates of gradual and partial contraction; still others, men who believed it possible to resume without reducing circulation. But unlike the motley band of Copperheads, labor reformers, congenital dissenters, and maverick businessmen whom they opposed, their sole end, one undisturbed by side issues, was the return to the gold standard. This does not mean that all men arrived at a hard money position by the same road. The motives of the conservatives were as mixed and complex as their adversaries'. Hard money men responded to conscience and duty as well as interest, and in their own way they were as receptive as their opponents to the cultural and intellectual influences which surrounded them.

If the Pendletonians and labor reformers drew strength from secular Agrarianism, hard money was infused with the values of American Protestantism. As we have seen, a Protestant concern with economic affairs was transmitted from Geneva to Britain and then transplanted to American soil by men of puritan outlook. The financial ferment after 1865 inevitably reawakened this concern. To the ministry, contemporary economic issues were moral issues, and they never doubted that the postwar money question came within their purview as moral guardians of the nation. They agreed with the Reverend Lyman Atwater that "economics and ethics largely interlock,"[1] and accepted Leonard Bacon's dictum that "any honest man" could "understand . . . financial questions because they are also, and equally, moral questions."[2] Among public issues of the day, only the fate of the freedmen was to engage the Protestant, and particularly the Calvinist, clergy and religious press so completely as the money question.

From the very first, the ministers and the religious editors were active partisans who identified hard money with virtue. The blunt declaration of the New York *Christian Advocate* that "atheism is not worse in religion than an unstable or irredeemable currency in political economy," expressed the settled conviction of the great majority of Protestant leaders.[3] Specifically, the religious indictment of soft money had two parts. Specie resumption was a question of common honesty. As the *Congregationalist and Boston Recorder* noted, expediency had become the country's guiding star with regard to the currency. Politics, momentary convenience, immediate economic advantage, all determined public policy. But these were "merely incidental and collateral." "The claims of justice and honesty come first and that which is just and honest is always expedient."[4] The paper system was also a danger to public morality. "It is hardly an exaggeration to say," declared the *Christian Examiner* of Boston, "that to the disordered condition of the currency we owe the chief part of the extravagance and dishonesty in mercantile circles, and so much of the corruption in public offices as is not due to our imbecile method of filling these offices."[5] "All other breaches of faith and morality which have been so pregnant with public and private disaster," wrote Atwater in 1874, "receive

---

[1] Atwater, "The Late Commercial Crisis," *The Presbyterian Quarterly and Princeton Review*, III (January 1874), 123-124.

[2] *Christian Mirror*, LII (Dec. 2, 1873), 68. See also the remark of the Chicago Congregational weekly, *The Advance:* "The paramount questions in politics are, it is true, financial, but they are moral at the same time. Christian newspapers, though in no sense partisan, cannot be silent in regard to them." *The Advance*, IX (Oct. 21, 1875).

[3] *The Christian Advocate* (New York), LIII (Aug. 8, 1878), 505.

[4] *Congregationalist and Boston Recorder*, quoted in *Reform League Broadsides*, Vol. I, No. 8 (July 28, 1869).

[5] *Christian Examiner*, LXXXVI (January 1869), 37.

stimulus and nutriment from the fundamental breach of faith and morality by the nation itself, in not taking steps to redeem with dollars its own promises to pay dollars."[6]

If the greenbacks evoked a moral judgment, the ethical import of the bond question was still plainer. The national debt "represent[ed] the national conscience," and the "first duty of the nation" was "to make its word good."[7] "If the nation should prove false to its present engagements, entered into before the whole world, and in circumstances peculiarly solemn," where was "the guarantee that it may not prove false to individuals in other things."[8] "The true course" was "to maintain the national faith by adhering to its sacred obligations."[9]

Nor in arguing the money issue could the agents of organized Protestantism refrain from publicly judging specific persons and policies. In the '60's McCulloch and his partisans were fulsomely praised. The widely circulated New York *Independent* applauded McCulloch's rebuke to Henry Carey in 1865 and added that "prices must continue to go *down, DOWN,* until the banks and the Government resume specie payments; and that glorious era cannot come a minute too quick."[10] The *Christian Mirror* of Portland, Maine, carried the Secretary's Fort Wayne speech under the heading "Sound & Hopeful Words," and later endorsed the contractionist recommendations in President Johnson's 1866 Annual Message.[11] The Ohio Idea, on the other hand, was a "base renunciation of our sacred honor";[12] Pendleton and Butler were "demagogues,"[13] and their scheme to tax the bonds and pay them in paper would "disgrace us in the eyes of all Christendom."[14] Henry Ward Beecher, the most popular pulpit orator of the day, preached a financial sermon on the text "thou shalt not steal," scolding the Democrats for adopting the Ohio Idea in their 1868 platform.[15] Pendleton's race for the Ohio Governor-

[6] Atwater, *op. cit.,* p. 100.
[7] *The Christian Advocate* (New York), LII (Dec. 20, 1877), 813.
[8] *Presbyterian Banner,* LIV (April 1, 1868), 1.
[9] *Christian Register,* XLVII (April 28, 1868), 2.
[10] *The Independent,* April 13, 1865, p. 8.
[11] *Christian Mirror,* XLIV (Oct. 31,

1865), 60; XLV (Dec. 11, 1866), 66.
[12] *The Christian Register,* XLVII (March 28, 1868), 2.
[13] *The Standard,* XVI (Dec. 31, 1868).
[14] *The Advance,* I (Oct. 17, 1867); I (March 19, 1868).
[15] Quoted in *WA,* Aug. 1, 1868.

ship in 1869 incited the Chicago *Advance* into bald political partisanship. "It is a matter of national import that Mr. Pendleton be defeated," editor A. B. Nettleton told his readers, "for his election . . . would be a blow to the public credit not to say a slight upon Ohio's patriotic dead."[16] Following Pendleton's defeat, Nettleton wrote his successful opponent, Rutherford Hayes, that "the overthrow of the greenback heresy . . . is really an event of national and historic import."[17]

The labor reformers were also rebuked for their currency views. Beecher's *Christian Union* decided that the interconvertible bond looked "remarkably like irredeemable paper currency."[18] The *Advance* was unbecomingly supercilious about the 1869 Labor Congress platform: "Of the English and the logic of these resolves we have not a word to say: they are matters to be wept over. The declaration that somebody is attempting to 'subvert the government of our fathers and establish in its ruins an empire,' etc. is such a happy cross between lunacy and comedy that we have no heart to criticize it soberly." In the end Nettleton complacently dismissed it as the work of "soft handed idlers," not the real workingmen of the nation.[19]

The Calvinist denominations took the lead in the religious attack on heretical financial ideas. Atwater was a Presbyterian, Bacon a Congregationalist; the *Advance*, the *Christian Mirror*, as well as the *Boston Recorder* and the *Presbyterian Banner* among those quoted above, were all Calvinist papers. Other Protestant groups opposed soft money. The New York *Christian Advocate* was the country's leading Methodist weekly, the Chicago *Standard* was Baptist, and one Baptist minister, the Reverend A. H. Strong of Cleveland, engaged in a loud public fracas with Butler over paying the 5-20's.[20] But throughout the debate, the Calvinist voice is heard most loudly. In addition to the orthodox Reformed weeklies, two of the papers quoted, the *Christian Examiner* and

[16] *The Advance*, II (Aug. 19, 1868).

[17] A. B. Nettleton to R. B. Hayes, Chicago, Oct. 19, 1869, Hayes MSS, Hayes Memorial Library, Fremont, Ohio.

[18] *Christian Union*, v, No. 9 (Feb. 28, 1872).

[19] *The Advance*, II (Aug. 2, 1869).

[20] See the clipping of Strong's sermon of Nov. 28, 1868, attacking Butler, and a draft of Butler's reply in the folder for November 1868, Benjamin F. Butler MSS, LC.

the *Christian Register*, were Unitarian and retained much of the old Calvinist concern for the moral public life. The *Independent* under Theodore Tilton was Congregationalist at its founding and did not abandon its Calvinist perspective with its disaffiliation. Beecher was originally a Congregationalist, and in the following decade his *Christian Union*, along with the Dutch Reformed *Christian Intelligencer*, was to uphold financial righteousness among New Yorkers.

This is not to suggest that the Arminian churches condoned economic unorthodoxy; they did not. In reality all of organized and official Protestantism in America upheld sound finance. It is largely a question of how much attention the non-Calvinist denominations devoted to public issues. The fact is that they were far less activist and far less interested in finance than the Reformed groups. If the Baptists and Methodists noticed the money question occasionally, the rural, fundamentalist churches, among whose communicants soft money views might be expected to flourish, were totally silent. In a thirteen-year run of the Campbellite weekly, the *Christian Standard*, for example, there is not a single reference to the nation's pressing money problems. Equally significant at the other extreme was the indifference of the Protestant Episcopal church, which then as now represented established wealth and social prestige. Traditionally opposed to zealotry, imbued with an often stultifying decorum, the Episcopal church eschewed all political controversy. Partisan involvement in public issues, declared the editor of the Hartford *Churchman*, was to be avoided. It often required "more true courage to be silent than to be noisy with the crowd."[21]

It is difficult to assess the impact of the churches on the financial debate. However, one clear effect was to endow hard money polemics with a moral vocabulary. According to Edward Atkinson, a prominent Massachusetts textile manufacturer, "God's will and the nature of things" ordained hard money.[22] The pious McCulloch, in his 1865 Fort Wayne speech, also claimed God's vote for honest finance.[23] The staid weekly, the *Financier*, saw "a

[21] *The Churchman*, v (April 1, 1871), 108.
[22] Atkinson to William B. Allison, Brookline, Mass., April 12, 1874,
Allison MSS, Iowa State Department of History and Archives.
[23] McCulloch had declared that gold and silver were "the necessary

connection between irredeemable paper money and the growth of financial dishonesty since the war."[24] "A bad currency" did "more to debauch public and private morals," wrote a Michigan friend to David A. Wells, than all other causes combined.[25] What started as pious partisanship sometimes slipped over into fanaticism. The Christian defense of hard money eventually led to a very unchristian fetishism that gave the precious metals almost supernal powers.[26] At its extreme it approached demonology. Wells's friend believed that paper money exerted an "influence for bad as subtle as the evil one."[27]

The Christian apology for hard money may seem little more than religion in the service of partisanship. True, the clergy took sides, but it is a mistake to question either their sincerity or the sincerity of those who echoed their arguments. Puritan values were deeply implanted in the American culture, and whether they were "church people" or agnostics, Americans could seldom disregard the stern commands of the Decalogue without emotional discomfort. When the stakes were high enough, men might subordinate the right to the profitable, but it was seldom without some sort of inner pain. In effect the Protestant conscience exacted a price for defiance and, all things being equal, defiance was avoided. The role of the churches, then, was to articulate what much of the public already believed and by constant reiteration make manifest what was latent. Under the ceaseless hortatory barrage of the pastors and the denominational press, hard money took on the odor of sanctity which gave it an immense competitive advantage with the respectable, church-going middle class.

That the Protestant divines were dangerous foes of monetary "heresy" was never doubted by the heretics themselves, and they

---

regulators of trade . . . prepared by the Almighty for this very purpose." Hugh McCulloch, *Men and Measures of Half a Century* (New York: Charles Scribner's Sons, 1900), p. 201.

[24] *The Financier*, III (May 17, 1873), 353.

[25] Willard Parker to David A. Wells, Detroit, April 10, 1877, Wells

MSS, LC.

[26] E.g., Joseph Medill, *Payment of the Debt: A Review of the Ohio Democratic Financial Departure . . . at Columbus, Ohio, Aug. 31, 1871* (Chicago, 1871), p. 6; Anonymous clipping in Thomas Bayard MSS, LC, Nov. 4, 1878.

[27] Willard Parker to Wells, Detroit, April 10, 1877, Wells MSS.

were quick to strike back at their clerical detractors. Cameron turned Beecher's "Thou Shalt not Steal" against the Brooklyn pastor's stylish congregation—full of "shady" contractors who had amassed fortunes during the War by cheating the government.[28] In the '70's Ignatius Donnelly's *Anti-Monopolist* called Beecher himself a "hollow old shell" for his attacks on the greenbacks, and hit below the belt by alluding to his notorious intrigue with Elizabeth Tilton.[29] The greenbackers scolded the editors of the church weeklies for making themselves a party to exploitation and injustice. "The religious press has almost without exception been the allies [sic] of the bondholders and bankers in their endless schemes to fleece the public, and the mouthpiece of the monopolists and the defender of the soulless corporations that fill their pockets by robbing the toiling people."[30] Even bankers and brokers occasionally supported labor reform, a writer in *Industrial Age* noted, but "the religious press has almost universally wheeled into line in support of the Shylocks and the sharpers."[31]

Allied with the clergy in the work of creating an "orthodox" financial view were the academic economists. Before the Civil War the clerical influence pervaded American higher education, and at most American colleges "political economy" was taught by a minister as a branch of "moral philosophy." In the 1850's Atwater had held the chair of metaphysics and moral philosophy at the College of New Jersey.[32] At Brown University President Francis Wayland, a Baptist minister, taught the course in political economy and wrote the most widely used introductory economics text of the prewar period.[33] The War did not suddenly end the clerical-academic association. After 1865 Atwater continued to indoctrinate young ministerial students at Princeton Theological Seminary, while at Yale William Graham Sumner, an ordained Episcopal clergyman, introduced several generations of

[28] *WA*, Aug. 1, 1868.
[29] *AM*, Aug. 9, 1877.
[30] *IA*, Oct. 31, 1874. See also *Labor Advance*, Feb. 2, 1878.
[31] "J. W." to *Industrial Age*, Allegan Co., Mich., in *IA*, May 1, 1876.
[32] Joseph Dorfman, *The Economic Mind in American Civilization, 1606-1865* (New York: The

Viking Press, 1946), II, 705. The College of New Jersey was, of course, the earlier name for Princeton.
[33] Michael J. L. O'Conner, *Origins of Academic Economics in the United States* (New York: Columbia University Press, 1944), pp. 172ff.

students to the mysteries of supply and demand, tariffs, and value, as well as banks, bonds, interest, and money.[34]

It is scarcely necessary to say that the "clerical school" of academicians saw economics as a branch of ethics. Atwater, as we have seen, believed that "economics and ethics largely interlock." Sumner told his students that God exercised "a political providence over the country . . . by the laws of political economy."[35] But even the lay professors in the postwar period were not entirely liberated from the traditional ethical perspective of their discipline. Francis Bowen, Alford Professor of "Natural Religion, Moral Philosophy & Civil Polity" at Harvard, was trying to combine the old faith in moral law with the fashionable new scientism when he noted that there was "a general science of Human Nature, of which the special sciences of Ethics, Psychology, Politics and Political Economy are so many distinct and coordinate departments."[36]

This ethical perspective was only reinforced by the dominant intellectual tradition of academic economics. The American professoriate accepted almost without question the dogmas of Classical Economics. Preponderantly free traders,[37] they also subscribed to Ricardo's and Mill's anti-mercantilist capital theories. Besides enjoying the prestige of European orthodoxy such theories confirmed, by emphasizing savings and self-denial, deep Calvinist prejudices. Capital, they held, must be distinguished from mere cash. The reward of frugality, real capital was the excess of production over consumption, and its abundance alone, not that of

[34] See Harris E. Starr, *William Graham Sumner* (New York: Henry Holt & Co., 1925), ch. xvi.

[35] Dorfman, *The Economic Mind in American Civilization, 1865-1918* (New York: The Viking Press, 1949), iii, 67.

[36] Francis Bowen, *American Political Economy, Including Strictures on the Management of the Currency and the Finances Since 1861* (New York: Charles Scribner's Sons, 1887), p. iv. This is a reprint of the 1870 edition.

[37] Bowen was an exception. For his mild protectionism see *op. cit.*, pp. 485ff. (Bowen's dissenting view

is, incidentally, another piece of evidence pointing to a rather loose connection between protectionist principles and soft money.) For the free trade views of several other prominent economists see Amasa Walker, *The Science of Wealth: A Manual of Political Economy* (4th ed.; Philadelphia: J. B. Lippincott & Co., 1875), pp. 91ff.; Arthur Latham Perry, *Elements of Political Economy* (New York: Charles Scribner & Co., 1866), pp. 77ff., 347-407; for Wayland's free trade views see O'Conner, *op. cit.*, p. 178.

currency, determined interest rates and the ease of borrowing.[38] "To increase the stock of money in the community," wrote Bowen, "is not thereby to augment the fund available for loans, or to diminish the difficulty of borrowing, or to lower the rate of interest."[39]

These principles the professors recited over their lecterns to the small elite in the nation's leading colleges. At Princeton, Yale, Williams, and Harvard, Atwater, Sumner, Perry, and Bowen respectively molded the financial thinking of the young. At Cornell President Andrew White illustrated the evils of currency experimentation from the lessons of French history.[40] Even in the West the academicians were "sound," and railed against the economic "vagaries" of their section.[41] But through their writings, particularly the widely circulated introductory texts, the professors' conservative teachings reached a far larger public. From 1837 on, Wayland's *Elements of Political Economy* shared the stage with Jean Baptiste Say's equally orthodox *Treatise*, as the most widely read "first principles" text. By the War it had gone through four editions and many printings and was to appear in six postwar editions.[42] In 1866 the introductory work of Professor A. L. Perry of Williams appeared, usurping first place from Wayland and running through a fantastic twenty editions before 1885.[43] Other prominent texts of the period which dispensed orthodoxy were Amasa Walker's *Science of Wealth* and Francis Bowen's *Principles of Political Economy*.[44]

[38] Bowen, *op. cit.*, pp. 245ff.; Bowen, *The Principles of Political Economy Applied to the Condition, the Resources, and the Institutions of the American People* (Boston: Little, Brown and Company, 1859), p. 309; Francis Wayland, *The Elements of Political Economy* (Boston: Gould & Lincoln, 1860), pp. 208-209.

[39] *Ibid.*, pp. 248-249.

[40] Andrew White to David A. Wells, Cornell University, April 6, 1876, Wells MSS.

[41] J. W. Andrews to Rutherford B. Hayes, Marietta College, Ohio, Dec. 10, 1877, Hayes MSS. At Illinois College and at Beloit, in Wisconsin, the Reverend Professors Julian M. Sturtevant and Aaron

L. Chapin respectively also upheld orthodoxy. But there were a few exceptions among the western academic contingent. For the details of these latter and Sturtevant and Chapin see Dorfman, *The Economic Mind, 1865-1918*, pp. 73-77.

[42] O'Conner, *op. cit.*, pp. 17, 174-178.

[43] *Ibid.*, pp. 314-315.

[44] Walker's book was first published in 1866. Bowen's *Principles* appeared in 1859; it was republished in 1870 as *American Political Economy*, with additional material on postwar finance. See n. 36 for full citation. On the question of the relative influence of the orthodox as opposed to the dissenting text writers, note the poll conduct-

On the specific question of fiat money the text writers followed the Ricardians. Walker's 1866 text condemned the issue of a legal tender as "a great usury," never "justified except in the most extreme case of national peril."[45] Perry declared that "a paper money is only tolerable when it is actually and instantly convertible on demand into gold and silver." Unlike Walker,[46] he praised the new national banking system and its issues, but concluded that "taking all things into consideration, every way the best money is the gold and silver which God has evidently designed for that purpose."[47] Bowen's revised text of 1870 observed that "the prolonged use of Paper Money" had "done even more harm to the morals of the country than to its commerce, its reputation, and its financial well being."[48] William Graham Sumner's *History of American Currency* pictured the issue of greenbacks as a great wartime error. "Whatever strength a nation has is weakened by issuing legal tender notes." "All history shows that paper money with a forced circulation is not a temporary resource. . . . It is a mischief easily done but most difficult to cure."[49]

Supported by a gifted corps of financial freelances and journalists, which included J. B. Hodgskin, Joseph Ropes, Gamaliel Bradford, Simon Newcomb, David Wells, and Edward Atkinson,[50] the academic economists allied themselves with the clergy

---

ed by *Publishers' Weekly* in 1876, which indicated that the ten leading works—which included the texts of Perry, Walker, Wayland, and Bowen, as well as of John Stuart Mill and Adam Smith—were all, without exception, orthodox on finance. See Dorfman, *The Economic Mind, 1865-1918*, p. 81.

[45] Walker, *op. cit.*, pp. 132-136.

[46] In 1866 Walker believed that the as yet untried national banking system would encourage the same instability as had the old state bank system. *Ibid.*, p. 236.

[47] Perry, *op. cit.*, pp. 249-256, 263.

[48] Bowen, *American Political Economy*, pp. 342ff.

[49] William Graham Sumner, *A History of American Currency* (New York: Henry Holt & Co., 1874),

p. 202.

[50] Hodgskin was a New York broker who wrote many of the financial articles for the *Nation*. Ropes was a Boston merchant, a Vice-President of the Boston Board of Trade in the '60's and '70's, and a gifted amateur financier. He wrote for *Banker's Magazine* and was prominent in the financial deliberations of the Social Science Association. Bradford was a Boston private banker and financial writer for the *North American Review* and other periodicals, as well as an advisor of Treasury Secretary Fessenden. Newcomb was a well-known astronomer who wrote on financial subjects for the *Nation, North American Review*, and other hard money publications.

to guard the country's financial purity and advocated heroic measures to return the nation to "sound" practices. Arguing, validly, that to succeed, resumption had to be preceded by deflation, which would bring American paper prices in line with those of Europe,[51] they stubbornly rejected every alternative to massive greenback destruction. *"I do not believe it possible to resume,"* Perry told his former pupil James A. Garfield, *"without further and large contraction."*[52] Bowen suggested in 1865 that one-fifth of the government's income be set aside in greenbacks "and publicly burned." At the end of eight or nine months "120 million would have been destroyed and gold would be down to 130."[53]

Originally Bowen's idea, this "cremation theory" is generally associated with the name of David A. Wells, Chairman of the Special Revenue Commission established in 1865 to review federal taxation policy.[54] Wells had been a protectionist early in his career. By 1868 his Reports as Special Commissioner had become tracts for both free trade and hard money, and he was the hero of the academicians and the educated public.[55] In 1870 his protectionist enemies forced him to resign his post, but they did not make him abandon the good fight. He became an aggressive and prolific pamphleteer for sound money and in 1875 published *The Cremation Theory of Specie Resumption,* advocating the draconian program of burning half a million greenback dollars weekly.[56]

Another influential champion of "honest finance" was the articulate and public-spirited Massachusetts cotton manufacturer Edward A. Atkinson, a man of immense industry and catholic

---

[51] Otherwise there would be a large and immediate outflow of gold to pay for cheap imported goods. See James K. Kindahl, "Economic Factors in Specie Resumption: The United States, 1865-79," *Journal of Political Economy,* LXIX, No. 1 (February 1961), pp. 29ff.

[52] A. L. Perry to James A. Garfield, Williams College, May 30, 1868, Garfield MSS, LC.

[53] Quoted in *The Independent,* March 23, 1865, p. 8.

[54] Herbert Ronald Ferleger, *David A. Wells and the American Revenue System, 1865-1870* (New York, 1942), pp. 17-21.

[55] *Ibid., passim.* Currency sections of Wells's reports will be found in *Report of the Special Commissioner of the Revenue for 1868,* pp. 13-20, 89-115; *Report . . . for 1869,* pp. iii-lix. In the latter, Wells characteristically declared, "the simple remedy for the evils of inflation would seem . . . to be *contraction, pure and simple, without artifice or indirection." Ibid.,* p. lix.

[56] Wells, *The Cremation Theory of Specie Resumption* (New York, 1875), pp. 5ff.

interests, whose views on finance and protection were to carry great weight with an important section of New England business-men. Atkinson encouraged McCulloch in his contraction policy[57] and advised Charles Sumner on financial problems.[58] Closely allied with the Yankee reformer element, he wrote numerous hard money pamphlets, and in both the '60's and '70's devoted much of his prodigious energy to leading the contractionist forces against the greenback attack.[59]

II

Wells and Atkinson are links between the academicians and the middle-class reform impulse of the postwar years. In the '70's this reform current would produce the Liberal Republican movement, and in the following decade men of similar outlook would be called Mugwumps. But in the '60's they generally referred to themselves as "independents" or "reformers" and championed a program of free trade, civil service reform, and hard money.

This genteel reformist current of the Reconstruction period was a complex phenomenon. Like all attempts to alter the *status quo*, it was fueled by discontent. But its appeal was not to the great mass of the underprivileged who filled the nation's urban and rural slums. It was largely the product of the social and political frustration of the middle and upper classes that was such an impressive source of the nineteenth-century American attempts to remake the world.

It is easy to see how post-Civil War America could frustrate educated young men of good family. To an ambitious, self-confident, young aristocrat like Henry Adams, America of the late '60's seemed an appalling place. Returning from England in 1868 intent on carving out a brilliant career in public affairs,[60] the

[57] Atkinson to Hugh McCulloch, Boston, June 1, 1867; July 26, 1867; Aug. 5, 1867, Atkinson Letter Books, Atkinson MSS, Massachusetts Historical Society.

[58] Atkinson to Charles Sumner, Boston, July 17, 1868, Sumner MSS, Houghton Library, Harvard University.

[59] See below, and Harold Francis

Williamson, *Edward Atkinson: The Biography of an American Liberal, 1827-1905* (Boston: Old Corner Book Store, 1934), pp. 81-98.

[60] He dreamed, while in London, of a "national set of young men . . . to start new influences not only in politics, but in law, in society and through the whole social organism of the country." See Ernest

young man found the places of power and honor in Washington occupied by political harpies, and public life "rotten with the servility of what was antiquated and the instability of what was improvised."[61] Adams' expectation that the new General-President would restore virtue to political life was cruelly disappointed. Grant's cabinet, with few exceptions, was composed of the new breed of political Neanderthals—men, Adams wrote, "who sprang from the soil to power . . . distrustful of themselves and others; shy, jealous, sometimes vindictive, . . . for whom action was the highest stimulant."[62] In such an environment the young Brahmin stifled, and after a short stint as a political reporter, he retreated behind the protective walls of Harvard.[63] If political life was closed to men of Adams' fastidious breed, so, too, was the world of commerce and industry. The vulgarity and moral shoddiness that had invaded politics was found double-distilled in American business. The worst scandals of eighteenth-century Britain paled beside the 1869 gold cornering operations of Jay Gould and Jim Fisk, Adams thought.[64] Henry's brother, Charles Francis, Jr., after a lifetime of observing the business scene close up, concluded that he had never encountered "a less interesting crowd" than the " 'successful' men." "A set of mere money-getters and traders, they were essentially unattractive and uninteresting."[65]

Indeed, there seemed little in American life that was not crass, venal, and vulgar. The young Englishman, Edwin L. Godkin, who established and edited the New York Nation, found America a "chromo civilization," with a social elite composed of half-educated dilettantes whose slim learning came from the "small colleges," the cheap periodicals, and desultory travel in Europe.[66] To the young Boston Brahmin, Charles Eliot Norton, writing in 1871 from the vantage of Europe, it appeared that "the Nation and Harvard and Yale Colleges" were "almost the only solid barriers against the invasion of modern barbarism and vulgarity."

Samuels, The Young Henry Adams (Cambridge: Harvard University Press, 1948), p. 78.

[61] Henry Adams, The Education of Henry Adams (Modern Library ed.; New York: Random House, 1931), p. 248.

[62] Ibid., p. 265.

[63] Ibid., pp. 291ff.

[64] Or at least later thought. Ibid., pp. 271-272.

[65] Charles Francis Adams, Jr., An Autobiography (Boston: Houghton Mifflin Co., 1916), p. 190.

[66] Nation, xix (Sept. 24, 1874), 202.

Nowhere in America did he see a "concentration of the forces of the upright and thoughtful part of the community."[67] Of an older generation, James Russell Lowell catalogued in verse the failure of the United States, entering the second century of nationhood:

> Columbia puzzled what she should display
> Of true home-make on her Centennial Day,
> Asked Brother Jonathan: he scratched his head,
> Whittled a while reflectively, and said,
> "Your own invention, and own making too?
> Why, any child could tell ye what to do:
> Show 'em your Civil Service and explain
> How all men's loss is everybody's gain;
> Show your new patent to increase your rents
> By paying quarters for collecting cents;
> Show your short cut to cure financial ills
> By making paper-collars current bills;
> Show your new bleaching-process, cheap and brief,
> To wit: a jury chosen by the thief;
> Show your State Legislatures; show your Rings;
> And challenge Europe to produce such things
> As high officials sitting half in sight
> To share the plunder and to fix things right;
> If that don't fetch her, why you only need
> To show your latest style in martyrs—Tweed:
> She'll find it hard to hide her spiteful tears
> At such advance in one poor hundred years."

How could the picture seem anything but bleak to the young aristocrats when even Walt Whitman, democrat to the core, judged American society "cankered, crude, superstitious and rotten."[68]

Cut off from the more congenial perquisites of place and power, some of the young men took refuge in the eastern universities with Henry Adams, Norton, and Francis A. Walker, son of the economist. Others took to journalism, an occupation that at once satisfied their literary instincts and kept them close to the

[67] Norton to Edwin L. Godkin, Dresden, Germany, Nov. 3, 1871, Godkin MSS, Houghton Library, Harvard University.   [68] From *Democratic Vistas*.

life of public affairs they so coveted. Godkin made the *Nation* into "a sort of moral policeman of . . . society . . . politics, and . . . art."[69] Norton and Henry Adams for a while edited the politico-literary *North American Review*, catering largely to the New England upper crust and the literati. Whitelaw Reid, Charles Nordhoff, Murat Halstead, Horace White, and Samuel Bowles found outlets for their talents with the more literate and respectable daily newspapers. Some, like David Wells and, for a while, Francis Walker, entered the civil service in technical capacities, only to discover how deeply partisan politics permeated even the most neutral functions of American government.[70] Almost all made minor careers of writing articles and reviews for the better periodicals and the more congenial daily newspapers. Few cared to stay away from politics, however. Excluded from leadership in the Gilded Age by an overdeveloped fastidiousness, unwilling or unable to court popularity or get along with the new type of politicians, they became political outsiders. As critics and gadflies they hovered at the fringes of public life, quick to pounce on transgressions, always ready to take on more active political roles when the opportunity appeared.[71]

Overwhelmingly the reformers were Yankees. Boston was the center of much of the reform agitation, and Boston men, or at least New Englanders, whether at home or transplanted to the numerous Yankee colonies in the West, supplied the brains, energy, and money for most of the reform program.[72] This New

---

[69] This was how Samuel Bowles of the *Springfield Republican* described the *Nation*. George S. Merriam, *The Life and Times of Samuel Bowles* (New York: The Century Co., 1885), II, 97.

[70] On Wells's public career as Special Commissioner of Revenue and the pressures which forced him out of government life see Ferleger, *op. cit.*, pp. 295-312. Walker originally served as Chief of the Bureau of Statistics and then as Indian Commissioner, only to resign from the latter post, convinced that government service under existing circumstances was no place for a young man of ability. James Phinney Monroe, *A Life of Francis Amasa Walker* (New York: Henry Holt & Co., 1923), pp. 141-149.

[71] The best examination in print of the nature and origin of these postwar reformers is Ari Hoogenboom's excellent article, "An Analysis of Civil Service Reformers," *The Historian*, XXIII, No. 1 (November 1960), *passim*. See also Hoogenboom, "Outlawing the Spoils: A History of the Civil Service Reform Movement, 1865-1883" (unpublished Ph.D. dissertation, Columbia University, 1957), pp. 34-35, 303ff.

[72] *Ibid.* If foreign born, they were also apt to be either English or German. The latter, it was often noted, like transplanted Yan-

England preponderance was doubtless related to the rapid falling away of Yankee political influence which followed the growth of the West and the ethnic revolution at home. The senior Charles Francis Adams, even from England, observed the decline and concluded that future national leadership lay with the West, while Boston and New England, their "intelligent and thrifty" Yankee population replaced by the "inferior celt," would be reduced to political and intellectual impotence.[73] For men of ability and energy, the decline of their region, and their role within that region, heightened the feeling of social and political futility and reinforced their disapproval of the state of the Union. But Calvinism was also an element in middle-class Yankee reform. Although the connection must not be pushed too far, both the Calvinist and the reformer possessed an ingrained penchant for judging men's actions and an irrepressible itch to improve and uplift. The old fear of hell-fire had long ago evaporated among the Yankee elite, but the puritan conscience and the puritan character remained to propagate a significant movement of social protest.

Yet the postwar reform impulse was not merely puritanism stripped of its supernatural element. Another ingredient in the mixture was a profound preoccupation with "science." Americans did not, of course, suddenly discover science in these years. There had been much interest in Natural Philosophy in both the Colonial period and the early Republic, and some original scientific work had been done by Amercians before the Civil War. But the advent of Darwinian biology, with its satisfying answers to age-old questions and its disturbing challenge to age-old beliefs, produced a large new public for scientific knowledge after 1865.[74] The universities, with Harvard in the lead, responded

---

kees, seemed to be highly resistant to soft money views even when surrounded by them. See James Shroeder to William Allison, Guttenberg, Iowa, Nov. 16, 1878, Allison MSS; *Indianapolis Sun*, July 1, 1876.

[73] Charles Francis Adams, Sr., to Charles Francis Adams, Jr., London, Feb. 4, 1868. See also Adams, Sr., to Adams, Jr., London, March 10, 1868; Adams, Sr., to Henry Adams, Boston, Feb. 24, 1869; Adams MSS, Massachusetts Historical Society.

[74] It is significant that such journals as the *Nation* and the *North American Review*, which represented the reform view in politics, were among the leaders in disseminating the new scientific ideas, particularly those connected

with courses in biology, chemistry, and physics.[75] By 1865 popular "scientific" magazines were being published, and "science" columns had begun to appear in the older periodicals.[76] The Astor Library in New York would find by 1872 that works in the natural sciences had become as popular among readers as "general literature."[77]

As used in the period, "science," of course, encompassed the study of natural phenomena. But by the '60's the term also came to be applied to what an earlier generation thought of as social philosophy.[78] The work of Auguste Comte and Herbert Spencer seemed to provide new insights by treating social events as scientific phenomena. Charles Francis Adams, Jr., later declared that reading Mill's essay on Comte "revolutionized in a single morning" his "whole mental attitude."[79] Spencer's *Social Statics* seemed to be a perfect analogue to the all-conquering Darwinian biology, bringing order and form into the apparently anarchic realm of human behavior.[80] Before long, the middle-class intelligentsia, acting at times as apologist for special interests, more often as sincere converts to a new way of explaining a puzzling world, began to claim for social theory the objectivity and precision of the natural sciences.

The new interest in the science of society found concrete expression in the fall of 1865 when, after three years of preliminary effort, a group of Boston intellectuals, philanthropists, and businessmen established a Social Science League modeled after the British "National Association for the Promotion of Social Science." Renamed the American Social Science Association, the organization dedicated itself to investigating and analyzing the "scientific"

---

with Darwin. Richard Hofstadter, *Social Darwinism in American Thought* (rev. ed.; Boston: The Beacon Press, 1955), pp. 20-25.

[75] *Ibid.*, pp. 19-22.

[76] Frank Luther Mott, *A History of American Magazines, 1865-1885* (Cambridge: Harvard University Press, 1938), pp. 104-105.

[77] *Ibid.*, p. 107.

[78] Sidney Fine notes, significantly, that the chief American outlet for Spencer's ideas during the '70's was Edward L. Youmans' *Popular Science Monthly*. Fine, *Laissez Faire and the General-Welfare State: A Study of Conflict in American Thought, 1865-1901* (Ann Arbor: The University of Michigan Press, 1956), pp. 41-42.

[79] This event, which he further explained changed his "intellectual and moral being," occurred, symbolically, in 1865. See Charles Francis Adams, Jr., *op. cit.*, p. 179.

[80] Hofstadter, *op. cit.*, ch. II; Fine, *op. cit.*, ch. II.

principles purportedly underlying society. The Association defined its province under four headings: "Education, Health, Economy and Jurisprudence"—subjects which were "confessedly susceptible of scientific treatment"—and established committees of "experts" to conduct discussions, disseminate information, and organize research in their special areas.[81] Like its British counterpart, however, the American Society was more than a collection of dispassionate investigators, for from the beginning, its founders sought to improve society. Social Science was conceived as a reform movement designed to "uplift whatever is low . . . by placing it on a firmer foundation." Distinguished from mere philanthropy, social science went "behind the effect to the cause," and attempted "to prevent, even more than relieve, the error existing among men."[82]

The new discipline was not morally neutral. Social Science was a new church which, like the old, sought to oversee the affairs of men. But the Calvinist fervor for moral guardianship conflicted with the concept of political economy advanced by the movement, for at the same time they sought to promote public righteousness, the men who made up the Association envisioned the neutral, detached state—honest, efficient, above politics, opposed to all special interests, and dedicated to strict *laissez faire* in economic matters. Such, they believed, had been the character of the conservative Republic of Washington, and Adams, and the Virginia Dynasty. It had been shaken by the rise of demagogy and the spoils system with the accession of King Andrew[83] and finally destroyed by greedy parvenus and political opportunists who, with "a certain amount of natural quickness of capacity" and "that sort of education picked up at hazard by the necessities of

[81] *Journal of Social Science*, I (June 1869), 1; Luther Lee Bernard and Jessie Bernard, *Origins of American Sociology: The Social Science Movement in the United States* (New York: Thomas Y. Crowell Co., 1943), pp. 527ff.

[82] *Journal of Social Science*, I (June 1869), 2-3.

[83] See the elder Charles Francis Adams' illuminating comment on the decline in the tone of national political life with the advent of Jackson. Adams, Sr., to Charles Francis Adams, Jr., Boston, Dec. 1, 1869, Adams MSS. Similarly, Charles Eliot Norton late in life longed for the old New England, "before the coming of Jacksonian Democracy and the invasion of the Irish." Kermit Vanderbilt, *Charles Eliot Norton, Apostle of Culture in a Democracy* (Cambridge: The Belknap Press, 1959), p. 212.

the moment" had come to the top in the postwar era.[84] Reform the Civil Service and restore government to those fitted by education, character, and ability to administer it. End the protective system, the nursery of irresponsible wealth. Bring the nation back to financial honesty and end the reign of "charlatans and quacks" who used the ignorance of the people to advance their political interests. These three themes—Civil Service Reform, free trade, and hard money—were to be endlessly debated at Association conventions and in the pages of the *Journal of Social Science* and the reformist New York *Nation*, and, with the later demand for ending Radical Reconstruction, were to become the platform of middle-class reform and political independency in the two decades following the War.[85]

During the '60's the Social Science Association served as an indispensable point of contact among the nation's middle-class dissenters. The list of Association officers and members in 1869 is a roster of the reform movements of the period. On the executive committee were David Wells, Amasa Walker, Arthur Latham Perry, and Daniel Coit Gilman of Yale.[86] Charles Francis Adams, Jr., was Treasurer, and among the members were Charles Francis Adams, Sr., the historian-diplomat John Lothrop Motley, Atkinson, E. L. Godkin, George William Curtis of *Harper's Weekly*, and William Cullen Bryant of the New York *Evening Post*.[87] In the following decade Wells and Curtis were both to serve as president of the Association; to the membership of the earlier decade were to be added Samuel Gridley Howe, Dorman Eaton, Horace White, Francis Walker, William Graham Sumner, and Gamaliel Bradford.[88]

[84] Charles Francis Adams, Sr., to Henry Adams, Boston, Dec. 30, 1868, Adams MSS. Adams was thinking specifically of Vice-President-elect Schuyler Colfax of Indiana and Massachusetts Senator Henry Wilson.

[85] Aside from Hoogenboom, "Outlawing the Spoils," which is primarily devoted to the Civil Service Reform movement, the only full treatment of the postwar middle-class reformers is the now inadequate work by Earl Dudley Ross, *The Liberal Republican Move-* ment (New York: Henry Holt & Co., 1919). Hofstadter's *The Age of Reform: From Bryan to F.D.R.* (New York: Alfred A. Knopf, 1956), ch. IV, contains some important insights into the Mugwump mind, but makes no attempt to treat the independents of the immediate postwar period exhaustively.

[86] He was later first president of Johns Hopkins.

[87] *Journal of Social Science*, I (June 1869), 195ff.

[88] See "Circular No. 1" of the *Financial Record*, I (March 5,

Professor Edward Chase Kirkland sees the Association as essentially dominated by businessmen,[89] and there were in fact a goodly number of New York and New England merchants and industrialists among the members.[90] But they were far outnumbered and outweighed by the university presidents and professors, the literary men, the rich Boston ladies,[91] and the professional reformers. Whitelaw Reid, urging Congressman Garfield to attend an Association meeting, noted that there was "a large amount of college respectability . . . concerned in it."[92] In the '70's with its largest single contingent from Massachusetts,[93] the Association was essentially the voice of New England professors, Boston Brahmins, and Yankee-born gentlemen interested in remaking America in their own image.

Two other organizations which were to bring the hard money reformers together were the Boston and New York Reform Leagues. The Boston group, organized in April 1869, played a particularly important role in the currency struggle. Unlike the Social Science Association, which at least had scholarly pretensions, the League was frankly designed for agitation and propaganda. Its membership included Atkinson, Charles Francis

---

1874), 9; *Journal of Social Science,* IX (January 1878), 166-167.

[89] Edward Chase Kirkland, *Dream and Thought in the Business Community, 1860-1900* (Ithaca, New York: Cornell University Press, 1956), pp. 15-17.

[90] Including Atkinson, William Endicott, Jr., William Gray, William E. Dodge, John Murray Forbes, and Anson Phelps Stokes. See *Journal of Social Science,* I (June 1869), 195ff.; *ibid.,* IX (January 1878), 166-167. Henry Villard, later organizer of the Northern Pacific Railroad, was Recording Secretary of the Social Science Association in the '60's, but his chief claim to fame at this time was that he was the son-in-law of William Lloyd Garrison.

[91] At various times before 1879, among the university presidents were: Daniel Coit Gilman of Johns Hopkins, Charles W. Eliot of Har-

vard, Theodore Dwight Woolsey of Yale, James McCosh of Princeton, and W. B. Rogers of M.I.T. Among the college faculty, in addition to those already mentioned, were: Charles F. Dunbar, Benjamin Pierce, and Louis Agassiz, all of Harvard; among the literary men: James Russell Lowell and Justin Winsor; among the Boston ladies: Mrs. John E. Lodge, Mrs. S. Parkman, and Miss Alice C. Hooper.

[92] Whitelaw Reid to Garfield, New York, Dec. 15, 1868, Garfield MSS. "College respectability" might be expected to appeal to Garfield, a Williams graduate and former President of Hiram College in Ohio.

[93] Some 36.5 per cent of the total membership in 1878, as compared with 31 per cent from New York and much smaller percentages from elsewhere. See Bernard and Bernard, *op. cit.,* p. 549.

Adams, Jr., William Endicott, Jr., John Murray Forbes, Henry Adams, and Joseph S. Ropes.[94] Although, like its sister group in New York organized two months later,[95] its chief concern was tariff reform, it made the "restoration of the specie standard of value" one of its most urgent concerns.[96]

It is not necessary to describe at length the financial doctrines of the reformers. They were the views of the prevailing academic orthodoxy, and ultimately of both the Classical Economists and the Protestant moral philosophers. In a word, they demanded the sort of doctrinaire contraction that made the reform brand of hard money politically unworkable.[97] The reformers' financial views were as moralistic as one would expect of those who found in social science what Professor Luther Bernard has described as "a substitute religion . . . for the ferocious and moss-grown old New England theology."[98] The theories of the inflationists not only violated "the universal natural laws which we cannot alter," Sumner told the Association in 1874, but their adoption would produce "a decline of national and mercantile credit, the deterioration of public morals, the contempt for patient industry as compared with smartness, [and] . . . the love of meretricious display."[99] "The law of God, the law of honesty, prudence and self denial," asserted Joseph Ropes, supported contraction and a quick return to hard coin.[100]

Joined with this almost sacerdotal response to public questions was a strange amalgam of apprehension and naïve optimism. The reformer as pessimist was given to horrendous visions of disaster. The triumph of the Pendletons, the Butlers, the labor reformers, the Careyites, and—later—the silverites, would usher in the rule

[94] Reform League Broadsides, No. 1 (June 1, 1869), p. 1.
[95] The Free Trader, III (July 1869), 17.
[96] Reform League Broadsides, loc. cit.
[97] See the paper of Joseph S. Ropes, "Restoration and Reform of the Currency," Journal of Social Science, v (1873), 48, 60-63. See also Nation, VI (March 5, 1868), 188-189; remarks by William Endicott, Jr., quoted in Henry Carey Baird, The British Credit System: Inflated Bank Credit as a Substitute for "Current Money of the Realm" (Philadelphia, 1875), pp. 5-6.
[98] Bernard and Bernard, op. cit., p. 545.
[99] This is from a paper read before the Association on May 21, 1874, and later published as a separate pamphlet called American Finance (Cambridge, 1874). See pp. 4-6.
[100] Joseph Ropes, op. cit., pp. 60-61.

of ignorance and villainy.[101] Disorder and venality would reign; unrestrained speculative mania would be followed by panic and total economic collapse. Civilization itself would be shaken, and honest, decent men would cower in their shelters awaiting the day when financial madness had run its course.[102] The reformer as optimist, on the other hand, however much he feared and despised the people's heroes, never lost faith in the people's ability to learn. In their ignorance they might follow the financial demagogues, but once informed they would embrace the truth. Through formal schooling, "popular lectures, and the distribution of books and pamphlets, the great mass of the people can be taught that there is a science of political economy," explained the *Nation*, and a "basis . . . laid for sound and rational" economic legislation.[103]

In June 1867 the reformers began to talk of "creat[ing] a public opinion" favorable to resumption,[104] and in the fall launched a vigorous propaganda campaign for this purpose. During the War the Loyal Publication Society, an organization of influential New Yorkers affiliated with groups in Philadelphia and New England, had bolstered the Union cause by distributing thousands of pamphlets and handbills to editors, patriotic groups, and soldiers in the field.[105] A revived Society now seemed to Atkinson and Norton ideally suited for their new purposes, and in September 1867 they resolved to organize an "Economic Club" to "publish broadsides containing short articles," which would be sent to some eight hundred papers and could be copied "without giving credit if the editor pleases."[106] A number of Atkinson's friends—John Murray Forbes, Charles Francis Adams, Jr., Francis Lieber of Columbia College,[107] and

---

[101] *Nation*, IX (July 22, 1869), 66.

[102] Edward Atkinson to William Allison, Boston, March 3, 1878, Allison MSS.

[103] *Nation*, IX (July 22, 1869), 66.

[104] Edward Atkinson to Edwin L. Godkin, Boston, June 14, 1867, Atkinson MSS.

[105] Frank Freidel, "The Loyal Publication Society: A Pro-Union Propaganda Agency," *MVHR*, XXVI, No. 3 (December 1939), pp. 359-375.

[106] Edward Atkinson to James W. Grimes, Boston, Sept. 10, 1867, Atkinson MSS. See also Hugh McCulloch to Atkinson, Washington, Jan. 3, 1868, *ibid.*

[107] Lieber, a noted political scientist of German birth, had been president of the Loyal Publication Society after its first year. See Freidel,

E. L. Godkin—were soon drawn into the campaign, and the facilities of Godkin's *Nation* were used for printing and distribution.[108] By March 1868 the first broadsides, articles by Atkinson refuting Sherman's recent heretical bond repayment plan, had begun to appear,[109] and the printing of other hard money copy—much of it drawn from the current Congressional debates[110]—was well under way.

With Norton's departure for Europe in July 1868 the campaign lost momentum—although not, Norton believed, before it had achieved valuable results.[111] At the least, the venture established an important precedent for other reformer efforts to educate the public on the money question, and the work was soon taken over by the Boston Reform League. In June 1869 this body began to publish a weekly *Broadside*, under the editorship of "Corresponding Secretary" Atkinson, devoted to "questions of Revenue and Financial Reform." This publication—actually a weekly one-page newssheet—carried on for two more years the work begun by Norton and Atkinson.[112] In the 39 weekly numbers which appeared, editorials supporting sound money and articles written for the occasion, or copied from the conservative press, along with free trade puffs, filled almost all the available space. By October 1870, when the *Broadside* suspended publication, Atkinson could claim that it had fulfilled its function and was no longer needed.[113]

By 1870 the combined efforts of the clergy, the academicians, and the reformers had forged out of two of the most potent

---

op. cit., p. 361. For Lieber's currency attitudes see Lieber to Martin Roscoe Thayer, New York, July 11, 1868, Lieber MSS, Henry E. Huntington Library.

[108] E. L. Godkin to Atkinson, New York, July 15, 1868, Atkinson MSS.
[109] These originally appeared in Bryant's *New York Evening Post* and were later published as a pamphlet, *Senator Sherman's Fallacies, Or Honesty the Best Policy* (Boston, 1868). See Charles Eliot Norton to Atkinson, Cambridge, Mass., March 21, 1868, and March 31, 1868, Atkinson MSS.
[110] Edward Atkinson to James

A. Garfield, Boston, May 23, 1868; July 21, 1868, Garfield MSS. A brief general description of the Loyal Publication Society revival can be found in *The League*, No. 11 (April 1868), p. 122.
[111] Norton to Atkinson, Cambridge, Mass., July 1, 1868, Atkinson MSS.
[112] In the last issue of the *Broadsides* Atkinson acknowledged that the publication was an attempt to imitate the "Loyal Publication Society technique." *Reform League Broadsides*, No. 39 (Oct. 28, 1870).
[113] *Ibid.*

dogmas of the age a powerful ideology for hard money. Here was no nineteenth-century war of Science and Religion, but Science and Religion harmonizing and reinforcing each other. "Sound and honest finance" to its adherents was a happy blend of ethics and wisdom that was rare indeed in an imperfect world. Neither pastor nor professor could keep all Americans on the path of righteousness, but they helped erect a formidable psychological barrier against greenbackism. They created, even in their opponents, a consciousness of what was legitimate, acceptable, and orthodox. Even men who rejected hard money goals sensed the power of hard money principles and responded with a stridency bred, perhaps, as much of guilt as of conviction. The Butlers and the Careys urged the public to reject the "old theories and commonplaces of the books,"[114] and railed at the "currency 'doctors,'" who "preached contraction as the straight and certain road to specie payments."[115] They complained bitterly at being called "heretics" by the "theorists" and "doctrinaires,"[116] and sought to clothe themselves in doctrinal garments as impeccable as their opponents'.[117]

But all to no avail. Articulate, affluent, and well-placed men—despite their proclaimed alienation—the hard money intelligentsia enjoyed ready access to a large and influential audience of the kind their opponents were denied. Among the respectable political leaders of New England (E. R. and George Frisbie Hoar, Justin Morrill, Charles Sumner) their views were economic gospel. They successfully cultivated such westerners as Garfield, Jacob Dolson Cox, and William Allison, whom they considered salvageable. Businessmen, floundering in the morass of conflicting financial opinion, read their books and recommended them to others.[118]

[114] Speech of Senator Oliver Morton of Indiana in Dec. 1873, quoted in *Nation*, xxvi (Jan. 17, 1878), 37.

[115] See Thomas Ewing, Jr., speech at Lancaster, Ohio, July 15, 1876, in *The Great Campaign*, July 25, 1876; *Iron Age*, v (July 23, 1868).

[116] *AM*, Oct. 10, 1878; speech of William D. Kelley in *WA*, June 12, 1875; Benjamin F. Butler to R. H. Williams, Boston, Nov. 4, 1875, Butler MSS.

[117] This meant, largely, quoting either the old mercantilists, or Jefferson and John Taylor.

[118] See, e.g., *Banker's Magazine*, "Banker's Library" listed on the back cover of Vol. xxx. See also the following: Charles Francis Adams, Sr., to John Pastorius, n.p., May 5,

In the end, in cooperation with the churches, they helped to make the financial conscience of the American people, and particularly the literate middle class. The reformers themselves plainly exhibited such a conscience. Atkinson emphatically rejected the "extravagant profits" in textiles that inflation had made possible because they were incompatible with right conduct.[119] The results among the less sophisticated were sometimes startling. "Paper money," wrote an impressionable correspondent of David Wells, "is the sum of all iniquity: specie is philosophy, morality and religion."[120]

III

A part of the business community not only read the reformers' and professors' financial works, but was mustered into the reform movement itself. The reformers' brand of free trade appealed to Republican merchants who balked at supporting free trade Copperhead Democrats. Civil service reform attracted many who feared the blackmail often extorted by corrupt politicians from legitimate merchants and manufacturers.[121]

The factors that made Yankee businessmen particularly receptive to the reformer financial philosophy are not hard to discern. Simple proximity to the center of reform agitation certainly played a role, but equally important was the puritan background the merchants and manufacturers of New England shared with the reformers. The region's chief industry, textile manufacturing, was controlled by men whose affiliations were overwhelmingly either Congregational or Unitarian,[122] and they

---

1874, Adams MSS; William B. Sears to David Wells, East Saginaw, Mich., Dec. 1, 1873, Wells MSS. Sears, Chief Engineer of the Père Marquette Railroad, told Wells that in order to inform himself on currency he had carefully read Perry and Mill.

[119] Edward Atkinson to Hugh McCulloch, Boston, Oct. 2[4?], 1865, Atkinson MSS. See also D. Currier, Cashier, Derry National Bank, Derry Depot, N.H., to Hugh

McCulloch, Nov. 16, 1865, McCulloch MSS, LC.

[120] Sam Reed to David Wells, Cincinnati, April 2, 1870, Wells MSS.

[121] Matthew Josephson, *The Politicos, 1865-1896* (New York: Harcourt, Brace & Co., 1938), ch. II.

[122] Over 62 per cent of a large sample of prominent textile manufacturers of the 1870 generation belonged to one of these two denominations. See Frances Gregory and

were sensitive to the same moral stimuli as the Yankee intelligentsia. But businessmen, unlike reformers, are concerned with profits as well as principles. Fortunately, the financial environment of New England and the special advantages of the textile industry permitted the Yankee manufacturer to indulge his sense of duty in a way that was seldom open to other businessmen. It must be remembered that unlike iron and steel, cotton textiles—and still more, woolens—had achieved relative maturity by 1870, with its period of most rapid growth and change behind them.[123] The need for new capital was not, therefore, as great in Massachusetts as in Pennsylvania and the West; yet at the same time, New England was better supplied with commercial banks, insurance and trust companies, and savings institutions than was any other part of the country.[124] Accordingly, both long- and short-term interest rates in the Boston money market were among the lowest in the nation,[125] and the section exported capital in large amounts. Also relevant was the competitive superiority of the textile industry to less mature industry. Even before the War, American cotton producers had achieved a virtual monopoly in supplying the coarser cloths for the domestic market, and they had even begun to develop a considerable export trade. The War, by raising labor costs and

---

Irene D. Neu, "The American Industrial Elite in the 1870's: Their Social Origins," in William Miller (ed.), *Men in Business: Essays in the History of Entrepreneurship* (Cambridge: Harvard University Press, 1952), Tables i, ii, and iv.

[123] Total capital investment in iron and steel grew from about $75 million in 1859 to $230 million in 1879. In cotton manufacturing, much of it in New England, the expansion in the same period was from $98 million to $208 million. Iron and steel capitalization, in other words, more than tripled during the period, while cotton capital doubled. These figures were derived from the U. S. Bureau of the Census, *Census of Manufactures* for 1860 and 1880. Special Commissioner Wells in 1868 estimated that the average annual increase in pig iron production since 1860 had been 8.35 per cent. By contrast, cotton textiles had declined between 1860 and 1864 and had grown only since the War's end. See *Report of the Special Commissioner . . . for 1868*, pp. 2-3.

[124] U. S. Comptroller of the Currency, *Report for 1876*, pp. 160ff.

[125] Joseph G. Martin, *A Century of Finance: Martin's History of the Boston Stock and Money Markets . . .* (Boston: the author, 1898), pp. 53-62. Henry Carey called attention on at least one occasion to the abundant capital and low interest rates of "Boston Capitalists" to explain New England opposition to raising the tariff. See Carey, *The Finance Minister, the Currency and the Public Debt* (Washington, 1868), p. 25.

other expenses, had—according to the cotton men—priced American textiles out of the world market and destroyed an important source of income.[126] Relatively indifferent to foreign competition, abundantly supplied with capital, but disturbed by high domestic costs, the Yankee cotton magnate could well afford to let his conscience be his guide in financial matters.

Thus principle and advantage alike disposed the New England textile men to orthodoxy. Atkinson, a cotton manufacturer himself,[127] William Gray of the Atlantic Cotton Mills, James M. Barnard, Charles W. Freeland, Treasurer of the Dwight Mills, along with John Murray Forbes, the railroad promoter, formed a circle of "radical" businessmen,[128] closely associated with the reform movement and the Social Science Association. True heirs of Calvin's Christian Tradesman, these men regarded the currency as "the great moral question of the day,"[129] and were constantly alert to financial error. But even conservative textile men, who had misgivings about the "radicals'" general reform program, were adamant for hard money. Amos A. Lawrence, scion of the mighty Massachusetts industrial family, detested the greenback and believed it would be the "greatest blessing" if one fifth "of that filthy currency were destroyed by fire."[130] Erastus Bigelow, a leading woolen manufacturer, in the mid-'70's attacked as a "wild scheme" an *"irredeemable* currency to be emitted by the government." "There can be no fit and stable currency," he wrote, "on any other than a gold basis."[131]

The outstanding dissenter among the textile men was the

---

[126] Some $10.9 million of cotton textiles had been exported in 1860. By 1870 this was down to $3.8 million, and the trade did not entirely recover until after 1880. See Melvin Thomas Copeland, *The Cotton Manufacturing Industry of the United States* (Cambridge: Harvard University Press, 1912), p. 17. See also Amasa Walker, *The National Currency and the Money Problem* (New York, 1876), p. 24; and remarks of Senator Charles Sumner, *Congressional Record*, 43 Cong., 1 sess., p. 143.

[127] Williamson, *op. cit.*, chs. i and ii.

[128] "Radical" was the term used for this group by Atkinson. See Atkinson to Charles Sumner, Boston, Feb. 19, 1868, Sumner MSS.

[129] Edward Atkinson to Henry Ward Beecher, Oct. 10, 1867, quoted in Williamson, *op. cit.*, p. 83.

[130] Lawrence to Charles Sumner, Boston, April 20, 1870, Sumner MSS.

[131] Reprinted in National Association of Woolen Manufacturers, *Bulletin*, vi (1876), 294-298.

young Senator William Sprague of Rhode Island, heir to a great textile empire, which by 1869 comprised nine mills and ten thousand operatives.[132] Sprague's career merely proves the rule. Though of distinguished New England stock, he resembles the villain in an old-fashioned cautionary tale. Born to immense wealth, he never developed that self-control and moral inflexibility that generally distinguished the Yankee business elite. Indeed, his whole career was marked by a certain ethical laxness and opportunism that suggests both a revolt against his heritage and the dangers of wealth and responsibility achieved too early. During the War, while still Governor of Rhode Island and commanding officer of a fashionable Rhode Island regiment, the young millionaire had played a dangerous game of trading in rebel cotton that bordered on treason. Later, William and his brother Amasa were heavy plungers in Texas and Kansas lands, water-power sites in South Carolina, timber lands and sawmills in Maine, and other chancy ventures.[133] Neither moral considerations nor economic advantage, then, disposed them to hard money, and understandably they rejected the contractionist views of their fellow textile men. In 1863 Sprague bought his way into Congress[134] where he joined Butler, William D. Kelley, and Stevens in resisting contraction.[135] As Lawrence superciliously, but accurately, noted, the Spragues were "the greatest speculators among the whole body of manufacturers in New England," and were terrified that resumption would ruin them.[136]

Turning to the currency views of the nation's merchants reveals a picture as variegated as the commercial community itself. Yet there is reason to place the traders in the hard

---

[132] *Iron Age*, VII (Dec. 16, 1869). Thomas Graham Belden and Marva Robins Belden, *So Fell the Angels* (Boston: Little, Brown & Co., 1956), pp. 52-54.

[133] Caroline F. Ware, *The Early New England Cotton Manufacture: A Study in Industrial Beginnings* (Boston: Houghton Mifflin Co., 1931), p. 159. Zechariah Chaffee, Jr., "Weathering the Panic of 1873: An Episode in Rhode Island Business History," *Dorr Pamphlet*, No. 4 (1942), p. 274.

[134] *Ibid.*, pp. 55-62, 100-102, 141-142, and ff.; and ch. v.

[135] Although he refused to accept their formula for paying the 5-20's in greenbacks. See Sprague, *Speech of ... Sprague in the United States Senate, March 15, 1869* (n.p., 1869), *passim.*

[136] Lawrence to Sumner, Boston, March 25, 1867, Sumner MSS.

money camp. After allowing for wide individual variation, the preponderance of mercantile opinion supported sound finance. Actually, from the standpoint of the postwar currency question, there are two significant groups among those who made their living buying, selling, and distributing goods. One of these was composed of the importers and exporters, commission merchants, brokers, and private bankers of New York, Boston, and Philadelphia who handled the country's foreign trade. The other included the jobbers, wholesale merchants, and dry goods dealers who distributed these wares to the interior cities and farms and conducted the nation's inter-regional exchanges.

The first of these groups, although confined to the three largest Atlantic coast cities, was the more influential. American foreign trade as a percentage of the gross national product was declining in these decades, and with it the influence of the great port merchants. To an increasing extent, moreover, as exports shifted from raw materials and agricultural produce to finished goods, the services of the large port city export-import houses were superseded by direct manufacturers' sales.[137] Nevertheless, through the '70's the foreign traders, particularly the New Yorkers, continued to enjoy great prestige. Morris K. Jesup, Elliot C. Cowdin, William E. Dodge, Abiel A. Low, Simeon Chittenden, Jonathan Sturges, and William Aspinwall, to name the best known, were men of national prominence and repute, often more influential than the contemporary industrialists and promoters we now identify as the great business movers of the era. The domestic merchants lacked the equivalent wealth, prestige, and political connections of their eastern colleagues and were less successful in making their voices heard.

With few, but important, exceptions the leading foreign traders favored a quick return to specie payments. Men of pre-

[137] In 1871 total foreign trade equaled $1.08 billion, about 16 per cent of estimated average GNP for the period 1869-1873. In 1879 it was $1.1 billion, about 12.2 per cent of GNP for the 1877-1881 period. Calculated from U. S. Bureau of the Census, *Historical Statistics of the United States* (Washington, 1960), p. 139, series F2; p. 538, series U1 and 2. For the shift in the export trade to direct manufacturers' sales abroad, see Edward Chase Kirkland, *Industry Comes of Age: Business, Labor, and Public Policy, 1860-1897* (New York: Holt, Rinehart and Winston, 1961), pp. 286-289.

ponderantly Yankee stock in New York as well as Boston, they were highly receptive to the moral appeal of hard money. The New York Chamber of Commerce solemnly insisted that it was the "great moral significance" of resumption that made it imperative. "All other reasons" were "secondary to this, and this alone [was] of really vital concern."[138] But as in the case of the textile men, conscience did not have to bear too heavy a burden. There were excellent, though complex, economic reasons reinforcing conviction. Of all the nation's businessmen, the port merchants were most visibly and directly affected by paper money. While internal commerce was conducted with paper, foreign trade was based on gold. This meant that foreign goods were bought with gold or its exchange equivalent and sold at home in greenbacks. As a consequence, a change in the gold premium affected the *importers*, to take half the picture at a time, in a number of disturbing ways. As we have seen in connection with the iron industry, a fall in gold, at least in the short run, immediately reduced the greenback price of imported goods. For American producers of goods competing with foreign manufactures—the ironmasters, for example—this meant a superior competitive position for foreign goods, equivalent to reducing the tariff. The effect on merchants and brokers, however, was much more complicated. Theoretically, the importers' fate, as gold changed value, should have been the simple converse of the manufacturers'—that is, they should have gained proportionately by a falling premium, since the competitive position of the imported wares they dealt in would have improved at home.[139] And in fact we can cite examples of importers who favored a declining gold premium so that they might undersell the home product.[140] But more often the great import houses

[138] New York Chamber of Commerce, *Tenth Annual Report for 1867*, p. 51. See also the moralistic tone of the 1868 hard money resolutions of the Boston Board of Trade, *Fifteenth Annual Report for 1868*, p. 54.

[139] This, indeed, is Dr. Robert P. Sharkey's assumption. See *Money, Class and Party: An Economic Study of Civil War and Reconstruction*

(Baltimore: The Johns Hopkins Press, 1959), p. 149, n. 31. See also the theoretical support given Sharkey's view by Frank D. Graham, "International Trade Under Depreciated Paper: The United States, 1862-1879," *Quarterly Journal of Economics*, xxxvi (February 1922), 220-227.

[140] See Lawton and White (crockery importers) to William P. Fessen-

of Boston and Philadelphia, and particularly New York, were engaged in a very different sort of trade, importing silks, glassware, embroidery, and fashions from France; china, hardware, woolens, fine cottons, and silver plate from England; tea and raw silk from China; coffee and sugar from Latin America.[141] These wares were either the products of tropical regions or "fancy goods," which did not compete directly with American manufactures.[142] As a result, a fall in their price did not particularly improve the competitive position of the importer; in fact, a fall in gold could seriously hurt him. Generally it deflated the value of all imported inventory. As George Stuart, a Philadelphia trader in British dry goods, told a Congressional committee in 1870, for his firm to make a profit on imported goods, gold had to be stable or rising. To illustrate, Stuart posed a hypothetical case for the Congressmen: "Our . . . house has purchased a large amount of goods with gold that cost us 21½ per cent. premium; the goods are in our possession; in order to get our money back we must sell upon a basis of 21½ per cent. premium. But if before these goods are disposed of, gold should go down to fifteen per cent., we should lose by the operation 6½ per cent." Stuart conceded that if gold rose so would the selling price of his inventory, but as he and most port merchants pointed out, the legitimate foreign trader was not in business to make a windfall from such a chance shift.[143]

---

den, New York, Nov. 2, 1864, Fessenden MSS, LC; and Edward Kinsley (of Hoswell, Kinsley, & French, Importers of Woolens) to Charles Sumner, Boston, Dec. 19, 1867, Sumner MSS.

[141] A representative group of import houses and their wares are advertised in the organ of the New York Free Trade League, *The League*, No. 4 (Sept. 1867), 41ff.

[142] In 1869 sugar was by far the largest American import, followed by wool and woolens—a large part of which was also non-competitive—then by the competitive iron and steel products, which in turn were followed closely by silk and coffee. Among the ten most important imported items, a decided minority competed with domestic goods. See U.S. Bureau of the Census, *Statistical Abstract of the United States for 1878*, pp. 58-77.

[143] U. S. House of Representatives, *Report No. 31* (The Gold Panic Investigation), 41 Cong., 2 sess., p. 189. See also *Nation*, III (Oct. 11, 1866), 290; and New York Chamber of Commerce, *Memorial . . . to the . . . Congress . . . for . . . Resumption of Specie Payments* (New York, 1873), p. 4. An interesting instance of a merchant attempting to capitalize on the fall in prices accompanying a gold decline appeared in an advertisement of a Pittsburgh "Wholesale and Retail House," Fleming and Company, in a religious weekly. The advertisement

Merchants with large inventories of foreign goods were naturally nervous at the prospect of a declining gold premium. John Murray Forbes, whose years in the China Trade placed him close to the Boston importers, predicted in late 1868 that the "mercantile public" would resist an early return to specie because it feared the effect on inventory values.[144] Indeed, a merchant with imported stock on hand, it was said, was almost compelled to become, "without intending it, a 'bull' in gold," that is, in effect, a speculator on a rising gold premium.[145]

Merchants and brokers engaged in the *export* of American staples and manufactured goods also found themselves enmeshed in the complexities of a double monetary standard. An exporter of cotton cloth, for example, might be injured by a falling gold premium, since goods sent abroad for sale in a gold standard currency would bring home fewer dollars than expected.[146] So unsettling was this regime to exporters, declared a New York Chamber of Commerce report, that many "prudent men will not willingly embark their money or their merchandise in ventures to distant markets . . . with the possibility of a fall [in gold] ere their return can be brought to market."[147]

---

read in part as follows: "The extensive fall in the price of gold and the consequent reduction in the price of goods in the East was not overlooked by such an enterprising firm as that of Fleming and Co. . . . This house, keeping, as it does, a stock always large, always fresh . . . is now able to offer its goods at greatly reduced rates." *Presbyterian Banner,* LVI (Nov. 6, 1870).

[144] Forbes to Charles Sumner, Boston, Nov. 16, 1868, Sumner MSS. The New York Chamber of Commerce in 1873 declared that "calculations on the part of the vendors of imported goods have been baffled by constant fluctuations [in gold]; the wholesale dealer being afraid to hold his merchandise, fearing a fall in the premium . . . and the retailer equally afraid to carry any considerable stock, for the same reason." New York Chamber of Commerce, *Memorial to Congress,* p. 4.

[145] *Nation,* III (Oct. 11, 1866), 29. The actual short-run interest of the individual merchant could vary a great deal, however, depending on the way he conducted his business. If he paid for the goods imported *after* they were sold for greenbacks, a rising premium, reducing the gold value of the paper dollar, would hurt him, since he would be able as a consequence to buy fewer francs or English pounds or ounces of gold to pay his European creditor. See the testimony of A. A. Low, U. S. House of Representatives, *Report No. 31,* p. 289.

[146] *Ibid.,* p. 290.

[147] New York Chamber of Commerce, "Report . . . on Resumption of Specie Payments," *Tenth Annual Report for 1867,* p. 52. This quotation appeared in my article, "Business Men and Specie Resumption," *Political Science Quarterly,* LXXIV, No. 1 (March 1959), where it was

Thus both importers and exporters found themselves at the mercy of a system that made foreign trade a game of chance, and the foreign traders often turned to hedging operations in order to protect themselves against fluctuations. At the time a foreign trade transaction was initiated, the trader would borrow coin at the Gold Exchange that had arisen on Wall Street shortly after suspension, and sell it immediately for greenbacks. If in the interval before the completion of the transaction the gold premium changed, its effects would be canceled by the hedge. If, because of a fall in gold, a merchant's return on his goods, whether sold abroad for gold or at home for greenbacks, were reduced, he could offset the loss by buying cheap gold; that is, he could replace the borrowed gold with fewer greenbacks than he had received when he first sold it. Thus a loss on his trade would be offset by a profit on the gold transaction. If gold should rise, on the other hand, he would gain on the trade, since his goods increased their paper prices, but he would now have to repay his gold loan at a higher greenback price.[148]

Hedging could indeed reduce the hazards of foreign trade,

---

ascribed, incorrectly, to importers. Falling gold quotations also produced difficulties for the export brokers who helped market the nation's agricultural staples. An English merchant, e.g., ordinarily gave a cotton order to a New York broker at a specific gold or sterling price per pound, delivered in England. The broker, who had to buy the cotton with paper, determined what the going greenback price was at Charleston or New Orleans or one of the other cotton ports. In order to make profitable delivery in England at the price agreed on, he of course had to consider insurance, freight, and other handling costs, but he also had to know the gold premium, since only if it were high enough could he make the purchase for the English importer at a profit. Assuming a sufficient gold premium—i.e., assuming he could buy paper dollars and hence the cotton at a low enough

price—the cotton would be shipped, and a bill of exchange drawn against the cargo. This would be brought to Brown Brothers, or some other private banking house dealing in exchange, to be discounted and converted into coin. If in the interval between the initial receipt of the order and the discounting of the bill—a period typically of a week or two—gold were to fall, the broker might find his coin reduced to fewer paper dollars than he paid for the cotton. An increase, on the other hand, would give him an unexpected windfall. See the testimony of James B. Hodgskin, U. S. House of Representatives, *Report No. 31*, pp. 26ff. A more compact description of the process by Hodgskin can be found in *Nation*, IX (Oct. 7, 1867), 294.

[148] A. A. Low, U. S. House of Representatives, *Report No. 31*, p. 290; Hodgskin, *ibid.*, p. 28.

but apparently it did not entirely solve the problem of fluctuating gold-paper ratios. Many merchants chose to take their chances rather than become involved in these complicated—and expensive—maneuvers.[149] On occasion, as during the 1869 gold corner engineered by Jay Gould, merchants who had to repay gold driven sky-high by the conspirators found themselves forced to default on contracts to brokers.[150] All told, through most of the 1860's and '70's, port city merchants would have agreed with the *Commercial and Financial Chronicle* that ever since the suspension, foreign trade had become "almost as uncertain as a ticket in a lottery."[151]

With gold fluctuations magnifying the normal hazards of business, it is not surprising that foreign traders detested the paper system. Eastern merchants wrote McCulloch and members of Congress complaining bitterly of the double standard and its annoyances.[152] More important politically, they mobilized the support of the Boards of Trade and Chambers of Commerce of the Atlantic coast ports. These bodies, among the oldest business associations in the country,[153] were not composed exclusively of merchants. But in the three most vocal—the New York Chamber of Commerce and the Boston and Philadelphia Boards of Trade—the bankers and manufacturers were far outnumbered by the "dry goods merchants," "importers," "wholesale grocers," "commission brokers," and "exporters-importers."[154] McCulloch's early contraction pronouncements were

[149] *Pomeroy's Democrat*, Nov. 23, 1870.

[150] See below, ch. v.

[151] *CFC*, IX (Nov. 6, 1869), 582.

[152] See the following: John K. Myers (of Halsted, Haines & Co., Importers and Jobbers of Dry Goods) to Hugh McCulloch, New York, Aug. 20, 1867, McCulloch MSS; Edward Kinsley (of Hoswell, Kinsley & French, Importers of Woolens) to Charles Sumner, Boston, Dec. 19, 1867, Sumner MSS; William E. Dodge to James A. Garfield, New York, June 12, 1868; and A. A. Low to Garfield, Brooklyn, Dec. 20, 1869, Garfield MSS.

[153] There is a list of the country's major trade associations—those which were members of the National Board of Trade—with their founding dates in National Board of Trade, *Proceedings of the Seventh Annual Meeting, 1875*, p. ix. The New York Chamber of Commerce, founded in 1768, was easily the oldest business association in America.

[154] In the case of the Philadelphia and Boston Boards there are complete listings of members by firm and type of business in the Annual Reports. I have deduced the complexion of the New York Chamber from lists of the officers and members of committees over a period of a decade. In many

warmly seconded by these associations,[155] and through the '60's they were among the most consistent upholders of hard money principles.[156] But there were dissenters even among the eastern merchants. Individual traders found that the paper standard created opportunities for profitable speculation. John Murray Forbes believed that much of the wave of imports in the last half of 1865 resulted from merchants gambling on a temporary rise in the gold premium.[157] Withdrawing the greenbacks would remedy the situation, but it "would raise a tremendous outcry . . . for there would be a slaughtering of the innocents who live and breathe by a *rise!*" In Forbes's estimation, "even men sound in theory who have been led into expansion will find some reason for waiting till *they* have got out."[158]

In New York a small faction in the Chamber of Commerce fought to keep that body on a moderate course. The leader of this group was George Opdyke, prominent merchant-banker and former Republican Mayor of the city, who in 1851 had written a book endorsing a government issued fiat money.[159] It also included dry goods merchant Horace B. Claflin, as well as Wallace Groom, editor of the New York *Mercantile Journal*, who had been one of the business supporters of the interconvertible bond, and others, representing an "anti-monopoly"

---

cases the industrialists and bankers were former merchants who continued to exhibit mercantile attitudes. Men like Samuel Babcock, William E. Dodge, and John Murray Forbes, though primarily involved in, respectively, banking, manufacturing, and railroad promotion in the postwar years, were still close to the mercantile interest and held financial views identical with their commercial colleagues'.

[155] Boston Board of Trade, *Twelfth Annual Report for 1865*, p. 55; Philadelphia Board of Trade, *Thirty-third Annual Report for 1865*, pp. 20-21; New York Chamber of Commerce, *Eighth Annual Report for 1865-1866*, p. 45.

[156] See Boston Board of Trade, *Fourteenth Annual Report for 1867*,

p. 67; *Fifteenth Annual Report for 1868*, p. 54; Philadelphia Board of Trade, *Thirty-sixth Annual Report for 1868*, p. 24; New York Chamber of Commerce, *Ninth Annual Report for 1867*, pp. 73-74; and *Eleventh Annual Report for 1869*, pp. 50-53.

[157] That is, merchants were buying goods abroad in anticipation of a rise in gold which would make their goods more valuable. In reality these men were to be disappointed, since the gold premium fell steadily during the period.

[158] Forbes to Hugh McCulloch, Naushon Is., Mass., Sept. 8, 1865, McCulloch MSS.

[159] George Opdyke, *A Treatise on Political Economy* (New York: G. P. Putnam, 1851), pp. 296ff., and Introduction, p. vi.

minority of the Chamber.[160] The cautious April 1867 resolution of the Chamber was designed to accommodate Opdyke and his group, who had dug in their heels against a stronger contractionist declaration.[161] The following year, Opdyke and his supporters were less successful in blunting resolutions demanding specie by 1869.[162] Eventually Opdyke so antagonized his colleagues of the Chamber that they forced him out,[163] but until 1875 he was occasionally able to moderate the ardent contractionist demands of the New York merchants.

The merchants of the West were less orthodox than their eastern brethren. In the first place they lacked the same material reasons for supporting contraction. As a committee of the New York Chamber admitted, "the inconveniences of a depreciated currency are most seriously felt on the seaboard, and the restraints and losses incidental to an abnormal condition of our foreign exchanges are most patent to those who are brought in contact with the pecuniary systems of England and continental Europe."[164] The inadequacy of credit facilities in the West and the higher prevailing interest rates also disposed western merchants toward a less dogmatic financial attitude. In general, moreover, there was an exuberance and permissiveness in western commerce, a "ballooning, kite-flying and go-aheadism" which encouraged a more liberal financial attitude.[165]

While the East Coast trade associations were endorsing contraction, a number of western Boards of Trade expressed fear that McCulloch had gone too far, too fast,[166] and individual western merchants occasionally demanded more circu-

---

[160] This group of New York merchants was later active in the cheap transportation movement that so closely paralleled the Grange-inspired attack on high railroad rates. See below, ch. IX.

[161] New York Chamber of Commerce, *Ninth Annual Report for 1867*, pp. 73-74.

[162] New York Chamber of Commerce, *Tenth Annual Report for 1868*, p. 20. See also *Eleventh Annual Report for 1869*, pp. 52-53.

[163] See below, ch. IX.

[164] New York Chamber of Commerce, *Tenth Annual Report for 1868*, p. 52.

[165] *NYT*, April 6, 1867.

[166] For the Detroit Board of Trade see *The Independent*, Feb. 14, 1867; for the apprehensions of several others, in general terms, see John F. Whitelaw to R. P. Spaulding, Cleveland, Feb. 4, 1867, quoted in Herbert S. Schell, "Hugh McCulloch and the Treasury Department," *MVHR*, XVII, No. 3 (December 1930), p. 408, n. 19.

lation.[167] Even in the West, however, commercial opinion was often conservative. Between 1865 and 1868 the Cleveland and Chicago Boards of Trade and the Cincinnati Chamber of Commerce several times endorsed speedy resumption.[168] In general, western tradesmen were divided and uncertain and would feel free to contradict their eastern colleagues to the end of the paper era.

These confused currents make the National Board of Trade, nineteenth-century precursor of the United States Chamber of Commerce, the nearest thing to a country-wide gauge of commercial attitudes toward finance. Organized in 1868, the Board admitted local boards of trade, chambers of commerce, and other trade groups and purportedly represented all sections of the trading community. From the outset, however, it expressed a conservative financial position, though only by dint of the unrelenting vigilance of the hard money men. At its organizing convention in February 1868 a fierce altercation over finance erupted which was to be typical of the Board's future financial deliberations. Fortunately for the conservatives, the organizing meeting was held in Boston and Atkinson's business "radicals" were present in force. Both in the convention itself and on the currency committee there were western majorities,[169] but the westerners were divided, and Atkinson, William Endicott, Jr., and Joseph Ropes succeeded in getting their way. The currency resolutions reported from committee recommended gradual contraction of legal tenders by funding, the legalizing of voluntary gold contracts, a moderate banknote redistribution, and free banking after resumption. The

[167] E.g., Horace Billings (merchant and provision dealer) to John Sherman, Beardstown, Cass Co., Ill., March 20, 1866, Sherman MSS, LC.

[168] Cleveland Board of Trade, *Annual Statement for 1867*, p. 6; for the Chicago Board of Trade see John F. Beatty to Hugh McCulloch, Chicago, Nov. 16, 1865, McCulloch MSS; for the Cincinnati Chamber of Commerce see John A. Gano to John Sherman, Cincinnati, March 29, 1866, Sherman MSS. See also Jesse Baldwin (of H. G. Baldwin, Dealers in Flour, Feed and Grain) to John Sherman, Youngstown, Ohio, Dec. 25, 1865, Sherman MSS.

[169] Some 144 of 244 delegates at Boston were accounted "westerners" by William Endicott, Jr., as were two-thirds of the currency committee. See Endicott to Charles Francis Adams, Jr., Boston, Feb. 11, 1868, Adams MSS.

committee also denounced attempts to pay the 5-20's in paper.[170] This was accompanied by a minority report from the future greenback leader Moses Field, which endorsed immediate free banking and an indefinite postponement of specie payments.[171]

Field's recommendations were rejected,[172] but the majority report provoked a full-scale debate in which the East-West division was brought into sharp focus. Ropes praised western committee members for supporting the majority resolution and repeated that what the country and the West needed was not more currency but more capital.[173] He was answered by several Chicago merchants, who asserted that western commerce was beset by chronic shortages of cash and exorbitant interest rates "not only on discounts but on commissions and acceptances."[174] Easterners must not be selfish or nearsighted in financial matters. "We claim that . . . domestic commerce may be worthy of some consideration as well as . . . foreign commerce. We find that these gentlemen on the seaboard base all their calculations on gold, to bring them to par with foreign countries, leaving us in the West to take care of ourselves."[175]

Endicott and Atkinson sought to soothe their opponents but betrayed no willingness to make concessions.[176] And in the end there was no need to. The Chicago group did not win over many of the delegates; on the final vote the majority resolutions were adopted "with but very few dissenting voices."[177]

During the rest of the decade the National Board of Trade remained under the tight control of the hard money forces, despite growing western dissent. At its first formal meeting,[178]

---

[170] National Commercial Convention, *Proceedings of the . . . Convention Held in Boston* (1868), p. 142.

[171] *Ibid.*

[172] *Ibid.*, p. 148. There was no roll call on this.

[173] *Ibid.*, pp. 159-160.

[174] A. V. Turpin of the Chicago Board of Trade, *ibid.*, pp. 161-162.

[175] John C. Dore of the Chicago Board of Trade, *ibid.*, p. 189.

[176] *Ibid.*, pp. 184-185, 190-191.

[177] *Ibid.*, p. 205. For the crucial role of the Atkinson group see

William Endicott, Jr., to Charles Francis Adams, Jr., Boston, Feb. 11, 1868; Charles Francis Adams, Jr., to Charles Francis Adams, Sr., Boston, Feb. 11, 1868, Adams MSS; E. Atkinson to Charles Sumner, Boston, Feb. 11, 1868, Sumner MSS; Atkinson to Charles Eliot Norton, Boston, Feb. 15, 1868, Norton MSS, Houghton Library, Harvard University.

[178] Actually there was an earlier meeting at Philadelphia in June, which formally launched the new National Board of Trade in accord-

held in Cincinnati in December 1868, the Board reiterated the Boston platform.[179] The following year at Richmond, much stiffer opposition to contraction was encountered, with Opdyke and W. S. Hastie of the Charleston Board of Trade attempting to block endorsement of immediate resumption and western delegates fighting a greenback funding plank. The westerners had their way on contraction by a vote of 36 to 24, but Opdyke was buried under an almost unanimous vote supporting the "restoration of the specie standard at the earliest practicable time."[180]

Till the end of the decade, then, the conservatives among the commercial class still retained the upper hand. What might have been the entire battle turned out to be only the opening round, however. The dissident westerners were forced to bow to the superior prestige, organization, and numbers of their conservative eastern colleagues,[181] but they did not capitulate. In later years there would be other occasions to attack the financial idols of the orthodox.

The bankers, like the merchants, divided along sectional lines. At first, however, they had welcomed contraction. Their response to McCulloch's Fort Wayne speech was almost unanimously friendly, with bankers from Chicago, Peoria, and

---

ance with the resolutions adopted by the Commercial Convention. This asymptotic approach to founding new voluntary associations was typical of Americans in these years.

[179] National Board of Trade, *Proceedings of First Annual Meeting . . . at Cincinnati, Dec. 1868*, pp. 214-223.

[180] National Board of Trade, *Proceedings of Second Annual Meeting, Richmond, Dec. 1869*, pp. 255-285.

[181] Aside from the deep divisions within the western trade associations, western attendance at National Board meetings, where the country's merchants put their currency views on record, was, with the exception of the Chicago, St.

Louis, and Cincinnati Associations, lax. Eastern cities tended, moreover, to be represented on the Board by several trade bodies, each having voting rights. Thus, besides the Boston Board of Trade there was the Boston Commercial Exchange; besides the Philadelphia Board of Trade there was the Philadelphia Commercial Exchange; in addition to the New York Chamber of Commerce there was the New York Produce Exchange, the largest single body in the National Board in the mid-'70's. On the makeup of the Board in the 1870's see the remarks of its President, Frederick Fraley, in U. S. House of Representatives, *Report No. 328*, 43 Cong., 2 sess., p. 115.

Columbus, as well as Philadelphia, Syracuse, and Buffalo writing to congratulate the Secretary on his courageous and farseeing position.[182]

The mood did not last. When the economy deflated following the Overend, Gurney panic, almost all businessmen had second thoughts about contraction. Among eastern national bankers little overt soft money sentiment appeared at this time, but there was much quiet dragging of feet. In 1868 George Coe of New York's American Exchange Bank predicted that the "great opposition" to quick resumption would "come from the National Banks, many of which will naturally dread any plan that looks toward the redemption of their notes."[183] Two years later U. S. Treasurer Francis Spinner noted that the national banks were still "not prepared, and manifest no disposition to prepare themselves for an honest resumption of specie payments."[184]

Coe and Spinner were being unnecessarily alarmist. The large eastern national banks, partly because of their intimate connection with foreign trade,[185] ultimately gave strong support to resumption. Far more serious opposition came from the eastern private investment bankers. These men, deeply involved in railroad and natural resources promotion, were westerners economically and temperamentally, whatever they were geographically. Their prototype was Jay Cooke with his large commitments to the Northern Pacific, but there were many lesser financiers equally fearful of contraction. Henry Clews, an early associate of Cooke, in 1867 was one of the many businessmen attacking McCulloch's

[182] H. R. Symonds to McCulloch, Chicago, Nov. 18, 1865; J. B. Smith to McCulloch, Peoria, Nov. 6, 1865; W. B. Hubbard to McCulloch, Columbus, Nov. 13, 1865; Thomas Smith and nineteen other Philadelphia bankers to McCulloch, Nov. ?, 1865; E. B. Judson to McCulloch, Syracuse, Dec. 8, 1865; E. G. Spaulding to McCulloch, Buffalo, Dec. 14, 1865, McCulloch MSS. Spaulding, of course, is the former Buffalo Congressman who had a hand in the issue of the first greenbacks.

[183] Coe to Garfield, New York, May 22, 1868, Garfield MSS. See also Atkinson to McCulloch, Boston, Nov. 8, 1867, Atkinson MSS.

[184] Spinner to H. B. Willson, Washington, April 18, 1870, Letters of U. S. Treasurer, Vol. VII (April 1870), National Archives (letter press copy).

[185] Coe believed that among the banks "no institution whose object is to become an auxiliary to true commerce and trade" could "reasonably object" to returning to gold. From context it is clear that Coe is speaking of foreign "commerce and trade." See Coe to Garfield, New York, May 22, 1868, Garfield MSS.

draconian policies.[186] John Cisco, a former U. S. Sub-Treasurer turned banker,[187] the same year prescribed a financial policy that foreshadowed the do-nothing approach of McCulloch's successor at the Treasury: "Stop all contraction of the legal tender notes; leave them where they are, in the pockets of the people, and take measures to make them good . . . thus avoiding the disturbance of business, which would re-act upon the public revenue and upon the prices of government securities. . . . I would not attempt to *force* specie payments, nor fix a day for them, but leave them to come about naturally."[188]

In the West even national bankers resisted contraction. "The only true and safe policy at the present time," pronounced an Ohio financier in early 1868, is "neither contraction nor expansion but to *let the currency alone.*"[189] "*Time* and patience," another wrote John Sherman, were needed "to get back to a specie basis."[190] Farther west the financial men were not content merely to complain. The National Bankers' Association in Iowa quite openly worked to undermine the Treasury's contraction policy. H. M. Kingman, Cashier of the First National Bank of Dubuque, wrote in late 1866 of "the efforts making against the old fogy notions of Sec. McCulloch in the matter of returning to specie payts. by retiring legal tenders." The Iowa bankers tried to get Congressman Allison, member from the Dubuque district, to manage the anti-contraction campaign. A holder of national bank stock himself, Allison had, Kingman noted, the "views of his constituents at heart" in the matter of the currency.[191]

The recruiting of Allison was apparently part of a concerted campaign launched by western bankers to get McCulloch's contraction power withdrawn. Sometime during 1866 these western financiers retained the Merchants' Union Law Company, a firm

[186] Clews to Hugh McCulloch, New York, March 9, 1867, *Banker's Magazine,* xxi (May 1867), 822. Clews, like Cooke, became overextended in his railroad ventures and failed in the 1873 panic. See *NYDT,* Sept. 30, 1873.

[187] Cisco was prominent in the early development of the Union Pacific.

[188] Cisco to W. P. Fessenden, New York, Feb. 8, 1867, Fessenden MSS.

[189] "J. B." of Jefferson County, Ohio, *Banker's Magazine,* xxii (March 1868), 737-738.

[190] T. P. Handy to John Sherman, Cleveland, Feb. 5, 1867, Sherman MSS.

[191] H. M. Kingman to Caleb Cushing, Dubuque, Dec. 26, 1866, Cushing MSS, LC.

of professional lobbyists, to guard their interests in Washington. The firm solicited contributions to fight further monetary curtailment and to quash legislation inimical to the banking interests. It also circulated a printed petition which charged that "further reduction of the volume of currency at present would prove highly injurious to the banking, manufacturing and mercantile interests of the country."[192] The firm's solicitations became so importunate that they provoked one Congressman—John Wentworth of Illinois—to denounce their activities on the floor of the House, a most unusual step.[193] This group may have been the "bankers' lobby" that later in the year was reported to be cooperating with the whiskey interests in an attempt to oust McCulloch from the Treasury.[194]

There was clearly an impressive amount of anti-contraction feeling among the nation's bankers. Nevertheless, the financial community, like the merchants, must be placed in the hard money camp.[195] Unfortunately there was no equivalent in the '60's of the National Board of Trade to speak for the bankers as a group. When, in 1875, the American Bankers' Association was established it declared unequivocally for resumption.[196] Even in the earlier decade, however, the leading financial journals—*Banker's Magazine* and the *Financier*—were sound money bulwarks. The aggressively hard money *Commercial and Financial Chronicle*, as its name suggests, reflected the conservative views of both the trading and banking communities.[197] With one notable exception—John Earl Williams of the Metropolitan Bank of New York—no American banker of these years was willing to give the greenbackers a serious hearing.[198]

[192] John Livingston to John Sherman, New York, Dec. 21, 1866, Sherman MSS.

[193] *Congressional Globe*, 39 Cong., 2 sess., p. 296.

[194] *Washington Daily Morning Chronicle*, Oct. 10, 1867.

[195] E.g., Elbridge Gerry Spaulding to James A. Garfield, Buffalo, May 18, 1868; John W. Ellis to Garfield, Dec. 16, 1867, Garfield MSS; Seth Gilman to D. Ferguson, New York, April 8, 1874; Alexander Mitchell MSS. State Hist.

Soc. of Wisc.; R. B. Minturn to William Allison, New York, April 28, 1874, Allison MSS.

[196] American Bankers' Association, *Reports of Proceedings at Conventions, 1875*, p. 135. For the later course of the Association see below, ch. x.

[197] Even the most casual perusal of these journals is enough to convince one of their strong hard money biases.

[198] Williams' views are hard to explain since little information is

These, then, were the hard money men. On the whole they were a socially superior breed, representing an older elite of eastern merchants, commercial bankers, textile manufacturers, professional men, gentlemen reformers, and respectable literati. By all the teachings of recent history they should have been as extinct in this era of spoilsmen and industrial primitives as perukes and small clothes; at the very most they might have been expected to survive as a frail, disorganized remnant. But although they were politically weaker than in the days when a gentleman sat in the President's mansion, they were to prove capable still, through the potent moral and intellectual force of puritan New England, of confounding the massed power of the new leaders of Industrial America.

---

available on him. For his views see Fritz Redlich, *The Molding of American Banking: Men and Ideas*, part ii (New York: Hafner Publishing Co., 1951), pp. 150-151; John E. Williams, *Short Road to Specie Currency* (New York, 1875), *passim;* Williams to Jacob Schuckers, New York, July 5, 1875, Schuckers MSS, LC.

EQUIPOISE (1869-1873)

I

THE election of Grant and Colfax in November 1868 opened a new phase of the postwar money struggle. The stolid, inarticulate soldier whom the Republicans nominated at their June convention caught the mood of the people with his slogan, "Let us have Peace," and the drubbing he gave Seymour and Blair reflected the popular desire for surcease and quiet at least as much as the adulation of a national hero. In turning to Grant, the public hoped to put the turmoil and controversy of the Johnson administration behind them. And events proved the wisdom of their choice, at least as far as the country's financial affairs were concerned. The new Chief Executive—although he was unable to quiet the tumult of Reconstruction—did manage for four years to keep the nation "dead center" financially.

Grant was totally unschooled in public finance, but he was, as his biographer remarks, peculiarly "plastic" and suggestible.[1] The Administration's financial policy until 1873 was dictated by Treasury Secretary George S. Boutwell, a reticent but canny Yankee, who before the War had risen by luck and political skill from a village store clerkship to the Governor's mansion in Boston. In 1863, after a short stint as the first Commissioner of Internal Revenue, Boutwell had gone to Congress, where he quickly joined the extreme Radicals. On the financial question he had been a moderate, attacking contraction but refusing to follow his fellow Radicals, Stevens and Butler, in supporting paper repayment of the 5-20's. In 1866 he fought to limit McCulloch's contraction power, suggesting instead that the financial problem would be solved by letting the natural growth of the

---

[1] William B. Hesseltine, *Ulysses S. Grant, Politician* (New York: Frederick Ungar Publishing Co., 1957), p. 1.

economy absorb the excess currency, bringing the nation automatically to specie payments.[2]

The choice of Boutwell for the Treasury[3] was dictated by the Radicals,[4] but he was his own man on financial matters. The new Secretary viewed the Treasury as the balance wheel of the economy. His goal was to preserve the settlement painfully forged by the Republican Congressional majority during the Fortieth Congress, which by repealing the Contraction Act and reaffirming the government's intention to pay the federal debt in gold,[5] had decreed that there would be neither contraction nor repudiation.[6] He discarded McCulloch's much criticized policy of selling gold at strategic times to aid Treasury refunding. Instead, surplus Treasury coin was sold to businessmen for paying customs and foreign balances at regular, announced intervals. With the greenbacks thus obtained, the Treasury bought up matured securities at a premium, reducing the debt while at the same time restoring currency to business channels.[7]

More important, Boutwell abandoned McCulloch's efforts to return the nation to specie. In his first *Annual Report* in December 1869, he announced that, in effect, inaction would be the theme of his administration. In a perfunctory way he requested

[2] *Congressional Globe*, 39 Cong., 1 sess., pp. 1458-1459, 1498.

[3] After a farcical episode involving the initial illegal appointment of New York dry goods tycoon, A. T. Stewart. Stewart, a heavy contributor to Grant's presidential campaign, was found ineligible under the 1789 statute establishing the Department, which prohibited any person "concerned . . . in trade or commerce" from holding the Treasury office. Despite Stewart's frantic efforts to find a formula to bypass the law, he was rejected. See Hesseltine, *op. cit.*, pp. 146-147.

[4] *The Diary of Gideon Welles* (Boston: Houghton Mifflin Co., 1911), III, 549.

[5] That is, by the Public Credit Act, which although originally passed in Johnson's Administration was vetoed by the outgoing Presi-

dent and did not become law until March 19, 1869, soon after Grant's inauguration. For details see Robert P. Sharkey, *Money, Class, and Party: An Economic Study of Civil War and Reconstruction*, pp. 123ff.

[6] For the construction of this settlement see above, ch. III, and my "Men, Money, and Politics: The Specie Resumption Issue, 1865-1879" (unpublished Ph.D. dissertation, Columbia University, 1958), chs. II and III, particularly pp. 100-101.

[7] See Boutwell's testimony before the House Banking and Currency Committee early in 1870, in U. S. House of Representatives, *Report No. 31*, 41 Cong., 2 sess., p. 354. See also Henry Adams, "The Session," *North American Review*, CXI (July 1870), 36ff.; *Nation*, VIII (May 20, 1869), 389.

contraction power to aid in resuming, but the rest of the *Report* was confined to his "growing-up to specie" approach, suggesting how little faith he really had in his predecessor's policy. "The ability of the country to resume specie payments will not be due to any special legislation upon that subject," the *Report* read, "but to the condition of its industries, and to financial relations to other countries." The War had exhausted the North and impoverished the South. An essential precondition to resumption was "the development of the nation both North and South and the subsequent accumulation of the movable products of industry to such an extent that our exports should be equal substantially to our imports."[8]

Thereafter, the *Annual Reports* became increasingly unfriendly to specie payments. In 1870 Boutwell ignored the resumption question entirely, and in 1871 he merely reiterated the "growing-up" theory. The following year the *Report* explicitly rejected contraction, which the country was "not prepared to sustain," and announced that it must "rely on the increase in population, the returning prosperity of the South, and the growing use of paper money in Texas and on the Pacific Coast to absorb the excess greenbacks and reduce the gold premium."[9]

The Administration's new, relaxed policy coincided with public feeling about the financial problem. By 1869 the country was experiencing a new burst of growth and prosperity, sparked by a railroad boom, and affluence brought its usual softening of controversy and a growing inertia. This effect was particularly striking among the hard money groups. Men who defended deflation before 1870 and who would later regain their hard money fervor were to be strangely blind to the failings of paper money during the bonanza years.

Businessmen, as chief beneficiaries of good times, seemed especially complacent. The National Board of Trade, which in 1868 and 1869 had gone on record—though not without opposition—for a no-nonsense resumption stand, by 1870 had begun to

[8] U. S. Treasury, *Annual Report of the Secretary of the Treasury on the State of the Finances for the Year 1869*, pp. xiii-xiv. Hereafter these Reports will be cited as U. S. Treasury, *Report for . . .* followed by the appropriate year.

[9] U. S. Treasury, *Report for 1871*, p. xi; U. S. Treasury, *Report for 1872*, p. xxii.

equivocate. At the Buffalo convention of that year a contraction resolution submitted by S. Lester Taylor, a Cincinnati merchant close to the reformers,[10] encountered stubborn resistance from New York, Philadelphia, Chicago, and Baltimore merchants who were now convinced that the paper system was essential to their prosperity. The opposition echoed Boutwell's faith in spontaneous, effortless resumption. "It is the labor of man applied to the soil and attention to economy in his expenditure" that would bring the nation to specie, asserted George Buzby of the Philadelphia Commercial Exchange. "You may legislate until the day of doom, . . . show the utmost subtlety if you please, devise the most ingenious plans, and you cannot frame one that shall be effective except that . . . labor shall go on accumulating the material which will create a balance of trade in our favor."[11] George Opdyke noted how, with little Congressional interference in money matters, the country had enjoyed "a rapid strengthening of [its] resources." If Taylor wanted to get back to specie he "would accomplish his object more certainly by letting well enough alone than by attempting to interfere."[12]

Dissent was not new for Opdyke. He had been a leader of the anti-contraction group in the New York Chamber of Commerce. But now, though perhaps for the last time, he was speaking for a majority of the Chamber. In his assault on Taylor's resolution he was joined by Simeon B. Chittenden, hitherto a confirmed hard money man, whose remarks—really a conversation with himself—beautifully disclose the tension between interest and principle that characterized so many of his type during the early '70's. Congress might have resumed immediately after the War, Chittenden reflected, but that opportunity was now past. Perhaps resumption would have been best, "but had we resumed we should not have had the great development of railroads which has come as an incident to our paper money, and which may yet prove, contrary to all history, that a great war and paper money

10 For Taylor's ties to the reformers see Taylor to David A. Wells, Avondale, Ohio, April 29, 1871, Wells MSS, LC; Taylor to Edward Atkinson, Avondale, Ohio, Nov. 30, 1868, Atkinson MSS, Massachusetts Historical Society; Taylor to Carl Schurz, Cincinnati, Feb. 13, 1874, Schurz MSS, LC.
11 National Board of Trade, *Proceedings of the Third Annual Meeting at Buffalo, Dec. 1870*, p. 182.
12 *Ibid.*, p. 184.

may possibly be a great blessing." The future might yet show "that the magnificent development of our country was an incident of the great rebellion and of the prodigious amount of paper which consequently was circulated through the country."[13] A man of stern principles, Chittenden was obviously uncomfortable with his new heresies. Later his conscience would reassert itself, and he would become a leader of the sound money wing in Congress,[14] but at this point, like so many other businessmen, he was riding the crest of the boom,[15] and scruples momentarily yielded to expediency.

Taylor's motion failed 29 to 24, with the rigidly conservative New England delegates and Taylor's own Cincinnati associates[16] voting affirmatively against the solid opposition of Philadelphia, Pittsburgh, Chicago, New York and Louisville, joined by a substantial part of the St. Louis and Baltimore boards.[17] Not that the merchant community had been converted to inflation; just before voting on the Taylor resolution the Board had first rejected a motion condemning "premature resumption"[18] and then had immediately endorsed resumption in principle.[19] But the endorsement was recognized as essentially meaningless,[20] and it was apparent that even the mercantile interests of the port cities —those, at least, outside New England—were content with the *status quo*.

Indeed, acceptance of things as they were was a pervasive mood in these years. On the other side of the business fence from the merchants, *Iron Age*, concluding that the Treasury ought to

[13] *Ibid.*, pp. 186, 189. For similar statements see the remarks of J. Price Wetherell of the Philadelphia Board of Trade and F. H. West of the Milwaukee Chamber of Commerce, *ibid.*, pp. 189, 211-212.

[14] During the Forty-fifth Congress. See below, ch. x.

[15] At various times during the late 1860's and 1870's Chittenden was President of the New Haven and New London, and Director of the Delaware, Lackawanna and Western and the Toledo, Wabash and Western railroads. *National Cyclopedia of American Biography* (New York: James T. White & Co., 1892 *et seq.*), xxx, 387; *Railroad Gazette*, vii, 522.

[16] Scattered votes from other western and a number of southern trade associations also supported the Taylor resolution.

[17] National Board of Trade, *Proceedings of the Third Annual Meeting*, pp. 213-214.

[18] *Ibid.*, pp. 176, 213.

[19] *Ibid.*, p. 214. There was no roll call on this motion.

[20] See the remarks to this effect by Richard Hawley of the Detroit Board of Trade, *ibid.*, p. 177.

let the currency issue alone, quoted Dr. Johnson's Tory adage: "Where we don't know what to do, we had better do nothing at all."[21] In the same spirit, Carey, as industry's philosopher, found Boutwell a vast improvement over McCulloch.[22] Even the reformers, though they felt only contempt for Boutwell's do-nothing policy,[23] had little hope of progress toward resumption. The elder Charles Francis Adams noted in June 1869 the effect of prosperity on financial opinion in Boston. "Everybody is going to sing at the Jubilee[24] 'Let us have peace,'" he wrote his son Henry, and a vigorous effort for resumption was now "utterly out of the question."[25] Amasa Walker resigned himself to the fact that the public was "not . . . ready for any great changes in our financial or political condition."[26]

During this period, Congress resisted every attempt to disturb the equilibrium. The national legislature, Representative John Coburn wrote shortly after the Forty-first Congress opened in 1869, "so far has done nothing as to our currency and will do nothing."[27] Garfield later complained that almost any money proposition introduced was apt to be denounced "by good men and true" as "idiotic and insane."[28] An inflammatory repudiation speech by Ohio Congressman William Mungen in December 1869 brought an immediate rebuke to any "proposition, direct or indirect, to repudiate any portion of the debt of the United States."[29] Congress had as little patience with contractionist legislation, and unceremoniously brushed aside a resumption measure

---

21 *Iron Age*, vii (June 2, 1870).

22 Carey to Boutwell, Philadelphia, Sept. 7, 1869, Treasury Dept., Misc. Letters Received by the Sec. of the Treasury, 1869, item no. 261, National Archives.

23 Charles Francis Adams, Sr., to Henry Adams, Boston, Nov. 24, 1869, Adams MSS, Massachusetts Historical Society; Joseph Ropes, "Restoration and Reform of the Currency," *Journal of Social Science*, v (1873), 60-61.

24 This was the Peace Jubilee at Boston, June 15-19, 1869, a great festival of music and oratory, to celebrate the ostensible end of Reconstruction.

25 Charles Francis Adams, Sr., to Henry Adams, Quincy, June 9, 1869, Adams MSS.

26 Amasa Walker to David A. Wells, North Brookfield, Mass., May 13, 1872, Wells MSS.

27 John Coburn to Henry Carey, Washington, April 9, 1869, Carey MSS, Historical Society of Pennsylvania.

28 Garfield to Carey, Washington, Nov. 30, 1869, *ibid.*

29 The bipartisan vote was 124 to one, with the extreme greenbackers abstaining. *Congressional Globe*, 41 Cong., 2 sess., pp. 185-195.

introduced by Sumner in December 1870.[30] Indeed, no legislation threatening to disturb the existing state of things could get by, and it seemed to Garfield, as to many contractionists, that the country was "drifting further away from specie payment every day."[31]

II

The Administration's concern for equilibrium paradoxically committed it to a vigorous fiscal policy. To maintain stability, the Treasury was forced to intervene frequently in the money market, since every major speculative operation, every serious international disturbance, and almost every important political development in these years threatened to upset the country's delicately balanced financial system. At times the Administration's behavior seemed arbitrary or politically motivated, but fundamentally it was designed to preserve the currency settlement that Grant had inherited from the Fortieth Congress.

Boutwell's policy received its baptism in the fall of 1869, before he had an opportunity to get fully settled in his new office. The use of gold by merchants for hedging and for paying customs and foreign balances put the commercial community at the mercy of speculators. Foreign traders were frequently "short" of gold— that is, they had borrowed gold to be sold as a hedge against a falling premium, pledging greenbacks as security.[32] This situation offered Jay Gould and Jim Fisk, two financial buccaneers already notorious for their Erie Railroad swindles, a rare opportunity to plunder the port merchants. If they could win control of the gold supply, they could squeeze the foreign traders who needed gold to meet short contracts or to pay customs fees.[33] The success of their operation depended on keeping the Administration neutral, since close to $100 million of gold lay in the Treasury vaults, an

[30] Sumner, blind as usual to political realities, failed to recognize the altered public mood following Grant's election, and scolded Atkinson for procrastinating on the resumption question. See Sumner to Atkinson, Washington, Jan. 4, 1869, Atkinson MSS. For Sumner's bill see *Congressional Globe*, 41 Cong., 3 sess., p. 2.

[31] Garfield to Henry Carey, [?],

March 11, 1871, Carey MSS. See also William Allison to Grenville Dodge, Washington, Dec. 16, 1869; and Horace White to Dodge, Chicago, May 4, 1870, Dodge MSS, Iowa State Department of History and Archives.

[32] See above, ch. IV.

[33] Testimony of James B. Hodgskin, *Report No. 31*, pp. 25-26, 28.

amount which far exceeded the conspirators' resources. If the Treasury decided to sell gold, the corner would instantly be smashed and its engineers buried in the ruins.[34]

How Gould and Fisk sought to influence the President; how they corrupted Grant's corruptible brother-in-law and the equally willing Assistant Treasurer in New York; how they cleverly concealed their gold purchases by operating behind dummy brokers —all this is part of a tawdry but classic story of these years.[35] It is enough to say that by Thursday, September 23, amid much frenetic activity, gold had been pushed up twelve points to 144, and merchants and brokers were being squeezed for more margin to cover their borrowing.[36] Commerce through New York was paralyzed, since foreign traders—those who had any choice— refused to buy gold for customs and remittances.[37] Bankers, merchants, and speculators showered Boutwell with telegrams and letters demanding that he sell coin,[38] and the Administration decided to break the corner. At noon of Friday the 24th, with gold now above 160, the Secretary ordered the sale of $4 million of coin. The premium, already undercut by private "bear" sales, collapsed, and in fifteen minutes fell to 133.[39]

The crisis was over quickly, but its effects were prolonged. Hundreds of traders found themselves committed to buying gold at panic rates and unable to meet their contracts.[40] The

---

[34] Henry Adams, "The New York Gold Conspiracy," in Charles Francis Adams, Jr., and Henry Adams, *Chapters of Erie* (Ithaca, N.Y.: Great Seal Books, 1956), p. 113.

[35] The story has been told many times, most notably in *ibid.*, pp. 101-136; Julius Grodinsky, *Jay Gould: His Business Career, 1867-1899* (Philadelphia: University of Pennsylvania Press, 1957), pp. 77-79; Matthew Josephson, *The Robber Barons: The Great American Capitalists, 1861-1901* (New York: Harcourt, Brace & Co., 1934), pp. 141-148.

[36] *Report No. 31*, pp. 185, 188; Adams and Adams, *op. cit.*, pp. 126-127.

[37] Boonen, Graves & Co. to Boutwell, New York, Sept. 4, 1869,

Misc. Letters Received by the Sec. of the Treasury, 1869, item no. 16, National Archives.

[38] Henry Clews to Boutwell, New York, Sept. 20, 1869, item no. 245; anonymous to Boutwell, Sept. 23, 1869, item no. 53; George H. Bond to [?], Sept. 18, 1869, item no. 117, *ibid.*; George S. Boutwell, "Black Friday—September 24, 1869—From the Standpoint of the Secretary of the Treasury Under Grant's First Administration," *McClure's Magazine*, xiv (November 1899), 33.

[39] *Report No. 31*, pp. 12-17.

[40] The conspirators were themselves able to escape their contracts with the help of the corrupt New York judiciary. Adams and Adams, *op. cit.*, pp. 133ff.

shock to the money market hurt thousands of general commercial borrowers and stock speculators, and adversely affected business for weeks.[41] An unexpected by-product—a sharp, permanent drop of gold to a new low plateau—hurt still others.[42]

Somehow, although it had confounded the conspirators, the Administration was forced to share the blame for the damage done. The Democratic *New York World* held Boutwell rather than Gould and Fisk responsible for the business derangement that followed the collapse of the corner.[43] When Congress investigated "Black Friday" the following January and February, the Democratic minority of the House Banking and Currency Committee attempted to implicate Grant and his Secretary in the debacle. Boutwell was called to testify regarding his part in the affair, and under sharp Democratic questioning protested that only the grave harm being done "legitimate" business induced him to intervene.[44] The Democrats were clearly trying to plant the suspicion that the Administration had hidden motives in moving against the corner, and with the ill-disposed they probably succeeded. But Boutwell was being candid. The picture of the government as protector of injured, defenseless business was overdrawn, but the move was entirely consistent with the Administration's policy of balance.

In October 1872, on the eve of the Presidential balloting, the Treasury again intruded into the money market, this time to break up a greenback "lock-up" that was once again creating severe hardship for eastern merchants. In Boutwell's absence, though with his approval, Assistant Secretary William Richardson injected some $5 million of McCulloch's $44 million "reserve" into the money market by buying up outstanding federal securities.[45] This "reissue" was similar to the "open market operations" that the Federal Reserve System undertakes frequently today, and indeed, under Grant, the Treasury was generally assuming

[41] *Report No. 31*, p. 129.

[42] The gold premium had averaged 35 most of 1869; by November it had fallen to 20. See Wesley Clair Mitchell, *Gold, Prices and Wages Under the Greenback Standard* (Berkeley: The University [of California] Press, 1908), Table I, pp. 309ff.

[43] *NYW*, Oct. 2, 1869.

[44] *Report No. 31*, p. 255.

[45] For details of this transaction see *CFC*, xv (Sept. 21, 1872), 373; (Oct. 16, 1872), 510; (Nov. 3, 1872), 582-583; *New York Herald*, Oct. 7, 1872.

some of the functions of a central bank. But in the 1870's the practice was unfamiliar and raised a storm of protest. Conservative financial journals were outraged by what they considered Richardson's usurpation of power.[46] The *New York Tribune*, organ of Grant's opponent, Horace Greeley, cried politics and suggested that the Administration was trying at the last minute to bribe the commercial community.[47] But the reissue, which was soon retired, was only another instance of the Treasury's firm policy. Boutwell was certainly not above trying to influence the New York merchants, but the Treasury's role as a financial gyroscope preceded the 1872 campaign and would continue after Grant's reelection.[48]

The Administration's concern for equilibrium also appears in its treatment of the Legal Tender Decisions of the Supreme Court. From the first there had been uncertainty regarding the constitutional authority of Congress to declare the greenbacks a legal tender. When the question of forcing the public to accept the federal notes through a legal tender clause was first broached in January 1862, constitutional objections were raised in the House Ways and Means Committee. Reassurances from the Attorney General satisfied Committee members,[49] but during the ensuing general debate Democrats again challenged the legal tender provision on constitutional grounds.[50] The issue came before the state courts some fifteen times between 1863 and 1869, and in almost every instance the courts held the law valid.[51]

[46] *CFC*, xv (Nov. 2, 1872), 585; *The Financier*, ii (Dec. 21, 1872), 528. Ultimately the Senate Finance Committee agreed, after an investigation, that the conservatives were right and the $44 million were permanently retired and not subject to reissue. The ruling had no legal force, however, and, as will be shown, was later ignored. See U. S. Senate, *Report No. 275*, 42 Cong., 3 sess., p. 6.

[47] *NYDT*, Oct. 8, 1872.

[48] That the Treasury's 1872 intervention was not primarily a political move was acknowledged shortly after by John Murray Forbes, and years later by John Young Scammon of Chicago, who testified that Boutwell's action enabled the Chicago banks to recover their reserves in time to aid crop movements. See Scammon's testimony in U. S. House of Representatives, *Miscellaneous Document No. 5*, 46 Cong., 2 sess., pp. 50-51. For the Forbes comment see Forbes to Charles Eliot Norton, Boston, Dec. 10, 1872, Norton MSS, Houghton Library, Harvard University.

[49] Elbridge Gerry Spaulding, *History of the Legal Tender Paper Money Issued During the Great Rebellion* (Buffalo: Express Printing Co., 1869), pp. 15-16.

[50] *Ibid.*, pp. 43-44, 53.

[51] Charles Fairman, *Mr. Justice Miller and the Supreme Court,*

The status of the Legal Tender Act was not merely an abstract constitutional question. By voiding the legal tender clause, the courts might throw the country's finances into chaos. Such a move would certainly increase the burden of all prewar debts still outstanding by making them payable in gold; furthermore, it might do the same for debts contracted after passage of the measure, and, conceivably, might reopen all debt settlements already made in paper.

During the '60's, each time it appeared that the Court would decide the constitutional issue once and for all, the public flinched. In early 1869 a Chicago real estate broker noted the "great and increasing feeling in our community that all indebtedness made now will have to be paid in Gold, the report having become current that the Judges . . . have decided . . . against the Constitutionality of the Legal Tender Act."[52] A manufacturer complained that he and his business colleagues "would like to know . . . where we are going to land."[53] Men as far apart as Henry Adams and Wallace Groom, the greenback editor of the New York *Mercantile Journal,* were appalled at the prospect that the Court might strike down the greenbacks. Groom thought that a constitutional amendment explicitly legalizing the greenbacks should be passed, "rather than . . . sacrifice the commercial, manufacturing, and agricultural interests of the Nation."[54] Adams, who had just set up in bachelor quarters in Washington and was in straitened circumstances, was afraid that an adverse decision would bankrupt the Indiana, Cincinnati, and Lafayette Railroad, and make his $4,000 of stock worthless.[55] Rumors afloat in November 1869, that a decision voiding the Act was imminent, terrified Congress as well as businessmen and debtors, and froze long-term credit.[56]

1862-1890 (Cambridge: Harvard University Press, 1939), pp. 152-153.

[52] G. S. Hubbard to James A. Garfield, Chicago, Jan. 4, 1869, Garfield MSS, LC.

[53] John Morris to James A. Garfield, Mineral Ridge, Ohio, Nov. 24, 1869, *ibid.*

[54] Groom to James A. Garfield, New York, Dec. 17, 1869, *ibid.*

[55] Adams to Charles Francis Adams, Jr., Washington, Nov. 23, 1868, Adams MSS. This did not keep Henry from being pleased at the Court's adverse decision once made. See below.

[56] *CFC,* IX (Nov. 6, 1869), 583; (Nov. 13, 1869), 614; (Nov. 27, 1869), 677; *New York Evening Post,* Dec. 9, 1868; Francis Perry to George Boutwell, Boston, Nov. 13, 1869, Misc. Letters Received by the

On February 7, 1870, Chief Justice Salmon P. Chase delivered the long awaited legal tender decision of the Court in the case of *Hepburn* v. *Griswold*. Chase initially accepted the fact that Congress indeed intended to make the United States notes a legal tender for debts contracted both before and after passage of the Act on February 25, 1862. The question now seemed to revert to whether or not the Act as a whole was constitutional. But the case at hand only involved a promissory note drawn in 1860, and the Chief Justice, by confining himself to the immediate issue, was able to avoid the larger question. Basing his decision on both the due process clause of the Fifth Amendment and the Contract Clause, Chase declared unconstitutional that part of the law applying to the pre-1862 debt.[57]

The motives of Chase and the Court majority in attacking the Legal Tender Act are obscure. Purely juridical considerations were doubtless involved, but probably there were also political and ideological factors at work. Professor Charles Fairman has observed that in the large number of state court decisions touching on United States notes before 1870, every Republican judge but one had upheld the legal tender clause, while every Democrat—with two possible exceptions—had pronounced it unconstitutional.[58] The Supreme Court majority, with the exception of Chase, who seemed to change his politics to suit his ambitions,[59]

Sec. of the Treasury, 1869, item no. 3245, National Archives. Business anxieties, at least regarding completed debt settlements, were probably exaggerated at this point. In 1869 the lower federal courts had upheld the right of Congress to issue Treasury notes and had asserted that the intent of the contracting parties determined the legality of debt settlements already made. This seemed to mean that debts already discharged in legal tenders without challenge, whether contracted before or after February 25, 1862, when the Legal Tender Act became law, would not be subject to review. But the issue had not been clearly determined, and in any case, debts pre-dating 1862, as yet unpaid, were still vulnerable. See Fair-

man, *op. cit.*, pp. 157-159; *CFC*, IX (Nov. 27, 1869), 677; X (Feb. 12, 1870), 198; *Nation*, IX (Dec. 9, 1869), 500.

[57] 8 Wallace 610ff. A recent discussion of Chase's decision will be found in Gerald T. Dunne, *Monetary Decisions of the Supreme Court* (New Brunswick, N. J.: Rutgers University Press, 1960), pp. 72-74.

[58] Some seventy justices were included in Professor Fairman's sample. See his excellent article, "Mr. Justice Bradley's Appointment to the Supreme Court and the Legal Tender Cases," *Harvard Law Review*, XIV, No. 7 (May 1941), p. 1131.

[59] Thomas Graham Belden and Marva Robins Belden, *So Fell the Angels* (Boston: Little, Brown & Co., 1956), *passim*.

were all Democrats; the minority with the possible exception of David Davis, all Republicans.[60]

The courts' cases were, then, actually miniature political contests, but contests in which current party financial positions were reversed. Republican jurists felt compelled to defend a major item of Republican wartime legislation; Democratic opposition reflected the party's traditional hostility to paper money and expanded federal functions—biases the judges did not abandon as readily as did the party's active politicians. In Chase's case the motives were probably more complicated. The Chief Justice had never really favored paper money, and if, as Treasury Secretary, he had condoned its issue, it was out of necessity, not conviction. His adverse decision eight years later was, from one point of view, a belated act of contrition. But it is also possible that Chase regarded the Hepburn case as a political opportunity. This strange man, a mixture of exalted principles and crude self-seeking, was a perennial candidate for President and had been a serious contender for the Democratic nomination in 1868. Chase's political instincts were never very sure. He apparently did not sense the new desire for financial quiet and may have believed he was ingratiating himself with the important sound money element.[61] Though he could well have confined his decision to questions of law and precedent, he took occasion to denounce in the most orthodox sound money fashion the "long train of evils which flow from the use of irredeemable paper money."[62]

Whatever the intended political effects, in the short run, at least, the purely financial consequences of the decision were modest. Businessmen received it with surprising calm. It seemed to affect only the pre-1862 debts, few of which were still out-

[60] Fairman, "Mr. Justice Bradley," *loc. cit.* Charles Francis Adams, Sr., told Henry that as the Court was then constituted "every political contest that may turn up will be decided pretty much as in Congress on a party vote." Adams, Sr., to Henry Adams, Boston, April 19, 1870, Adams MSS.

[61] The elder Adams suspected that Chase's political ambitions lay in back of his decision, but then he did not like Chase. On Adams' sus-picions see Adams, Sr., to Henry Adams, Boston, April 19, 1870, *ibid.;* for Chase's regrets about his role in issuing the legal tenders see Chase to Nathaniel Sargent, Narragansett, R. I., Oct. 24, 1874, quoted in Robert E. Warden, *An Account of the Private Life and Public Services of Salmon Portland Chase* (Cincinnati: Wilstach, Baldwin & Co., 1874), p. 273.

[62] 8 Wallace 621.

standing.[63] Only long-term obligations of states, municipalities, and—among business firms—railroad corporations, together totaling some $350 million, were involved.[64] The common opinion, moreover, was that the decision would not stand for long. Gold quotations, which should have reflected the Court pronouncement by a rapid rise, barely stirred, closing about as high at the end of the week as they had the Saturday preceding the ruling.[65] Though the railroads were among the few businesses that appeared certain to suffer by the Hepburn decision, railroad stocks were only momentarily depressed and soon rose to new high levels in a buoyant market.[66] Before the week was out, the financial editor of the *New York Herald* was remarking on how quickly the decision had been forgotten.[67]

This initial indifference did not last. Though limited in scope, the Hepburn decision caused difficulties for some firms. As one New Yorker complained, the "commercial community" was "not prepared for any change" and the decision promised to "cause widespread ruin over the whole of the United States."[68] According to one railroad official, the roads would now have to pay their bond interest in gold, though confined by their charters to fixed fares and rates.[69] Actually, railway directors did not know whether to take the Court ruling seriously, ignore it entirely, or defer a decision on interest payments until further clarification. A few roads decided to continue paying their bond coupons in currency;[70] several agreed to pay in gold at a 20 per cent premium;[71] others paid their current interest in paper, promising to

[63] Fairman, "Mr. Justice Bradley," p. 1148.

[64] *CFC*, x (Feb. 12, 1870), 199.

[65] *Ibid.*, 205; also Fairman, "Mr. Justice Bradley," p. 1147.

[66] *CFC*, x (Feb. 12, 1870), 204.

[67] *New York Herald*, Feb. 14, 1870, quoted in Fairman, "Mr. Justice Bradley," p. 1148.

[68] T. C. Minturn to Salmon Chase, New York, Feb. 12, 1870, Chase MSS, LC.

[69] This was S. S. L'Hommedieu, president of three railroads in Ohio, who went on to acknowledge, however, that Chase was "doubtless right." See L'Hommedieu to Salmon Chase, Clifton, [N. J.], Feb. 9, 1870, *ibid.*

[70] This was true of the Chicago, Burlington and Quincy, the Erie, and the Lehigh. See Charles Fairman's data on the debt repayment policies adopted by the railroads after *Hepburn v. Griswold*, "Mr. Justice Bradley," pp. 1149-1150.

[71] These included the Boston and Maine, the Eastern Railroad of Massachusetts, and the Illinois Central. *Ibid.*, pp. 1149, 1152.

make up the difference in gold when and if the Hepburn decision was sustained.[72]

But if businessmen demurred, sound money doctrinaires rejoiced. The court had apparently broken the currency deadlock by bypassing the popular branch of government—a judicial role that has become increasingly familiar today. Henry Adams—like a true Adams—rose above his personal interests and remarked that the ruling was the "single step which has been taken by any department of the government since the close of the war towards the restoration . . . of a solid basis to the currency."[73] S. Lester Taylor, the Cincinnati merchant-reformer, applauded the decision as likely to put an end to a great deal of uncertainty, though he believed it only the first step toward resumption.[74]

The Administration, however, was deeply disturbed. Grant and Boutwell had sought to stabilize the currency situation. Now the Court's ruling threatened to upset it. Nor were the Republicans better pleased by what seemed a deliberate attempt to repudiate the party's war policies. The Hepburn ruling, Greeley wrote, had "stirred up" the Radicals, and they would fight to get it reversed.[75] Administration organs like *Harper's Weekly* and the *New York Times* also denounced the decision,[76] and in the Senate, Administration stalwart Henry Wilson, intent on a reversal, prepared a measure to increase the Court to eleven justices.[77]

Grant did not need additional legislation, however. Two openings already existed on the Court,[78] and he proceeded to fill them with men (William Strong of Pennsylvania and Joseph Bradley of New Jersey) whose opinions on the legal tender question were

---

[72] These roads included the Camden and Amboy, the Philadelphia and Reading, and the Pennsylvania, at least at first. *Ibid.*, pp. 1141, 1150, 1151.

[73] Henry Adams, "The Session," p. 47.

[74] Taylor to David A. Wells, Avondale, Ohio, April 29, 1871, Wells MSS. See also *CFC*, x (Feb. 12, 1870), 199.

[75] Fairman, "Mr. Justice Bradley," p. 1016.

[76] Charles Warren, *The Supreme Court in United States History* (Boston: Little, Brown & Co., 1926), ii, 515.

[77] Fairman, "Mr. Justice Bradley," p. 1016.

[78] One of these vacancies had occurred through the retirement of Justice Grier and the death of his replacement, Edwin M. Stanton; the other was a new position authorized by a recent act of Congress. For the details of this complicated shifting of openings and nominees see *ibid., passim.*

known.[79] Attorney General E. R. Hoar promptly asked the reconstituted Court to consider two new cases involving debts contracted after February 1862. On April 1, with Chase and the Democratic members dissenting, the Court agreed to reconsider the issue; and exactly thirteen months later,[80] Strong handed down the majority decisions in *Knox* v. *Lee* and *Parker* v. *Davis*. The new rulings reversed the Hepburn decision regarding prewar contracts and also upheld the constitutionality of the Act as it applied to all debts contracted after 1862.[81]

Strong's decision was the fine-spun argument of a skilled constitutional lawyer, but its most arresting feature concerned the expediency of voiding the legal tender currency. Since passage of the 1862 Act, he stated, all debts had been contracted with the understanding that they might be discharged in legal tenders. If the Court now held the legal tender clause invalid, the government would become the "instrument of the grossest injustice; all debtors are loaded with an obligation it was never contemplated they should assume; a large percentage is added to every debt, and such must become the demand for gold to satisfy contracts, that ruinous sacrifices, general distress and bankruptcy may be expected."[82]

The President and Justices Strong, Bradley, Miller, Swayne, and Davis may well have had deep constitutional convictions regarding the extent of federal powers, but it is apparent that they also wished to preserve the financial balance that had been so painfully achieved.

The Administration's readiness to spare businessmen the hazards of financial instability, nevertheless, did admit of exceptions. Neither Grant nor Boutwell had pushed the 1870 Redistribution Act, which, by authorizing an additional $54 million bank circulation, had in a modest way altered the *status quo;* but the re-

[79] It now seems reasonably clear that Grant knew what Chase's decision would be before it was announced, and that hope of a quick reversal was an important consideration in the choice of Strong and Bradley. See Sidney Ratner, "Was the Supreme Court Packed by President Grant?" *Political Science Quarterly,* L, No. 3 (September 1935), *passim; Fairman,* "Mr. Justice Bradley," pp. 977ff.

[80] The long delay resulted in part from a change of case after the appellants in the original suits withdrew. Warren, *op. cit.,* II, 523.

[81] 12 Wallace 529; and Dunne, *op. cit.,* pp. 76-81.

[82] 12 Wallace 529-530.

funding problem which pressed upon the Treasury after 1868 did force Boutwell to risk ruffling the financial calm. This one positive effort of his regime placed the government in opposition to important business groups for the sake of sound budgeting policy. In effect, administrative—or bureaucratic—considerations triumphed over interest-group pressures.

When Boutwell came to the Treasury, the urgent problem of refunding the 6 per cent 5-20's and 5 per cent 10-40's was still unsettled as a result of the defeat of the 1868 funding measure.[83] Over $1.6 billion of "six percents" would be payable before July 1873, and although the government was not obliged to redeem them,[84] with its credit so enormously improved since the War years, it would have been patently derelict not to replace them with a lower paying security.[85] In his December 1869 *Report* Boutwell recommended the conversion of up to $1.2 billion of the 5-20's into several types of new bonds, paying at most 4½ per cent interest.[86] On February 3 Sherman reported enabling legislation from the Senate Finance Committee. The bill authorized three classes of bonds paying 5, 4½, and 4 per cent interest, in amounts of $400 million each, to be sold or exchanged at par for 5-20's, 10-40's, and other outstanding obligations. The principal and interest of the new bonds were to be "payable in coin of the standard value of the United States," and were to be exempt from all taxation, federal or local.[87]

The measure immediately came under attack from two directions. Believing that the greenbacks as well as the interest-bearing obligations could be funded into the new bond issues, *Workingman's Advocate* denounced the bill as a means of forcing contraction and resumption by the back door. Moreover, the provisions for tax exemption and repaying principal in "coin" perpetuated an injustice that had been imposed on the country by

---

[83] See above, ch. II.

[84] The 5-20's, it will be recalled, were not "redeemable," as distinguished from "payable," before twenty years from issue date. Since they first appeared in 1862, the government was not obliged to pay any of them before 1882.

[85] For a general description of the debt picture in 1869 see Robert T.

Patterson, *Federal Debt-Management Policies, 1865-1879* (Durham, N. C.: Duke University Press, 1954), pp. 78-81.

[86] U. S. Treasury, *Report for 1869*, p. xvii.

[87] John Sherman, *Recollections of Forty Years in the House, Senate and Cabinet* (Chicago: The Werner Co., 1895), I, 451-452.

the Public Credit Act.[88] The bill, declared a petition circulated among National Labor Union men, was "a public enemy."[89] At the other extreme, bondholders, and particularly the national bankers, thought the measure endangered their dividends. The bankers complained that their profits were so low that reducing interest on bonds held for note security would drive them out of business. The bill was "confiscatory" and would destroy any incentive for capital to remain in the national banking system.[90] In their anxiety to explain their position they overreached themselves and unwittingly admitted that their profits were often excessive. As the director of the First National Bank of Jefferson, Ohio, explained, his bank had made 10 per cent profit the previous year by the "closest economy," and "because we are receiving 9 per ct on our Bonds."[91] With the gap between gold and paper narrowing, and the banks forced to accept reduced interest, his institution would have to surrender its charter.[92]

Impelled by the unavoidable obligation to save the government money, Congress ignored these complaints. The bill was thoroughly debated in the Senate but cleared the Congressional hurdles substantially as introduced.[93]

III

As Grant's first term drew to a close, there appeared in the na-

[88] WA, Feb. 19, 1870; April 9, 1870.

[89] John Magwire, Response . . . to a Resolution of the National Labor Council (St. Louis, 1874), pp. 24-25.

[90] See the following series of letters, all in the Garfield MSS: J. P. Robinson, Director of the First National Bank of Cleveland to Garfield, Cleveland, March 13, 1870; Joseph Pool, President of the American National Bank of New York, to Garfield, New York, March 18, 1870; Thomas Robins of the Philadelphia National Bank to Garfield, Philadelphia, March 21, 1870; J. F. Whitelaw, Cashier of the National City Bank of Cleveland to Garfield, Cleveland, March 24, 1870; Don P. Eels, President of the Chemical National Bank of Cleveland to Comptroller Hulburd, Cleveland, March 25, 1870.

[91] That is, 9 per cent when the gold was converted into greenbacks.

[92] U. S. Simonds to James A. Garfield, Jefferson, Ohio, April 4, 1870, ibid.

[93] At the insistence of the House, however, the amounts of the various new securities were changed to $200 million of five percents, $300 million of 4½ percents, and $1 billion of four percents; and the provision of a sliding scale of "callability" and/ or repayment, as with the 5-20's, was eliminated. This eventually saddled the country with a high-interest debt. See Sherman, op. cit., I, 452-456.

tion an insurgent political impulse which threatened to topple the President and his party from power. Though not primarily financial in inspiration, the movement was to have important implications for several groups active in the monetary struggles of these years.

The first of these was the labor reformers, who in the early '70's found themselves irresistibly drawn into politics. This trend was an ironic by-product of good times. Prosperity stimulated union growth,[94] as it had during the War. Instead of staying in the National Labor Union, however, workingmen turned to pragmatic trade-unions. Such defections of trade-unionists left the National Labor Union increasingly in the hands of the reformers, and instead of weakening the Union's greenback orientation, propelled it into greenback politics.

Not that this was a complete change of course. At its very first convention in 1866 the N. L. U. had endorsed the principle of a labor party to secure the eight-hour day.[95] The interest in national currency problems by itself implied political action at the federal level, and in 1867 and 1868 the Union endorsed labor party action, this time to help enact the new financial program.[96] By 1870, in Massachusetts, where Wendell Phillips ran for Governor on a Labor Reform Party ticket,[97] labor-greenback politics had advanced beyond the planning stage.

It was in 1870, however, at the N. L. U. convention, that the first serious steps were taken to form a national labor party. As yet, neither prosperity nor Sylvis' death the previous year, which removed from the scene a respected greenback-reformer of authentic trade-union background,[98] had driven the "practical" men away. Almost all the old labor reformers were there—Trevellick, Campbell, Cameron, Magwire, Troup—but a number of younger trade-unionists, including William Saffin of the Molders' International and John Siney of the Pennsylvania Miners, also at-

[94] John R. Commons and associates, *History of Labour in the United States* (New York: The Macmillan Co., 1946), II, 46-47, 151-152.

[95] *Ibid.*, II, 99; John R. Commons and John B. Andrews (eds.), *A*

Documentary History of American Industrial Society (Cleveland: The Arthur H. Clarke Co., 1910), IX, 135.

[96] *Ibid.*, pp. 122, 129-130.

[97] Sharkey, *op. cit.*, pp. 199-206.

[98] Commons and associates, *op. cit.*, II, 151-153.

tended.[99] The convention squabbled over the tariff, immigration, and the seating of delegates, but it agreed on the main point: a new labor party was to be formed, and to this end the delegates chose a committee to draw up the appropriate resolutions and a "call."[100] In January 1871 the committee met in Washington and issued a manifesto condemning the banking and money monopoly for concentrating the "products of human labor" in "the hands of non-producers" through "ruinous rates of interest."[101] This is familiar Campbellism. But besides the usual anti-bank and interchangeable bond recommendations, there were demands for regulation of railroads, a revenue tariff, and a renewed and enlarged emphasis on laws to protect the homesteader against land monopoly.[102] The committee also unequivocally endorsed paying the bonds in greenbacks and attacked resumption.[103] The platform reflects a broadening of the labor reform program to suit the needs of a national political party with a mass appeal. Here the separate strands of Agrarian dissent of the 1860's are beginning to merge into the omnibus greenback movement of the later '70's.

Long before the National Labor Reform Convention assembled at Columbus in February 1872, the reformers were beating the bushes for likely Presidential candidates. For a while ex-Senator George W. Julian, an old abolitionist egalitarian and reformer, seemed a possibility, but he apparently was not interested.[104] Far more serious was the candidacy of Thomas Ewing, Jr., son and namesake of a prominent prewar Ohio Whig. The elder Ewing had served all four Whig Presidents in various Cabinet posts, including the Treasury. Like most northern Whigs, after his party's demise he had drifted over to the Republicans. During

[99] Commons and Andrews, *op. cit.*, IX, 257-259.

[100] Commons and associates, *op. cit.*, II, 144-146; WA, Feb. 4, 1871.

[101] *Ibid.*, Dec. 3, 1870; Feb. 4, 1871.

[102] At the 1867 Chicago Congress non-monetary monopolies had been mentioned, but rather perfunctorily. Homestead legislation had first been touched on at the 1868 N. L. U. convention. Commons and Andrews,

op. cit., IX, 178, 139-140.

[103] WA, Feb. 4, 1871. Actually, this was the first time the labor greenbackers had specifically rejected resumption, although it was always implicit in their financial position. See e.g. Trevellick's 1868 remarks, Commons and Andrews, *op. cit.*, IX, 209.

[104] Andrew Cameron to Julian, Chicago, Feb. 15, 1871, George W. Julian MSS, Indiana State Library.

the War the elder Thomas and his family had supported the Lincoln administration. Radical "usurpations" after 1865 antagonized the Ewings, and the former Secretary and his four sons—Tom, Jr., Hugh, Charles, and Philemon—apparently converted as a group to the Democracy.[105]

To the Ewings and a group of Ohio Democrats who acknowledged their leadership, the labor reform movement seemed to hold great political promise. In 1867 they had watched Samuel F. Cary, a Cincinnati lawyer and temperance reformer, defeat both major party candidates for Congress with the endorsement of the Cincinnati Trades Assembly.[106] The Ewings believed Cary's victory foreshadowed the future drift of politics and they hastened to ally the Ohio Democracy with the rising power of labor.

This orientation was only one strand in the Ewings' greenbackism. The family's history peculiarly epitomizes the tangled origins of soft money. Thomas, Sr. had been a determined opponent of Jacksonian finance and as Secretary of the Treasury under Harrison and Tyler, he had helped draft two bills for rechartering the Bank of the United States.[107] Most men of such impeccably Whiggish antecedents were resumptionists after the War. The exceptions were found among the Careyite group of promoters and enterprisers, and it was, indeed, to this element that the Ewings really belonged. Like many of the men who preached the business brand of soft money, the Ewings were caught up in the postwar "paroxism [*sic*] of improvement" that was sweeping Ohio and the nation. "Nothing is talked of" in the state, the elder Ewing wrote in 1870, "but coal and iron and RRs—and engineers and Geologists are our only aristocracy."[108] The Ewings were in on the ground floor of all the frenetic new growth. They had acquired important coal land investments in southeastern Ohio, which in 1869 were "advancing rapidly in value."[109] In 1871 Tom,

[105] Thomas Ewing, [Sr.], *An Address by Hon. Thomas Ewing to the Unpledged Voters of the United States* (Columbus, 1868), pp. 3-5.

[106] *WA*, Sept. 21, 1867; *Cincinnati Commercial*, Oct. 1, 1867; Oct. 6, 1867; *Cincinnati Times*, Oct. 9, 1867; *New York Herald*, Sept. 19, 1867.

[107] Allen Johnson and Dumas Malone, *Dictionary of American Biography* (New York: Charles Scribner's Sons, 1931), vi, 237-238.

[108] Thomas Ewing, Sr., to Hugh Ewing, Lancaster, Ohio, June 19, 1870, Ewing Family MSS, LC.

[109] Thomas Ewing, Sr., to Hugh Ewing, Lancaster, Dec. 25, 1869, *ibid*.

Jr. was offering his brothers Hugh and Charles a share in the Columbus and Fenora railroad project, which was to be "connected with a speculation in coal lands along the line."[110] He was also involved in another road in distant Southern California, and in later years the Ewings' interests were to spill over into iron manufacturing and real estate speculation.[111]

Had private profit been their sole concern, the Ewings—like the Careyites—might, in their financial principles, have stopped at free banking. But politics, Democratic politics, was another major ingredient in their soft money sympathies. Thomas, Sr., in his seventies by 1865, had no political ambitions for himself. But he had large plans for his able and ambitious namesake. The younger Tom had gone to Kansas with his new bride in 1856 to make his fortune and had become first Chief Justice of the new state's Supreme Court while still in his thirties. In 1862 he marched off to war as Colonel of the Eleventh Kansas Volunteers and returned a Brevet Major General and a hero. After Appomattox he tried his hand at law in Washington, but returned to Ohio in 1870 and settled down in his native town of Lancaster.[112] Like his Republican counterparts, Hayes and Garfield, Ewing turned to politics as a suitable career for an ambitious man and made himself a force in the Ohio Democratic party.

The elder Ewing, experienced in finance, was the guiding spirit behind his son's monetary views. He sought to further Tom's career by identifying the Ewing name with a broad financial program combining appeals to traditional Democrats, labor reformers, and promoter business interests. While the General was at the 1868 Democratic National Convention, his father warned him that Cary "and his working men must have some consideration, for they will perhaps hold the balance of power."[113] In a letter to John Magwire the elder Ewing pledged to support a modified version of the interconvertible bond as a means of preventing excessive paper issues.[114]

[110] Thomas Ewing, Jr., to Hugh Ewing, Lancaster, Nov. 17, 1871, ibid.

[111] Thomas Ewing, Jr., to Hugh Ewing, Lancaster, July 29, 1871; Thomas Ewing, Jr., to Charles Ewing, Lancaster, July 14, 1873, ibid.

[112] Dictionary of American Biography, vi, 239.

[113] Thomas Ewing, Sr., to Thomas Ewing, Jr., Lancaster, June 23, 1868, Ewing MSS.

[114] Thomas Ewing, Sr., to John Magwire, Washington, April 26, 1870, ibid.

His chief contribution to the currency position of the Ohio Democracy, however, was a clear note of enterpriser dissatisfaction with the Republican hard money policy. To resume[115] now, he wrote in 1869, "would be productive of much hardship and injustice to the debtor class of our community—the class made up of our active young business men, merchants, manufacturers, shippers, in short the producing class—those who combine their own personal energies with borrowed capital, and thus build up gradually an independence for themselves, while they give prosperity to the country. Now if we resume specie payments . . . we ruin this whole class of business men at once and drive them to bankruptcy." Ewing, like a good Agrarian, asserted the superiority of the "producers" over the "capitalists," although he was unwilling to abuse the latter, who on the whole were a "worthy and meritorious class of citizens." Still, they should not be "singled out from all other classes and made the object of especial favors."[116]

This eclectic credo the younger Ewing accepted as his own and with it he tried to convert the Ohio Idea from an essentially narrow attack on the banks and the bondholders into a broad platform for labor and growing enterprise as well. Soon after returning to his native state, he sought to enlist Ohio labor under the Democratic banner. In 1870 he addressed a letter to Trevellick and Campbell endorsing every major point of the labor reform money platform.[117] The following year Ewing succeeded in committing the Ohio Democracy to the labor reform version of soft money over the opposition of the old Copperhead chieftain, Clement Vallandigham, and the other party bullionists. Confronted by the attempt, in Vallandigham's "New Departure," to return the party to its original Jacksonian hard money principles, Ewing and his friends made the state convention reaffirm the Ohio Idea and add a clause endorsing greenbacks "convertible into 3 per cent. bonds . . . said bonds to be redeemed in greenbacks on demand."[118] Ewing's political

---

[115] In a printed letter of Aug. 2, 1869, in *ibid.*, repeal of the Legal Tender Act is substituted for resumption as the danger.

[116] Thomas Ewing, Sr., *Letters* . . .

to the Finance Committee of the Senate (Washington, 1869), p. 6.

[117] *WA* (supplement), Aug. 27, 1870.

[118] *NYDT*, May 19, 1871; June 2,

activities and speeches were reported favorably in the *Workingman's Advocate*, which in the 1871 state campaign urged Ohio wage earners to support the Democracy.[119]

The presence of Democrat Ewing at the Columbus labor reform convention represents the continuing trend toward fusion among soft money groups. Also in Columbus were such old labor-greenback regulars as Hinchcliffe, Campbell, and Cameron of the regular Illinois contingent, and Trevellick and Alexander Troup, who was now editor of the greenback New Haven *Union*. Siney of the Miners, and E. M. Chamberlain of the Knights of St. Crispin, were among the important active union officials present. In addition, professional greenback-reformers like L. De Wolf, Horace Day, and Moses Field attended; and for the first time, the soft money business element of New York in the persons of Wallace Groom and Pliny Freeman appeared alongside the labor men.[120]

The work of the convention as well as its personnel reflects this homogenizing tendency. The platform committee placed the interconvertible bond, with the 3.65 per cent interest that the New York group had popularized, first among the planks. Additional provisions suggested taxing the wartime bonds and paying the debt "according to the original contract," and endorsed the Granger-type legislation already called for in the Washington manifesto. The discussion that followed revolved around the novel 3.65 figure, which both Day and Trevellick considered too high. Groom counseled against being too niggardly with the security holders, since too low a rate would repel "farmers and men in moderate circumstances," and by preventing sale of the bonds keep the scheme from working. In the end, the convention adopted only the financial and strictly labor resolutions, including the 3.65 bond. The rejection of the rest, despite talk of "farmers," was an unimaginative rejection of the Granger program and postponed a farmer-labor

1871; *CDT*, June 2, 1871; Eugene H. Roseboom, *The Civil War Era, 1850-1873*, Vol. IV of *The History of the State of Ohio* (Columbus: Ohio State Archeological and Historical Society, 1944), p. 476.

[119] *WA*, May 27, 1871; Aug. 26, 1871; June 10, 1871; Sept. 2, 1871.

[120] De Wolf and Field had been at the 1869 N. L. U. convention, but had played minor roles; Groom and Freeman allied themselves with labor for the first time at this meeting.

alliance four years. The bond and tax resolutions, however, reflected the attempted merging of the Democratic and labor reform financial platforms that was to mark the rest of the decade.[121]

In its choice of standard-bearer this first political convention of the greenback forces was as unlucky as its successors. Ewing was not personally interested in the labor party Presidential nomination.[122] Like many other delegates, he supported Supreme Court Justice David Davis,[123] whose chief hold on the labor reformers was his acknowledged interest in running for President and his minority stand against Chase's Legal Tender decision.

What the labor reformers did not recognize was that Davis had little use for their financial program. An old friend and political associate of Lincoln, his loyalty to the Lincoln Administration, and not his love of paper money, had led him to uphold the Legal Tender Act. At this point his interest in the labor greenbackers, whose existence he barely knew of, was purely political. Like Chase, Davis wore the judicial ermine under protest; after a decade on the Court he was restless and tempted by an active political career. With the national revolt against Grantism growing stronger every day, Davis, and even more his ambitious friends, were anxious to collect any support they could. They hoped the labor reform nomination might be snowballed into a succession of nominations that would sweep him into office as the anti-Grant, fusion candidate.[124]

Yet there were dangers in the labor nomination. It might indeed ignite the Presidential train; it might also brand Davis as a financial crank. The Judge—or his friends—apparently tried to

---

[121] WA, March 2, 1872; Edward Topping James, "American Labor and Political Action, 1865-1896: The Knights of Labor and Its Predecessors" (unpublished Ph.D. dissertation, Harvard University, 1954), pp. 57ff.

[122] He did, however, consider the Vice-Presidential position. See Alexander Campbell to David Davis, La Salle, Ill., Feb. 29, 1872, Davis MSS, Illinois State Library.

[123] Thomas Ewing, Jr., to David Davis, Lancaster, Feb. 22, 1872, ibid.

[124] Willard L. King, Lincoln's Manager: David Davis (Cambridge: Harvard University Press, 1960), pp. 271-278. King makes Davis rather too innocent of any conscious seeking of the nomination and also throws most of the blame for his later lack of candor on his friends.

postpone the Columbus convention until after the independent-reformer meeting (representing the middle-class, good-government element) scheduled for the spring in Cincinnati.[125] When this attempt failed he seems to have decided to work for the nomination. Actually Davis had little serious opposition. Horace Day placed himself in the running, but his personal eccentricity, his colossal ego, and above all, his obscurity outside greenback circles, crippled his chances. Ewing's indifference made Davis the only acceptable figure of national reputation who seemed available. By the time the balloting began on the twenty-second, his candidacy was already far advanced.[126] On the first ballot he won a plurality; on the third an almost unanimous vote. To balance off the ticket with an eastern man and a Democrat the convention named Governor Joel Parker of New Jersey for Vice-President.[127]

Now followed a rare political tragi-comedy. While still in session the convention dispatched a telegram to Davis formally tendering the nomination. Davis was now on the spot, almost certainly just where the labor men hoped to put him.[128] How could he accept the proffer without accepting the platform? The wily judge[129] was equal to the challenge. "Be pleased to thank the Convention for the unexpected honor which they have conferred upon me," he wired back. "The Chief Magistracy of the Republic should neither be sought nor declined by an American citizen."[130]

Had Davis accepted the nomination, or merely announced a political principle? Had he accepted the platform? Of course,

[125] Thomas Ewing, Jr., to David Davis, Lancaster, Feb. 22, 1872, Davis MSS.

[126] Ewing had buttonholed prominent delegates the evening of the 21st and had built up a strong following for Davis. *Ibid.*

[127] *WA*, March 2, 1872.

[128] Campbell, a Davis supporter who in all of this was clearly an unconscious dupe of more experienced men, had been commissioned to prevent such a telegram being sent. He had stepped out of the hall momentarily, however, and in his ab-

sence the deed was done. Campbell to Davis, La Salle, Ill., Feb. 29, 1872, Davis MSS.

[129] Or his acquaintance and later secretary, James E. Harvey. King says the response, a paraphrase of a reply of Congressman William Lowndes of South Carolina to a similar offer years before, was suggested by Harvey and accepted by Davis. King, *op. cit.*, p. 279.

[130] Davis to E. M. Chamberlain, Washington, Feb. 22, 1872, Davis MSS.

publicly, the reformers had to assume that he had accepted both, and they promptly wired back their congratulations.[131] Still, they were uneasy and appointed a committee of five including Day, Groom, Campbell, Chamberlain, and A. M. Puett of Indiana, to carry the formal nomination to the candidate in Washington and to extract from him assurances of his good faith.[132]

At this point the Davis forces resorted to procrastination and the most shameless duplicity. Campbell was summoned to the Davis home in Bloomington and told by the judge's friends, as one of them archly explained, that "there were some planks in . . . [the] platform," that, while they *had no doubt* Davis "agreed to . . . (awful lies) [,] it would be very bad policy" to make him publicly endorse. It would "raise up and provoke" premature opposition. Campbell, in turn, tried to convince the Davis men that it would be unwise to hold additional conventions. Let all other opponents of Grant enlist under the labor reform banner. Taking advantage of Campbell's political innocence, they flattered him into doing what they wanted. "The eyes of Illinois were on him," they said, and he alone could save the state's candidate from unnecessary attack. Campbell was thoroughly taken in and promised to head off the committee's attempt to make Davis declare himself.[133]

At this point the story becomes confused. Apparently, Campbell was unable to quiet his colleagues' fears.[134] The committee, minus Chamberlain who could not attend, and Day who had bolted the party,[135] came to the capital in late April or early May. But again the Davis men were able to keep the reformers from their candidate. All the committee got for their

[131] Alexander Campbell to Davis, Columbus, Feb. 23, 1872; Alexander Troup to Davis, New Haven, Feb. 24, 1872, *ibid.*

[132] Samuel Parks to David Davis, Lincoln, Ill., Feb. 26, 1872, *ibid.*

[133] Clifton H. Moore to Davis, Clinton, Ill., Feb. 28, 1872; Lawrence Weldon to Davis, Bloomington, Ill., Feb. 28, 1872, *ibid.*

[134] In the weeks following the convention, *Workingman's Advocate* kept reassuring its readers that Davis was reliable, an action which, of course, suggests fears of the very opposite. WA, April 6, 1872; April 13, 1872.

[135] Why he did so is not clear. Cameron charged that it was out of pique at not getting the nomination himself, but there is some reason to believe that he foresaw Davis' betrayal. *Ibid.*, April 6, 1872; April 26, 1872; May 11, 1872.

trouble was a public statement from the judge that his high judicial position forbade him from taking an open political stand. This evasion they had to accept, and despite lingering dissatisfaction, they reported back that they had fulfilled their mission.[136] By now the greenback men must have known that they were being used by Davis to further his candidacy at the Cincinnati convention. Although beset by doubts, they went to Cincinnati prepared to fight for their taciturn and inaccessible candidate.

Middle-class reform was the soul of the Cincinnati movement, although eventually the mugwumps, like their labor counterparts, were outmaneuvered by the shrewder politicians who climbed aboard. Nominally Republican, the reformers had at first been enthusiastic about the new soldier-President, who they hoped would rise above mere party politics and bring an elevated tone to the national government. They had become disillusioned with Grant when it appeared, by his associates and his appointments, that he intended to favor Republican time-servers and doctrinaire Radicals.[137]

Boutwell, and the Administration's financial record, contributed to the growing disaffection. From the outset, the reformers had misgivings about the Massachusetts Congressman, a man close to the spoilsmen, who had supported the detested Ben Butler against their candidate in the 1868 Congressional campaign.[138] They felt contempt for the social and intellectual origins of the former grocery clerk.[139] Nevertheless, they were at first pleased

---

[136] *Ibid.*, May 11, 1872; May 12, 1872; July 6, 1872.

[137] "It's the old regime," Henry Adams wrote his older brother a few weeks after the inauguration, "and Grant is—between ourselves—less capable than Johnson." Henry Adams to Charles Francis Adams, Jr., Washington, March 29, 1869, Adams MSS.

[138] The respectable element and the reformers in the Massachusetts Republican party had supported Brahmin author Richard Henry Dana against Butler. Butler had won

a thumping victory, for which Boutwell, who had campaigned for his fellow Radical, was held partly responsible. *Nation*, VIII (March 11, 1869), 184; Samuel Shapiro, "Aristocracy, Mud and Vituperation: The Butler-Dana Campaign in Essex County—1868," *New England Quarterly*, XXXI, No. 3 (September 1958).

[139] Henry Adams to Charles Francis Adams, Jr., Washington, May 3, 1869; Charles Francis Adams, Sr., to Henry Adams, Boston, Jan. 12, 1870, Adams MSS.

with his "intelligible business-like purposes, frankly announced in advance and faithfully adhered to."[140] But they turned on him angrily when he and the Administration became entangled in the gold machinations of Gould and Fisk. His intervention to save the merchants violated the reformers' laissez faire scruples, and they found it difficult to understand or forgive him.[141]

An even more serious disagreement concerned Boutwell's "growing-up to specie" doctrine. Actually, a good theoretical case can be made for the policy.[142] Boutwell was certainly guided as much by a desire to avoid a ticklish issue as by profound financial insight, but assuming—as most men did—that the money stock was stationary, doing nothing made good sense. Deflation brought about by the country growing into its monetary skin promised to be relatively painless;[143] to impose further direct contraction seemed unnecessary, and in fact cruel.[144] Yet as captives of the current academic orthodoxy, which was skeptical of any resumption process short of remorseless greenback destruction,[145] the reformers had only contempt for Bout-

---

[140] This refers largely to his scrupulous gold-selling policy. *Nation,* IX (July 1, 1869), 5.

[141] The usually judicious *New York Evening Post* called the intrusion "the greatest defeat the Treasury has met under the present administration." *Post,* Sept. 25, 1869. See also *Nation,* IX (Sept. 23, 1869), 244; (Sept. 30, 1869), 261.

[142] And, indeed, has in recent years. See James K. Kindahl, "Economic Factors in Specie Resumption: The United States, 1865-1879," *Journal of Political Economy,* LXIX, No. 1 (February 1961), *passim;* also Roy Harrod, *The Dollar* (London: Macmillan & Co., 1953), p. 30.

[143] Boutwell's policy of repaying the debt with government surpluses, however—probably without his full realization—was deflationary, since he was retiring the bonds which served as the basis for national bank issue. On the other hand, since the debt did not fall below $2 billion until after 1880, it can be argued that in the period under consideration here debt reduction had little

contraction effect, and indeed, that given Treasury surpluses, it was less deflationary to put the money back into circulation than to hoard it in government vaults.

[144] George F. Hoar, brother of Grant's first Attorney General, later wrote of Boutwell's policy that it was "wiser . . . and more successful than that proposed by the economists who condemn him. He knew the exact extent to which the governing and prevalent forces in our public affairs would permit him to go in the direction of specie payment and payment of the debt. Of these forces the doctrinaires of the press who condemn him seem to me utterly [ignorant?]." George F. Hoar to Charles Eliot Norton, Washington, Feb. 16, 1877, Norton MSS.

[145] Besides the discussion in ch. IV of the contractionist views of the academic economists, see the interesting long letter of English economist J. E. Cairnes to E. L. Godkin, in which Cairnes shows utter contempt for the "growing-up" theory as contrary to all sound doctrine.

well's inertia. They received his first *Annual Report* coolly. Gamaliel Bradford ridiculed the Secretary's proud display of his debt reduction as "highly praiseworthy" in a "private citizen," but idiotic for the Treasury, which instead should have been redeeming its "overdue" and "dishonored" legal tender notes.[146] Henry Adams, in an essay dripping condescension, assailed the self-made Boutwell as a man with little respect for knowledge not "narrowly practical," a man who "believed in common schools and not political economy, in ledgers and cash books but not in Adam Smith or Mill." His only policy seemed to be a simple-minded devotion to reducing the debt, and to this program, which "appealed directly to the lowest order of intelligence and struck with the greatest possible force the mind of the voting public," Boutwell had sacrificed "currency reform, revenue reform and every hope of relief from taxation."[147]

Nor did the reformers' opinion of Administration policies improve with time. Boutwell's 1871 *Report* was dismissed by the *Nation* as of little consequence;[148] the following year he was reproved for asserting the Treasury's right to manipulate the money market—a power, Godkin wrote, never recognized by the "old political economy" of Smith, Mill, and Ricardo.[149]

At Cincinnati the reformers were prepared to do more for sound finance than scold the taciturn Secretary. The convention of independents, intellectuals, gentlemen reformers, disgruntled politicians, and opportunists which convened in May 1872 to form the Liberal Republican party, agreed on little besides the currency. There was squabbling over the tariff and a hard fight over nominations, but, to the labor group's dismay, a strong statement favoring "speedy" specie payments was adopted without a murmur.[150] Nor were Campbell, Cameron, Puett, Trevellick, and the rest any happier with the candidate of the

---

Economists had obviously not yet learned humility. Cairnes to Godkin, Aix-les-Bains, France, May 19, 1869, Godkin MSS, Houghton Library, Harvard University.

[146] Gamaliel Bradford, "The Treasury Reports," *North American Review*, cx (January 1870), 210.

[147] Adams, "The Session," pp. 36-37.

[148] *Nation*, xiii (Dec. 7, 1871), 362.

[149] *Ibid.*, xv (Dec. 12, 1872), 376-377.

[150] Earl Dudley Ross, *The Liberal Republican Movement* (New York: Henry Holt & Co., 1919), pp. 85-105; *Nation*, xiv (May 9, 1872), 203; *WA*, May 11, 1872.

new party. Setting aside their misgivings, they gave Davis what support they could from the sidelines, only to see the nomination go to Horace Greeley, a past friend of labor, but an arch resumptionist.[151]

Soon after, almost the last hope for a labor reform ticket vanished when the bewildered Democrats at Baltimore embraced Greeley and the Liberal Republican platform.[152] A few leaders refused to surrender, however. Cameron noted on June 1 that Davis was still officially in the race and recommended that the labor party go it alone.[153] Then, at the end of the month, the two labor reform candidates announced that they had withdrawn.[154] In August a small, disconsolate contingent met again in Columbus and formally abandoned the campaign.[155]

Still, the election was not a total disaster for soft money, whatever it was for the labor greenbackers. At their Philadelphia convention the Republicans, like the Liberals, had denounced repudiation. But they praised the greenback, and in a clause cleverly worded in the passive voice, implied that resumption would come about spontaneously without contraction or government interference.[156] The Republicans had become "softer" on finance than their opponents!

The different emphases of the parties became a factor in the vituperative campaign that developed. Although the election did not turn on the money issue, Greeley's oversimplified and doctrinaire financial views, summed up in his oft-repeated slogan, "the way to resume is to resume," hurt him with nervous businessmen, who were fearful lest he disturb the country's economic adjustment. As the aristocratic *North American Review* remarked, Greeley's election would not be "regarded as favorable to the national finances" by the timid public. His victory, it was believed, would "involve a change, and no change is wanted, least of all by a President who believes a card

[151] *Ibid.*
[152] Ross, *op. cit.*, pp. 140-141.
[153] *WA*, June 1, 1872.
[154] *Ibid.*, June 22 and 29, 1872.
[155] *Ibid.*, Aug. 24, 1872.
[156] The platform declared: "[We]
confidently expect that our excellent national currency will be perfected by a speedy resumption of specie payments." *Appleton's Annual Cyclopedia and Register of Important Events of the Year 1872*, p. 779.

tacked upon the Treasury doors would accomplish the instant resumption of specie payments."[157]

Weeks before the Republican national convention, the New York business community had come to Grant's support. In mid-April Henry Clews, soft money banker and Wall Street operator, organized a large meeting of prominent businessmen to endorse Grant's renomination.[158] Shortly before the October elections, a group of New York business leaders, including Clews, Chittenden, and Opdyke, issued a manifesto endorsing Grant on financial grounds. The President's reelection, they declared, would further the "general welfare of the country, the interests of its commerce and trade, and the consequent stability of public securities."[159]

The Liberal debacle which followed cannot be explained by any single factor. Greeley, an erstwhile Radical and an early free-soiler, was a noisome dose for Democrats to swallow, and many stayed at home on election day. His erratic personality also made him vulnerable to Republican ridicule, and many voters found it difficult to take him seriously.[160] But at bottom, complacency and the desire for economic tranquillity were probably decisive.[161] No specific issue that the Liberals raised could overcome the Republican advantages of good harvests, full employment, and high profits. A few intransigent greenbackers and a few unwavering upholders of public virtue might fuss over finance, but as yet the electorate was content to let well enough alone. Boutwell's course at the Treasury did not ensure Republican victory, perhaps, but it helped convince the public, which wished only to go about its business undisturbed, that with Grant in office the national finances were in good hands.

[157] *North American Review*, cxv (October 1872), 419; Ross, *op. cit.*, pp. 170-171.

[158] Clews, *Twenty-Eight Years in Wall Street* (New York: Irving Publishing Co., 1888), pp. 315-324.

[159] *NYT*, Oct. 16, 1872.

[160] Ellis Paxson Oberholtzer, *A History of the United States Since the Civil War* (New York: The Macmillan Co., 1926), iii, 44ff.

[161] My account of the election generally follows Eugene H. Roseboom, *A History of Presidential Elections* (New York: The Macmillan Company, 1958), pp. 224ff.

CHAPTER VI

THE FARMER (1865-1873)

PAPER money inevitably summons up images of insurgent farmers; yet thus far nothing has been said about rural financial attitudes. There is a simple reason for this omission: not until after 1873[7] do substantial numbers of farmers support paper money. It is important to understand that the Granger uprising of the prepanic years was an attack upon the supposed malpractices of railroads, agricultural processors, grain-elevator corporations, manufacturers, and "middlemen" in general, and had little directly to do with the money problem.

Nevertheless, Grangerism and greenbackism overlapped in a significant way. Primarily, both movements were deeply imbued with the Agrarian, anti-monopoly faith of prewar America. While not in origin a grass-roots creation, philosophical Agrarianism, not surprisingly, permeated rural thinking. Farm leaders, farm organizations, and farm journalists alluded endlessly to the nobility of husbandry, the special virtue of the producer, the complete dependence of society on agriculture. In the words of the 1873 National Grange constitution: "The soil is the source from whence we derive all that constitutes wealth; without it we would have no agriculture, no manufactures, no commerce. Of all the material gifts of the Creator, the various productions of the vegetable world are of the first importance. The art of agriculture is the parent and precursor of all arts, and its products, the foundation of all wealth."[1]

This agricultural "fundamentalism" is the brighter, more generous side of rural Agrarianism. But there was a darker

---

[1] Jonathan Periam, *The Groundswell: A History of the Origin, Aims, and Progress of the Farmer's Movement* . . . (Cincinnati: E. Hanneford & Co., 1874), pp. 168-169. See also the speeches of Dudley W. Adams of the National Grange and W. C. Flagg of the Illinois Farmers' Association, *IA*, Aug. 30, 1874, and April 4, 1874 respectively; also *AM*, April 3, 1877; William Finch to Ignatius Donnelly, Richfield, Minn., June 13, 1873, Donnelly MSS, Minnesota Historical Society.

aspect as well. The countryside was steeped in latent hostility toward the traditional enemies of the "industrial classes." Long before the Granger movement swept through the prairies, "bond-holders," "capitalists," "the money power," had become the focus of rural fears and suspicions.[2] Such attitudes, which had abounded during the War in Copperhead areas of the North-west,[3] with the advent of the greenback issue blossomed into a pervasive uneasiness which affected even Republican country folk. In December 1868 the "Citizens of Eden Illinois" wrote Benjamin Butler: "While we may not be able to properly ap-preciate the magnitude of the difficulties to be met and over-come and of the sacrifices to be made by those who assume the responsibility of opposing the nefarious scheme of the money oligarchy to rob and enslave the industrial classes. Yet we are not ignorant of nor insensible to the fact that their power is well nigh omnipotent and that they will employ every means at their command however base to accomplish their vile pur-pose and crush those who dare stand up for the people."[4]

These rural fears served as fertile ground for the soft money Democracy, which from the very beginning sought support for its financial program among western farmers. The earliest post-war efforts by western Democrats to contrive a winning financial issue were linked with farmers' grievances. Henry Clay Dean, for one, at the outset of his postwar greenback career, was an active missionary among western farm groups. At a meeting at Monmouth Courthouse, Illinois, in December 1865, resolutions were adopted at Dean's behest which began with an emotional statement of farmer grievances, progressed to an indictment of Republican wartime finance, and concluded with an early version of the Ohio Idea. Agriculture, this statement read, had been sacrificed to the "lust of Eastern power." Con-

[2] For an interesting discussion of the "radical" Northwestern anti-monopoly tradition up to 1865, see Chester M. Destler, "Western Radi-calism, 1865-1901: Concepts and Origins," in *American Radicalism, 1865-1901: Essays and Documents* (New London, Conn.: Connecticut College, 1946), pp. 3-4.

[3] Frank Klement, "Middle West-ern Copperheadism and the Genesis of the Granger Movement," *MVHR*, xxxviii, No. 4 (March 1952), pp. 679ff.

[4] Citizens of Eden, Ill., to Ben-jamin F. Butler, Dec. 14, 1868, But-ler MSS, LC.

gress had irresponsibly bestowed public land on speculators and had "locked up in idleness the entire available capital of the United States and placed it in the keeping of monopolists who draw from it a ruinous rate of interest which has to be paid by the laboring classes of the country." Congress must abolish the national banks and redeem their bonds by "Treasury notes," which would then replace the "unsafe" national bank-note currency. With Dean's prompting, the "people of Warren County" pledged themselves "to unite with other people of the Mississippi Valley and all the agricultural districts of the United States to resist the invasion of their rights." They would "vote for no man" who would "subordinate the interests of agriculture for the exclusive benefit of the bondholders."[5]

This meeting was not an isolated event. A year later an anonymous "Democrat," in a three-and-a-half-column article in the *Chicago Times,* brought under one program the Ohio Idea and resistance to the dangerous "transport monopolies" which were currently "drawing so strongly upon the farmers of the West."[6] Throughout 1867 numerous Democratic meetings in rural townships of Indiana and Iowa endorsed the Pendleton Plan and protested discriminatory federal taxation that enriched the tax exempt bondholders at the expense of the producers.[7] Small-town weeklies in Illinois were at the same time demanding "equal taxation" and an end to special privileges for the "bondholding aristocracy."[8]

The bondholders' supposed favored treatment, widely advertised by the Democrats in the West,[9] seems to have been especially resented in the rural regions. Possessing highly visible property, the farmer noted that he, a poor man, carried most of the tax burden of the nation. As one Wisconsinite complained: "I am a common farmer of Steuben Co. in Debt for one third of my land and have to pay tax on the whole, whereas the

---

[5] *Cincinnati Enquirer,* Jan. 4, 1866.
[6] *Chicago Times,* Dec. 21, 1866.
[7] *Cincinnati Enquirer,* Jan. 24, 1867; April 24, 1867; Aug. 19, 1867; Aug. 20, 1867. See also M. Suitliff to B. F. Butler, Warren, O., Oct. 8,
1867, Butler MSS.
[8] Max Shipley, "The Greenback Issue in the Old Northwest, 1865-1880" (unpublished Ph.D. dissertation, University of Illinois, 1929), pp. 70ff.
[9] See ch. III.

capitalist with his hundreds of thousands, escapes taxation altogether, is this just."[10] Such grievances the Democrats sought to convert into votes during the 1868 Presidential election. The Democratic platform, with its professed concern for the "people," the "laborer," and the "producer," was more than a ceremonial evocation of old Democratic themes; it was designed to appeal directly to the rural voters of the country, a tactic the Republicans recognized and feared. Joseph Medill of the *Chicago Tribune*, no friend of "repudiation" himself, warned his associates that the Democrats would garner thousands of western rural votes with their charge that Republican financial policies had "rob[bed] the plow-holders to gorge and fatten the bondholders."[11]

And they probably did. Seymour lost the election, of course, but this tells us little about the farmers' reception of the Democratic financial plank. Though Seymour and Blair did not win a single electoral vote in the old Northwest, the Democratic candidates received a larger percentage of the vote in many predominantly rural counties of Ohio and Indiana, to choose two examples, than they had in 1864, or would in 1872.[12] These results are admittedly ambiguous. There is no way of isolating the appeal of the money issue from all the other elements in so complex a phenomenon as an American Presidential election. But in this contest, unlike the ones preceding

[10] J. R. Decker to Benjamin F. Butler, Avoca, Wisc., Oct. 28, 1867, Butler MSS. Also A. B. Easton to Butler, Bardolph, Ill., Dec. 14, 1868, *ibid.*; Benjamin Close to E. B. Washburne, Fulton, Ill., Jan. 4, 1868, Washburne MSS, LC.

[11] Medill to John Sherman, Chicago, June 25, 1868, Sherman MSS, LC.

[12] In Ohio, out of a state total of 88 counties, 54 gave one or the other party a larger vote in 1868 than in either 1864 or 1872. In all but six cases these were Democratic, with both urban and rural counties registering larger Democratic totals than in either the preceding or the following elections. In Indiana the pattern was almost identical. In Illinois, however, the Republicans received a larger vote in 1868 in more counties than the Democrats. Since the two more easterly states were generally more strongly Democratic than Illinois, this would support the view that Seymour, and possibly the greenback platform, brought out Democratic voters, both urban and rural. The results also accord with the general conclusion reached below that farmers not already committed to the Democrats were not interested in paper money, and only with the advent of silver, turned in any number to monetary answers to their problems.

and following it, soft money was a prominent Democratic plank, and its presence may well explain the superior Democratic turnout in the rural West.

But who were these extra voters for Seymour and Blair? There was, as we have seen, some Republican Agrarianism, and no doubt some Republicans crossed party lines. But the 1868 Democratic financial plank was probably more effective in bringing out the old rural Jacksonians than in making converts of Republican farmers. For Indiana, at least in a later period, there is indeed evidence that the greenback platform largely attracted transplanted rural southerners who voted Democratic almost by reflex action.[13] Elsewhere in rural Indiana, and in other parts of the rural Northwest, where Republican-voting Yankees—and Germans[14]—resided, soft money ideas were clearly heterodox. The predominantly rural parts of Ohio's Western Reserve which sent Garfield to Congress remained an enclave of hard money pressed against Lake Erie by a perimeter of greenback territory.[15]

It was, then, primarily as a Democrat, or a Copperhead, or at least as an Agrarian and anti-monopolist—in a word as a political or intellectual being—that the western farmer endorsed heretical financial views in the years before 1873. As a member of an economic class, as a producer of commercial crops for sale in a world market, his attitudes differed. Unhappily, such a formulation raises the slippery question of "role," one of the most difficult problems for the social investigator to deal with satisfactorily. When does a man represent a party; when does he speak for an occupational group, for a section of the country, for a particular religious group? Specifically, who spoke for the farmer as a farmer? It has seemed best for present purposes to assume that the agricultural press and generally

[13] William Carlton, "Why Was the Democratic Party in Indiana a Radical Party, 1865-1890?" *Indiana Magazine of History*, XLII, No. 3 (September 1946), pp. 222ff.

[14] See James Shroeder to William Allison, Guttenberg, Clayton Co., Iowa, Nov. 16, 1878, Allison MSS, Iowa State Department of History and Archives.

[15] With the exception of Mahoning County which contained Youngstown, an industrial city, the rest of the 19th Congressional district had few towns of any size. On the resistance to paper money of the Yankee-inhabited Reserve, see below, ch. VIII.

recognized farm leaders come close to voicing the sentiments and aspirations of the dirt farmers of their states or region. By this yardstick it appears that the farmer, even in the West, remained suspicious of paper money. "The Greenback of today is not a real value," wrote a correspondent of the *Ohio Farmer* in 1868. "It is only a partial one and hence . . . instead of not having enough of Greenbacks we have still too many."[16] *Iowa Homestead* in 1870 criticized the "currency tinkerers" in Washington who were pandering to an ill-considered and ignorant demand for expansion.[17] Ignatius Donnelly, soon to lead the greenbackers of Minnesota, noted in 1873, that "we have no interest in an inflated money market. . . . As we have to sell our wheat at the world's price, it is our interest that everything we buy should be at the world's price."[18] The same year, Willard C. Flagg, President of the Illinois Farmers' Association, told a farm audience that he doubted whether "our present system of finance . . . is one from which the farmer . . . derives any advantage." "The resumption of specie payment" was "for the best interests of the laboring, honest and non-speculative masses of the country."[19]

It is difficult to explain this support of specie payments by economic considerations alone. Donnelly, to be sure, had suggested a plausible economic motive for an agricultural defense of sound money—one which paralleled the port merchants' argument for a single world gold standard. On the other hand, these immediate postwar years were generally prosperous in the Northwestern farm belt. In Iowa, 1868 was hailed as the state's "Golden Year."[20] Wheat in Minnesota the same year was bringing an outstanding $1.65 to $1.70 a bushel; oats were at 75 to 80 cents.[21] Farm prices had indeed fallen from their inflated war-

[16] *Ohio Farmer*, Feb. 15, 1868.
[17] *Iowa Homestead*, Feb. 25, 1870. See also *Western Rural*, Dec. 21, 1872.
[18] Quoted in Solon J. Buck, *The Agrarian Crusade: A Chronicle of the Farmer in Politics* (New Haven: Yale University Press, 1920), p. 81.
[19] *IA*, Aug. 30, 1873; also *Western Farmer*, Jan. 11, 1868; *Kansas Farmer*, March 1868.
[20] *Iowa Homestead*, Aug. 5, 1868; and Aug. 12, 1868.
[21] John Rhodes to McCormick Brothers, Hastings, Minn., Jan. 6, 1868, Cyrus H. McCormick MSS, State Hist. Soc. of Wisc.

time peaks, but more slowly than the general price level.[22] Similar conditions in business had encouraged conservative acquiescence in the paper money regime, not agitation for returning to gold. Why was the farmer not similarly affected by prosperity? The answer probably lies in the greater persistence of older modes of thought among rural than among urban Americans. From the advent of the American party system, anti-monopoly had been wedded to bullionism. Rural Agrarians had distrusted attempts to declare paper slips equal to God's good coin and had been among the most loyal supporters of Jefferson and "Bullion" Benton. Rural isolation, the basically conservative nature of all rural attitudes, the financial naïveté of farm folk, apparently all combined to protect these older attitudes in rural areas long after they had suffered erosion elsewhere.

Yet the seeds of greenbackism among farmers as a class were present even in these generally good years. If farmers had not yet suffered the painful experience of declining prices, they had other grounds for discontent. One of the failings of so much that has been written on the farm problem is that it draws large conclusions from little data. The whole farm uprising is sometimes explained by a few imperfect statistical series for wheat, corn, and cotton, and a few impressionistic statements about interest and freight rates. But even in his narrowly occupational role, not to mention his status as citizen, or Agrarian, or country-dweller, the farmer had other concerns besides profit and loss.[23] Noting the rarity of farmer representation in state legislatures and Congress, he was concerned about his political impotence.[24] He deplored the steady exodus of the talented young men and women from the farms.[25] He was uneasy about

[22] See Wesley Clair Mitchell, *Gold, Prices and Wages Under the Greenback Standard* (Berkeley: The University [of California] Press, 1908), Table 16, pp. 49-51.

[23] Significant in this connection is the "Country Life Movement" of the early twentieth century which expressed discontent with the quality of rural life even though farm prosperity was general and acknowl-edged. See Liberty H. Bailey, *The Country-Life Movement in the United States* (New York: The Macmillan Company, 1911).

[24] Solon J. Buck, *The Granger Movement: A Study of Agricultural Organization and Its Political, Economic and Social Manifestations, 1870-1880* (Cambridge: Harvard University Press, 1913), pp. 34-36.

[25] *Iowa Homestead*, May 20, 1868.

the growing economic gap between country and city.[26] When
Willard Flagg told a Missouri Grange audience that the rural
share of the total national wealth had declined from 56 to 37
per cent between 1860 and 1870, he was cheered by men deeply
disturbed by the apparent decay of agriculture.[27]

Much of this may be summed up as resentment of the city—
a feeling that was not new. The tension between town and
country is as old as the ancient world. In America it had existed
before the Civil War. For the period after 1865 it has already
been noted in the polemics of Dean and Pomeroy. But the growing ease of communication, the increasing—though scarcely
complete—breakdown of rural isolation, the spread of the agricultural press,[28] amplified these grievances still further. Ironically, the Grange itself, bringing farm leaders to the cities for
conventions and lobbying expeditions, probably stimulated discontent by exposing rural men to the startling advances of the
urban centers.[29]

Beyond this was another problem that unsettled and disturbed
the farmer: the loss of control over his economic fate. As agriculture moved farther away from the population centers of the
East, a growing portion of the agricultural community became
entangled in a web of intermediaries between itself and the
consumer of its product. Lee Benson notes that the opening of
the continental interiors to agricultural exploitation in the years
after 1870 generated movements of farm discontent on both
sides of the Atlantic. The "Communication Revolution," he
writes, produced "an international agrarian market, an inter-
ternational agrarian depression, and, as a climax, international
agrarian discontent."[30]

---

[26] *IA*, Oct. 23, 1875.

[27] *Ibid.*, Nov. 27, 1875.

[28] On this last see Frank Luther
Mott, *A History of American Magazines, 1865-1885* (Cambridge: Harvard University Press, 1938), p. 151.

[29] Buck writes as follows of this
phase of Grange activities: "The
educational advantages to those who
went as delegates to meetings of
state and national granges are obvious. The travelling expenses were
always paid out of grange treasuries

and thus many farmers were enabled
to take trips which would have been
impossible for them otherwise."
Buck believes these contacts with
the urban world were liberalizing,
but I think it more likely that they
helped reinforce rural prejudices.
See Buck, *The Granger Movement*,
pp. 286-287.

[30] Lee Benson, *Turner and Beard:
American Historical Writing Recon-
sidered* (Glencoe, Ill.: The Free
Press, 1960), p. 48.

In this country the discontent assumed the traditional anti-monopoly form of social protest movements. Oliver Kelley, who traveled through the Northwest in 1867-68 organizing granges for the new Patrons of Husbandry, was surprised to discover how concerned the farmers were about "every kind of monopoly." They were not particularly interested in the educational functions of the Grange, he reported, but did see the organization as a possible weapon against the monopolies.[31]

For the prairie farmer, discontent initially was directed at the railroads. In the first place, while the railroad made his grassland agriculture possible, it also wielded a frightening life-or-death power over him. The change of an established rate to a major rail center might blight a large flourishing farm region, itself perhaps carved out of a railroad land grant and settled through railroad colonization enterprise. His fear, moreover, was mixed with the disappointment that followed the collapse of his expectations. The western farmer had had high hopes for the railroads. For subsistence farmers, unable to export their surpluses of corn and wheat and forced to accept a primitive living standard, the railroads promised assimilation to civilized, modern living. To farmer-speculators who bought land in excess of their needs for reselling at a profit, the railroads promised the windfalls they had gambled on. To landless men in densely settled, older areas, they meant the opening of new, cheaper virgin lands for a new start. States, towns, and counties in the West had all courted the roads in the early years, pledging township and county taxes for guarantees of service. In the years 1866-73, Carter Goodrich reports, 29 states granted over 800 authorizations for local aid to railroad corporations.[32] Thousands of farmers personally invested their savings in railway securities.[33]

[31] Oliver H. Kelley, *Origin and Progress of the Order of the Patrons of Husbandry* . . . (Philadelphia: J. A. Wagenseller, 1875), pp. 96, 113.

[32] Carter Goodrich, *Government Promotion of American Canals and Railroads, 1800-1890* (New York: Columbia University Press, 1960), p. 241 and ff.; *Kansas Farmer*, February 1865.

[33] Fred A. Shannon, *The Farmer's Last Frontier: Agriculture, 1860-1897* (New York: Rinehart & Company, 1945), p. 175. See also Theodore Saloutos, "The Agricultural Problem and Nineteenth Century Industrialism" in Joseph T. Lambie and Richard D. Clemence (eds.), *Economic Change in America: Readings in the Economic History of the United States* (Harrisburg: The Stackpole Company, 1954), pp. 328-329.

The glowing vision quickly dimmed. The roads seemingly created as many problems as they solved. Although they made possible the commercial agriculture of the prairies, they did so at painful cost. Shipping wheat 1,600 miles to the Atlantic seaboard absorbed much of the price of a bushel. Railroad rates actually fell steadily during the postwar period, but inconsistencies, discrimination, and the arrogance and "bad manners" of railway corporations, superimposed on the cruel realities of distant, inaccessible markets, all tended to create bad will for the roads among their chief western customers.[34] And the farmer had no recourse. The giant "soulless" corporations which possessed such power over him could not be dealt with individually; nor could the "warehouse monopolies," the grain-elevator subsidiaries of the railroads which charged him exorbitant storage rates and misgraded his grain.[35]

It was in the newer West, with its large-scale commercial farming and its great distances from markets, that these grievances and these frustrations were most keenly felt. In 1858 in Illinois we encounter one of the earliest meetings of farmers addressed to the railroad problem. This was an assemblage at Centralia which asserted the "supremacy" of the "producing classes" and attacked the power of the middleman who kept the farmer and consumer too far apart.[36] During the War the entire Northwest was rife with attacks on the railroads, the banks, and the "vested interests" which foreshadowed in a startling way the later Granger movement.[37]

Two-dollar wheat and dollar corn effectively smothered this embryonic uprising. But after 1870, in a great swathe of prairie country from Illinois through Kansas and Minnesota, these grievances, now greatly amplified by hard times, provoked a formidable movement against railroads and "middlemen" under the auspices of the Grange, the Patrons of Husbandry. Along

[34] Charles Francis Adams, Jr., "The Granger Movement," *North American Review*, cxx (April 1875), passim; Saloutos, *op. cit.*, p. 329; Arthur Bentley, *The Condition of the Western Farmer as Illustrated by the Economic History of a Nebraska Township* (Baltimore: The Johns Hopkins Press, 1893), p. 45.

[35] *Prairie Farmer*, Dec. 3, 1870; Henrietta M. Larson, *The Wheat Market and the Farmer in Minnesota, 1858-1900* (New York, 1926), p. 86.

[36] Periam, *op. cit.*, pp. 204-206.

[37] Klement, *op. cit.*, pp. 681-687.

with other farm organizations—most notably the Illinois Farmers' Association—through cooperative marketing, buying, and production, through railroad rate regulation, and agricultural education, the Grange sought to tip the economic balance the farmers' way.[38] These farm organizations also had social purposes. But quite clearly few of the Grange founders had any interest in the money question.

Nevertheless, there was a significant connection between organized farmer protest and greenbackism. Dean and other Democrats had obviously tried to link the railroads and the bondholders in one indictment. Apparently they had failed to convince those farmers not already predisposed by Democratic leanings. But from the very outset, particularly in Illinois, there were signs of incipient greenbackism among *bona fide* farmers. In June 1866 "a mass meeting of Farmers and others opposed to the present Money Monopoly" convened at Bloomington to take action on the financial question. Campbell and L. De Wolf were present, and the resolutions, including demands for more greenbacks and the interconvertible bond, an attack on warehouse and railroad monopolies, and a suggestion that a "just monetary system" would encourage the building of new railroads and destroy the transportation monopoly—all bear Campbell's unmistakable eclectic stamp. Before adjourning, the meeting voted to set up county and township societies and a state anti-monopoly organization.[39] In September of this same year the *Workingman's Advocate* noted a meeting of the State Anti-Monopoly Association, to be held at La Salle, Campbell's home town. An invitation was extended to everyone who favored repeal of the National Banking Act and who wished to see the "proper legislative restrictions upon railroads, ware house and other corporate monopolies of whatever kind or nature."[40]

While it is true that Campbell had a hand in these matters, unlike the earlier assemblage at Monmouth presided over by Dean (a violently partisan Democrat), these meetings seem to

[38] Buck, *The Granger Movement, passim.*

[39] *WA*, June 30, 1866. Dr. Sharkey notes this meeting, but for reasons he does not explain, believes that the farmers' "influence and interest" in it were "slight." See Robert P. Sharkey, *Money, Class and Party: An Economic Study of Civil War and Reconstruction*, p. 192, n. 72.

[40] *WA*, Sept. 1, 1866.

have been authentic gatherings of farmers. It is true that farm organizations, like labor groups, often accepted—as they still do—the leadership of intellectuals, or at least educated men. It is also true that much of the so-called Granger legislation of the 1870's originated in the agitation of urban merchants, and even eastern urban merchants.[41] But something similar seems to be characteristic of all American reform movements. Frequently, the most articulate and sophisticated malcontents, often men drawn from the fringes of the aggrieved group—or opportunists seeking to profit by the general distress—take charge of the movement. At all events, the Illinois Anti-Monopoly Association appears to have been the immediate precursor of the Illinois State Farmers' Association,[42] an organization as representative of the dirt farmer as such a body ever is.

The Illinois case was apparently unique, however. Until mid-1873, farmer interest in finance remained slight. Even the deteriorating markets after 1870 had little noticeable effect in stimulating farmer discussion of the money question. Many of the elements of agricultural greenbackism existed in solution but refused to precipitate out. Anti-monopoly sentiment flourished in the Northwest, but where farmers *qua* farmers were involved it continued to be aimed primarily at the railroads.[43] Even the formation in January 1873 of the Illinois Farmers' Association, soon to be the most militantly soft money of all farmer pressure groups, did not at first change the picture. In its first statement of principles the Association attacked the railroad monopoly and endorsed lower tariffs, but entirely disregarded finance.[44] At its second meeting in April it declared that "all chartered monopolies, not regulated and controlled by law, have proved . . . detrimental to the public prosperity,

[41] See Lee Benson, *Merchants, Farmers and Railroads: Railroad Regulation and New York Politics, 1850-1887* (Cambridge: Harvard University Press, 1955), *passim*, but especially pp. 25 and 256, n. 116; George H. Miller, "Origins of the Iowa Granger Law," *MVHR*, XL, No. 4 (March 1954), pp. 657-680.

[42] On the agricultural ferment in Illinois see A. E. Paine, *The Granger Movement in Illinois*. The University [of Illinois] Studies I, No. 8 (Urbana, 1904), *passim*.

[43] Buck, *The Granger Movement*, chs. III-VI; Fred E. Haynes, *Third Party Movements Since the Civil War with Special Reference to Iowa: A Study of Social Politics* (Iowa City: The State Historical Society of Iowa, 1916), pp. 51-53.

[44] *Prairie Farmer*, Jan. 25, 1873.

corrupting in their management, and dangerous to republican institutions."[45] This was the congenial philosophical milieu of greenbackism, but it was not greenbackism itself.

The Grange also was silent on finance both at the national and state levels. Neither at the 1873 nor 1874 Annual Sessions of the national body, the first regular meetings of the Patrons, was the issue discussed, though at the later meeting, railroad abuses, middlemen's charges, interest rates, and the high cost of agricultural implements all received attention.[46] So general was farmer neglect of the money question that it seriously disturbed the labor reformers. In Illinois, the *Workingman's Advocate* in January 1873 expressed "surprise" that one local Grange speaker, in recounting the farmer's grievances, "left out the centre or base—the pivotal point around which all robbery centres and revolves—we mean the financial question."[47] Indeed, during these years, while the conservative business community grew increasingly reconciled to the paper system, farm organizations and anti-monopoly associations regularly endorsed specie payments![48]

Abruptly, in the middle of 1873, rural financial conservatism began to give way. Significantly, the first important break occurred in Illinois, where the ground had been well prepared by Campbell in the 1860's. The first intimation of change appears in a July 4th speech by S. M. Smith. Although, in his own words, "a plain uneducated farmer," Smith had obviously read Campbell closely. Following the stereotyped indictment of middlemen and railroads, he launched into an attack on the banks as the source of all special interests and noted that the 30 per cent interest they charged was ten times the annual increase in national wealth. This might have been lifted from the pages of the *Workingman's Advocate*, and indeed, Smith told his audience that in their crusade against the bank monopoly

[45] John R. Commons and John B. Andrews (eds.), *A Documentary History of American Industrial Society* (Cleveland: The Arthur H. Clarke Co., 1910), x, 52-59.

[46] National Grange, *Journal of Proceedings of the Sixth Annual Session* (1873); *Journal of Proceedings of The Seventh Annual Session* (1874), pp. 12ff.

[47] *WA*, Dec. 15, 1873.

[48] Haynes, *op. cit.*, p. 55; Buck, *The Granger Movement*, p. 81.

they would have the support of the labor reformers.[49] Soon after, a rash of resolutions by local farm organizations attacking the banking monopoly appeared in Illinois.[50] By August the *Chicago Tribune* was complaining, a bit prematurely, that "nearly all the Granges are resolving to abolish the National Banks."[51]

This attack on the national banking system cannot be explained as a direct response to provocation. It is difficult to see what the farmer's legitimate grievance against the national banks might be. True, by law, the banks could not lend on real estate, generally the only security the farmer had; nor could they supply the long-term credit agriculture needed.[52] But to blame them for this failure was to blame a dog for not performing like a horse. If the commercial banks did not suit the farmer's needs, this would seem to call for changing the law, not destroying the system.[53] Eventually, farmer agitation was to produce an elaborate structure of federal land and intermediate credit banks equipped to supply cheap rural credit.[54] But aside from occasional endorsements of free banking, which, given the nature of the national banks, could scarcely have improved the farm credit situation,[55] farmer groups in this period had no constructive alternatives to the mortgage loan companies which imperfectly supplied their needs.[56]

[49] *Prairie Farmer*, July 12, 1873. See also the report of a farmer convention in Topeka, Kansas in April 1873, attacking the banking business as legalized robbery. *Western Rural*, April 5, 1873.

[50] E.g., the farmers' meeting in Jefferson Co., Aug. 30, 1873, *CDT*, Sept. 3, 1873; farmers' anti-monopoly meeting at Rock Island, Sept. 6, 1873, *ibid.*, Sept. 8, 1873; farmers' meeting at Bloomington, Sept. 1873, *ibid.*, Sept. 18, 1873.

[51] *Ibid.*, Aug. 20, 1873.

[52] Although they did make some short-term loans on "personal and chattel security." See Earl Sylvester Sparks, *History and Theory of Agricultural Credit in the United States* (New York: Thomas Y. Crowell

Company, 1932), p. 312.

[53] But see Fred Shannon, who as a strong partisan of the prairie farmer, believes this failure somehow justifies the farmers' anti-bankism. Shannon, *op. cit.*, p. 315.

[54] Clara Eliot, *The Farmer's Campaign for Credit* (New York: D. Appleton & Co., 1927), chs. II and IX.

[55] E.g., *Kansas Farmer*, March 1868; *IA*, Aug. 20, 1873; *CDT*, Sept. 8, 1873.

[56] But not as imperfectly as western farmers believed. For recent reevaluations of western mortgages and credit see Allan G. Bogue, *Money at Interest: The Farm Mortgage on the Middle Border* (Ithaca: Cornell University Press, 1955); Margaret Beattie Bogue, *Patterns*

No, the banks, and particularly the federal banks, were the symbolic rather than the real enemy of the post-Civil War farmer. Faced with a complex world he did not understand, beset by difficulties beyond his control, like others before and after him, the husbandman sought a scapegoat. To some extent the railroads served this purpose—surely they were blamed for too much.[57] But after the disappointing results of Granger railroad legislation, owing to resistance by the roads and court action, they lost their appeal as villains. Given the old Agrarian tradition, given the influence of the labor reformers, given the propaganda of the Democracy, the shift to the banks is easy to explain. The fact that most national banks, with their high legal capitalization requirements, were confined to the larger towns and the cities made it possible to create the needed image. The national banker was a stranger to the farmer,[58] and it was easy to convert him into a figure of pure malevolence.

This symbolization of the national banking system was a progressive phenomenon. From valid—if exaggerated and misguided—complaints about the failure of the system to provide cheap farm credit, there is an ever-growing allusion to "usurers," "money lenders," and the "money power." Increasingly, the old Jacksonian rhetoric is adapted to describe the farmers' circumstances,[59] and there is even a very explicit resurrection by farm leaders of Jacksonian writings on monopoly and banks.[60] In the course of the discussion a tendency develops to see the world in dualistic terms, much as would the later Populists and their

---

from the Sod: Land Tenure and Use in the Grand Prairie, 1850-1890 (Springfield: Illinois State Historical Library, 1959), ch. IX.

[57] Recent scholarship suggests that the farmer exaggerated the problem of railroad rates, which during the period fell rapidly. See, e.g., Saloutos, *op. cit.*, p. 329; Larson, *op. cit.*, pp. 63-66. Buck ascribes these reductions to the Granger agitation, yet they were national, occurring even in the East and South where agitation was less energetic, and are probably due more to the general decline of prices than to farmer action. See Buck,

The Granger Movement, pp. 231-232.

[58] Sparks, *op. cit.*, pp. 307-308; Ivan Wright, *Bank Credit and Agriculture Under the National and Federal Reserve Banking Systems* (New York: McGraw-Hill Book Co., 1922), pp. 46-47.

[59] See *Western Rural*, May 3, 1873.

[60] See the Illinois Farmers' Association's publication, *Industrial Age*, quoting William Leggett on the dangers of "chartered monopolies," *IA*, Sept. 6, 1873; Sept. 27, 1873.

still more recent academic defenders, even to the extent of seeing the Civil War, Beard-like, as the triumph of industry, over agriculture. According to Donnelly's St. Paul *Anti-Monopolist*, the War overthrew a Southern aristocracy resting on an enslaved black population. But now a new aristocracy—or, more properly speaking, a plutocracy—had risen in the North to enslave the "producing population." "Its headquarters are established in Wall Street," Donnelly wrote, "where . . . through non-taxed bondholders, subsidized banking monopolies and the monopolies in business which have grown out of these financial monopolies, [it] rules the nation more despotically than under the old pro-slavery régime."[61]

Eventually the money monopoly was blamed for all of agriculture's difficulties. It was the mother of all monopoly—warehousing, manufacturing, transportation, and communication—wrote one farmer. "Back of all these and more potent for evil than these and all like monopolies is a vicious monetary system of which the national banks are the source."[62] The ultimate charge was not long delayed. "Banks of issue are an ingenious contrivance of the devil to get everyone in debt so deeply that they can't pay, and then break everybody up."[63]

At its most unbalanced, rural anti-bankism of the 1860's and 1870's was tinged with anti-Semitism. For some time, Agrarian anti-Semitism has been recognized as a phenomenon of the 1890's,[64] but like so much else in the ideology of Populism it originated in the money discussion of the immediate post-Civil War period. Although at the time many American Jews were

---

[61] Quoted in *ibid.*, Aug. 20, 1873.
[62] "Granger" to editor, Tonica, Ill., Sept. 13, 1873; *CDT*, Sept. 18, 1873.
[63] *IA*, April 22, 1876.
[64] See the following for descriptions of Populist anti-Semitism: Oscar Handlin, "American Views of the Jew at the Opening of the Twentieth Century," *Publications of the American Jewish Historical Society*, XL, part 4 (June 1951), *passim;* Richard Hofstadter, *The Age of Reform: From Bryan to F.D.R.* (New York: Alfred Knopf, 1956), pp. 77-81; Jeannette P. Nichols, "Bryan's

Benefactor: Coin Harvey and His World," *Ohio Historical Quarterly*, LXVII, No. 4 (October 1958), 315-316. But also see the following dissents, which, while acknowledging some rural anti-Semitism deny its importance: Norman Pollack, "Hofstadter on Populism: A Critique of 'The Age of Reform,'" *Journal of Southern History*, XXVI, No. 4 (November 1960); Pollack, "The Myth of Populist Anti-Semitism," *AHR*, LXVIII, No. 1 (October 1962); John Higham, "Anti-Semitism in the Gilded Age: A Reinterpretation," *MVHR*, XLIII, No. 4 (March 1957).

craftsmen or manual laborers,[65] farm folk and even industrial workers outside the few great cities knew the Jew, if at all, largely as a storekeeper or peddler. More often the Jew was a semi-mythical figure, sometimes identified favorably with Old Testament heroes and prophets; often associated, negatively, with the deeply imbedded Anglo-Saxon folk-image of the usurer and sharp trader.[66] For the American Agrarian there was a special reason for suspicion of Jews. They were aliens, outside the charmed circle of the "producing classes." "Brick" Pomeroy, who for all his years in New York and Chicago was perfectly attuned to the rural mind, attacked the Jews as men who "do not pay much attention to farming or to raising hogs for market, but who from their peculiarities are skimmers, gleaners, gatherers who can scent a dollar as far as a Yankee politician can a carpet bag."[67] The Jew was a non-producer, one of the detested middlemen.[68] More immediately, for the greenbacker he was a "capitalist"; a money lender and a banker. Unlike the Jewish storekeeper, perhaps, the Jewish banker was clearly beyond the direct experience of most Americans, but they learned from the greenback leaders of the great international banking houses of the Seligmans, Speyer, and Belmont, and above all Belmont's backers, the Rothschilds. The Jew came to represent the money power of "Wall Street," itself the personification of sinister forces. "Wall Street Jews" became a common epithet of the

[65] See e.g., the following on the Jews of Rochester, N. Y.: Blake McKelvey "The Jews of Rochester: A Contribution to their History During the Nineteenth Century," *Publications of the American Jewish Historical Society*, XL, part 1 (September 1950), pp. 65, 70.

[66] For example, in defending the Jews from attack after the 1877 Grand Union Hotel incident, Henry Ward Beecher noted "that it is said that the Jews are crafty and cunning, and sometimes dishonest in their dealings." Carey McWilliams, *A Mask for Privilege: Anti-Semitism in America* (Boston: Little, Brown and Company, 1948), p. 6.

[67] *The Great Campaign*, Aug. 22, 1876.

[68] This Jeffersonian observation has a curious echo in the Nazi distinction between "productive national capitalism" and "Jewish parasitic capitalism." See Oscar Handlin, "Prejudice and Capitalist Exploitation: Does Economics Explain Racism?" *Commentary*, VI, No. 1 (July 1948), 82-83. For an interesting linking of unorthodox money views with the "radical right" in recent America see Victor C. Ferkiss, "Populist Influences on American Fascism," in Sidney Fine and Gerald S. Brown (eds.), *The American Past: Conflicting Interpretations of the Great Issues* (New York: The Macmillan Co., 1961).

soft money men,[69] and even the national banks were held to be dominated by "the same corporate Jew class."[70]

It would be a mistake to make too much of this anti-Semitism. It was not pervasive; nor was it the exclusive affliction of Agrarians. Anti-Semitism has flourished in many environments, and in America it has had several distinct strands. In the notorious case of the manager of Saratoga's Grand Union Hotel who refused to accept banker Joseph Seligman's patronage, it is doubtful whether that gentleman's profession was at issue. In the New York slums old immigrant urban Irish clashed with new immigrant Jews without either side alluding to the money monopoly. Henry Adams and Charles Eliot Norton disliked Jews about as much as they disliked inflationists.

Yet the phenomenon is interesting out of proportion to its incidence. Anti-Semitism, we are told, is often a displaced expression of frustration. The fear of Jews by rural Agrarians is significant not because it dominated the insurgent farmer movement, but because it was symptomatic. It was an extreme manifestation of the same irrationalism that made the banks the rural scapegoat, and like most irrationalism it reveals an inability to deal with problems realistically. Scapegoatism, like the abstractions of the labor reformers' interconvertible bond, was an attempt to find an easy answer to a difficult question. At the opposite financial extreme, its irrationality resembles the gold fetishism of the neo-Calvinist clergy or the visions of social apocalypse that victorious soft money suggested to the reformers.

Thus, by the fall of 1873, the farmers of the Northwest were beginning to move along the road to greenbackism. Few had as yet espoused paper money, but by translating their discontents into Agrarian, anti-bank, anti-monopoly terms, they were taking the necessary preliminary steps. Bullionist convictions, however, remained strong among the nation's agriculturists. In former years, anti-monopoly and hard money had been closely joined, and it would require more than one blow to tear the two apart. The first of these was about to strike the nation.

[69] See William Wilkeson to Thaddeus Stevens, Buffalo, June 23, 1868, Stevens MSS, LC; IA, Dec. 13, 1873; January 16, 1875.
[70] Ibid., May 2, 1874.

PANIC AND INFLATION

(1873-1874)

I

THE railroad boom collapsed abruptly in the fall of 1873, and hard times settled over the nation. The September panic and the five years of depression which followed destroyed business complacency and intensified farmer and wage earner grievances. For the remainder of the decade the currency problem once again became a major public concern, agitating and unsettling the nation's political life.

The blow caught the country by surprise. By 1872 the careful observer might have noted a decline in new rail construction and in manufacturing output. Since the "lock-up" of the previous fall, the money market had been tight. But almost no one suspected how seriously overextended the economy had become, and the eruption of business failures culminating in the suspension of Jay Cooke and Company on September 18, 1873, stunned the nation. Stock prices dropped from five to ten points in the next few days, and the wave of selling forced the Board of Governors to close the New York Stock Exchange on the 20th. Important trust companies and banking houses suspended during the first few days of the panic; scare withdrawals of deposits threatened the remainder. Only recourse to clearing-house certificates for paying inter-bank debts saved the New York banks from total ruin.[1]

The financial writers and columnists, fighting to preserve confidence, feigned optimism in those first few days. But from

[1] Rendigs Fels, *American Business Cycles, 1865-1897* (Chapel Hill: University of North Carolina Press, 1959), pp. 92-98; Henrietta M. Larson, *Jay Cooke, Private Banker* (Cambridge: Harvard University Press, 1936), p. 397; *CFC*, xvii (Sept. 20, 1873), 383; (Sept. 27, 1873), 410-411; O. M. W. Sprague, *History of Crises Under the National Banking System*, U. S. Senate, *Miscellaneous Document No. 538*, 61 Cong., 2 sess., pp. 38-53.

the beginning the Treasury knew how grave the crisis really was. Almost immediately Secretary William Richardson, Boutwell's successor and disciple,[2] began pumping Treasury surplus funds into the money market by buying federal securities for the sinking fund.[3] On the 20th Grant and Richardson hurried to New York to view the scene of the disaster. That evening and the following morning they conferred at the Fifth Avenue Hotel with the leading businessmen of the city. Many of these men had already been badly hurt and almost all feared further blows. A few, like Cornelius Vanderbilt and George Opdyke, were fighting fiercely to keep from going under. Vanderbilt had lost heavily in the stock crash;[4] Opdyke's speculative New York and Oswego Midland Railroad had just suspended, and his other business affairs were in a precarious state.[5] All these men, the desperate and the merely uneasy, looked to the Treasury for relief. Even such pillars of the business community as Frederick Tappan of the Gallatin National Bank, the Seligmans, and Henry Vail of the Bank of Commerce urged Grant to do more than buy bonds. The more conservative wanted the Treasury to lend the banks $20 million of the "reserve" on some sort of collateral. The more extreme urged the government to restore the reserve permanently by "reissuing" it.[6] Grant listened sympathetically to the agitated men who came to his suite, but perhaps remembering the outcry that the small reissue of the previous fall had aroused, refused to commit himself. When

[2] Boutwell had resigned in March 1873 to take Henry Wilson's place in the Senate. Boutwell, *Reminiscences of Sixty Years in Public Affairs* (New York: McClure, Phillips & Co., 1902), II, 221.

[3] U. S. Treasury, *Annual Report of the Secretary of the Treasury on the State of Finances for the Year 1873*, p. xv. Hereafter the Treasury Reports will be referred to as U. S. Treasury, *Report for . . .* , followed by the appropriate year.

[4] *CFC*, XVII (Sept. 20, 1873), 383.

[5] *Ibid.*, 388; *Nation*, XVII (Sept. 25, 1873), 201.

[6] It is not clear how the green-backs were to be gotten into circulation, whether by buying outstanding bonds or by accelerating government spending. On the question of who were the instigators of the plan to have the government inflate, banker-merchant Robert Minturn later claimed that only the "stock gamblers" among the New York businessmen wanted the Treasury to reissue. The legitimate bankers, he claimed had "begged" the President "not to draw upon the 'reserves.'" See Minturn to William B. Allison, New York, April 27, 1874, Allison MSS, Iowa State Dept. of History and Archives.

the Presidential party left New York late on the 21st Grant had promised only to continue the bond purchases.[7]

The pressure on the Administration did not end with the President's return to Washington. In the next few days businessmen and citizens from every corner of the country bombarded the White House with telegrams and letters pleading for relief.[8] Several of Grant's close advisers urged him to inflate the currency,[9] and despite the opposition of Secretary of State Hamilton Fish, Grant began to waver. On September 27 he publicly reassured businessmen that if the bankers themselves adopted a lenient loan policy he would treat the reserve "as money in the Treasury to meet the demands of public necessity as the circumstances of the country may require."[10] Early in October Richardson made the first of the actual reissues, which continued until mid-January when the Treasury had restored to circulation $26 million of the retired greenbacks.[11]

It was obvious that the Forty-third Congress, due to meet in December, would spend most of its time on the economic crisis. But no one foresaw a financial debate that would range so widely, persist so long, or finally accomplish so little as the one that soon erupted. Most of this energy could have been conserved if the Administration had taken the initiative in proposing a financial program. Congress was solidly Republican and probably would have followed the President's lead. But Grant and Richardson were both timid and indecisive. Both men favored resumption,[12] but were afraid to defy the strong expansionist pressures that had revived since the panic. In the

[7] The following contain several complete accounts of the Presidential visit to New York: NYDT, Sept. 22, 1873; New York Evening Post, Sept. 22, 1873; NYW, Sept. 22, 1873.

[8] See the response of Interior Secretary Columbus Delano. Delano to F. D. Sturges, Washington, Sept. 23, 1873; Delano to Benjamin Tathan, Washington, September 26, 1873, Delano MSS, Ohio Historical Society.

[9] That is, Secretary Delano and the President's private secretaries, Generals Orville Babcock and Hor-

ace Porter. See William B. Hesseltine, *Ulysses S. Grant, Politician* (New York: Frederick Ungar Publishing Co., 1957), p. 328; MS diary of Hamilton Fish, Sept. 30, 1873, Fish MSS, LC.

[10] Grant to H. B. Claflin and Charles H. Anthony, Washington, Sept. 27, 1873, *Banker's Magazine*, xxvii (Dec. 1873), 478.

[11] *New York Evening Post*, Oct. 10, 1873; *CFC*, xvii (Oct. 11, 1873), 479; xviii (Jan. 17, 1874), 571.

[12] Fish Diary, *loc. cit.*

weeks before Congress assembled, the President scattered financial suggestions in all directions, at various times advocating free banking, a postal savings system, currency flexibility, and even silver resumption.[13] His Annual Message reflected his indecision, and only succeeded in further confusing Congress and the public, who could not tell what the Administration wanted. The President described the greenback circulation as "the best that [had] ever been devised," though it was insufficient for the busiest parts of the year and should be made flexible, even if this meant expanding it in time of need. But in the next breath he assured Congress that he was sound. The nation must avoid "undue" inflation, which might give "temporary relief" to business but would in the long run only lead to a general price rise. He then detailed a confused scheme for making the circulation flexible, concluding weakly that he did not expect Congress to adopt his suggestions "literally."[14] Richardson's *Report* was equally feckless. An arid rehearsal of the well-known failings of the nation's financial system, it too resigned responsibility for a clear program, although it referred vaguely to both elasticity and resumption.[15]

In the absence of Administration leadership, finance became everybody's business. Congress was immediately buried under an avalanche of monetary proposals. On the first day of the session, which was to witness the most extensive financial discussion since the days of Jackson,[16] a score of private currency bills were introduced in the Senate alone.[17] In a week, however, the Finance Committee of the upper house, under Chairman Sherman, had taken charge of the legislative program. On December 10 Sherman introduced two resolutions, representing both majority and minority committee viewpoints, which were

[13] *Ibid.;* Hesseltine, *op. cit.,* 329-330.

[14] James D. Richardson (ed.), *A Compilation of the Messages and Papers of the Presidents, 1789-1902* (n.p.: Bureau of National Literature and Art, 1903), VII, 243-246. Cf. Hesseltine, *op. cit.,* pp. 331-332.

[15] U. S. Treasury, *Report for 1873,* pp. xvi-xx.

[16] Charles Francis Adams, Jr., later estimated that the financial discussion consumed over 1700 columns of the *Congressional Record,* or between three and four thousand octavo pages. See Adams, "The Currency Debate of 1873-1874," *North American Review,* CXIX (July 1874), 112.

[17] *Congressional Record,* 43 Cong., 1 sess., pp. 2, 3, 51-52. For the remainder of this chapter, unless otherwise specified, all references to the *Record* will be to volumes for this Congress and session.

intended to feel out the attitude of the Senate and aid the committee in drafting final legislation.[18] The majority resolution was the usual evasive formula endorsing the earliest "practicable" resumption, with the amount of currency "so adjusted as to meet the changing wants of trade and commerce." The minority proposal demanded an immediate return to specie.[19] On December 15, Thomas Ferry, a Michigan Republican, submitted a third resolution which endorsed a substantial greenback increase and free banking.[20]

These three proposals, ranging from stubborn contraction to outright inflation, remained before the Senate while a general financial debate raged. In February the discussion temporarily shifted to the subject of reapportioning the national bank notes.[21] By the end of March the committee was ready with a serious legislative proposal. This bill, which attempted to synthesize the divergent views,[22] was a hodgepodge of expansionist, resumptionist, and free banking elements that pleased no one entirely. The first of its four important sections set a $382 million ceiling on the total greenback issue, in effect legalizing the $26 million that Richardson had reissued. Section two provided for specie payments on January 1, 1876, and permitted the Treasury to redeem greenbacks in either coin or a new 5 per cent gold bond. The measure also authorized expanding the bank-note allotment of each state and territory to the per capita circulation of New York. The following section offset this increase by requiring that for each $100 million of new bank notes the Treasury withdraw $70 million of greenbacks until outstanding greenbacks had been reduced to $300

[18] *Ibid.*, p. 295.
[19] *Ibid.*, pp. 123, 192. Actually this was the proposal of only one member, conservative Democrat Thomas F. Bayard of Delaware.
[20] *Ibid.*, p. 192. Like the majority proposal of the committee, Ferry's suggestion called for an elastic circulation, but this was to be achieved by removing the bank-note ceiling. A final clause was frankly expansionist, allowing a total new greenback issue of $100 million, including the $44 million reserve.

[21] *Ibid.*, pp. 1141, 1175, 1382, 1476.
[22] *Ibid.*, p. 2350. On the Committee itself, three members—Justin Morrill of Vermont, Reuben Fenton of New York, and Thomas Bayard of Delaware—were firm contractionists; Sherman was opposed to both expansion and contraction; while Thomas Ferry of Michigan, John Scott of Pennsylvania, and George Wright of Iowa were expansionists. *New York Evening Post*, Dec. 9, 1873.

million.[23] This measure, amended out of recognition, would become the basis for the later "Inflation Bill."

Currency legislation in the House also evolved in leisurely stages. Early in the session Clinton Merriam of New York introduced a bank-note redemption measure.[24] In January a Ways and Means Committee bill, restoring the $400 million greenback limit and thereby returning the entire reserve to circulation, was debated. This bill actually passed the House but was shunted aside by more comprehensive legislation and never got to the Senate.[25]

Before bringing in its own measure, the House Banking and Currency Committee, unlike its Senatorial counterpart, went through the motions of sampling public opinion. Beginning on January 2, the Committee held three weeks of hearings designed to acquaint Congress with the views of businessmen, experts, and the general public. If they accomplished nothing else, these hearings disclosed that the easy tolerance of the *status quo* that characterized the boom period had disappeared. The panic had intensified old fears, revived earlier demands, and reawakened the sharp conflicts of the '60's.

The eastern bankers were partly responsible for Richardson's reissues, but by January they had reverted to orthodoxy. Tappan, a leading pleader for reissue in September, George Coe, and Henry P. Kidder of Boston's Kidder, Peabody and Company, now told the Committee that paper money was responsible for the panic.[26] The reformers and the academicians were at the hearings to speak for doctrinal orthodoxy and monetary ethics.[27] A small contingent of industrialists—including Carey's Detroit friend, Eber Ward—testified to the high interest rates paid by manufacturers and the blessings of an elastic currency.[28] Eastern merchants, including a delegation from the National Board of Trade, were on hand to urge immediate specie payments.

---

[23] *Congressional Record*, pp. 2386, 2387, 2391. There was also a provision to forbid the depositing of country bank reserves in New York, and a final, purely procedural section.

[24] *Ibid.*, p. 62; *CFC*, XVII (Dec. 13, 1873), 789.

[25] *Congressional Record*, pp. 2376-2378.

[26] U. S. House of Representatives, *Report No. 328*, 43 Cong., 1 sess., pp. 140, 172, 63-74.

[27] Including Amasa Walker, John Murray Forbes, and S. Lester Taylor, *ibid.*, pp. 8-13, 121-122, 134.

[28] *Ibid.*, pp. 15, 46-48, 124-133.

Simeon Chittenden, who had recently spoken for a do-nothing policy, now declared that the "present amount of currency" was "beyond the requirements of all the legitimate business that [would] be done in 1874," and it could readily be reduced without harm to business.[29]

If the hearings had any influence on the House it cannot be detected. The House measure, introduced on January 29, like that of the Senate, was designed to be all things to all men and was a similar jumble of elements pointing simultaneously in different directions. The bill authorized a modest expansion by eliminating greenback reserves hitherto required against bank-note circulation. Another section established a 5 per cent central bank-note redemption fund in New York for currency elasticity. The two most important clauses provided for gradual specie payments beginning July 1876 and for immediate free banking.[30]

Senate bill 617 and the free banking H. R. 1572 between them stimulated enough oratory to fill several volumes of the *Congressional Record*, but very little was added to the debate of the preceding decade. Butler, now joined by Kelley, continued to push the interconvertible bond. Western and southern Democrats reopened the attack on the banks, and clamored, despite the Public Credit Act, for repayment of the 5-20's in legal tenders. New York, New Jersey, and New England Representatives defended the "national honor" against the ignorant country members. The compromisers and the moderates talked again of letting natural growth take care of the resumption problem.[31]

But while the panic had not altered the conventional ingredients of the debate, it had changed the proportions. There was a new note of urgency in the discussion. Never before had western and Pennsylvania Republicans been so willing to support undisguised expansion. They continued to reject the label "inflationist," but they did not deny that they favored a "moderate increase of the currency."[32] In both houses the expansionists included the acknowledged party leaders, men close to the

[29] *Ibid.*, pp. 77-78.
[30] These are only the most important provisions. *Congressional Record*, p. 1007.
[31] See, respectively, *ibid.*, pp. 1009, 3005-3007; 2741-2742, 2582, 2585-2587; 2934-2935; 2939, 2969-2971, 2708; 295-296, 652, 2931.
[32] Remarks of Senator John Logan, *ibid.*, pp. 865-866.

Administration who reputedly spoke for the President on important political matters. In the Senate the inflation program was pushed by a powerful inner circle of Republican leaders—Ferry of Michigan, John "Black Jack" Logan of Illinois, and Oliver P. Morton of Indiana.[33] Leading House expansionists included Butler, Kelley, Chairman Horace Maynard of the Banking and Currency Committee, and Charles Farwell of Illinois. Among western Congressmen of both parties the expansionist majority was overwhelming. Garfield was to complain that only he and one other member of the Ohio delegation in the House were willing to fight inflation.[34]

II

While Congress debated, public excitement over the perennial money problem reached a new peak of intensity. The acute phase of the crisis passed in a few weeks, but it was enough to destroy the public confidence which had sustained the boom. A six-year depression followed—the longest on record—[35] and as the economy spiraled downward, businessmen, wage earners, and farmers once more made the currency issue the focus of their fears and discontents.

Among businessmen, the railroad promoters, the advance agents as well as the chief beneficiaries of prosperity, were the first victims of the crisis. In the early weeks many roads—eastern and western, established and speculative—were forced to the wall. In September, *Railroad Gazette* reported 5 major companies in imminent danger of bankruptcy. Soon after, the Chesapeake and Ohio defaulted. By November, 55 roads, including such giants as the Santa Fe, the Burlington, and the

[33] Morton, though earlier opposed to contraction, had also been opposed to additional greenback issues. His role in the Forty-third Congress is a measure of the panic's effect. For Morton's anti-greenback phase, see his speech of Aug. 27, 1867 in the Morton MSS, Indiana State Library.

[34] Garfield to Burke A. Hinsdale, Washington, March 26, 1874, in

Theodore Clarke Smith, *The Life and Letters of James Abram Garfield* (New Haven: Yale University Press, 1925), i, 513.

[35] Though not the most severe. See Asher Achinstein, "Economic Fluctuations," in Seymour E. Harris (ed.), *American Economic History* (New York: McGraw-Hill Book Co., 1961), tables 1 and 2, pp. 165, 167; Fels, *op. cit.*, *passim*.

Kansas Pacific, with securities representing one-eighth of the total national railroad debt, were in default; in a year 108 roads, with some $500 million of outstanding securities, had failed to meet their interest payments.[36]

The fall and winter of 1873-74 were particularly harrowing. The underwriting of the Northern Pacific had been the proximate cause of the Jay Cooke failure, and falling freight traffic and the general business uncertainty threatened to pull down the other railroad promoters. Thomas Scott, First Vice-President of the Pennsylvania, who was raising funds for the highly speculative Texas and Pacific when the panic struck, was threatened with total ruin. Scott "nearly collapsed mentally as well as financially" under the strain of keeping the road out of the receiver's hands and escaped bankruptcy only through the forbearance of his creditors.[37] Collis P. Huntington, one of the "Big Three" of California railroading, and Scott's chief rival, was almost as severely shaken by the collapse of his eastern road, the Chesapeake and Ohio.[38]

As might be expected, the railroad men were among the noisier exponents of currency relief in the months following the panic. Vanderbilt and Opdyke had been prominent among the New York businessmen who had urged Grant and Richardson to reissue the reserve. Scott was quoted as saying that business would remain stagnant "until our people are assured of some permanent financial relief, by which there will be money enough in the country to do its work."[39] What was specifically needed, he later told a newspaper reporter, was a new issue of federal notes.[40] Huntington, Russell Sage of the Chicago, Milwaukee and St. Paul, John Newell of the Illinois Central, and other, lesser railroad men also became advocates of more money,

[36] *Railroad Gazette*, v (Sept. 27, 1873), 392ff.; *CDT*, Nov. 1, 1874; John F. Stover, *The Railroads of the South, 1865-1900: A Study in Finance and Control* (Chapel Hill: University of North Carolina Press, 1955), pp. 122-123.

[37] C. Vann Woodward, *Reunion and Reaction: The Compromise of 1877 and the End of Reconstruction*

(Boston: Little, Brown & Co., 1951), pp. 75-76; *CDT*, Nov. 6, 1873.

[38] *Ibid.*, Nov. 1, 1873.

[39] Quoted in T. H. Carter, *The Financial Problem: Easy Mode of Paying the National Debt* (n.p. [1874]), pp. 13-14. This pamphlet seems, from internal evidence, to have been commissioned by Scott.

[40] *NYDT*, Dec. 6, 1873.

though they did not always agree on how to get it.[41] There was no doubt, the *Louisville Courier-Journal* declared in April, that "the strongest influence at work in Washington upon the currency proceeded from the railroads. . . . The great inflationists after all," the paper concluded, with some exaggeration, "are the great trunk railroads."[42]

The panic that punctured the railroad boom also devastated the closely linked iron industry. Rail production, which reached one million tons in 1872, fell by more than one fourth in 1874. Rail prices, between April 1873 and April 1874 declined from $82 to $60 a ton and were to go much lower in succeeding months. General iron prices soon followed, with Pittsburgh pig iron deflating one-third in the year following the panic. By late 1874, 295 of the country's 677 furnaces were idle.[43]

The ironmasters responded to falling prices and profits as they had during the 1867-68 recession. In eastern Pennsylvania, where rail and rolling-stock cutbacks had produced acute distress, they were convinced that only expansion could save them from ruin. If Congress "decided that we are to have an extended currency," railroads could resume their orders and the iron industry would recover. The "question of inflation" would determine whether the industry would survive.[44] Daniel Morrell, complaining bitterly of high interest rates, once more demanded free banking.[45] In the Youngstown district of Ohio the iron men were reported in open revolt against Representative Garfield's sound money position.[46] As in the previous decade, the industry's trade organizations and trade publications spearheaded the soft money drive. Even before Congress convened, the American Iron and Steel Association demanded "a financial system adequate to the largely increased and increasing business needs of

[41] *CDT*, April 23, 1874; *NYDT*, April 23, 1874; John Newell to William B. Allison; Chicago, Feb. 21, 1874, Allison MSS; D. D. Dykeman (Vice-President of the Logansport, Crawfordsville and Southwestern RR) to Daniel D. Pratt, Logansport, Ind., Feb. 16, 1874, Pratt MSS, Indiana State Library.

[42] Quoted in *Financial Record*, I (April 10, 1874), 25.

[43] Victor S. Clark, *History of Manufactures in the United States* (New York: Peter Smith, 1929), II, 329, 157.

[44] Pottsville (Pennsylvania) *Miner's Journal*, April 3, 1874.

[45] *Iron Age*, XIII (Feb. 5, 1874).

[46] C. E. Henry to James A. Garfield, Pond Sta[tion], Ohio, April 8, 1874, Garfield MSS, LC.

the country."[47] The Union Meeting of American Ironmasters, in February 1874, urged restoring the $400 million legal tender issue and lifting the bank-note ceiling.[48] Similar proposals of moderate greenback expansion coupled with free banking were being pushed by *Iron Age, American Manufacturer*, the *Bulletin of the Iron and Steel Association*, and *Industrial Bulletin*, journal of the Pennsylvania Industrial League.[49]

The extractive industries shared the plight of iron manufacturing[50] and responded similarly. In the eastern Pennsylvania coal districts the "bullionists and money changers," who cried "for resumption and oppose[d] an increase in the volume of currency," were attacked, and the revived currency discussion welcomed as an opportunity to refute the views of English and American "theorists."[51] In the young petroleum industry, the hard-pressed Thomas Wharton Phillips, a pioneer oil refiner, told his friend Garfield that he hoped Congress would provide two or three hundred millions more circulation, an amount that would just compensate for what the South and West had absorbed since the War.[52]

One result of the panic was to push some of the ironmasters temporarily into greenbackism. Free banking had been the characteristic program of soft money industrialists in the '60's. Unlike the small group of merchants and insurance underwriters who had been attracted by the interconvertible bond, with its greenback accompaniment, the manufacturers had eschewed "fiat" money. The shock of the crisis made them receptive to new ideas, and when, in October 1873, the 3.65 per cent bond was

[47] *CFC*, xvii (Nov. 22, 1873), 681; also *Iron Age*, xii (Nov. 27, 1873.

[48] *Ibid.*, xiii (Feb. 12, 1874).

[49] See the following: *ibid.*, xii (Oct. 2, 1873); (Dec. 25, 1873); xiii (March 26, 1874); *Bulletin of the Iron and Steel Association*, vii (Nov. 15, 1873), 460; *American Manufacturer*, xiii (Nov. 16, 1873), 3; xiv (Nov. 6, 1873), 3; xiv (Nov. 13, 1873), 3; *Industrial Bulletin*, iv (January 1874), 1; (February 1874), 1; (March 1874), 1; (April 1874), 4. See also the expansionist suggestions

of John B. Sherriff, a Pittsburgh brass and bell founder, to James A. Garfield, Pittsburgh, Jan. 1, 1874, Garfield MSS.

[50] *Coal and Iron Record*, iv (Oct. 15, 1873), 162; (Oct. 29, 1873), 186; *Engineering and Mining Journal*, xvi (Oct. 14, 1873), 245.

[51] *Miner's Journal*, April 24, 1874; April 10, 1874. See also *Engineering and Mining Journal*, xvi (Nov. 4, 1873), 296.

[52] T[homas] W[harton] Phillips to James A. Garfield, Pittsburgh, March 26, 1874, Garfield MSS.

taken up by both Kelley and Carey's nephew, Henry Carey Baird,[53] it was endorsed by a substantial group of iron men.[54]

For most of the manufacturers this was a brief flirtation. To the men who had long done the thinking for them, however, the change was more fundamental. Kelley remained faithful to the new scheme past resumption.[55] By 1874 Carey himself had become a convert to the labor reform program and remained so to his death.[56] By 1876 Baird was calling the national bank notes the money of "the great and powerful," and had come out for their replacement by greenbacks.[57] Both he and Kelley would move further away from the ironmasters and industrialists whose spokesmen they had long been and cast their lot with the political greenbackers and silverites of the later '70's.

Even among the more conservative business groups the panic initially reawakened quiescent soft money tendencies. Western bankers, who had long ceased their agitation for free banking and "elasticity," resumed it during the months of the Congressional debate.[58] For a while the shock of the economic collapse also threatened to wring a soft money endorsement out of the National Board of Trade. After the panic, the merchants, like the financial men of New York, pursued an erratic course. In the weeks following the suspension of Jay Cooke, commercial affairs had become chaotic. Credit tightened as the banks,

[53] William D. Kelley, *The Finances . . . Correspondence . . . Giving the Views of Hon. Wm. D. Kelley . . . Oct. 3, 1873* (Philadelphia, 1873), pp. 6ff.; Kelley, *Judge Kelley on the Crisis* (Philadelphia, 1874), p. 6; Henry Carey Baird, *Letters on the Crisis, the Currency and the Credit System* (Philadelphia, 1873), p. 7.

[54] *Bulletin of the Iron and Steel Association*, vii (Oct. 15, 1873), 460. *IA*, Dec. 19, 1874, records a meeting of ironmasters held in Philadelphia which endorsed the 3.65 per cent bond scheme.

[55] Kelley borrowed from Pliny Freeman, Philadelphia labor groups, and Campbell as well. Kelley, *Judge Kelley on the Crisis*, p. 6; W. D. Kelley to James A. Garfield, Philadelphia, Nov. 6, 1875, Garfield MSS;

Congressional Record, p. 2806.

[56] Henry C. Carey, *Currency Inflation . . . . Letters to the Hon. B. H. Bristow . . .* (Philadelphia, 1874), pp. 15-16.

[57] Henry Carey Baird, *Money and Its Substitutes . . .* (Philadelphia, 1876), pp. 12ff.; Baird, *The Eastern and Western Questions . . .* (Philadelphia, 1877), p. 13.

[58] See John Williams (Pres., First National Bank of Springfield, Ill.) to Richard Oglesby, Springfield, Jan. 19, 1874, Oglesby MSS, Illinois State Historical Library; William B. Fairchild (Fairchild and Balch, Bankers), to William B. Allison, Charles City, Iowa, Feb. 3, 1874; Samuel Merrill (Pres., Citizen's National Bank of Des Moines) to Allison, New York, March 23, 1874, Allison MSS.

hard-pressed to meet their own obligations, refused to renew loans. Money went into hiding and interest rates soon went to one and a quarter per cent a day. Jobbers and wholesalers could not make collections, and trade stagnated.[59] This was the situation when the regular annual National Board of Trade convention assembled in Chicago. Many western merchants had been skeptical of specie payments, and now a three-way contest developed between doctrinaire hard money Yankees, a western group equally determined to stop specie payments at all costs, and a middle-of-the-road element which favored resumption but was willing to make concessions to the West. It proved impossible to reconcile these factions, and the convention adjourned without taking action, to meet again that winter in Baltimore.[60]

The move to Baltimore was really a shrewd hard money stratagem. Charles Randolph, the Board's Secretary, later explained that the Chicago meeting had been adjourned to prevent a panicky endorsement of inflation.[61] Baltimore was an eastern port city, close to Washington and far from the heresies of the West. More eastern delegates would be present, and in such an atmosphere there was reason to hope that the members would regain their balance. In any event the conservatives could keep an eye on Congress and, if all went well, perhaps influence currency legislation.[62]

As expected, the currency discussion at Baltimore was more to the conservatives' liking. Over the opposition of a dozen western delegates, the Board condemned Richardson's reissue and demanded that it be retired, urged the government to retrench, and suggested that the national banks be required to accumulate gold against resumption.[63] Shortly thereafter, President Frederick Fraley, Vice-President Benjamin F. Nourse, S. Lester Taylor, and John Austin Stevens turned up at the House

[59] *CFC*, xvii (Sept. 20, 1873), 382; Sprague, *op. cit.*, pp. 77-80.
[60] National Board of Trade, *Proceedings of the Sixth Annual Meeting at Chicago, October 1873*, pp. xii, 139, 196ff.
[61] National Board of Trade, *Proceedings of the Adjourned Meeting at Baltimore, January 1874*, pp. vii-

viii; *American Manufacturer*, xiii (Nov. 30, 1873), 3.
[62] See the remarks of John A. Gano, National Board of Trade, *Proceedings of the Sixth Annual Meeting*, p. 245.
[63] National Board of Trade, *Proceedings of the Adjourned Meeting*, passim.

currency hearings to press for the Baltimore resolutions.[64]

Businessmen, of course, bore the brunt of the business crisis. The clogging of the commercial wheels had instantaneous and highly visible effects on their sales and receipts, their debt position, their profits and losses. The plight of wage earners was almost as grim. Mass unemployment on the post-1929 scale did not develop during the depression of the 1870's,[65] but there was to be suffering in many parts of the nation. The abrupt end of railroad building threw thousands of unskilled workers out of jobs; the slowdown of heavy industry meant more thousands unemployed in the coal and iron areas of Ohio, Pennsylvania, and Illinois.[66] The depression spread to trade, building construction, services, and light industry and created difficult welfare problems in the cities. During the first winter following the panic, the New York Society for Improving the Condition of the Poor reported 93,000, or one-fourth of the New York labor force, out of work. In Troy, New York, a "soup house" was set up for the jobless. In Chicago 20,000 destitute men besieged the Common Council demanding relief. Here and there violence flared as jobless men gathered to protest conditions, frightening the middle class and the police into hasty acts of repression.[67]

The disaster caught organized labor in an already weakened condition. The political fiasco of 1872 had destroyed the National Labor Union.[68] The attempt the following year to reconstruct a national trade-union at Cleveland was formally successful, but the new Industrial Congress was scarcely two months old when the panic struck and had little reserve strength to withstand hard times.[69]

---

[64] *Report No. 328*, pp. 107-116.

[65] Fels, *op. cit.*, p. 108.

[66] Herbert George Gutman, "Social and Economic Structure and Depression: American Labor in 1873 and 1874" (unpublished Ph.D. dissertation, University of Wisconsin, 1959), pp. 6-7, chs. IV, VI, and VII.

[67] As in the "Tompkins Square Riot" of January 1874 in New York when the police charged a demonstration of the city's unemployed with, happily, no serious casualties on either side. See *ibid.*, ch. XII. For the other material in this paragraph see Samuel Rezneck, "Distress, Relief and Discontent in the United States during the Depression of 1873-1878," *Journal of Political Economy*, LVIII, No. 6 (Dec. 1950), 498-499; and Gutman, *op. cit.*, ch. XI.

[68] John R. Commons and associates, *History of Labour in the United States* (New York: The Macmillan Company, 1946), II, 153-155.

[69] *Ibid.*, pp. 157ff.

Labor greenbackism had fared even worse in the last months of prosperity. To begin with, the collapse of the N. L. U. deprived the greenbackers of a valuable forum. Then Cameron and the *Workingman's Advocate* faltered. While continuing to advertise the interconvertible bond, the Chicago editor now began to apologize for riding his hobby so hard.[70] Finally, it proved difficult to sell the greenback to the new national union. The Industrial Congress, at the behest of Cameron and Trevellick, endorsed paper money, but the greenback plank was the last of twelve and the only one not adopted unanimously. Many of the younger labor leaders present were simon-pure trade-unionists, who rejected "utopianism." Only one, German-born Robert Schilling of the Coopers' International, had absorbed the greenback faith.[71] As first President of the Congress, however, Schilling was to become an important agent for transmitting the old creed to the labor movement during the remainder of the decade.

Into this generally bleak scene hard times now intruded, producing diametrically opposite effects on labor unionism and labor greenbackism. Organized labor virtually disintegrated under the strain of the long depression. Many trade-unions went out of existence; others lost most of their members. The 30 or more national trade-unions of 1873 were reduced to 9 by 1877. Total union membership dropped to 50,000 by the following year.[72] On the other hand, deteriorating economic conditions reinvigorated the old labor greenbackers. Shortly after the panic, Campbell, responding, so he claimed, to many requests, prepared a revised version of *The True American System* that ran for seven consecutive weeks in *Workingman's Advocate*.[73] Cameron considered the disaster a vindication of his money views and took new heart. He now warned the nation's legislators that the

---

[70] WA, issue of Feb. 22-March 1, 1873.

[71] *Ibid.*, issue of July 19-July 26, 1873; Commons, *op. cit.*, II, 159-161; Edward Topping James, "American Labor and Political Action, 1865-1896: The Knights of Labor and Its Predecessors" (unpublished Ph.D. dissertation, Harvard University, 1954), pp. 76-79.

[72] Rezneck, *op. cit.*, p. 507; Gerald Grob, *Workers and Utopia: A Study of Ideological Conflict in the American Labor Movement, 1865-1900* ([Evanston, Ill.]: Northwestern University Press, 1961), pp. 34-35.

[73] Beginning Dec. 13, 1873.

people had "come to see what our banks are, and the Congress that fails to abolish it [sic] and substitute greenbacks in lieu of bank notes, will never assemble but once."[74] Soon after the Congressional session opened, Cameron sent his subscribers printed petitions urging the labor reform financial program. Presumably to encourage Congress to grant greenback relief, these were to be mailed to Senator Ferry and Moses Field, the Detroit merchant-greenbacker, now representing Michigan in the lower House.[75] The last months of the gloomy year also produced a rash of greenback speeches and writings by reformers and labor leaders connected with the old National Labor Union or the Labor Reform Party.[76]

Besides stirring up the old believers, the depression created something a little closer to mass labor support for greenbacks. As trade-unionism declined, reformist solutions once more attracted labor leaders. At the second meeting of the National Industrial Congress in April 1874 President Schilling asked for a redoubled emphasis on the money question. Included in the previous Congress platform largely out of respect for Cameron and Trevellick, the greenback plank now received enthusiastic support. A full interchangeable bond platform was adopted and greenback resolutions sent to Congress, then in the throes of the financial debate.[77]

The panic was the catalyst that transformed farmer Agrarianism into farmer greenbackism. Not that an irresistible current for soft money suddenly appeared in rural America. On the contrary: most farmers, in most parts of the nation, where not simply indifferent to finance, remained as suspicious as ever of paper money. But for the first time, in a few places in the Northwest, a decided inflationist note became audible.

In this catalytic role the panic's action was more psychological than economic. There was no sudden change in farm prices, no

---

[74] WA, Oct. 4, 1873.

[75] Ibid., Jan. 17, 1874.

[76] See E. M. D[avis], The "Labor Reform" View of Money (n.p., 1873); R. F. Wingate, An Address by Hon. R. F. Wingate on American Finance . . . (St. Louis, 1874); John Magwire, Response of John Mag-

wire to a Resolution of the National Labor Council . . . (St. Louis, 1874). But Magwire, an old-line labor reformer, now dropped the 3.65 bond and plumped for a great new issue of greenbacks to pay off the whole national debt!

[77] WA, April 25, 1874.

abrupt shift from prosperity to hard times in the prairies after September 1873. The price decline of the decade had already begun, and would continue slowly, punctuated by temporary rallies, for the next twenty years. Gross farm income in the nation was actually higher in 1874 than in the four previous years. Wheat prices held up well until 1875.[78] To be sure, for a short while after the panic eastern loan capital went into hiding, but there is no evidence for any leap in farm mortgage rates, or any permanent change in the availability of mortgage funds in the West.[79] The real, though clearly limited, shift in farmer attitudes detectable after the panic was prompted by the general public apprehension, the renewed attack on resumption, and the nationwide financial excitement, rather than by any specific immediate injury to the Northwestern farmer himself.

The process of change, if not the causes, may be seen in capsule form in the pages of *Industrial Age,* organ of the Illinois Farmers' Association. Founded jointly in August 1873 by S. M. Smith and J. A. Noonan, a Wisconsin anti-monopolist long active in the railroad regulation fight,[80] the paper at first reflected more closely Noonan's conservatism than Smith's militant Agrarianism. In its prospectus the new weekly promised "to protect and defend the industrial classes of the West from the onerous exactions of monopolies." But monopolies at this point meant only the railroads.[81] In his first mention of money, Noonan concluded, curiously, that either specie payment or an exclusive greenback currency was required by the times. The paper issues of "a monopoly banking system" at all events had been a failure

[78] U. S. Department of Agriculture, *Technical Bulletin No. 703* (*Gross Farm Income and Indices of Farm Production and Prices in the United States, 1869-1937*), Table 8, p. 24; Table 13, p. 36.

[79] Margaret Bogue remarks that farm interest rates in Illinois went down steadily from the late '60's on. Following the panic, demand for mortgage money exceeded supply. By early 1874 money once again became available and by the end of the year the terms had decidedly

shifted in favor of the borrower. See Margaret Beattie Bogue, *Patterns from the Sod: Land Use and Tenure in the Grand Prairie, 1850-1900* (Springfield: Illinois State Historical Library, 1959), pp. 147, 188, 198-199.

[80] For Noonan's earlier career see New York *Daily Graphic,* May 8, 1873; J. A. Noonan to James R. Doolittle, Milwaukee, Sept. 25, 1871, Doolittle MSS, State Hist. Soc. of Wisc.

[81] *IA,* Aug. 20, 1873.

and should be canceled.[82] On October 4, however, Noonan declared without reservation that "a stable . . . currency is what the people need. . . . Make a paper dollar worth a gold one as soon as possible and we shall all know where we are. A debased currency is a design of the devil to fleece the arm of labor [*sic*], and no class loses more by it than the farmers."[83]

In the next few weeks Noonan painfully reformulated his money views. On November 15, after opening its pages to several letters and articles on the interconvertible bond, *Industrial Age* acknowledged that "the scheme has many able advocates."[84] Three weeks later Noonan printed a typical greenback speech of Horace Day, but felt called upon to deny that the greenback resembled the old "wildcat" bank notes.[85] Well into the new year *Industrial Age* printed hard money contributions from readers, as well as greenback articles by De Wolf,[86] serving for a while as a neutral forum for conflicting views. But by this time Noonan had become a full convert to the interconvertible bond and soft money and would soon throw the *Age* behind the greenback forces in Congress.

Noonan's odyssey paralleled—if it did not simply reflect—the journey of the Illinois Farmers' Association itself. Secretary Smith had already foreshadowed the radical money position in his July 1873 speech attacking the bank evil. In October, M. M. Hooton, a Vice-President of the Association, prefaced a jeremiad against banks with a pure Campbellite analysis of the disastrous effects of high interest rates.[87] The end of the road was finally reached at the Decatur meeting of the Association in December, where delegates listened to frank greenback speeches by Hooton and guest Horace Day, and passed resolutions demanding repeal of the National Bank Act, a further federal legal tender issue, and a low interest, interconvertible bond.[88]

[82] *Ibid.*, Sept. 27, 1873.
[83] *Ibid.*, Oct. 4, 1873.
[84] *Ibid.*, Nov. 15, 1873.
[85] *Ibid.*, Dec. 6, 1873.
[86] *Ibid.*; and Dec. 13, 1873; Dec. 20, 1873; Dec. 27, 1873; Jan. 3, 1874.
[87] Speech at Northwestern Farmers' Convention at Chicago, Oct. 22,

1873, in Jonathan Periam, *The Groundswell: A History of the Origins, Aims, and Progress of the Farmers' Movement* (Cincinnati: E. Hannaford & Co., 1874), pp. 354-355.
[88] *CDT*, Dec. 18, 1873; *IA*, Dec. 27, 1873.

Similar movements occurred in Iowa and Indiana. In the former state the move to soft money at first affected only a few opinion leaders. *Iowa Homestead,* dubious of "currency tinkers" in 1870,[89] and thereafter generally indifferent to finance, took note of the panic in a lead editorial soon after it occurred.[90] On January 16, after six weeks of the excited Congressional debate, the *Homestead*[91] plumped for outright inflation. "The conviction is gaining upon the public mind," its editor declared, "that there is not currency enough afloat; that a business so vast and constantly increasing requires a corresponding increase in circulating medium."[92] On the other hand, the Iowa State Grange, some weeks before this editorial, had declared itself "satisfied with the policy of the administration," though willing to support a state free banking law.[93]

In Indiana, with its powerful Democratic party and its large erstwhile Copperhead element, the change was more thoroughgoing. There, one man, A. E. Olleman, was to serve almost single-handedly as midwife to farmer greenbackism. A farmer and anti-monopolist of Morgan County, Olleman suddenly emerges from obscurity in November 1873 as the newly appointed assistant editor of the *Indiana Farmer.*[94] Already a confirmed greenbacker, in his new post Olleman remade the influential state farm journal into a powerful soft money organ, taking an unusually frank stand for forthright inflation to lower interest rates and raise farm prices.[95] At the Indiana State Grange meeting held shortly before Congress convened, Olleman was responsible for the resolution labeling contraction a "mistaken policy," and the existing banking system "prejudicial to labor." Strong convention opposition prevented anything more radical than a free banking recommendation,[96] but Indiana farmer opinion moved quickly beyond what the timid State Grange would endorse. By mid-January the Council of the Tipton County Grange was praying Congress "to have the circulat-

[89] See above, ch. vi.
[90] *Iowa Homestead,* Oct. 3, 1873.
[91] Its name was now changed to the *Western Farm Journal.*
[92] *Western Farm Journal,* Jan. 16, 1874.
[93] *IA,* Dec. 20, 1873; *CDT,* Dec. 14, 1873.
[94] *Indiana Farmer,* Nov. 8, 1873.
[95] *Ibid.,* Dec. 20, 1873; Dec. 27, 1873.
[96] *Ibid.,* Dec. 6, 1873.

ing medium of . . . [the] country increased to . . . one billion, five hundred millions of dollars by redeeming a similar amount of United States Bonds."[97]

Yet the process of converting rural Agrarianism into green-backism moved sluggishly even after the panic. If the Illinois Farmers' Association succumbed to Campbellite views, the Illinois State Grange did not. At its state convention in December 1873 the Grange attacked the national banks as monopolies, but also recommended "some policy . . . looking ultimately to a return to a specie basis."[98] Nor did the flourishing Illinois agricultural press support soft money. *Western Rural* as well as the influential *Prairie Farmer* continued to defend the State Grange's financial conservatism against Smith's "incendiarism."[99]

Elsewhere the picture was the same. The resistance to green-backism in both the Iowa and Indiana State Granges has already been noted. In Minnesota, although by mid-1873 anti-bank sentiment was flourishing,[100] state farm leaders continued to resist soft money. Donnelly remained a bullionist until the middle of 1875.[101] The Wisconsin Reform Party, made up of grange elements, soon after the panic endorsed "honest" repayment of the public debt.[102] Both the Ohio and Michigan State Granges, meeting in early 1874, refused to consider the money problem.[103]

It was clear that the farmer, despite the trauma of the panic, would not readily surrender his old-fashioned bullionism. The more militant elements in Illinois, Iowa, and Indiana had broken with the past, but old traditions and prejudices, particularly rural traditions and prejudices, die hard. Jacksonian hard money still cast its spell over the country's rural citizens. The

[97] See petition enclosed in Joel Reece to Daniel D. Pratt, Tipton, Indiana, Jan. 27, 1874, Pratt MSS.

[98] *IA*, Dec. 12, 1873.

[99] *Western Rural*, Aug. 16, 1873; Sept. 20, 1873; May 9, 1874.

[100] See W. W. Mays to Ignatius Donnelly, St. Paul, July 21, 1873; Donnelly MSS, Minnesota Historical Society.

[101] See Martin Ridge, "Ignatius Donnelly and the Greenback Move-ment," *Mid-America, An Historical Review*, xxxix, No. 3 (July 1957), 157, for a fuller discussion of Donnelly's money views in 1873-1874.

[102] Solon J. Buck, *The Granger Movement: A Study of Agricultural Organization and Its Political, Economic, and Social Manifestations, 1870-1880* (Cambridge: Harvard University Press, 1913), p. 90.

[103] *Western Rural*, March 14, 1874; Jan. 31, 1874.

developments in Indiana and Illinois, especially, where farmer greenbackism now began to take root, can probably be explained by exceptional circumstances. In the former, Olleman's efforts, the state's Copperhead past, and the appearance of an aggressive and opportunistic group of greenback leaders[104] help account for the change. In Illinois the proximity of the Chicago labor reformers was almost certainly significant. Hooton and Smith borrowed at length from Campbell. Campbell himself had attended the State Farmers' Association meeting at Springfield in April 1873. He did not succeed in imposing his views on the convention, but the meeting did adopt an exceptionally strong anti-monopoly platform.[105] When the Association finally embraced greenbackism at Decatur, Hooton explicitly acknowledged his debt to "Judge Campbell."[106] By early 1874, then, the prairies were beginning to stir. Farmer greenbackism had been born, and Northwestern farmers would soon join businessmen and labor groups in the legislative drive for soft money.

III

The Congressional currency debate of 1873-74 inevitably mirrored these turbulent currents of public opinion. Westerners, and for the first time, Southerners waved the Agrarian banners. Rural Democrats supported Representative James Beck's unsuccessful attempt to convert the Republican sponsored House free banking bill into an anti-bank, greenback measure.[107] Republicans from Pennsylvania and the older, industrialized West, claimed that "plenty of money" made "business active and prosperous," and promoted "the growth and development of the nation."[108] Reformers Charles Sumner and Carl Schurz spoke against every attempt to inflate.[109] One or two Congressmen were themselves caught in the general business disaster and had

[104] For this last development see below, ch. IX.

[105] *Prairie Farmer*, XLIV (April 12, 1873), 115.

[106] *IA*, Dec. 27, 1873.

[107] For Beck's classic Agrarian views see *Congressional Record*, pp. 2927-2928. The text of the Beck amendment is in *ibid.*, p. 3015, and the vote is on p. 3019. See Appendix B.

[108] The phrase is Oliver P. Morton's. *Congressional Record*, p. 1388. For other western and Pennsylvania Republican statements see *ibid.*, pp. 1511, 2103, 2667, 2933.

[109] *Ibid.*, pp. 143, 1720-1721.

a strong personal interest in expanding the circulation. The panic almost destroyed Senator William Sprague, and alone among New England Senators he defended inflation.[110] But most Congressmen had more conventional political motives. Whatever their own financial convictions, an irresistible tide seemed to be running for currency expansion. They had left home for the session at the tail-end of the panic, when everyone seemed to be clamoring for monetary relief and even conservatives were willing to desert gold. A few members may have picked up the cues—the Banking and Currency Committee hearings, for example—that indicated returning conservatism. But many remained convinced, apparently, that the public wanted easy money. It seemed expedient to ride the soft money current, or at the very least, to offer no resistance. Many Congressmen, Schurz wrote, would support sound money "were they not afraid of their constituents."[111]

In such an atmosphere, soft money legislation moved methodically over the parliamentary hurdles. In the Senate S. 617, the Finance Committee's bill, was quickly amended into an inflationist measure. On March 26 an attempt by Schurz to return the greenback limit to the amount in circulation before Richardson's reissue was voted down by 40 to 18.[112] Soon after, an amendment to raise the greenback ceiling to $400 million, the total before McCulloch's contraction, was carried 31 to 26. Several days and much debate later the soft money men struck out the bill's original specie resumption section.[113] They then took up the bank note limitation of S. 617 and presumably would have attacked each hard money clause in turn. But this piecemeal assault was abandoned in favor of a substitute for the entire bill,

---

[110] Eventually the Spragues failed for $20 million. See Zechariah Chaffee, Jr., "Weathering the Panic of 1873: An Episode in Rhode Island Business History," *Dorr Pamphlet*, No. 4 (1942), pp. 276ff.; *CFC*, xvii (Nov. 1, 1873), 581-582. On Sprague's stand in Congress see the remarks of Senator Ferry, praising Sprague for being the only New England Senator daring to dissent from the view of his section. *Congressional Record*, p. 2103.

[111] Carl Schurz to Manton Marble, Washington, Feb. 1, 1874, Marble MSS, LC. See the similar remarks of Representative Mark Dunnell of Minnesota, *Congressional Record*, p. 2940.

[112] *Ibid.*, pp. 2440, 2484.

[113] *Ibid.*, pp. 2524, 2610.

and on April 6, against adroit and desperate opposition, the Senate passed the substitute proposal 29 to 24.[114]

The House had been debating its own measure for some months, and House Republican leaders were uncertain what course to take with the Senate bill. Speaker Blaine, fearing an open break between hard and soft factions, called an informal meeting of leading Republicans on April 13 in an attempt to reconcile differences. The conservatives—Garfield, Joseph Hawley of Connecticut, the brothers E. R. and George F. Hoar, and Henry Dawes of Massachusetts—agreed to support the House free banking bill if the soft money men[115] would accept modifications.[116] On the floor the next day, however, the expansionists refused to abide by their agreement. Over the opposition of Garfield and many eastern Republicans the House first passed the straight free banking bill and then took up and passed the Senate measure by the decisive majority of 140 to 102.[117]

This measure—soon called the Inflation Bill—was a product of the same coalition of western and Pennsylvania Republicans which had dominated currency legislation since the War's end. It was clearly not an offspring of western Agrarianism. Almost half the voting western Democrats and about one-third the southern Democrats opposed it. Pennsylvania Republicans favored the measure 13 to 5. Delegates of both parties from New York, New Jersey, and New England voted almost solidly against the bill.[118]

Although S. 617 would create an enormous furor, it was not an extreme measure. It provided for a $46 million increase in the national bank circulation, to be distributed to new institutions. It also expanded the legal tenders, but only to $400 million—some $18 million more than were currently outstanding, and only enough to bring it back to the total before McCulloch's

---

[114] *Ibid.*, pp. 2719, 2819, 2829ff.

[115] These included James Colwin of Indiana, Butler, and Kelley.

[116] Namely, a provision to retire $25 of greenbacks for each $100 of new bank notes. This amendment had been suggested by Charles Foster of Ohio, one of the confer-ees. See *NYW*, April 15, 1874. For a report of this meeting see *ibid.* and Garfield MS Diary, April 13, 1874, Garfield MSS.

[117] *Congressional Record*, pp. 3075-3078; Garfield Diary, April 14, 1874, Garfield MSS.

[118] See Appendix C.

contraction.[119] The new Inflation Bill could have enlarged the circulation—both national bank and greenback—by at most a moderate $64 million. Indeed, several well-informed observers were certain that through a minor clause changing bank reserve requirements, it would contract.[120] But to most conservatives it was the entering wedge for an inflation that would soon drown the country in paper money, and all the forces of financial rectitude rallied to keep it from becoming law.

Spearheading the attack were the reformers and the sound money intelligentsia. In November the *Nation* solemnly warned its readers against the greenback folly and attacked the proponents of "flexibility."[121] Through the remainder of the winter and into the spring, Godkin fired away at the soft money men in and out of Congress,[122] claiming, as usual, to speak for the country's "intelligence," its "leading scholars, thinkers, merchants, traders, manufacturers, bankers and administrators—in short, nearly the whole body of those by whose labors it maintains itself in civilization."[123] Atkinson urged his friend, Senator William B. Allison of Iowa, who leaned toward soft money, not to "join the black sheep." "Your people will damn you within two years," he wrote, "if you don't give them good money. Truth is truth and will prevail."[124]

The most active figure among the reformers was John Murray Forbes. At the January House Currency Committee hearings both Forbes and S. Lester Taylor had spoken out against expansion. Forbes returned from the capital shocked by the financial ignorance and irresponsibility of Congress, his reformer soul aching to dispel the darkness.[125] He had been impressed by the experience of Norton and Atkinson with the Loyal Publication

[119] *Congressional Record*, p. 2981. One other important clause was designed to prevent the practice of depositing country bank reserves with New York banks, by providing that not more than one-fourth of circulation reserves could be kept outside the banks' own vaults, and on this no interest could be paid.

[120] E.g., this was the view of Comptroller of the Currency, John Jay Knox. See *NYDT*, April 15, 1874.

[121] *Nation*, xvii (Nov. 13, 1873), 316; (Nov. 27, 1873), 350-351.

[122] *Ibid.* (Feb. 5, 1874), 86-87; (Feb. 19, 1874), 116; xviii (April 16, 1874), 243.

[123] *Ibid.* (April 2, 1874), 214.

[124] Atkinson to William B. Allison, Boston, March 23, 1874, Allison MSS.

[125] See Charles Eliot Norton to E. L. Godkin [Cambridge, Mass.] Feb. 8, 1874, Godkin MSS, Houghton Library, Harvard University.

Society revival of the '60's, and his first move was to establish a propaganda periodical. For this purpose he enlisted the resources of the existing reformer organization. The new journal, the *Financial Record*, was to be published weekly by the "Financial Department" of the Social Science Association, a group consisting at this point of Wells, Sumner, Gamaliel Bradford, Forbes himself, Francis Walker and Frank B. Sanborn. Sanborn, Secretary of the Association, was to edit the new periodical.[126]

In early February the first issue of the *Record* appeared. The publication contained anti-inflation editorials, polemical pieces borrowed from the orthodox economists or written for the occasion by Association members, surveys of conservative editorial opinion from all parts of the nation, and extended reports of the Congressional currency debates.[127] The journal was "intended as a Document for sowing seed among constituents,"[128] and Forbes saw to it that it got into the hands of newspaper editors as well as members of Congress and local politicians.[129] The *Record* ran for 39 weekly issues—until long after the session ended—and undoubtedly helped to enspirit the waverers in Congress and among the public.

The whole purpose of the reformer campaign was once again to rally the forces of respectability—and on the whole it succeeded. As in former years, the Protestant churches stood as a rock against error. To the ministers the new inflationist threat, like the Ohio Idea, was the call to a crusade. The religious press saw the panic in Old Testament terms as God's punishment for the extravagance and dishonesty engendered by the paper system, and as a divine signal for repentance and reform.[130] During the months following, ministers and religious editors admonished the country against heeding the siren call of more greenbacks.[131] The passage of the Inflation Bill shocked

[126] *Ibid.*

[127] *Financial Record*, Feb. 5, 1874-Oct. 30, 1874, *passim*. A complete file of this ephemeral publication can be found in the New York Public Library Reference Collection.

[128] Forbes to Carl Schurz, Boston, Feb. 15, 1874, Schurz MSS, LC.

[129] *Ibid.*; Forbes to William E. Chandler, Feb. 5, 1874, Chandler

MSS, LC.

[130] *Chicago Advance*, VII (Oct. 2, 1873), 8; *Christian Union*, VIII (Oct. 15, 1873), 310-311; *The Methodist*, XIV (Nov. 8, 1873), 356.

[131] *Christian Intelligencer*, XLV (March 12, 1874), 16. See also Leonard Bacon, quoted in *Christian Mirror*, LII (Dec. 2, 1873), 68.

and disgusted the editors of the religious weeklies. The bill's "perfidy to solemn pledges" was "equalled only by its financial stupidity."[132] A step had "been taken in the wrong direction," and if it was not "speedily retraced" the country would "soon be advancing upon the double quick toward bankruptcy."[133]

Not content with mere declaiming, the religious press urged its readers to place pressure on Congress and the President to prevent the bill's enactment into law.[134] Congress and the President were themselves urged to consider the consequences of their actions. Writing before the House had acted on the Senate bill, the *Independent* warned that the Republican party would have "outlived its usefulness" if "the measure finally adopted . . . shall . . . launch the people out upon the high seas of an irredeemable, depreciated and fluctuating paper currency."[135]

Among the merchants, bankers, and textile manufacturers, the reformers found willing subjects for their organizing efforts. Once past their early scare, many conservative businessmen had reverted to their normal hard money position. In February the Chicago Merchants' Exchange protested against inflation,[136] as did the powerful Chicago Board of Trade,[137] and the Chicago Clearing House, in April.[138] Sherman had earlier presented to Congress a resumption petition from the New York Importers' and Grocers' Board of Trade.[139] Another came from the New York Chamber of Commerce. Hard money petitions from trade bodies in Baltimore, Portland, Maine, Milwaukee, and Cincinnati, as well as from other groups of merchants, bankers, and brokers, poured in between December and April.[140]

[132] *Independent*, April 23, 1874, p. 16.

[133] *The Christian Register*, LIII (April 11, 1874), 2.

[134] *Watchman and Reflector*, LV (April 2, 1874), 6.

[135] *Independent*, April 9, 1874, p. 16.

[136] *NYDT*, April 23, 1874.

[137] See Charles Randolph to Richard Oglesby, Chicago, April 7, 1874, Oglesby MSS.

[138] B. B. Hale to Richard Oglesby, Chicago, April 10, 1874, *ibid.*

[139] *Congressional Record*, p. 2349.

[140] See the following: New York Chamber of Commerce, *Sixteenth Annual Report for 1873-1874*, pp. 87-94; for the Baltimore Board of Trade, *Congressional Record*, p. 139; for Baltimore Shoe and Leather Board of Trade, *Shoe and Leather Reporter*, XVII (Jan. 15, 1874), 1; for the Portland Board of Trade, *NYW*, April 15, 1874; for the New York Cotton Exchange, *Congressional Record*, p. 2349; for the Milwaukee Chamber of Commerce, *CDT*, April 23, 1874; Cincinnati Board of Trade, *Fifth Annual Report for 1873*, p. 46. See also *Banker's Magazine*, XXVIII (May 1874), 891; *Con-*

The soft money element among the merchants did not allow the conservatives to have it all their own way. The opposition almost defeated the Chicago Board of Trade's hard money petition.[141] The financial discussion at the Cincinnati Board of Trade was protracted by the soft money groups for seven sessions, and the memorial that was finally sent represented a watered-down version of the original forthright attack on inflation.[142] In New York two sets of resolutions were sent by the Chamber of Commerce. The majority adopted the sort of no-nonsense contractionist statement that had become standard for the Chamber; the dissenting Opdyke-Groom-Claflin wing sent a separate resolution warning against immediate resumption.[143]

Despite this persistent undercurrent of dissent, the panic, on balance, had strengthened hard money opinion among the merchants. Business opposition to the orthodox financial position had been more formidable in the prosperous years just before the panic; the depression once more made it a distinctly minority voice. The remaining dissenters were to be shunted aside as the conservatives mobilized to block the Inflation Bill.

As the Bill moved toward final passage, the merchants, bankers, and reformers joined hands to wage a counteroffensive. Atkinson, with the help of Taylor and other western business friends, launched a letter and a petition campaign which swamped the White House with western business protests against inflation.[144] In March and April the reformers collaborated with the commercial and financial men to stage two great protest rallies in New York and Boston. The New York meeting was held on March 24 at Cooper Institute and included A. A.

gressional Record, pp. 1031, 2704. The index of the Record for this session includes scores of currency petitions on both sides of the issue, from organizations and individuals.

[141] CDT, April 8, 1874.

[142] Cincinnati Board of Trade, Fifth Annual Report, pp. 6, 46. See also S. Lester Taylor's remarks to the Banking and Currency Committee, Report No. 328, p. 134.

[143] George Opdyke, Memorial: Minority Report of the Chamber of Commerce Committee, pp. 2ff.; New York Chamber of Commerce, Sixteenth Annual Report, pp. 95-98. The minority memorial also recommended an interconvertible bond, but without any greenback increase.

[144] Edward Atkinson, "Veto of the Inflation Bill of 1874," Journal of Political Economy, i (December 1892), 17-19; NYDT, April 18, 1874; S. Lester Taylor to Alexander Mitchell, Cincinnati, April 1, 1874, Mitchell MSS, State Hist. Soc. of Wisc.

Low, Opdyke, Chittenden, Cyrus Field, August Belmont, and other leading traders and financiers of the metropolis. Also on hand was a contingent of local reformers: Whitelaw Reid, Parke Godwin, and Dorman Eaton. Atkinson was there representing the Boston business-reformer group, and Francis Walker and Charles Francis Adams, Sr., sent letters of encouragement. With the exception of Opdyke and a small band of allies, the assemblage was intensely hostile to soft money and adopted resolutions denouncing inflation as "demoralizing to all who buy and sell . . . borrow and lend."[145]

The Boston meeting, held early in April, was wholly staged by the reformers. Charles Backus, a Detroit newspaperman employed by the Social Science Association, was given the task of organizing the rally, as well as the larger task of mobilizing business opinion nationally. At Faneuil Hall on April 4 were some 3,000 of Boston's most prominent merchants, bankers, reformers, and political leaders. Atkinson, Forbes, Charles Francis Adams, Jr., and John Quincy Adams; banker Henry Kidder; and cotton manufacturers William Gray and William Amory, were among the speakers. The meeting adopted resolutions warning that any measure to increase the circulation would be a breach of the government's pledged word. Grant was exhorted to veto any inflation measure, and a group was selected to present these views in person to Congress and the President.[146]

Backus planned to have delegations from other parts of the country join the Faneuil Hall group in Washington to impress the nation with business unity. "We hope by thus exercising a combined pressure of mercantile and financial men from the West and East," he wrote, "to influence the Senate, or if that be too late, then the President—whose veto can perhaps in this way be secured."[147]

The actual passage of the Inflation Bill was the signal for a second round of meetings. On April 15 a group of New York businessmen, "including the majority of the presidents of the

[145] [Cooper Institute], *Proceedings at the Mass Meeting of Citizens in the Cooper Institute. . . , passim.*
[146] *NYT*, April 5, 1874; *New York Evening Post*, April 22, 1874.
[147] Charles Backus to Carl Schurz, Boston, March 28, 1874, Schurz MSS.

banks in the Clearing House Association," met at Cyrus Field's Gramercy Park home and arranged to send their own delegation to Washington.[148] Meetings were also held in Cincinnati, Milwaukee, and other western cities.[149] The Cincinnati rally, according to the *Enquirer*, was composed of "theoretical and visionary" lawyers, editors, bankers, and holders of bank stock—which, after allowing for the *Enquirer's* biases, was not a bad description of the conservative business-reformer group. "The house builders, the boat builders, the machine builders, the city builders," the paper noted, "were not there."[150]

In the end, however, only New York and Boston sent delegations to Washington, and only after the Inflation Bill had passed both houses. By this time, of course, nothing but a veto could stop the bill, and the delegations went directly to the President. They could not have expected success. It was generally believed that Grant favored the bill,[151] and their chilly reception by the President only confirmed their fears. The chairman of the Boston delegation, William Gray, saw Grant on April 16. The President took exception to several statements made at Faneuil Hall which were critical of the Administration's financial record, and the interview deteriorated into an angry and undignified wrangle.[152] The New York group, which included Low, Chittenden, Field, and R. B. Minturn, inauspiciously saw the President the following day. They found Logan, Ferry, and Matthew Carpenter, the soft money Senator from Wisconsin, already with Grant. While the delegates were making their representations, Butler, who had been kept informed of the reformers' activities,[153] shouldered his way into the room and took the President off to a corner, leaving the New Yorkers cooling their heels. The presence of the inflationist Senators, Butler's rude interruption, and Grant's inattention and informal demeanor, all appeared deliberately insulting. But the President's hostility was

[148] *New York Evening Post*, April 16, 1874.

[149] *NYW*, April 15, 1874; *CDT*, April 23, 1874.

[150] *Cincinnati Enquirer*, April 15, 1874.

[151] *NYW*, April 15, 1874; *New York Evening Post*, April 18, 1874;

NYDT, April 16, 1874.

[152] *New York Evening Post*, April 22, 1874.

[153] See James M. Shute to Butler, Boston, April 1, 1874; R. G. Usher to Butler, Boston, April 6, 1874, Butler MSS, LC.

unmistakable when, at the end of the New Yorkers' remarks, he lectured the group on their manners, alluding to the previous day's interview with Gray. The disheartened delegates withdrew "with anything but a pleasant impression of Mr. Grant and his financial intentions."[154]

Soft money opinion, of course, was pushing Grant the other way. The labor reformers, expansionist rural groups, speculators, ironmasters—the latter currently going through their brief greenback phase—urged enactment of the law.[155] Grant knew, moreover, that it would be dangerous to defy the powerful expansionist element in the party.[156] Accordingly, he planned to sign the bill, convinced, as was Secretary Richardson, that there was little inflation in it, and fearing a veto would be put down to anti-western prejudice.[157] He "earnestly desire[d] to give his approval," Secretary Fish wrote, but when forced to compose a message to accompany his signature he found the reasons he could marshal in the bill's favor all "fallacious and untenable," while the opposing arguments now seemed impressive.[158] Grant, therefore, turned on his heel and wrote a veto message instead, the final draft of which was revised during the April 22 Cabinet meeting and released the same day.[159] In the end the conservatives had gotten through to the President. His truculent behavior toward the merchant delegations probably betrayed a painfully tender conscience rather than a firm commitment to soft money. He was rude to Gray and the New Yorkers because they were repeating the inconvenient and po-

[154] NYW, April 18, 1874; New York Evening Post, April 17, 1874; R. B. Minturn to David Wells, New York, April 20, 1874, Wells MSS, LC; Minturn to William B. Allison, New York, April 20, 1874, Allison MSS.

[155] WA, March 28, 1874; S. Cadwallader to Alexander Mitchell, Madison, Wisconsin, April 4, 1874, Mitchell MSS; R. Spencer (Secty. of the Macon Co. Farmers' Assoc.) to Richard Oglesby, Macon Co., Ill., April 15, 1874, Oglesby MSS; IA, April 18, 1874; Henry Stivers to William B. Allison, Osceola, Iowa, April 9, 1874, Allison MSS; Iron

Age, XIII (April 2, 1874); (April 16, 1874).

[156] In Grant's official family, Navy Secretary George M. Robeson, Attorney General George Williams, and Interior Secretary Columbus Delano all warned that a veto would hurt the party. Fish Diary, April 21, 1874, Fish MSS.

[157] Ibid., April 15, 1874.
[158] Ibid., April 21, 1874.
[159] Ibid., April 22, 1874. The message, circuitous and unconvincing in its reasoning, reflected the President's own mental confusion and uncertainty. Richardson, op. cit., pp. 268-271.

litically inexpedient promptings of his own conscience. Ultimately even the obtuse and insensitive old soldier could not deny the impelling conservative image of soft money as "the sum of all iniquity"; specie as "philosophy, morality and religion."

The veto was a bombshell. The reformers were jubilant, if surprised. "Ulysses the unwise," wrote a friend of David Wells, had been "obstinate enough to stick at that point," and the carping Wells should be grateful.[160] Soft money opinion was, of course, outraged. *Iron Age*, which had been newly won to the greenback, regretted that the "promise of relief to commerce and manufactures still remain[ed] unfulfilled."[161] The *Western Farm Journal* (*Iowa Homestead* under a new name) called the vetoed bill a token of good faith with the West and its defeat the work of the Eastern money interest.[162] The *Cincinnati Enquirer* proclaimed the veto "a victory for Wall Street and the New England National Bankers and bondholders," and warned Grant that he had opened a Pandora's box that would be as deadly as the repeal of the Missouri Compromise. It would lead to an uprising of the West that would destroy those responsible.[163]

[160] Estes Howe to David Wells, Cambridge, April 24, 1874, Wells MSS. Samuel Bowles's *Springfield Republican* called Grant's act "one of the great and good things of his administration." The *Nation* heaped praise on Grant for defying Morton, Logan, and Butler—three of the most powerful men in Washington. The eastern commercial and banking interests and the religious press also applauded the President, as did some western business groups. See George S. Merriam, *The Life and Times of Samuel Bowles* (New York: The Century Co., 1885), II, 230; *Nation*, XVIII (April 30, 1874), 278; Philadelphia Board of Trade, *Forty-Second Annual Report for 1874*, p. 11; New York Chamber of Commerce, *Seventeenth Annual Report for 1874-1875*, p. 27; *Banker's Magazine*, XXVIII (May 1874), 917; *The New York Observer*, LII (April 30, 1874); *Christian Intelligencer*, XLV (April 30, 1874), 16; *Christian Union*, IX (April 29, 1874), p. 2; *The Advance*, VII (April 30, 1874), 8; *The Standard*, XXI (April 30, 1874), 8; R. P. Lane (Pres. of Second National Bank of Rockford, Ill.) to Richard Oglesby, Rockford, April 27, 1874, Oglesby MSS.

[161] *Iron Age*, XIII (April 23, 1874). See also *Weekly Miner's Journal*, May 1, 1874; *IA*, April 25, 1874, claimed the veto proved that the producing classes could not expect justice from the traditional parties.

[162] *Western Farm Journal*, May 1, 1874. See also *Indiana Farmer*, June 27, 1874; A. M. Jones to Richard Oglesby, Warren, Ill., April 25, 1874, Oglesby MSS.

[163] *Cincinnati Enquirer*, April 25, 1874.

And it looked as if the veto would indeed cause serious trouble for the Republicans. To soft money Congressmen, faced with an election in the fall, it threatened political disaster. The inflation managers in the Senate were struck "dumb with surprise" when the message was read. The paralyzed Morton, it was reported, looked as if he had suffered a second stroke. Senator Timothy Howe of Wisconsin confessed that the veto "scared" him.[164] In the House "all work stopped and members gathered in knots to discuss the problem."[165] If the inflationists were angry at Grant's sacrifice of his closest political friends, party moderates were appalled at the conspicuous public display the veto made of Republican disunity. For a while a complete party schism appeared a serious possibility. Morton, Logan, Ferry, and Cameron talked of a manifesto denouncing the President. They would save the party in the West and their own futures by dissociating themselves from his policy. In the House, eastern conservatives and westerners exchanged threats and epithets, and the western men boasted that they would override the veto.[166] Speaker Blaine, whose concern for the party was reinforced by his own Presidential ambitions for 1876, rushed about frantically, trying to patch things up.[167] The inflationists would undoubtedly try to override, and the immediate problem was to avoid further ruffling of tempers. Blaine and other peacemakers promised the soft money men another opportunity at financial legislation when the House banking bill came before the Senate. They also referred ominously to Charles Sumner's fate three years before when he had crossed Grant.[168]

The peacemakers succeeded in holding the would-be insurgents in check by this combination of cajolery and threat. The soft money men got their chance to revote, but only after agreeing to dispense with further debate. While the Democrats made sarcastic remarks about the independence of Republican Sena-

---

[164] Timothy O. Howe to Grace T. Howe, Washington, May 7, 1874, Howe MSS, State Hist. Soc. of Wisc. Howe was a moderate opposed to all extreme positions and in favor of free banking. See *Congressional Record*, p. 671.

[165] *NYW*, April 23, 1874.

[166] *Ibid.*

[167] *Ibid.*, April 27, 1874.

[168] *Ibid.*, and April 24, 1874. Sumner had been removed as Chairman of the Foreign Affairs Committee when he defied Grant over Santo Domingo and other Administration foreign policies.

tors and the "great unshaken and intrepid" Republican party, the grim-faced inflationists voted on the motion to override.[169] The vote was almost identical with the original one—far short of the necessary two-thirds.[170]

IV

As Blaine had promised, Congress was to have another try at currency legislation before adjournment. The House financial measure had evolved into a straight free banking bill, and the House soft money leaders were prepared to carry this measure through to the President. The more conservative upper chamber refused, however, to accept the bill without some alterations,[171] and after a good deal of sparring it was referred to a joint conference committee.[172] While the committee met, the Administration for the first time asserted its policy-making role. Shortly before June 1, Grant, after conferring with Sherman, Maynard, and Carpenter[173] decided to intervene in the pending legislation by stating his precise financial position. On June 3 he consulted conservative Senators Conkling of New York, Lot Morrill of Maine, and John P. Jones of Nevada, as well as the newly appointed Secretary of the Treasury, Benjamin Bristow.[174] Bristow and the Senators approved, and on June 4 the President's views appeared as a memorandum to Senator Jones.[175]

Grant declared that he wished to see a clause repealing the Legal Tender Act attached to the pending legislation. The bill should also provide that after July 1, 1875, all contracts would be made in coin; and after July 1, 1876, greenbacks would be

[169] *Ibid.*, April 29, 1874.
[170] *Ibid.*, April 23, 1874; April 25, 1874; *NYDT*, April 23, 1874. The attempt to override the veto was defeated in the Senate by a vote of 30 to 34. *Congressional Record*, p. 3436. The defeat in the Senate was final; no attempt was made to revote in the House.
[171] The only significant change was a provision that for each $100 of new national bank notes, $25 of greenbacks be retired. *Ibid.*, pp. 3880-3896.
[172] For the twists and turns of the free banking bill to this point see *CFC*, xviii (May 30, 1874), 537.
[173] Representing Morton, who apparently was still angry and *"felt that he could not come."* Fish Diary, June 1, 1874, Fish MSS.
[174] Richardson, a man of modest talents at best, had been removed because of his connection with the notorious Sanborn contract frauds in Boston.
[175] The details of the Memorandum's evolution are described in the Fish Diary, June 1 and 3, 1874, Fish MSS.

redeemable in a 4½ per cent bond. He also expected Congress to withdraw all United States notes of denominations below ten dollars.[176] Grant certainly knew that so draconian a measure was not politically realistic,[177] but he was warning Congress that any bill that came from the conference committee would have to meet a strictly conservative test if it was to escape a veto.

The Jones memorandum raised another political tempest. The President seemed determined to offend the westerners and drive them out of the party. Republican inflationists denounced Grant's intervention as unprecedented, and predicted that he would irreparably damage the party if he persisted.[178] "A glycerine explosion," remarked one Washington observer, "could hardly have shattered the Republican party . . . more than the failure of the currency bill, the veto and the memorandum."[179]

Angered by what they considered a second breach of party faith, the conference committee's Republican majority ignored the Jones letter. On June 13 its bill, a moderate free banking measure, was submitted to the upper chamber. This passed, but met difficulties in the House. Blaine, after learning that Grant was adamantly opposed to the new legislation, intervened to prevent a second veto which he was certain would irretrievably split the party.[180] When the conference measure came before the House he used his influence to bring about its defeat.[181] The bill went back to committee, was revised to accommodate several of the President's suggestions, and was resubmitted. This time it passed both houses by large bipartisan majorities,[182] and was signed by Grant on June 20.

Thus, after seven months, Congress had finally produced a financial measure. But for so great a labor, the new legislation was ludicrously trivial. The bill made minor concessions to the soft money men. The national banks were freed from the requirement of a reserve against note circulation; Richardson's

---

[176] *NYW*, June 6, 1874.
[177] *Iron Age*, for example, raised strong objections to the plan. See *Iron Age*, XIII (June 11, 1874).
[178] *NYW*, June 6, 1874.
[179] "Special Correspondent" of *ibid.*, June 15, 1874.
[180] *Ibid.*, June 14, 1874.

[181] In this move he got the support of most of the Democrats, who of course had never been partial to free banking. *Ibid.*
[182] The vote in the Senate was 43 to 19, in the House 221 to 40. *Congressional Record*, pp. 5189, 5316. See Appendix D.

reissue was legalized; and western Republicans got a redistribution of $55 million of bank notes from New York and New England to newer areas. But the conservatives also won concessions. The greenback limit was fixed at $382 million, ending for good the threat of another reserve reissue, while another clause—one with unexpected consequences—permitted the banks voluntarily to surrender all or part of their note issue.[183]

With the June Banking Act, Congress finished its last important business and soon after adjourned. In the seven months since the opening of the session, financial prospects had revolved full circle. When Congress assembled in December, soon after the panic, the public was frightened and there was every reason to expect massive inflation. Although the expansionists faced stiff opposition from the beginning they succeeded in carrying both free banking and greenback expansion. At this point the reformers, the clergy, and the conservative commercial and financial interests, shaken by early inflationist successes, hastily mobilized to check the threat to monetary stability. The counterattack had been too late to influence Congress which remained, in June as in December, in the hands of the expansionists. It was the conservatives' ability to get to the President, an impressionable man who basically disapproved of soft money, that restored the nation's normal balance of soft and hard forces

---

[183] The effects of this last clause are discussed below, ch. VIII. There were also minor provisions regarding a central redemption agency and various procedural matters. For the text, as passed, see Charles F. Dunbar, *Laws of the United States Relating to Currency, Finance, and Banking from 1789 to 1896* (Boston: Ginn & Co., 1897), pp. 210-214. So close a balance of "hard" and "soft" elements produced curiously mixed reactions in the press. *Banker's Magazine* regarded the new law as the least objectionable financial legislation introduced during the session, but warned, in a somewhat mixed metaphor, that its mild redistribution provisions threatened "the foundations of the banking fabric on which our whole financial machinery moves." The *Commercial and Financial Chronicle* was relieved that the bill introduced so few changes. The *Cincinnati Enquirer* felt the inflationists had suffered a loss. "They have accepted a compromise on the currency question which must be regarded in the light of a defeat." On the other hand, the *Philadelphia Press*, a voice of the Pennsylvania soft money interest, predicted that "the whole effect of the law should be decidedly favorable to every form of business activity." See *Banker's Magazine*, XXIV (July 1874), 1; *CFC*, XVIII (June 27, 1874), 46; the *Enquirer* is quoted in *Financial Record*, I (July 3, 1874), 70; the *Press* is quoted in *ibid.*

disturbed by the September panic. This was achieved only at the cost of Republican harmony, however. By vetoing the major legislation of the western Senatorial leaders, Grant had created strains and resentments that were to shape the resumption battle for the next half-decade.

CHAPTER VIII

THE RESUMPTION ACT:

PASSAGE AND TRIAL (1874-1875)

I

THE political reverberations of the Inflation Bill veto could be heard long after Congress adjourned. Congressional elections were scheduled for 1874, and after two years of political scandal that reached high into the President's official family itself, it promised at best to be a difficult year for the Republicans. The veto now seemed likely to be the final blow to the party's chances in the fall, with serious consequences, perhaps, for 1876.[1] In the West, Republicans found themselves everywhere on the defensive, forced either to explain away Grant's action or openly repudiate the party's leader. Morton struggled manfully in Indiana to excuse Grant, arguing ingeniously that the vetoed measure would have produced less expansion and consequently less real relief than the June banking measure the President signed.[2] In both Indiana and Ohio the Republicans, with moderate soft money platforms,[3] confronted militant Democratic greenbackers,[4] and were forced to bear the onus of the Grant veto—ordered, Daniel Voorhees charged, by the bondholders, the railroads, and the bankers.[5] Elsewhere in the West Democrats gleefully reminded the voters that their opponents "had no unity of sentiment" on the currency issue.[6]

The veto not only exposed the Republicans to Democratic attack; in several western states it came close to tearing the

---

[1] See Matthew Carpenter to Richard Oglesby, Milwaukee, Aug. 5, 1874, Oglesby MSS, Illinois State Historical Library.

[2] William Dudley Foulke, *Life of Oliver P. Morton* (Indianapolis: The Bowen-Merrill Co., 1899), II, 345-347.

[3] Both of these platforms endorsed

a form of free banking. *The American Annual Cyclopedia and Register of Important Events of the Year 1874*, pp. 414, 668.

[4] *Ibid.*, 415, 667.

[5] *CDT*, Aug. 8, 1874.

[6] *IA*, Oct. 17, 1874, quoting John Farnsworth, former Republican Congressman from Chicago.

party apart. Michigan conservatives, led by Senator Zachariah Chandler, collided with Ferry's soft money followers at the August state convention, and a serious breach was barely averted.[7] In Illinois, where the Republicans expected a hard fight, the conflict between the hard money men and the Logan forces seemed likely to throw the election to the Democrats.[8] In Ohio, party unity deteriorated to the point where conservative Republicans openly demanded the defeat of Congressmen of either party who had supported inflation in the last session.[9] Everywhere in the Northwest, the veto made Republicans painfully aware of the problem of internal cohesion.[10]

Although they expected Democratic gains, the Republicans fought hard to keep control of Congress—to no avail. Early Democratic victories in the October states foreshadowed defeat, but the extent of the Republican debacle when the November returns were counted was startling. For the first time since 1861 the House of Representatives passed into Democratic control, an overwhelming Republican majority converted into a Democratic majority of sixty. In Illinois, Missouri, and elsewhere, local Democratic victories ensured the defeat of several prominent Republican Senators, although the Senate remained Republican by a small margin. Democratic Governors were elected in Massachusetts, Missouri, New Jersey, and New York. These calamitous results, a product in part of Republican disunity, would profoundly influence the events of the next few months.

The lame-duck Congressional session that convened in the shadow of the fall elections enacted into law the measure by which the nation resumed gold payments in January 1879. In passing the Resumption Act, the second session of the Forty-third Congress took an unexpected course, one that still raises some knotty problems. Why at this juncture in the decade-long currency battle, so soon after the Inflation Bill, should Congress take the momentous final step to resumption? What had pro-

---

[7] *CDT*, Aug. 27, 1874; Harriette M. Dilla, *The Politics of Michigan, 1865-1878* (New York: n.p., 1912), pp. 162-166.

[8] *Nation*, xviii (June 25, 1874), 404.

[9] *The Cleveland Leader*, June 27, 1874.

[10] See, e.g., David Atwood to Timothy O. Howe, Madison, Wisc., Aug. 18, 1874, Howe MSS, State Hist. Soc. of Wisc.; John Beveridge to Richard Oglesby, Springfield, Ill., May 2, 1874, Oglesby MSS.

duced such a revolution in Congressional opinion in less than a year?

The traditional explanation of this apparent about-face sees the fall defeats as a sobering rebuke to Republican radicalism which made the majority party see the error of its ways. Once back in the conservative fold, the Republicans were anxious to secure the national honor against their Democratic successors and hurriedly enacted the 1875 Resumption Act.[11] The Beardian explanation simply transposes the terms of this argument. The Republicans, contrite after a momentary agrarian lapse, rushed to secure resumption for their industrial and financial allies against the expected farmer-labor dominated Forty-fourth Congress.[12]

Neither of these explanations stands up under close scrutiny. When Congress reconvened there was every expectation of financial peace. A number of Republicans blamed their defeat on the currency issue,[13] and a few still favored a monetary relief measure,[14] but the Congressional leaders were determined to avoid further currency legislation for the session. The party, they felt, could not afford to enter the 1876 Presidential campaign weakened by further dissension.[15]

Events soon made such a course impossible. The Administra-

[11] E.g., Ellis Paxson Oberholtzer, *A History of the United States Since the Civil War* (New York: The Macmillan Co., 1922), III, 119-120; Don Carlos Barrett, *The Greenbacks and Resumption of Specie Payments, 1862-1879* (Cambridge: Harvard University Press, 1931), pp. 180-181; William B. Hesseltine, *Ulysses S. Grant, Politician* (New York: Frederick Ungar Publishing Co., 1957), p. 340; Martin Ridge, "Ignatius Donnelly and the Greenback Movement," *Mid-America: An Historical Review*, XXXIX, No. 3 (July 1957), 157.

[12] For Beard's own analysis see Charles A. and Mary R. Beard, *The Rise of American Civilization* (rev. 1 vol. ed.; New York: The Macmillan Co., 1944), I, 330-331. See also Louis M. Hacker, *The Triumph of American Capitalism* (New York: Columbia University Press, 1947), pp. 386-387.

[13] John Quincy Smith to John Sherman, Oakland, Ohio, Oct. 22, 1874, Sherman MSS, LC; *New York Herald*, Dec. 7, 1874. Butler, one of the defeated Republicans, later blamed his defeat on the "money lenders of Massachusetts" who opposed him because he had "warned the people" that contraction meant ruin. See Butler to Benjamin Pitman, Washington, Feb. 2, 1876, Butler MSS, LC.

[14] *New York Herald*, Dec. 7, 1874.

[15] *NYW*, Dec. 7, 1874; *CDT*, Dec. 14, 1874. Garfield wrote Jacob Schuckers, Chase's former secretary: "I should be glad if the Republican Party could take some conservative step toward specie payments, but I doubt if anything can be secured this winter." James A. Garfield to Schuckers, Washington, Dec. 19, 1874, Schuckers MSS, LC.

tion's financial recommendations, as embodied in the President's Message and Secretary Bristow's *Annual Report*, seemed designed to provoke the soft money men. Grant and Bristow called for repeal of the Legal Tender Act and funding of the greenbacks into a long-term bond[16]—demands that together were so rigorously deflationary that they even disturbed conservatives.[17] On December 8, the day following the Message, Kelley unexpectedly brought in an interconvertible bond bill, which he defended in a long, excited speech.[18] He was followed by Butler, who also "exhibited the inflation doctrine full blast."[19] Garfield and Henry Dawes were stung into replying, and a full-scale debate, with all its political risks, seemed imminent.[20]

The threat of another party feud dismayed Republican leaders. They were enveloped in gloom "in consequence of the hopeless division on the question of the currency," Garfield wrote the next day.[21] But at this point the instinct for self-preservation asserted itself. The debate, which threatened to revive on the tenth, was suspended by mutual consent, and it was agreed to hammer out some sort of general party measure away from the glare of publicity. The militant House soft money men, who at first refused to cooperate, came around when it was made clear that any bill they might get through Congress was certain to be vetoed.[22]

In the next few days Republican leaders worked overtime to put their house in order. The Morton-Logan-Ferry faction met several times to discuss the currency problem and its political ramifications. Blaine and Dawes sought to reach an advance understanding with the President, so as to avoid another demoralizing veto, while Dawes, joined by Sherman, began to work on a

[16] James D. Richardson (ed.), *A Compilation of the Messages and Papers of the Presidents, 1789-1902* (n.p.: Bureau of National Literature and Art, 1903), VII, 285-286; U. S. Treasury, *Annual Report of the Secretary of the Treasury on the State of the Finances for the Year 1874*, pp. xiv-xvi.

[17] See Benjamin F. Nourse to Carl Schurz, Washington, Dec. 12, 1874, Schurz MSS, LC; *NYW*, Dec. 15, 1874; *NYT*, Dec. 8, 1874.

[18] *Congressional Record*, 43

Cong., 2 sess., pp. 20-22. Hereafter all references to the *Record*, unless otherwise indicated, will be to this Congress and session.

[19] James A. Garfield MS Diary, Dec. 8, 1874, Garfield MSS, LC. For Butler's speech see *Congressional Record*, pp. 22-24.

[20] *Ibid.*, pp. 24-26; *NYW*, Dec. 9, 1874.

[21] Garfield MS Diary, Dec. 9, 1874, Garfield MSS.

[22] *NYW*, Dec. 10, 1874.

compromise measure.[23] On December 14 Senator Howe reported that he had been one of fifteen "serious minded" Republicans who had met to consider what the party "shall do to be saved." The question had "not been satisfactorily answered," but there would be another session in a week and he hoped for better progress.[24]

Howe's group was probably the parent of the Senatorial caucus committee, which sometime before the 19th assumed command of currency legislation for the session.[25] With Sherman as its chairman, this group of eleven Senators represented every important shade of Republican opinion. On one side were the western soft money triumvirate, all of whom were members. In the middle were moderates like Howe, and at the other extreme were such arch conservatives as Roscoe Conkling of New York and George F. Edmunds of Vermont.[26] Whatever the political merits of such an arrangement, it was not conducive to harmony, and almost immediately the committee ran into difficulties. Asked to outline their individual views of resumption, the Senators advanced a set of seemingly irreconcilable proposals, and it soon appeared that nothing would be accomplished. Another untidy public wrangle was now in prospect. But at this point Sherman came forward with a formula which succeeded in uniting the committee.[27]

[23] CDT, Dec. 13, 1874; NYW, Dec. 11, 1874; Dec. 15, 1874.

[24] He added that his information was to be kept confidential. See Timothy Howe to Grace Howe, Washington, Dec. 14, 1874, Howe MSS.

[25] If indeed it was not simply a larger version of the same group. Note that Howe was on the Caucus Committee as finally constituted.

[26] Besides Morton, Logan, Ferry, Conkling, Edmunds, and Howe, they were: William Allison of Iowa, Boutwell, Frederick T. Frelinghuysen of New Jersey, and Aaron Sargent of California. John Sherman, Recollections of Forty Years in the House, Senate, and Cabinet (Chicago: The Werner Co., 1895), i, 509.

[27] Sherman's responsibility for this scheme has been disputed by Professor Don Carlos Barrett, who sees George F. Edmunds as its author. (See Barrett, op. cit., pp. 182-184.) Contemporaries, however, generally gave Sherman credit, a claim he never denied, although there were times when it was in his interest to do so, and I believe his authorship to be more probable. See the following letters, ascribing the measure to Sherman: A. Sidney Biddle to Samuel J. Randall, Philadelphia, Jan. 14, 1875, Randall MSS, University of Pennsylvania Library; Rutherford B. Hayes to John Sherman, Fremont, Ohio, June 29, 1875, Hayes MSS, Hayes Memorial Library, Fremont, Ohio.

The first two sections of this scheme, replacing the worn fractional paper currency with a new silver coinage and repealing the seignorage charge for converting gold bullion into coin, were minor and non-controversial. The heart of the plan was contained in the two final proposals. The first of these enacted free banking, but with the proviso that for each $100 of new bank notes, $80 of greenbacks were to be "redeemed," down to a minimum of $300 million. Thereafter, presumably, the bank-note issue could expand indefinitely without affecting the volume of legal tenders. The last section, composed jointly by Sherman and Edmunds, balanced free banking with specie payments. This clause permitted the Treasury to acquire gold by selling bonds authorized by the 1870 Funding Act and by direct purchase, this reserve to be used to redeem the greenback issue on January 1, 1879.[28]

Little in this set of proposals was new. Free banking with a prorated reduction of greenbacks and resumption by accumulating a gold reserve had been thoroughly discussed in the daily press, the financial journals, and most recently, in Congress the previous session. The scheme strongly resembled Senate Bill 617, the original Finance Committee measure of the first session, which Sherman had introduced. But the new proposals were more generous to soft money. S. 617 had proposed resumption on January 1, 1876; the caucus scheme set the date exactly three years later. The bank-note redistribution feature of S. 617, moreover, was expanded to full free banking, to become operative not after resumption, but at passage. Indeed, the bill was as much a victory for soft as for hard money. While the caucus plan did fix a date for resumption, and this was an important concession to sound money opinion, the provision meant little by itself. It would not be the first time Congress had piously announced its intention to resume. Neither the Alley Resolution nor the 1869 Public Credit Act—the two previous instances—had brought the country any closer to resumption,[29] and there was little reason to expect more of the new measure. Most academic opinion, it must be remembered, held that successful resumption must be pre-

[28] Sherman, *op. cit.*, I, 510-511.
[29] Neither of these two measures, however, had specified a date for resumption.

ceded by a drastic contraction of the outstanding greenbacks, and the ill-defined borrowing powers given the Treasury as its sole means to resume would only confirm conservative opinion that the specie payments clause was an empty promise. At all events, the soft money Republicans received immediate free banking, for which they had long agitated, in exchange for a problematical resumption in 1879, four years away.

The caucus committee plan was not, then, a conspicuous triumph for sound money. It was a compromise measure, containing what appeared at the time to be strong expansionist features to set against a weak resumption clause. Still, it is inconceivable that even so tepid a resumption measure could have emerged from a representative Republican caucus the previous session. In the winter of 1873-74 Morton, Logan, and Ferry were in no mood to talk of specie payments, even specie payments in 1879. With the coming of spring, public opinion had indeed calmed. After adjournment, members quickly learned of the altered atmosphere. If Morton in Indiana found his constituents as receptive to expansion as ever, Congressmen from other states detected a cooling of soft money ardor. Senator William Windom told a reporter in August that Minnesotans were largely indifferent to the money issue. He had voted for the Inflation Bill under a misconception of opinion at home, and now regretted it.[30] According to Samuel S. Cox, a New York sound money Democrat, Congress as a whole was more conservative in the new session. Hard money sentiment, he noted in December, had revived in the previous six months, and inflation opinion was now "very much modified."[31]

Nevertheless, when this is conceded, a problem still remains. In a word, the shift of public opinion is not great enough to account for the measure. Nothing in the press or surviving political correspondence suggests a buildup of hard money strength. The bill, it is clear, was at heart political in origin, as isolated from public opinion as any political event can be where universal male suffrage prevails. The fall election debacle, though it did not produce the alleged Republican contrition, did

[30] *Nation,* xix (Aug. 6, 1874), 81.   Washington, Dec. 8, 1874, Marble
[31] S. S. Cox to Manton Marble,   MSS, LC.

display the folly of disunity. Failure to heal the financial breach seemed to Republican leaders certain to ensure the party's defeat in the 1876 Presidential contest. It is significant that it was not among the lame ducks of the House, but in the Senate—the body that represented political continuity in Congress—that the Resumption Act originated. The very vagueness of the scheme supports a political interpretation. It lacked consistency and, it would soon become apparent, clarity as well. In the eyes of its supporters it more than compensated for these defects by its potentially broad political appeal. No one could really be certain of its consequences—either financial or political. But to most moderate Republicans its long-run results were irrelevant: it was sufficient that it promised momentary party peace.

Once past the caucus committee the bill moved quickly. On December 19 it was submitted to the full Senate caucus, and after careful scrutiny was adopted without change.[32] Sherman encountered stiff opposition in the Senate itself, however, when the bill was brought in on December 21. Much of the resistance came from the root-and-branch resumptionists, who would have been overjoyed with a strong specie payment measure. Carl Schurz, who as a Liberal Republican was not bound by the caucus decision, immediately called the bill a fraud. It was unworkable as a resumption measure, since it would be impossible to raise a gold fund sufficient to redeem $300 million in greenbacks. Unless supplemented by a drastic prior withdrawal of legal tenders it would be worthless.[33]

In the course of his attack Schurz succeeded in baring Republican motives with probing questions about the greenback "redemption" intended to offset the new bank note issue. Could these notes, he asked, be kept as a "reserve" to be recirculated at the Treasury's discretion as Richardson had just done with McCulloch's reserve?[34] Hard money Democrats Allen Thurman of Ohio, Bayard of Delaware, and William Hamilton of Maryland immediately joined Schurz in demanding to know what was to be done with the retired greenbacks.[35]

[32] Sherman, *op. cit.*, I, 511; *CDT*, Dec. 20, 1874.
[33] *Congressional Record*, pp., 205-
206.
[34] *Ibid.*, pp. 196, 205-206.
[35] *Ibid.*, pp. 198, 202-203.

Schurz and his fellow conservatives had succeeded in spotting one of the major ambiguities of the caucus bill. This very problem had caused difficulties when the measure was being prepared, and for the sake of harmony it was agreed that when reporting the bill, Sherman would sidestep the embarrassing reissue question.[36] When called to account by Schurz, the Ohio Senator confessed that the question of the redeemed notes had been deliberately left open to avoid controversy. But confident of a disciplined Republican majority, he peremptorily refused to discuss the question further. He would not, he told the Senate, permit so necessary a measure to bog down over a minor issue of this sort.[37]

Opposition Senators protested Sherman's steam roller tactics. The bill was being pushed through with indecent haste, complained Thurman; there should be at least two weeks for thorough debate.[38] Bayard protested that he had not even had the time to read the bill.[39] Sherman replied that the issues raised in the measure had already been fully discussed, and that delay would only prolong public uncertainty.[40] In the end the Democratic outcry failed to move the Republicans. After a few frustrating hours the opposition gave way, and the measure was passed by a strict party vote of 32 to 14, with 27 Senators abstaining.[41] Bayard, for one, was so disgusted with Sherman's highhanded tactics that he did not bother to stay for the roll call.[42]

The Republican managers tried to get the lower chamber to take immediate action on the bill. Sherman and other leaders were on the House floor on December 23, holding earnest consultation with House committee chiefs. But the pending civil rights legislation had priority, and consideration was postponed until after the Christmas recess.[43]

Although Congress was inactive, the new financial legislation continued to concern the politicians in the next few weeks. In general the more intransigent sound money Republicans found it

---

[36] Sherman, *op. cit.*, I, 510.
[37] *Congressional Record*, p. 196.
[38] *Ibid.*, pp. 186, 198.
[39] *Ibid.*, p. 186.
[40] *Ibid.*

[41] *Ibid.*, p. 208.
[42] Thomas Bayard to Manton Marble, Washington, Dec. [29?], 1874, Marble MSS.
[43] *CDT*, Dec. 24, 1874.

difficult to swallow the caucus scheme. Eastern Republicans representing the money centers of Boston and New York objected to the free banking clause, fearing it would dilute the value of existing national bank stock.[44] The New England "honest money" element, as certain as Schurz that contraction must precede specie payments, thought the resumption clause fraudulent. Representative E. Rockwood Hoar, for one, rejected the proposed bill despite assurances from his less fastidious fellow Republicans that the resumption clause would be reinforced with more adequate legislation.[45] Dawes was warned that he would hurt his chances for the vacant Massachusetts Senate seat if he voted for such a dishonest measure.[46] Eastern sound money Democrats were also skeptical of the bill. One Pennsylvania Democrat likened it to the Pope's bull against the comet; it was a futile gesture which would only give the country four more years of uncertainty.[47]

Significantly, those western Republicans who had long been on the defensive at home over finance were far more friendly to the pending bill. Garfield convinced himself that it took "steps in the direction of specie payments." Although admittedly it was "not very decisive . . . it does do something," and, more important, he wrote, it promised "something that approaches a union in the party."[48] Western greenbackers, however, attacked the bill. The *Cincinnati Enquirer* warned that it conferred immense powers on the Treasury and reinforced the monopolistic national banking system. Western Democrats, the paper predicted, would oppose it "as a cheat, a false promise," which would "perpetuate and enlarge" the powers of the detested national bankers.[49]

Clearly, extremists at either end of the spectrum disliked the measure; it was just as clear that it would have the support of

[44] *Ibid.*, Jan. 4, 1875.
[45] Hoar to John Murray Forbes, Washington, Jan. 8, 1875, quoted in Moorfield Storey and Edward D. Emerson, *Ebenezer Rockwood Hoar, A Memoir* (Boston: Houghton Mifflin Co., 1911), p. 237.
[46] Samuel Bowles to Henry L. Dawes, Jan. 6, 1875, quoted in George S. Merriam, *The Life and Times of Samuel Bowles* (New York: The Century Co., 1885), II, 344.
[47] Jonathan M. Hildeburn to Samuel J. Randall, West Chester, Pa., Dec. 29, 1874, Randall MSS.
[48] Garfield MS Diary, Dec. 23, 1874, Garfield MSS.
[49] *Cincinnati Enquirer*, Dec. 24, 1874.

the large moderate Republican element. Both "hards" and "softs" were to be found in this group, but these men were not ideologues and were unwilling to endanger the party for what they considered an abstraction. The resumption bill would pass the House handily, the *Chicago Tribune* predicted on January 4, because the Republicans who would not vote for it on its merits would support it for reasons of party strategy. Western Republicans, confronting militant Democratic greenbackers in their home districts, believed it would help defer a showdown on the money issue. Moderate Republicans of both East and West hoped the bill would remove the disturbing money question from politics, at least until after the Presidential contest.[50]

When Congress reconvened, the Republican chiefs, anxious for quick passage, resorted to some fancy parliamentary sleight-of-hand. After encountering resistance on his Banking and Currency Committee, Chairman Horace Maynard agreed to permit amendment and debate in return for an agreement making the resumption measure the special order of business for January 7. But once the bill had been brought up he demanded an immediate vote. Dawes and Democrat Samuel J. Randall were bitingly sarcastic about Maynard's "generosity" when he agreed to permit the dissenters to record their protests in the *Congressional Record*, but party machinery functioned smoothly and the bill passed 136 to 98.[51]

The House vote, like that of the Senate, was strongly partisan, with only two Democrats supporting the measure. But Maynard was less successful than Sherman in maintaining party discipline. Twenty-two Republican Representatives, half of them easterners, voted against the bill. Nine of the twenty-two voting New England Republicans, all stubborn conservatives—including Dawes and the Hoar brothers—opposed passage. Butler, the only New England soft money man, abstained, while Kelley was one of the five middle-state Republicans who voted no. As predicted, the bill had been passed by the moderate Republicans with the Democrats and the Republican extremists opposed.

[50] *CDT*, Jan. 4, 1875.
[51] *Ibid.*, Jan. 8, 1875; *Congressional Record*, p. 319.

Whatever motives modern historians have detected, the political origin of the 1875 Resumption Act was an open secret to contemporaries. In sharp contrast to the weeks preceding the previous session, there had been little demand for new financial legislation prior to the opening of the lame-duck session in December. General public interest in finance had slackened following the veto. Although the Democrats had made capital of Grant's conservatism during the Congressional campaign, there had been little serious demand for another inflation bill. Nor were conservatives interested in stirring up another hornet's nest. Businessmen in particular, after the uncertainty of the past year, wanted financial peace. Merchants, bankers, and manufacturers alike agree, *Banker's Magazine* reported, that the "country needs rest; that the turmoil of congressional meddling with the currency should cease."[52]

Businessmen could be objective about the new measure, since they had taken no part in its passage. Generally they recognized its political function. The organs of the respectable financial community—*Banker's Magazine*, the *Financier*, and the *Commercial and Financial Chronicle*—found little to say in its favor. Central monetary management was suspect in the United States, and the conservative financial writers feared that the Resumption Act gave the Treasury a dangerous, unsupervised control of the currency system.[53] At the same time, no adequate machinery for resuming had been established. Despite its grant of discretionary powers, the law was useless. As for its immediate results, it was not at all clear whether it would expand or contract. All in all, the measure seemed to be a political trick, not to be taken at face value.[54]

These views were not confined to the financial editors. John E. Williams, President of the Metropolitan National Bank of New York, considered the resumption measure a "game of bluff" designed primarily "to make a show of cohesion in the republican party which the other side asserted did not exist"; and second-

[52] *Banker's Magazine*, xxix (January 1875), pp. 492-493.
[53] *The Financier*, vii (Jan. 16, 1875), 36-37; *Banker's Magazine*, xxix (February 1875), 65-70;

CFC, xx (Jan. 16, 1875), 49-50.
[54] *Ibid.*, xx (Feb. 20, 1875), 172-173; *Banker's Magazine*, xxix (March 1875), 710-711; Sherman, *op. cit.*, i, 519-520.

arily "to force the democrats to vote against it that the oligarchic [i.e., Administration] organs might proclaim to the world that the democrats opposed specie payments."[55] The journal of the Industrial League observed that the Republicans had proved "that they could come to agreement upon the finances by adopting a measure to which nobody is really agreed." Everyone "finds something in it he don't like, but it pleases him to think that it must be disgusting to someone else; and there is a desire at all events to get the whole subject out of the way which is temporarily gratified."[56] The measure, the *Financier* concluded, "gives no assurance whatever that resumption will be reached at the date named and . . . it is entirely disregarded by the business community in its calculations."[57]

Democrats and Liberals were, of course, quick to point out the political purposes of the new legislation. Manton Marble called it a purely partisan declaration of "not much more value . . . than to say Christmas shall fall on the 4th of July."[58] It was "Sherman's Sham,"[59] an epithet that was soon used by Democrats all over the country. Less partisan, and hence more interesting, was the attitude of the Liberals and reformers, who for all their contempt for stalwart Republicanism, would have applauded what they could accept as an honest resumption law. The new measure was "got up," observed the *Nation*, to "produce both an appearance of union where no real union exists and an appearance of doing something where nothing is done."[60] David Wells belittled the "Sherman Financial Bill" as "utterly senseless and impracticable."[61] Atkinson, who spoke for both the Liberals and a part of the Boston business community, wrote Speaker Blaine that the bill, which had then just passed the Senate, was "a dead letter already in the public estimation." "It declares for specie payment at a fixed date but makes no *operative* provision to

[55] Quoted in John G. Drew to Samuel J. Randall, Elizabeth, New Jersey, Dec. 31, 1874, Randall MSS.

[56] *Industrial Bulletin*, v (January 1875), 1.

[57] *The Financier*, VIII (Nov. 27, 1875), 358-359.

[58] Marble to Bayard, Dec. 27, 1874, quoted in Charles C. Tansill, *The Congressional Career of Thomas Francis Bayard, 1868-1885* (Washington: Georgetown University Press, 1946), p. 96, n. 118.

[59] *NYW*, Dec. 23, 1874.

[60] *Nation*, XIX (Dec. 31, 1874), 427, 432.

[61] David A. Wells, *The Cremation Theory of Specie Resumption* (New York, 1875), pp. 11, 15.

bring it about." It would "do harm rather than good because it . . . [would] not restore confidence and confidence is the one thing now needed. . . . That the bill is rubbish and a sham is the inside verdict of everyone that pretends to know anything."[62]

Such ridicule was almost universal.[63] Republican motives were too transparent for either businessmen or the general public to take the measure seriously as a solution of the nation's financial problems. Designed by the Republican Congressional leadership "as a party necessity under the whip and spur of the previous question,"[64] it contained little to attract men outside the narrow circle of Republican orthodoxy. Western Democrats, eastern Democrats, and Liberals alike held it in contempt; its only support came from the strong Republican "party" men. In New York the Administration organ, the *Times*, welcomed it as a step in the right direction.[65] Logan's paper, the *Chicago Inter-Ocean*, was even mildly enthusiastic, though for reasons the hard money *Times* would have deplored. "The bill gives the country free banking," an *Inter-Ocean* editorial noted. "Naming a day four years hence on which to resume is really an expression of opinion by the gentlemen comprising the Senate."[66]

These conflicting interpretations confirm the political success of the new law. It could unite the most diverse elements. Reformers and businessmen might cavil, but Republicans could congratulate themselves on having saved the party. As Senator Howe wrote his niece shortly after passage, "The Republican party has been scared to death. But the color is coming back. It

---

[62] Atkinson to James G. Blaine, Boston, Dec. 29, 1874, Atkinson MSS, Massachusetts Historical Society.

[63] For example: *Iron Age*, xv (Jan. 21, 1875); *New York Herald*, Dec. 24, 1874; Amasa Walker to Manton Marble, North Brookfield, Mass., Dec. 25, 1874, Marble MSS. The London *Times* of Dec. 26, 1874, called the bill, which had just passed the Senate, a measure "to provoke the laughter of all mockers," while the Washington reporter of the *Independent* bluntly referred to it as a partisan political measure condemned by "every bank

president and practical financier." See the *Times* clipping in the letter of J. H. Wilson to Benjamin Bristow, London, Dec. 26, 1874, Bristow MSS, LC; and the *Independent*, Dec. 31, 1874, p. 3.

[64] This was S. S. Cox's description during a financial debate in the following Congress. *Congressional Record*, 44 Cong., 1 sess., p. 5219.

[65] *NYT*, Dec. 21, 1874.

[66] *Chicago Inter-Ocean*, Dec. 24, 1874. At the time this editorial was written the bill had as yet passed only the upper house, hence the reference to the Senate alone.

will be all right as soon as their teeth stop chattering."[67] Eventually, the 1875 legislation did bring the country back to the gold standard, and it is this result that gives to its passage the specious appearance of a great sound money victory. But this was probably neither foreseen nor intended by most of its sponsors. Acting with largely political ends in view, the Republican moderates foisted on the nation an unwanted measure. Far from submitting meekly to the postwar business interests, the politicians acted despite the general business desire for financial quiet. The 1875 Act illustrates not the triumph of the businessman, but the ubiquity of the great American game of politics.

II

Ironically, the measure that Congress had just passed for a while threatened to produce the very trouble it was designed to prevent. Secretary Bristow, a hard money man close to the reformers, from the outset agreed with his friends that the bill was weak and unworkable,[68] and Congressmen were told during the Christmas recess that although Grant would sign it, he would request supplementary legislation to make it effective.[69] When the bill was returned with Grant's signature, it was accompanied by a recommendation that the Treasury be permitted to retire $80 million of greenbacks prior to January 1, 1879.[70] This amounted to returning to McCulloch's contraction, and Congress would not hear of it. Despite Congressional opposition, however, Bristow soon discovered how to convert the new law into the contraction measure he wanted.

Under the Act, the Secretary of the Treasury was required to retire $80 of greenbacks for each $100 of new bank notes issued. Sherman had refused to say what would be done with these retired notes, but under Bristow they were kept from circulating. Nevertheless, the process of expanding the bank-note issue prom-

---

[67] Howe to Grace Howe, Washington, Jan. 14, 1874, Howe MSS.

[68] *NYW*, Dec. 25, 1874.

[69] E. R. Hoar to J. M. Forbes, Washington, Jan. 8, 1875, quoted in Storey and Emerson, *loc. cit.*

[70] This was to be accomplished by tax changes designed to yield additional revenue out of which the $80 million might be taken. *Congressional Record*, p. 459.

ised a small increase in the total circulation[71] and from the point of view of the business expansionist, at least, would have been a net gain. But now that free banking was won it proved an empty victory. The country's growing commercial maturity since the War had made creation of a deposit for borrowers an increasingly common form for bank loans. National bank deposits grew 30 per cent between 1865 and 1875, and based on the new practice, the state banking system, which had been eclipsed after 1865, enjoyed a great revival in the early '70's.[72] The new importance of checking accounts made circulation less necessary and profitable. It encouraged the national banks to sell federal bonds for the sake of the high premiums they had begun to command, and—as permitted by the June 1874 Banking Act—retire their notes.[73] By November 1875, bond sales had led to voluntary surrender of over $20 million of circulation.[74] New institutions in the West and South, first under the redistribution feature of the 1874 measure, and then under the new free banking clause, might have made up this loss; but the response to the new law proved disappointing. With business depressed, banks were not profitable, and neither measure gave rise to more than a small amount of new notes.

To make matters worse, Bristow's interpretation of the 1875 Act served simultaneously to contract the *greenback* circulation. The Resumption Act clause requiring a proportionate withdrawal of greenbacks for new bank notes, meant, he claimed, that regardless of the *net* change in bank note volume he must continue to withdraw $80 of greenbacks for each $100 of new bank notes issued under the Act. Consequently, the limited issues that new western and southern institutions acquired served to reduce the

[71] Much of this would be offset by the reserves which the new banks, like the old, were required to keep against note issue.

[72] The increase in national bank deposits was from $695 million to $897 million. State banks grew in number from 325 to 1,260 between 1870 and 1875; their deposits from a minuscule $70 million to $1.1 billion. U. S. Bureau of the Census, *Historical Statistics of the United*
States: *Colonial Times to 1957* (Washington: Government Printing Office, 1960), p. 627, series X56; p. 621, series X64; p. 629, series X78.

[73] U. S. Treasury, *Annual Report for 1876*, p. xxiii.

[74] U. S. Treasury, *Annual Report for 1875*, pp. xxiv-xxv. Between 1874 and 1877, *total* national bank circulation declined from $339 million to $290 million. *Historical Statistics*, p. 627, series X61.

total greenback issue.[75] By the summer of 1875, the 1874 banking law, the Resumption Act, and Benjamin Bristow had together managed to contract the total currency by $13 million, half of Richardson's reissue.

The unexpected reduction coincided with falling prices, profits, and employment, as the depression of the '70's tightened its grip on the nation. Railroad construction, which had reached almost 7500 miles in 1872, fell to 1600 in 1875.[76] Measured by total business failures, 1875 was far worse than the panic year 1873.[77] With the decline in railroad building came a sharp drop in rail orders.[78] Coal production dropped five million tons and pig iron production fell off a half-million tons between 1873 and 1875.[79]

The depression was particularly severe in the industrial areas of Ohio and Pennsylvania. In the coal and iron regions of the Mahoning Valley of northeastern Ohio, the mining areas of the Hocking Valley, and the industrial regions adjoining the Ohio River, production declined sharply. The year 1875 was "one of great uncertainty" in the Ohio iron producing areas, with prices for No. 1 "hot blast charcoal" down from $34 a ton in January to $28 in August 1875.[80] In the mining regions, coal lands worth $10 million in 1872 had fallen to $6 million by 1877.[81] "The iron and coal trade," wrote an official of one of the largest Youngstown rolling mills in December 1874, "is in a state of terrible depression, great numbers of Iron workers and coal miners being absolutely without work." It would be "a bitter winter for

[75] Between passage of the Resumption Act in January and Bristow's December 1875 *Report*, the $10.9 million of new bank notes issued under the free banking clause had served to retire $8.7 million of greenbacks. U. S. Treasury, *Annual Report for 1875*, pp. xxiv-xxv. For a description of Bristow's policy see the *Nation*, xxi (Dec. 2, 1875), 349.

[76] *Historical Statistics*, p. 428, series Q43.

[77] There were 5,183 failures in 1873; in 1875 there were 7,740. N. S. B. Gras and Henrietta M. Larson, *Casebook in American Business History* (New York: Appleton-Century-Crofts, Inc., 1939), p. 723.

[78] Rendigs Fels, "American Business Cycles, 1865-1879," *American Economic Review*, xli, No. 3 (June 1951), 347-348.

[79] U. S. National Monetary Commission, *Statistics for the United States, 1867-1909*, p. 13.

[80] Ohio Secretary of State, *Annual Report for 1875*, p. 427.

[81] Ohio Bureau of Labor Statistics, *Annual Report for 1877*, pp. 116-117.

thousands" unless something were done.[82] In the eastern Pennsylvania anthracite districts a general wage slash, forced on the
operators by declining prices, precipitated a six months' strike
marked by flare-ups of violence.[83] Hard times in the Pittsburgh
iron region erupted into an industry-wide lockout, which thoroughly demoralized the iron trade of the western part of the
state.[84]

These conditions played into the hands of the soft money interests in both states. In Ohio it produced a resurgence of the
Democratic greenbackism which had subsided since the 1871
gubernatorial defeat. In 1873, in a campaign emphasizing
personalities rather than finance Democrats had elected to the
Governorship "Rise Up" William Allen, a relic of the Jacksonian
era.[85] Under normal circumstances there would have been little
incentive to take up the greenback again. But the depression,
joined with the immediate political situation in 1875, shifted attention to the money question and made Ohio once more the
nation's financial cockpit.

The appeal of easy money as a relief measure in Ohio would
seem obvious, particularly since labor spokesmen had helped
fan the soft money excitement preceding the Inflation Bill session. Yet, strangely, for months after the veto, labor nationally
was passive; labor editors barely noticed the Resumption Act
at the time of passage. This indifference began to vanish by the
spring of 1875, and the Republican measure soon came under
heavy attack as the chief obstacle to recovery. Leading the assault in Ohio was Clevelander Robert Schilling, President of the
Industrial Congress. Schilling, who had imbibed his money views
from the labor reformers,[86] tried in June to get the Cleveland
Democracy to take a stand against the Resumption Act. He failed
with the local leaders[87] and soon turned to the state convention.

[82] Brown, Bonnell and Company to James A. Garfield, Youngstown, Dec. 16, 1874, Garfield MSS.

[83] NYDT, June 4, 1875; Iron Age, xv (April 1, 1875).

[84] Ibid. (March 25, 1875).

[85] Reginald C. McGrane, William Allen: A Study in Western Democracy (Columbus: The Ohio Archeological and Historical Socie-

ty, 1925), ch. viii. Only during the last week or two of the campaign, following the panic, was finance mentioned by the Democrats, and then by Thurman, not Allen himself.

[86] See above, ch. vi.

[87] The Cleveland Democracy explicitly endorsed hard money instead. CDT, June 13, 1875.

Shortly before this assembled, he wrote the *Cleveland Leader* that the wage earners of Ohio would never be "caught by the shining but hollow bait of specie resumption," and warned the Democrats that meaningless pronouncements on finance would alienate thousands of the state's labor voters.[88]

In his attempt to sell the Resumption Act issue to the Democrats Schilling had the active support of the younger Ewing. As usual, the latter's motives were simultaneously political and entrepreneurial. He was still trying to advance his political career by an alliance with labor that would give him control of the Ohio Democracy. Murat Halstead was probably right when he warned the conservative Democrats that if given a chance the Ewing group would "occupy and possess" the Ohio Democracy and use it in a bid for the Presidency in 1876.[89] But Ewing also hoped to save his family from a business disaster. The Ewings had been badly hurt by the crash. With large investments in railroads— including the Chesapeake and Ohio, one of the roads which defaulted[90]—they were hard pressed, and during the remainder of the decade fought a losing battle to avoid bankruptcy. Ewing sincerely believed he could save the family fortunes by a timely repeal of the Resumption Act. "If that infernal law were repealed or amended," he later explained, the family "coal and iron lands would sell at once."[91]

Ewing and Schilling together represented enterprise and labor, two powerful interests whose demands the Democrats could not easily ignore. But there were also immediate political factors working powerfully for an anti-Resumption Act campaign. During the previous state legislative session, John J. Geghan, an Irish Democratic member of the lower house, had introduced a bill authorizing Catholic chaplains at state hospitals and penal institutions. Catholics had reputedly put pressure on the Demo-

---

[88] *WA*, June 19, 1875. There is an interesting letter in the David A. Wells MSS, LC, from an acquaintance and apparently fellow countryman of Schilling's, which describes the latter's financial views and those of Ohio labor in general. See W. Vingst[?] to David A. Wells, Cincinnati, June 8, 1874. See also *Cooper's Monthly Journal*, VI (June

1875), 157-158.

[89] *Cincinnati Commercial*, July 15, 1875. See also the *Cleveland Leader*, Oct. 7, 1875.

[90] Thomas Ewing, Jr., to Charles Ewing, Lancaster, Ohio, Oct. 29, 1873, Ewing MSS, LC.

[91] Thomas Ewing, Jr., to Charles Ewing, Lancaster, Aug. 13, 1877, *ibid.*

cratic General Assembly to secure passage of the bill. Together with an insistent Catholic demand for state aid to parochial schools, the Geghan bill had aroused the latent nativism of the state's Protestant majority and revived the perennial "No Popery" cry as a major political issue.[92] At their convention the Republicans happily seized on the Catholic issue. Their platform denounced any attempt to break down the wall between church and state, and upheld free, public, tax supported education.[93] Turning from Judge Alphonso Taft, a man unpopular with the party bigots,[94] they nominated for Governor Rutherford B. Hayes, who had already served two terms in the state house. It was clear to most observers that they intended to "make the main fight" on the religious question.[95]

The incendiary religious issue, added to hard times, made the Democrats receptive to the Ewing-Schilling program at their Columbus convention. To offset the anti-Catholic attack, they permitted Ewing and the labor group,[96] aided by Governor Allen, to make contraction the major campaign issue. The platform read to the delegates did not mention the Resumption Act specifically, but condemned the Administration's financial policy, particularly Bristow's unauthorized contraction. By forcing resumption, the Republicans had brought "disaster to the business of the country." The Treasury's deflationary policies must be "abandoned, and . . . the volume of currency be made and kept equal to the wants of trade, leaving the restoration of legal tenders to par with gold to be brought about by promoting the industries of the people, and not by destroying them." In addition, the platform repeated the old Pendletonian slogans about the dangers of a money monopoly and urged withdrawing the national bank cur-

[92] NYT, Aug. 7, 1875; Harry Barnard, Rutherford B. Hayes and His America (Indianapolis: The Bobbs-Merrill Co., 1954), pp. 272-273.

[93] NYDT, June 3, 1875.

[94] Taft's unpopularity resulted from a decision he had handed down as Judge of Cincinnati's Superior Court, upholding the right of the Cincinnati School Board to prohibit use of the Protestant Bible in the city schools. Lewis Alexander Leonard, Life of Alphonso Taft (New York: Hawke Publishing Co., 1920), pp. 128, 145-146; Barnard, op. cit., pp. 273-274.

[95] NYDT, June 3, 1875.

[96] In addition to Schilling, Martin A. Foran, a predecessor of Schilling's as President of the Coopers' International, now City Attorney of Cleveland, was actively working for a Democratic greenback plank. See Cleveland Leader, June 15, 1875.

rency.[97] There was no serious opposition to the plank. Conservatives like Allen Thurman, who might have resisted it, submitted meekly out of fear of destroying the party's only chance of victory.[98]

With the campaign issue settled, the convention renominated Governor Allen, and in another bid for the labor vote, chose Sam Cary, the labor reform Congressman, as his running mate.[99]

The Ohio canvass became the first political test of the Resumption Act. From the outset the Democrats made finance the keynote of their campaign. At the giant Democratic ratification meeting on June 17, Ewing told his listeners that the Democracy was gathered at Columbus to launch more than a local political contest. The Republicans would concentrate on state issues and play on religious bigotry, but the Democrats knew that Ohio was only the preliminary for the Presidential race and they must turn to national questions. The Republicans had failed woefully to provide the country with adequate government, but nowhere had their policy been so bankrupt as in the area of finance. Spreading his net wide to capture businessmen as well as other economic groups, Ewing rehearsed the failures of past Republican financial policy. Contraction had laid an immense burden of debt on individuals, corporations, and local governments, and under this burden "the industries of the nation are being crushed, the laborers brought to poverty, the producing capitalists to bankruptcy."

Now the resumption measure hung like a sword over the heads of the "producing classes." Great Britain had attempted to resume specie payments in 1819 at a time when her industries were prosperous, her trade balance favorable, and gold at a premium of only 3 per cent. The attempt produced "wide spread ruin through all branches of industry and trade," and was soon abandoned. In the face of this lesson America was being "led blind fold to specie payment," with gold "at seventeen per cent. premium and rising," "industries already bankrupt," and "the

[97] Annual Cyclopedia for 1875, pp. 606-607.
[98] Michael Kerr to Manton Marble, Manitou Springs, Colorado, Sept. 1, 1875, Marble MSS.
[99] Annual Cyclopedia for 1875, p. 607.

balance of trade steadily against us." Specie payment meant contraction of $400 million, and would involve us in "general and inevitable bankruptcy and ruin."[100]

As the campaign gathered momentum, Ewing carried this theme out to the hustings, hammering home his attack in every industrial region of the state. At Ironton he specifically arraigned the Resumption Act for the prevailing distress.[101] The free banking clause—"the tub thrown to Morton, Logan and such other Western or Southern Republicans as demanded an increase of the currency"—had been the instrument for contracting the circulation more than $16 million in the first 75 days of the law's operation. "Capitalists know that if the contraction policy be pursued the bottom is not yet reached, and will not be for years after resumption; that most industrial pursuits . . . cannot survive the strain of the further contraction necessary to resumption in 1879."[102] Later in the campaign, Ewing toured the towns of Shawnee, Lancaster, Galion, Upper Sandusky, Circleville, Wilmington, and Tiffen, debating the money issue with Stewart Woodford of New York, an imported Republican speaker. At Wilmington, Ewing's rebuttal was a close paraphrase of his father's earliest soft money statement, emphasizing the currency needs of the "active young business men" on whose broad shoulders rested the nation's economic future.[103]

If Ewing aimed his words primarily at the state's industrialists, the Democrats, generally, did not neglect the labor vote. Cary spoke to large working-class audiences in the industrial and

[100] *Speeches of Governor William Allen, Hon. Geo. H. Pendleton, Hon. A. G. Thurman, Gen. Thomas Ewing, Gen. Samuel F. Cary . . . before the Democratic Ratification Meeting . . .* (Columbus, 1875), pp. 9-10. Pendleton, too, made a point of Republican finance, which had "paralyzed all enterprise and checked all adventures." *Ibid.*, p. 6.

[101] Ewing with some exaggeration later claimed that this speech was the first public allusion in the West to the Resumption Act. It is the point of this chapter that the 1875 Ohio campaign, and Ewing in par-

ticular, helped make the Act notorious; but Shilling, at least, had preceded Ewing. See Ewing to James R. Doolittle, Lancaster, Ohio, March 28, 1876, Doolittle MSS, State Hist. Soc. of Wisc.

[102] [Thomas Ewing, Jr.], *Speech . . . Delivered at Ironton, Ohio, July 24, 1875* (Columbus, 1875), pp. 4-10.

[103] [Thomas Ewing, Jr., and Stewart L. Woodford], *Joint Discussion Between Gen. Thomas Ewing of Ohio and Gov. Stewart L. Woodford of New York on the Finance Question* (Columbus, 1876), p. 9.

mining regions.[104] Richard Trevellick and Moses Field came to Ohio and made effective appeals for Allen and Cary in the Hocking Valley and Ohio River industrial towns.[105] The *Workingman's Advocate*, while unhappy over the failure of the Democrats to adopt the interconvertible bond, did concede that they had taken "a long step in the *Right* direction," and urged its Ohio readers to support the Democratic cause.[106]

The situation in the farm regions was less promising. To be sure, several soft money farm leaders had already been frightened by the Resumption Act. Shortly after its passage in the Senate, Noonan had described it as "a corrupt combination between the Republican bullionists and Republican bankers who have united upon this financial monstrosity for the purpose of saving the Republican party from destruction."[107] Olleman, too, had expressed serious misgivings concerning the new measure.[108] At the February 1875 National Grange session the Maryland State Grange tried unsuccessfully to get the Act condemned.[109] In Ohio itself, however, though Hooton of the Illinois Farmers' Association actively campaigned for the Democrats,[110] and Noonan and Donnelly gave their editorial support,[111] slow progress was made in overcoming rural conservatism. Important farm journals, such as the *Ohio Farmer*, refused to support paper money.[112] The Grangers, too, were skeptical of the Democratic platform.[113] Not even the sanguine Ewing expected the Demo-

---

[104] *NYDT*, Sept. 14, 1875; *NYT*, Aug. 13, 1875; Aug. 18, 1875; Aug. 26, 1875; Sept. 18, 1875.

[105] *WA*, Sept. 4, 1875; *IA*, Sept. 11, 1875.

[106] *WA*, June 26, 1875; July 10, 1875; Aug. 9, 1875.

[107] *IA*, Jan. 2, 1875.

[108] *Indiana Farmer*, Dec. 31, 1874.

[109] It was tabled by a vote of 18 to 13, on the grounds that the currency was rapidly becoming a political question and hence outside the proper sphere of the Patrons. National Grange, *Proceedings of the Ninth Meeting*, pp. 175-177.

[110] Hooton to editor of *Industrial Age*, Dayton, Ohio, Oct. 3, 1875; *IA*, Oct. 9, 1875. S. M. Smith may also have campaigned for Allen. See J. A. Noonan to Joseph H. Osborn, Chicago, Sept. 25, 1875, Osborn MSS, State Hist. Soc. of Wisc.

[111] *IA*, Aug. 7, 1875; J. A. Noonan to Donnelly, Chicago, Sept. 16, 1875, Donnelly MSS, Minnesota Historical Society; *AM*, July 19, 1875.

[112] *The Ohio Farmer*, July 17, 1875.

[113] See J. H. Pallerston [?] (Purchasing Agent of the Mercer County Patrons of Husbandry) to R. B. Hayes, St. Marys, Ohio, Sept. 14, 1875, Hayes MSS.

crats to do more than hold their own in the purely agricultural counties.[114]

Despite the gray areas, by mid-campaign the Democrats were feeling confident of victory. Both labor and "producing capital" seemed to be rallying to Allen: "A great revolution is going on in . . . the manufacturing and mining districts," wrote George W. Morgan.[115] "Businessmen, generally, are awakening to the fact that the real issue is between dead capital on the one side, and active capital and labor on the other. They are beginning to understand that specie resumption and bankruptcy mean the same thing. Our platform is therefore freed from unmeaning phrases and the consequence is that thousands of business men are uniting with us on business grounds." Morgan reported that Henry Blanding of Zanesville, one of the leading ironmasters of southeastern Ohio, was canvassing the state for Allen. The Blanding brothers had always been Republican, and their defection would "bring . . . a powerful following of men who think as they do."[116] In Mahoning County, it was said, "leading Republicans engaged in the iron business" would rally to the Democrats.[117] In mid-September Sam Cary was prophesying large Democratic gains in the coal and iron districts. One Lawrence County "capitalist with 300 workers" who had been obliged by the hard times to shut down would vote Democratic this year. So would his men.[118]

Eastern observers on the scene confirmed these optimistic reports. A New York correspondent, observing in the Mahoning Valley, noted that the Democratic rallies were composed largely of "the rolling mill owners who want more money and the workmen whose wages are reduced to $1 a day." The Democrats could expect the votes of the unemployed and the "manufacturers and businessmen who had incurred risks, had notes to pay, and

[114] Thomas Ewing, Jr., to Samuel J. Randall, Lancaster, Ohio, Sept. 14, 1875, Randall MSS.

[115] Morgan, a former Union officer, had been the Democratic gubernatorial nominee in 1865.

[116] Morgan to Samuel J. Randall,

Mt. Vernon, Ohio, Aug. 19, 1875, Randall MSS.

[117] George W. Morgan to William Allen, Cleveland, Ohio, July 4, 1875, Allen MSS, LC.

[118] NYDT, Sept. 14, 1875.

look[ed] to inflation or speculation as their only hope to un-load."[119]

Allen's victory seemed assured when the Democrats of Penn-sylvania took up the anti-contraction cause at their September convention. As early as July there were reports that the Ohio Democrats would be discreetly pushing an anti-resumption plank at the Erie meeting,[120] and by the eve of the convention soft money had won considerable support among the Pennsylvanians. The western delegates were said to be almost to a man for an end to contraction, and they were seconded by a "considerable number of delegates from the lumber regions along the upper Susquehanna and from the coal and iron districts." Together these groups could probably command a majority of the conven-tion, though the conservatives who controlled the party ma-chinery might be able to offset soft money strength by shrewd maneuvering.[121]

When the convention finally assembled, political circumstances in the shape of a serious factional conflict favored the soft money men. On one side was the "Ring," a clique of corrupt politicians affiliated, through State Senator William Wallace, with the Penn-sylvania Railroad. On the other was the group of honest govern-ment men led by Samuel J. Randall, a veteran Congressional Democrat who was eager to win the Speakership of the incoming Forty-fourth Congress.[122] A third group, as the New York press had noted, was composed of delegates from western and indus-trial counties who supported some version of the Ohio platform.

At Erie the "Ring" threw its support to the anti-contractionists in order to defeat Randall's gubernatorial candidate.[123] After first rejecting a soft money plank, the Resolutions Committee shifted ground and submitted an almost verbatim copy of the Columbus platform. In the open convention the platform was pushed through over determined opposition, and the Pennsylvania De-mocracy went on record against the Resumption Act.[124]

[119] *Ibid.*, Sept. 13, 1875; Sept. 21, 1875.
[120] *NYT*, July 19, 1875.
[121] *NYDT*, Sept. 8, 1875.
[122] Albert V. House, "Men, Mor-als, and Manipulation in the Penn-sylvania Democracy of 1875," *Penn-sylvania History*, xxiii, No. 2 (April 1956), 251ff.
[123] *Ibid.*, p. 262; *CDT*, Sept. 11, 1875.
[124] *NYW*, Sept. 10, 1875.

The campaign in Pennsylvania closely duplicated the Ohio pattern. In the Keystone state, too, the Democratic platform seemed to attract the "industrial classes." Working-class support, however, came only through the spontaneous endorsement of individuals. Organized labor, represented by the Knights of Labor, was at best equivocal on the money question. The Knights originated in Pennsylvania, having been founded in 1869 by Uriah Stephens to advance the interests of the Philadelphia garment cutters. By 1875 much of its strength was concentrated in Pittsburgh where John M. Davis, editor of the *National Labor Tribune* was the union's western organizer. Unfortunately for the Democrats, Davis blew hot and cold on soft money, and although he finally came down on the right side, he never endorsed the Democratic ticket.[125] Nevertheless, as in Ohio, laboring men seemed ready to vote Democratic. The coal, the iron, and the lumber regions, it was reported shortly after the Erie convention, were all solidly anti-resumption. In the anthracite counties both capital and labor would be found in the soft money ranks. The same was true of the iron districts along the Lehigh and Schuylkill Rivers in the eastern part of the state. In the lumber regions, a report ran, "the cry 'more greenbacks' carries everything before it, the lumberman believing that inflation will set everybody to building houses and thus bring their product into brisk demand." In the soft coal regions, "wherever you find a coal miner, whether he be owner, boss or digger in the pit, you find an inflationist." The iron and steel district of Pittsburgh, the petroleum counties south of Erie—these, too, were soft money. Only in the agricultural south-central part of the state and in Philadelphia was there strong hard money sentiment, and even in the state's metropolis, "while the mercantile and financial classes . . . [are] solid for a specie basis, the manufacturers are two to one the other way."[126]

The Erie convention gave a further lift to Democratic hopes in Ohio. Ewing was "delighted" with the action of the Pennsylvanians and believed it would "greatly strengthen" the common cause in Ohio. "We will carry Ohio, I am sure," he wrote Randall. Still, he admitted, there were hazards remaining. The re-

---

[125] See *National Labor Tribune,* July 3, 1875; July 10, 1875; July 31, 1875; Aug. 7, 1875.   [126] *NYDT,* Sept. 18, 1875; *NYT,* Oct. 17, 1875.

ligious issue would lose the Democrats votes. Losses might also be expected in most of the Western Reserve, and in Cleveland. Democratic gains would come largely in the iron counties. The whole contest would turn on the money issue. "If there were no disturbing questions," he declared, "I would confidently expect to carry Ohio by 30 to 40 thousand."[127] By late September, Washington observers, too, were predicting an Allen victory.[128]

This was to be the Democratic high-water mark. The Republicans had indeed been thrown off balance by their opponents' attack. Hayes and other leaders had been reluctant to defend the party's financial record and had been cagey on the Resumption Act.[129] At one point they even imported Kelley to allay fears among businessmen of the party's intentions.[130] But Republican courage returned as national support for Hayes began to materialize. With each day it became clearer that the Ohio contest might have repercussions far beyond the borders of the state. All sorts of dangerous consequences were predicted by conservatives, Republicans and Democrats alike, if Allen won, from wild Congressional inflation to a greenback President in 1876.[131] The New York Democracy saw Allen as a major threat to Governor Tilden's Presidential aspirations.[132] The reformers were particularly alarmed. Murat Halstead, though he had few illusions about Republican courage or reliability, thought the Democrats, hopelessly benighted on the currency, deserved defeat.[133] Outside the

---

[127] Ewing to Randall, Lancaster, Ohio, Sept. 14, 1875, Randall MSS.
[128] Garfield MS Diary, Sept. 22, 1875, Garfield MSS.
[129] John Quincy Smith to John Sherman, Oakland, Ohio, Oct. 18, 1875, and Nov. 12, 1875, Sherman MSS; Edward D. Mansfield to James Williams, Morrow, Ohio, August [?] 1875, Hayes MSS.
[130] (Kelley, of course, had voted against the Resumption Act.) On the incident see Hayes to John Sherman, Fremont, Ohio, July 5, 1875, Sherman MSS. For Kelley's later explanation of his role in the Ohio canvass see *Congressional Record*, 45 Cong., 1 sess., p. 385.
[131] *The Financier*, VII (Sept. 25, 1875), 212-213; *Cincinnati Com-*

mercial, Sept. 13, 1875; Thomas Bayard to Samuel J. Randall, Wilmington, Del., Sept. 21, 1875, Randall MSS.
[132] James E. Broome to Samuel J. Tilden, Sept. 13, 1875, Tilden MSS, New York Public Library; Ellicott Evans to David A. Wells, Clinton, N.Y., Dec. 17, 1875, Wells MSS.
[133] Murat Halstead to Carl Schurz, Cincinnati, Sept. 10, 1875, Schurz MSS. Roeliff Brinkerhoff, a prominent Ohio Liberal, believed the "only healthy prescription for the Ohio Democracy" was "defeat in heroic doses." See Brinkerhoff to David A. Wells, Mansfield, Ohio, July 27, 1875, and Sept. 29, 1875, Wells MSS.

state, the reformers, who had had nothing but contempt for Sherman's bill, now began to see the measure in a new light. If nothing else they began to love it for the enemies it had made. William Grosvenor, a Missouri associate of Schurz's, came to Ohio and stumped for the Republicans and hard money.[134] Schurz himself was dragged back from a European visit by the entreaties of Halstead, Charles Francis Adams, Jr., and other Liberals, who knew Schurz's power to charm his fellow German-Americans and the educated, independent voters.[135]

Shouting support from the sidelines were the forces of organized Protestantism. According to Princeton Theological Seminary's Lyman Atwater, it was "scarcely possible to conceive a greater national catastrophe" than the repeal of the Resumption Act. Making an easy leap from repeal to inflation, he saw an Allen victory as a threat to "public morality," to the "cause of religion in all its departments," and even to the stability of the social order. Allen was close to the labor reformers who were "constantly invading the rights of capital and claiming a redistribution of the latter in some form among those now destitute of it."[136] "We are not blind to the dangers that beset this country from this inflation madness," Lyman Abbott wrote in the *Christian Union*, "but we must indulge the hope that the people of Ohio will resist and defeat it."[137] In Ohio itself the Protestant clergy rallied to Hayes. At Oberlin, the College, the Theological seminary, and the churches were all supporting the Republicans.[138] Ohio students at Princeton Theological Seminary told Hayes they were praying for his success.[139]

Some time in late August the Republicans themselves began to

[134] *Pittsburgh Daily Dispatch,* Aug. 13, 1875.

[135] George Hoadly to Carl Schurz, Cincinnati, Sept. 24, 1875, Schurz MSS; Frederic Bancroft (ed.), *Speeches, Correspondence and Political Papers of Carl Schurz* (New York: G. P. Putnam's Sons, 1913), III, 157, 161; Henry Adams to Charles Milnes Gaskell, Beverly Farms, Mass., Oct. 4, 1875; Worthington C. Ford (ed.), *Letters of Henry Adams, 1858-1891* (Boston: Houghton Mifflin Co., 1930), p.

272. See also M. F. Force to R. B. Hayes, Court House, [Ohio?], July 13, 1875, Hayes MSS.

[136] *Presbyterian Quarterly and Princeton Review*, IV (1875), 721ff.

[137] *Christian Union,* XII (Oct. 6, 1875), 282. See also *Watchman and Reflector,* LVI (Aug. 26, 1875).

[138] [E. M. Leonard] to *Workingman's Advocate*, Oberlin, Ohio, Oct. 14, 1875; WA, Oct. 23, 1875.

[139] John A. Ewalt to R. B. Hayes, Princeton, N. J., Sept. 13, 1875, Hayes MSS.

see that evading the financial issue would ensure Allen's victory and only transfer the resumption question to the national arena, subjecting the party once more to dangerous internal strains. The Ohio contest now seemed the point to dig in and confront the soft money forces with a united stand on the resumption measure. Republican stalwarts were soon hurrying into the state to enter the fray. Boutwell used his prestige as former Treasury head to bolster the Republican campaign. Senator Dawes, John Ingalls of Kansas, and Congressman Eugene Hale of Maine stumped the state for Hayes. Even Morton, whose party regularity had by now overcome his recent principles, spoke for Hayes and sound money.[140] The Republicans, Ewing reported in mid-September, were "spending money freely" to support their "great effort."[141] "The whole power of the Administration was used against us," one Ohio Democrat later recalled. Never before had he seen such an outpouring of energy in a local contest.[142] Local Republicans regained confidence and for the first time turned to face the currency issue squarely. Soon Hayes, former Governor Edward Noyes, Sherman, Judge Taft, Garfield, and other Ohio Republicans were striking out boldly against the "rag baby."[143]

Democratic prospects faded as the contest entered its last weeks and the immense Republican effort began to tell. On September 27 Schurz made his first campaign address to a crowd that overflowed Cincinnati's Turner Hall. In quick succession he made six more speeches, both in English and German, to large and enthusiastic audiences.[144] Republican mass meetings in various parts of the state became ever more exuberant as election day approached. One at Warren, in the Reserve, was attended by some 25 thousand Ohioans who listened to 15 brass bands blaring patriotic music; cheered speeches by Noyes, Ben Wade, and Taft; goggled at maneuvering artillery and fire companies;

[140] *NYDT*, Sept. 18, 1875; *NYT*, Oct. 6, 1875; *Nation*, xxi (Aug. 12, 1875), 93.

[141] Ewing to Samuel J. Randall, Lancaster, Ohio, Sept. 14, 1875, Randall MSS.

[142] Milton I. Southard to Randall, Zanesville, Ohio, Nov. 15, 1875, *ibid.*

[143] *NYDT*, Sept. 4, 1875; Oct. 6, 1875; *CDT*, Sept. 6, 1875.

[144] *Ibid.*, Sept. 28, 1875; Oct. 5, 1875; *NYT*, Oct. 1, 1875; Carl Schurz, *The Reminiscences of Carl Schurz* (New York: The McClure Co., 1908), ii, 363-364.

and marched in procession carrying banners inscribed "In Hayes we Trust, In Allen we Bust," and "Allen and Cary, Not a Vote Nary." It was, a reporter wrote, one of the most colossal affairs in the political history of the state.[145]

The rest of the Hayes campaigners, both the imported and the domestic varieties, were out in force in the weeks before the election. The campaign entered a new phase as the Republicans and Liberals, playing on middle-class fears and religious conservatism, turned the anti-contraction platform of their opponents into a wild inflation scheme threatening capital, property, and social stability. "Inflation means the repudiation of all debts public and private, the utter destruction of credit, and a long lapse toward barbarism";[146] "a vote for the Democratic ticket is encouragement . . . to communist revolution";[147] the Democratic platform was "a bare faced bid for the communistic elements of the state";[148] every man with a house or land mortgage who voted for Allen and inflation voted for foreclosure of that mortgage.[149]

The "inflationists" were accused bluntly of inciting class war. Cary's speeches were "calculated to do the greatest possible mischief in stirring up strife between what he is pleased to call 'classes' of the people."[150] The Democratic campaign reminded the *Cincinnati Gazette* of the French Revolution, "when such men as Cary, Ewing, Pendleton and Kelley rose to the surface . . . appealing to the masses against property and capital."[151] The Hayes papers, now that the Republicans had stopped running from the money question, made much of Kelley's supposedly intemperate address to the ironmasters at Ironton. Kelley was accused of wishing "to set up a division of classes, to divide the laboring class from the rest, and to persuade the working men that their interests [are] hostile to the rest."[152] In its issue of August 9, Halstead's *Commercial* featured a four-column Nast cartoon depicting Kelley releasing a "rag baby" jack-in-the-box

[145] *CDT*, Sept. 24, 1875.

[146] *Cincinnati Commercial*, Sept. 12, 1875.

[147] *Cincinnati Daily Gazette*, Oct. 12, 1875.

[148] C. E. Henry to James A. Garfield, Pond Station, Ohio, Aug. 8, 1875, Garfield MSS.

[149] *Cleveland Leader*, Oct. 5, 1875.

[150] *Cincinnati Commercial*, Aug. 4, 1875.

[151] *Cincinnati Daily Gazette*, Aug. 4, 1875.

[152] *Ibid.*, Sept. 7, 1875.

as he brandished "a bullionist heart" on a spear; surrounding his head was inscribed "Vive la Guillotine," "Tremble Tyrants," "The Sans Culottes are coming," and "more greenbacks or death."[153]

Taking their cue, perhaps, from the clergy, the Republicans skillfully played upon all the social and religious prejudices that permeated late nineteenth-century, midwestern America. The Democrats were disreputable, dishonest, and immoral; Cary was guilty of "dirty harangues" in one of which, it was alleged, he charged the daughters of "rich men" with "curvature of morals."[154] Hayes asserted that "overtrading and fast living" always went with the sort of financial views held by the Democrats.[155] The Democracy, Schurz told his Cincinnati audience, was attempting to force the state of Ohio to endorce a financial policy "which, if followed by the National Government . . . would make our political and business life more than ever a hot-bed of gambling and corruption, and plunge the country into all those depths of moral . . . bankruptcy and ruin . . . which never fails [*sic*] to follow a course so utterly demented in its wickedness." To entrust to any government the power to increase or decrease the national currency at will, as the inflationists intended, would have disastrous consequences. "The private fortune of every citizen is placed at the mercy of the government's arbitrary pleasure" by such a course. No business venture would be safe, no contract secure: only speculators and gamblers would gain. "The rings would thrive and honest men would pay the cost."[156]

By the last days of the contest the Democrats began to lose confidence. Increasingly beset by the foot-dragging of the hard money group led by Thurman,[157] secretly undermined by the

---

[153] *Cincinnati Commercial*, Aug. 9, 1875.

[154] *Ibid.*, Aug. 8, 1875.

[155] *Cincinnati Daily Gazette*, Aug. 2, 1875.

[156] *CDT*, Sept. 28, 1875. What passed for satire in this simple age was also used by the Republicans. The humorist, David R. Locke, nationally known under his pseudonym, Petroleum V. Nasby, composed a set of letters from "Confederit X Roads," ridiculing the Ohio Democrats. These circulated in both Ohio and Pennsylvania. See Petroleum V. Nasby, *Inflation at the Crossroads, Being a History of the Rise and Fall of the Onlimited Trust and Confidence Company, of Confederit X Roads* (New York: American News Co., 1875).

[157] Thurman, a Presidential aspirant who inclined to hard money, was placed in a peculiar dilemma by the Democratic platform. He could not afford to break with his own party, but neither could he risk an Allen victory, which would deliv-

Tildenites who were reported "putting money in the fight . . . on the wrong side,"[158] the Allen men sent urgent appeals to their Pennsylvania brethren. They dangled the Speakership of the House before Randall. He could expect the solid support of the Ohio Democratic delegation when the new Congress opened if he could mobilize the Pennsylvania Democracy for Allen.[159] Randall had been maneuvering for the Speakership at least since March[160] and eagerly accepted. By the end of September a long list of Pennsylvanians had taken the stump for Allen in Ohio.[161]

Aid came too late. Although the first returns received on October 13 were inconclusive, by the 16th Hayes's victory was clear. But the results were close; only 5,000 votes separated the candidates out of a total of almost 600,000 cast.[162]

The Pennsylvania results duplicated those of Ohio. The contest had gotten off to a slow start. Both sides believed the race would be determined by the early October vote in Ohio, and the result was a sluggish, lackadaisical campaign.[163] Allen's defeat might have been expected to rouse the Democrats to a new sense of urgency. Instead, it destroyed whatever will to win they possessed. The various factions immediately took to squabbling. The Randall reformer wing considered Allen's defeat a repudiation of the Columbus platform and urged shifting the campaign emphasis to honest government and

---

er the party into the hands of the Ewing group. During the campaign, Thurman cursed the greenbackers in private, but temporized in public, at one point getting into hot water when his candid opinion of the Columbus platform leaked out. Even Pendleton, despite his earlier enthusiasm, set about quietly undermining the Allen campaign. *NYDT*, Sept. 18, 1875; *Cleveland Leader*, Aug. 20, 1875; C. W. Wooley to Thomas Bayard, Aug. 14, 1875, in Tansill, *op. cit.*, p. 105; Bayard to Manton Marble, Wilmington, Del., Aug. 19, 1875, Marble MSS.

[158] A. M. Gibson to Samuel J. Randall, Washington, Sept. 21, 1875, Randall MSS.

[159] John G. Thompson to Randall, Columbus, Sept. 15, 1875; Sept. 29,

1875; Oct. 4, 1875; A. M. Gibson to Randall, Washington, Sept. 21, 1875, *ibid.*

[160] See Thomas MacDonnell to Randall, Harrisburg, Pa., March 3, 1875, *ibid.*

[161] Including Andrew Curtin, Edgar Cowan, Victor Piollett—the Democratic nominee for Lt. Governor—and Hiester Clymer. See J. G. Thompson to Randall, Columbus, Ohio, Sept. 29, 1875; Clymer to Randall, Cincinnati, Ohio, Oct. 3, 1875, *ibid.*

[162] *NYDT*, Oct. 14, 1875; Oct. 23, 1875; *Annual Cyclopedia for 1875*, p. 607.

[163] A. M. Gibson to Chauncey Black, Washington, Sept. 25, 1875; Jeremiah Black MSS, LC; *NYDT*, Oct. 8, 1875; Oct. 13, 1875.

civil service reform.[164] The soft money *Harrisburg Patriot,* organ of the "Ring," was convinced that the Catholic issue had defeated Allen, and asked for redoubled attention to finance.[165] Beset by such internal friction, the Democratic campaign, never very energetic at best, slowed to a crawl. Both parties, it was reported, acted as if they were under sedation—the Democrats rendered spiritless by the certainty of defeat; the Republicans unwilling to exert themselves needlessly.[166] And in Pennsylvania, too, the Democrats were beaten. Republican Governor Hartranft and the entire state ticket were carried into office by a majority of over twelve thousand.[167]

I I I

The defeated Democrats of both states indulged in the usual post-election soul-searching. The conservatives in Ohio believed the defeat a just punishment for the party's desertion of Jacksonian principles.[168] The soft money men in both states, thinking of August Belmont as much as of Republican financiers, blamed the "money power." "The eastern banking and bondholding rings have poured out their money," declared the *Enquirer,* enabling the Republicans to "perfect such organization as they never had before."[169] The Ewing men were livid at the "treachery" of the eastern Democracy. *New York World* editorials belaboring Allen and Cary had been circulated as Republican campaign documents and had weakened the Democrats much as Grant's veto had hurt western Republicans during the 1874 Congressional race. These "eastern gentlemen"—Tilden, Belmont, and Manton Marble—the *Enquirer* promised, "will not be forgotten. They have built up a good account which will be settled in good time."[170]

The hostility of the party's New York wing may have hurt the

[164] A. M. Gibson to Randall, Harrisburg, Oct. 14, 1875, Randall MSS; W. W. Denny to Randall, Doylestown, Pa., Oct. 16, 1875, *ibid.*
[165] *Harrisburg Patriot,* Oct. 14, 1875; Oct. 23, 1875; Oct. 24, 1875.
[166] *NYDT,* Oct. 22, 1875.
[167] *Philadelphia Press,* Nov. 12, 1875.

[168] *NYDT,* Oct. 14, 1875.
[169] Quoted in the *NYW,* Oct. 15, 1875.
[170] *Cincinnati Enquirer,* Oct. 13, 1875. The truth of these charges is impossible to determine. They were so widely made by both Democrats and Republicans, however, that they are difficult to dismiss. See, e.g.,

Ohioans but the most important single factor in the election was probably the successful mobilization of middle-class urban, Protestant, Yankee opinion against the Democracy. The Ohio contest brought out the largest vote of any election in the state's history, and it was Cleveland, Columbus, and Cincinnati, the centers of "trade and culture," that gave the Republicans their majority.[171] The fight, the *New York Times* noted, was "won in the cities, the larger towns, and the populous intelligent counties where daily newspapers, good schools, and speakers like Schurz [and] Garfield . . . got in their good work."[172] In the more rural areas it was the northern tier of the Western Reserve, a part of the state settled by New Englanders and retaining much of the Yankee ethical approach to political affairs, that turned out in force for Hayes and Young. Ashtabula County, "the most Puritanical part" of Ohio, the Democratic *Chicago Times* claimed, carried the state for the Republicans.[173] In Pennsylvania the drastic shift of the Pittsburgh vote, added to the increased majority of some five thousand in Philadelphia, accounted for the largest part of Hartranft's margin over Democrat Pershing.[174]

The political puritans—the Liberals, the reformers, the honest government men, who voted for Greeley in 1872—apparently supported Hayes three years later. Carl Schurz had been invaluable in getting out the old Liberal vote. His speeches circulated by the thousands, and wherever the former Senator appeared in the state, crowds gathered to hear him denounce sinful inflation.[175] Without Schurz—that "crout-eating Greeleyite"[176]—Ohio would have gone Democratic, it was said, by a fifty-thousand majority.[177] Schurz had aroused the Germans and the great mid-

Thomas Ewing, Jr., to James R. Doolittle, Lancaster, March 28, 1876, Doolittle MSS; Hawkins (?) Taylor to William B. Allison, Washington, Oct. 18, 1875, Allison MSS, Iowa Dept. of History and Archives.

[171] Forrest William Clonts, "The Political Campaign of 1875 in Ohio," *Ohio Archeological and Historical Publications*, xxxi (1922), 86; NYDT, Nov. 1, 1875.

[172] NYT, Oct. 14, 1875.
[173] Quoted in the *Cleveland Leader*, Nov. 26, 1875. See also *ibid.*, Nov. 21, 1875.
[174] *Philadelphia Press*, Nov. 12, 1875.
[175] NYT, Oct. 2, 1875.
[176] The phrase is that of J. M. Cooper. See Cooper to Chauncey Black, Harrisburg, Pa., Oct. 21, 1875, Black MSS.
[177] NYT, Oct. 15, 1875.

dle-class public receptive to the reformer moral appeal,[178] and they responded at the polls. The margin of victory in Ohio was small, Henry Adams wrote an English friend, "but every man of that five thousand was one of us."[179]

But the soft money platform had not been a total failure, at least in Ohio. The anti-contraction slogans successfully converted hard times into Democratic votes in the industrial districts. As the dispatches reporting Democratic defeat pointed out, the party had made advances over 1873 in the coal and iron regions. In the manufacturing towns of Steubenville, Youngstown, Canton, and Wooster substantial gains for Allen were recorded.[180] Pennsylvania Democrats, nervously scanning the Ohio returns for a forecast of their own faltering campaign, noted with relief that the anti-contraction platform had carried the mining districts.[181]

In all six of the largest coal-producing counties of Ohio the Democrats had improved their relative standing over 1873, when they had carried the state for Allen. In a close contest, characterized by a remarkable stability of traditional voting patterns, two important industrial counties—Belmont and Mahoning—were turned from the Republican to the Democratic column. Against the trend in the state as a whole, and the three major metropolitan centers in particular, industrial Ohio voted Democratic.[182]

If these results show Democratic success in winning Ohio industrial labor, they tell nothing about the numerically insignificant group of ironmasters, mine operators, and other industrialists. Other evidence suggests, however, that a revolution in the outlook of industrial leaders took place during the campaign. Whatever their intention in June and July, they eventually rejected the Democrats, partly out of fear of disturbing the social equilibrium. During the course of the Ohio campaign, several

---

[178] See the interesting analysis of Schurz's moral appeal in the *Christian Union*, xii (Oct. 6, 1875), 282.

[179] Henry Adams to Charles Milnes Gaskell, Beverly Farms, Mass., Oct. 15, 1875, in Ford, *op. cit.*, p. 272. An Ohio Liberal, William B. Sloan, wrote Hayes shortly after the latter's victory: "Of the 10,129 Liberals of the State, I do not know of 20 that were prominent that worked for the Democratic ticket." Sloan to Hayes, Clinton, Ohio, Oct. 16, 1875, Hayes MSS.

[180] *NYDT*, Oct. 13, 1875; Oct. 14, 1875.

[181] J. M. Cooper to Chauncey Black, Harrisburg, Pa., Oct. 21, 1875, Black MSS.

[182] See Appendix E.

ironmasters announced their support for Hayes.[183] In Pennsylvania the Industrial League turned its back on the past and broke with Carey and Kelley. In a manifesto of September 25 the League's Executive Committee, consisting of the three old Carey disciples, Joseph Wharton, William Sellers, and Henry C. Lea,[184] expressed anxiety over "the unsettled state of opinion concerning the currency." Kelley's greenbackism and 3.65 bond scheme were "revolutionary" and "intrinsically, and in the highest degree unsound." "Sooner or later," the statement read, "the country must return to the standard of value that no legislation can change." Iron men were cautioned "not to be so carried away by vague promises . . . nor to venture upon a campaign . . . under leaders who have no fitness for the great task they would undertake."[185]

Iron Age, too, broke with its soft money past. In July, when the currency issue in Ohio first began to attract attention, editor Williams noted—inaccurately—that there had been a time when the financial debate had been confined to men of intelligence and education. It had since become a political sport, with the "people taking sides . . . without any clearer idea of the consequence of extreme legislation upon either side than is gained from partisan and ingenuous discussion in the political newspapers and upon the stump."[186] After the Ohio election, Williams noted that a "success [for Allen] . . . would have . . . created an uncertainty as to the future legislation of Congress on the currency question. . . . While a majority of our manufacturers and business men do not favor any experimental financial legislation, and are averse to a sudden contraction, they believe that the whole policy of the government should point steadily to resumption." The Resumption Act might require some minor modifications, but on the whole it was a wise piece of legislation whose operation must not be hindered.[187] Neither Williams, nor the

---

[183] These were: John Tod of Cleveland, John Campbell of Ironton, and James Botsford of Youngstown. See *CDT,* Sept. 22, 1875; *Cincinnati Commercial,* Aug. 4, 1875; and James Botsford to Hayes, Youngstown, September [?] 1875, Hayes MSS.

[184] In addition, Lea, the later historian of witchcraft and the Spanish Inquisition, was Carey's nephew.
[185] *Philadelphia Press,* Sept. 27, 1875.
[186] *Iron Age,* xvi (July 29, 1875).
[187] *Ibid.* (Oct. 14, 1875).

Wharton-Sellers-Lea group spoke for the whole industry, and in the next few years individual iron men would continue to take a soft money stand, but never again would the ironmasters present the same unbroken front against specie resumption.

The campaigns were an equally important turning point for the Republicans. Before June it was impossible to tell whether western Republicans would stand by the Resumption Act; by November the party as a whole was committed to the measure. Among Ohio Republicans, the confirmed hard money men rejoiced that the election had "exorcized the devil of inflation from the . . . party."[188] Western Republicans, driven by desperation rather than conviction to support the party's financial position, suddenly found that sound money paid political dividends. In Illinois Logan, and his Senate colleague Richard Oglesby, leading expansionists in the months following the panic, conceded that they had mistaken the drift of public opinion.[189] Morton, whose soft money views had begun to waver during the 1874 Congressional campaign, enthusiastically championed the resumption measure during his speaking tour of Ohio and Pennsylvania. The campaign, the *New York Tribune* noted, had "thoroughly educated the Republican party on the currency question, lifted it up to firm ground, converted the numerous inflationists in its ranks, or driven them into the Democratic camp."[190]

The *Tribune* exaggerated; the dissemblers, the dissenters, and the timid souls had not all departed. But after November the Republicans were to stand as a party united behind the 1875 Resumption Act.

[188] D. W. McClung to R. B. Hayes, Woodsdale, Ohio, Oct. 14, 1875, Hayes MSS.

[189] *NYDT*, Nov. 9, 1875.
[190] *Ibid.*, Oct. 11, 1875.

THE ELECTION OF 1876

I

IN the wake of the Ohio and Pennsylvania victories, jubilant conservatives talked as if resumption were assured.[1] The soft money men had indeed been handed another stinging rebuff, but the narrow Ohio victory did not warrant overconfidence. Resumption day was more than three years off, and any realistic reading of the past decade pointed to three more years of struggle. If nothing else, the new Congress was certain to be unfriendly to resumption. Grant and the Republican Senate could, of course, stop the Democrats, who would attack the Resumption Act mostly for political effect, but 1876 was an election year, and there was no telling what would happen in the excitement of a Presidential campaign.

Yet the prospects for "sound" finance were clearly brighter than in the dark days of early 1874. The Inflation Bill veto, the Resumption Act, and the Ohio and Pennsylvania victories, coming in quick succession, had restored the courage of the hard money forces and shaken their opponents. There would never again be a serious threat of paper inflation. Agrarian greenbackism did not die; in fact, it grew more vigorous. But paper money, whether bank notes or legal tenders, would no longer attract respectable business support on a large scale. After 1875 we hear little of the organized business clamor for more circulation that had marked the '60's and the immediate post-panic period. Yet businessmen most emphatically did not welcome "forced" resumption. Even the more conservative among them shrank from returning to specie too fast and too soon. Chicago merchants and manufacturers, an informal survey in August 1875 revealed, were reluctant to accept either expansion or immediate resump-

---

[1] Edward Atkinson to David Wells, n.p., Nov. 9, 1875, Wells MSS, LC; *NYDT*, Nov. 3, 1875; *CFC*, xxi (Oct. 23, 1875), 381.

tion.[2] In both Ohio and Pennsylvania, despite the fall elections, businessmen were reported six months later still in favor of repealing the Resumption Act.[3] One Cleveland industrialist warned Congressman Garfield in June 1876 that the "Sherman Resumption Act" was a "dead weight for the Republican Party to carry" and "should be gotten out of the way as soon as possible."[4]

In the more orthodox East the traditionally conservative port merchants continued to agitate for specie payments. In late 1875 and early 1876 the New York Chamber of Commerce, the New York Produce Exchange, the New York Grocers' Board of Trade, the Boston Board of Trade, and the Newark Board of Trade, all endorsed resumption.[5] Yet even eastern businessmen had serious misgivings about moving too quickly. At the National Board of Trade convention in June 1876, delegates from Philadelphia, Scranton, and New York attacked the contraction policy which they held the 1875 Act implied.[6] New England manufacturers were reported looking "with great suspicion on any contraction of the currency or any measure . . . to make the act of last January operative." Secretary Bristow's recent request for supplementary enabling legislation[7] had caused concern among the New Englanders, who found their sound money convictions at odds with their fear of a stringent money market. Their attitude, it was said, might even bring several New England Congressmen into the anti-resumption camp.[8]

[2] *CDT*, Aug. 20 and 21, 1875. See also E. W. Cummings to Cyrus McCormick, in William T. Hutchinson, *Cyrus Hall McCormick* (New York: The Century Co., 1935), II, 336.

[3] J. J. Faran to William Allen, [?], Feb. 3, 1876, Allen MSS, LC; S. Burke to Thomas Ewing, Jr., Cleveland, Feb. 15, 1876, Ewing MSS, LC; A. Burrows to Samuel J. Randall, Philadelphia, June 9, 1876, Randall MSS, University of Pennsylvania Library.

[4] W. C. Andrews (of Andrews, Hitchcock & Co., Coal and Iron) to James A. Garfield, Cleveland, June 24, 1876, Garfield MSS, LC.

[5] New York Chamber of Commerce, *Eighteenth Annual Report for 1875-1876*, pp. 86-91; New York Produce Exchange, *Annual Report for 1875-1876*, p. 16; *New York Evening Post*, March 8, 1876; Boston Board of Trade, *Twenty-third Annual Report for 1876*, pp. 20-21; Newark Board of Trade, *Eighteenth Annual Report for 1875*, p. 31.

[6] The delegates were George Buzby of the Philadelphia Board of Trade, J. A. Price of the Scranton Board of Trade, and George Opdyke of the newly organized New York Board of Trade. See National Board of Trade, *Proceedings of the Eighth Annual Meeting, 1876*, pp. 65-76.

[7] See U. S. Treasury, *Report of the Secretary of the Treasury on the State of the Finances for the Year 1875*, pp. xix-xx.

[8] *NYDT*, Jan. 6, 1876.

One reluctant eastern business group which, against the general trend, was to figure in the greenback movement of the next three years, was composed of the dissidents of the New York Chamber of Commerce. In mid-1875, after years of fighting contraction from within, this faction finally seceded from the Chamber.[9] Shortly after the break, a number of the dissenters—including George Opdyke, Horace Claflin, Peter Cooper, Wallace Groom, Francis B. Thurber, and Pliny Freeman—organized the New York Board of Trade in competition with the Chamber.[10] With Opdyke as President, Freeman as Vice-President, and Groom as Secretary, the new body seemed to some a "regular

[9] The occasion for the break was Opdyke's defeat for election to the Presidency of the Chamber. As First Vice-President his nomination in April 1875 was a matter of form, since the First Vice-President normally succeeded without a contest. But this time a group of self-styled "independents," including some of the more prominent merchants and bankers of the city, placed another slate in the field, headed by former Chamber President Samuel D. Babcock, a dry goods merchant turned banker. The usefulness of the Chamber, the independents argued, required that its "chief officers should have the reputation of sound and practical views on the subject of finances and trade, instead of speculations and doubtful theories." On May 6, with crowds of members present, most of whom had not attended a meeting in years, the Opdyke slate was defeated. *Ibid.,* May 6, 1876; *New York Herald,* Feb. 3, 1876; *NYW,* May 7, 1876; New York Chamber of Commerce, *Eighteenth Annual Report for 1875-1876,* pp. 5ff.

[10] I have not been able to determine the precise date of the new body's organization, but it was sometime before September 1875. The Board should not be confused with the Cheap Transportation Association, with which it shared members. The two bodies were distinct until September 1877 when they joined to form the Board of Trade and Transportation. There was an elusive relationship between the two groups from the very beginning, however. The Cheap Transportation Association, which favored lower railroad rates between Atlantic ports and the Mississippi Valley, had affiliations with western anti-monopolists. It was organized at an 1873 "Farmers' Convention" in New York attended by Horace Day, Noonan, and Henry Bronson of the Douglas County (Kansas) Farmers' Union, as well as by numerous eastern merchants. Claflin and Thurber were members of the Association, and the latter, at least, was in close touch with such western greenbackers as Joseph Osborn of Wisconsin. It is difficult, under the circumstances, not to suspect some connection between the Association's Agrarian convictions and the Board's heterodox money views. See *Western Rural,* May 17, 1873; R. H. Ferguson to Joseph Osborn, n.p., May 22, 1874; F. B. Thurber to Osborn, New York, Feb. 25, 1875, Osborn MSS, State Hist. Soc. of Wisc. There is an interesting discussion of the Association, the Board, and the later National Anti-Monopoly League, whose most prominent early leaders were Thurber and Peter Cooper, in Lee Benson, *Merchants, Farmers*

greenback concern."[11] It was radical only by contrast with the hide-bound Chamber, however. In 1876 the Board sent a memorial to Congress which attacked the Resumption Act as a "standing menace against all business enterprise," criticized Bristow's use of the measure to contract, and called for $50 million of interconvertible bonds. But the Board also suggested a plausible resumption scheme of its own and eschewed any increase in greenbacks in connection with the suggested interconvertible bonds.[12] In reality the new body represented a range of opinion from the outright greenbackism of Groom, Cooper, and Freeman, to the rather conservative views of Thurber.[13] The memorial was a moderate document of a moderate group which revealed how completely anxiety over resumption permeated the business community.

All told, the Resumption Act—assailed since the Ohio campaign by western Agrarians, labor groups, and now by a large part of business—was highly vulnerable, and no sooner did Congress convene in December 1876 than it came under furious attack.

The offensive began in the House. The first business of the lower chamber was also the beginning of the drive to repeal the unpopular measure. The Democrats had a clear majority of over 60 but were, as usual, sharply divided over finance. Westerners and the important Pennsylvania group favored repeal. Yankees, New Yorkers, and far westerners, while not averse to embarrassing the Republicans, were openly friendly to specie payment; southern delegations, representing rural constituencies, were split. Both sides realized that committee appointments would be crucial in the repeal fight, and the sharp skirmish which occurred

---

and Railroads: Railroad Legislation and New York Politics, 1850-1887 (Cambridge: Harvard University Press, 1955), *passim,* but especially chs. II and VIII.

[11] This was the description, however, of greenbacker Samuel Leavitt, a later historian of soft money, and it must be discounted heavily. See *WA,* Sept. 4, 1875. For the conservatives' comments see *New York Evening Post,* March 2, 1876; *The Public,* IX (Dec. 12, 1876), 102.

[12] New York Board of Trade, *Memorial to Congress on the Currency of the United States* (1876), *passim.*

[13] It is significant that in 1875 the Board sponsored a series of financial debates at which David Wells and Sherman, as well as Butler, Kelley, and soft money Senator John B. Gordon of Georgia appeared. S. Leavitt to editor, *Anti-Monopolist,* New York, Sept. 3, 1875; *AM,* Sept. 25, 1875.

over choice of Speaker, who in this period had almost unlimited control over committee assignments, had an important financial aspect. In the end, Michael Kerr of Indiana, a hard money man,[14] defeated Samuel Randall, who as promised got the support of the Ohio delegation for recent services rendered.[15]

Kerr's election proved to be a serious obstacle to the plans of the anti-resumptionists. After consulting with Manton Marble,[16] the new Speaker appointed William Morrison of Illinois Chairman of Ways and Means and Samuel "Sunset" Cox Chairman of Banking and Currency—the two House committees directly concerned with financial legislation. To make certain of conservative control, both committees were packed with hard money men.[17] These moves enabled the conservatives to block currency legislation for weeks. Bills aimed at repeal disappeared into committee pigeonholes,[18] and attempts to bypass the committees were beaten down by Speaker Kerr or the two chairmen. On February 1 Kerr infuriated greenbacker John Atkins of Tennessee by persistent refusal to recognize him when he rose to introduce a currency measure.[19] Later in the month, Cox, as Speaker *pro tem* in Kerr's absence, smothered a similar motion by William Holman of Indiana. As the waggish New Yorker explained it, "without *exactly* intending it we adjourned the Ho[use] before the slush came in."[20] Similar tactics stopped passage of a resumption repeal resolution introduced by Atkins some weeks later.[21]

Attempts to bypass the committees failed repeatedly. House rules required a two-thirds majority for passage of a measure introduced outside the regular committee time. On March 20 a motion by Atkins to repeal part of the Resumption Act received

---

[14] A. M. Gibson of the *New York Sun* referred to Kerr as a "decent man," but "the candidate of the self-glorified hard money men." Gibson to Samuel J. Randall, York, Pa., Nov. 11, 1875, Randall MSS.

[15] See the *New York Herald*, Dec. 2, 1875, for the Ohio Democrats' work on Randall's behalf. The caucus vote taken on Dec. 4 was 90 for Kerr to 60 for Randall. *NYW*, Dec. 5, 1875; *NYDT*, Dec. 6, 1875.

[16] Kerr to Marble, Washington, Dec. 7, 1875, Manton Marble MSS, LC.

[17] *NYDT*, Dec. 20, 1875.

[18] See the following for the measures that died in committee: *Congressional Record*, 44 Cong., 1 sess., pp. 207, 318, 1577, 2356, 3432. All references to the *Record* in this chapter, unless otherwise specified, will be to this Congress and session.

[19] *NYDT*, Feb. 2, 1876.

[20] S. S. Cox to Manton Marble, Washington, Feb. 28, 1876, Marble MSS.

[21] *NYDT*, March 21, 1876; *New York Herald*, Feb. 28, 1876.

a majority of one on a roll-call vote, but failed of passage because of the House rule.[22] Efforts to force through a repeal motion during the morning hour on Monday, under suspension of the rules, were blocked by the conservative Democratic leaders with motions for adjournment and other dilatory maneuvers.[23]

While effective, these tactics were politically risky, for they threatened to set up the same internal stresses that had earlier shaken the Republicans, and at a time when the stakes were higher. The hard money Democrats could antagonize their anti-resumptionist colleagues only at the risk of weakening the party on the eve of a Presidential election. Conservative strategy, moreover, by revealing party dissension, risked providing ammunition for the enemy. Complicating the issue were the fears of a number of conservative Democrats that resumption, successfully carried out under the 1875 measure, would be a political coup for the Republicans.[24]

Eventually, events outside Congress forced the gold men to relent. Besides business and labor pressure for repeal, rural groups, slow to respond to the Democratic agitation of the fall, were growing uneasy at the prospect of resumption. Among agricultural spokesmen the money question had not by any means been settled. In Illinois Willard Flagg continued to reject paper money,[25] and the *Prairie Farmer*, the state's most influen-

[22] The vote was 110 to 109, with 74 abstentions. Some 63 Republicans, 45 Democrats, and 1 Liberal voted against the measure. Every Democrat from the New York, Massachusetts, Mississippi, Maryland, California, and Texas delegations opposed the bill. On the other hand, 8 of 9 Democrats from Illinois, all 8 of the Virginia Democrats, 9 of 10 Missourians, 11 of 12 Ohioans, all 9 of the Tennesseeans, 8 of the 13 Pennsylvanians, and all 3 of the Wisconsin Democrats voted in the affirmative. Some 14 Republicans voted with the Democrats for the bill: 4 from Indiana, 2 each from Illinois, Pennsylvania, and Ohio, and 1 each from Kansas, Alabama, and North Carolina. *Congressional Record*, p. 1815. A slightly different breakdown can be found in *NYDT*, March 22, 1876.

[23] *Ibid.*, March 21, 1876.

[24] August Belmont to Manton Marble, [New York, May or June], 1876; Thomas Bayard to Marble, Washington, Jan. 16, 1876. Marble MSS.

[25] Willard Flagg to David Wells, Moro, Ill., April 27, 1876, Wells MSS, LC; *IA*, Nov. 13, 1875. It is significant, I think, that Flagg, unlike most Grange leaders, was the product of the best eastern education. He was a Yale graduate who had contacts with the Social Science Association. In a word, he was a farmer-mugwump, much as S. Lester Taylor was a merchant-mugwump.

tial farm journal, remained a bastion of conservatism.[26] But slowly rural opinion in the prairie states began to move behind repeal. The change seems connected with the weakening of the granger impulse. The Patrons had reached their peak in 1874 with over 20,000 local Grange bodies. Thereafter, with much of their regulatory program enacted and their cooperative efforts bankrupt, they began to decline. It was in this period of ebbing fortunes that several influential Grange leaders first began to worry about finance.[27] By late 1875 *Industrial Age* of the Illinois Farmers' Association was agitating for repeal of the Resumption Act. Noonan still felt uneasy about a purely paper issue and continued to reject inflation;[28] but he saw resumption as calamitous for the farmer. "The farms of many of those who have braved the dangers and hardships of the wild west and contributed to the wealth and glory of the nation," he wrote melodramatically, "will empty their occupants into beggary, and capital will mock the tear which trickles down the sunburned cheeks of the despoiled."[29] His chief competitor for grange leadership in the region, the Chicago *Western Rural*, also newly converted to anti-resumption, put it more succinctly: farm debts contracted at 80 cents would have to be repaid at a dollar, which "would be rank injustice and, in many cases, ruin."[30] The *Rural's* unsentimental directness represented a new farm pragmatism which in our own day would culminate in the drive for parity.

By the opening of the Forty-fourth Congress, farm leaders and farm organizations elsewhere were also in full cry against the Resumption Act. In Minnesota, Donnelly finally moved to an unequivocal soft money position. As late as December 1874 he had called Wendell Phillips "crackbrained" and had defended the national banks.[31] He was still talking about the farmer's need

---

[26] *Prairie Farmer,* Oct. 16, 1875.

[27] In Wisconsin, Joseph Osborn, Granger leader and official of the State Board of Railroad Commissioners, began about this time to read Edward Kellogg and to disseminate among his associates Kellogg's message of salvation through cheap money. See J. E. Follett to Osborn, Milwaukee, Nov. 30, 1874, Osborn MSS.

[28] *IA,* May 20, 1876. On the other hand, in February Noonan published a special supplement containing a lengthy summary of Campbell's money views. See *ibid.,* Feb. 19, 1876.

[29] *Ibid.,* Dec. 18, 1875.

[30] *Western Rural,* Nov. 20, 1875; also Oct. 16, 1875; and Oct. 23, 1875.

[31] *AM,* Dec. 31, 1874. He did want them reformed, however.

to use the "world's money," in April 1875. But by this time the Sage of Nininger was listening to the advice of Noonan and greenbacker Joseph Goar on currency matters[32] and had begun to entertain serious doubts about resumption.[33] By early 1876 the *Anti-Monopolist* was offering its readers anti-bank, anti-resumption, and even pro-greenback editorials.[34] In Wisconsin, Michigan, and Indiana the Resumption Act had also become the target of farmer groups.[35] Although the National Grange still refused to discuss the money question,[36] it was clear that western farmers, while not prepared to endorse greenbacks, were ready to resist "forced" resumption.

Congressional inaction in the face of this growing distrust of the Resumption Act generated serious political discontent, and for the second time since the War the existing parties were threatened by a national third-party movement. The initial impulse for the new party came from Indiana, where early in 1873 a group of farm leaders and reformers including A. E. Olleman broke with the major parties. Calling themselves "Independents," they set up a separate political organization. This group was only one of a handful of anti-monopoly or "independent" Granger parties that had appeared in the early '70's[37] and does not at first seem to have differed much from the general run in its anti-railroad orientation. After the panic, however, the emphasis changed. The driving force behind the Indiana group came from James Buchanan, a 300-pound Indianapolis lawyer,

---

[32] Noonan to Donnelly, Chicago, March 16, 1875; April 26, 1875; May 16, 1875; Goar to Donnelly, Faribault, Minn., Jan. 20, 1875; and Jan. 21, 1875, Donnelly MSS, Minnesota Historical Society.

[33] *AM*, March 2, 1876; March 30, 1876.

[34] *Ibid.*, Jan. 13, 1876; Feb. 24, 1876; March 2, 1876; March 9, 1876.

[35] *IA*, Jan. 22, 1876; May 13, 1876; March 25, 1876.

[36] National Grange, *Journal of Proceedings of the Ninth Meeting, 1875*, pp. 175-177. Grand Master

Dudley W. Adams acknowledged, however, that farmers were "deeply interested" in the money question.

[37] For these see Fred E. Haynes, *Third Party Movements Since the Civil War, with Special Reference to Iowa: A Study in Social Politics* (Iowa City: The State Historical Society of Iowa, 1916), ch. VI; Solon J. Buck, *The Granger Movement: A Study of Agricultural Organization and Its Political, Economic and Social Manifestations, 1870–1880* (Cambridge: Harvard University Press, 1913), ch. III.

and his brother Thomas, who edited the weekly *Indianapolis Sun.*
The Buchanans were ardent disciples of Campbell and soon imposed their financial views on the new organization. Between
October and December 1873, while the nation reeled from the
recent shock to the economy, the Indiana Independents sponsored several meetings of workingmen and "citizens and business
men" to petition Congress for monetary relief.[38] The following
June an Independent convention nominated a state ticket on the
interconvertible bond platform.[39] By this time the Indiana leaders had become ambitious, and in August 1874 they issued a call
to all greenback men to meet in Indianapolis to organize a new
national party.[40]

The call fell on fertile ground. Ever since the collapse of the
National Labor Union and the 1872 labor party effort, greenbackism had been without a home. In the panic's wake there appeared a busy ferment of currency and labor reform groups and
financial clubs interested in saving the world through paper
money. In Washington there was the National Labor Council led
by A. E. Redstone, pledged to a platform of National Bank Act
repeal, the interconvertible bond, cheap transportation, free education, and the protective tariff.[41] New York had Edward Nieuwland's International Financial Improvement Society.[42] In Philadelphia Henry Carey Baird and E. M. Davis presided over the
National Reform League.[43] Early in 1875 a secret Order of
United Reformers, reminiscent of the ante-bellum Friends of

---

[38] *CDT*, Dec. 6, 1873; *Indiana
Farmer*, Nov. 8, 1873; Dec. 27,
1873; *Indianapolis Sentinel*, Dec. 6,
1873; Dec. 21, 1873; Henry C.
Guffin to Daniel D. Pratt, Indianapolis, Nov. 10, 1873; James Buchanan to Pratt, Indianapolis, Jan.
1, 1874, Pratt MSS, Indiana State
Library.
[39] *The American Annual Cyclopedia and Register of Important
Events of the Year 1874*, pp. 412-
413.
[40] *IA*, Dec. 15, 1874. Two
months later Trevellick made a
similar suggestion for a unified
greenback organization, which was
enthusiastically endorsed by Cameron. *WA*, Oct. 3-10, 1874; Oct. 24,

1874.
[41] Printed letter of A. E. Redstone, President of the National
Labor Council, Washington, Jan. 23,
1874, in the Matthew W. Ransom
MSS, Southern Historical Collection,
University of North Carolina. Redstone had been associated with the
1872 labor reform movement, but
had dropped out of sight until this
point. See Redstone to David Davis,
Washington, March 11, 1872, Davis
MSS, Illinois State Library.
[42] Nieuwland to Peter Cooper,
n.p., June [?] 1874, Peter Cooper
MSS, The Cooper Union Library.
[43] *Indianapolis Sun*, March 11,
1876.

Universal Reform, was organized to "secure increased social, intellectual and pecuniary benefits for the industrial classes" through "the advancement of all *Reforms* . . . calculated to promote the interests of the industrial classes, increase the prosperity of the nation and eventually to secure the greatest good to all."[44]

Too new and too isolated, these groups at first remained outside the new political movement. Indeed, the assemblage that gathered in November 1874 in answer to the call, although conceived as a microcosm of soft money, represented relatively few of the currency reform elements. To be sure, the large Indiana contingent was not monolithic. In addition to the Buchanans, who were reformers before anything else, there were Olleman and several other important Grange leaders and an assortment of independent-minded politicians.[45] Unfortunately, the small representation from outside the state was too heavily weighted on the side of labor leaders. The western reform group of Cameron, Campbell, and Robert Schilling attended. Alexander Troup of the New Haven *Union* and the stubborn and egotistical reformer Horace Day of New York came, ostensibly as delegates of eastern labor. The representation of other soft money elements proved disappointing, however. S. M. Smith of the Illinois Farmers' Association was the only bona fide out-of-state farm leader present, and although letters of endorsement were received from Wallace Groom and Henry Carey Baird, there were no actual delegates from the small but important business greenback groups.[46] The convention adopted the orthodox interconvertible bond platform, but conscious perhaps of its unrepresentative character, wisely postponed plans for a new party. Instead, an exaggerated succession of new meetings, committees, and "calls" was prescribed as preliminary to launching the new organization. The convention chose an Executive Committee of thirteen to draft a declaration of principles and fix a time for a national

[44] Printed broadside, Order of United Reformers, n.d., Osborn MSS. According to this document, the "International Senate" of the group was established at Toledo, April 6, 1875.

[45] William G. Carleton, "The Money Question in Indiana Politics, 1865-1890," *Indiana Magazine of History*, XLII, No. 2 (June 1946), 184ff.

[46] *IA*, Dec. 5, 1874.

convention. This in turn was to compose another platform and set the date for a national nominating convention.[47]

This stately progression was doubtless intended to provide time for sweeping in all the unaffiliated greenback elements, but the delay came perilously close to destroying any possibility of a united party. By the time the Committee of Thirteen had issued its call for a March convention at Cleveland, some serious obstacles had appeared. The call itself was attacked as too narrow by Noonan and other farm leaders, who could not shake off their suspicion of paper money. The "people's movement," *Industrial Age* declared, "must have more scope—more breadth of beam—than it can obtain by planting itself on but one idea, and that an idea that the country at large doesn't understand."[48] More serious was the defection of Horace Day, who, angered at the Indianapolis group for not electing him Chairman of the Executive Committee[49] and concerned with the poor representation of eastern labor, tried to set up a competing organization.

Day's opportunity came when an anti-monopoly convention, composed largely of Pennsylvania labor leaders and coal dealers, with a sprinkling of grangers and professional reformers, met in Harrisburg in early March. The primary purpose of this meeting, apparently, was to fight the strangle hold on the coal trade exercised by Franklin Gowen, President of the powerful Philadelphia and Reading Coal and Iron Company.[50] But Day somehow inveigled the convention into issuing a call for a "national conference of farmers and workingmen." An ambitious invitation committee, including most of the country's prominent Grange

[47] *Ibid.*

[48] *Ibid.*, Feb. 6, 1875; Feb. 20, 1875.

[49] This, at least, was Cameron's explanation. See *WA* for successive issues from July 17, 1875, through August.

[50] Dr. Edward Topping James believes that the Harrisburg convention was called almost entirely for the purpose of stopping Gowens. Yet the presence of state farm leaders and reformers casts doubt on so narrow an interpretation. Among the reformers were C. Os-borne Ward of New York and E. M. Davis, the ex-abolitionist, Philadelphia Quaker. S. M. Smith represented the Illinois Farmers' Association, while Victor Piolett represented the Pennsylvania Grange. See James, "American Labor and Political Action, 1865-1896: The Knights of Labor and Its Predecessors" (unpublished Ph.D. dissertation, Harvard University, 1954), p. 112; C. Ben Johnson, Pottsville, Pa., to editor, *Workingman's Advocate*, July 3, 1875; *WA*, July 17, 1875.

leaders and labor greenbackers, was hopefully drawn up, although a less illustrious group from the convention itself assembled in Philadelphia two weeks later to issue the formal call for a September meeting at Cincinnati. Day usurped control of this group and set about trying to exclude the western labor reformers from the third-party movement.[51]

Meanwhile, the Cleveland convention had met on schedule and unobtrusively established the National Independent Party. M. M. Hooton of the Illinois State Farmers' Association, and Noonan—despite his reservations—were present. But the Chicago labor reformers and the Indiana group dominated the proceedings. The convention adopted an interconvertible bond-greenback platform, with an incidental nod to farmers' demands for railroad regulation and preservation of the public domain. After selecting St. Louis as the place for a national nominating convention, the group adjourned, leaving the actual meeting time for the Executive Council to determine.[52]

The political alliance ostensibly concluded at Cleveland eventually exhibited considerable vitality, but for the next few months the very survival of the new party was in doubt. The attacks of Day and his eastern labor friends hurt the Independents.[53] The ambitious New York reformer succeeded in convincing the farm element that the Cleveland group had little to offer them. S. M. Smith of the Illinois Farmers' Association disparaged the work at Cleveland. The meeting the Clevelanders planned, if it ever came off, would have little significance, he believed. On the other hand, he had great hopes for Day's Cincinnati conference, "the first meeting," as he saw it, "where labourers from every department of industry will have met for a union and a confederation for a common defense." "Shysters and politicians," he noted, would "be excluded and the great interests of labour and

---

[51] Day's own explanation of his actions was that the Cameron-Campbell-Trevellick group were not bona fide labor men. The westerners, on the other hand, saw the move as an attempt to give control of any new greenback party to the easterners, and to further Day's persistent Presidential ambitions. For further details of the controversy see *ibid.*, April 3, 1875; July 17, 1875; Aug. 14, 1875; *National Labor Tribune*, June 5, 1875; July 31, 1875. A copy of the official call for the Cincinnati meeting can be found in the Osborn MSS for April 1875.

[52] *WA*, March 30, 1875; *IA*, March 20, 1875.

[53] *WA*, April 13, 1875.

not politics will be the theme for discussion."[54] Even Noonan was critical of the Cleveland meeting, believing the resolutions adopted were still "too much in the monetary groove."[55]

For a while the discontent of the farm leaders seemed about to erupt into still another convention. John R. Winston, a North Carolina Granger, who like Noonan was disturbed by the over-emphasis on finance at Cleveland, issued a call in July or early August for a political meeting of farmers at Indianapolis. As soon as Winston got wind of Day's group he abandoned this separate enterprise. "The eastern [Day] movement," he wrote Joseph Osborn, a Wisconsin Grange leader, "so far as I can see fills my idea of what is needed especially among farmers."[56] At first Winston tried to talk Day into accepting a merger of all three groups, but when the latter balked he agreed to unite with the Cincinnati movement.[57]

At Cincinnati Day's atempt to consign the Cleveland element to political oblivion failed. When the conference convened on September 7, the Clevelanders were on hand demanding admission to the deliberations. Day and his eastern labor supporters fought to exclude them, but their attempt backfired. Day's mulish insistence on his own way alienated many of the Cincinnati people who saw no reason to sacrifice advantages of a united "producer" front to Day's vanity and ambition. The meeting turned into a free-for-all as the majority of the moderates and the Cleveland element "took possession of the chair by force, lifting day [sic] out bodily," and depositing the pro-Day door-keeper in a corner of the hall with orders to keep his peace. "The most kindly . . . expressions were used by each to the other," a facetious Wisconsin Granger reported of the rowdy convention: "damn liars, infernal thieves and sons of bitches . . . among the most polite."[58] In defiance of the Day faction, Smith, Cameron,

[54] S. M. Smith to Joseph Osborn, Kewanee, Ill., Aug. 6, 1875, Osborn MSS.

[55] IA, March 20, 1875. But he also refused to follow Day whom he considered "a broken minded demagogue," interested only in the Presidency, a position for which he was "about as fit . . . as Geo. Francis Train." See Noonan to Joseph Os-

born, Chicago, Aug. 18, 1875, Osborn MSS.

[56] Winston to Osborn, Milton, N. C., Aug. 18, 1875, ibid.

[57] Horace Day to Joseph Osborn, New York, Aug. 15, 1875, ibid.

[58] See W. J. Orledge to Joseph Osborn, Kenosha, Wisc., Sept. 16, 1875, ibid.

and Schilling were all elected officers of the convention, and another Committee of Thirteen was selected to join with the Cleveland Committee to conduct the business of the National Independent Party. At this point Day and his followers resigned in a bloc and stormed out of the conference.[59]

As a show of "producer" unity the meeting was scarcely a triumph. Even men who had little affection for Day found the performance unedifying. John M. Davis of the *National Labor Tribune* criticized the majority for their high-handed treatment of the minority and pronounced the convention a complete failure.[60] Nevertheless, it proved to be a milestone for political greenbackism, and despite Day's defection, it ended the threat of a second "third party." For Day it meant the end of labor reform: rather than continue the fight he simply left the greenback movement.[61] With that source of discord gone, the committee selected to cooperate with the Cleveland Executive Council soon put an end to the schism that had been opened. The convention also made an important change in the greenback program by demoting the interconvertible bond to second place on the platform. In an effort to broaden its appeal, particularly to rural groups, the Kellogg-Campbell scheme, which since 1867 had represented the heart of the greenback reform philosophy, was subordinated to "immediate and absolute" repeal of the Resumption Act. Thereafter, until 1879, repeal remained the major demand of the Greenback men.

The convention was a turning point in still another way. For the first time, substantial numbers of farm and labor leaders were brought together for joint political action. This time the Grange and other farmer protest groups were well represented by S. M. Smith, Ebenezer Ayres of Minnesota, John and Julia Garretson of Iowa, and A. S. Piatt of Ohio. Part of the eastern labor delegation departed with Day. But others remained. John

[59] *Ibid.*; John Winston to Joseph Osborn, Milton, N. C., Sept. 20, 1875, *ibid.*; *National Labor Tribune*, Sept. 18, 1875; Sept. 25, 1875; *Miners' National Record*, October 1875, pp. 203-204.

[60] *National Labor Tribune*, Sept. 18, 1875. Noonan and Osborn, however, believed that "at the up-

shot . . . the convention . . . was the best thing" that could be done "under the circumstances." W. J. Orledge to Osborn, Kenosha, Wisc., Sept. 16, 1875, Osborn MSS.

[61] John R. Commons and associates, *History of Labour in the United States* (New York: The Macmillan Co., 1946), II, 170.

Siney of the Pennsylvania anthracite miners not only stayed but was chosen to preside over the meeting. E. M. Chamberlain of the flourishing Sovereigns of Industry was one of the thirteen chosen to cooperate with the Independents. John E. Welsh, another Pennsylvania mine leader, also played a prominent part. As one New York delegate, Samuel Leavitt, wrote, "for the first time . . . that old dream [of unity] of the earnest mechanics and laborers of the East and the farmers of the West [had] been realized."[62]

One important group, the small but articulate and influential business greenback element, was still outside the coalition, however. An attempt was now made to draw them into Greenback politics. At a meeting called by Moses Field in Detroit in late August, the Indiana group, Grange leaders, labor men, and a few representatives of eastern and western business greenback groups were brought together. Kelley delivered a speech; Henry Carey sent a friendly letter; E. P. Allis, a rich Milwaukee ironmaster soon to become prominent in Wisconsin Greenback circles attended, as did John Young Scammon, a Chicago banker; and, possibly, Pliny Freeman.[63] The convention adopted the usual greenback platform, demanded repeal, and adjourned without taking further action.[64] Although no mention was made of the Independents, it is difficult not to see this curiously inconclusive meeting as an attempt to bring a group of wealthy and influential businessmen into the new party's orbit.

Following the Cincinnati conference, the planning of a Presidential ticket in the field was never in doubt, although the number of additional steps that were considered necessary was ludicrous. The merger of the Cincinnati and Cleveland executive committees was effected sometime in early fall. On November 10, S. M. Smith, as chairman of the joint committee,

[62] Leavitt to Ignatius Donnelly, New York, Sept. 16, 1875, in AM, Oct. 11, 1875. See also the following for the convention in general: IA, Sept. 11, 1875; Sept. 18, 1875.

[63] Freeman was listed among the officers of the convention, but so was Peter Cooper, who almost never attended conventions. There was a tendency to include among the announced officers of such meetings the names of all prominent sympathizers with the movement, an understandable attempt to give importance to otherwise obscure gatherings.

[64] NYT, Aug. 26, 1875; Aug. 28, 1875; IA, Aug. 28, 1875; WA, Sept. 4, 1875.

called a meeting in Chicago to decide on a time and place for nominating a national ticket.[65] The committee finally chose May 17 and Indianapolis for the great event.[66] Soon after, the Independent National Executive Committee issued an address "to the Electors of the United States," spelling out to the public once more the aims of the new party.[67]

This was the actual beginning of the party organization drive, which during the next few weeks gained considerable momentum. Smith proved to be an energetic organizer. His chief aim during the winter was to awaken grass-roots support for the Independent movement so that the Indianapolis convention would be a meeting of representatives of real constituencies, not merely the self-appointed as at Cleveland and Cincinnati.[68] Under his leadership much was accomplished to prepare the ground for Indianapolis. Greenback clubs, pledged to support the new party, were organized throughout the West.[69] In January the Illinois Farmers' Association and the Indiana State Grange came as close to endorsing the Independents as their pledge of political non-partisanship would permit.[70] Some half-dozen state Independent conventions met, established state organizations, selected state tickets in some cases, and nominated delegates to the Indianapolis meeting.[71] Labor, too, rallied to the Independents. John M. Davis of the Knights of Labor, critical at first of the majority's tactics at Cincinnati, by April had become more friendly. At the Pittsburgh National Labor Convention the Knights of Labor element succeeded in getting a close paraphrase of the Independent platform adopted over the protests of the Socialists,[72] and thereafter the Knights supported

[65] IA, Nov. 27, 1875.

[66] Ibid., Dec. 4, 1875; Western Rural, Dec. 11, 1875. The choice of Indianapolis represented, of course, a change from St. Louis, the site for the convention as originally announced by the Cleveland gathering.

[67] IA, Jan. 22, 1876.

[68] S. M. Smith to Joseph Osborn, Kewanee, Ill., Nov. 16, 1875, Osborn MSS.

[69] IA, Oct. 1, 1875; N. C. Martin to Ignatius Donnelly, Litch-field, Minn., Feb. 25, 1876 and April 17, 1876; O. H. Page to Donnelly, Pleasant Grove, Minn., April 10, 1876, Donnelly MSS; AM, March 2, 23, and 30, 1876.

[70] Prairie Farmer, Jan. 29, 1876.

[71] See Indianapolis Sun, March 25, 1876; April 15, 1876; April 22, 1876; May 6, 1876; May 13, 1876.

[72] This convention was called by the Junior Sons of '76, a Pennsylvania labor group with strong greenback leanings. The meeting, which originally convened at Ty-

the new party.[73] Progress was also made in winning over the business greenbackers. Smith corresponded with Baird, Peter Cooper, Moses Field, and Ewing, and was optimistic about drawing them into the new party.[74]

The advent of the Independents was a disturbing element on the political scene. The Democrats felt particularly threatened. With a constituency already deeply imbued with greenbackism, the Democracy appeared certain to lose more votes to the new party than their opponents, and in a close race such losses might well turn victory into defeat. Greenback Democrats warned that the party faced disaster unless the Independent threat could be contained.[75] It was evident that the Independents themselves were aware of their advantage and were actively proselytizing among soft money Democrats.[76]

The Democracy moved in several directions simultaneously to meet the danger. Ewing believed it best to try stealing the Independents' thunder. The Democratic State Central Committee in greenback ridden Ohio must call an early convention to take a strong line against the "Sherman Law," he wrote. The General said nothing directly about the new party, but his haste betrayed his hope of heading off the movement in that state.[77] Later in the year Ewing tried to get the Independents to abandon their Indianapolis meeting in favor of one at St. Louis, immediately after the Democratic convention.[78] This was obviously a move to have the new party merely rubber stamp the

rone, Pa., in December 1875, reconvened at Pittsburgh with Socialists, Knights of Labor men as well as Junior Sons present. There was a fight over the platform with the two latter groups succeeding in getting greenback resolutions adopted, whereupon the Socialists withdrew from the convention. *National Labor Tribune*, April 22, 1876; Commons, *op. cit.*, II, 201-202, 235-239.

[73] The secret nature of the Knights at this time makes it impossible to tell if it officially supported the Independents. My conclusion is based on the efforts of prominent individuals in the union.

[74] S. M. Smith to Joseph Osborn, Kewanee, Ill., Nov. 16, 1875, Osborn MSS.

[75] For example, C. Bonsall to Thomas Ewing, Jr., Salem, Ohio, Feb. 29, 1876; H. Blandy to Ewing, Zanesville, Ohio, March 17, 1876, Ewing MSS.

[76] *IA*, Jan. 22, 1876; April 15, 1876.

[77] *Ibid.*, April 1, 1876.

[78] D. H. Pinney to Ignatius Donnelly, Joliet, Ill., April 14, 1876, Donnelly MSS.

Democratic nominee, although Ewing may also have been trying to influence the choice of the Democratic ticket.

Ewing's call for an early state convention was not heeded, but he did succeed in neutralizing the third-party effort in Ohio. A meeting of state Independents in mid-April calling for a separate party organization was ill-attended, with most greenbackers reported waiting to see what the Democrats would do.[79] When the Democrats did meet in May, the soft money forces won an effortless victory. Ewing and his followers forced through a platform recommending repeal, a flexible currency system modeled after the interconvertible bond, and a measure to substitute legal tenders for national bank notes. The convention also bypassed Thurman and pledged Ohio to Allen at the St. Louis convention.[80] Under the circumstances, the state Independents were seriously undercut and conducted a weak, ineffectual campaign in the succeeding months.

Similar attempts to neutralize the third party by appropriating its program occurred in Kentucky, Missouri, and Kansas,[81] but in other western states the conservative Democrats gained control of the party machinery and defied the Greenbackers. In Iowa the state convention chose as delegates to St. Louis men pledged to New York Governor Samuel J. Tilden and adopted a strong sound money platform, although it was conceded that most of the state's Democratic voters were strong greenback men.[82] In Wisconsin the conservative machine defeated an insurgent greenback group and was able to send a full roster of Tilden delegates to the convention unencumbered by a repeal pledge.[83] In Michigan and Minnesota, too, the Democratic

[79] IA, April 15, 1876; Indianapolis Sun, April 15, 1876.

[80] NYDT, May 18, 1876; May 19, 1876; Charles Bonsall to Thomas Ewing, Jr., Salem, Ohio, May 20, 1876; John T. Blair to Ewing, Columbus, May 23, 1876, Ewing MSS. Also Durbin Ward to David Wells, Lebanon, Ohio, June 10, 1876, Wells MSS; Durbin Ward to Allen G. Thurman, Lebanon, May 21, 1876; Henry Bohl to Thurman, Marietta, Ohio, May 23, 1876; Thurman MSS, Ohio Historical Society.

[81] For Kentucky: Henry Watterson to Samuel J. Tilden, Louisville, June 10, 1876, Tilden MSS, New York Public Library; Annual Cyclopedia for 1876, pp. 436, 557. In the case of Kentucky, Tilden delegates were chosen to go to St. Louis.

[82] John P. Irish to Manton Marble, Iowa City, May 19, 1876; W. W. Witmer to Marble, Des Moines, May 23, 1876, Marble MSS.

[83] Horace Samuel Merrill, William Freeman Vilas, Doctrinaire Demo-

platforms made no concessions to greenback sentiment.[84]

Despite these conservative victories, the growing Greenback strength could not be ignored by the Democrats in Congress. Belmont reported in February that the western hard money men, including Speaker Kerr, were "getting weak in the knees."[85] But even Belmont was by now willing to accept compromise for the sake of party unity.[86] Goaded by Independent taunts of disunity and impotence, Democratic leaders sought, as had the Republicans the year before, to find common ground between hard and soft factions. Beginning in early February and continuing intermittently for over a month, a joint House-Senate caucus committee held sessions in an effort to forge an agreement. The committee was too deeply divided. Indianans William Holman and Franklin Landers, along with Tennesseean John M. Bright, demanded immediate and unconditional repeal of the resumption clause and a measure substituting greenbacks for national bank notes. A group of Texans and easterners refused to consider repeal; while a middle group—led by Henry Payne of Ohio—was prepared to accept postponement of resumption to some later date.[87] Eventually, two proposals—one resembling the Payne compromise, and the other recommending unqualified repeal—went to the full caucus. There, neither scheme made headway. For two weeks the Democrats worried the currency problem with no sign of agreement. Gradually, seeing the futility of the sessions, members ceased to attend, and on March 15 the caucus adjourned sine die.[88]

Following this failure the greenback wing made one last effort to get the House to vote on repeal. This move was stopped in committee, and when an attempt was made to call it up from the floor, it was blocked by Cox and other conservatives.[89] As

crat (Madison, Wisc.: State Historical Society of Wisconsin, 1954), p. 38.

[84] Annual Cyclopedia for 1876, pp. 552, 557.

[85] Belmont to Manton Marble, Washington, Feb. 14, 1876, Marble MSS.

[86] See Perry Belmont to Thomas F. Bayard, New York, Feb. 18, 1876, Bayard MSS, LC.

[87] NYDT, Feb. 5, 1876; Feb. 18, 1876; Feb. 21, 1876.

[88] Ibid., Feb. 28, 1876; March 3, 1876; March 6, 1876; March 13, 1876; March 21, 1876; David Wells to Henry B. Payne, Norwich, Conn., Feb. 3, 1876, Wells MSS; Payne to Manton Marble, Washington, March 1, 1876, Marble MSS.

[89] NYDT, June 27, 1876; Congressional Record, pp. 4157-4158.

Congress adjourned for the national conventions, the Democrats faced the unpleasant prospect of having to thrash out the financial issue at St. Louis before the eyes of the whole country.

II

The Independent convention was the first of the three to meet. Some 230 delegates from 18 states, including almost all the greenback regulars and the business greenbackers, were on hand at Indianapolis on May 17. In the large Illinois delegation were Hooton, Smith, Cameron, Hinchcliffe, and Campbell— the latter now a vocal member of the Forty-fourth Congress and, to the other delegates, something of a celebrity.[90] Michigan sent Trevellick and Moses Field;[91] Ebenezer Ayres and Donnelly represented Minnesota. Pliny Freeman, Wallace Groom, and Samuel Leavitt came from New York. From Pennsylvania there were Siney of the anthracite miners, and Frank Hughes, a greenbacker from Pottsville. A. E. Redstone of the National Labor Council represented California.[92] The Indiana delegation included Olleman and the two Buchanans. Troup of Connecticut, apparently reconciled to the Independent leadership; John Drew, the New Jersey utopian reformer; D. Wyatt Aiken, an important National Grange official of South Carolina; Winston of North Carolina; and E. P. Allis, the Wisconsin manufacturer, were also present. Some notable new faces were to be seen as well. Solon Chase, greenback editor from Turner's Falls, Maine; General James B. Weaver of Iowa; Adlai E. Stevenson of Illinois, were to be important leaders in later soft money politics.

Historians have generally identified the Independents of 1876 as insurgent farm leaders and have drawn a clear distinction between the platform adopted at Indianapolis and the National

[90] He had been elected as a Democrat-Independent in the Democratic sweep of 1874, and during the Forty-fourth Congress had spent most of his time agitating for repeal of the Resumption Act.

[91] Field was now Chairman of the Executive Committee, following S. M. Smith's resignation because of ill health. *IA*, April 15, 1876.

[92] This was probably a case of proxy representation, a common occurrence at such conventions for distant states. He was not a Californian.

Labor Union platform of the 1860's.[93] Unfortunately, there is no surviving list of all 230 delegates, but from the tone of the speeches and resolutions, and from what we know of the leading participants, it is possible to deduce the nature of the group. The 1876 convention was not, of course, primarily a labor gathering; but neither was it dominated by the Grangers. Both pragmatic trade-unionists and farm leaders who had little faith in money panaceas came to Indianapolis obviously hoping that the new party, whatever its avowed program, would serve the "producer" cause. But to see the convention as an assemblage of economic pressure groups would be a mistake. At bottom it consisted of True Believers—greenback ideologues who had converged on the movement from many directions. The meeting was the culmination of the process of encounter and mutual recognition that had been taking place since the late '60's. Businessmen, labor reformers, lawyers, marginal politicians, as well as farm leaders, were present at Indianapolis. But the central core was composed of men who, whatever their professional callings, were greenbackers—labor greenbackers, reformer greenbackers, business greenbackers, agricultural greenbackers, Democratic greenbackers—before everything else. They all shared a common vision that transcended their origins and their day-to-day occupations. From the beginning, greenbackism had the quality of a transfiguring faith, but its quasi-religious nature had never emerged so clearly as it did at Indianapolis.

By now, of course, the greenback program had been defined *ad nauseam*, and the actual work of the convention was quickly accomplished. After the formal admission of delegates and the selection of a committee on permanent organization, the platform was reported. It repeated almost word for word the formulas of the recent farmer-labor conventions, with "immediate and unconditional repeal of the specie resumption act" taking precedence over the interconvertible bond. The only new plank was a blast at the clause of the Resumption Act authorizing a new fractional currency. It was a mistake to substitute coin for paper, and besides, the move was a "job" to "enrich the owners of silver mines."

[93] Commons *op. cit.*, II, 170-171; Reginald C. McGrane, "Ohio and the Greenback Movement," *MVHR*, XI, No. 4 (March 1925), 534.

The platform was adopted amid cheers and applause, but at this point a Michigan delegate got the floor and proposed the following additional plank: "We . . . declare that justice demands the payment of . . . coin obligations in either gold or silver at the option of the government." Here was something new. In the orthodox greenback canon, silver was as much "hard money" as gold, a view reflected in the last of the regular platform planks. Was the convention, then, to go on record as endorsing coin payment for coin obligations? At the very best this must have seemed redundant; at worst, even though few green-backers denied that where specifically enjoined coin obligations had to be paid in specie, it must have seemed gratuitously bullionist. The delegates were confused and hesitated. Hinch-cliffe now insisted that the platform was being overloaded with detail, and succeeded in getting the proposal tabled. The convention then proceeded to nominations. After the candidates were chosen, James Buchanan returned to the question and proposed making the old silver dollar a legal tender. By this time the delegates, or at least their leaders, had been briefed on the significance of the silver question, and the motion car-ried. Only as an afterthought was the most momentous domestic issue of the next quarter-century injected into American politics![94]

In its choice of standard bearers the new party erred as badly as its predecessor in 1872. David Davis was again available, but after rejecting this *ignis fatuus*, the convention nominated the elderly New York ironmaster-philanthropist, Peter Cooper, an almost equally foolish choice. Certainly Cooper deserved well of the greenbackers. An old Locofoco, he had been one of the few men of wealth to befriend labor before the War.[95] As early as 1867, moreover, he had apparently championed the inter-convertible bond[96] and in 1869 had been commended by the

[94] The silver resolution was not, however, included in the official platform of the party as published. See *AM*, Aug. 24, 1876.

[95] For Cooper's prewar politics and benefactions see Edward C. Mack, *Peter Cooper, Citizen of New York* (New York: Duell, Sloan & Pearce, 1949), especially ch. VIII.

[96] See Cooper's 1867 statement to the Union League Club in the Cooper MSS. Edward Mack be-lieves that this pronouncement has been misdated and was not really made until 1876. From Cooper's

National Labor Union for his financial views.[97] But the venerable New Yorker was 85 in 1876 and could scarcely have been expected to fire the public imagination or wage a vigorous campaign. Indeed, Cooper at first refused to run at all and had to be persuaded to accept the nomination.[98] Undoubtedly, he did represent respectability, a commodity sorely needed by the greenbackers, but ultimately it was Cooper's wealth that made the poverty-stricken Independents choose him.[99] To restore some political realism to the ticket, the vigorous anti-monopoly Senator from California, Newton Booth, was given the Vice-Presidential nomination.[100] After presumably carrying the ticket to victory, Cooper, it was hoped, would resign in favor of his youthful running-mate![101]

The money question was not a major concern of the Republicans at their June convention. Butler and Kelley were on hand to preach the greenback doctrine,[102] but as usual they were not given a serious hearing. At Cincinnati both the financial plank and the nomination of Rutherford Hayes reaffirmed the party's basic conservatism on finance.[103]

At St. Louis, on the other hand, the divided Democrats got into just the sort of dogfight over finance they had feared. The conservatives had expected little trouble in controlling the resolutions committee,[104] but the repeal faction, led by Ewing and Daniel Voorhees of Indiana, almost proved their match.

---

earlier connection with Groom and Freeman, however, it seems to me highly likely that he actually did entertain these views in 1867. See Mack, *op. cit.*, p. 419, n. 2.

[97] At its Philadelphia convention of August 1869 the N. L. U. had passed a resolution commending Cooper for his "well-timed defense of our American monetary system." Commons *op. cit.*, II, 241.

[98] Mack, *op. cit.*, p. 367.

[99] Groom, who acted as Cooper's representative at Indianapolis, though probably without Cooper's permission, apparently made promises that the New York millionaire would contribute generously to the party campaign fund if nominated. *Ibid.*, p. 366.

[100] Booth had been anti-railroad Governor of California in 1871, and was elected United States Senator against the opposition of the powerful California railroad corporations.

[101] The most complete reports on the convention may be found in *AM*, May 25, 1876; *WA*, May 20, 1876.

[102] In the months before the Indianapolis convention Butler was in touch with James Buchanan. See Butler to Buchanan, Boston, Nov. 11, 1875; and Washington, Feb. 2, 1876, Butler MSS, LC.

[103] *NYT*, June 16, 1876.

[104] Thomas Bayard to David Wells, Washington, May 27, 1876, Wells MSS.

Tilden's lieutenant, William Dorsheimer, who led the conservatives' fight on the committee for Manton Marble's financial plank, proved inept at the in-fighting. Hoping to pacify the westerners and avoid an open floor battle, he agreed to accept a demand for repeal of the resumption date. But after taking this concession Ewing and Voorhees submitted a minority report demanding total repeal.[105]

The soft money faction could not, however, overcome the conservative majority on the convention floor. The two reports touched off a debate between Dorsheimer and Henry Watterson on the one side and Ewing and Voorhees on the other, that ended in a severe drubbing for the total repeal men. Though short, the debate was acrimonious and revealing—more revealing than was politically expedient. If the hard money men were to be permitted some chance to carry their states, Dorsheimer declared, the convention must stand by the majority report. Voorhees retorted that similar considerations applied to the westerners. The debate threatened to become a frank discussion of party weaknesses when Watterson interrupted and reminded his colleagues that the public was watching them. This ended the discussion, and when the vote was taken, the majority report carried 505 to 219.[106]

The currency plank as finally adopted, though demanding less than total repeal, arraigned the Republicans for "financial imbecility and immorality." In the eleven years since the War, the opposition had controlled the Administration and yet had made no serious preparation for resumption; in fact they hampered the return to sound money. "As such a hindrance," the platform read, "we denounce the Resumption Clause of the act of 1875, and we demand its repeal."[107] Despite Dorsheimer's concessions the platform was essentially a conservative statement. The Democrats questioned only the date of resumption. By implication the rest of the measure, with its provision expanding the "monopolistic" national banking system, its grant

[105] Manton Marble to Samuel J. Tilden, Bedford [?], July [?], 1876; Marble to Tilden, n.p., June [?], 1876, Marble MSS.

[106] NYT, June 29, 1876; Nation,

xxiii (July 7, 1876), 1; NYDT, June 29, 1876; New York Herald, June 29, 1876.

[107] Annual Cyclopedia for 1876, pp. 785ff.

of extraordinary loan powers to the Treasury, and its endorsement of resumption in principle, was accepted; and even the resumption clause, as Ewing pointed out, had been attacked only because it purportedly hindered ultimate resumption.[108]

The victory of the hard money men was completed by the swift nomination of Tilden, while in an obvious move at peace-making, the convention chose former Senator Thomas Hendricks of Indiana, a soft money man, as his running mate.

Second place and an ambiguous platform pronouncement did not satisfy the Democratic greenbackers, and in Congress they tried to force the party to make good on the repeal plank. The conservatives were "embarrassed," wrote Congressman Randall Gibson of Louisiana, "by demands of our Western friends for the repeal of the resumption clause." They insist "that the St. Louis Platform commits the party to its repeal."[109] In this claim the westerners had the support of Hendricks. His acceptance was said to be contingent on fulfillment of the platform pledge,[110] and he was using his influence with members of Congress to force repeal,[111] telling everyone that it would remove the uncertainties of the platform.[112]

Both factions were playing the frankest sort of politics with the currency. The soft money men knew that they could not get repeal through the Republican Senate, but hoped to commit the Democracy to the currency program they felt would win votes in the West and South in November.[113] The conservatives for the moment were concerned largely with avoiding embarrassment to Tilden, who had retired to Saratoga after the convention and, in his deliberate and cautious way, was still composing his letter of acceptance a month later. It would be awkward, to say the least, if the Democrats in Congress and the party nominee were to collide over a central issue of the campaign.[114]

[108] *NYT*, June 29, 1876.

[109] Gibson to Marble, Washington, July 5, 1876, Marble MSS. For details of the struggle see *Congressional Record*, p. 4506.

[110] *NYT*, July 18, 1876.

[111] William Morrison to Manton Marble, Washington, July 4, 1876, Marble MSS.

[112] Interview with a reporter for the *Nashville American*, quoted in *NYT*, July 9, 1876.

[113] *Ibid.*, July 5, 1876.

[114] Randall Gibson to Manton Marble, Washington, July 26, 1876; Marble to Gibson, New York, July 12, 1876, Marble MSS.

Conservative Democrats sent anxious appeals to Tilden and his close advisors urging an end to the delay. From Washington, Gibson wrote that it was becoming difficult to restrain Congress. If the inflationists were to be stopped Tilden must furnish a guide to House leaders.[115] Morrison, fearing a public breach between Tilden and Hendricks, urged Marble to get the two men together,[116] and a conference was arranged at Saratoga.[117] This accomplished little. The candidates' acceptance letters, released August 4, only advertised the basic party split. Tilden condemned the Resumption Act as "a barren promise," but studiously avoided endorsing repeal. Hendricks called for unqualified repeal of the resumption clause.[118]

Tilden's letter was not the ringing hard money manifesto that the conservatives had hoped for, and its weakness helped the greenback Democrats. Up to this point Cox had resisted pressure for a repeal measure, hoping for either adjournment or strong support from Tilden.[119] He now felt it expedient to move with the tide and called the Banking and Currency Committee into immediate session to vote on a repeal bill. On August 5 he brought before the House a report recommending passage of two distinct measures. The first called for repeal of the resumption date but did not suggest any alternate time. The second—actually a concurrent resolution—provided for a House-Senate committee, with three non-political experts, to inquire into both the resumption problem and the new silver question. To justify reopening the currency question, Cox claimed that public opinion was almost unanimously agreed that the Resumption Act was "hopeless of execution and a steady threat to . . . prosperity."[120]

Despite the usual attempts at evasion and delay, both measures were brought to an immediate vote, and passed by a

---

[115] Gibson to Marble, Washington, July 13, 1876; July 26, 1876; August Belmont to Marble, [?], Long Island, July 23, 1876, *ibid.* On July 20 *The Public* (formerly *The Financier*) reported that Hendricks and his friends were trying to force Tilden at least to endorse the platform repeal plank. *The Public*, x (July 20, 1876), 36.

[116] Morrison to Manton Marble, Washington, July 4, 1876, Marble MSS.

[117] Marble to Morrison, New York, July 12, 1876, *ibid.*

[118] *NYDT*, Aug. 5, 1876.

[119] *Ibid.*

[120] *Congressional Record*, pp. 5218-5220.

majority of 106 to 86, with 93 abstentions.[121] They were then reported to the Senate and the repeal bill was referred to committee. The concurrent resolution, providing for an investigatory commission, passed;[122] though as predicted, and probably as intended, Congress adjourned before action could be taken on repeal.

The Presidential campaign was already under way as Congress wound up its business for the session. Democratic success seemed assured in a solid bloc of "redeemed" southern states, and even the Republicans conceded that Tilden would have to capture only two or three major northern states to win.[123] A shift of a few thousand votes in a few key places might well decide the election. Democratic hopes centered on New York, Indiana, and Ohio, where in recent contests the Democracy had made a strong showing. In the two western states soft money had long shown its political potential, and with the new greenback party on the scene the currency problem became a major campaign issue.

The Independents were first in the field. From the outset they faced towering difficulties. To begin with, money was hard to find, for Cooper proved less generous than expected. An unwilling candidate at best, who even after accepting the nomination talked of withdrawing if the Democrats nominated Allen,[124] he was more willing to pay for greenback pamphlets than to contribute to the party campaign chest.[125] All through the campaign, poverty hampered the third-party effort. When the Indiana Independents held their state convention, they could not even afford to rent a hall and met in an open field.[126] Moreover, the whole Independent campaign was marked by hard luck and ineptitude. Senator Booth rejected the Vice-Presidential nomination, and the Executive Committee had to choose an alternate. The Committee, meeting in the East, failed

[121] *Ibid.*, p. 5232.
[122] *Ibid.*, p. 5245.
[123] Harry Barnard, *Rutherford B. Hayes and His America* (Indianapolis: The Bobbs-Merrill Co., 1954), p. 308.
[124] *IA*, July 1, 1876. He also called at Tilden's home and told him he would vote for him if he would endorse the greenback platform! See Mack, *op. cit.*, p. 367.
[125] *Ibid.*, pp. 366, 368-369.
[126] *Indianapolis Sun*, Aug. 19, 1876.

to keep the western group informed of their deliberations, and for a while the westerners were driven to the point of revolt by rumors that another easterner would be selected to run with Cooper. In the end Noonan was not even informed of the choice of Sam Cary, and had to learn it from the Chicago daily press.[127]

A bad mistake was made in giving Brick Pomeroy a major place in the campaign. Unable to swallow Tilden, leader of his archenemies, Pomeroy had joined the Independents after St. Louis. By this time he had sold his New York paper and reestablished the *Democrat* in Chicago. As editor of a popular daily, he could be valuable to the Independents and was promptly made chairman of the party's Organization Committee.[128] Unfortunately, in his new role he exhibited, along with his usual vigor, his usual extravagant humbuggery. One of his first moves was to establish a weekly campaign paper, *The Great Campaign*, to enspirit the workers in the vineyard, attract converts, and spread the word of the party's doings and triumphs.[129] He also took over the organizing of greenback clubs for Cooper and Cary and pushed the task with great energy.[130] But he probably hurt the cause more than he helped it. The anti-Semitism of *The Great Campaign*, if nothing else, raised unnecessary side issues.[131] Pomeroy was always extravagant in his language, and his violent attacks on the Republicans—"political harlots"—and Tilden—"the paid tool of the jews who control the gold market"—scarcely could have recommended the Independent ticket to soft money men in the major parties.[132] Nor was Pomeroy above transparent mendacity in advancing the cause. In October *The Great Campaign* published a sensational "confidential circular," purportedly by the "Chairman of the National Executive Committee of the Bankers' Association," implicating the American Bankers' Association in a plot to destroy American democracy and return the nation to

[127] *IA*, July 15, 1876; July 29, 1876.
[128] *The Great Campaign*, Sept. 5, 1876.
[129] This ran for 16 issues, between July 18, 1876 and Oct. 31, 1876. There is a file of the paper at the Hayes Memorial Library, Fremont, Ohio.
[130] *IA*, Sept. 23, 1876.
[131] See above, ch. VI.
[132] *The Great Campaign*, Aug. 8, 1876; Sept. 5, 1876.

the conservative class society of Federalist days. The unnamed Chairman talked contemptuously of the ignorant childlike populace, praised Hamilton and the Bank of the United States as a bulwark against social unrest, and hinted broadly at using violence to rid the country of "any noisy, worthless scamps who go about talking about the money power."[133] This was a crude forgery, obviously growing out of the "soliloquies" Pomeroy had composed the previous decade. Now they were being passed off as the truth and could have fooled no one not already far gone in greenback fanaticism. Even his work in organizing greenback clubs turned out to be controversial. By late September, before the campaign ended, Noonan was charging that Pomeroy was using the clubs to advance his own personal ambitions.[134]

Despite mismanagement and bad luck, the Independents got off to a fast start. State conventions met in Illinois, Kansas, Indiana, Michigan, New York, Connecticut, and other states to ratify the Indianapolis results and nominate electors and state tickets.[135] The new party apparently appealed strongly to the groups ostensibly represented at Indianapolis. Farmers, told that Cooper was their candidate,[136] seemed to respond. In rural areas of the West open-air rallies, complete with picnic baskets, brass bands, and the florid oratory popular with western audiences, whipped up enthusiasm for Cooper and Cary.[137] Small-town, midwestern newspapers flocked to the Independent cause;[138] county and township grange groups endorsed the Independent platform.[139]

Labor, too, was courted with some success. In Chicago the Independent Greenback Party organized Cook County ward by ward to woo wage earners and the unemployed.[140] In Pennsylvania the "currency reformers" of the Philadelphia National

[133] *Ibid.*, Oct. 10, 1876; *Indianapolis Sun*, Oct. 28, 1876.

[134] *IA*, Sept. 23, 1876.

[135] These are described in *IA* and *Indianapolis Sun* for June to Sept. 1876.

[136] *Indianapolis Sun*, June 17, 1876.

[137] *AM*, June 22, 1876; Aug. 10, 1876; *Indianapolis Sun*, Sept. 2, 1876.

[138] *The Great Campaign*, July 18, 1876 and Sept. 19, 1876, containing lists of pro-Cooper papers.

[139] *Indianapolis Sun*, July 1, 1876.

[140] See the MS Record Book of this group in Labor Collection, Political Parties, State Hist. Soc. of Wisc.

Financial Reform League and old labor reformers joined with elements from the Knights of Labor to campaign for Cooper.[141] The Knights were also active in the Scranton area where Terence Powderly worked hard for the Independent ticket.[142] In the Pittsburgh region editor John M. Davis, as Independent Executive Committee Sub-Chairman, propagandized among the miners and mill workers.[143] Even in New York, the heart of the enemy camp, the combined support of labor and the soft money reformers created an active Independent organization with a state ticket and some newspaper support.[144]

Indeed, within the ranks of labor the only audible sour note came from the Socialists. Long opposed to greenbackism as a mere social palliative, as recently as April 1876 they had tried unsuccessfully to defeat the greenback platform proposed at the Pittsburgh National Labor Convention. Now, under editor J. P. McDonnell of the *Labor Standard*, organ of the Marxist Social-Democratic Workingman's Party of North America, they struck out at the Independents. Cooper and Cary, a millionaire and a politician, could not truly represent labor. Such people, and the Greenbackers as a group for that matter, were middle-class men who had little sympathy for labor's troubles. Greenbackism as a solution of the labor problem was chimerical. "The disease from which we suffer is not the want of currency, but a planless system of production."[145]

Despite the blunders, despite the opposition, for a while

[141] On the background and activities of this group see William C. Crooks to Samuel J. Randall, Philadelphia, Jan. 14, 1875; A. H. Owen to Randall, Philadelphia, April 19, 1875; and the broadside entitled "Monetary Reform," in the Randall MSS. See also Ralph R. Ricker, "The Greenback-Labor Movement in Pennsylvania" (unpublished Ph.D. dissertation, Pennsylvania State University, 1955).

[142] Powderly MS Diary, entries for Oct. 3, 12, 13, and Nov. 6, 1876, Powderly MSS, Catholic University of America.

[143] *National Labor Tribune*, May 20, 1876; June 10, 1876; July 21,

1876; Sept. 16, 1876; Sept. 30, 1876; Oct. 21, 1876.

[144] Clipping on last page of MS Record Book, Independent Greenback Labor Party, 1876-1877, Labor Collection, Political Parties, State Hist. Soc. of Wisc.; *AM*, Sept. 14, 1876; *NYDT*, Sept. 27, 1876; *IA*, Nov. 4, 1876. The *Indianapolis Sun* listed three greenback newspapers in New York City: Groom's *New York Mercantile Journal*, the *New York New Republic*, and the *Irish World*. Quoted in *The Great Campaign*, Sept. 19, 1876.

[145] *Labor Standard*, Aug. 12, 1876; Sept. 2, 1876; Oct. 7, 1876.

Independent hopes ran high. B. G. Chace of the National Committee actually believed that although the party was hard pressed for funds, it would carry enough "central western states" to throw the election into the House and elect Cooper.[146] Equally optimistic was R. M. Springer, Secretary of the Illinois State Central Committee.[147]

Wild as these predictions now appear, the major parties took the money question seriously. In the East the Republicans told businessmen that a Tilden victory would mean uncontrolled inflation and repudiation of the federal debt;[148] in the West, burdened with a sound money national platform, they ran from the currency issue. "*A bloody shirt campaign with money* and Indiana is safe for us, a *financial* campaign and no money and we are beaten*,*" an electioneering Republican wrote Hayes in August.[149] In Ohio few Republican speakers would touch finance. With the exception of Schurz and Sherman they concentrated on the "Southern Question"—a euphemism for the bloody shirt.[150]

For the Democrats the money issue was an equally grave, though more equivocal, danger. Tilden's nomination had been a bitter disappointment to the soft money wing and had driven some of them over to the Independents. In Indiana, for example, Republican journals were certain that the Independents would cut into Democratic strength,[151] a conviction shared by Republican state boss Oliver Morton who sought to encourage the movement by secretly subsidizing a local Greenback paper.[152] In Ohio, despite Ewing's efforts to keep the greenback wing

[146] Chace to Donnelly, Providence, R. I., July [?], 1876, Donnelly MSS.

[147] R. M. Springer to Donnelly, Chicago, Sept. 15, 1876, *ibid.*

[148] *NYT*, July 3, 1876; July 5, 1876; *NYDT*, Sept. 22, 1876; Nov. 6, 1876. In mid-October a *New York Evening Post* dispatch asserted that the London syndicate underwriting Secretary Bristow's 4½ per cent funding loan would stop subscriptions if the Democrats won. The article produced consternation among Democratic leaders. Abram Hewitt, National Chairman, wrote to Belmont, whose firm represented the English Rothschilds in the syndicate, that he must issue an emphatic denial of the *Post* statement at once to save Tilden from serious harm. See Hewitt to Belmont, n.p., Oct. 18, 1876, Marble MSS.

[149] This was General Judson Kilpatrick. Kilpatrick to Hayes, n.p., Aug. 21, 1876, in *Annual Cyclopedia for 1876*, pp. 410-411.

[150] *NYDT*, Sept. 26, 1876.

[151] *NYT*, July 30, 1876.

[152] Barnard, *op. cit.*, p. 301.

loyal,[153] a few defections occurred among local Democratic leaders and Democratic voters early in the campaign.[154] Hayes, not otherwise optimistic about his chances, believed that while in the October state contests soft money Democrats would remain loyal, in November a considerable number of them would vote for Cooper out of hatred for Tilden, whom they held responsible for Allen's defeat the previous year.[155]

But in the end the Independent campaign collapsed. Besides Cooper's age, Pomeroy's clumsiness, the Socialists' antipathy, and the crippling dearth of cash, traditional party loyalties were ties too strong to break. Americans once again proved that a political fight intrigued them more than the class struggle. If a few Democratic soft money men defected, most held their noses and swallowed Tilden. The *Cincinnati Enquirer* remained loyal to the party, despite Independent predictions.[156] Both Ewing and Allen resisted Greenback blandishments, as did Voorhees in Indiana.[157]

In areas of greenback strength the Democrats kept their adherents loyal by successfully copying the Independents' program. Ewing, himself a candidate for Congress, had held the Democrats in line at the May state convention; and in the fall the local Democratic campaign was almost indistinguishable from the Greenbackers'.[158] The Indiana Democracy, too, aped their radical opponents and provided a shelter for greenback sentiment.[159] The Illinois Democrats went so far as to adopt Louis Steward, the Independent gubernatorial candidate, as their own.[160]

[153] Thomas Ewing, Jr., *Speech . . . at Lancaster, Ohio, July 15, 1876*, p. 3.

[154] *NYT*, July 1, 1876; July 23, 1876.

[155] Charles R. Williams (ed.), *Diary and Letters of Rutherford Birchard Hayes, Nineteenth President of the United States* (Columbus: The Ohio State Archeological and Historical Society, 1924), III, 360, diary entry for Sept. 16, 1876.

[156] *NYDT*, Sept. 5, 1876; *WA*, July 1, 1876.

[157] A. E. Olleman to William Allen, Indianapolis, Aug. 10, 1876; W. O. Waggoner to Allen, Toledo, Sept. 6, 1876; J. J. Faran to Allen, Cincinnati, Oct. 22, 1876, Allen MSS; *NYDT*, Sept. 5, 1876.

[158] John T. Blair to Thomas Ewing, Jr., Columbus, May 23, 1876; Ewing MSS; R. B. Hayes to Edwards Pierrepont, Columbus, Sept. 16, 1876, in Williams, *op. cit.*, III, 360.

[159] *Annual Cyclopedia for 1876*, p. 408.

[160] *IA*, Nov. 4, 1876.

Realizing the danger of being swallowed up, the Independents had made the Democracy their chief target. They scored the procrastination of the Democratic House and blasted Tilden's record as Governor and as leader of the New York Democracy.[161] The Democrats, they charged, with all their talk, were betrayers of the people.[162] These efforts availed little. Toward the end the Independent campaign fell apart. In Indiana Anson Wolcott, the party's gubernatorial nominee, abruptly withdrew from the race less than a week before the election, charging that the Indiana Independents were nothing more than a stalking-horse for the Democrats.[163] Although they managed to get another ticket in the field before election day,[164] the betrayal ended whatever slim chance the Greenbackers may have had in the state. Steward in Illinois turned out to be an opportunist who had sought the Independent nomination only to use it to pry a similar nomination out of the Democrats. He refused to endorse the Independent state platform and was repudiated by Noonan before November.[165] At the very end, Redstone of the National Executive Committee even proposed withdrawing the national ticket itself on condition that Hayes promise to support legislation to increase the legal tender circulation![166]

It was scarcely a surprise, then, that the new party made a pitiful showing at the polls. In Illinois, Campbell himself, "father of the greenback," was defeated for reelection to Congress.[167] In the country as a whole only 80,000 votes were officially credited to the Cooper-Cary ticket. Obviously, this vote did not reflect the full Independent electorate. Powderly later recalled how in his Pennsylvania district the local election board simply counted hundreds of Cooper votes for Tilden, since they were

[161] *The Great Campaign*, July 18, 1876; *IA*, July 29, 1876, quoting the *Indianapolis Sun*; *WA*, July 15, 1876.

[162] *Indianapolis Sun*, April 22, 1876.

[163] *NYDT*, Oct. 6, 1876; *Annual Cyclopedia for 1876*, pp. 410-411.

[164] This was the second change. Franklin Landers, the soft money Democrat, had been the original Independent nominee. After he declined, Wolcott, the candidate for Lt. Governor, had been moved up to first place. *Indianapolis Sun*, April 29, 1876; May 27, 1876.

[165] Though not by the State Executive Committee. *IA*, Nov. 4, 1876.

[166] A. E. Redstone to R. B. Hayes, Washington, Oct. 13, 1876, Carl Schurz MSS, LC.

[167] *WA*, Dec. 9, 1876.

"naturally Democratic."[168] But even doubling the vote does not make the Independent showing very impressive.

Such as it was, the Cooper-Cary vote did in fact reflect the coalition the new party claimed to represent. In Pennsylvania the bulk of the 7100 votes recorded for Cooper were concentrated in Allegheny, Beaver, Berks, Dauphin, Fayette, Luzerne, Mercer, Schuylkill, Venango, Washington, and Westmoreland counties—all prominent in coal mining and iron manufacturing. Ohio's disappointing 3058 votes also came from the wage earners of the industrial centers. Ohio manufacturers continued to oppose resumption apparently,[169] but there is no evidence that they voted for Cooper. In Iowa, Kansas, and Illinois, on the other hand, the Independent vote was largely rural, and seemingly represented the support of isolated, single-crop farmers tilling the poorer soils. In Indiana depressed farmers and the urban unemployed voted Independent.[170]

But obviously the overwhelming majority of farmers and wage earners retained their traditional party loyalties; what little change occurred represented defection from the Republicans. In Indiana the Independent gubernatorial candidate received

[168] Harry J. Carman, Henry David, and Paul N. Guthrie (eds.), *The Path I Trod: The Autobiography of Terence V. Powderly* (New York: Columbia University Press, 1940), pp. 67-68. The outright theft of votes resulted in such ludicrous totals for Cooper as 10 votes in Philadelphia, and 93 in Pittsburgh—though more in Allegheny County as a whole—and 21 in Cincinnati. See James, *op. cit.*, pp. 119-120.

[169] Henry Safford Neal to John Sherman, Ironton, Ohio, June 9, 1876, Sherman MSS, LC; W. C. Andrews to James A. Garfield, Cleveland, June 24, 1876, Garfield MSS.

[170] The figures on which these general conclusions are based come from W. Dean Burnham, *Presidential Ballots, 1836-1892* (Baltimore: The Johns Hopkins Press, 1955). The conclusion regarding isolated, single-crop farmers is drawn from

Clyde O. Ruggles, "The Economic Basis of the Greenback Movement in Iowa and Wisconsin," *Proceedings of the Mississippi Valley Historical Association for the Year 1912-1913*, VI, 160-161. There is little point in a close statistical analysis of the Cooper vote. As I have suggested, it is unreliable as recorded and also far too scattered. In the vote for state-wide office in Indiana, however, where despite Wolcott's treachery there was a sizable Independent turnout, Ruggles's conclusions, although drawn largely from the Presidential statistics for 1880, and largely concerned with Iowa and Wisconsin, seem to be borne out. But the 1876 Indiana state statistics do show one significant divergence from Ruggles. The whopping 31 per cent turnout for the Greenback ticket in Vigo County clearly represents a substantial labor turnout in industrial Terre Haute city.

more than twice the vote in counties normally Republican than in those normally Democratic,[171] and this pattern seems to have held for the other states of the Northwest.[172] In effect, then, the Independents' failure consisted to a large extent of their inability to attract any sizable part of the large Democratic greenback contingent. Democratic greenbackers did well in the West— Ewing, for example, won in Ohio—while Independents everywhere ran a very poor third. The Democrats retained their House majority. Although accident was to give Hayes the Presidency, Democratic greenbackers, by providing soft money men with an alternative to Cooper, had served the party well.

As the nation began the agony of the disputed election, the currency question receded into the background. A few Ohio Democrats believed that the bankers, fearing insurrection and resulting repudiation, would "demand a fair count."[173] In a curiously oblique way the Independents actually tipped the election to Hayes. Briefly, a coalition of Independents and Democrats in the Illinois state legislature elected David Davis United States Senator. Davis, the one non-partisan on the Electoral Commission chosen to count the disputed election returns for President, promptly resigned his Supreme Court Justiceship. His replacement, Justice Bradley, was a Republican who, as the fifteenth member of an otherwise evenly divided body, cast the deciding vote which threw out all the disputed Tilden returns and elected Hayes President.[174] To say the least, the Greenbackers had played a marginal role in the disputed election. Unlike railroads and patronage the country's finances scarcely entered into the intrigues and arrangements of the 1876 electoral compromisers.[175]

---

[171] Haynes, op. cit., p. 119.

[172] It is significant that with only one exception, in neither Ohio nor in Illinois did any sizable block of Cooper votes come from the southern tier of counties, normally Democratic. In Iowa, too, the Independents drew largely from the Republicans. Ibid., p. 154.

[173] Hugh Ewing to Charles Ewing, Hillsdale, Ohio, Dec. 9, 1876; Charles Bonsall to Thomas Ewing,

Jr., Salem. Ohio, Nov. 24, 1876, Ewing MSS.

[174] Willard L. King, Lincoln's Manager: David Davis (Cambridge: Harvard University Press, 1960), pp. 291-293.

[175] The foremost authority on the inner history of the Disputed Election, Professor C. Vann Woodward, does not suggest any connection between the financial question and the "Compromise of 1877." Wood-

For the Greenbackers the financial calm was the quiet of the tomb. A stunning blow to Independent morale, the election almost destroyed the new party. Leaders and followers alike melted away. Pomeroy, though he soon relented, virtually read himself out of the party in a post-mortem issue of *The Great Campaign*, in which he accused the National Executive Committee of incompetence and mismanagement.[176] *Industrial Age* did not long survive the debacle. Noonan's attack on Steward for treachery alienated many of the paper's readers and financial supporters in Illinois. On February 24, the last issue of the *Age*, full of Noonan's self-pity over the trials of greenback journalism, appeared. Thereafter both Noonan and his paper disappear from view. At the end of the year, Donnelly, expecting the Independents to be "swallowed up in the great national struggle over the Presidency," tried to sell the *Anti-Monopolist*, and presumably retire from greenback politics.[177] Even the *Workingman's Advocate*, for over a decade a bastion of soft money doctrine, faltered. By December it had become a bi-monthly, and for a time could not even meet this limited schedule.

This was not, of course, the end of soft money. Viewed in the perspective of the entire postwar generation, however, it marks the end of one phase of the financial debate which began in 1865. By the opening session of the Forty-fifth Congress the money question would be transfigured by a glittering new issue which had barely emerged during the campaign just concluded.

---

ward, *Reunion and Reaction: The Compromise of 1877 and the End of Reconstruction* (Boston: Little, Brown & Co., 1951), *passim*.

[176] Actually it was before the national election, though after the disastrous state defeat in Indiana, and the handwriting was clearly on the wall. *The Great Campaign*, Oct. 31, 1876.

[177] Donnelly to [?], St. Paul, Dec. 12, 1876, Donnelly MSS.

SHERMAN AND SILVER (1877-1878)

I

AFTER the long, anxious months of the disputed Presidential election, most Americans were probably relieved to see Rutherford Hayes safely installed in office. The hard money men, however, had special reason to feel pleased. As a Congressman in the '60's, Hayes had wavered on national finance, but the 1875 gubernatorial campaign had established him as a hard money man. So clear was his position, he personally felt, that there was no reason to mention finance in accepting the nomination, and he had finally declared himself only on Carl Schurz's strong urging.[1] In his inaugural address the new President repeated the views he had expressed as a candidate. "The feeling of uncertainty inseparable from an irredeemable paper currency is one of the greatest obstacles to a return to prosperous times." Only gold-convertible paper money was "safe" paper money, and he intended, he said, to ask Congress for early resumption legislation.[2]

After such a beginning, Hayes's choice of John Sherman for the Treasury was a distinct shock to the hard money purists. At best, Sherman's record on finance was spotty. He had flirted with the Ohio Idea and in general had not been averse to cutting corners when it appeared expedient. To contractionist die-hards he seemed "a trickster by birth, and habit," who had "been on all sides of the financial question."[3]

[1] Hayes to Carl Schurz, Columbus, June 26, 1876, in Charles Richard Williams (ed.), *Diary and Letters of Rutherford Birchard Hayes, Nineteenth President of the United States* (Columbus: The Ohio State Archeological and Historical Society, 1924), III, 329. See also *ibid.*, pp. 331-332; and Williams, *The Life of Rutherford Birchard Hayes, Nineteenth President of the United States* (Columbus: Ohio State Archeological and Historical Society, 1918), I, 461.

[2] *Ibid.*, II, 9.

[3] Burke A. Hinsdale to Garfield, Hiram, Ohio, Feb. 28, 1877, in Mary L. Hinsdale (ed.), *Garfield-*

To the more practical conservatives, however, the appointment seemed an augury of safe and steady progress toward resumption,[4] and in this case the moderates proved wiser than their more intransigent allies. Sherman was certainly not doctrinaire. A hard money man by conviction, he was a political pragmatist who opposed moving too far beyond public opinion. In 1868 he had advocated an interconvertible bond, believing the principle wise and the theory popular. By 1872 he had concluded that growing up to specie was the best policy.[5] This was not consistency, but who could blame Sherman? It was safe enough for a New York or New England politician to be a sound money crusader, but for an Ohioan the alternative to pliancy was oblivion. Although he had learned to adjust to the shifting wind of Ohio monetary politics, Sherman had little love for the periodic greenback upsurges that disturbed state and national politics. The Resumption Act, which he had hoped would end the soft money agitation, had thus far only amplified it. Only by returning to specie could the disrupting currency issue once and for all be removed from political life. Fortunately, his years in the Donnybrook of Ohio politics, his long Congressional career, his experience as Chairman of both the House Ways and Means and the Senate Finance Committees, gave the Secretary a suppleness of method, a knowledge of the Congressional mind, and, on the most practical level, the important connections in banking circles that admirably fitted him for the delicate and exacting task of resumption which lay ahead.

Sherman faced towering difficulties as he entered on the duties of his new office. Nothing had been done by his predecessors Benjamin Bristow and Lot Morrill[6] to implement the Resumption Act, beyond exhorting Congress to provide supplementary

---

Hinsdale Letters: Correspondence between James Abram Garfield and Burke Aaron Hinsdale (Ann Arbor: University of Michigan Press, 1949), pp. 364-365. See also *Nation*, xxvi (June 20, 1878), 375; Charles Nordhoff to David A. Wells, Washington, May 5, 1878, Wells MSS, LC.

[4] *CFC,* xxiv (March 10, 1877),

212; *The Public*, xi (March 8, 1877), 147.

[5] See Sherman's long and revealing letter to David Davis, Mansfield, Ohio, Nov. 9, 1872, Davis MSS, Illinois State Library.

[6] Morrill succeeded Bristow as Grant's last Secretary of the Treasury.

legislation.[7] Deeply divided, distracted by the disputed election, and reluctant to stir up further controversy, Congress had done nothing, and Sherman knew that he would face resumption day without better means than the 1875 Act provided.

Nor was the state of public opinion likely to inspire easy confidence. Through the last months of 1877 and into 1878, business conditions, unhealthy for four years, had worsened perceptibly. Business failures were a third greater for the first half of 1878 than for the corresponding period of 1877.[8] Under the circumstances a large part of business still shied away from resumption. True, gold had fallen to 105 by January 1877, the lowest point in fifteen years, but many businessmen still dreaded the final drop to convertibility—and many would remain apprehensive until the very end. Merchants and manufacturers, it was said, feared that in preparing for resumption the banks would curtail loans, ruining many "who are strictly solvent but are engaged in operations which they cannot carry forward without credit."[9]

The first intimations, early in 1877, that the Treasury was about to borrow gold for resuming, produced consternation among western businessmen. Oliver Morton reported in May that the news of the Treasury's impending move had caused alarm "almost approaching a panic" among Indianapolis "bankers and businessmen."[10] A month later Senator William Allison of Iowa told Sherman that many western railroads with "heavy floating debts held by the banks" would be totally ruined if, as was feared, he locked up currency for resumption during the fall crop moving season.[11] At least one western trade association, the Cincinnati Chamber of Commerce, urged the Treasury to abandon "forced" resumption, which was already "working . . .

[7] Unless Bristow's deliberate interpretation of the June 1874 Banking Act and the free banking clause of the Resumption Act to produce a contraction is considered positive action. For the exhortation see U.S. Treasury, *Report of the Secretary of the Treasury on the State of the Finances for the Year 1875*, p. xx; *ibid. for 1876*, pp. xiv-xvi.

[8] There were 4,749 bankruptcies involving $99 million in capital in the first half of 1877. For the same period of 1878, failures totaled 5,825 and involved $130 million. See Dun & Company Report in the *Nation*, xxvii (July 18, 1878), 33; and also xxvi (May 2, 1878), 283.

[9] *NYDT*, Sept. 12, 1877.

[10] Morton to John Sherman, Indianapolis, May 25, 1877, Sherman MSS, LC.

[11] Allison to Sherman, Dubuque, June 21, 1877, *ibid.*

hardships to the industrial and financial interests of the country, creating apprehensions of depression and disaster."[12]

Nevertheless, there were signs of a thaw in some areas of business opinion hitherto hostile to specie payments. Paradoxically, the depression itself contributed to the hopeful if limited change. By 1877 the economy had almost reached the "hard pan" that businessmen had long feared. Many of the most vocal supporters of easy money had already been forced to the wall, and others saw little point in holding out against the last few inches of contraction. "The country has already suffered all or nearly all the hardships incident to the restoration of the specie standard," one Albany banker believed. "To go back would be to necessitate . . . travelling the same ground over, and suffering anew all its evils."[13]

The general picture during 1877-78 was confused, however. Many businessmen fought specie down to the line; others, full of doubts and anxieties, longed for peace and an end to uncertainty. In a situation strongly reminiscent of the earliest postwar years, bankers in the East continued to oppose those in the West, although in 1876 and 1877 the newly organized American Bankers' Association went on record for early resumption.[14] Yet there was a distinct drift in the direction of hard money. This was clearest among the ironmasters. *Iron Age*, which had already moved decisively toward a more orthodox position during and just after the 1875 Ohio campaign, in December 1875 approved the hard money recommendation of Grant's Annual Message.[15] In 1877 and 1878 the paper avoided the money question, apparently out of deference to such intransigents as Carey and Kelley, who for so long had voiced the aspirations of the ironmasters,[16] editor Williams being content to note that resumption

[12] Cincinnati Chamber of Commerce, *Twenty-ninth Annual Report for 1877*, p. 23.

[13] G. P. Williams (President of the National Albany Exchange Bank) to James A. Garfield, Albany, N. Y., Dec. 12, 1877, Garfield MSS, LC.

[14] American Bankers' Association, *Report of Proceedings for 1876*, p. 63; *Report of Proceedings for 1877*, pp. 83-84. For western opinion see J. Whiting to William B. Allison, Mt. Pleasant, Iowa, Jan. 10, 1877, Allison MSS, Iowa State Department of History and Archives.

[15] *Iron Age*, xvi (Dec. 9, 1875); see also *ibid.*, xvii (Feb. 10, 1876).

[16] The deference is detectable in the journal's guarded editorial comment on an interconvertible bond polemic of Kelley's. *Ibid.*, xx (Aug. 30, 1877).

seemed inevitable.[17] But after resumption, Williams could not suppress a shout of glee. "Once more on solid ground contracts of all kinds have a definite basis which they never could have when the value of the currency of commerce was subject to sudden and violent fluctuations."[18] The *American Manufacturer*, which spoke for the trans-Allegheny iron interests, from a very explicit soft money position in the early '70's, became evasive and conciliatory by 1876.[19] By early 1877 the *Manufacturer* was resigned to resumption and in a January editorial demonstrated how a favorable trade balance would make specie payments possible.[20] A similar movement can be observed among other manufacturers. John S. Perry of the Stove Manufacturers' Association, in June 1874 had assailed resumption as "in theory . . . superb," but in practice "a fallacy."[21] His successor in 1877 looked forward eagerly and hopefully to gold payments. "Our currency (if left alone) will soon be exchangeable for gold on an equal basis. Prices of all commodities are already adjusted to that level so that the reaction from the times of inflation is almost complete." Henceforth "the natural growth and resources of the country" would be developed "without restraint."[22]

Although generally defenders of conservative finance, the seaboard merchants, particularly the smaller, produce dealers, had been suspicious of the Resumption Act at the time of passage; and for a year or two thereafter they had been unusually skeptical of specie payments. At the 1876 National Board of Trade convention a group of New York, Baltimore, and Philadelphia produce merchants, as well as a few westerners, resisted a Boston Board of Trade resolution endorsing contraction. In an angry debate, the anti-contractionists accused the hard money men of sacrificing the West and the smaller businessmen to the golden calf. The Boston resolution was finally carried, but a third of the delegates, representing the Baltimore Corn and Flour Exchange, the New York Produce Exchange, the Philadelphia Board of Trade, and the Cincinnati Chamber of Commerce, voted against

---

[17] *Ibid.*, xxi (Jan. 17, 1878); (April 25, 1878).
[18] *Ibid.*, xxiii (Jan. 9, 1879).
[19] *American Manufacturer*, xix (July 20, 1876), 3; (June 22, 1876), 11.
[20] *Ibid.*, xx (Jan. 8, 1877), 3.
[21] *Metal Worker*, i (Feb. 14, 1874), 2.
[22] *Iron Age*, xix (Jan. 25, 1877).

it.[23] The following year the hard money element quickly disposed of the dissenters. Soft money resolutions from the Chicago Board of Trade were considered but voted down 27 to 4, and the convention endorsed a scheme to fund $10 million of greenbacks monthly into forty-year gold bonds.[24] Thereafter, through 1877 and 1878, local trade associations, including the previously balky New York Produce Exchange, supported returning to the solid ground of gold.[25]

Taken together, the state of business opinion was only moderately encouraging to Sherman. He had reason to believe he could count on the port merchants' support, and perhaps he could now rely on the iron men as well. If nothing else, fatigue had done its work, and businessmen as never before were willing to give resumption a chance. But there were dark patches, too. Westerners, in particular, remained suspicious of resumption, and many other businessmen were still uncertain. It was clear, at the very least, that the Treasury would have to proceed slowly and with tact.

The political climate in the spring of 1877 also disposed Sherman to caution. Although Cooper's poor showing in the Presidential race had spread gloom among the Greenbackers, it had not destroyed the Independents as a functioning third party. In January 1877 the Independent National Executive Committee issued a manifesto calling for a renewed attack on the money power. Reorganization on a state and local level, a fund-raising drive, and a national Greenback paper were proposed to reinvigorate the soft money forces.[26] By spring there were signs of third-party revival in the West. In April the Indianapolis "workingmen" joined the Independents in the city mayoralty cam-

[23] National Board of Trade, *Proceedings of the Eighth Annual Meeting at New York, 1876*, pp. 65-76, 127.

[24] National Board of Trade, *Proceedings of the Ninth Annual Meeting at Milwaukee, 1877*, pp. 154-163. This analysis cannot be carried further since the Board did not meet again until after resumption.

[25] Boston Board of Trade, *Twenty-fifth Annual Report for 1878*, pp. 6-7; New York Chamber of Commerce, *Twentieth Annual Report for 1877-1878*, p. 89; New York Produce Exchange, *Annual Report for 1876-1877*, p. 4; Philadelphia Board of Trade, *Forty-fourth Annual Report* (1877), p. 22; *Forty-fifth Annual Report* (1878), p. 34. For the Charleston, S. C. Chamber of Commerce see *Nation*, xxvi (Jan. 24, 1878), 49.

[26] *WA*, Feb. 3, 1877. See also *Indianapolis Sun*, March 31, 1877.

paign.[27] In May, Independents in Iowa and Wisconsin held well-attended conventions, adopted greenback platforms, and made arrangements to run candidates in the fall campaigns. There were simultaneous stirrings in Minnesota and Ohio, and in early June both states held Independent conventions. The Minnesota meeting adopted a platform but postponed nominations. The small Ohio gathering nominated Stephen Johnston, a retired lawyer and farmer, as Independent gubernatorial candidate.[28]

At this point it was still too early to tell how formidable the revived movement would be, and what it would mean for resumption. But Sherman could be certain that the Greenbackers would be among his more obstreperous foes. Even before the Secretary had a chance to show his hand, he had become the target of the paper money politicos. In March, Alexander Troup attacked him in conventional soft money billingsgate as "a champion of monopoly, salary grabs, subsidies, and railroad jobs." He had fathered the "so-called resumption act of 1875, . . . a scheme to contract the legal tender circulation, thereby strengthening the bank monopoly."[29] Western Independents also flayed the new Secretary,[30] and it seemed possible that before long—certainly by the fall elections—Sherman would be facing a serious challenge from the greenback radicals.

I I

But a revived demand for paper money would not be the gravest danger that resumption faced. Overriding and complicating all the other difficulties of the Treasury was the silver issue, which by the beginning of the new administration had become an urgent political problem. The question of remonetizing the

[27] *Ibid.*, April 28, 1877.
[28] *AM*, May 17, 1877; May 31, 1877; June 14, 1877; June 28, 1877; *Indianapolis Sun*, June 9, 1877; Ebenezer Ayres to Ignatius Donnelly, Cottage Grove, Minn., May 28, 1877, Donnelly MSS, Minnesota Historical Society; *WA*, May 5, 1877; *National Labor Tribune*, June 14, 1877; Edward Topping James, "American Labor and Political Action, 1865-1896: The Knights of Labor and Its Predecessors" (unpublished Ph.D. dissertation, Harvard University, 1954), p. 138.
[29] Quoted in *AM*, March 22, 1877.
[30] For example, see the attack of the *Hammond* (Wisconsin) *Independent,* quoted in *ibid.*, April 13, 1877; May 10, 1877; and *Indianapolis Sun*, May 19, 1877; June 2, 1877; and June 30, 1877.

old 412.5 grain silver dollar was still new in March 1877. At no time during the comprehensive financial debate following the panic had there been a whisper of the "dollar of the daddies," either in or out of Congress. While silver was overvalued in the world market in relation to gold, as it had been since the 1830's, it held no attraction for soft money men. When the Act of 1873, dropping silver from the list of coins issued by the Treasury, came to the House from the upper chamber, William Kelley, as Chairman of the Coinage Committee, gave it his active support. It passed the lower house by a vote of 110 to 13, meaning, of course, that almost every soft money man supported it.[31] In fact, until well into 1876 and even 1877 silver was regarded as just another variety of specie, of hard money. When, in early 1876, a resolution implementing the fractional coinage provision of the Resumption Act came before Congress,[32] the greenbackers called the measure a "silver resumption fraud."[33] Senator John P. Jones of Nevada, who was one of the resolution's sponsors and who was remembered as an active gold man in 1874, was attacked as a "silver millionaire" and a "bonanza king," interested primarily in selling his wares to the government.[34]

But by this time the picture had already begun to change. Under the simultaneous impact of a spurting production of silver and its demonetization in Germany and the "Latin Union,"[35]

[31] Albert S. Bolles, *The Financial History of the United States from 1861 to 1885* (New York: D. Appleton & Co., 1894), II, 377-380. It was passed without a roll call and so the identity of the thirteen opposed and their financial positions cannot be determined.

[32] This measure originated as a House Joint Resolution 109 authorizing $10 million of silver coin to replace an equal amount of paper fractional currency ("shinplasters"). Earlier in the session Senator Aaron Sargent of California had introduced a measure to demonetize the overweight "trade dollar." Shortly after the joint resolution Samuel J. Randall proposed still another silver bill designed to add $20 million of silver coin to the nation's stock. Both the Sargent and Randall pro-

posals stirred up a debate that foreshadowed the more extended silver discussion of the next two years. The Randall Bill (H. R. 3398) and the Sargent measure (S. 263) may be followed through the index of the *Congressional Record*, 44 Cong., 1 sess.

[33] *IA*, March 4, 1876; May 13, 1876.

[34] *Ibid.*, May 6, 1876; May 13, 1876; Britton Hill, *Specie Resumption and National Bankruptcy, Identical and Indivisible* . . . (St. Louis, 1876), p. 25. See also the following for initial greenbacker reactions to silver: *Indianapolis Sun*, April 1, 1876; April 8, 1876; April 22, 1876.

[35] I.e., France, Italy, Belgium, Switzerland, and Greece.

world silver prices began to drop just as the 1873 coinage bill became law. The 412.5 grain silver dollar, nine-tenths pure, fell below par for the first time in 1874, and in 1875 declined to 96 cents in bullion value. This was still not enough to attract much attention, but the following year the standard silver dollar dropped to 90 cents in gold.[36] Now the changed relation of silver to gold from the legally defined 16 to 1 ratio was publicly noticed. On March 2, 1876, the *Boston Globe* published a letter by George M. Weston, a former Republican newspaper editor of Maine, which called attention to the change and set out almost the whole of the later silverite line.

Weston's most arresting—and ultimately most fertile—idea was the notion that the 1873 demonetization of silver was a plot to defraud the American people for the sake of the creditor interests. The Constitution, Weston asserted, made gold and silver coin alike legal tenders, and in effect established the double, or bimetallic, standard.[37] Disregarding the fact that, whatever the law decreed, actual bimetallism had never really worked in the United States,[38] he claimed that this double standard had prevailed until the 1873 law. Then, "without discussion in or out of Congress and without notice or warning," the silver dollar was discontinued. This legislation, and the later 1874 law formally demonetizing silver,[39] "was as selfish in its origin as it

[36] U. S. Bureau of the Census, *Statistical Abstract of the United States, 1907*, p. 564, Table 191.

[37] Actually, the Constitution (Article I, Section 10, paragraph 1) only prohibits the *states* from making "anything but gold and silver coin a tender in payment of debts." It does not apply to the federal government, and of course, does not prohibit even the states from making gold alone a legal tender. Paradoxically, what Weston—a man clearly in the Jeffersonian-Agrarian tradition—ascribed to the Constitution was actually the bimetallic view of Alexander Hamilton! See Arthur Nussbaum, *Money in the Law, National and International* (Brooklyn, N. Y.: The Foundation Press, Inc., 1950), p. 572.

[38] Since, with but a few exceptional years, the American legal gold-silver ratio had diverged from world market ratios in favor of one or another of the two metals. When gold was overvalued legally, as it was before 1834, it did not circulate: when undervalued—after 1853—silver disappeared from circulation. J. Laurence Laughlin, *The History of Bimetallism in the United States* (New York: D. Appleton & Co., 1897), pp. 26ff., 52ff., 86ff.

[39] The 1873 measure discontinued the minting of further silver dollars, but did not demonetize those already issued. This was not formally done until the Act of June 22, 1874, which deprived all silver of its legal tender quality for sums of

was surreptitious in the manner of its introduction." It was "the most flagrant and audacious of the manifestations of the control exercised by foreign and domestic bankers over national legislation in these recent and evil days."[40]

Weston's conspiracy theory was, of course, groundless. There was nothing collusive about the discontinuance of silver. In the 1860's a strong, world-wide current for an international gold standard had set in, but the rational needs of a developing international economy, rather than the demands of scheming creditors, seem to have been behind the trend.[41] Weston was on firmer ground, however, when in this letter and his later voluminous silver writings he pointed out that demonetization deprived the country of an important avenue of relief from the heavy burden of public debt. "The people who are to pay this debt, and who received nothing for it but depreciated paper, are entitled to the benefit resulting from the richness and abundance of newly discovered silver mines." Demonetization, combined with the Public Credit Act, he wrote, had made expensive gold the only legal medium for paying the federal creditors, and would crush the taxpayers for the profit of a minority.[42]

Weston's exposé opens the great American silver controversy.[43] The letter attracted immediate attention. On March 23 Horace White gave it wide publicity by attacking it in the pages of the influential financial weekly *The Public*.[44] It was noticed elsewhere and soon became the center of a noisy discussion which

over $5. Charles F. Dunbar, *Laws of the United States Relating to Currency, Finance and Banking* (Boston: Ginn and Company, 1897), pp. 244-245.

[40] The *Boston Globe* letter is reprinted in George M. Weston, *The Silver Question* (New York, 1878), as paper no. 1, pp. 105-109.

[41] Henry B. Russell, *International Monetary Conferences: Their Purposes, Characters and Results . . .* (New York: Harper & Bros., 1898), ch. II; Ernest Seyd, *Bullion and Foreign Exchanges, Theoretically and Practically Considered* (London, 1868), pp. 20f. This is not to endorse the development as either wise or necessary, however.

[42] Weston, *op. cit.*, p. 109; paper no. 2, pp. 110-115.

[43] Weston's is apparently the first full development of the free silver argument. As early as 1875, however, Congressman John Bright of Tennessee attacked the Act of 1873 as "unnecessary, expensive and in the interest of the money power." While words such as these were common among later silverites, Bright's remarks are confused, and do not reveal a full comprehension of the implications of the silver question. *Congressional Record*, 43 Cong., 2 sess., Appendix, pp. 5-10.

[44] *The Public*, IX (March 23, 1876), 198-199.

Weston himself happily fanned with articles and letters published, literally, from coast to coast.[45]

Fortunately, the new issue offered a range of possible positions which could accommodate a wide spectrum of financial opinion. The label "silverite" would come to mean many things. At their most conservative the silver men were "bimetallists" who wanted silver "remonetized"—restored as a legal tender—only after an agreement among the major nations to establish an international gold-silver exchange rate had been reached. Such an agreement alone, this group asserted, would make it possible to maintain a dual standard. Other bimetallists believed a treaty unnecessary if silver coinage were limited in amount.[46] Such conservative silverites opposed a devalued dollar but were equally hostile to the contraction they believed an exclusive gold standard imposed. More extreme were those silverites who demanded "free and unlimited coinage at sixteen to one," that is, the coinage, at the old ratio, of all silver bullion brought to the mint. Some "free silver" men denied that this practice would prevent the return to a gold standard. Most probably realized— as conservatives insisted—that gold, the dearer metal at 16 to 1, would be driven from circulation and the nation left with devalued silver. It was not always easy—nor is it easy today—to keep these distinctions clear. In practice, the silver dollar, as the greenback earlier, became an emotionally charged symbol which engendered noisy polemics rather than precise and temperate discussion.

Much of the silver debate of the next three years parallels the battle over greenbacks. Once past their initial prejudice against coin,[47] the paper money men almost universally embraced the new panacea. The greenback ideologues saw it as a renewed opportunity to put off the evil day of resumption and at the same

[45] Many of Weston's replies to his critics, originally published in nationally prominent newspapers and periodicals, are to be found in Weston, *op. cit., passim.*

[46] Still other bimetallists would accept silver in unlimited amounts if the silver dollar were made heavier to compensate for its depreciation.

[47] A process that was completed for most greenbackers by mid-1876. See *Indianapolis Sun,* May 27, 1876; *Indiana Farmer,* July 29, 1876.

time scale down the federal debt without hurdling the barrier of the 1869 Public Credit Act.[48] The more pragmatic greenbackers hoped for relief to private debtors from the new form of "cheap money."[49] Among the soft money men of the prairies, silver seemed the answer to the problem of rural taxes and rural debts.[50]

It must not be supposed, however, that the greenbackers abruptly abandoned paper money for silver. The old beliefs were too firmly embedded. For men like Alexander Campbell, silver, indeed, was largely a stalking horse for legal tenders. The people were not likely to use much of the proposed new coinage, he admitted privately to Ewing, but once "get silver . . . made applicable to payment of the national debt and you will see the 'rag baby' stepping out in its holiday dress."[51] Other greenbackers welcomed silver as a useful supplement to paper, though they believed there was not enough of it to meet the country's monetary needs.[52] The paper money men accepted, then, the added strength that silver brought but retained their earlier allegiance. To the end of the decade and beyond, third-party politics remained tied to greenbacks, with silver a mere adjunct.

The greenback response to silver was predictable and could be easily met. More dangerous from Sherman's point of view were the surprising silver sympathies of the business community. At the precise moment that business opinion was shifting perceptibly, if unevenly, to resumption, silver was winning converts among commercial men and industrialists. Among the merchants the traditional rift between East and West once again appeared. In the West the Cincinnati and St. Paul Chambers of Commerce endorsed remonetization,[53] as did individual mer-

[48] *WA*, Aug. 27, 1876.
[49] See *National Labor Tribune*, June 30, 1877.
[50] See, for example, *Western Rural*, April 8, 1876; April 20, 1878; *IA*, May 13, 1876; *Indiana Farmer*, Aug. 19, 1876.
[51] A[lexander] Campbell to Thomas Ewing, Jr., La Salle, Ill., Jan. 30, 1878, Ewing MSS, LC.
[52] Thomas Ballinger to William

B. Allison, Oskaloosa, Iowa, April 9, 1878, Allison MSS.
[53] For Cincinnati, see Cincinnati Chamber of Commerce, *Twenty-ninth Annual Report*, p. 23; George Ward Nichols to David Wells, Cincinnati, April 18, 1877; S. Lester Taylor to Wells, Cincinnati, July 5, 1877, Wells MSS. For St. Paul see Martin Ridge, "Ignatius Donnelly and the Greenback Movement,"

chants of Chicago, Toledo, and St. Louis.[54] In the East, while there was some support for bimetallism, the overriding realities of foreign trade limited its appeal. As one member of the Boston Board of Trade noted, neither he nor his colleagues could forget that "their transactions" were "not simply domestic but foreign."[55] In every case, in the trade bodies of port cities, the conservatives succeeded in beating down the silver men.[56] The National Board of Trade, representing all sections, gave bimetallism a better hearing, however. At the 1877 annual meeting, a majority of the delegates, including the Cincinnati, Dubuque, and Chicago, as well as the Baltimore and Trenton associations,[57] voted to recommend a $50 million issue of new silver. The motion did not receive the necessary two-thirds vote and so did not go with the Board's annual memorial to Congress.[58] But with this ballot the nation's merchants came a long way toward endorsing the silver movement.

Other business groups fell to squabbling over silver in 1876 and 1877. *Iron Age* applauded the defeat of an 1876 remonetization attempt, referring to the rejected measure as "retrograde legislation" in the "interest of the Bonanza mine owners."[59]

Mid-America: An Historical Review, xxxix, No. 3 (July 1957), 162.

[54] See, respectively, J. V. Farwell to William Henry Smith, Chicago, Jan. 23, 1878, Smith MSS, Ohio Historical Society; Lyman Robinson to William B. Allison, Toledo, Dec. 13, 1877, Allison MSS.

[55] W. W. Warren to James A. Garfield, Boston, Feb. 4, 1878, Garfield MSS. The same point was made by A. A. Low before the Monetary Commission in October 1876. U. S. Senate, 44 Cong., 2 sess., *Report No. 703*, pt. 2, pp. 171ff.

[56] In Boston and New York the Board of Trade and the Chamber of Commerce respectively memorialized Congress against hasty and unilateral remonetization by the United States. Any Congressional silver legislation, they declared, must be made contingent on an in-

ternational monetary conference to fix the world gold-silver ratio. This position suggests a conservative bimetallism, but at this point was actually an attempt to delay any action at all on silver. Boston Board of Trade, *Twenty-fourth Annual Report for 1877*, p. 43; New York Chamber of Commerce, *Nineteenth Annual Report for 1876-1877*, pp. v-vi, 3-4, 68-72, 106.

[57] Most of the negative votes came from the three largest eastern port cities: New York, Boston, and Philadelphia.

[58] The details of the currency discussion at the Milwaukee meeting can be found in National Board of Trade, *Proceedings of the Ninth Annual Meeting*, pp. 188-218.

[59] *Iron Age*, xviii (Aug. 3, 1876); (July 20, 1876). See also W. Hastings (of the Wilmington Plate Iron Rolling Mills) to Thomas Bayard,

American Manufacturer, on the other hand, favored restoring silver "to the place it so long beneficially held," for at least a trial period, and even subscribed to the Crime of '73 conspiracy thesis![60] Remonetization also won the support of other industrialists, real estate brokers, at least some of the "speculators in lands, railroads, coal and iron mines," who earlier had supported free banking, and even, in a qualified way, some bankers.[61] Indeed, for a movement traditionally identified with rural Agrarian forces, silver remonetization was urged with surprising warmth by the business community.

One hitherto obscure group of businessmen played a particularly controversial role in the silver discussion. These were the "Bonanza Kings," to use the contemporary pejorative label—the western silver miners whose profits were directly linked to the silver question. Of course, the mine operators had much to gain from restoring silver, particularly if they could pocket the difference between the market price of silver and its par value. Free and unlimited coinage, which implied such a process, would have been a sizable gift to the silver men.[62] But even a limited Treasury purchase program promised some relief from the low prices that the deluge of precious metal from Nevada had produced.

Needless to say, the miners and their friends in Congress supported remonetization. No clearer evidence of the political role of personal interest can be found than the abrupt switch from gold and sound money to silver and easy money of Nevada Senator Jones, an acknowledged silver millionaire. Such shifts made plausible the hard money view that there was a western

---

Wilmington, Del., Feb. 6, 1878, Bayard MSS, LC.

[60] *American Manufacturer,* XXI (June 28, 1877), 3; XX (Feb. 22, 1877), 3.

[61] See the following: James Austin to Rutherford B. Hayes, New York, Dec. 21, 1877, Hayes MSS, Hayes Memorial Library, Fremont, Ohio; *Independent,* Feb. 7, 1878, p. 13; George Walker to John Sherman, New York, Dec. 25, 1876,

Sherman MSS; George Van Allen to William B. Allison, Mt. Pleasant, Iowa, Dec. 25, 1877, Allison MSS; James F. Wilson (President of the First National Bank of Fairfield) to Allison, Fairfield, Iowa, Aug. 21, 1877, *ibid.* Wilson was a former Republican United States Senator.

[62] A gift of between $3 and $4 million per year in the late '70's, or about 10 per cent on all the silver produced in the United States.

mine owner behind every Congressional move to remonetize.[63] Yet there were often ambiguities in the mine operators' attitudes that make all generalization dangerous. Sometimes the miners were pulled two ways. "Louis McLane and the principals of the Bank of Nevada," for example, were "against unqualified remonetization"; since they held large amounts of 5-20's, they favored only a "moderate coinage" of silver.[64] This is only one case, perhaps, but it underscores the dangers of accepting uncritically the familiar stereotypes.

Up to this point, apart from the silver miners, there is little to distinguish the pro-silver, cheap money interest from the soft money coalition of the '60's. Western business groups, Agrarian ideologues, and confirmed anti-resumptionists were to be found in both movements. But silver was destined to win a far wider following than paper money ever attained. Within a few months of Weston's letter, "silver" had seized the public imagination and, undefined and half-understood, become a popular craze threatening to sweep all before it.

Unlike the greenback, the silver dollar was hard coin which seemed to possess the same claim to "intrinsic" value as gold. Clearly, until 1873, Congress had never distinguished between the two metals in matters concerning the federal debt. The 5-20's, under the terms of the Public Credit Act, as well as the bond issues authorized for refunding in 1870, were all payable in "coin," not gold. If silver had depreciated since 1870, that appeared to many reasonable men to be one of the legitimate risks that public creditors faced. To redefine "coin" to mean gold for the sake of protecting creditors seemed to represent excessive zeal for a special interest. Old Jacksonians, latter-day puritans, even gentlemen-reformers, found it possible to call themselves silverites, or at least bimetallists, without serious qualms. Moreover, it must be remembered that demonetizing silver had made gold the sole support for all future American currency. After January 1, 1879, the country's circulation would be presumably

---

[63] The view was also to be adopted by conservative financial scholars of a later period. See Laughlin, *op. cit.*, pp. 223-224.

[64] James W. Simonton to John Sherman, New York, Dec. 29, 1877, Sherman MSS.

tied, not to coin, but to gold coin exclusively, and so subject, it was felt, to the rigid confines of the world's limited gold stock.[65] Even men who detested greenbackism viewed this prospect with alarm. Conservative politicians like Thurlow Weed, the old Whig boss of New York; former New York Governor John A. Dix; and Jacob D. Cox, Grant's upright and fastidious first Secretary of the Interior; warned that negating half the world's money stock would produce economic convulsions that would rend the very fabric of capitalist society.[66] As Chicago merchant-prince John V. Farwell put it, if the nation insisted "on *gold* liquidation of present liabilities" it would have "French communism inside of two years."[67]

The new controversy even split apart the academic-reform community, hitherto a mighty bulwark against financial heterodoxy. Wells; Atkinson; Forbes; Henry Varnum Poor, the railroad economist; the English economist Stanley Jevons; and Francis Bowen, to name only the most prominent, were foes of silver in any guise, unwilling even to consider the possibility of bimetallism through international agreement.[68] But other members of the respectable intelligentsia—Francis A. Walker, B. F. Nourse, S. Dana Horton—had deep misgivings about demonetization.[69] Walker, whose heresy foreshadowed the more general

[65] Men of this viewpoint were, of course, ignoring the monetary role of bank deposits.

[66] For Weed, see the newspaper clipping in W. Dennison to W. K. Rogers, n.p., Nov. 30, 1877, Hayes MSS; for the others, see John A. Dix to Rutherford B. Hayes, New York, Aug. 11, 1877, *ibid.*; J. D. Cox to David Wells, Washington, Feb. 28, 1878, Wells MSS.

[67] Farwell to William H. Smith, Chicago, Jan. 25, 1878, Smith MSS, Indiana Historical Society.

[68] David A. Wells, *The Silver Question: The Dollar of the Fathers versus the Dollar of the Sons* (New York, 1877), *passim;* Wells to Thomas F. Bayard, Norwich, Conn., March 27, 1878, Wells MSS; Atkinson to William B. Allison, Boston, March 3, 1878, Allison MSS; J. M.

Forbes to Allison, Boston, Jan. 5, 1878, *ibid.;* Henry Varnum Poor, *Resumption and the Silver Question . . .* (New York, 1878), pp. 16ff., 133-134; Stanley Jevons, "The Silver Question," *Journal of Social Science,* IX (January 1878), *passim;* Francis Bowen, *Report No. 703*, pp. 139-160. Bowen was one of the non-political "experts" appointed under the monetary commission measure of August 1876.

[69] Benjamin F. Nourse, "The Silver Question," *Journal of Social Science,* IX (January 1878), *passim;* S. Dana Horton, *The Monetary Situation: An Address Delivered by Request of the American Social Science Association . . .* (Cincinnati, 1878), pp. 14ff. See also the pro-silver article in the reformist *Public,* XII, No. 1 (July 5, 1877), p. 5.

pro-silver bent of the intellectuals in the 1890's,[70] wrote shortly after resumption: "Moralists and economists rightly visit their severe condemnation upon all schemes for 'scaling down debts' by means of paper money inflation. Is it any the less reprehensible morally—is it not even more a blunder economically—to adopt measures which must seriously aggravate the pressure of all existing obligations, public, corporate and private throughout Christendom?"[71]

But what gave silver its enormous political potential was the fire it lit in the West and South. Despite the most impassioned argument of western greenbackers like Noonan and Donnelly, the farmer had never lost his respect for hard coin. Greenbackism had not achieved a mass rural following and had not even won all the militant farm insurgents. Noonan and Donnelly had themselves been reluctant converts to soft money, and such important farm leaders as Willard Flagg and Dudley W. Adams of the National Grange refused to endorse paper money. No doubt the progressive deepening of the agricultural depression[72] made rural America generally more receptive to monetary schemes as time passed, but equally important in finally enticing the farmer away from gold were the special qualities of the silver dollar. The American farmer was not a European peasant, of course, but when it came to money his reactions were often identical. He valued hard cash—something he could heft, something that

[70] When even Henry Adams became a silverite!

[71] Francis A. Walker, "The Monetary Conferences of 1867 and 1878," *Princeton Review* (January 1879), p. 42. Among the academicians, it may be noted, the battle of the standards is still very much alive. Economic historians continue to debate the causes of the "Great Depression" of 1873-1896, and often argue the influence of demonetization in depressing world price levels. For a recent discussion see W. W. Rostow, *British Economy of the Nineteenth Century* (Oxford: at the Clarendon Press, 1948), chs. III and VII.

[72] Although whether it was getting worse or better is actually diffi-

cult to determine. Contemporaries disagreed. One citizen of central Illinois wrote Senator Richard Oglesby: "Times are terrible in Illinois . . . : corn rotting in the fields . . . cattle ruinously low, real estate without any market value, and a cloud of almost utter despair brooding over the people." On the other hand wheat and flour prices, responding to the Russo-Turkish War, in 1877 reached levels unequaled since 1864-1865. For these conflicting views see respectively James A. Connally to Oglesby, Springfield, Ill., Feb. 9, 1878, Oglesby MSS, Illinois State Library; and *Ohio Farmer*, May 5, 1877; *American Agriculturist*, October 1877.

would not tear, and could be hoarded against the day of reckoning or celebration.[73] In the most literal sense silver was "hard money" with just these qualities; besides it was a more familiar form of cash to the farmer than gold, little of which had been seen in the agricultural areas before the War. As the Ohio correspondent of the *New York Tribune* wrote, "the bigness and tangibility of the silver dollar" were proving irresistible to the rural West and South. The farmers were convinced that "silver is money, not a mere promise to pay" and were being "swept completely off their feet by the new mania for the short weight silver dollar."[74]

The appeal of silver in the hinterland was nourished by a devil theory of the kind which is always congenial to the unsophisticated. The greenbackers had an analogous doctrine but the silverite version of conspiracy had a particularly dramatic mythology. In its final form, the 1873 Coinage Act became the "Crime of '73," planned by one Ernest Seyd, an English financier who—so the tale went—was the agent of foreign holders of United States securities. Seyd was reputed to have arrived in America with $500,000 for the express purpose of inducing Congress to demonetize silver; and his success, it was said, was embodied in the 1873 Coinage Act.[75] The English

[73] See J. Fred Meyers to William B. Allison, Denison, Iowa, Jan. 28, 1878, Allison MSS.

[74] *NYDT*, Jan. 3, 1878. See the following for enthusiastic rural support of remonetization: *Western Rural*, Aug. 19, 1876; Sept. 2, 1876; April 4, 1877; Dec. 15, 1877; *IA*, Aug. 12, 1876; *Indiana Farmer*, Dec. 22, 1877; Jan. 26, 1878; Indiana State Grange, *Proceedings of the Seventh Annual Meeting* (December 1877), p. 19. In November 1877, the National Grange broke its long-standing rule against "political activity" to endorse both re-monetization and repeal of the Resumption Act. It is significant that the silver resolution passed with a substantially larger majority than the repeal motion. National Grange, *Proceedings of the Eleventh Session, 1877*, pp. 69, 82.

[75] The earliest attack on Seyd as instigator of the Coinage Act that I have discovered is in a letter by Stephen Johnston, the 1877 Ohio Independent gubernatorial candidate. This is dated August 20, 1877, and is printed in the *Anti-Monopolist* of Sept. 27, 1877. There is evidence, however, that Pomeroy, with his sure feel for what would appeal to farmers, had earlier made the same charges. See *ibid.*, Sept. 13, 1877, quoting *Pomeroy's Democrat*. The germ of truth in the charge is that in 1872 Seyd had helped draft the bill submitted by Samuel Hooper of Massachusetts which eventually evolved into the Coinage Act. Paradoxically, although a bullionist of almost fanatic intensity, Seyd was a bimetallist, who in 1868 believed that the 1867 Paris Monetary Conference recommendation of single

financier's work was seen, however, only as part of the larger conspiracy of the "colossal Hydra of the Gold Ring," which, in the new silverite lexicon, soon became the successor in villainy to the national bank "monopoly."[76] Eventually the conspiracy theme took its apparently inevitable course and became overtly anti-Semitic. By 1877 some silverites were charging that the "combination to depreciate silver has been perfected by the great Jew bankers of the world."[77]

Silver's allure for the farmer raised the South for the first time to a prominent place in the postwar financial discussion. War-time devastation and postwar social dislocation had widened the economic gap separating the South from the rest of the country. Both the region's share of the national income and its total pro-ductivity dropped disastrously between 1860 and 1880, and the former did not significantly improve until the twentieth cen-tury.[78] During the pre-silver years, southerners had voiced the usual rural complaint about insufficient money. In 1875 Clement Claiborne Clay, former secessionist Senator from Alabama, wrote Judge Jeremiah Black from his Madison County plantation: "There is no money to be had as a loan in this vicinity, except from the banks on 60 to 90 days, or of Shylocks at exorbitant

---

world gold standard would "prove injurious to the best and truest in-terest of mankind." His advice to Congressman Hooper, it seems, was pro-, not anti-silver, but it was ig-nored. For Seyd's monetary views see Ernest Seyd, *Bullion and For-eign Exchanges, Theoretically and Practically Considered* (London, 1868), pp. 611-614, and Seyd, *Sug-gestions in Relation to the Metallic Currency of the United States* (Lon-don, 1871), pp. 4-6. Paul M. O'Leary recently revived the crime of '73 thesis while shifting the blame to Henry Linderman of the mint, who supposedly foresaw the decline in silver. He does not blame Seyd, nor does he suppose a general conspir-acy. See "The Scene of the Crime Revisited . . . ," *Jour. of Polit. Econ-omy*, 68 (Aug. 1960).

[76] See Hill, *op. cit.*, pp. 3ff.; *Western Rural*, April 20, 1878; *In-*

dianapolis Sun, July 22, 1876; *In-diana Farmer*, Aug. 26, 1876.

[77] Washington correspondent of the *New York Graphic*, as quoted in *AM*, July 12, 1877. See also *The Telegram*, VII, No. 38 (September 1878). This last was a rabid greenback-free silver sheet pub-lished in Washington, D. C., which seems to have been associated in some way with one Telemachus Ti-mayenis, an unstable Greek-Ameri-can who later became a professional anti-Semite. On Timayenis see John Higham, "Anti-Semitism in the Gilded Age: A Reinterpretation," *MVHR*, XLIII, No. 4 (March 1957), 576.

[78] Richard A. Esterlin, "Regional Income, 1840-1950," in Seymour E. Harris (ed.), *American Econom-ic History* (New York: McGraw-Hill Book Co., 1961), p. 529, figure 2; p. 535, table 2; p. 538, table 4.

usury—Indeed, if the report of the Sec. of the Treasury be looked to . . . I need not assure you that our circulation is very small. By the same authority there seems to be an excess of currency in the middle and N. Eng. States."[79] Clay was complaining about the maldistribution of national banks, an object of only a little less resentment in the South than in the West. De Bow's Review, mouthpiece of James D. B. De Bow, the prominent southern economist-publicist, deplored government issued paper money,[80] but charged that a "wanton spirit of sectionalism" had deprived the South of its share of banks and bank notes.[81] At various times during these years, southerners who saw "the great evil of the South" as "want of money" also endorsed additional greenback issues.[82]

Yet on the whole the South was not sympathetic to cheap money. During the '60's southern Democrats had little patience with the Ohio Idea.[83] Later, southern Granges were more often than not proponents of deflation.[84] Until 1873 at least, if we except a few prominent Radicals like Horace Maynard of Tennessee, southern Congressmen took a distinct back seat on national finance. This was not mere financial conservatism, although the prewar South, particularly the commercial centers, had generally subscribed to sound finance.[85] Southern political en-

[79] Clay to Jeremiah Black, Gurleyville, Ala., Nov. 8, 1875, Black MSS, LC.

[80] De Bow's Review, After the War Series, I (January 1866), 77-87; (February 1866), 148ff.

[81] Ibid., VIII (April-May, 1870), 350.

[82] W. G. Cazanove to Benjamin F. Butler, Alexandria, Va., March 9, 1869; also H. N. Perry to Butler, Middlebrook, Va., n.d., Butler MSS, LC.

[83] Conservative Indiana Democrat William English described a little scene in 1868 which illustrates this rejection of Pendletonism. On his way to the Democratic National Convention in New York, English traveled with a train full of southern delegates. "Dirty Shirt" Henry Clay Dean was also aboard haranguing the "unsophisticated southern men

on the greenback issue." "His eloquence," English noted, "seemed to be 'wasted on the desert air' as they didn't pay much attention to him." English to "loved ones at home," New York, July 1, 1868, English MSS, Indiana Historical Society.

[84] Despite the role of North Carolina Grange leader John Winston in organizing the Independent party in 1876. Theodore Saloutos, Farmer Movements in the South, 1865-1933 (Berkeley: University of California Press, 1960), pp. 35-36.

[85] The ante-bellum state banking systems of Louisiana and South Carolina, states where the influence of the port merchants and the bankers who helped finance them was significant, were considered models of stability in their day. See Bray Hammond, Banks and Politics in America from the Revolution to the Civil War

ergies were almost wholly absorbed by the intractable problems of Reconstruction and race adjustment, and there was little left over for financial matters.[86]

This indifference began to give way after the panic. During the Inflation Bill session, southern Democrats—Senators Augustus Merrimon of North Carolina and John B. Gordon of Georgia, and Representative James Beck of Kentucky—responding to some home pressure,[87] had been active allies of Butler, Morton, and Logan. During the following Congress, Landers and Atkins of Tennessee, as well as other southerners, collaborated with western Democrats in the effort to repeal the Resumption Act.[88] In the 1876 campaign the Independents had attracted some support in the South.[89] But not until 1877, with Reconstruction safely behind and silver exerting its special appeal for rural folk, did the South fully enter the financial lists. By 1878 southerners were totally immersed in the great debate,[90] and cheap money had gained a powerful accession of strength.

The new silver movement won the unexpected support of two great western dailies, Joseph Medill's *Chicago Tribune* and Murat Halstead's *Cincinnati Commercial*. These were among the country's most influential papers, and their attack on the "rag baby" had done much to make greenbackism disreputable beyond the Alleghenies. Neither Medill nor Halstead now suddenly embraced paper money or inflation. Bimetallism and greenbackism, they insisted, were distinct propositions. Silver "is the money

---

(Princeton: Princeton University Press, 1957), pp. 168, 680-685.

[86] For a similar estimate of the South's financial passivity until 1873 see Saloutos, *op. cit.*, pp. 46ff.

[87] At least there was some grass-roots demand in the South. See, for example, C. W. Grandy to "Mack," E[lizabeth] City, N. C., Sept. 7, 1873; J. J. Sommerel to Matthew W. Ransom, Salisbury, N. C., April 14, 1874, both in the Ransom MSS, Southern Historical Collection, University of North Carolina.

[88] On the House vote of Aug. 5, 1876, repealing the Resumption Act, the South divided 43 yeas to 15 nays. See Appendix F.

[89] *AM*, Oct. 12, 1876; *IA*, Sept. 9, 1876; Sept. 23, 1876.

[90] See, for example, R. Y. McAden to Matthew Ransom, Charlotte, N. C., Nov. 7, 1877; Joseph B. Cherry to Ransom, Windsor, N. C., Feb. 18, 1878, Ransom MSS; J. S. H. to Alexander Stephens, Augusta, Ga., Jan. 1, 1878, Stephens MSS, LC; W. A. Montgomery to Thomas F. Bayard, Jackson, Miss., Jan. 22, 1878; W. Frazier to Bayard, Staunton, Va., Feb. 11, 1878; J. L. M. Curry to Bayard, Richmond, Va., Oct. 12, 1878, Bayard MSS; Joseph Medill to Richard Oglesby, Chicago, Jan. 28, 1878, Oglesby MSS.

that shines and sings and endures," wrote the rhapsodic Halstead. Any attempt to associate "this old-fashioned hard money doctrine with financial wickedness" was "worthy of those who seek to make out that sticking to contracts is repudiation."[91] Both editors pledged their continued support for resumption, and insisted that remonetization was essential to specie payments. "Any scheme for resumption . . . on a single gold basis . . . could not be brought about without a serious contraction and a great danger to the business interests of the country," the *Tribune* argued.[92] If the gold men persist in their "warfare against silver," declared Halstead, "they become allies of the Greenbackers."[93]

There is no reason to doubt that both Medill and Halstead sincerely believed that changing the currency rules was economically risky as well as unjust to taxpayers and debtors. To the extent that they propagated their honest convictions they helped create the enthusiasm for silver which they shared. But the two editors were as much products as authors of the public mood. As good Republicans,[94] they feared the political repercussions of resisting the silver movement. With the whole trans-Allegheny region and the South caught up in the frenzy, they saw remonetization as an immediate political problem, not an abstract exercise in ethics or theory. As Medill noted during the 1876 campaign, "self-preservation is the first law of nature, and I feel we cannot afford to throw away this state [i.e., Illinois] in a vain fight on behalf of an exclusive gold dollar."[95] Such pragmatism was to be widespread among western Republicans and would help make silver the political force it shortly became.

Silver made its first appearance on the political stage, as

---

[91] See Halstead's letter to the editor, *The Public*, XII (Jan. 17, 1878), 37.

[92] *CDT*, March 5, 1877; also April 4, 1877; July 5, 1877.

[93] *Cincinnati Commercial*, Oct. 1, 1877.

[94] By 1877 Halstead, who had been a leader of the Liberal Republican revolt, was back in the Republican fold, while Medill, who had remained a good Republican, had

taken the *Tribune* editorship back from Liberal Horace White.

[95] Joseph Medill to James A. Garfield, Chicago, Aug. 27, 1876, Garfield MSS. (This item is filed under 1875, but from internal evidence it clearly belongs to 1876.) See also the 1877 letter of Samuel Bowles to Halstead in George S. Merriam, *The Life and Times of Samuel Bowles* (New York: The Century Co., 1885), II, 419-420.

noted, early in 1876 in connection with the fractional silver bill. Later in this same Congress, Kelley introduced a bill to remonetize the silver dollar at the pre-1873 ratio and make it a legal tender.[96] This was one of a half-dozen silver proposals introduced, some of which were overtly inflationist.[97] At one point, just before recessing for the national conventions, both houses actually approved a remonetization measure which was later emasculated by a joint conference committee and reduced to the Monetary Commission with its purely investigatory powers.[98] In the short session beginning December 1876, while the nation was convulsed by the disputed election, the silverites again pushed through a remonetization bill in the House, only to see it smothered in the Senate.[99]

This legislative activity coincided with the rise of silver as a party issue during the 1876 campaign. As noted earlier, the Indianapolis convention—as an afterthought—had endorsed free silver. This was in May, only a short time after Weston had thrown his spotlight on the silver question, and the hesitation at Indianapolis had reflected the traditional soft money dislike of all hard coin. Thereafter, as they became more familiar with the implications of the new question, the Independents grew more confident of silver.[100] Cary in particular made the Crime of '73 and the old silver dollar major campaign issues[101] and sent his unprepared opponents fleeing for cover.[102]

Cooper's defeat, of course, did not still the silverites. The January meeting of the Independent National Executive Committee endorsed remonetization, as did the early Greenback state conventions in the West and the later ones in Massachusetts, Pennsylvania, and New York.[103] In almost every case, however,

[96] Laughlin, op. cit., pp. 211-212.
[97] For example, Congressional Record, 44 Cong., 1 sess., pp. 1348, 2861, 5168.
[98] NYT, July 1, 1876; July 14, 1876. Also see above, ch. ix.
[99] Laughlin, op. cit., pp. 212-213.
[100] Ridge, op. cit., p. 160; Joseph Goar to Ignatius Donnelly, Faribault, Minn., Aug. 7, 1876, Donnelly MSS.
[101] Samuel F. Cary, On the Aims of the Independent Greenback Party: The Issues of the Campaign (New York, 1876), pp. 3-4; AM, Aug. 24, 1876; IA, Sept. 2, 1876.
[102] Joseph Medill to James A. Garfield, Chicago, Aug. 27, 1876; W. Townsend to Garfield, West Chester, Pa., Aug. 17, 1876, Garfield MSS; R. L. Gibson to Manton Marble, Washington, July 5, 1876, Marble MSS, LC; IA, Sept. 23, 1876.
[103] WA, Feb. 3, 1877; AM, May 31, 1877; June 14, 1877; June 28,

repeal of the Resumption Act was given priority. The Independents were still primarily paper money men and would remain so for the rest of the paper era.

Western Democrats were more friendly to silver. In Ohio Ewing told fellow Democrats that the Republicans were certain to support silver. It could not, therefore, be made an issue between the parties. On the other hand, their opponents were captives of their own unpopular resumption measure, and sound strategy called for the Democrats to emphasize repeal.[104] His advice was taken by the Ohio Democracy the following month, but on the whole, western Democrats could not resist the silver craze, and in the fall remonetization was prominently displayed in their state platforms.[105]

Ewing was right about the Republican response to silver. They seized the "dollar of the daddies" as a drowning man clutches his rescuer. In Iowa and Minnesota, where the Democrats endorsed the greenback as well as free silver, the Republicans responded with their own silver plank.[106] In Ohio Garfield found himself forced to come to terms with political reality and accept at least qualified remonetization.[107] At the 1877 Republican state convention, to the disgust of the purists, he helped push through an endorsement of "both silver and gold as . . .

1877; Sept. 13, 1877; *National Labor Tribune*, June 14, 1877; Sept. 22, 1877; Ralph R. Ricker, "The Greenback-Labor Movement in Pennsylvania" (unpublished Ph.D. dissertation, Pennsylvania State University, 1955), pp. 47ff.

[104] *AM*, June 28, 1878.

[105] See *Annual Cyclopedia and Register of Important Events for the Year 1877, passim,* for state party platforms.

[106] *Annual Cyclopedia for 1877,* pp. 398-399, 524-525. Actually, in Minnesota the Democrats adopted the Greenback candidate for Governor, banker William Banning, although they did not accept the other Independent candidates. *AM,* Sept. 13, 1877; Oct. 4, 1877.

[107] In August 1876 he wrote in his diary: "We are struggling . . . every day to keep off the silver bill . . . . I see signs of a coming storm on this question among the people. But I will not give way to the passion and folly [of] this new and most dangerous form of inflation and speculation." Garfield MS Diary, Aug. 9, 1876, Garfield MSS. In late 1877, however, he tried to procure a copy of Enrico Cernuschi's *Or et Argent,* a bimetallist tract that was becoming the bible of the moderate silver men. He had difficulty finding the book, but some of Cernuschi's arguments proved so convincing that for a while Garfield became a qualified silverite. See George Walker to Garfield, New York, Dec. 3, 1877, *ibid.;* Burke A. Hinsdale to Garfield, Hiram, Ohio, Nov. 6, 1878, Hinsdale, *op. cit.,* p. 389.

legal tender . . . except where otherwise provided by law."[108] The platform did not represent the "wiser sentiments" of the party, one hard money critic claimed, but was adopted "simply as a . . . device to tickle the crude fancy of the inflationists who seem to be a terror to the Republican leaders of [the] state."[109]

In Wisconsin the conservatives were made of sterner stuff, and the resulting struggle over silver almost shook the party apart. Normally, the Republicans had little to fear in the state. The Democrats could muster considerable strength in some areas, but they seldom captured the state house. Now, with the rise of the Independents, political prospects changed. In 1877 the Independent gubernatorial candidate was the dynamic E. P. Allis, the rich Milwaukee iron manufacturer, who had been active for some time in greenback politics. Here was a man who might appeal to Republican voters, and who, if he could not win himself, might draw off enough strength to throw the election to the Democrats who had taken up greenbacks, Resumption Act repeal, and silver in an attempt to keep their soft money wing loyal.[110]

At their Madison convention the Republicans were forced to recognize the danger, and while taking a strong stand for resumption, they also adopted a silver plank,[111] believing, as Senator Howe explained to Horace Rublee, Republican State Chairman, that there was "no better antidote to Allis than Silver."[112] But Rublee, a conservative, was not convinced and called a ratification meeting at Milwaukee, attended by prominent conservative businessmen, which repudiated the Madison

[108] *Annual Cyclopedia for 1877*, pp. 619-620. For Garfield's part in the convention see the letter from a fellow member of the Cleveland resolutions committee. *NYDT*, Sept. 15, 1877.

[109] *Ibid.*

[110] See D. C. Fulton to Wendell A. Anderson, Hudson, Wisc., Aug. 20, 1877; John Ringle to Anderson, Wausau, Wisc., Sept. 18, 1877; J. N. Brundage to Anderson, Grand Rapids, Wisc., Oct. 17, 1877, Anderson MSS, State Hist. Soc. of Wisc.; Thomas Lynch to William Vilas, Chilton, Wisc., Oct. 5, 1877, Vilas MSS, State Hist. Soc. of Wisc.

[111] *AM*, Aug. 2, 1877; W. W. Chadwick to Elisha Keyes, Monroe, Wisc., Aug. 30, 1877, Keyes MSS, State Hist. Soc. of Wisc.; *CDT*, Sept. 12, 1877; *Annual Cyclopedia for 1877*, pp. 769-770; Ellis B. Usher, *The Greenback Movement of 1875-1884 and Wisconsin's Part in It* (Milwaukee, 1911), pp. 32-33.

[112] Timothy Howe to Rublee, Green Bay, Wisc., Sept. 18, 1877, Howe MSS, State Hist. Soc. of Wisc.

platform. The meeting adopted a new set of resolutions denouncing as "dangerous, delusive and disreputable all schemes . . . that do not contemplate the honest payment of the public debt and the speedy attainment of . . . a gold basis."[113] Almost alone in the West, the Wisconsin Republicans were ready to fight the campaign on an unequivocal sound money platform.

The fall campaigns were vastly encouraging to the friends of cheap money. Wisconsin Republicans excepted, erstwhile conservatives, everywhere sensing a new public mood, retreated to some form of political heresy. For the third-party men the drought finally appeared to be over as thousands of miners, mill hands, and laborers rushed to vote for Independent, or Greenback, or Greenback-Labor tickets in Pennsylvania, Ohio, Illinois, Iowa, Wisconsin, and Minnesota.

This new working-class support sprang from the great railroad disorders of the summer—upwellings of hatred and violence against the great trunk roads which, to offset declining revenues during these hard times, had sought to cut wages. Beginning in July, the desperate engineers, firemen, and brakemen tried to restore their wages by blocking the movement of trains, only to meet the smoking muskets of the state militia. From Martinsburg, West Virginia, waves of arson, riot, and looting, fueled by four years of working-class misery, spread out in all directions along the routes of the major eastern railroads. In Baltimore, Pittsburgh, Buffalo, Chicago, and many other smaller places, strikers and militia, as well as foolhardy bystanders, were shot down; trains were derailed and roundhouses and stations gutted. With order ruthlessly restored and the trains rolling again, industrial strikes, marked by further violence, continued to sputter through the nation, particularly in the coal and iron regions of eastern Pennsylvania.[114]

The summer social upheaval was a blessing for the Greenbackers. They were quick to urge embittered laboring men to take up the Independent ticket as the workable escape from bondage to all-powerful capital.[115] Across the country, from

[113] Usher, *op. cit.*, pp. 33-34.
[114] Robert V. Bruce, *1877: Year of Violence* (Indianapolis: The Bobbs-Merrill Company, 1959).

[115] Dennis Geary to Terence Powderly, Reading, Pa., Sept. 4, 1877, Powderly MSS, Catholic University of America. See also *Indian-*

Pennsylvania westward, the Independents were infused with a new confidence, convinced that for the first time they would have a sympathetic hearing from labor. In the Keystone State, Davis and Powderly of the Knights of Labor joined with Independent politicos Frank Hughes and F. P. Dewees and a handful of farm leaders to organize the United Greenback-Labor Party. Although short of funds, by early fall the new party was putting on an energetic campaign with its leaders confident of a large state vote.[116] In Ohio the feeble Independent beginnings of spring had grown into a formidable movement by the fall. The Ohio campaign, with Ohioans in both White House and Treasury, attracted national attention. Again the Democrats were worried that they would lose votes to the Independents[117] and adopted Machiavellian tactics to meet the danger. Where labor normally voted Democratic they shouted louder for greenbacks than their third-party opponents. In normally Republican areas they tried to split the labor vote by secretly subsidizing the separate Independent ticket.[118] Republicans countered by touting silver as a powerful cure-all for resumption. Sherman, brought home to help the party, explained how resumption could easily be achieved by a gold and silver reserve without withdrawing a single greenback. Only Garfield, despite his earlier convention role, refused to surrender completely to silver to quiet public fears.[119] In Indiana, Illinois, Wisconsin, Iowa, and Minnesota separate Independent-Labor tickets, or Democratic-Independent coalitions, were in the field, vigorously canvassing for labor, farm, and even business votes.[120]

---

apolis Sun, July 28, 1877; Labor Advance, Aug. 11, 1877.

[116] Indianapolis Sun, Sept. 29, 1877; Frederick Turner to Terence Powderly, Philadelphia, Sept. 3, 1877; F. P. Dewees to Powderly, Pottsville, Pa., Sept. 27, 1877; Dewees to Powderly, Pottsville, Oct. 1, 1877; T. V. Walker to Powderly, Carbondale, Pa., Oct. 13, 1877; Dewees to Powderly, Pottsville, Oct. 6, 1877; V. Rutledge to Powderly, Carbondale, Nov. 1, 1877. All these are in the Powderly MSS.

[117] See Thomas Ewing, Jr., to James R. Doolittle, Lancaster, Ohio, Sept. 15, 1877, Doolittle MSS, State Hist. Soc. of Wisc.

[118] J. S. Robinson to Sherman, Columbus, Sept. 24, 1877; J. M. Case to Sherman, Columbus, Oct. 2, 1877, Sherman MSS.

[119] John A. Gano to Garfield, Cincinnati, Sept. 30, 1877, Garfield MSS.

[120] Indianapolis Sun, Sept. 29, 1877; CDT, Oct. 6, 1877; Usher, op. cit., pp. 48-50; John McCartney

No amount of Republican soothing syrup could deaden the pain of hard times, unemployment, and class hostility. Everywhere, the Independents and Independent-Labor coalitions made great gains. Stephen Johnston in Ohio got over 30,000 votes. The Iowa Independents increased their vote from 900 in 1876 to 33,000. Allis received 26,000 votes out of 175,000 cast in Wisconsin; while in Pennsylvania, the Greenback-Labor candidate for State Treasurer, James L. Wright, received 53,000 votes, almost 10 per cent of the total. Even in Maine the Independents showed some strength. Throughout the nation the third-party turnout more than doubled over 1876.[121]

The Democrats also made gains and carried off several choice plums. Narrowly beaten in Wisconsin, they won in Ohio, a result widely interpreted as a rebuke to Sherman and resumption.[122] Sound money men blamed the currency issue for the defeat,[123] and to many Republicans the lesson seemed unmistakable. The party would find peace from the money problem only after resumption. The Ohio setback was temporary, one of Sherman's friends noted, but the incessant greenback propaganda was winning converts even among Ohio Republicans, some of whom were beginning to view the Resumption Act as an "evil measure." The only "permanent relief" from the constant agitation lay in "an early resumption . . . and . . . destruction of the greenbacks as a *legal tender* . . . so as to put it [*sic*] beyond the reach of the demagogue as a topic of annual appeal to the ignorant masses."[124]

---

to William B. Allison, Vinton, Iowa, Sept. 3, 1877; C. C. Carpenter to Allison, Fort Dodge, Iowa, Oct. 15, 1877, Allison MSS; AM, Oct. 4, 1877.

[121] *Indianapolis Sun*, Oct. 13, 1877; *Labor Advance*, Oct. 13, 1877; AM, Nov. 15, 1877; James, *op. cit.*, pp. 129-143; F. P. Dewees to Powderly, Pottsville, Pa., Nov. 30, 1878, Powderly MSS; Fred E. Haynes, *Third Party Movements Since the Civil War, With Special Reference to Iowa: A Study in Social Politics* (Iowa City: The State Historical Society of Iowa, 1916), p. 124.

[122] *Annual Cyclopedia for 1877*, pp. 768, 621; T. C. James to Rutherford B. Hayes, Delaware, Ohio, Oct. 12, 1877, Hayes MSS; Charles Conant to John Sherman, London, England, Oct. 10, 1877, in U.S. House of Representatives, *Executive Document No. 9*, 46 Cong., 2 sess., p. 167.

[123] J. W. Case to John Sherman, Columbus, Oct. 12, 1877, Sherman MSS; C. E. Poorman to Carl Schurz, Bellaire, Ohio, Oct. 25, 1877, Hayes MSS.

[124] Warner Bateman to John Sherman, Cincinnati, Oct. 11, 1877, Sherman MSS. See also MS

III

The public excitement over silver and the hazards of a resurgent greenback movement were the setting for Sherman's early resumption moves. At every turn, the Secretary had to consider political realities, and only remarkable agility saved him from disaster. There were also difficult problems of a technical nature to overcome, and these required still other skills. The only resumption machinery available was the 1875 Act which did nothing more than give the Treasury authority to sell bonds for gold. It made no provision for reducing the volume of notes that could be brought for conversion on January 1, 1879, beyond requiring that $80 of legal tenders be "redeemed" for each $100 of new bank notes. Without specific power to retire greenbacks, it was said, the Treasury could be compelled on resumption day to convert to gold all the legal tenders, plus an equal volume of bank notes, and about a billion dollars of bank deposits as well.[125] A coin reserve sufficient to convert even the whole greenback issue dollar for dollar was out of the question and would have made resumption without substantial contraction impossible. Almost certainly Sherman would have preferred some means of reducing the Treasury's obligations before resumption day. But he was a realist. He knew that the West, and for that matter eastern businessmen, would not tolerate any attempt to cancel greenbacks and if pushed too hard might frustrate all chance of bringing resumption off.[126] Specie payments, however difficult, would have to come without contraction, and by the frail instrument of a

Diary of George W. Julian, entry for Feb. 10, 1878, Julian MSS, Indiana State Library. For a forceful statement of the same view in the preceding decade see Samuel J. Kirkwood to Grenville M. Dodge, Iowa City, Jan. 10, 1869, Dodge MSS, Iowa State Dept. of Hist. and Archives.

[125] The logic of this view was that although neither bank notes nor deposits were legally payable in gold, both were convertible into greenbacks. Greenbacks brought for redemption and not retired but paid out again, could serve as an endless belt to draw gold from the Treasury. *Bankers' Magazine*, xxxii (May 1878), 889; Henry C. Carey, *Resumption: When and How Will It End?* (Philadelphia, 1877), p. 8; George Coe, remarks before the American Bankers' Association, in American Bankers' Association, *Reports of Proceedings*, i, 38-39.

[126] Jacob D. Cox to Rutherford B. Hayes, Toledo, Feb. 10, 1877, Hayes MSS.

modest gold reserve, most of which would have to be borrowed.

It was at this point that the silver question intruded, threatening to undercut the entire resumption effort. Soon after taking office, Sherman had begun to negotiate a gold loan. At this time a contract for refunding the national debt was in force between the Treasury and a syndicate of international bankers composed of Seligman Brothers; Morton, Bliss and Company; August Belmont and Company, acting on behalf of the English Rothschilds; and Drexel, Morgan and Company, representing Junius Spencer Morgan of London. This contract provided for the sale of $40 million of 4½ per cent bonds for gold, 5-20 bonds, and other matured securities. Since the gold proceeds of this sale were to be applied exclusively to refunding the 5-20's, Sherman renegotiated the contract in April and May to permit part of the gold received to be set aside for the resumption coin reserve. In all, under this modified arrangement, the Treasury acquired $15 million of coin in the next few months.[127] Soon after, a completely new contract was drawn with the syndicate, joined now by the First National Bank of New York, to market 4 per cent bonds. Some of the proceeds of this sale were also to be applied to the resumption reserve.[128] But just before public subscriptions were opened by the banks, the silver issue almost ruined the whole carefully worked out scheme.

Sherman himself was partly responsible for this near disaster. Like other western Republicans, he feared repeal more than remonetization. As Senator he had not been afraid of limited silver coinage although, as he explained to former Secretary McCulloch, he favored a full legal tender silver dollar only with a concurrent withdrawal of greenbacks.[129] As Secretary of the Treasury he was, if anything, still more friendly to silver, realizing that to resume under the 1875 Act he would need all the political support he could get. Accordingly, he tried hard

[127] John Sherman, *Recollections of Forty Years in the House, Senate and Cabinet, An Autobiography* (Chicago: The Werner Co., 1895), I, 566-578; *Exec. Doc. No. 9*, pp. 2-4; Don Carlos Barrett, *The Greenbacks and Resumption of Specie Payments, 1862-1879* (Cambridge: Harvard University Press, 1931), pp. 206-207; *CFC*, xxv (Feb. 8, 1877), 542.

[128] Sherman, *Recollections*, I, 571-573.

[129] Sherman to Hugh McCulloch, Washington, Dec. 21, 1876, McCulloch MSS, LC.

not to alienate the moderate bimetallists and whenever possible appeared cordial to their pet scheme. In June 1877, at the beginning of the political season, Sherman told western newspaper correspondents that he opposed both the extreme silver men and the doctrinaire gold bugs. A certain amount of silver to replace the greenbacks would actually help the Treasury resume by reducing the volume of paper redeemable on resumption day. But free coinage, he warned, "would destroy our public credit," disturb the funding of the debt, and drive gold abroad, leaving the country with an exclusive silver standard.[130]

This statement was moderate enough in itself, but when followed by Ohio Senator Stanley Matthews's report that Hayes, a close friend, favored paying the bonds in silver,[131] the interview stirred up a tempest. Almost immediately, American investors took fright and domestic loan subscriptions stopped.[132] English capitalists, too, were reported reconsidering decisions to take American securities. "Our credit," wrote Charles F. Conant, United States Treasury Agent in London, "would be absolutely ruined here if silver were made a legal tender in any large amount."[133]

The syndicate bankers were frantic at the turn of events. On June 9 they had agreed to take $25 million of the new bonds for resale, and they had visions of having to make the contract good out of their own pockets. Belmont, Joseph Seligman, and the other syndicate members dispatched appeals to Sherman urging him to deny categorically Administration approval of legal tender silver.[134] Though willing to reassure the bankers privately, Sherman was reluctant to irritate the silver men and at first refused to make any public declaration.[135] On June 19, however, after a Cabinet session, he issued an explicit denial of the Treasury's authority to pay either principal or interest of

---

[130] *CDT*, June 12, 1877; Jeannette Nichols, "John Sherman and the Silver Drive of 1877-1878: The Origin of the Gigantic Subsidy," *Ohio State Archeological and Historical Quarterly*, XLVI (1937), 152-153.

[131] *CDT*, June 13, 1877; Nichols, *op. cit.*, p. 153.

[132] *Nation*, XXIV (June 21, 1877), 357.

[133] Charles Conant to Sherman, London, England, June 16, 1877, *Exec. Doc. No. 9*, p. 78.

[134] *Ibid.*, pp. 76-80; August Belmont to Sherman, [New York], June 14, 1877, Sherman MSS.

[135] Sherman to August Belmont, Washington, June 16, 1877, *Exec. Doc. No. 9*, p. 76.

the coin bonds in anything but gold.[136] This letter had its intended effect, and with confidence restored, the loan moved quickly. In a month over $77 million of the "four percents" had been sold and a substantial amount of gold added to the resumption reserve.[137]

Through the remainder of the summer the state elections proved a headache to Sherman. As we have seen, he had to take valuable time off to campaign in Ohio—and to little effect at that. The Republican defeat in his home state had been judged a vote of no confidence, although it probably only encouraged him to push through his plans all the faster.

A far graver threat now appeared as the Forty-fifth Congress assembled in special session in October to vote the military appropriations that had been neglected in the previous Congress. The Army remained unpaid, as free coinage men, bimetallists, greenbackers, anti-resumptionists, and gold bugs turned the session into a financial free-for-all. The organization of the Democratic House was favorable to cheap money this time. Samuel J. Randall, who was elected Speaker to succeed the recently deceased Michael Kerr, was beholden to the Ohio Democracy,[138] and gave the Ohioans control of the strategic Banking and Currency Committee. The new Chairman of the Committee[139] was Aylett Buckner of Missouri, an anti-resumption, free silver man; but the real power in the Committee was Ewing, who, although a freshman member, had powerful support from the Ohio Democrats and was given second place. Several sound money men, including Simeon Chittenden, the New York merchant-enterpriser, and Benjamin Eames of Rhode Island, secured places, but they were outnumbered by the soft money group.[140]

All through the preceding summer, western Congressmen

---

[136] *Nation*, xxiv (June 21, 1877), 357; Sherman, *Recollections*, i, 580.

[137] *Ibid.; Exec. Doc. No. 9*, p. 4. By April some $25 million had been raised for the resumption fund under this contract.

[138] See above, ch. viii. Randall was not a soft money man himself, and his election was not related in any direct way to the money question. *NYDT*, Oct. 15, 1877.

[139] S. S. Cox, who had been Chairman during the preceding Congress, had found the Committee's work uncongenial and refused reappointment. *Ibid.*, Oct. 29, 1877.

[140] *Ibid.*, Oct. 30, 1877.

had been sharpening their knives for the Resumption Act, and on October 29, after committee appointments were announced, thirteen repeal measures were submitted in the House. These were referred to the Banking and Currency Committee, and on October 31 Ewing reported back H. R. 805, repealing the crucial third section—the resumption clause—of the Act. Slightly modified to preserve the free banking provision which was part of the third section, this measure won consistent majorities of from 10 to 20 on an early series of test votes,[141] and apprehensive resumptionists began to fear that a Presidential veto would be the only way to stop repeal.[142]

At this juncture, Ewing, an inexperienced parliamentarian, fumbled. Hoping to force an immediate vote, he ineptly lodged the bill in the morning hour where the sound money men, by dilatory tactics, were able to keep it from coming to a vote. To escape from this limbo, it was necessary to make the measure the special order of business, a move requiring a two-thirds majority, which once accomplished exposed the repeal bill to amendment and debate. This was precisely what Ewing had tried to avoid, but it was the only way out and he was forced to take it. Turning to the anti-repeal silverites, he apparently promised to expedite pending silver legislation in return for parliamentary concessions, and on November 5, by similar roll calls, the Bland free silver bill and a motion making H. R. 805 the special order for the following Tuesday passed the House in quick succession. Twenty-two members who voted for the Bland Bill opposed the special order resolution, but the support of a small group of moderates gave Ewing the needed two-thirds vote.[143]

Several weeks of debate followed, with Ewing and his fellow committee member William Phillips of Kansas, a maverick

---

[141] Ibid.; Congressional Record, 45 Cong., 1 sess., Index, p. 149, under heading "Resumption of Specie Payments"; ibid., pp. 203-205, 225-226; Nation, xxv (Nov. 8, 1877), 277. Hereafter, all references to the Record, unless otherwise indicated, will be to this Congress and session.

[142] Garfield MS Diary, Oct. 31,

1877, Garfield MSS.

[143] Congressional Record, pp. 212, 225-226, 228-229, 241-242; NYDT, Nov. 1-3, 1877; Nov. 5, 1877. The Bland Bill passed by a vote of 163 to 34; repeal by 143 to 47. The moderate group can be distinguished by their later course on repeal. See below.

Republican, pushing for quick repeal, and Chittenden and Eames defending both the justice and practicality of resumption under the 1875 measure.[144] These two wings of the Banking and Currency Committee represented the extremes of House opinion, but a third group held the balance of power. This faction consisted of moderates, many of whom had joined the anti-resumptionists in extricating the repeal bill from the morning hour. Western bimetallist Republicans, these men were the Congressional equivalents of Medill and Halstead, supporting specie payments but convinced that resumption in gold alone would cripple commerce and industry. Jacob D. Cox, the most articulate of this group, believed, as we have seen, that without remonetization resumption would be defeated and the forces of "communism" released. But Cox supported silver for strategic reasons as well, having seen from the beginning "that prompt remonetization was the only hope of escaping wild experiments which would convulse the country." Men like Ewing, Butler, and Voorhees, he explained to his anti-silver friend David Wells, could be thwarted only by a diversionary movement.[145]

Although this group voted for the November 5 legislative package, they deserted Ewing in the debate, and joined the eastern resumptionists in an attempt to hamstring and delay the repeal measure. Their efforts were unavailing, however. On November 23 the long string of amendments that had accumulated in the seventeen-day debate were disposed of and the bill passed 133 to 120.[146]

Even as the House debated repeal, public attention was turning once more to silver. The decisive House majority for the Bland Bill seemed to foreshadow the success of remonetization and promised once again to wreck Sherman's plans. "The threatening position of the silver question," Belmont warned on November 7, would "check completely" sales of the 4 per

[144] *Congressional Record*, pp. 258-262, 382-383, 427, 617-621; Garfield MS Diary, Nov. 22, 1877, Garfield MSS.

[145] Cox to David Wells, Washington, Feb. 28, 1878, Wells MSS.

[146] Garfield MS Diary, Nov. 14, 15, and 21, 1877, Garfield MSS;

Congressional Record, pp. 266, 429-432, 462-463, 632-633. The vote represented the familiar coalition of southern and western Democrats, joined by a majority of the Pennsylvania members. For the vote of the crucial moderate silverites see Appendix G.

cent resumption bonds both at home and in Europe. Two days later the "four percents" fell below par, and the syndicate was compelled to repurchase $750,000 worth to support the market. The bankers could not, of course, continue to shore up prices indefinitely, and the same day, after conferring in New York, they suspended sales.[147]

The syndicate bankers naturally were not happy with this turn of events and joined with the commercial bankers, the insurance underwriters, and New York and Philadelphia merchants in sending a delegation to the Senate silver hearings scheduled for November 13.[148] They also needled Sherman into issuing another statement denying the Treasury's intention to pay the bonds in anything but gold coin.[149] But investors continued wary, and the bond sales remained stalled while the silver legislation pended in the Senate.

One cause for apprehension was the uncertainty regarding the President's intentions. Senator Matthews had been assuring friends and the press that Hayes would sign a free silver bill, and the affirmative vote on the Bland measure by Charles Foster and Jacob Cox, both old Ohio friends of the President, was considered a straw in the wind.[150] The syndicate bankers demanded that Hayes guarantee to stop the silver drive with a veto if necessary,[151] but his actual intentions remained obscure until his first Annual Message on December 3.

In the Message the President lectured Congress on the dangers of full remonetization at 16 to 1 and urged that the legislators refrain from restoring silver as a legal tender. But, like Sherman, reluctant to antagonize the silver resumptionists,

---

[147] Belmont to John Sherman, New York, Nov. 7, 1877, *Exec. Doc. No. 9*, p. 183; Sherman, *Recollections*, II, 605; Belmont to Sherman, New York, Nov. 9, 1877, *Exec. Doc. No. 9*, p. 186.

[148] Anthony Drexel, Joseph Seligman, J. P. Morgan, and Francis O. French—the latter of the First National Bank—were members of the delegation to Washington. See French to John Sherman, Nov. 12, 1877, Sherman MSS; Morris K. Jesup to William B. Allison, New York, [?], 1877; J. S. Kennedy to Allison, New York, Nov. 10, 1877, Allison MSS; *NYDT*, Nov. 14, 1877.

[149] See Sherman's letter to Colgate and Company, Washington, Dec. 1, 1877, *Exec. Doc. No. 9*, pp. 201-209.

[150] Nichols, *op. cit.*, p. 154; Samuel J. Randall to Manton Marble, Washington, Nov. 3, 1877, Marble MSS.

[151] Harris C. Fahnestock to John Sherman, New York, Nov. 7, 1877, Sherman MSS.

Hayes held out hope that silver could somehow be fitted into the national coinage.[152] Sherman's *Annual Report* seconded the President's position, warning that free coinage would cripple the Treasury's efforts to refund the debt at lower interest rates.[153]

Though the Administration now seemed committed to defending the public credit, the Senate was at first strongly disposed to follow the radical course of the House. In October, during the special session, Jones of Nevada had officially opened the Senate silver discussion by introducing a free coinage bill.[154] At the same time, he circulated among his colleagues the report just submitted by the Monetary Commission authorized by the previous Congress, recommending remonetization as a necessary preliminary to resumption.[155] Now, in the regular session, soon after the President's Message was received, Stanley Matthews introduced a concurrent resolution giving Congressional sanction to repaying the federal debt in silver. "All bonds of the United States," this declaration read, "are payable principal and interest . . . in silver dollars . . . containing 412½ grains each of standard silver." Restoring the pre-1873 silver dollar as legal tender, it specified, was "not a violation of the public faith, nor a derogation of the public creditors."[156]

Congress recessed for Christmas before acting on the Matthews Resolution, but news of the new peril soon reached Europe and

[152] James D. Richardson (ed.), *Messages and Papers of the Presidents, 1789-1902* (n.p.: Bureau of National Literature and Art, 1903), VII, 462.

[153] U. S. Treasury, *Report for 1877*, pp. xi, xxi-xxiv.

[154] Nichols, *op. cit.*, p. 154.

[155] These were the majority recommendations of Bland, Jones, William Groesbeck of Ohio, Senator Lewis Bogy of Missouri, and Representative George Willard of Michigan. The minority, consisting of Boutwell, Randall Gibson of Louisiana, and Professor Francis Bowen of Harvard, claimed that it would be impossible to maintain a bimetallic standard; that silver would drive gold out, and the nation would revert to silver monometallism. The Commission had held hearings in New York and elsewhere at which it had interviewed businessmen, bankers, academicians, experts, etc. But as was often the case with such committees, the hearings only confirmed the members' previous prejudices, and the Commission split along the lines that had existed at the outset. The conclusions and recommendations of the majority were already foreshadowed by the appointment of George Weston as Commission Secretary! The Report is U. S. Senate, *Report No. 703*, 44 Cong., 2 sess.

[156] Laughlin, *op. cit.*, pp. 231-232.

investors began to sell their United States holdings. In the next few weeks American bonds sagged badly, as individuals and fiduciary institutions in England and on the Continent rushed to convert their American securities into gold.[157]

During the recess and the weeks of Senate debate that followed, public excitement over finance rivaled that of the Inflation Bill period. Throughout the nation the pro-silver men attempted to make as much noise as possible to impress Congress with the strength of silver sentiment. From the West came the insistent voice of Agrarian soft money. On January 16 the Minnesota State Senate, prodded by Donnelly, voted 35 to 3 to endorse remonetization. A large convention at Springfield, Illinois, sent pro-silver resolutions to Congress. In Indianapolis a joint Democratic-Independent rally demanded free and unlimited coinage. Medill and Halstead stepped up their propaganda barrage.[158] The eastern silverites were active also. In New York a packed meeting of businessmen, labor leaders, and soft money professionals passed resolutions declaring that remonetization would restore wages and property values.[159] Even Carey, now in his eighty-fourth year, did his part for the cause, telling a reporter that Congress should insist on passage of the Bland Bill even if Hayes vetoed it.[160]

The House soft money men themselves, not trusting to a spontaneous upwelling of public support, met in a special caucus to help work up pressure for silver. The meeting, chaired by

[157] Charles Conant to John Sherman, London, England, Dec. 15, 1877 and Dec. 29, 1877, *Exec. Doc. No. 9*, pp. 213, 218-219; *CFC*, xxiv (Dec. 29, 1877), 632. On Dec. 18 Andrew White of Cornell University sent Hayes an advertisement from a Stuttgart paper by a German investment house advising holders of U. S. bonds "before the final passage of such a [silver] law to exchange such bonds for other securities." See White to Hayes, Stuttgart, Germany, Dec. 18, 1877; also Charles Conant to Sherman, London, England, Jan. 3, 1878, Hayes MSS. Needless to say the resolution

also frightened the syndicate bankers. See Levi Morton to William B. Allison (cablegram), London, England, Dec. 14, 1877, Allison MSS; August Belmont to Thomas F. Bayard, New York, Dec. 18, 1877, Bayard MSS.

[158] *AM*, Jan. 24, 1878; *CDT*, Jan. 16, 1878; *Indianapolis Sun*, Jan. 19, 1878; Joseph Medill to Hayes, Chicago, Jan. 15, 1878, Hayes MSS; *The Public*, xiii (Jan. 17, 1878), 37.

[159] *NYDT*, Feb. 2, 1878; *AM*, Feb. 21, 1878.

[160] *Ibid.*, Feb. 14, 1878.

Buckner, was bipartisan and included Republicans Butler and Kelley, Greenbury Fort and Joseph Cannon of Illinois, as well as Democrats Ewing, Bland, Springer of Illinois, and other prominent soft money men. A "League" was organized to press for silver and repeal and an executive committee of seven chosen to collect funds to finance a propaganda campaign. Another meeting a week later resolved to distribute pro-silver documents in the eastern states to counteract the prevailing hard money sentiment.[161]

The hard money forces immediately lighted a backfire. Once again organized respectability rallied for sound and honest finance. The religious press, although riddled with pro-silver heresy,[162] lectured Congress, Sherman, and the President himself on the duty of the hour. The contest, one editor declared, was "between honor and dishonor, between integrity of purpose and repudiation."[163] The reformers raised their voices to cry down the evil measure which was as dangerous, as demented, as dishonest as the Inflation Bill had been.[164] Through late December and early January the trade associations of the port cities, including the hitherto greenback tainted New York Board of Trade, passed resolutions condemning the Bland Bill.[165]

[161] *Ibid.*, Feb. 7, 1878; *Nation,* xxvi (Jan. 24, 1878), 49; (Jan. 31, 1878), 69. A third avowed purpose, besides silver and repeal—repeal of the National Banking Act—was postponed in deference to the Republicans.

[162] The *Christian Advocate* of New York, a leading Methodist paper, on Jan. 10, 1878, came out in a defense of remonetization reminiscent of Halstead's and Medill's. For a while, in 1877, even the Dutch Reformed *Christian Intelligencer* supported silver, although by 1878 second thoughts had put the paper back on the sound money track. These defections are added confirmation that silver enjoyed greater appeal than greenbacks. See *Christian Advocate,* liii (Jan. 10, 1878), 25; *Christian Intelligencer,* xlviii (Oct. 25, 1877), 9.

[163] *Ibid.*, xlix (Jan. 10, 1878), 16; also (Feb. 14, 1878), 9; *The*

Advance, xii (Feb. 7, 1878), 81; *Christian Union,* xvii (Feb. 13, 1878), 135; *Christian Register,* lvii (Feb. 2, 1878), 2; *The Independent,* Jan. 10, 1878, p. 22.

[164] See *Nation,* xxvi (Feb. 7, 1878), 91; (Feb. 14, 1878), 106-107; *Journal of Social Science,* ix (January 1878), pp. 14-20, 21-43.

[165] Boston Board of Trade, *Twenty-fifth Annual Report for 1878,* pp. 37-40; New York Chamber of Commerce, *Twentieth Annual Report for 1877-1878,* pp. 112-113; for the New York Board of Trade see *NYDT,* Feb. 5, 1878; for the Importers' and Grocers' Board of Trade of New York, George W. Lane to R. B. Hayes, New York, Feb. 14, 1878, Hayes MSS; for Philadelphia mercantile opinion see *NYDT,* Jan. 12, 1878; for the Mobile Board of Trade see Leslie E. Brooks to Thomas F. Bayard, Mobile, Ala., Jan. 16, 1878,

Perhaps the most apprehensive businessmen were the national bankers and insurance men. They held for investment and as security against circulation, as much as $600 million of federal bonds and would face a substantial loss of capital if these were made payable in depreciated silver.[166] On January 9 the New York bankers, led by the aggressive George Coe of the American Exchange Bank, drew up plans for mobilizing eastern businessmen against the silver bill. A committee composed of New York, Boston, Philadelphia, and Baltimore bankers, together with eastern merchants and representatives of trust and insurance companies, was to be organized to coordinate the fight against remonetization. The committee would communicate with banks all over the country, inviting them to join with the eastern institutions. In addition, merchants and manufacturers would be urged to put their affairs on a gold basis as soon as possible in preparation for specie payments.[167] By the end of the month, Hayes and Congress were receiving anti-silver memorials from committees representing the leading banks and fiduciary institutions of the four major Atlantic coast cities, as well as the Clearing House Associations of New Orleans and Milwaukee.[168]

The action of the eastern bankers helped restore British confidence in American securities and had a generally soothing effect on the bond market.[169] But the improvement was only temporary. Shortly after Congress reconvened, the Matthews Resolution was passed,[170] and the Senate was soon engaged in a full-dress debate on the silver bill itself. More anxious days for the hard money

---

Bayard MSS. On the other hand, one Philadelphia ironmaster when interviewed said he preferred silver and greenbacks to gold as they were not exportable. See *NYDT*, Jan. 12, 1878.

[166] *The Public*, XII (Dec. 20, 1877), 388-389.

[167] *NYDT*, Jan. 10, 1878; Committee of the Banks of . . . New York, Boston, Philadelphia and Baltimore, *The Silver Question: Memorial to Congress, January 1878*, pp. 1-2.

[168] *Ibid.*, pp. 3ff.; George Coe to R. B. Hayes, New York, Jan. 31, 1878, Hayes MSS; clipping in E.

C. Palmer to Thomas F. Bayard, New Orleans, Jan. 8, 1878, Bayard MSS; *NYDT*, Feb. 4, 1878.

[169] Charles Conant to Sherman, London, England, Jan. 12, 1878, *Exec. Doc. No. 9*, pp. 223-224; George N. Henlee to Thomas F. Bayard, London, England, Jan. 8, 1878, Bayard MSS.

[170] It passed the Senate on Jan. 25, 1878, and the House three days later by overwhelming majorities. *Congressional Record*, 45 Cong., 2 sess., pp. 564-628. Hereafter all references to the *Record*, unless otherwise indicated, will be to this Congress and session.

men followed. It looked for a while as if nothing would stop the silverites. The only energetic men at the capitol, wrote Charles Nordhoff, were either "Godless scoundrels, or ignorant . . . children," who would make the silver bill "the entering wedge for the commune."[171] John Murray Forbes feared that the silver men—"lunatics and fanatics"—were using remonetization as a cover for outright inflation.[172]

The syndicate bankers again became panicky as United States bonds fell sharply on the London market.[173] Morton, Seligman, and Morgan wrote Hayes from the British capital that English investors would consider the Bland Bill a "breach of public honor." Fahnestock of the First National despaired of stopping the silverites and proposed a compromise that would eliminate free coinage and make remonetization contingent on the common conservative formula—an international agreement fixing gold-silver ratios.[174]

To outsiders, the Administration appeared curiously passive during the crucial Senate debate. Even Belmont was annoyed by the waiting game both Sherman and the President seemed to be playing.[175] In fact, Hayes had interceded for the moderate position supported by Allison of Iowa, although with little apparent effect.[176]

Fortunately for the resumption program the Senate moderates were able to blunt the edge of the Bland Bill. Allison and William Wallace of Pennsylvania succeeded in cutting the free coin-

[171] Charles Nordhoff to Edward Atkinson, Washington, Feb. 19, 1878, Atkinson MSS, Massachusetts Historical Society.

[172] Forbes to Hugh McCulloch, Boston, Jan. 24, 1878, McCulloch MSS.

[173] Charles Conant to Sherman, London, England, Jan. 24, 1878, *Exec. Doc. No. 9*, p. 243. On Jan. 14, Sherman, for reasons not connected with the silver bill, decided to terminate the syndicate contract as it applied to bond sales in the United States. The syndicate continued to market bonds in Europe, however. Sherman, *Recollections*, II, 627-628.

[174] Morton, Morgan and Selig-

man to Hayes, London, England, Feb. 15, 1878, *Exec. Doc. No. 9*, pp. 261-262; Fahnestock to Sherman, New York, Feb. 1, 1878, Hayes MSS.

[175] Belmont to David Wells, New York, Jan. 29, 1878, Wells MSS.

[176] Williams, *Diary and Letters*, III, 479, diary entry for April 14, 1878. Sherman had also written a letter to his friend Allison on Dec. 10, but Allison's biographer does not believe it had any influence on the Senator's course. Leland L. Sage, *William Boyd Allison: A Study in Practical Politics* (Iowa City: State Historical Society of Iowa, 1956), pp. 152-153.

age provision out of the House measure.[177] The bill passed by the Senate on February 16 made the standard silver dollar a legal tender for all public and private debts, but saved the gold standard by limiting the amount of silver to be coined to no more than $4 million nor less than $2 million monthly. Sherman, in other words, was to have the option of buying as little as $24 million of silver a year and accordingly could keep the inflationary effects of the Bland Act well under control. In addition, the Treasury, not the mine owners, would pocket the difference between the market and mint value of silver.[178]

Returned to the House on February 21, the silver bill was quickly disposed of. The Ewing faction called it a sham, but most western and southern silverites followed Bland's lead and were willing to take it as a first installment.[179] The pro-resumption silver men, believing they could "defeat the inflationists and all comers on this silver bill and stop the greenbackers on the silver line,"[180] voted with the anti-resumptionists to pass the Senate bill 205 to 72.[181]

No sooner did the bill reach the White House than the President came under the barrage that earlier had landed on Congress. A large part of Hayes's mail during the week the bill lay on his desk urged him to take a prudent course. Halstead warned that if the bill failed "there would be disastrous agitation" and business would "perish" in the uncertainty.[182] Medill added lurid details to Halstead's picture: "If the veto is *sustained* the country will be convulsed with excitement and indignation and wild, desperate men will get control of popular feelings and make mischief. Ultra measures will be forced thro Congress, and Repeal of the Resumption act will be attached to vital appropriations bills: vast and incalculable injury may result from thwarting popular will on the silver bill."[183] Even the clergy were troubled

---

[177] *Ibid.*, pp. 152-155; Nichols, *op. cit.*, pp. 159-161; *Nation*, xxvi (Feb. 21, 1878), 123.
[178] The other important clause of the bill provided for calling an international monetary conference to consider establishing an international bimetallic standard. Dunbar, *op. cit.*, pp. 246-248.
[179] *CDT*, Feb. 20, 1878; Feb. 22, 1878.

[180] Murat Halstead to John Sherman, Cincinnati, Feb. 26, 1878, Sherman MSS.
[181] *Congressional Record*, pp. 1284-1285.
[182] Halstead to R. B. Hayes, Cincinnati, Feb. 20, 1878, Hayes MSS.
[183] J. Medill to R. B. Hayes, Washington, Feb. 25, 1878, *ibid.*

by the possible consequences of a veto. Editor Francis Hoyt of the *Western Christian Advocate* wrote that while he was opposed to the short-weight silver dollar, he feared the strife that would follow a veto.[184] A surprisingly large part of the President's mail from both eastern and western businessmen also urged him to sign to avoid prolonging the silver agitation.[185]

There was, of course, pressure from the other side. One Wisconsin minister assured Hayes that "the larger part of the Congregational clergymen in the state . . . are opposed to the silver bill and hope it may never become a law."[186] Businessmen, bankers, college professors also demanded that the President rebuke "dishonesty."[187] Still, if Hayes had been a practical politician he would almost certainly have decided to sign. Indeed, western greenbackers did not think him "cheeky enough to veto"[188]—but veto he did. Though earlier in his career no more proof against expediency than other politicians, Hayes, as President, was the puritan in politics. On February 17, with passage certain, he resolved to veto so that the nation could avoid "a stain on its honor." On February 26 he read the veto message to his Cabinet. Schurz, now serving as Secretary of the Interior, approved striking down the "immoral" measure. Equally in character, Sherman, concerned with practical consequences, balked. But in the end he too agreed that the message should be sent.[189]

[184] Francis Hoyt to R. B. Hayes, Cincinnati, Feb. 27, 1878, *ibid.*

[185] For example: L. Austin, of Austin Powder Co., to Hayes, Cleveland, Feb. 18, 1878; H. C. Brown of A. H. Brown & Co., Bankers, to Hayes, New York, Feb. 23, 1878; William H. Andrews and nineteen other businessmen to Hayes, Cincinnati, Feb. 25, 1878, *ibid.*

[186] William Crawford to Hayes, Green Bay, Wisc., Feb. 19, 1878, *ibid.* Crawford's description was probably accurate and seems to have applied equally to other states and other denominations as well. See the following congratulatory letters after the veto: Theodore L. Cuyler to Hayes, Lafayette Avenue Church, Brooklyn, N. Y., March 1, 1878; Rev. Henry M. Storrs of the American Home Missionary Society, New York, March 2, 1878; Rev. G.

S. Dickerman, Pine Street Congregational Church, Lewiston, Me., March 4, 1878; George W. Wainright, Congregational Church, Raymond, Wisc., [July?], 1878, *ibid.*

[187] For example: S. H. Tingley, Cashier of the Mechanics' National Bank of Providence, Providence, R. I., Feb. 15, 1878; C. E. Bessey, Iowa Agricultural College, Ames, Iowa, Feb. 18, 1878; H. A. Grey, Chicago, Feb. 23, 1878; C. P. Williams, President National Albany Exchange Bank, Albany, N. Y., Feb. 23, 1878, *ibid.*

[188] A. Babcock to Luman Weller, New Hampton, Iowa, Feb. 21, 1878, Weller MSS, State Hist. Soc. of Wisc.

[189] Williams, *Diary and Letters,* III, 460-461. Hayes did not think the veto would be sustained, however.

On February 28 Hayes returned the vetoed bill and, as expected, it was promptly repassed by both chambers.[190] In the House the negative votes, or even the simple abstention, of the silver men who favored resumption would have been sufficient to sustain the veto.[191]

I V

The moderates, then, had saved the Bland Bill; it remained to be seen if, as they had promised, they could now save resumption. In the next few weeks Halstead and Medill threw themselves into the task of putting over Sherman's resumption scheme. The new double standard, Halstead told his readers, not only settled the silver question, but had greatly eased the return to specie. In the ten months until January 1879 the Treasury could issue up to $40 million of new silver coin. This would serve to cushion the shock of returning to gold, and the country could rest assured that convertibility would come without serious disturbance.[192] Medill's *Tribune* noted that whatever value the Ewing repeal bill might have had in October when the country was threatened by forced resumption on a narrow gold base, was now canceled, and the repeal measure might "wisely be left where it is without any action."[193]

As part of the campaign to save resumption, Medill, apparently, also tried to provoke a quarrel between the silverites and the repeal men. The *Tribune* gave publicity to Senator Allison's view that by depressing the paper dollar below silver, repeal would keep the new coins from circulating. With resumption imminent, Allison pointed out, the paper dollar was worth 97 cents. Silver was currently cheaper and so would circulate readily. Without the prospect of resumption, the paper dollar would collapse, causing the now more valuable silver to be hoarded much as gold had been hoarded for the past decade.[194]

[190] *Congressional Record*, p. 1420.

[191] Had only 19 of the Cox-Garfield group abstained the bill would have failed. See Appendix H.

[192] *Cincinnati Commercial* editorial quoted in *CDT*, March 2, 1878. On March 6, 1878, Halstead wrote Hayes: "I shall not be less [energetic?] in opposing the repeal of the Resumption act than I was urgent in advocacy of the silver law. . . ." Halstead to Hayes, Cincinnati, Hayes MSS.

[193] *CDT*, March 8, 1878; March 13, 1878.

[194] *Ibid.*, March 8, 1878. This was, of course, merely a restatement of Gresham's Law.

Allison's remarks reflected a serious split that had developed in the soft money ranks since passage of the Bland-Allison Act. Whether a spontaneous development or part of the plan hinted at by Halstead and Cox, a group of western Senators—men who earlier favored repeal—now agreed to delay the repeal issue until the effects of the silver bill had become apparent. House Resolution 805, which had been pushed aside by the Bland Bill in January and February, consequently remained bottled up in the Finance Committee for weeks after Congress had settled the silver question.[195]

In the meantime, the repeal men watched helplessly while the resumptionists won a series of striking victories. The first of these was as much a triumph for Sherman as for his policy. Summoned before the Banking and Currency Committee on April 1 and 4 to defend his resumption program, the Secretary submitted to a barrage of hostile questions from Buckner and his own kinsman, Ewing.[196] He replied with cool assurance and authority, displaying an impressive command of Treasury detail and great agility in handling cross-examination. The burden of Sherman's defense was that the 1875 Act was workable as it stood without additional contraction. The silver agitation had stopped the 4 per cent loan, he admitted, but if necessary he could negotiate at higher rates to ensure the needed coin reserve. He denied Ewing's assertions that on January 1 the Treasury would become liable not only for the outstanding greenbacks but for bank notes as well and pointed out that the Bank of England was able to maintain specie payments with a smaller proportionate coin reserve than the Treasury contemplated.[197]

The Secretary's performance created a highly favorable impres-

[195] *Ibid.*, March 3, 1878; April 16, 1878. The only action on repeal taken by the Finance Committee was a short interview with Sherman on March 19, 1878. See U. S. Senate, Committee on Finance, *Interview of the Committee on Finance . . . with John Sherman . . . in Regard to the Repeal of the Resumption Act.* Hereafter this document will be cited as Finance Committee, *Interview with Sherman.*

[196] John's older brother, William Tecumseh, was adopted by Thomas Ewing, Sr. after the death of Charles Robert Sherman in 1829. The General, moreover, later married one of Ewing's daughters.

[197] U. S. House of Representatives, 45 Cong., 2 sess., *Misc. Doc. No. 62, passim.*

sion. Chairman Buckner, Sherman later wrote, who had considered him a hopeless visionary before the interview, was disposed at the end to let the Treasury proceed without Congressional interference.[198] The hearing received much attention in the newspapers and helped convince the public that resumption under the 1875 measure was not a dangerous experiment.[199]

More important victories for the Treasury soon followed. Immediately after passage of the silver bill, the syndicate had finally canceled the June 4 per cent contract that had been suspended since November.[200] By late March the bankers' confidence had been at least partially restored, and Sherman was able to negotiate another resumption loan. Before this could be concluded, however, the Treasury was compelled to meet a threat from an unexpected quarter.

The banking community, like every other segment of American business, had pursued an erratic course on the resumption question. Bankers had been doctrinaire contractionists, moderate resumptionists, growing-up-to-specie men, and even outright greenbackers. Nevertheless, the banking fraternity as a whole had been a bulwark of sound money. Unfortunately for Sherman, the domestic commercial bankers, whose cooperation was vital to success, drew back when confronted by the imminent return to gold. Like many other businessmen, the New York national bankers—the most important domestic financiers—disliked the Treasury's resumption plans, though for special reasons of their own. They were annoyed by Sherman's apparent partiality for the international financiers[201] and deeply resented his seeming indifference to the problems of the commercial banks. The reserve scheme threatened to withdraw large amounts of gold from commercial channels, placing the banks, which were themselves liable for gold payments after January 1, in a difficult position. To protect themselves, it might become necessary for the banks to bring their greenbacks to the Treasury on resumption

[198] Sherman, *Recollections*, II, 634-635.
[199] *Ibid.*, p. 636.
[200] August Belmont and Company to Sherman, New York, March 1, 1878, *Exec. Doc. No. 9*, p. 266.
[201] Warner Bateman to John Sherman, Cincinnati, July 23, 1877, Sherman MSS; Sherman, *Recollections*, II, 637.

day—a move, they ominously pointed out, which would place a severe burden on the reserve.[202]

Protesting loudly that they did not oppose specie payments, they demanded that the Treasury consult them at every stage of the resumption process. Under Coe's leadership, the American Bankers' Association proposed in September 1877 to aid the Treasury with a $50 million gold loan against federal bonds. Accepting the policy Salmon Chase had rejected in 1862,[203] the Treasury would allow the banks to retain the gold, drawing against it only as needed to meet resumption demands. While it was in the banks' vaults, the gold would function as both Treasury and bank reserves, and both the banks and the government would be protected.[204]

The bankers' plan appealed as little to Sherman as it had to Chase, though for different reasons. As late as April 1878 Sherman still hoped to reopen the 4 per cent loan and did not want to pay the 4½ per cent that Coe and his New York colleagues were asking. Equally important, perhaps, was the control the syndicate could exercise over international gold flows, which, if they ran against the United States, might cancel out the effect of a loan.[205] Under the circumstances, he felt he must stay with the syndicate and therefore turned down the offer.

This rejection, and a remark Sherman made in mid-March to the effect that the banks would have to take care of themselves at resumption,[206] provoked the bankers into an ill-concealed, and ill-advised, threat against the Treasury. This was given wide publicity when Ewing and Chittenden, visting New York on minor Banking and Currency Committee business,[207] discussed

[202] See the remarks of George Coe, American Bankers' Association, *Reports of Proceedings*, pp. 318ff.; *CFC*, xxv (Sept. 15, 1877), 245ff.; Poor, *op. cit.*, p. 10.

[203] See above, ch. i.

[204] *CFC*, xxv (Sept. 15, 1877), 245ff.; *NYDT*, Oct. 17, 1877; *Banker's Magazine*, xxxii (October 1877), 257-261. There is a good brief discussion of the Coe plan by Fritz Redlich, "Translating Economic Policy into Business Policy," *Bulletin of the Business History*

Society, xx (1946), p. 191. See also Coe to James A. Garfield, New York, Nov. 17, 1877, Garfield MSS.

[205] *Misc. Doc. No. 62*, p. 10; *The Public*, xiii (April 18, 1878), 245.

[206] This was on March 19, when Sherman briefly appeared before the Senate Finance Committee. See Finance Committee, *Interview with Sherman*, p. 11.

[207] They were in New York checking Sherman's recent report on the Treasury's gold reserve.

resumption with the New York bankers. They discovered that almost without exception the financiers were skeptical of Sherman's plans. B. B. Sherman of the Mechanics' Bank and J. D. Vermilye of the Merchant's National Bank predicted large gold exports for the next few months and doubted the Treasury's ability to amass a sufficient reserve. Coe, and Frederick Tappan of the Gallatin National, smarting under the Treasury's rebuff, virtually presented Sherman with an ultimatum. If the New York banks were expected to fend for themselves at resumption, they would have no choice but to raid Treasury gold. Tappan remarked that he "would like to 'pre-empt' the head of the line" at the sub-Treasury door on resumption day. Coe pointedly observed that first place on that line would be worth $50,000 to any man.[208] The bankers were holding their greenback reserves as a club over Sherman's head.

During his testimony before the Banking and Currency Committee, Sherman had dismissed these threats as bluster since the Treasury could easily retaliate by withdrawing government deposits from the banks, or by in its turn presenting bank notes for greenbacks.[209] But of course, he preferred to avoid a test of strength with the bankers and laid his plans accordingly. In late February he held about $70 million of coin: he had set $120 or $130 million as his goal.[210] This meant once more turning to the bankers for aid, and by the end of March Sherman had decided that it was again possible to resume specie loans. But this time he was careful to include the New York national bankers in his calculations.

On April 5 Sherman arranged to meet with the members of

---

[208] CDT, March 17, 1878; March 29, 1878; The Public, XIII (April 18, 1878), pp. 246-247. Coe claimed that his views and those of Tappan had been misunderstood by both Sherman and the public. The bankers, he claimed, would support resumption, though he admitted that they disagreed with Sherman about the banks' responsibilities. See George Coe to Jacob Schuckers, New York, April 2, 1878, Schuckers MSS, LC. It is amusing that Henry Carey Baird sided, this time, with the bankers, holding that they were "to a certain extent acting with the people while the [Treasury] department is against them, and has . . . been so since the war." Baird, Resumption of Specie Payments: Testimony . . . before the Committee on Banking and Currency (Philadelphia, 1878), pp. 3-4.

[209] Misc. Doc. No. 62, pp. 9-10.

[210] Finance Committee, Interview with Sherman, pp. 4-5, 11.

the old syndicate and the leading New York commercial bankers to discuss a new $50 million resumption loan. On the eighth, in an interview with members of the syndicate in New York, he proposed to sell "four percents" at par for gold. This proposition, he was told, was unrealistic at the moment, and the financiers suggested that the Treasury offer the "four-and-a-halfs" instead. When Sherman offered to negotiate the "four-and-a-halfs" at 103, the syndicate countered with a tentative offer of 101. The meeting adjourned at this point until the next day, while the bankers consulted their European correspondents.[211]

The following afternoon Sherman and his entourage met with the leading New York commercial bankers including Vermilye, Coe, Tappan, James Buell, Moses Taylor, and B. B. Sherman. The Secretary presented the bank presidents with the same offer he had made to the syndicate. The bankers were not interested. They talked of uncertainty in the money market and the silver threat, and refused even to consider the "four-and-a-halfs" at par before consulting the Philadelphia and Boston banks—and then only on condition that any coin advanced would be retained on deposit in their vaults.[212]

This was essentially the Coe scheme and was no more acceptable to Sherman now than the previous fall. But he preferred to disarm rather than antagonize the national bankers. Accordingly, before breaking off negotiations, he informed the New Yorkers of the syndicate's tentative terms. Was it not his duty, he asked, to accept an offer of 101 for the "four-and-a-halfs"? The bankers were forced to concede that the Treasury could not turn down such a liberal proposal, and Sherman politely ended the meeting.[213] He had not gotten the national bankers' cooperation, and probably had not expected to on terms favorable to the Treasury, but by giving them the opportunity to share in the loan he had helped salve their wounded pride and in the end had tempered their hostility to his plan.

[211] *Exec. Doc. No. 9,* p. 290; Sherman, *Recollections,* II, 638.

[212] The fullest surviving account of this much reported meeting is Sherman's frank letter to Hayes of the same day. Sherman to Hayes, New York, April 9, 1878, Hayes

MSS. Sherman's later account, published in his autobiography, deals more gently with the bankers. Sherman, *Recollections,* II, 638-639.

[213] *Exec. Doc. No. 9,* pp. 291-292.

Later that day Sherman saw the syndicate men and final terms were arranged. The Treasury would sell $50 million of "four-and-a halfs" for gold at 101½, allowing a one-half per cent commission. The syndicate would assume responsibility for all sales expenses. After a twenty-four-hour delay, while cablegrams passed between New York and London, these terms were accepted and the contracts signed.[214]

The successful negotiation of this loan was hailed as the turning point of resumption. With the powerful international banking houses guaranteeing to deliver European gold to the Treasury, the return to specie seemed assured. President Hayes now saw specie payments as possible "long before the first of January," and offered up thanksgiving for the end of the paper regime.[215] The arrangement, pronounced the *Commercial and Financial Chronicle*, "practically put at rest all doubts with regard to the fact that on or before the first day of January 1879, anyone, on application at the office of the Assistant Treasurer in New York, can obtain gold and silver for greenbacks."[216] Quoted at about 104 for most of 1877, gold declined to 101.2 in March 1878 and, soon after the 4½ per cent loan was announced, reached the purely nominal premium of one-eighth of 1 per cent.[217]

Fortunately, the April contract also created a highly favorable impression in Europe. With Morgan and the Rothschilds underwriting United States securities, there was an immediate revival of investor confidence. The dumping of American bonds by English investors ceased,[218] and a brisk market soon developed for the new four-and-a-halfs. Although the contract called for only $10 million to be taken in the first month, in three weeks some $20 million were sold at above 102, and early in May the syndicate anticipated its June subscription.[219] By the end of May, seven months before the contract expired, the books were closed.[220] Over $50 million of coin had been added to the Treasury reserve.

[214] Sherman, *Recollections*, II, 640-642.
[215] Williams, *Diary and Letters*, III, 279, entry for April 13, 1878.
[216] *CFC*, xxvi (April 13, 1878), 361; *The Public*, xiii (April 18, 1878), 245.
[217] Wesley Clair Mitchell, *Gold,* *Prices and Wages Under the Greenback Standard* (Berkeley: University [of California] Press, 1908), pp. 6ff.; *CFC*, xxvi (May 4, 1878), 432.
[218] *Ibid.*, p. 431.
[219] *NYDT*, May 6, 1878.
[220] *CFC*, xxvi (May 25, 1878), 513.

The new loan was a hard blow to the anti-resumptionists. It "knocked the bottom out of the soft money fabric," wrote Garfield in a rather dubious metaphor. If the Treasury could resume before the fall elections, the greenbackers would "find themselves without occupation."[221] Sherman's coup had a sobering effect on the less extreme repeal men, and in the next few weeks they displayed a more conciliatory attitude. But to the die-hards the loan was only a spur to new effort. The April contract seemed to confirm every Agrarian suspicion of bankers in general, international bankers in particular, and—since Belmont, the Seligmans, and the Rothschilds were involved—Jewish international bankers above all.[222] Everything possible was done to discredit it with the public. It contained secret clauses which gave one-sided advantages to the syndicate; it placed American finance at the mercy of foreigners; it was a corrupt bargain by which Sherman hoped to add to his great personal fortune.[223] Phillips of the House Banking and Currency Committee was reported at one point to be pressing a measure designed to terminate the contract by act of Congress.[224]

The real hope of the extremists lay in the Senate, where in April the House repeal measure was still pending. Few of even the most optimistic anti-resumption men still expected to get a repeal measure passed over a certain Presidential veto. Nevertheless, there remained the outside chance that they could wreck the Treasury loan by frightening foreign investors. Their immediate task was to force the bill out of committee, where it had been lodged since November, but here they were opposed by all the force of the Administration. Sherman used his personal influence with doubtful members of the Finance Committee,[225] while Hayes, in one of his few effective efforts to influence Congress, used the patronage to whip Senators into line.[226] Daniel Voorhees, who represented the extreme soft money faction on the

[221] Garfield to Edward Atkinson, Washington, April 16, 1878, Atkinson MSS; also *CDT*, April 13, 1878.

[222] *Labor Advance*, April 20, 1878.

[223] *NYDT*, April 23, 1878, Sherman, *Recollections*, II, 648-649.

[224] *NYDT*, April 30, 1878.

[225] Sherman, *Recollections*, II, 647-648.

[226] This little known instance of Hayes's use of the patronage was recorded many years later by Hayes in his diary. See Williams, *Diary and Letters*, V, 6, entry for May 15, 1891.

Finance Committee, saw his supporters drop away one by one and soon found himself virtually alone.[227]

On April 17 the Finance Committee reported a substitute for the House bill which reflected the new situation. This measure included a 4 per cent bond exchangeable for legal tenders at par; a clause making greenbacks receivable for customs after October 1, 1878; repeal of the 80 per cent contraction feature of the Resumption Act; and an explicit provision for reissuing legal tenders converted after January 1.[228] It immediately became the basis for a series of involved negotiations among the factions. The Treasury opposed all but the provision authorizing greenback reissue.[229] The intransigent soft money men continued to demand repeal and refused to concede publicly that there was no longer any chance of such action during the session.[230] The uncompromising resumptionists—men like Justin Morrill and Thomas Bayard—resisted even the one concession that the Treasury was willing to grant.[231]

But despite all the outward bristling, neither side, apart from the few doctrinaires, had much heart for continuing the financial wrangle. On May 21 the Finance Committee reported a bill which fixed the legal tender limit at the current $346 million and provided that all redeemed greenbacks be returned to circulation after January 1, 1879.[232] This measure duplicated one sponsored by Greenbury Fort which had passed the House in late April,[233] and Fort now tried to make it the basis for a final settlement. In talks with Sherman, he promised that if the Administration accepted this bill the more reasonable soft money men would stop the repeal agitation. In effect the Administration

[227] *CDT*, April 6, 1878; April 14, 1878.

[228] *Congressional Record*, p. 2599; *CDT*, April 16, 1878.

[229] *NYDT*, April 22, 1878. In his first *Annual Report* Sherman had sought to appease soft money opinion by acknowledging the Treasury's responsibility for reissuing redeemed greenbacks if the volume fell below $300 million. He repeated this assurance to both the Finance and Banking and Currency Committees in the spring of 1878. But with almost $350 million of greenbacks still circulating a substantial contraction was still possible after Jan. 1, 1879, and his statements failed to quiet soft money fears. See U. S. Treasury, *Report for 1877*, pp. xiii-xiv; Finance Committee, *Interview with Sherman*, p. 19; *Misc. Doc. No. 62*, pp. 12-13.

[230] For example, *Congressional Record*, pp. 3083ff.

[231] *Ibid.*, pp. 5631ff., 4539.

[232] *Ibid.*, p. 3596.

[233] *Ibid.*, p. 2928.

would concede $46 million of extra greenbacks—an additional burden on resumption day—and would be given a free hand to press its plans.[234]

Hayes and Sherman were willing to go along with Fort, but the Senate conservatives attacked the measure. The moderates on both sides, as well as the Voorhees men who approved any blow against contraction, fell in behind the bill, and it passed 41 to 18.[235] Hayes fulfilled his part of the bargain and to the disgust of the conservatives,[236] signed the measure.

With the passage of the Fort Bill, all serious currency discussion ended for the session. Neither Voorhees nor Ewing was ready to surrender,[237] but their activities came to nothing, and Congress adjourned on June 20 with the Resumption Act intact. Many problems remained before the country returned to the gold standard, but the politicians had tacitly consented to let Sherman try his hand at resuming gold payments.

[234] *CDT*, May 22, 1878; *NYDT*, May 24, 1878; May 30, 1878; *Nation*, xxvi (May 30, 1878), 350.
[235] *Congressional Record*, pp. 3861ff., 3871.

[236] *Nation*, xxvi (June 6, 1878), 366.
[237] *CDT*, June 14, 1878; June 20, 1878; *NYDT*, June 19, 1878.

RESUMPTION ACCOMPLISHED
(1878-1879)

I

THE new administration had made remarkable progress toward resumption since taking office. Yet from Sherman's vantage there were still shoals ahead. The gold premium had fallen below 1 per cent following the April bond sales, but there it hovered for many months, mutely testifying to the final residue of public distrust. With any gap at all between coin and paper on January 1, a run on the Treasury's gold remained a frightening possibility. The Fort Bill also created a hazard, for by requiring the Treasury to recirculate the redeemed notes, it could act as an open drain on the reserve gold.[1] Finally there was silver. Though it was unlikely that the monthly bullion purchase under the Bland Act could stop resumption, by January it would add at least $20 million to the circulation redeemable in gold.[2] After January 1 the volume of convertible cash would grow steadily as the Treasury accumulated silver, and without a corresponding increase in the gold reserve, permanent resumption would be precarious at best.[3]

More immediate, and more disturbing, was the perennial political problem. The Congressional election intervened between the second and third sessions of the Forty-fifth Congress, and an electoral triumph for soft money might still revive the repeal

[1] *Banker's Magazine*, xxxii (May 1878), 886ff.; *CFC*, xxvi (June 1, 1878), 533; G. P. Kenyon to John Sherman, New York, Sept. 17, 1878, Sherman MSS, LC.

[2] Actually, neither the silver dollars nor the silver certificates into which they could be converted were directly redeemable in gold coin, but a kind of quasi-redemption existed, since silver certificates were receivable in lieu of gold for customs. Particularly in times of stress, therefore, when business uncertainty prevailed and gold was apt to be hoarded, the government would tend to receive silver coin alone while paying out gold or gold convertible paper in its general disbursements. See J. Laurence Laughlin, *The History of Bimetallism in the United States* (New York: D. Appleton & Co., 1897), pp. 253-254.

[3] *Banker's Magazine*, xxxiii (December 1878), 435.

threat in the lame-duck session. Early in the year there were intimations that the fall canvass would once again turn on the money question. Sherman was warned that "the people [were] moving as they did in the anti-slavery movement in 1855-56," and would demand "vengeance on the bondholders."[4] During the spring and summer, while the Secretary negotiated with the bankers and wrestled with Congress, soft money sentiment mounted to a new pitch. The political greenbackism of the year was compounded of several elements. In one respect it was a typical depression movement, for 1878 was the last full year of the long economic downturn and before the year was out, wholesale farm prices and general wage levels would touch all-time postwar lows.[5] Greenbackers, far more than in previous years, would play on the stimulating effect of more money. Important in attracting the labor vote was the jolt of the previous summer's railroad disorders, with their nasty undertone of class war. Coming late in the 1877 state campaigns, their full political impact had not been felt; by 1878 their lesson had burned deeply into the minds of wage earners, and labor was ready, as never before, to vote as a class-conscious body. Finally, the very success of Sherman's efforts in bringing close the dreaded resumption generated political antibodies.

The labor phase of the 1878 political uprising was sparked by the Knights of Labor, a group which had already played a small role in the 1876 Cooper-Cary campaign. In 1877 individual Knights—Schilling in Ohio, Ralph Beaumont in New York, and John M. Davis, James L. Wright, and Terence V. Powderly in Pennsylvania—had been in the thick of the state Independent campaigns. As an organization, moreover, the Knights had been politically active in the anthracite coal fields of eastern Pennsylvania, where their work accounted for most of the state's large third-party vote. The following February the residue of the fall political enthusiasm carried Powderly into office as Mayor of Scranton.[6]

[4] B. M. Failon to General W. A. Knapp, Clayton, Ill., Jan. 29, 1878, enclosed in Knapp to John Sherman, Washington, Feb. 11, 1878, Sherman MSS.

[5] U. S. Bureau of the Census, *Historical Statistics of the United States, Colonial Times to 1957* (Washington: Government Printing Office, 1960), p. 115, series E 2; for wheat and cotton p. 123, series E 101 and 104; p. 90, series D 574 and D 578-588.

[6] Edward Topping James, "Ameri-

In both its trade-union and its political roles the Knights had been handicapped by loose organization and resulting internal friction. This condition was partly remedied in January 1878, when for the first time a permanent directorate of national officers was established. At the same time, under the aegis of Powderly, Beaumont, and Schilling, a constitution was drawn up which contained, along with "practical labor proposals," a greenback plank, though without the interconvertible bond.[7]

Other hands, however, were responsible for launching the 1878 Greenback campaign. The impetus was supplied by D. B. Sturgeon of Toledo, a hydropathic physician, formerly active in Republican politics. Under Sturgeon's leadership in 1877, Lucas County, normally Republican, had given a majority to the Independents, or the "Nationals," as the third-party ticket was labeled in Ohio; at the same time, Sturgeon himself was elected to the State House of Representatives. These results, produced as much by voter disgust with local Republican and Democratic corruption and indifference as by cheap money sentiment, surprised everyone, including the Nationals, and immediately filled Sturgeon's head with ambitious plans.[8] In December a call was issued by Sturgeon and the Ohio Nationals, signed by many of the old-line greenbackers, for a national convention to discuss the financial question.[9]

can Labor and Political Action, 1865-1896: The Knights of Labor and Its Predecessors" (unpublished Ph.D. dissertation, Harvard University, 1954), pp. 141-149. Apparently there was also an ethnic factor in the Scranton Mayoralty campaign. Powderly's opponent was a Welshman named Jones who attempted to rally anti-Irish sentiment to his cause, an effort that in the end backfired. See "Mary Josephine" to Terence Powderly, Brooklyn, N. Y., March 4, 1878, Powderly MSS, Catholic University of America.

[7] The phrase quoted is Edward Topping James's. See his "American Labor and Political Action," pp. 149-154. See also John R. Commons and associates, *History of Labour in the United States* (New

York: The Macmillan Co., 1946), II, 336-337. The greenback plank recommended establishing "a purely national circulatory medium based on the faith and resources of the nation, and issued directly to the people without the intervention of any system of banking corporations, which money shall be a legal tender in payment of all debts, public or private."

[8] *Indianapolis Sun*, Sept. 22, 1877; Sept. 29, 1877; Oct. 13, 1877; C. Ben Johnson to Terence Powderly, Wilkes Barre, Pa., Dec. 27, 1877, Powderly MSS.

[9] Among the signers were: Alexander Campbell, Thomas Buchanan, Thomas J. Durant, Moses Field, Alexander Troup, Peter Cooper, John Magwire, Wendell Phillips, Ignatius Donnelly, B. G. Chace, S.

The meeting, which assembled on February 22 at Toledo's Wheeler Opera House, closely resembled the 1876 Indianapolis convention. It is usually treated as a new political beginning for soft money,[10] but this is a gross exaggeration. Both its personnel and its work leave a strong impression of *déjà vue*. Present and active were such original greenback reformers as Campbell, Troup, Cary, Moses Field, Trevellick, and John Drew. Pomeroy, too, having decided to stay in third-party politics after all, was there, as was the post-panic reformer contingent of Donnelly, Allis, Stephen Johnston of Ohio, S. M. Smith, Frank Hughes, Solon Chase, Blanton Duncan, the Buchanans, Frank Dewees, and James B. Weaver. In addition, there was a smaller group of trade-unionists, many of whom had first been carried into third-party politics by the labor upheaval of the previous summer. Among the Knights of Labor were Beaumont, James L. Wright, Thomas J. Armstrong, and Grand Master Workman, Uriah Stephens. Men like Trevellick, Robert Schilling, and John Siney, unionists of an earlier day, helped bridge the gap between the newer labor men and the older reformers. Although the labor group would make its weight felt, the convention was dominated by the reformers and ideologues who had been active in greenback politics since the '60's.[11]

The platform differed little from previous greenback political pronouncements in its Agrarian tone and its emphasis on the crucial place of finance for the nation's well-being. Even the rejection of the interconvertible bond was not a complete innovation: it had already been relegated to second place by the In-

---

M. Smith, James B. Weaver, Solon Chase, and R. M. Springer. Only one Knights of Labor man— Thomas J. Armstrong, John Davis's successor as editor of the *National Labor Tribune*—was a sponsor of the meeting. AM, Jan. 17, 1878; *Indianapolis Sun*, Jan. 19, 1878.

[10] See the following: Commons, *op. cit.*, II, 244; James, *op. cit.*, pp. 158-159; Norman J. Ware, *The Labor Movement in the United States 1860-1895: A Study in Democracy* (Gloucester, Mass.: Peter Smith, 1959), p. 50; Fred E. Haynes, *Third Party Movements*

Since the Civil War, With Special Reference to Iowa: A Study in Social Politics (Iowa City: The State Historical Society of Iowa, 1916), pp. 120-121.

[11] For the continuity with the past see *Labor Advance*, March 3, 1878; *Indianapolis Sun*, Feb. 2, 1878. The *Advance* under editor Robert Schilling, after listing the names of the most prominent delegates, finished with "and many of the old guard who fought the battles of the people at a time when the people themselves stoned those who advocated their rights."

dependents in 1876.[12] Yet it was jettisoned only under pressure. All that we know of the decision is that it was made by a caucus of leaders, against strong resistance, the evening before the convention formally opened.[13] In view of later events and the Knights' own recent action, it seems certain that the trade-unionists were responsible for the change. As a substitute for the usual Kellogg-Campbell bond formula, a statement was adopted enjoining Congress to supply money "adequate to the full employment of labor, the equitable distribution of its products and the requirements of business, fixing a minimum amount per capita . . . and . . . regulating its volume . . . so that the rates of interest will secure to labor its just reward." There were also brief endorsements of free silver, taxation of federal bonds, a government issued paper money without bank intermediaries, and planks for a federal income tax, Chinese exclusion, homestead legislation, and government aid to agriculture.

Each of these planks was unanimously endorsed, but the first, the money plank, aroused "vociferous and long continued cheering." Clearly the majority at Toledo were still greenbackers. But the convention was not the love feast that this applause implies. The trade-union element was still not satisfied with the financial emphasis, and when Pomeroy, with his talent for sowing discord, proposed that no candidate for office be endorsed who was not an actual laborer, there was a flareup of submerged resentment. Trade-union men charged that the "industrial party" had been snubbed on the platform. The "greenback idea had almost excluded the working class from any part in the convention." The trade-union men were mollified, however, by passage of Pomeroy's resolution, and with the singing of the Doxology, the convention adjourned in apparent harmony.[14]

Before the campaign ended, the reform fusion of the trade-union men and Greenbackers would come unstuck in a number

[12] Although some greenbackers, most notably Thomas Buchanan, fought to retain the bond. See *Indianapolis Sun*, Sept. 5, 1877; Oct. 26, 1877.

[13] The Nationals were, naturally, reticent about this meeting. The *Indianapolis Sun* coyly referred to it as "a friendly little gathering among the arrived delegates." *Sun*, March 2, 1878.

[14] The best accounts of the convention are *ibid.*, and *AM*, Feb. 28, 1878.

of places. But at first, in the usual manner of greenback political campaigns, the Nationals put on a good performance. The spring brought local victories in Maine, New York, and Michigan, the Greenbackers winning in the latter state 200 out of 700 assessors' places in the town elections.[15] In the wake of these successes, literally from Maine to California, local National—or, frequently, "Greenback-Labor"—groups sprang to life, sweeping up and absorbing stranded greenback clubs and other surviving soft money organizations. The National Executive Committee attempted to provide over-all coordination for the party effort,[16] but during the campaign the various state groups acted autonomously.

In New England and the Middle States the growth of Greenback strength was impressive, far outstripping the 1877 achievement. In Maine Solon Chase, taking advantage, as one Republican put it, of the injured feeling "of all the soreheads we have made in 22 years," put together a powerful alliance of rural Republicans and office-hungry Democrats which for the first time in a generation threatened the tight Republican grip on the Pine Tree State.[17] Under Troup, Connecticut Nationals put a strong ticket in the field and forced the state's generally conservative Democrats to fish for greenback votes,[18] to the disgust of a group associated with Yale College which considered running a rival Democratic candidate.[19] In Massachusetts Butler, who wore his Republicanism lightly despite his earlier power in the party, snatched both the National and Democratic gubernatorial nominations[20] and threatened to make deep inroads into Republican

[15] Henry Carey Baird to Jacob Schuckers, Philadelphia, April 8, 1878, Schuckers MSS, LC; *Indianapolis Sun*, March 16, 1878; *NYT*, April 7, 1878; George W. Cooper to Thomas Ewing, Jr., Elmira, N. Y., April 10, 1878, Ewing MSS, LC.

[16] See the address of Sturgeon, Chairman of the National Executive Committee, March 12, 1878, in *AM*, March 14, 1878.

[17] S. L. Milliken to James A. Garfield, Belfast, Me., Sept. 18, 1878, Garfield MSS, LC; Charles R. Williams (ed.), *Diary and Letters of Rutherford Birchard Hayes*,

Nineteenth President of the United States (Columbus: Ohio Archeological and Historical Society, 1924), III, 496; *AM*, June 27, 1878; July 18, 1878; Aug. 22, 1878.

[18] *Ibid.*, Aug. 29, 1878; A. E. Burr to David Wells, Hartford, Sept. 19, 1878, Wells MSS, LC; James R. Hawley to James A. Garfield, Hartford, Oct. 14, 1878, Garfield MSS.

[19] *NYT*, Oct. 14, 1878.

[20] Butler declared in August that he would run for Governor without a formal party endorsement if petitioned by 20,000 voters. In a few weeks he had gotten twice that

strength in Boston and the other big towns.[21] The badly frightened Republicans had to call in all the outside support they could get to lure back the labor vote.[22] Even in dour, Congregational Vermont, there appeared during the summer surprising Greenback stirrings.[23]

In the Middle States the Nationals' progress was rockier, but nonetheless formidable. In both New York and Pennsylvania deep rifts developed between the reform and trade-union elements. In New York, moreover, the issue was further complicated by urban-rural differences. The strong third-party sentiment, which spawned a series of local Greenback victories in early spring, soon began to dissipate as a result of internal bickering. Upstate, where the spring successes had been won, the Nationals were united. In the City there was political Babel. One faction, with Peter Cooper and his lieutenant Walter Shupe, editor of the greenback *Advocate*, at its head, derived directly from the Independent-National line. Another, led by Eugene Beebe, for years Secretary of the Legal Tender Club,[24] was apparently a survivor of Pomeroy's stay in the city and shared Pomeroy's irascibility and uncooperativeness. A third, headed by George Blair in the city, but closely allied with John Junio of Syracuse, represented trade-unionist sentiment still unreconciled to either the reformist platform or reformist control.[25] These

number of signatures, and in September won the Independent-Greenback (National) nomination as well. He and his followers, over the opposition of the party leaders, then captured the Democratic convention at Worcester. The regular Democrats now withdrew and nominated their own state ticket. The Butler Democrats and the Nationals combined on Congressional candidates. Butler, it should be noted, refused to call himself a National, and in an interview in July kept evading when asked about his formal political affiliations. See *American Annual Cyclopedia and Register of Important Events of the Year 1878*, pp. 530-531; AM, Aug. 1, 1878.

[21] Horace N. Fisher to James A. Garfield, Boston, Oct. 28, 1878, Garfield MSS.
[22] Garfield, Schurz, and conservative Democrat Francis Kernan, Senator from New York, came to speak against Butler. *Ibid.*; NYW, Oct. 25, 1878; Oct. 28, 1878.
[23] AM, Aug. 29, 1878.
[24] Beebe was also close to Butler. On Beebe see IA, Sept. 4, 1875; Benjamin F. Butler to Beebe, Boston, Aug. 10, 1875; Oct. 22, 1875, Butler MSS, LC.
[25] NYDT, Aug. 3, 1878; James, *op. cit.*, pp. 162-163; NYW, July 16, 1878; Edward C. Mack, *Peter Cooper, Citizen of New York* (New York: Duell, Sloan, & Pearce, 1949), pp. 370-371.

groups appeared together at the two large rallies of May and June organized by the National Executive Committee,[26] but they split at the July Syracuse convention with all three city groups bolting the meeting.[27]

This squabble virtually destroyed the Nationals in the city, but upstate they developed considerable strength as the Congressional and state[28] campaigns progressed. "Glib tongued demagogues," one nervous Republican reported, were going "from village to village and school house to school house advocating an unlimited issue of 'Fiat Money'—the immediate payment of the whole interest bearing debt—of the Govt—the repeal of the National Bkg law & the appointment of U. S. loan Commissioners to receive greenbacks from the Nat. Treasy. & loan them at low rates of interest to borrowers—very tempting propositions to that class of which there are many in this locality [central New York] which has been heavily bonded for non paying Railroads."[29]

In Pennsylvania,[30] where the Nationals were expected to develop great strength,[31] the reformist-labor split was kept under control, though only by great effort. From the outset of the campaign, the Knights of Labor faction was determined to prevent the reformers from controlling either the platform or the state nominations. "The whiley [sic] Politicians," wrote James Wright, must be kept "from placing men on the State Ticket who look upon the labor element [as] an old glove to be taken off and on

[26] At the May 10 meeting Solon Chase, clad in "thread bare homespun," made his famous remark about the bondholders stealing two years' growth from his steers. From then on he was called "them steers" Chase, a sobriquet which unaccountably seems to have amused contemporaries. See AM, May 23, 1878; June 27, 1878.

[27] Mack, op. cit., p. 371; James, op. cit., p. 163; AM, July 25, 1878; NYDT, Aug. 17, 1878; Indianapolis Sun, July 27, 1878.

[28] The Syracuse convention, after the walkout, nominated Gideon Tucker for Judge of the Court of Appeals, the only state-wide office being contested.

[29] S[ilas] B. Dutcher to John Sherman, Oneonta, N. Y., Oct. 12, 1878, Sherman MSS. Dutcher was the New York Customs House Appraiser. For other reports of the National threat in New York see Edmund Johnson to John Sherman, New York, Oct. 7, 1878, ibid.; NYW, Oct. 6, 1878.

[30] The Nationals also showed some strength in New Jersey where, in the First Congressional District, they came close to capturing the Democratic endorsement for their nominee. Morris H. Stratton to Thomas F. Bayard, Salem, N. J., Sept. 27, 1878, Bayard MSS, LC.

[31] C. Ben Johnson to Terence Powderly, Wilkes Barre, Pa., March 21, 1878, Powderly MSS.

to be used for there [*sic*] pleasure."[32] The labor men apparently united for Governor on Congressman Hendrick B. Wright, a nominal Democrat with strong labor and greenback sympathies,[33] and prepared to support him at the state convention. But the greenback-reformers—most of them in the business, rather than the Agrarian, soft money tradition[34]—more than held their own against Stephens, Armstrong, Wright, and Powderly. In the end, the platform issue was resolved by evasion,[35] but the reformers had their way on candidates.[36]

Nevertheless, the Pennsylvanians remained united. The *National Labor Tribune*, under Armstrong, gave the state ticket full support.[37] Powderly, though still angry at "pure greenbackers," campaigned vigorously for the National ticket.[38] Stephens accepted a National Congressional nomination in a Philadelphia district.[39] By summer the campaign was progressing well in the coal and mining counties and in the oil and lumber regions, though lagging in Philadelphia.[40]

In the West and South the public mood was particularly receptive to the third-party appeal. "The people witness the continued shrinkage of their property, the decline of their products, the loss of their fortunes, the loss of their homes," wrote a friend of Sherman from Kansas. Banks, insurance companies, and bond-

[32] Wright to Powderly, Philadelphia, March 23, 1878, *ibid.*
[33] Powderly to James Wright, Scranton, March 25, 1878; F. Turner to Powderly, Washington, April 11, 1878, *ibid.*
[34] These included Henry Carey Baird; David Kirk, an oil man who later became organizer and president of the Pure Oil Company; and Frank Hughes, a land developer and railroad promoter. See Ralph R. Ricker, "The Greenback-Labor Movement in Pennsylvania" (unpublished Ph.D. dissertation, Pennsylvania State University, 1955), pp. 62-69.
[35] The convention simply reiterated the Toledo platform and also called for repeal of the Resumption Act.
[36] They nominated for Governor Samuel R. Mason, a lawyer. Details

of the convention will be found in Ralph R. Ricker, *op. cit.*, pp. 62-76; James, *op. cit.*, pp. 163-166; *AM*, May 16, 1878.
[37] *National Labor Tribune*, Oct. 12, 1878; Oct. 19, 1878; Nov. 2, 1878.
[38] Powderly to J. S. Coxey, Scranton, Sept. 16, 1878; Powderly to Anthony McNulty, Scranton, Sept. 28, 1878, Powderly MSS.
[39] Powderly to Uriah Stephens, Scranton, Sept. 13, 1878; Powderly to Stephens, Scranton, Sept. 16, 1878, *ibid.*
[40] *AM*, Aug. 15, 1878; C. E. Cooper to James A. Garfield, Oil City, Pa., June 26, 1878, Garfield MSS; D. A. Dengler to John Sherman, Philadelphia, Sept. 21, 1878, Sherman MSS; Ricker, *op. cit.*, p. 102.

holders were prospering by cheating the farmers, while the latter, "the producers of wealth, look in vain for any Relief."[41] Such grievances, Chairman Sturgeon told a reporter, the Nationals would turn into a flood of votes in Indiana, Michigan, Ohio, and Illinois, as well as parts of the South.[42]

And for a while it looked as if the Nationals were heading toward a major political upset in the West. From Ohio, Republicans peppered Sherman with letters, sometimes hopeful but often despairing, regarding local National strength. In February J. S. Robinson, Chairman of the State Committee, wrote that the Nationals were pushing their "organization with a good deal of vigor," and it looked "as though the party would pull a large vote."[43] The following month a Republican publisher warned that the "Republican workmen" were being enticed away "in great numbers with the argument that when during and after the war, we had a vast volume of irredeemable paper currency, we had plenty of work and business was good."[44] In the northwestern lake counties, particularly, trouble was expected. Fremont, for example, the President's home, was a place of "wonderful" greenback growth.[45] "The financial question," Robinson wrote in August, "overshadows all other questions, and *must be met.*"[46]

The danger brought Sherman hurrying home to save the state —with unfortunate consequences. At Toledo, "headquarters of 'Nationalism,'"[47] Sherman attempted to deliver a speech to a large crowd of what the apologetic Republican city Solicitor later called "toughs" and "bullies."[48] According to the published text, it was a surprisingly forthright defense of the stable dollar,

[41] C. Davenport to John Sherman, Ottowa, Kans., Jan. 18, 1878, Sherman MSS.

[42] AM, July 4, 1878.

[43] Robinson to John Sherman, Kenton, Ohio, Feb. 21, 1878, Sherman MSS.

[44] Wilson J. Vance to John Sherman, Canton, Ohio, March 24, 1878, *ibid.*

[45] Charles Eaton to James A. Garfield, Toledo, June 6, 1878, Garfield MSS; J. S. Robinson to John Sherman, Kenton, Ohio, June 27, 1878, Sherman MSS.

[46] Robinson to John Sherman, Kenton, Ohio, Aug. 10, 1878, Sherman MSS. There is a full description of the 1878 Ohio campaign in Reginald C. McGrane, "Ohio and the Greenback Movement," MVHR, XI, No. 4 (March 1925), 536-540.

[47] The phrase is J. S. Robinson's. See Robinson to John Sherman, Kenton, Ohio, Aug. 13, 1878, Sherman MSS.

[48] J. K. Hamilton to John Sherman, Toledo, Aug. 29, 1878, *ibid.*

limited silver, and resumption,[49] which doubtless reflected Sherman's confidence that he could not now be stopped. But little of it was ever heard by the audience. The Secretary was heckled unmercifully. When he referred to a possible scarcity of money, he was interrupted by "the poor man haint got no money" and "you've burnt it all." Jeers, groans, whistles, and stamping at times drowned him out entirely. Sherman kept his temper and at least won some personal respect, but his invasion of enemy territory could scarcely be called a triumph for the hard money cause.[50]

Ominous signs of National strength also appeared farther west. Indiana and Illinois had formidable greenback groups[51] with the Nationals in the latter state described as "zealous and determined" men, who were in the movement out of "convictions that bind them all with . . . the force of fanaticism."[52] In Iowa, which was to be the banner National state, despite poverty and a slow start, the third party campaign moved into high gear by summer.[53] In Wisconsin the Greenbackers threatened to lure large numbers of farmers away from their traditional Republican ties. Party loyalty had lost much of its charm in the rural districts, lamented one Republican, and it would actually be necessary to choose first-rate men to win the farmers back.[54]

[49] John Sherman, *Speech . . . Delivered at Toledo, Monday, August 26, 1878* (Washington, 1878), *passim*.

[50] *AM*, Sept. 5, 1878; John Sherman, *Recollections of Forty Years in the House, Senate and Cabinet* (Chicago: The Werner Co., 1895), II, 661-663.

[51] For Indiana: *Indianapolis Sun*, Sept. 7, 1878; Oct. 5, 1878; William H. English to Thomas Bayard, in Charles C. Tansill, *The Congressional Career of Thomas Francis Bayard, 1868-1885* (Washington: Georgetown University Press, 1946), p. 216; for Illinois: John B. Hawley to John Sherman, Rock Island, Ill., Sept. 25, 1878, Sherman MSS.

[52] James Connelly to Richard Oglesby, Springfield, Ill., March 27, 1878, Oglesby MSS, Illinois State Historical Library.

[53] A. W. McCormick to Luman Weller, Nashua, Ia., Aug. 10, 1878; D. Fichthorn to Weller, Waverly, Ia., May 2, 1878; Fichthorn to Weller, [n.p.] July 29, 1878; W. F. Daniels to Weller, Lime Springs, Ia., Aug. 28, 1878, Weller MSS, State Hist. Soc. of Wisc.; J. W. Alfree to William B. Allison, Newton, Ia., March 16, 1878; W. S. Russell to Allison, Perry, Ia., April 30, 1878; N. A. Reed, Jr., to Allison, Muscatine, Ia., Sept. 16, 1878, Allison MSS, Iowa State Department of History and Archives.

[54] R. L. Potter to Elisha Keyes, Wantoma, Wisc., Aug. 15, 1878; Angus Cameron to Keyes, La Crosse, Wisc., July 8, 1878, Keyes MSS, State Hist. Soc. of Wisc.

The Michigan fight proved particularly hot, despite the fact that for a while the Nationals were split into two wings, one led by Moses Field and one by Pomeroy men.[55] These merged, however, and were soon making things lively for the Republicans. Even in the state's Yankee-populated region, which had always been a Republican sound money stronghold, the Greenbackers were becoming a grave threat by early fall.[56] In Minnesota, where the crusade against the Grain Association monopoly complicated issues,[57] the Nationals claimed to be winning converts from among businessmen and mechanics as well as farmers.[58] In Missouri, home of Bland and Buckner, the third-party movement developed considerable strength.[59] On to the Pacific Coast,[60] and down into parts of the South—particularly Texas[61]—there appeared vigorous Greenback movements.

Not that the Nationals did not have their own serious problems. Money, as usual, was in very short supply. In Iowa the

[55] AM, July 4, 1878.

[56] E. G. Reynolds to James A. Garfield, Hillsdale, Mich., Sept. 28, 1878, Garfield MSS. See also J. W. Stone to Garfield, Grand Rapids, Mich., Sept. 2, 1878, ibid.; and John Curtis to John Sherman, Bonds Mills, Wexford Co., Mich., Sept. 23, 1878, Sherman MSS; AM, Aug. 29, 1878.

[57] Martin Ridge, "Ignatius Donnelly and the Greenback Movement," Mid-America: An Historical Review, xxxix, No. 3 (July 1957), 163ff.; John D. Hicks, "The Political Career of Ignatius Donnelly," MVHR, viii, Nos. 1 and 2 (June-September 1921), p. 98.

[58] C. F. Rowe to Ignatius Donnelly, n.p., Sept. [?], 1878; E. A. Cramsie to Donnelly, Minneapolis East, Aug. 14, 1878, Donnelly MSS, Minnesota Historical Society.

[59] F. B. Mitchell to James A. Garfield, St. Louis, April 27, 1878; George H. Shields to Garfield, St. Louis, Sept. 23, 1878, Garfield MSS; J. A. Leach, "Public Opinion and the Inflation Movement in Missouri, 1875-1879," The Missouri Historical Review, xxiv (1929-1930), 571ff.

[60] R. C. Percival to James A. Garfield, Monmouth, Ore., Jan. 29, 1878, Garfield MSS; The (Indianapolis) Daily Sun, April 6, 1878. In California Denis Kearney's Workingmen's Party demanded a system of finance "uncontrolled by rings, brokers and bankers." Annual Cyclopedia for 1878, p. 74.

[61] William C. Wicham to John Sherman, Richmond, Va., Oct. 12, 1878, Sherman MSS; J. L. M. Curry to Thomas Bayard, Richmond, Va., Oct. 12, 1878, Bayard MSS; Andrew J. Keller to William Henry Smith, Louisville, Ky., Aug. 23, 1878, Smith MSS, Ohio Historical Society; Roscoe Martin, "The Greenback Party in Texas," The Southwest Historical Quarterly, xxx, No. 3 (January 1927), 165-168; G. Schleicher to Thomas Bayard, Cuero, Tex., Aug. 19, 1878, Bayard MSS. Also, according to National Chairman Sturgeon, Louisiana—where the Nationals were being supported by a group called the American Alliance—and Arkansas, Kentucky, West Virginia, and Mississippi as well. See AM, July 4, 1878.

editor of *The People's Right*, "the only greenback paper in Chicasaw County," having "collected all of 70 cents in subscriptions during the week," pleaded for $15 to carry the paper through the month.[62] As we have seen, in some states there were crippling party schisms. Pomeroy was responsible for most of these and was soon *persona non grata* to the more level-headed Greenbackers, as much for his irrepressible scurrility as for his egotism and arrogance.[63] In March, after he had attacked the Toledo platform, he was read out of the party by the Indiana Nationals. Yet he seems to have maintained at least nominal affiliations till the end, although a continuing source of embarrassment.[64]

A less easily settled problem concerned relations with the Democrats. One clause of the Pomeroy resolution at Toledo had pledged the party to run candidates only on separate tickets, distinct from both major parties.[65] But particularly in places where the Democrats were the perennial minority, the temptation to join forces—the only possible way to beat the Republicans —was irresistible. Despite the resolution, from Maine to Kansas, wherever the Democrats were weak, mergers on Congressional candidates took place.[66] Even in Pennsylvania, where the Democracy was a going concern, pressures for fusion built up toward the end.[67] In Minnesota Donnelly, who was at first appalled by the fusion movement, could not resist accepting the Democratic nomination for Congress.[68]

As in past years, the major parties were forced to take the Greenbackers seriously. In Indiana, Iowa, Michigan, Missouri, and Ohio, the Democrats aped the Nationals,[69] and the two

[62] A. W. McCormick to Luman Weller, Nashua, Ia., Aug. 10, 1878, Weller MSS.

[63] See J. Porter to Luman Weller, Harding City, Ia., Aug. 1, 1878, *ibid.*

[64] *Indianapolis Sun*, March 9, 1878; *Labor Advance*, March 16, 1878.

[65] *AM*, Feb. 28, 1878.

[66] For example, in Iowa, Massachusetts, Maine, Michigan, and other states. In Missouri, where the relative strength of the parties was reversed, it was the Republicans who sought fusion, although they had been consistently hard money. See Leach, *op. cit.*, pp. 583-584.

[67] Terence Powderly to F. Dewees, Scranton, Oct. 23, 1878; Dewees to Powderly, Philadelphia, Oct. 25, 1878, Powderly MSS.

[68] *AM*, May 23, 1878; July 4, 1878; Sept. 17, 1878.

[69] *Annual Cyclopedia for 1878*,

groups competed for followers, to the joy of their common enemy[70] The Republicans almost everywhere held fast to resumption—and in the West to silver[71]—and here at least the fight was reasonably clear cut. Republican tactics included the usual visits of distinguished national leaders to critical areas: Sherman's unsuccessful foray into Ohio was one example. Garfield, who this time made a straight fight for honest money, was much in demand in threatened Republican districts. Blaine and Schurz were also in constant motion bolstering the Republican cause.[72]

A valuable ally of the Republicans during the campaign was the Honest Money League of the Northwest. This organization had grown out of the 1877 Wisconsin gubernatorial campaign, when the Republicans seemed about to turn tail on the money question. Despite the later reversal of the Madison platform, most Republicans had balked at defending the gold standard in the face of the vigorous Democratic and Independent soft money campaigns.[73] To save Wisconsin and the party from "dishonesty," a group of conservative businessmen, lawyers, and politicians hired Thomas Nichol, a former manufacturer of Fort Scott, Kansas, to tour the state and alert the public to the dangers of inflation.[74] Nichol set out for himself a prodigious itinerary of lectures and debates with Greenbackers in a score of Wisconsin towns.[75] The narrow Republican victory, plucked from what had seemed certain disaster, impressed the businessmen and politicians with Nichol's value and he was retained for further work.[76]

---

pp. 441, 451, 561, 578, 667. In Ohio, Ewing angered the Nationals by again claiming that the platform of the state Democracy made it unnecessary for greenback men to vote for the third party. See *Indianapolis Sun*, July 6, 1878; *Labor Advance*, Oct. 5, 1878.

[70] J. S. Robinson to James A. Garfield, Columbus, Sept. 17, 1878, Garfield MSS; McGrane, *op. cit.*, pp. 538-539.

[71] *Annual Cyclopedia for 1878* is the most convenient source for state party platforms.

[72] George H. Shields to James A. Garfield, St. Louis, Sept. 23, 1878; J. W. Stone to Garfield, Grand Rapids, Mich., Sept. 2, 1878; Thaddeus C. Pound to Garfield, Madison, Wisc., Sept. 13, 1878; James G. Blaine to Garfield, Augusta, Me., Sept. 24, 1878, Garfield MSS; *Nation*, xxvii (Oct. 3, 1878), 205.

[73] *Wisconsin State Journal*, Oct. 19, 1877; *NYDT*, May 10, 1878.

[74] *Ibid.;* Thomas A. Bones to Elisha Keyes, Racine, Wisc., Oct. [?], 1877, Keyes MSS.

[75] *Wisconsin State Journal*, Oct. 3, 1877; Oct. 5, 1877; Oct. 6, 1877; Oct. 12, 1877; Oct. 15, 1877; Oct. 27, 1877; Nov. 2, 1877.

[76] Jerome Case to Elisha Keyes, Racine, Wisc., Nov. 10, 1877, Keyes MSS; *NYDT*, May 10, 1878.

In the winter of 1877 Nichol traveled east to Washington and New York to raise the alarm among complacent—and affluent—conservatives. By this time "a plan [had] been fully digested" to establish a permanent anti-greenback organization. The new body would avoid any connection with "eastern *bondholders*" or "*money powers*," Nichol wrote, but would launch "an honest, honourable and . . . sensible effort to do a great public duty and save the government from the hands of the most unmitigated set of scoundrels that ever lived."[77]

By January a group calling itself the Honest Money League had been organized in Milwaukee, with George Allen, a prominent leather manufacturer, as President.[78] In March, this group, including Allen and Alexander Mitchell, a Milwaukee banker-politician high in the ranks of the Wisconsin Bourbon Democracy, called a meeting at Chicago to enlarge the scope of the League's operations to the whole Northwest. Invitations were issued to businessmen, editors, civic leaders, and sound money politicians to join in forming a permanent association, "the object of which shall be to disseminate sound views upon the subject of money and medium of exchange, and thereby counteract the influence of those organized agitators, who would lead the nation to the adoption of irredeemable paper money."[79]

On March 15 the Honest Money League of the Northwest officially came into being, with Nichol as Secretary. The new League was perhaps not composed of the eastern "money powers," but its membership looked suspiciously like the western "money powers." Allen continued as President, and Chicago banker Lyman J. Gage was made Treasurer. On the Executive Committee were Mitchell, Chicago traction magnate Moses W. Scudder, Charles Randolph, Secretary of the Chicago Board of Trade, and F. W. Hayes, Vice-President of Detroit's Merchants' and Manufacturers' Bank.[80]

During the next few weeks the League, largely run by Scudder

[77] Thomas Nichol to Keyes, New York, Dec. 31, 1877, Keyes MSS.

[78] George Allen to Rutherford B. Hayes, n.p., Jan. 7, 1878, Hayes MSS, Hayes Memorial Library, Fremont, Ohio.

[79] Honest Money League of the Northwest, Chicago, March 8, 1878, printed circular in Hayes MSS; *CDT*, March 16, 1878.

[80] Thomas Nichol, *An Argument in Favor of Honest Money and Redeemable Currency* (Chicago, 1878), inside front cover.

and its chief employee, Nichol, was a blur of activity. Anti-greenback meetings of businessmen were called in Milwaukee, Chicago, Detroit, and Cleveland; local leagues were organized in Detroit, Cincinnati, and other western cities and at least projected for Baltimore; several hard-hitting hard money pamphlets were commissioned; the press was approached for publicity; prominent Republicans, including Garfield and Sherman, were solicited for aid.[81] It was a high-pressure campaign that would have done credit to a modern advertising agency.

But the League's road was not smooth. Despite the rallies and the publicity, public response was disappointing. Not all businessmen wanted to be saved from the "organized agitators," or at least not enough to dig into their pockets.[82] In the process of raising the needed cash to finance the League's campaign, even "eastern bondholders," or their agents in any case, had to be approached. In April, when the League's first broadsides and pamphlets were ready for the printers, Nichol solicited the syndicate for an advertisement to help defray costs.[83] Fahnestock, with more political insight than the League itself, refused to associate the syndicate publicly with a domestic political problem, but instead sent $250 through Sherman to aid in distributing League documents.[84] About the same time, the Milwaukee business community, at a large public meeting, voted to contribute $1000.[85]

The League also, inevitably, collided head-on with the Greenbackers. The Nationals, needless to say, showed little love for the

[81] *NYDT*, Feb. 15, 1878; *The Milwaukee Daily Sentinel*, March 19, 1878; M. L. Scudder to James A. Garfield, Chicago, March 21, 1878 and March 25, 1878, Garfield MSS; Scudder to John Sherman, Chicago, March 21, 1878; Thomas Nichol to Sherman, Chicago, March 25, 1878, Sherman MSS; Honest Money League, April 2, 1878, Garfield MSS. This last item is a League-printed letter signed by Chicago businessmen including Philip Armour and Nelson Morris requesting Garfield's appearance at Chicago to address the group on the dangers of inflation.

[82] Nichol to Sherman, Chicago,

March 25, 1878 and April 8, 1878, Sherman MSS; F. W. Hayes to David Wells, Detroit, April 18, 1878, Wells MSS.

[83] Nichol to Sherman, Milwaukee, April 11, 1878, Sherman MSS.

[84] H. C. Fahnestock to John Sherman, New York, April 16, 1878 and April 20, 1878, *ibid.*

[85] Nichol to Sherman, Chicago, April 17, 1878, *ibid.* Apparently the local League officials were expected to underwrite Nichol's expenses when he came to visit and speak. See Nichol to William Henry Smith, Detroit, June 28, 1878, Smith MSS, Indiana Historical Society.

new organization. Sam Cary aptly, if a little harshly, described it as composed of "national bankers, gold gamblers, coupon clippers" who were "alarmed at the rapid growth . . . and power of the Nationals."[86] Thomas Buchanan called it "the hard-pan and hard-times league."[87] The Republicans, of course, were much more friendly, particularly since it was clear, as Nichol privately observed, that the League was "a powerful adjunct to the republican party."[88] Sherman and Garfield in particular gave the League what help they could, the Secretary with some attempt to conceal his interest.[89] But some Republicans thought the new organization likely to cause unnecessary trouble. "If those so-called honest money men will keep still and not go to extremes," wrote Senator Angus Cameron from Washington in March, "I think the present Congress can be held where it is, but if they go and force the issue there will be more radical legislation than has yet been seen."[90]

As the 1878 campaign unfolded, the League concentrated all its efforts on electing a hard money Forty-sixth Congress. The first task was to keep the Republicans, and if possible the Democrats, from surrendering to greenback pressures. Scudder pointed out in April that though the Nationals were strong in their own right in Michigan, Indiana, Illinois, and Wisconsin, the really serious danger through much of the West was that one or both of the major parties would take up their cause.[91] Through the spring and early summer Nichol made the rounds of the western state conventions, trying to stiffen the backs of conservatives of both parties. The Democrats proved hopeless, but in Iowa and Michigan in particular the League claimed some success in help-

[86] AM, Oct. 31, 1878.

[87] Indianapolis Sun, June 22, 1878. See also Schilling's Labor Advance, March 23, 1878.

[88] Nichol to Elisha Keyes, Chicago, March 11, 1878, Keyes MSS.

[89] Aside from soliciting the syndicate for an advertisement, Sherman sent a private letter to Nichol to be used at the Milwaukee meeting. He also sent Nichol a hundred copies of the printed account of his Banking and Currency Committee interview. Nichol to Sherman, Chicago, April 17, 1878 and April 19, 1878, Sherman MSS; Milwaukee Daily Sentinel, June 12, 1878.

[90] Angus Cameron to Elisha Keyes, Washington, March 18, 1878, Keyes MSS.

[91] M. L. Scudder to James A. Garfield, Chicago, April 17, 1878, Garfield MSS.

ing to keep the Republican platforms sound and conservative.[92]

During the campaign itself, the League performed valiantly for the Republican cause. Nichol was in a constant whirl by August, speaking in Maine, Illinois, Pennsylvania, and Michigan. League pamphlets circulated widely, although money for printing was hard to come by, owing—in Nichol's ironic words—to the "fiat" and "irredeemable" promises of Milwaukee businessmen.[93] The most effective of these publications indicted the Nationals as profligates, communists, and traitors, citing as evidence two scurrilous pamphlet series by Pomeroy, *Hot Drops* and *Meat for Men*, originally written for the 1877 state campaigns. Pomeroy was quoted—accurately—as calling on "young men of the West and South" to organize Greenback Clubs "with bayonets in reserve," and describing "wives of Cabinet officers as "political prostitutes to rob the Treasury for the benefit of plundering pimps of power."[94] The generous extracts from Pomeroy's writings made the League pamphlet as sensational as the works it condemned; and with the added appeal of an improving purpose, it became immensely popular.[95]

The League's attack on Pomeroy as a communist and an incendiary was part of a broader conservative attempt, reminiscent of the 1875 Ohio campaign, to brand the soft money men as social radicals.[96] Coming so soon after the railroad riots, while the public was still jumpy, it put the Nationals on the defensive. Donnelly felt called on to deny that the party had any interest

[92] Thomas Nichol to Elisha Keyes, Chicago, June 9, 1878 and June 24, 1878, Keyes MSS; Nichol to Sherman, Chicago, June 27, 1878, Sherman MSS; M. L. Scudder to Garfield, Chicago, July 1, 1878, Garfield MSS.

[93] Nichol to Elisha Keyes, Chicago, Aug. 1, 1878, Keyes MSS; *CDT*, Sept. 19, 1878.

[94] Honest Money League of the Northwest, *Extracts from Some of the Communistic, Inflammatory, and Treasonable Documents Circulated by the National Greenback Party* (Chicago, 1878), pp. 5-6. The extracts quoted were both verbatim and in context.

[95] Nichol to Elisha Keyes, Chicago, Aug. 1, 1878, Keyes MSS. Other League pamphlets included: Nichol, *op. cit.*; C. K. Backus, *The Contraction of the Currency* (Chicago, 1878); John Johnston, *An Address on the Currency Delivered before the Literary Society and Citizens of Bay View* (Chicago, 1878).

[96] For example, George Wilson, Jr., *The Greenbackers and Their Doctrines* (Lexington, Mo., 1878), pp. 53-54; 75-87; George Walker, "Communism and Greenbacks," *Banker's Magazine*, xxxiii (October 1878), 248ff.

in "direct action" to carry out its program. Turning the public case of nerves to his own account, he noted that communism battened on poverty and despair. "Produce good times by putting an end to the contraction of the currency and . . . restore confidence and set the wheels of enterprise and industry in motion once more," and the danger of revolution would cease.[97]

Until September, despite both the dire predictions and the confident claims, no one could really tell how strong the Nationals were. Then on September 9 the National-Democratic coalition scored a brilliant victory in Maine, electing two out of five Congressmen, and winning a large enough portion of the popular vote to throw the gubernatorial election into the legislature.[98] Nichol, who had been campaigning in Maine just before the debacle, did not think the result a fair test of hard money sentiment and advised Sherman to wait until the Michigan contest before drawing conclusions.[99] But for Yankee Maine to go National was too rude a jolt to allow for calm appraisal, and shuddering at what might happen in the West, Republican leaders hurried to appease soft money opinion. Soon after the Maine results reached the capital, Sherman was telling a Washington editor in a widely reported interview that after resumption he saw no reason why greenbacks should not replace the national bank circulation: he himself preferred a government issue to bank notes![100] Simultaneously, George C. Gorham, Secretary of the Republican Congressional Election Committee, presumably speaking for the party, publicly upbraided the contractionists and the national bankers.[101]

[97] *AM*, May 16, 1878; May 30, 1878.

[98] *Indianapolis Sun*, Sept. 14, 1878; *NYW*, Sept. 10, 1878; Sept. 11, 1878; *Nation*, xxvii (Sept. 12, 1878), 153; *Annual Cyclopedia for 1878*, pp. 514-516. In the gubernatorial race Joseph Smith, the National, won 41,000 votes, enough to keep the Republican candidate, Cormer, from getting a popular majority. Under the law, this threw the election into the legislature where the Democrat, although originally last in the field, was elected.

[99] Nichol to Sherman, Washington, Sept. 16, 1878, Sherman MSS; also Nichol to Garfield, Chicago, Sept. 13, 1878, Garfield MSS; Nichol to Keyes, Chicago, Sept. [?], 1878, Keyes MSS. As he told Sherman, the Republicans had blundered badly by not organizing against the Greenbackers, who "sowed tares in our field . . . while *we* slept."

[100] See *NYW*, Sept. 16, 1878; Sept. 17, 1878.

[101] *Ibid.*

Conservatives immediately demanded the blood of both Sherman and Gorham.[102] Donnelly, at the other end, chortled that "the bottom is out of the hard money party at last."[103] Neither response could have been very pleasing to the two men,[104] but it is possible that their statements helped save the party. Compared to Maine, the results in the "October" states and then in November were a great triumph for sound finance. The total national Greenback-Labor vote was impressive. It is usually given as over a million, divided approximately three to two between West and East.[105] But as a measure of actual third-party strength, this figure is misleading, since it includes hundreds of thousands of Democratic votes for fusion candidates. In Iowa, for example, with the largest National turnout, the total Greenback-Labor vote is generally recorded at almost 125,000. Yet the two Congressional victories—which sent James B. Weaver and A. H. Gillette to the Forty-sixth Congress—were won by fusion with the Democrats.[106] The Nationals finally claimed between 24 and 26 Congressmen,[107] but most of these were Democrats running with National endorsement. In only one case, in fact, did a National running in a three-cornered race succeed.[108] In perhaps four or five others coalition candidates were primarily Nationals.[109] A more realistic measure of third-party strength in

[102] E.g., J. M. Bundy (of the *New York Daily Mail*) to W. K. Rogers, New York, Sept. 18, 1878, Rutherford B. Hayes MSS; J. W. Stone to Garfield, Grand Rapids, Mich., Sept. 23, 1878, Garfield MSS; see *NYW*, Sept. 17, 1878, for the adverse comments of the *Boston Advertiser*, the *New York Times*, and the *New York Evening Post*.

[103] *AM*, Sept. 19, 1878.

[104] Sherman angrily denied the report that the Administration intended to abandon resumption on January 1, but was silent about replacing national bank notes with greenbacks. See Sherman to Nichol, newspaper clipping enclosed in John Long to Sherman, St. Louis, Sept. 22, 1878, Sherman MSS.

[105] Haynes, *op. cit.*, p. 124; James, *op. cit.*, p. 166, n. 18.

[106] Haynes, *op. cit.*, p. 167.

[107] *AM*, Nov. 14, 1878; Dec. 5, 1878 quoting the New Haven *Union; National Labor Tribune*, Nov. 16, 1878. Troup, in the *Union*, even included Kelley in his total! Buchanan was more conservative, claiming only 15. See *Indianapolis Sun*, April 12, 1879.

[108] Thompson Murch in Maine was the sole exception. In Pennsylvania, in similar three-cornered races, several Nationals came in second, very close behind the winning candidates. Moreover, in several places in the South—North Carolina and Texas—where the Republican party scarcely existed, Nationals defeated Democratic opponents.

[109] These were, besides Murch: James B. Weaver and A. H. Gillette in Iowa, Gilbert De La Matyr in Indiana, and G. W. Ladd in Maine.

1878 is the 870,000 votes that separate National state tickets received.[110]

In the usual post-election assessments, Greenbackers, not surprisingly, emphasized the great advance over 1877 and talked of capturing the White House in 1880.[111] Conservatives generally saw the results as a popular vindication of their position. One religious weekly, characteristically, pictured the election result as a great moral triumph exhibiting the hand of Providence. "The men who wished to commit the nation to financial dishonesty," wrote the editor of the Dutch Reformed *Christian Intelligencer*, "and those who aimed at the destruction of rights of property, and the enthronement of indolence, and recklessness, and unthrift, seemed . . . about to succeed. . . . But He who trims the hearts of men according to His will has given a spirit of wisdom and understanding, has given the people a sound mind, and dishonesty has been rebuked and defeated. . . . 'Praise God from whom all blessings flow.' "[112] On a less exalted level, the election seemed to confirm estimates that nothing could stop resumption. The greenback movement had clearly been overestimated. Though the money radicals might win local successes, they could not,

---

The *Commercial and Financial Chronicle* credited the Nationals with 11 Congressmen: 2 each from Maine and Iowa, and 1 each from Vermont, New Jersey, Pennsylvania, Indiana, Georgia, North Carolina, and Texas. Republican William Henry Smith conceded 5 victories to the Greenbackers. See *CFC*, xxvii (Nov. 9, 1878), 471; Smith to Rutherford B. Hayes, [Chicago], Nov. 12, 1878, Smith MSS, Ohio Historical Society.

[110] Murray S. Stedman, Jr., and Susan W. Stedman, *Discontent at the Polls: A Study of Farmer and Labor Parties, 1827-1948* (New York: Columbia University Press, 1950), pp. 37-38, 173. The realistic Thomas Buchanan, at the outset at least, claimed 800,000 votes for the Nationals. *Indianapolis Sun*, Nov. 16, 1878. As for the composition of the National electorate, it appears to have been largely rural. West of the Alleghenies, only Ohio and In-

diana delivered a sizable labor vote for the Nationals. Even in the East a large part—though probably not a majority—of the National vote was cast by farmers. The Maine vote was clearly rural. In Pennsylvania farmers in the western counties were a significant part of the electorate. In New York the National candidate for Judge of the Court of Appeals received most of his vote from such rural counties as Oswego, Oneida, Allegheny, and Warren, although Albany and Rensselaer, both industrial, were first and second respectively in total National turnout. McGrane, *op. cit.*, pp. 536-539; Ricker, *op. cit.*, pp. 102ff.; *NYDT*, Nov. 30, 1878.

[111] *National Labor Tribune*, Oct. 19, 1878; Nov. 16, 1878; *AM*, Nov. 14, 1878; Uriah Stephens to Terence Powderly, n.p., n.d., Powderly MSS.

[112] *Christian Intelligencer*, xlix (Nov. 28, 1878), 8.

in a national election, draw farmers and wage earners in large numbers away from their traditional party loyalties. They were not formidable, the *New York World* noted, and hereafter they could be ignored.[113] "The result of the elections," the *Nation* summarized, "is likely to be very healthy in giving the Republicans practical assurances that in their present stand on the currency question they are on safe and winning ground."[114]

II

During the weeks of the Congressional race, besides campaigning for the ticket, Sherman was busy with important last-minute preparations for resumption. He had done much to conciliate banking opinion in the last few months, but he still had not come to a clear-cut understanding with the New York financial men. The central question in 1878 as in the previous year was whether the bankers, to protect themselves, would draw gold from the Treasury reserve. At the beginning of December the metropolitan bankers held over $40 million in greenbacks,[115] which if brought for redemption on January first would, in one observer's homely phrase, "suck up the Treasury gold as a siphon exhausts a cistern."[116] By late October Sherman, who had once told the bankers to look after themselves, had concluded he must come to an understanding with them or risk losing his reserve on resumption day.

On the 29th Sherman broached a scheme to have the Treasury made a member of the New York Clearing House Association.[117] This would permit the government to settle balances with the banks without either party having to disburse more than a minimum of gold and would prevent the Treasury and the bankers from raiding each other's specie reserves. Sherman also

[113] *NYW*, Oct. 10, 1878.
[114] *Nation*, xxvii (Nov. 7, 1878), 277.
[115] *CFC*, xxvii (Dec. 11, 1878), 580. Comptroller John Jay Knox later estimated the total greenback holdings of all national banks on January 1, 1879 at $125 million. Knox, *Address . . . to the Annual Convention of the American Bank-*

ers' Association, August 1879 (New York, 1879), p. 7.
[116] *New York Sun* correspondent reported in *CDT*, Nov. 15, 1878.
[117] Sherman to Assistant Secretary Henry F. French, Washington, Oct. 29, 1878, in U. S. House of Representatives, 46 Cong., 2 sess., *Executive Document No. 9*, p. 393.

wanted the bankers to abandon their policy of keeping separate gold accounts for depositors, since this helped preserve the gold premium.[118]

Shortly thereafter, Comptroller John Jay Knox told the Clearing House Association members of the Treasury's wishes,[119] and on November 8 a conference was held in Washington to negotiate an agreement. The Treasury proposal, promising to protect the reserves of both the banks and the government, seemed mutually advantageous and was cordially received.[120] The government was welcome to enter the Clearing House, the financiers said, and the banks would do all they could to end the distinction between gold and paper. But there was one condition. The Secretary must remember that after January 1 the burden of resumption would rest largely on the banks, and their position would have to be secured. The bankers' chief anxiety at this point was the silver circulation. In February, when the Bland-Allison measure became law, the bullion value of the standard silver dollar was a little over 93 cents in gold.[121] By November it was about 83 cents and gave promise of declining still further.[122] If the banks were compelled to take silver coin on regular deposits, they might easily find themselves drained of their reserves by speculators demanding gold for silver deposited. This could be prevented, however, if silver were received on "special account" only; that is, if it were segregated on the banks' accounts so that only silver coin need be returned to a silver depositor.[123]

But this unilateral action by the banks, it was felt, could only be a palliative. The final solution, barring repeal of the Bland Act,

---

[118] NYW, Nov. 13, 1878.

[119] Knox, op. cit., p. 7.

[120] Resistance to resumption had by this time almost entirely broken down. At its August 1878 convention the American Bankers' Association had unanimously endorsed resolutions favoring cooperation with the Treasury, although the bankers were still unwilling to make the pledge of support very specific. American Bankers' Association, Reports of Proceedings at Conventions . . . (New York, 1890), pp. 48-56.

[121] This was Sherman's figure. Actually silver had risen in 1877 and apparently was still higher than the average for 1876 at the time of the Bland Bill's passage. It soon fell, however, bringing the 1878 average a little below 1876. Sherman, Recollections, II, 692. See U. S. Bureau of the Census, Statistical Abstract of the United States for 1907, p. 564, table 191.

[122] NYW, Nov. 13, 1878.

[123] Ibid.; New York Herald, Nov. 12, 1878.

was to restrict the silver coinage to the minimum $2 million monthly and to retire greenbacks of small denomination, replacing them with silver dollars. In this way silver would be kept constantly circulating through many hands and could not be used to draw off the banks' gold reserves. If Sherman would encourage such a policy, the banks implied, they would wholeheartedly cooperate with the Treasury.[124] Not wishing to antagonize the silver men, Sherman refused to commit the Treasury formally, but apparently gave some sort of private assurances. It was soon "an open secret at the Treasury" that he would accommodate the bankers within legal limits.[125]

On November 11 the request for admission to the Association was formally made, and the following day the New York Assistant Treasurer became a member of the New York Clearing House.[126] At the same time, the banks promised to end the distinction between gold and paper on their books after December 31 and agreed to pay and receive balances between the banks and the Clearing House in either gold or legal tenders. But they also insisted on discriminating against silver by refusing to treat it as anything but subsidiary coin.[127]

This last move naturally infuriated the silverites and soft money men. Donnelly declared that it was the bankers' pound of flesh for aiding resumption.[128] Even Republican silverites were angered by what they considered the banks' arbitrary action. It was "an attempt to obstruct the use and remonetization of silver against the declared policy of the government," one of Sherman's Ohio friends wrote,[129] while one of the President's correspondents warned that if the bankers succeeded in frustrating the Bland Act they "would kill the Republican party beyond any power to resurrect it."[130] Sherman denied that he had condoned the

[124] *Ibid.; CDT,* Nov. 15, 1878.
[125] *Ibid.*
[126] *New York Herald,* Nov. 13, 1878.
[127] For a complete account of the Clearing House resolutions see *NYW,* Nov. 13, 1878; *The Public,* xiv (Nov. 14, 1878), p. 309.
[128] *AM,* Nov. 21, 1878; also *In-dianapolis Sun,* Nov. 23, 1878.
[129] Warner Bateman to John Sherman, Cincinnati, Nov. 14, 1878; also Samuel J. Kirkwood to Sherman, Iowa City, Ia., Nov. 13, 1878, Sherman MSS.
[130] William H. Smith to Hayes, [Chicago], Nov. 12, 1878, Smith MSS, Ohio Historical Society.

move,[131] and in December he tried to get the banks to reconsider their decision—but without success. If Congress would take action to prevent the silver dollar from becoming "a disturbing element," they would gladly rescind their resolution, they told him. But to do so without protection "would be to stultify themselves [and] strengthen the unlimited silver people."[132] Thereafter, the combined action of the banks and the Treasury, which restricted its silver purchases to the legal minimum, kept silver effectively demonetized.[133]

The arrangement with the New York Clearing House Association[134] represented yet another obstacle overcome.[135] Still, December was an anxious month for the Treasury. Sherman believed public confidence on resumption day absolutely essential for success, and in his *Annual Report* he sought to present specie payments as an accomplished fact. He briefly rehearsed the Treasury's loan operations and noted that $142 million in gold lay in the government's vaults. In reviewing the arrangements with the syndicate, he remarked that "every step in these preparations" had "been accomplished with increased business confidence." The stockpiling of reserve gold, rather than boosting the premium as had been feared, had actually reduced it, so that it was currently "merely nominal."[136] "The present condition of our trade, industry, and commerce, . . . our ample reserves, and the general confidence inspired in our financial condition," he declared, "seem to justify the opinion that we are prepared to commence and maintain resumption from and after the first day of January, A. D., 1879."[137]

[131] *CDT*, Nov. 14, 1878; Sherman to Thomas Lamb, Washington, Nov. 18, 1878, *Exec. Doc. No. 9*, p. 411.

[132] H. C. Fahnestock to Sherman, New York, Dec. 11, 1878, Sherman MSS.

[133] On the Treasury's policy see the *New York Sun* statement, reported in *CDT*, Nov. 15, 1878. In August, it should be noted, the International Monetary Conference at Paris which, under the terms of the Bland Act had been called to settle the question of an international gold-silver ratio, adjourned sine die, with nothing accomplished. *CDT*, Aug. 31, 1878.

[134] The agreement was shortly extended to the Boston Clearing House. *Exec. Doc. No. 9*, pp. 408-409.

[135] Comptroller Knox later declared that it ended all doubts of resumption. Knox, *op. cit.*, p. 7.

[136] On Nov. 12, 1878, gold was quoted in New York at 100⅛. *New York Herald*, Nov. 12, 1878.

[137] U. S. Treasury, *Report of the Secretary on the State of the Finances for the Year 1878*, pp. viii-xv.

Conservatives hastened to second the Treasury's efforts to nurture public confidence. The *Nation* told its readers that the change from paper to coin would come as smoothly as the daily "transition from night to day."[138] "The advocates of sound currency may . . . lay aside their fears," declared the *Commercial and Financial Chronicle*.[139] Lyman Abbott, editor of the important New York religious weekly, the *Christian Union*, arranged to have his paper publish reassuring statements by the leading New York bankers just before resumption day. "We believe that such publication will go far among our circle of readers to make it a success," he explained to Sherman. "I am sure the press can do nothing more effective to second your successful work in leading us out of the financial wilderness than by thus echoing God's message to Israel. Be of good courage."[140]

Fortunately the general drift of public opinion in the last weeks of 1878 was favorable to resumption. Resistance was not suddenly snuffed out, of course. On November 30 the Executive Committee of the National Party fired one last shot at resumption as "a fraud and a delusion, impracticable in theory in any civilized country."[141] Many businessmen were still jittery. The Cincinnati business community while "anxious for success," would not "feel assured until the experiment shall be finally tried."[142]

On the whole, however, the public seemed prepared to take the plunge. Seven out of ten men in the West, an Ohio Republican believed, now thought resumption would come without ill effects, at least "*immediately.*"[143] Even Greenbackers, the National Executive Committee notwithstanding, seemed willing to give Sherman a chance. One prominent Kentucky National, Blanton Duncan, wrote that he would "be grateful to see a change for the better, come from whatever cause it may."[144] Most important of all, Congress proved acquiescent. Two new

[138] *Nation*, xxvii (Dec. 26, 1878), 393.
[139] *CFC*, xxvii (Nov. 30, 1878), 550.
[140] Abbott to Sherman, New York, Dec. 22, 1878, Sherman MSS.
[141] *National Labor Tribune*, Dec. 7, 1878.

[142] Richard Smith (of the *Cincinnati Gazette*) to John Sherman, Cincinnati, Dec. 14, 1878, Sherman MSS.
[143] Rush Sloan to Sherman, Chicago, Dec. 13, 1878, *ibid.*
[144] Blanton Duncan to Sherman, n.p., Dec. 3, 1878, *ibid.*

silver bills were introduced during the short December session,[145] but the legislators went home for Christmas before acting on either.[146]

Only one more hurdle remained—the persistent gold premium. In January 1878 gold was quoted at about 102; by June it was down to 100.7, and it had fallen to 100.1 by December 1.[147] With the Treasury continually withdrawing gold from commercial channels, the steady decline, as Sherman had remarked, was an unexpected occurrence—one made possible by the remarkable export balance that had developed since 1876.[148] But while nominal, the premium worried Treasury officials. So long as it remained, a profit could be made by exchanging paper for gold, and the prospect of a run on gold on January 1 loomed as a frightening possibility. In mid-December the Treasury suspected that a clique of speculators was deliberately maintaining the gap between coin and paper.[149] In an attempt to close it, Sherman threw Treasury gold on the market by authorizing prepayment of the January bond interest.[150] This show of strength was suffi-

[145] One by Greenbury Fort forbade the banks to refuse silver; the other, introduced by Aylett Buckner, provided for an additional $7 million monthly of silver purchases. *NYDT*, Dec. 10, 1878.

[146] In 1882, however, Congress passed a measure denying charter renewal to any national bank which refused to accept silver coin in settlement of balances. This, too, proved ineffective in forcing the banks to use silver. Fritz Redlich, *The Molding of American Banking: Men and Ideas* (New York: Hafner Publishing Company, 1951), part II, p. 432.

[147] Wesley Clair Mitchell, *Gold, Prices and Wages under the Greenback Standard* (Berkeley: The University [of California] Press, 1908), p. 13.

[148] This brought back to America a steady flow of federal securities, but also made it possible for the country to retain its gold supply. Without such a favorable balance of payments it is difficult to see how Sherman could have accumulated his coin reserve. For the relationship between the trade balance and Sherman's refunding and resumption policies see Don Carlos Barrett, *The Greenbacks and Resumption of Specie Payments, 1862-1879* (Cambridge: Harvard University Press, 1931), pp. 176, 213-214; *NYDT*, March 12, 1878; and Frank D. Graham, "International Trade Under Depreciated Paper: The United States, 1862–1879," *Quarterly Journal of Economics*, XXXVI (February 1922), 230-233, 248.

[149] See Assistant Treasurer Thomas Hillhouse to John Sherman, New York, Dec. 14, 1878, *Exec. Doc. No. 9*, p. 421. For a detailed description of the October move against resumption see Sherman, *Recollections*, II, 669; and for the one in early December, *CFC*, XXVII (Dec. 7, 1878), 577.

[150] John Sherman to Thomas Hillhouse, Washington, Dec. 18, 1878, *Exec. Doc. No. 9*, p. 426.

cient to scatter the gamblers, and on December 17 the gold premium, which had first appeared in December 1861, finally disappeared. Shortly thereafter, cases were reported of business-men, legally entitled to gold, accepting greenbacks in normal commercial transactions.[151]

January 1, 1879, was a bank holiday, a fact that the Republican Forty-third Congress in its haste to get a financial bill on the books had overlooked, and resumption, already delayed for a decade and a half, was postponed still another day. On the second, New York, the legal place of redemption, wore a festive air in anticipation of the great financial reform. The Customs House and the banks were covered with bunting, and flags flew from many public buildings. The gold room at the Stock Exchange was deserted, and across the great board, on which for seventeen years had been chalked the latest gold quotations, somebody had scrawled in large letters, "PAR."[152] At the Sub-Treasury large bags of coin were piled up at the redemption counter ready so that no delay need occur to set loose rumors of the Treasury's inability to pay. In the vaults lay over $100 million in coin reserves.

The Sub-Treasury doors opened at 10 a.m., accompanied by a salute from the Navy Yard; but the rest of the day was anti-climactic. One person was on hand at opening to demand coin. He was paid $210, and by noon, less than $3000 had been paid out. At the close of business, $132,000 in notes had been redeemed and $400,000 in gold exchanged for the more convenient paper.[153]

At the banks the story was the same. The tellers, well supplied with coin, had paid out virtually nothing. At the First National less than $50 was exchanged for paper; at the Mechanics' Bank Association not one dollar was redeemed the entire day,[154] and by evening the bankers were congratulating Sherman and themselves on the end of the paper era.[155]

---

[151] *CFC*, xxvii (Dec. 21, 1878), 645; *NYDT*, Dec. 19, 1878; Dec. 23, 1878.
[152] *Ibid.*, Jan. 3, 1879; *NYT*, Jan. 3, 1879.

[153] *NYDT*, Jan. 3, 1879.
[154] *NYT*, Jan. 3, 1879.
[155] Beard remarks at this point in his account of resumption "the captains of business enterprises and the

During the next few days jubilation reigned among the hard money men. Letters and telegrams poured into Sherman's office offering congratulations on "the magnificent success of the greatest event of modern times."[156] The Honest Money League Executive Committee met and passed resolutions praising Sherman.[157] The conservative press burst into ringing hosannas. To the *Commercial and Financial Chronicle* resumption meant "that the farmer's grain, the planter's cotton, the Chinaman's tea are all interchangeable anywhere on a common basis of value, and as every venture is thus relieved of the element of uncertainty, enterprise becomes less hazardous and therefore freer."[158] *Banker's Magazine* saw it as a great victory for self-discipline over "demagogism," made possible only by a secure banking system.[159] The *Nation* called it the triumph of the "rational, reflective, remembering element in society" over "folly and ignorance."[160] The religious press hailed it as a great moral triumph and a credit to the American people, brought to see the light through the "practical instruction of the American pulpit in the fundamental principles of national honor and honesty."[161] To *Harper's Weekly* it was another great victory of the Republican party, one which could be placed alongside the abolition of slavery and the preservation of the Union.[162]

These responses, full of the exuberance of the moment, are actually capsule statements of historical causation. Sherman, the

---

financiers heaved a sigh of relief." His suggestion, of course, is that specie payments were a triumph for the new business element. Actually his phrase was borrowed from the resumption account of the *New York Daily Tribune* for Jan. 3, 1879, where it referred only to the New York bankers, and merely suggested the pleasure of the New York financial men at escaping a run on their gold. See Charles A. and Mary R. Beard, *The Rise of American Civilization* (Revised college edition, New York: The Macmillan Company, 1944), II, 331.

[156] C. H. Baldwin to John Sherman, Charleston, S. C., Jan. 1, 1879, Sherman MSS. See also the following in *ibid.*: William Dennison to Sherman, Columbus, Jan. 1, 1879; Levi P. Morton to Sherman, New York, Jan. 2, 1879; Thomas Nichol to Sherman, Chicago, Jan. 4, 1879; Schuyler Colfax to Sherman, n.p., Jan. 4, 1879.

[157] See Daniel L. Shorey to John Sherman, Chicago, Jan. 3, 1879, *ibid.*

[158] *CFC*, XXVIII (Jan. 4, 1879), 1.

[159] *Banker's Magazine*, XXXIII (Jan. 1879), 489ff.

[160] *Nation*, XXVII (Dec. 26, 1878), 394. This was, of course, anticipatory.

[161] *Christian Union*, XIX (Jan. 8, 1879), 25; also *Christian Intelligencer*, LIII (Jan. 16, 1879), 1; *The Advance*, XIII (Jan. 9, 1879), 17.

[162] *Harper's Weekly*, XXIII (Jan. 18, 1879), 42.

foreign traders, the bankers, the educated elite, the pulpit, the Republican party, are all given credit, directly or by implication, for the great consummation. Much of this may be put down to rhetoric or self-importance, but taken together it is a remarkable composite description of the forces which actually carried resumption through.

Any analysis of these years which fails to note the crucial role of strategically placed individuals grossly distorts reality. On the soft money side, Alexander Campbell shaped the course of events by implanting an attractive theoretical abstraction in the fertile soil of working-class and rural discontent. Carey, by making accessible the submerged mercantilist thought of an earlier day, translated the needs of the industrialists into soft money terms. At the opposite end of the spectrum, McCulloch seriously crippled the hard money cause at the outset by identifying resumption with the remorseless burning of the people's money. But above all, it is impossible to exaggerate the role of John Sherman, the supple master of accommodation. Following in the footsteps of his great Whig predecessors, he subordinated the ideal to the workable and succeeded where men more righteous, perhaps, had failed.

The hard money businessmen, the seaboard merchants and bankers, the Yankee textile magnates, all had reason to congratulate themselves on resumption day. Against the great and growing power of a class of businessmen identified with postwar industrial expansion and western development, they had carried their point. Resumption was a victory for A. A. Low, the transplanted Yankee and China Trader, and for A. A. Lawrence, second generation Brahmin Lord of the Loom; it was a defeat for Jay Cooke, the upstart Ohio railroad promoter, and the self-made western industrialist Eber Ward.

The political parties, with their separate traditions, their distinctive textures, their individual inner compulsions and needs, were also movers of events. The Democrats, thrust from leadership into persistent minority status, possessing deep Jeffersonian roots, drawing their strength in the West from the southern-born and the immigrant, were susceptible to Agrarian greenback appeal and coalition with dissident labor and farmer elements. The

Republicans, not so much as the instrument of rising industrial capitalism, but as the majority party and the party of the Yankee and the Teuton, the respectable middle class, the erstwhile Whig, the church-goer, the professional man, proved resistant to green-backism, though not to free banking—the respectable version of soft money.

The intellectual and moral leaders of the community also added considerable weight to the scales. Soft money and hard money were far more than congeries of economic interests, or even economic *cum* political interests. They were also competing intellectual and ethical systems. On the moral plane, Agrarianism confronted Calvinism; on the intellectual, a revived mercantilism confronted the prevailing economic orthodoxy. In both cases the hard money position, reinforced by the prestige of the Protestant Churches and the academy respectively, enjoyed an immense advantage over the soft money ideology so often identified with quacks, visionaries, and charlatans.

The conservative post-mortem reveals, then, an impressive grasp of contemporary reality. In rough outline it identifies the leading actors in the drama of specie payments. They were not the "rising" industrial capitalists. In a strict economic sense, measured by shares of the national income contributed, manufacturing had indeed outstripped, individually, agriculture, construction, transportation, and services by the mid-'80's. But in the previous decade, if their role in the currency fight is any measure, there was a significant gap between the dynamism of American industrial progress and the social power and prestige of American industrialists.

The composite conservative estimate is also a remarkably penetrating general overview of post-Civil War America. It recognizes, in the first place, a society deeply divided internally. There was not, indeed, the conflict over the political and social fundamentals that often turned nineteenth-century Europe into a battleground of irreconcilable elements ready to resort to bombs and barricades. The American struggle was always tamer, and to this extent, the recent discovery of a continuing American "consensus"[163] is surely valid. Political democracy, an expanding

[163] See John Higham, "Beyond Consensus: The Historian as Moral Critic," *AHR*, LXVII, No. 3 (April 1962).

economy, and a relatively fluid social system softened class asperities and narrowed the area of disagreement among Americans. Yet conflict there was, and often it generated frustrations and aggressions just short of the social flash point. Men have a way, in the absence of truly fundamental issues, of turning lesser differences into matters of life and death.

The men who congratulated themselves on January 2 were close enough to events to comprehend also the intricacy of what they observed. If it is hard to see the consensus in post-bellum America, it is also difficult to detect a simple Beardian polarity. On the money question there were not two massive contending interests; there were many small ones. If the financial history of Reconstruction reveals nothing else of consequence, it does disclose a complex, pluralistic society in which issues were resolved —when they were not simply brushed aside—by the interaction of many forces. And yet the ghost of dualism still lingers. It has been impossible to avoid using the terms "hard money" and "soft money," although the intent has always been to tag coalitions rather than the homogeneous entities posited by Beard. This seems to return dualism through the back door after it has been ejected through the front. But it does only in a verbal sense, I think. The need for stylistic shorthand, the demands of rational organization, and the very laws of thought, perhaps, impose a kind of dualism on the historian even when he rejects it as a true picture of reality. Each coalition was not, however, a tug-of-war team, pulling against its opponent along a single axis. Instead, each was a jostling crowd, full of seeming random activity, which nonetheless managed to move in a consistent direction.

While at most points conservative contemporaries and modern historians disagree, they do share one serious illusion: resumption, they believed, was a conclusive victory for hard money. In the momentary jubilation at reaching gold, conservatives did not notice that their triumph was more symbolic than real. The enemy had not surrendered, a fact that was indeed recognized by the more acute among them. In December 1878 Garfield noted that the Nationals were showing more life than before the

Congressional election.[164] The Honest Money League felt it necessary to continue its work after resumption, sponsoring a series of lectures during the winter in major western cities on the dangers of inflation;[165] and to counteract continuing greenback agitation conservative Congressmen took steps to nationalize the League and move its headquarters to Washington.[166] To look beyond the decade, in 1880 Weaver, on a Greenback Presidential ticket, would win over 300,000 votes. In 1884 Butler would run for President on a paper money platform.[167] Not until the late '80's when, with the advent of Populism, free silver rose once more, did greenbackism go into a steep decline. Even then, however, the Populists would salvage much of the ideology, platform, and general outlook of their greenback predecessors.[168]

On January 2, 1879, the conservatives won only the opening round of a thirty-five-year struggle. And even this victory was qualified. The country was back on the gold standard, but $346 million of wartime greenbacks, augmented year by year by $24 million of silver certificates, still circulated as the price exacted by the cheap money forces for acquiescence. As long as the nation remained prosperous, Sherman's reserve preserved the gold standard. But after the 1893 recession, the great inverted pyramid of fiat money, resting on the narrow apex of 100 million gold dollars, threatened to topple. Only the quick work of another hard money administration—this time headed by a New York gold Democrat—and another syndicate of international bankers, kept the greenbackers from winning a belated victory a decade and a half after resumption.

[164] Garfield MS Diary, Dec. 4, 1878, Garfield MSS.

[165] M. L. Scudder to Garfield, Chicago, Nov. 2, 1878, *ibid*. Garfield delivered one of these lectures to a large gathering in Chicago. Garfield, *Suspension & Resumption of Specie Payments. Address of . . . Garfield . . . at Chicago* (Chicago, 1879).

[166] Garfield MS Diary, Dec. 4, 1878, Garfield MSS. The move was not made, however. The League remained at Chicago where it apparently survived into the 1890's as an "educational" agency for sound money during the momentous struggles over silver which characterized the decade. See references to the League in 1895 and 1896 in Harry Barnard, *Eagle Forgotten: The Life of John Peter Altgeld* (Indianapolis: The Bobbs-Merrill Company, 1962), pp. 352, 379.

[167] Solon J. Buck, *The Agrarian Crusade: A Chronicle of the Farmer in Politics* (New Haven: Yale University Press, 1920), pp. 92-97.

[168] Note, for example, the concern for the "producing classes" which permeates William Jennings Bryan's "Cross of Gold" speech.

This study, finally, may help us reevaluate the concept of the Civil War as the great watershed of the nation's history. Does the War in fact divide American history into an older rural-agrarian and a newer urban-industrial phase? Did a new society, transformed in its political, cultural, economic, and social life, emerge from the ashes of fratricidal strife? It has been suggested here that until 1880 continuity was at least as characteristic of the nation's history as cataclysm. To be sure, the flash of Union and Confederate guns signaled a physical and human destruction such as the country had never experienced before. But when quiet returned, much remained of the old America. Many of the old centers of power and social prestige survived. The prewar commercial-financial community remained influential. The power of the South and West as revealed in the silver struggle remained formidable. The clergy, the educated elite, and the professoriate continued to exercise intellectual and moral leadership. Nor had ideas or norms changed drastically. The economic orthodoxy of Ricardo and Mill continued to compete with mercantilistic doctrines, as it had in different terms for a century previously. Calvinism, surprisingly little altered in its general fervor for a moral society from the days of Cotton Mather, continued to battle Agrarianism, virtually unchanged from John Taylor's *Arator* and Jefferson's *Notes On Virginia*. Even the ante-bellum humanitarian impulse, translated into monetary reform, persisted.

This is not to say that America in 1880 was identical with America in 1860. The nation has never stood still for two decades. But if this historical test boring bears true witness, it seems a little less certain, perhaps, that the Civil War was the momentous turning point we have all supposed.

APPENDICES

APPENDIX A

Tally Showing Vote Overlap for
Contraction Repeal and Public Credit Act

	Democrat	Republican	Total
Middle of the Road[1]	3	61	64
Soft Money[2]	12	27	39
Hard Money[3]	5	14	19
Vacillating[4]	4	1	5
Total	24	103	127

[1] Voted for contraction repeal and for Public Credit Act.
[2] Voted for contraction repeal and against Public Credit Act.
[3] Voted against contraction repeal and for Public Credit Act.
[4] Voted against contraction repeal and against Public Credit Act.

APPENDIX B

Beck Amendment to Change Free Banking Bill
to Greenback Measure[1]

I. For bill, 68.

	Democrat	Republican	Other[2]	Total
East (including Md. and Del.)	4	4	0	8
West (including Mo.)	16	8	0	24
South (including Ky. and W. Va.)	30	4	2	36
Pacific (including Nev.)	0	0	0	0
Total	50	16	2	68

II. Against bill, 163.

	Democrat	Republican	Other[2]	Total
East	11	60	1	72
West	0	60	0	60
South	3	24	0	27
Pacific	1	3	0	4
Total	15	147	1	163

[1] House vote of April 11, 1874, *Congressional Record*, 43 Congress, 1 session, p. 3019.
[2] This group includes "Conservatives," "Liberals," etc.

APPENDIX C

Inflation Bill[1]

I. For bill, 140.

	Democrat	Republican	Other[2]	Total
East[3] (including Md. and Del.)	1	15	0	16
West (including Mo.)	11	61	0	72
South (including Ky. and W. Va.)	23	28	0	51
Pacific (including Nev.)	0	1	0	1
Total	35	105	0	140

II. Against bill, 102.

	Democrat	Republican	Other[2]	Total
East[3]	17	50	1	68
West	8	9	0	17
South	11	3	0	14
Pacific	1	2	0	3
Total	37	64	1	102

III. Pennsylvania.

	Democrat	Republican	Total
For	0	13	13
Against	4	5	9
Total	4	18	22

---

[1] House vote of April 14, 1874, *Congressional Record*, 43 Congress, 1 session, p. 3078.

[2] This group includes "Conservatives," "Liberals," etc.

[3] Includes the Pennsylvania vote.

APPENDIX D

Joint Conference Committee Banking Bill[1]

I. For bill, 221.

	Democrat	Republican	Other[2]	Total
East (including Md. and Del.)	8	49	0	57
West (including Mo.)	21	72	0	93
South (including Ky. and W. Va.)	31	36	3	70
Pacific	0	1	0	1
Total	60	158	3	221

II. Against bill, 40.

	Democrat	Republican	Other[2]	Total
East	11	20	1	32
West	0	0	0	0
South	4	0	0	4
Pacific	3	1	0	4
Total	18	21	1	40

[1] House vote of June 20, 1874, *Congressional Record*, 43 Congress, 1 session, p. 5316.

[2] This group includes "Conservatives," "Liberals," etc.

APPENDIX E

1875 Ohio Gubernatorial Election

I. Leading Ohio Coal Mining Counties (Bituminous)

County	Production in Thousands of Tons[1]	No. of Miners Over 16	Total Pop. of County	Percentage Changes of Democratic Vote from 1873[2]
Perry	913	1694	28,218	+4.4
Trumbull	722	2014	44,880	+2.7
Columbiana	524	1198	48,602	+3.1
Belmont	399	707	49,638	+1.5
Meigs	359	984	32,325	+13.5
Stark	357	1563	64,031	+1.7

II. Leading Ohio Iron and Steel Producing Counties

County	Capitalization in Thousands of Dollars[1]	Workers in Industry Over 16	Total Pop. in 1880	Percentage Changes of Democratic Vote from 1873[2]
Lawrence	$4,010	3278	39,068	+4.1
Mahoning	3,781	2774	36,158	+4.7
Cuyahoga[3]	2,839	2788	196,943	−1.4
Trumbull	1,330	1516	44,880	+2.7
Belmont	1,200	864	40,638	+1.5
Scioto	1,130	859	33,511	+0.1
Jefferson	1,130	1267	33,018	+4.1
Perry	913	644	28,218	+4.4
Franklin[4]	800	1149	86,797	−7.1

[1] Production and capitalization data, as well as population statistics, are from United States Bureau of the Census, *Tenth Census of the United States: 1880.*

[2] Election figures are from Ohio Secretary of State, *Annual Report for 1875 to the Governor of Ohio* (Columbus: Nevins and Myers, 1876), pp. 283ff.

[3] Includes the city of Cleveland.

[4] Includes the city of Columbus.

APPENDIX F

Repeal of the Resumption Act[1]

I. For bill, 106.

	Democrat	Republican[2]	Total
East (including Md. and Del.)	18	0	18
West (including Mo.)	35	9	44
South (including Ky. and W. Va.)	43	0	43
Pacific (including Nev.)	1	0	1
Total	97	9	106

II. Against bill, 86.

	Democrat	Republican[2]	Total
East	17	29	46
West	3	20	23
South	5	10	15
Pacific	0	2	2
Total	25	61	86

[1] House vote of August 5, 1876, *Congressional Record*, 44 Congress, 1 session, p. 5232.
[2] Includes "Liberals."

APPENDIX G

Men Who Voted for the Bland Bill
but Against Resumption Repeal

*Aldrich	R	Ill.	Monroe	R	Ohio
*Brentano	R	Ill.	*Morrison	D	Ill.
*Burdick	R	Iowa	Pacheco	R	Cal.
*Cain	R	S. C.	Page	R	Cal.
*Rush Clark	R	Iowa	Patterson	R	N. Y.
*Conger	R	Mich.	Pound	R	Wisc.
*J. Cox	R	Ohio	*Price	R	Iowa
*Cummings	R	Iowa	Rainey	R	S. C.
*Cutler	D	N. J.	*Randolph	R	Tenn.
Danford	R	Ohio	*Sampson	R	Iowa
*Deering	R	Iowa	Stewart	R	Minn.
Dunnell	R	Minn.	John Stone	R	Mich.
*Ellsworth	R	Mich.	*Thornburgh	R	Tenn.
Foster	R	Ohio	Amos Townsend	R	Ohio
*Henderson	R	Ill.	*Welch	R	Neb.
*Hubbell	R	Mich.	Charles Williams	R	Wisc.
*Ittner	R	Mo.	Richard Williams	R	Ore.
Keightley	R	Mich.	*Wren	R	Nev.
Luttrell	R	Cal.			
*McKinley	R	Ohio	*Total*: 38		

* Voted to make Repeal the special order of business: 22.

APPENDIX H

The Pro-resumption Silverites and the Vote to Override
Hayes's Veto of the Bland Allison Bill[1]

I. Voted with the majority to override, 31.

Aldrich	Cutler	McKinley	John Stone
Brentano	Danford	Morrison	Thornburgh
Burdick	Deering	Page	A. Townsend
Cain	Henderson	Patterson	Welch
Rush Clark	Hubbell	Pound	Charles Williams
Conger	Ittner	Price	Richard Williams
J. Cox	Keightley	Rainey	Wren
Cummings	Luttrell	Sampson	

II. Voted to sustain veto or no vote recorded, 3.

Ellsworth
Pacheco (no vote recorded)
Stewart

[1] House vote of February 28, 1878, *Congressional Record*, 45 Congress, 2 session, p. 1420.

BIBLIOGRAPHY

I. SOURCE MATERIALS

A. MANUSCRIPTS

Adams Family Papers. Massachusetts Historical Society.

Allen, William. Papers, Library of Congress.

Allison, William B. Papers, Iowa State Department of History and Archives, Des Moines.

Anderson, Wendell A. Papers, State Historical Society of Wisconsin.

Atkinson, Edward A. Papers, Massachusetts Historical Society.

Barlow, S. L. M. Papers, Henry E. Huntington Library, San Marino, California.

Bayard, Thomas F. Papers, Library of Congress.

Black, Jeremiah S. Papers, Library of Congress.

Blaine, James G. Papers, Library of Congress.

Bright, John M. Papers, Southern Historical Collection, University of North Carolina.

Bristow, Benjamin. Papers, Library of Congress.

Bromberg, Frederick G. Papers, Southern Historical Collection, University of North Carolina.

Butler, Benjamin F. Papers, Library of Congress.

Carey, Henry C. Papers, Historical Society of Pennsylvania.

Chandler, William E. Papers, Library of Congress.

Chandler, Zachariah. Papers, Library of Congress.

Chase, Salmon P. Papers, Historical Society of Pennsylvania.

————. Papers, Library of Congress.

Colfax, Schuyler. Papers, Library of Congress.

Colwell, Stephen. Papers, University of Pennsylvania.

Cooke, Jay. Papers, Historical Society of Pennsylvania.

Cooper, Peter. Papers, The Cooper Union, New York City.

Curtis, George William. Papers, Harvard University.

Cushing, Caleb. Papers, Library of Congress.

Davis, David. Papers, Illinois State Library, Springfield.

Dawes, Henry L. Papers, Library of Congress.

Delano, Columbus. Papers, Ohio Historical Society, Columbus.

Dix, John A. Papers, Columbia University.

Dodge, Grenville M. Papers, Iowa State Department of History and Archives, Des Moines.

Donnelly, Ignatius. Papers, Minnesota Historical Society.

Doolittle, James R. Papers, State Historical Society of Wisconsin.

English, William H. Papers, Indiana Historical Society, Indianapolis.

Ewing Family Papers. Library of Congress.

Fessenden, William Pitt. Papers, Library of Congress.

Fish, Hamilton. Papers, Library of Congress.

Garfield, James A. Papers, Library of Congress.

Godkin, Edwin L. Papers, Harvard University.

Grant, Ulysses S. Papers, Library of Congress.

Hassaurek, Friedrich. Papers, Ohio Historical Society, Columbus.

Hayes, Rutherford B. Papers, Hayes Memorial Library, Fremont, Ohio.

————. Papers, Library of Congress.

Howe, Timothy O. Papers, State Historical Society of Wisconsin.

Johnson, Andrew. Papers, Library of Congress.

Julian, George W. Papers, Indiana State Library, Indianapolis.

Keyes, Elisha. Papers, State Historical Society of Wisconsin.

Labor Collection. Political Parties, State Historical Society of Wisconsin.

Lawrence, Amos A. Papers, Massachusetts Historical Society.

Lieber, Francis. Papers, Henry E. Huntington Library, San Marino, California.

Logan, John A. Papers, Library of Congress.

McCormick, Cyrus H. Papers, State Historical Society of Wisconsin.

McCulloch, Hugh. Papers, Library of Congress.

Marble, Manton. Papers, Library of Congress.

Mitchell, Alexander. Papers, State Historical Society of Wisconsin.

Morrill, Justin. Papers, Library of Congress.

Morton, Levi P. Papers, New York Public Library.

Morton, Oliver P. Papers, Indiana State Library, Indianapolis.

Norton, Charles Eliot. Papers, Harvard University.

Oglesby, Richard J. Papers, Illinois State Library, Springfield.

Osborn, Joseph H. Papers, State Historical Society of Wisconsin.

Powderly, Terence V. Papers, Catholic University of America, Washington, D.C.

Pratt, Daniel D. Papers, Indiana State Library, Indianapolis.

Randall, Samuel J. Papers, University of Pennsylvania.

Ransom, Matthew W. Papers, Southern Historical Collection, University of North Carolina.

Schilling, Robert. Papers, State Historical Society of Wisconsin.

Schuckers, Jacob W. Papers, Library of Congress.

Schurz, Carl. Papers, Library of Congress.

Seymour, Horatio. Papers, New York Historical Society.

Sherman, John. Papers, Library of Congress.

————. Papers, Ohio Historical Society, Columbus.

Smith, William Henry. Papers, Indiana Historical Society, Indianapolis.

————. Papers, Ohio Historical Society, Columbus.

Sovereigns of Industry. Papers, State Historical Society of Wisconsin.

Stephens, Alexander H. Papers, Library of Congress.

Stevens, Thaddeus. Papers, Library of Congress.

Sumner, Charles. Papers, Harvard University.

Thurman, Allen G. Papers, Ohio Historical Society, Columbus.

Tilden, Samuel J. Papers, New York Public Library.

Trumbull, Lyman. Papers, Library of Congress.

United States Congress. House and Senate Committee Papers, National Archives.

United States Secretary of the Treasury. Series K, Letters Received, National Archives.

Vilas, William F. Papers, State Historical Society of Wisconsin.

Wade, Benjamin F. Papers, Library of Congress.

Washburne, Elihu B. Papers, Library of Congress.

Watterson, Henry. Papers, Library of Congress.

Weaver, James B. Papers, Iowa State Department of History and Archives, Des Moines.

Weller, Luman H. Papers, State Historical Society of Wisconsin.

Wells, David A. Papers, Library of Congress.

————. Papers, New York Public Library.

B. GOVERNMENT PUBLICATIONS

Ohio Bureau of Labor Statistics. *Annual Report for 1877.*

Ohio Secretary of State. *Annual Report to the Governor of Ohio for 1875.*

United States Bureau of the Census. *Census Reports for 1860, 1870, 1880.*

United States Comptroller of the Currency. *Annual Reports for 1874, 1875, 1881.*

United States Department of Agriculture. *Technical Bulletin No. 703; Gross Farm Income and In-*

dices of Farm Production and Prices in the United States, 1869-1937.

United States House of Representatives. Report No. 31 (Gold Panic Investigation). 41 Congress, 2 session.

——. Report No. 328 (Views Expressed Before the Committee on Banking and Currency). 43 Congress, 2 session.

——. Miscellaneous Document No. 62 (Testimony Before the Committee on Banking and Currency in Relation to the Resumption of Specie Payments). 45 Congress, 2 session.

——. Executive Document No. 9 (Specie Resumption and Refunding of the National Debt: Letter from the Secretary of the Treasury). 46 Congress, 2 session.

——. Miscellaneous Document No. 5 (Investigation . . . Relative to the Causes of the General Depression in Labor and Business

. . .). 46 Congress, 2 session.

United States National Monetary Commission. Statistics for the United States, 1867-1909.

United States Senate. Miscellaneous Document No. 100. 39 Congress, 1 session.

——. Report No. 275. 42 Congress, 3 session.

——. Report No. 703 (Report of the Monetary Commission). 44 Congress, 2 session.

——. Finance Committee (Interview of the Committee on Finance . . . with the Hon. John Sherman . . . in Regard to the Repeal of the Resumption Act). Washington: Government Printing Office, 1878.

United States Special Commissioner of Internal Revenue. Reports No. I-IV, for 1866-1869.

United States Treasury. Annual Report of the Secretary of the Treasury on the State of the Finances for the Years 1865-1879.

C. NEWSPAPERS AND PERIODICALS

1. THE DAILY AND POLITICAL PRESS

Chicago Daily Tribune.
Chicago Inter-Ocean.
Chicago Times.
Cincinnati Commercial.
Cincinnati Enquirer.
Cincinnati Gazette.
Cleveland Leader.
The Great Campaign.
Harrisburg Daily Patriot.
Indianapolis Sentinel.
Indianapolis Sun.
La Crosse Democrat.
New York Daily Tribune.
New York Evening Post.
New York Herald.
New York Times.
New York World.
Ohio State Journal.
Philadelphia Press.
Pittsburgh Daily Dispatch.
Pomeroy's Democrat (New York).
Pottsville Miners' Journal.
The Telegram (Washington).
Washington Daily Morning Chronicle.
Wisconsin State Journal (Madison).

2. JOURNALS OF GENERAL OPINION

Harper's Weekly.
The Nation.
North American Review.

3. AGRICULTURAL PRESS

American Agriculturist.
American Farmer.
The Anti-Monopolist.
Country Gentleman.
The Grange Visitor and Farmer's Monthly Magazine.
Indiana Farmer.
Industrial Age.
The Iowa Homestead (and Western Farm Journal).
Kansas Farmer.
The New England Farmer.
Ohio Farmer.
The Practical Farmer
Prairie Farmer.
Western Farmer (Wisconsin Farmer).
Western Rural.

4. LABOR PRESS

Coopers' Monthly Journal.

Fincher's Trades' Review.
The Labor Advocate (The Labor Advance).
Labor Standard.
The Miners' National Record.
National Labor Tribune.
The Workingman's Advocate.

5. RELIGIOUS PRESS

The Advance.
The American Presbyterian and Theological Review.
The Baptist Quarterly.
The Christian Advocate (New York).
The Christian Examiner.
The Christian Intelligencer.
Christian Mirror.
The Christian Register.
Christian Standard.
The Christian Union.
Christian World.
The Church Journal.
The Churchman.
Congregational Review.
The Episcopalian.
Examiner and Chronicle.
The Golden Age.
The Independent.
The Methodist.
Methodist Quarterly Review.
New York Observer.
Presbyterian Banner.

Princeton Review.
Protestant Churchman.
St. Louis Christian Advocate.
The Southern Churchman.
Southern Presbyterian Review.
The Southern Review.
The Standard.
Watchman and Reflector.

6. TRADE, COMMERCIAL, AND ECONOMIC PRESS

American Manufacturer and Trade of the West.
The Banker's Magazine.
The Coal and Iron Record.
The Commercial and Financial Chronicle.
De Bow's Review.
The Financial Review.
The Financier (The Public).
The Free Trader.
Gunton's Magazine (Social Economist).
The Industrial Bulletin.
Iron Age.
The League.
Manufacturer and Builder.
Merchant's Magazine and Commercial Review (Hunt's).
The Metal Worker.
Railroad Gazette.
Shoe and Leather Reporter.

D. PROCEEDINGS AND MEMORIALS

American Bankers' Association. Reports of Proceedings at Conventions, 1875-1879.

American Iron and Steel Association. Annual Reports for 1868-1879.

American Social Science Association. Journal of Social Science, 1869-1878.

Baltimore Board of Trade. Annual Reports for 1867 and 1868.

Boston Board of Trade. Annual Reports for 1864-1878.

Chicago Board of Trade. Annual Reports for 1866-1879.

Cincinnati Board of Trade. Annual Reports for 1869-1878.

Cincinnati Chamber of Commerce. Annual Reports for 1869-1879.

Cleveland Board of Trade. Annual Statement of the Trade, Commerce and Manufactures of the City of Cleveland for the Year 1867.

Committee of the Banks of . . . New York, Boston, Philadelphia and Baltimore. The Silver Question: Memorial to Congress, January 1878.

Cooper Institute. Proceedings at the Mass Meeting of Citizens in the Cooper Institute . . . March 24, 1874 on National Finances.

Indiana State Grange. Proceedings, 1876-1878.

National Association of Wool Manufacturers. Bulletin of the National Association of Wool Manufacturers for 1869-1878.

National Board of Trade. Proceedings of Annual Meetings for 1868-1879.

———. Debates and Action on the Subject of Currency and Finance by the National Board of Trade at its Sessions in the City of Baltimore . . . Jan. 14 and 15, 1874.

National Commercial Convention. Proceedings of the National Commercial Convention Held in Boston, Feb. 1868.

National Democratic Convention. Official Proceedings of the National Democratic Convention Held in New York, July 4-9, 1868.

National Grange. Journal of Proceedings of the National Grange (1873-1879).

Newark Board of Trade. Annual Reports for 1873-1875.

New England Cotton Manufacturers' Association. Transactions for 1866-1878.

New York Board of Trade. Memorial to Congress on the Currency of the United States (1876).

New York Board of Trade and Transportation. Proceedings of the Annual Meeting, Jan. 14, 1880.

New York Cheap Transportation Association. Proceedings of the Annual Meeting, Jan. 1877.

———. Minutes of Meetings (From Oct. 1873-Dec. 1878).

New York Produce Exchange. Reports for the Years 1872-1879.

New York State Chamber of Commerce. Annual Reports for 1865-1878.

———. Centennial Celebration at Irving Hall, April 6, 1868.

———. Memorial . . . to the Congress of the United States for the Resumption of Specie Payments, Dec. 2, 1873.

Philadelphia Board of Trade. Annual Reports for 1865-1879.

E. PAMPHLETS, PRINTED SPEECHES, AND POLEMICAL LITERATURE

Allen, William, et al. Speeches of . . . Allen . . . Pendleton . . . Thurman . . . Ewing . . . Cary . . . Southard Before the Democratic Ratification Meeting in . . . Columbus . . . June 17, 1875. Columbus, 1875.

Anonymous. The Money Agitation. New York, 1879.

———. Opinions of John C. Calhoun and Thomas Jefferson on the Subject of Paper Currency. n.p., n.d.

Atkinson, Edward. Address of Mr. Edward Atkinson on the Export of Cotton Goods at the Meeting of the New England Cotton Manufacturers' Association, April 26, 1876. n.p., 1876.

———. Senator Sherman's Fallacies; Or Honesty the Best Policy. Boston, 1868.

———. Speech Delivered by Edward Atkinson of Brookline, Mass. at a Republican Meeting in Salem. Salem, 1868.

Backus, Charles K. The Contraction of the Currency. . . . An Argument Founded on Figures and Quotations from Official Reports. . . . Chicago: Honest Money League of the Northwest, 1878.

Baird, Henry Carey. The British Credit System. Inflated Bank Credit as a Substitute for "Current Money of the Realm." Philadelphia, 1875.

———. Brief Tracts on Some Economic Questions. Third Series (1871-1888). Philadelphia, 1888.

———. Criticisms on the Recent Financial Policies of the United States and France. Philadelphia, 1875.

———. The Eastern and Western Questions. . . . Philadelphia, 1877.

———. Letters on the Crisis, the Currency, and the Credit System. Philadelphia, 1873.

———. Money and Its Substitutes. Commerce and Its Instruments of Adjustment. Philadelphia, 1876.

———. The National Finances. The Views of Henry Carey Baird. . . . n.p., n.d.

———. Political Economy. Philadelphia, 1888.

——. *Remonetization of Silver. Testimony of . . . Baird Before the United States Monetary Commission . . . October 31, 1876.* Philadelphia, 1878.

——. *The Results of the Resumption of Specie Payments in England, 1819-1823. A Lesson and a Warning to the People of the United States.* Philadelphia, 1874.

——. *Resumption of Specie Payments. Testimony of . . . Baird Before the Committee on Banking and Currency in Relation to the Resumption of Specie Payments.* Philadelphia, 1878.

Beecher, Henry Ward. *Hard Times.* Philadelphia, 1877.

Bland, Richard P. *Injustice of Monopolies: Speech . . . in the House of Representatives, June 4, 1874.*

Butler, Benjamin F. *The Currency Question. General Butler's Letter to the Editor of the Boston Daily Advertiser, Oct. 12, 1867.* n.p., n.d.

——. *Reduction of the Currency. Speech of . . . Butler . . . in the House. . . . Nov 26 and 27, 1876.* n.p., n.d.

——. *Speech of. . .Butler Upon his Bill to Authorize the Issue of a National Currency. . . . Jan. 12, 1869.* n.p., n.d.

Campbell, A[lexander]. *The True American System of Finance; the Rights of Labor and Capital, and the Common Sense Way of Doing Justice to the Soldiers and Their Families. No Banks: Greenbacks the Exclusive Currency.* Chicago, 1864.

——. *The True Greenback, Or the Way to Pay the National Debt Without Taxes and Emancipate Labor.* Chicago, 1868.

Carey, Henry C. *Appreciation in the Price of Gold: Evidence of Henry C. Carey Before the Congressional Committee for Ascertaining the Causes of Recent Changes in the Prices of the Precious Metals.* n.p., n.d.

——. *Contraction or Expansion? Repudiation or Resumption? Letters to the Honorable Hugh McCulloch, Secretary of the Treasury.* Philadelphia, 1866.

——. *The Currency Question. Letters to the Hon. Schuyler Colfax.* Chicago, 1865.

——. *Currency Inflation: How It Has Been Produced, and How It May Profitably Be Reduced. Letters to the Hon. B. H. Bristow.* Philadelphia, 1874.

——. *The Finance Minister, the Currency and the Public Debt.* Philadelphia, 1868.

——. *The Harmony of Interests, Agricultural, Manufacturing and Commercial.* Philadelphia, 1890.

——. *Monetary Independence: Letter of . . . Carey to the Hon. Moses Field.* n.p., n.d.

——. *Money.* Philadelphia, 1860.

——. *The Past, the Present and the Future.* Philadelphia, 1848.

——. *Of the Rate of Interest and Its Influence on the Relations of Capital and Labor.* Philadelphia, 1873.

——. *Reconstruction: Industrial, Financial, Political. Letters to the Hon. Henry Wilson.* Philadelphia, 1867.

——. *Resumption! How It May Profitably Be Brought About.* Philadelphia, 1869.

——. *Resumption: When, and How, Will it End? Letters to the President of the United States.* Philadelphia, 1877.

——. *Review of the Farmer's Question.* n.p., 1870.

——. *The Senate Finance Bill. Letters to the Honorable Horace Maynard, Chairman of the Committee of Banking and Currency.* Philadelphia, 1875.

——. *Shall We Have Peace? Peace Financial and Peace Political? Letters to the President-Elect of the United States.* Philadelphia, 1869.

——. *The Unity of Law; As Exhibited in the Relations of Physical, Social, Mental and Moral Science.* Philadelphia, 1872.

Carter, T. H. *The Currency Question: A Plan of Permanent Relief.* Boston, 1875.

————. *The Financial Problem: Easy Mode of Paying the National Debt.* n.p., 1874.

Cary, Samuel F. *On the Aims of the Greenback Party. The Issues of the Campaign.* New York, 1876.

Clews, Henry. *Our Monetary Evils; Some Suggestions For Their Remedy.* New York, 1872.

Cloud, D. C. *Monopolies and the People.* Davenport, Iowa, 1873.

Colwell, Stephen. *Remarks and Suggestions Upon the State and National System of Banks.* Philadelphia, 1864.

————. *The Ways and Means of Payment.* . . . Philadelphia, 1860.

D[avis], E. M. *The "Labor Reform" View of Money.* n.p., 1873.

Dean, Henry Clay. *Crimes of the Civil War and Curse of the Funding System.* Baltimore, 1868.

Deshler, John G. *A Financial System For the Granger.* . . . Columbus, 1874.

Elder, William. *Questions of the Day: Economic and Social.* Philadelphia, 1871.

Esterly, George. *A Consideration of the Currency and Finance Question.* Whitewater, Wisc., 1874.

————. *A Plan For Funding the Public Debt.* n.p., 1875.

Ewing, Thomas, Sr. *An Address by the Hon. Thomas Ewing, to the Unpledged Voters of the United States.* Columbus, 1868.

————. *Letters of the Hon. Thomas Ewing of Ohio to the Finance Committee of the Senate on the Public Debt and Currency.* Washington, 1869.

Ewing, Thomas, Jr. *Discussions by Thomas Ewing, 1829-1896.* n.p., n.d.

————. *Speech of Thomas Ewing, Jr. at Capitol Square, Columbus, Ohio, August 11, 1871.* n.p., n.d.

————. *Speech of Gen. Thomas Ewing Delivered at Ironton, Ohio, July 24, 1875.* Columbus, 1875.

————. *Speech of General Thomas Ewing at the Democratic Ratification Meeting at Lancaster, Ohio, July 15, 1876.* n.p., n.d.

————. *Speech of General Thomas Ewing Delivered at Findlay, Ohio, August 14, 1875.* n.p., n.d.

————, and Woodford, Stewart L. *Joint Discussions Between Gen. Thomas Ewing of Ohio and Gov. Stewart L. Woodford of New York on the Finance Question.* Columbus, 1876.

Freeman, Pliny. *Correspondence on National Finance from 1862 to 1875.* New York, 1876.

————. *The National Standard. Rate of Interest as a Regulator. Correspondence Between. . .Freeman . . . and . . . Hugh McCulloch.* . . . *March 20, 1865 to Nov. 22, 1865.* New York, 1872.

Gallatin, James. *Letter to the Hon. Samuel Hooper of Massachusetts.* . . . n.p., n.d.

Garfield, James A. *Suspension and Resumption of Specie Payments.* Chicago, 1879.

Green, Duff. *A Memorial and Bill Relating to Finance, National Currency, Debt, Revenue, Etc.* Memphis, 1869.

Greene, William B. *Mutual Banking. Showing the Radical Deficiency of the Recent Circulating Medium, and the Advantages of a Free Currency.* Worcester, Mass., 1870.

Groom, Wallace P. *Currency Needs of Commerce. National Paper Money Interchangeable with Government Bonds Advocated.* New York, 1873.

Grubb, Joseph. *The National Finances.* n.p., 1873.

Hazard, Rowland G. *Finance and Hours of Labor.* New York, 1868.

Heywood, E. H. *Hard Cash. An Essay to Show That Financial Monopolies Hinder Enterprise and Defraud Both Labor and Capital.* . . . Princeton, Mass., 1875.

Hill, Britton A. *Absolute Money. A New System of National Finance Under a Cooperative Government.* St. Louis, 1875.

————. *Specie Resumption and National Bankruptcy, Identical and Indivisible.* . . . *A Final Appeal for* the Repeal of the "Specie Resumption Act." St. Louis, 1876.

Honest Money League of Cincinnati. Address, Constitution and Platform of the Honest Money Leagues of Cincinnati and Franklin County. Columbus, 1879.

Honest Money League of the Northwest. Extracts from Some of the Communistic, Inflammatory and Treasonable Documents Circulated by the National Greenback Party. Chicago, 1878.

Horton, S. Dana. The Monetary Situation. An Address Delivered by Request of the American Social Science Association in Cincinnati, May 21, 1878. Cincinnati, 1878.

Hughes, Robert W. A Popular Treatise on the Currency Question Written from a Southern Point of View. New York, 1879.

Johnston, John. An Address on the Currency Delivered Before the Literary Society and Citizens of Bay View [Wisconsin]. n.p., 1878.

Kelley, William D. Conversation with Horatio Seymour on the National Debt and Taxes. Speech of . . . Kelley at Spring Garden Hall, Sept. 8, 1868. Philadelphia, 1868.

———. The Finances. Washington Correspondence of the Philadelphia Press, Giving the Views of the Hon. Wm. D. Kelley. . .Oct. 30, 1873. Philadelphia, 1873.

———. How and When Our War Debt Can Be Paid. Washington, 1867.

———. Judge Kelley on the Crisis. Philadelphia, 1874.

———. Speeches, Addresses and Letters on Industrial and Financial Questions. Philadelphia, 1872.

———, et al. Opinions of Our National Banks. . . Expressed by William D. Kelley, Demas Barnes. . . . Washington, 1868.

[Kellogg, Edward]. Currency: The Evil and the Remedy. n.p., 1844(?).

———. Labor and Other Capital: The Rights of Each Secured and the Wrongs of Both Eradicated. New York, 1849.

———. A New Monetary System: The Only Means of Securing the Respective Rights of Labor and Property and Protecting the Public from Financial Revulsions. New York, 1868.

———. Remarks Upon Usury and Its Effects: A National Bank a Remedy. New York, 1841.

Knox, John Jay. Address of John Jay Knox to the Annual Convention of the American Bankers' Association, August 1879. New York, 1879.

Leavitt, Samuel. Our Money Wars. The Example and Warning of American Finance. Boston, 1896.

[Locke, David R.]. Inflation at the Crossroads, Being a History of the Rise and Fall of the Onlimited Trust and Confidence Company, of Confederit X Roads, by Petroleum V. Nasby. New York, 1875.

Low, A. A. Address by Mr. A. A. Low Before the Chamber of Commerce of the State of New York . . . and Resolution Adopted by the Chamber, Feb. 24, 1876. New York, 1876.

McCabe, James Dabney. History of the Grange Movement: Or the Farmer's War Against Monopolies. Chicago, 1874.

McCulloch, Hugh. Our National and Financial Future: Address of Hon. Hugh McCulloch, Secretary of the Treasury, at Fort Wayne, Indiana, Oct. 11, 1865. Fort Wayne, 1865.

Magwire, John. Response of John Magwire to a Resolution of the National Labor Council . . . Giving His Views of a Just System of American Finance. St. Louis, 1874.

Mason, John. An Exposition of the Principles of Money. San Francisco, 1877.

Medill, Joseph. Payment of the Debt. A Review of the Ohio Democratic Financial Departure Before the Young Men's Republican Club at Columbus, Ohio, August 31, 1871. Chicago, 1871.

Nichol, Thomas. An Argument in Favor of Honest Money and Redeemable Currency. Chicago, 1878.

———. Fiat Money, Or Resumption for Workingmen, Considered from the Standpoint of their Own Self-Interest. Boston, 1878.

———. The Labor Question in Its Relation to Political Parties: An Address to Workingmen. Milwaukee, 1886.

Nieuwland, Edward J. Political and Financial Independence from Ring Rule. n.p., 1878.

Oaksmith, Appleton. Southern State Debts and the National Currency System. Baltimore [1874].

Opdyke, George. Letter on National Finances. . .to Hon. Roscoe Conkling. New York, 1869.

———. Memorial. Minority Report of the Chamber of Commerce Committee. n.p., n.d.

"A Patriot." The Financial Situation. [New York, 1865].

———. Our National Finances. A Review. . .of the Report of the Secretary of the Treasury. New York, 1865.

———. Our National Finances No. 10. Plain Facts for the Plain People. New York, 1865.

Pendleton, George H. Payment of the Public Debt in Legal Tender Notes. Speech of the Hon. George H. Pendleton, Milwaukee, Nov. 2, 1867. n.p., n.d.

Periam, Jonathan. The Groundswell. A History of the Origins, Aims and Progress of the Farmers' Movement. . . . .Cincinnati, 1874.

Pomeroy, Marcus Mills. Hot Drops Nos. 1-4. n.p., n.d.

———. Soliloquies of the Bondholder, the Poor Farmer, the Soldier's Widow . . . and Other Political Articles. New York, 1866.

Poor, Henry Varnum. Resumption and the Silver Question. . . . New York, 1878.

Preadmore, James Harker. A Treatise on Finance and Currency. . . . Sacramento, 1873.

Price, Bonamy. The Principles of Currency; and the Error of Inflation. New York, 1875.

———. Currency and Banking. New York, 1876.

[Randolph, Charles]. The Future Currencies of the United States. . . . Chicago, 1877.

Reform League Broadsides, Nos. 1-39; June 1, 1869-Oct. 29, 1870.

Richardson, D. M. Policy of Finance. A Plan for Returning to Specie Payments, without Financial Revulsion. Detroit, 1869.

Ropes, Joseph. The Currency. Boston, 1868.

Sanborn, J. K. Currency, Money, Coin: How Made and Why Used. Williamsport, Pa., 1874.

Schuckers, Jacob W. The Currency Conflict. n.p., n.d.

———. The Finances: Panics and Specie-Payments. Philadelphia, 1874.

Seyd, Ernest. Bullion and Foreign Exchanges Theoretically and Practically Considered. London, 1868.

———. Suggestions in Reference to the Metallic Currency of the United States of America. London, 1871.

Sherman, John. The New Departure. Washington, 1871.

———. Public Debt and Currency. Washington, 1867.

———. Speech of Hon. John Sherman of Ohio on the Financial and Other Issues of the Times. Delivered at Portland, Maine, July 23, 1879. n.p., n.d.

———. Speech Delivered by Hon. John Sherman, Secretary of the Treasury at Mansfield, Ohio . . . August 17, 1877. Washington, 1877.

———. Speech of John Sherman, Secretary of the Treasury Delivered at Toledo. . .August 26, 1878. Washington, 1878.

Sherwood, Isaac R. The Currency. n.p., n.d.

Smith, Matthew Hale. Twenty Years Among the Bulls and Bears of Wall Street. Hartford, 1870.

Sumner, William Graham. American Finance. Cambridge, 1874.

Walker, Amasa. *Corn, Cotton and Currency.* n.p., n.d.

———. *The Currency Question.* New York, 1876.

———. *The National Currency and the Money Problem.* New York, 1876.

Walker, John Brisben. *An American System of Finance.* Washington, 1878.

Warren, Marvin. *American Labor: Its Great Wrongs, and How It Can Redress Them.* . . . St. Joseph, Mo., 1877.

Wells, David A. *Contraction of Legal Tender Notes vs. Repudiation and Disloyalty.* New York, 1876.

———. *The Cremation Theory of Specie Resumption.* New York, 1875.

———. *Robinson Crusoe's Money.* New York, 1892.

———. *The Silver Question. The Dollar of the Fathers versus the Dollar of the Sons.* New York, 1877.

"The West and the South." *Governor Dix on the Currency.* n.p., n.d.

"A Western Farmer." *Our Finances. Inflation, Expansion or Contraction, Which Shall It Be?* The East versus the West and South. Hartford, 1874.

Weston, George M. *The Silver Question.* New York, 1878.

Wilkeson, Samuel. *How Our National Debt May Be A National Blessing.* Philadelphia, 1865.

Williams, John E. *Short Road to Specie-Currency.* New York, 1875.

Willson, Hugh Bowlby. *A Plea for Uncle Sam's Money; Or Greenbacks versus Bank Notes.* New York, 1870.

Wilson, George, Jr. *The Greenbackers and Their Doctrines.* Lexington, Mo., 1878.

Winder, W. H. *An Exposition of Currency and Free Trade. Specie Payment and Free Trade Inseparable.* New York, 1877.

Wingate, R. F. *An Address by Hon. R. F. Wingate on American Finance; Its Evils and Remedies.* St. Louis, 1874.

Winsor, Henry. *Our Currency. By A Merchant.* Philadelphia, 1871.

Woodhull, Victoria. *A Speech on the Principles of Finance. . .Delivered at Cooper Institute.* New York, 1871.

F. AUTOBIOGRAPHIES, MEMOIRS, AND COLLECTIONS OF PRINTED LETTERS

Adams, Henry. *The Education of Henry Adams.* New York: Random House, 1931.

Bancroft, Frederic (ed.). *Speeches, Correspondence and Political Papers of Carl Schurz.* New York: G. P. Putnam's Sons, 1913.

Boutwell, George Sewall. *Reminiscences of Sixty Years in Public Affairs.* New York: McClure, Phillips and Co., 1902.

Brinkerhoff, Roeliff. *Recollections of A Lifetime.* Cincinnati: The Robert Clarke Company, 1904.

Butler, Benjamin F. *Autobiography and Personal Reminiscences of Major-General Benjamin F. Butler: Butler's Book.* Boston: A. M. Thayer and Co., 1892.

Carman, Harry J.; David, Henry; and Guthrie, Paul N. (eds.). *The Path I Trod: The Autobiography of Terence V. Powderly.* New York: Columbia University Press, 1940.

Cater, Harold Dean (ed.). *Henry Adams and His Friends: A Collection of His Unpublished Letters.* Boston: Houghton Mifflin Company, 1947.

Clews, Henry. *Twenty-Eight Years in Wall Street.* New York: Irving Publishing Co., 1888.

Ford, Worthington Chauncey (ed.). *Letters of Henry Adams, 1858-1891.* Boston: Houghton Mifflin Company, 1930.

Hinsdale, Mary L. (ed.). *Garfield-Hinsdale Letters. Correspondence Between James Abram Garfield* and Burke Aaron Hinsdale. Ann Arbor: University of Michigan Press, 1949.

Hoar, George F. *Autobiography of Seventy Years.* New York: Charles Scribner's Sons, 1906.

Hughes, Sarah Forbes (ed.). *Letters and Recollection of John Murray Forbes.* Boston: Houghton Mifflin and Company, 1899.

McCulloch, Hugh. *Men and Measures of Half a Century.* New York: Charles Scribner's Sons, 1900.

Schurz, Carl. *The Reminiscences of Carl Schurz.* New York: The McClure Co., 1908.

Sherman, John. *Recollections of Forty Years in the House, Senate and Cabinet.* Chicago: The Werner Co., 1895.

Thorndike, Rachel Sherman (ed.). *The Sherman Letters: Correspondence Between General and Senator Sherman from 1837 to 1891.* New York: Charles Scribner's Sons, 1894.

Williams, Charles Richard (ed.). *Diary and Letters of Rutherford Birchard Hayes, Nineteenth President of the United States.* Columbus: The Ohio State Archeological and Historical Society, 1924.

G. BOOKS, TEXTS, AND ARTICLES
BY CONTEMPORARIES

Adams, Henry. "The Session," *North American Review,* cxi (July 1870).

Bowen, Francis. *American Political Economy; Including Strictures on the Management of the Currency and the Finances Since 1861.* New York: Charles Scribner's Sons, 1887.

———. *The Principles of Political Economy. . . .* Boston: Little, Brown and Company, 1859.

Bradford, Gamaliel. "The Treasury Reports," *North American Review,* cx (January 1870).

Carey, Henry C. *Principles of Political Economy.* Philadelphia: Carey, Lea and Blanchard, 1837-1840.

———. *Principles of Social Science.* Philadelphia: J. B. Lippincott Company, 1888.

Garfield, James A. "The Currency Conflict," *Atlantic Monthly,* xxxvii (February 1876).

Kelley, Oliver H. *Origin and Progress of the Order of the Patrons of Husbandry.* Philadelphia: J. A. Wagenseller, 1875.

Opdyke, George. *A Treatise on Political Economy.* New York: G. P. Putnam, 1851.

Perry, Arthur Latham. *Elements of Political Economy.* New York: Charles Scribner and Company, 1866.

———. *An Introduction to Political Economy.* New York: Charles Scribner's Sons, 1877.

Say, Jean-Baptiste. *A Treatise on Political Economy; Or the Production, Distribution, and Consumption of Wealth.* Philadelphia: J. B. Lippincott and Co., 1860.

Smith, E. Peshine. *A Manual of Political Economy.* New York: G. P. Putnam and Sons, 1868.

Sumner, William Graham. *A History of American Currency.* New York: Henry Holt and Company, 1874.

Walker, Amasa. *The Science of Wealth, A Manual of Political Economy.* Boston: Little, Brown and Company, 1866.

Walker, Francis A. *Money.* New York: Henry Holt and Company, 1877.

Wayland, Francis. *The Elements of Political Economy.* Boston: Gould and Lincoln, 1860.

H. MISCELLANEOUS PRIMARY

Bryce, James. *The American Commonwealth.* London: Macmillan and Company, 1891.

Commons, John R. *et al. A Documentary History of American Industrial Society.* Cleveland: The Arthur H. Clark Company, 1910.

Merchants' and Bankers' Almanac for 1870.

National Democratic Convention. *Official Proceedings. . .July 4-9, 1868.* Boston, 1868.

Richardson, James D. (ed.). *A Compilation of the Messages and Papers of the Presidents.* n.p. Bureau of National Literature and Art, 1903.

U.S. Bureau of the Census. *Historical Statistics of the United States. Colonial Times to 1957.* Washington: Government Printing Office, 1960.

Wallace, John William (Reporter). *Cases Argued and Adjudged in the Supreme Court of the United States.* Vols. VIII and XII. Washington: W. H. and O. H. Morrison, 1870 and 1872.

II. SECONDARY MATERIALS

A. BOOKS: GENERAL HISTORIES, SPECIAL STUDIES, MONOGRAPHS AND COLLECTION OF ESSAYS

Abell, Aaron Ignatius. *The Urban Impact on American Protestantism, 1865-1900.* Cambridge: Harvard University Press, 1943.

Acworth, Angus W. *Financial Reconstruction in England, 1815-1822.* London: P. S. King and Son, 1925.

Adams, Charles Francis, Jr., and Adams, Henry. *Chapters of Erie.* Ithaca, New York: Great Seal Books, 1956.

Ashton, T. S., and Sayers, R. S. (eds.). *Papers in English Monetary History.* Oxford: at the Clarendon Press, 1953.

Bailey, L[iberty] H[yde]. *The Country Life Movement in the United States.* New York: The Macmillan Co., 1911.

Barrett, Don Carlos. *The Greenbacks and Resumption of Specie Payments, 1862-1879.* Cambridge: Harvard University Press, 1931.

Beale, Howard K. *The Critical Year: A Study of Andrew Johnson and Reconstruction.* New York: Harcourt, Brace and Company, 1930.

Beard, Charles A., and Mary R. *The Rise of American Civilization.* Revised one volume college edition. New York: The Macmillan Co., 1944.

Beer, M. *Early British Economics from the XIIIth to the Middle of the XVIIIth Century.* London: George Allen and Unwin, Ltd., 1938.

Bell, Daniel. *The End of Ideology.* Glencoe, Ill.: The Free Press, 1960.

Benson, Lee. *Turner and Beard: American Historical Writing Reconsidered.* Glencoe, Ill.: The Free Press, 1960.

———. *Merchants, Farmers and Railroads: Railroad Regulation and New York Politics, 1850-1887.* Cambridge: Harvard University Press, 1955.

Bentley, Arthur F. *The Condition of the Western Farmers as Illustrated by the Economic History of a Nebraska Township.* Baltimore: The Johns Hopkins Press, 1893.

Bernard, Luther Lee, and Bernard, Jessie. *Origins of American Sociology: The Social Science Movement in the United States.* New York: Thomas Y. Crowell Company, 1943.

Binkley, Wilfred E. *American Political Parties, Their Natural Histo-*

ry. New York: Alfred Knopf, 1945.

Blinkoff, Maurice. *The Influence of Charles A. Beard Upon American Historiography.* The University of Buffalo Studies: Vol. xii, Monographs in History No. 4, May 1936.

Bodo, John R. *The Protestant Clergy and Public Issues, 1812-1848.* Princeton: Princeton University Press, 1954.

Bogart, Ernest Ludlow, and Thompson, Charles Manfred. *The Industrial State, 1870-1893.* Vol. iv of *The Centennial History of Illinois.* Springfield: Illinois Centennial Commission, 1920.

Bogue, Allan G. *Money At Interest: The Farm Mortgage on the Middle Border.* Ithaca, New York: Cornell University Press, 1955.

Bolles, Albert Sidney. *The Financial History of the United States from 1861 to 1885.* New York: D. Appleton and Co., 1894.

Bruce, Robert V. *1877: Year of Violence.* Indianapolis: The Bobbs-Merrill Company, 1959.

Bruckberger, R. L. *Image of America.* London: Longmans, Green and Co., 1959.

Buck, Paul H. *The Road to Reunion, 1865-1900.* Boston: Little, Brown and Company, 1937.

Buck, Solon Justus. *The Agrarian Crusade, A Chronicle of the Farmer in Politics.* New Haven: Yale University Press, 1920.

————. *The Granger Movement: A Study of Agricultural Organization and Its Political, Economic and Social Manifestations, 1870-1880.* Cambridge: Harvard University Press, 1913.

Cannan, Edwin. *The Paper Pound of 1797-1821.* London: P. S. King and Son, Ltd., 1919.

Catterall, Ralph C. H. *The Second Bank of the United States.* Chicago: The University of Chicago Press, 1903.

Clapham, J. H. *An Economic History of Modern Britain.* Vol. i: *The Early Railway Age.* Cambridge

(England): Cambridge University Press, 1950.

————. *The Economic Development of France and Germany, 1815-1914.* Cambridge (England): Cambridge University Press, 1951.

Clark, Victor S. *History of Manufactures in the United States.* Vol. ii, 1860-1893. New York: Peter Smith, 1949.

Cochran, Thomas C. *Railroad Leaders, 1845-1890: The Business Mind in Action.* Cambridge: Harvard University Press, 1953.

————, and Miller, William. *The Age of Enterprise: A Social History of Industrial America.* New York: The Macmillan Company, 1942.

Cole, Arthur Charles. *The Era of the Civil War, 1848-1870.* Vol. iii of *The Centennial History of Illinois.* Springfield, Illinois Centennial Commission, 1919.

Cole, Arthur Harrison. *The American Wool Manufacture.* Cambridge: Harvard University Press, 1926.

Cole, Charles C. *The Social Ideas of the Northern Evangelists, 1826-1860.* New York: Columbia University Press, 1954.

Coleman, Charles H. *The Election of 1868: The Democratic Effort to Regain Control.* New York, 1933.

Commons, John R. and associates. *History of Labour in the United States.* New York: The Macmillan Co., 1918-1935.

Copeland, Melvin Thomas. *The Cotton Manufacturing Industry of the United States.* Cambridge: Harvard University Press, 1912.

Curti, Merle. *The Growth of American Thought.* New York: Harper and Brothers, 1951.

Davis, Andrew McFarland. *The Origins of the National Banking System.* Washington: Government Printing Office, 1910.

Destler, Chester McArthur. *American Radicalism, 1865-1901: Essays and Documents.* New London, Conn.: Connecticut College, 1946.

Dewey, Davis Rich. *Financial History of the United States.* New York: Longmans Green and Company, 1934.

Dorfman, Joseph. *The Economic Mind In American Civilization.* New York: The Viking Press, 1946-1959.

Dunne, Gerald T. *Monetary Decisions of the Supreme Court.* New Brunswick, N. J.: Rutgers University Press, 1960.

Eiselen, Malcolm Rogers. *The Rise of Pennsylvania Protectionism.* Philadelphia: the Author, 1932.

Eliot, Clara. *The Farmer's Campaign for Credit.* New York: D. Appleton and Company, 1927.

Esary, Logan. *History of Indiana From Its Exploration to 1922.* Dayton, Ohio: Historical Publishing Co., 1924.

Fels, Rendigs. *American Business Cycles, 1865-1897.* Chapel Hill: University of North Carolina Press, 1959.

Ferleger, Herbert Ronald. *David A. Wells and the American Revenue System, 1865-1870.* New York, 1942.

Fine, Nathan. *Labor and Farmer Parties in the United States, 1828-1928.* New York: Rand School of Social Science, 1928.

Fine, Sidney. *Laissez Faire and the General-Welfare State: A Study of Conflict in American Thought, 1865-1901.* Ann Arbor: The University of Michigan Press, 1956.

Fite, Emerson D. *Social and Industrial Conditions in the North During the Civil War.* New York: Peter Smith, 1930.

Foner, Philip. *History of the Labor Movement in the United States.* New York: International Publishers, 1947.

Gardner, Charles M. *The Grange: Friend of the Farmer.* Washington: The National Grange, 1949.

Gibson, Florence E. *The Attitudes of the New York Irish Toward State and National Affairs, 1848-1892.* New York, 1951.

Gouge, William M. *A Short History of Paper Money and Banking in the United States. . . .* Philadelphia, 1833.

Gras, N. S. B., and Larson, Henrietta M. *Casebook in American Business History.* New York: Appleton-Century-Crofts, Inc., 1939.

Green, Robert W. (ed.). *Protestantism and Capitalism: The Weber Thesis and Its Critics.* Boston: D. C. Heath and Co., 1959.

Greer, Thomas H. *American Social Reform Movements. Their Pattern Since 1865.* New York: Prentice-Hall, Inc., 1949.

Grimes, Alan Pendleton. *The Political Liberalism of the New York Nation, 1865-1932.* Chapel Hill: University of North Carolina Press, 1953.

Griswold, A. Whitney. *Farming and Democracy.* New York: Harcourt, Brace and Company, 1948.

Grob, Gerald. *Workers and Utopia: A Study of Ideological Conflict in the American Labor Movement, 1865-1900.* [Evanston, Ill.]: Northwestern University Press, 1961.

Hacker, Louis M. *The Triumph of American Capitalism.* New York: Columbia University Press, 1947.

Hammond, Bray. *Banks and Politics in America, from the Revolution to the Civil War.* Princeton: Princeton University Press, 1957.

Harris, Seymour E. (ed.). *American Economic History.* New York: McGraw Hill Book Company, 1961.

Harrod, Roy. *The Dollar.* London: Macmillan and Company, 1953.

Haynes, Fred E. *Third Party Movements Since the Civil War, with Special Reference to Iowa: A Study in Social Politics.* Iowa City: The State Historical Society of Iowa, 1916.

Hepburn, A. Barton. *History of Coinage and Currency in the United States and the Perennial Contest for Sound Money.* New York: The Macmillan Co., 1903.

Hicks, John D. *The Populist Revolt: A History of the Farmer's Alli-*

ance and the People's Party. Minneapolis: The University of Minnesota Press, 1931.

Hoffer, Eric. The True Believer: Thoughts on the Nature of Mass Movements. New York: Harper Brothers, 1951.

Hofstadter, Richard. The Age of Reform, From Bryan to F.D.R. New York: Alfred Knopf, 1956.

————. The American Political Tradition and the Men Who Made It. New York: Alfred Knopf, 1949.

————. Social Darwinism In American Thought. Boston: The Beacon Press, 1955.

Hoogenboom, Ari. Outlawing the Spoils: A History of the Civil Service Reform Movement, 1865-1883. Urbana: University of Illinois Press, 1961.

Hubbart, Henry Clyde. The Older Middle West, 1840-1880. New York: D. Appleton-Century, 1936.

Hunt, R. L. A History of Farmer Movements in the Southwest, 1873-1925. n.p., n.d.

Johnson, E. A. J. American Economic Thought in the Seventeenth Century. London: P. S. King and Son, Ltd., 1932.

————. Predecessors of Adam Smith. The Growth of British Economic Thought. New York: Prentice-Hall, Inc., 1937.

Johnson, Emory R. et al. History of Domestic and Foreign Commerce of the United States. Washington: Carnegie Institution of Washington, 1915.

Jordon, Phillip D. Ohio Comes of Age, 1873-1900. Vol. v of The History of the State of Ohio. Columbus: Ohio State Archeological and Historical Society, 1943.

Josephson, Matthew. The Politicos; 1865-1896. New York: Harcourt, Brace and Co., 1938.

Kirkland, Edward Chase. Business in the Gilded Age. Madison: University of Wisconsin Press, 1952.

————. Dream and Thought in the Business Community, 1860-1900.

Ithaca, N.Y.: Cornell University Press, 1956.

————. Industry Comes of Age. Business, Labor, and Public Policy, 1860-1897. New York: Holt, Rinehart, and Winston, 1961.

Klement, Frank L. The Copperheads in the Middle West. Chicago: The University of Chicago Press, 1960.

Knox, John Jay. A History of Banking in the United States. New York: Bradford Rhodes and Company, 1900.

————. United States Notes: A History of the Various Issues of Paper Money by the Government of the United States. New York: Charles Scribner's Sons, 1884.

Kramer, Dale. The Wild Jackasses: The American Farmer in Revolt. New York: Hastings House, Publishers, 1956.

Laughlin, J. Laurence. The History of Bimetallism in the United States. New York: D. Appleton and Company, 1897.

McNeill, George E. (ed.). The Labor Movement: The Problem of Today. Boston: A. M. Bridgeman and Co., 1887.

McWilliams, Carey. A Mask for Privilege: Anti-Semitism in America. Boston: Little, Brown and Company, 1948.

Madeleine, Sister M. Grace. Monetary and Banking Theories of Jacksonian Democracy. Philadelphia, 1943.

Marget, Arthur. The Theory of Prices: A Reexamination of the Central Problems of Monetary Thought. New York: Prentice-Hall, Inc. 1938.

Martin, Joseph G. A Century of Finance. Martin's History of the Boston Stock and Money Markets. . . . Boston: the Author, 1898.

Merrill, Horace S. Bourbon Democracy of the Middle West, 1865-1896. Baton Rouge: Louisiana State University Press, 1953

Merrill, Louis Taylor. General Benjamin F. Butler and the Campaign of 1868. Private edition distributed by the University of Chicago Libraries, 1939.

Miller, Harry E. *Banking Theories in the United States Before 1860.* Cambridge: Harvard University Press, 1927.

Miller, Perry. *The New England Mind: From Colony to Province.* Cambridge: Harvard University Press, 1953.

Miller, William (ed.). *Men in Business: Essays in the History of Entrepreneurship.* Cambridge: Harvard University Press, 1952.

Mints, Lloyd W. *A History of Banking Theory in Great Britain and the United States.* Chicago: University of Chicago Press, 1945.

Mitchell, Wesley Clair. *Gold, Prices and Wages under the Greenback Standard.* Berkeley: The University [of California] Press, 1908.

———. *A History of the Greenbacks, With Special Reference to the Economic Consequences of their Issue, 1862-1865.* Chicago: University of Chicago Press, 1903.

Mott, Frank Luther. *A History of American Magazine, 1865-1885.* Cambridge: Harvard University Press, 1938.

Mudge, Eugene Tenbroek. *The Social Philosophy of John Taylor of Caroline.* New York: Columbia University Press, 1939.

Myers, Margaret G. *The New York Money Market.* New York: Columbia University Press, 1931.

Niebyl, Karl H. *Studies in the Classical Theories of Money.* New York: Columbia University Press, 1946.

Noyes, Alexander Dana. *Forty Years of American Finance: A Short Financial History of the Government and People of the United States Since the Civil War, 1865-1907.* New York: G. P. Putnam's Sons, 1909.

Nussbaum, Arthur. *Money in the Law, National and International.* Brooklyn: The Foundation Press, Inc., 1950.

Nye, Russel Blaine. *The Cultural Life of the New Nation, 1776-1830.* New York: Harper and Bros., 1960.

Oberholtzer, Ellis Paxson. *A History of the United States Since the Civil War.* New York: The Macmillan Co., 1926.

O'Conner, Michael J. L. *Origins of Academic Economics in the United States.* New York: Columbia University Press, 1944.

Paine, A. E. *The Granger Movement in Illinois.* Urbana: The University [of Illinois], 1904.

Parrington, Vernon Louis. *The Beginnings of Critical Realism in America.* Vol. iii of *Main Currents in American Thought.* New York: Harcourt, Brace, and Company, 1930.

Patterson, Robert T. *Federal Debt-Management Policies, 1865-1879.* Durham, N. C.: Duke University Press, 1954.

Perlman, Mark. *Labor Union Theories in America: Background and Development.* Evanston, Ill.: Row, Peterson and Company, 1958.

Plunkett, Sir Horace. *The Rural Life Problem of the United States.* New York: The Macmillan Company, 1912.

Porter, George H. *Ohio Politics During the Civil War Period.* New York, 1911.

Powell, Thomas E. (ed.). *The Democratic Party of Ohio.* n.p., The Ohio Publishing Co., 1913.

Pressly, Thomas J. *Americans Interpret Their Civil War.* Princeton: Princeton University Press, 1954.

Randall, Emelius O., and Ryan, Daniel J. *History of Ohio: The Rise and Progress of An American State.* New York: The Century History Co., 1912.

Ratner, Sidney. *American Taxation: Its History as a Social Force in Democracy.* New York: W. W. Norton and Co., 1942.

Redlich, Fritz. *Essays in American Economic History.* n.p., 1944.

———. *History of American Business Leaders: A Series of Studies.* Ann Arbor: Edwards Brothers, 1940.

——. *Molding of American Banking: Men and Ideas.* New York: Hafner Publishing Company, 1951.

Rhodes, James Ford. *History of the United States from the Compromise of 1850 to the Final Restoration of Home Rule at the South in 1877.* New York: The Macmillan Company, 1893-1927.

Rist, Charles. *History of Monetary and Credit Theory from John Law to the Present Day.* New York: The Macmillan Company, 1940.

Roll, Eric. *A History of Economic Thought.* New York: Prentice Hall, Inc., 1942.

Roseboom, Eugene. *A History of Presidential Elections.* New York: The Macmillan Company, 1958.

——. *The Civil War Era, 1850-1873.* Vol. IV of *The History of the State of Ohio.* Columbus: Ohio State Archeological and Historical Society, 1944.

Ross, Earle Dudley. *The Liberal Republican Movement.* New York: Henry Holt and Company, 1919.

Rostow, W. W. *The British Economy of the Nineteenth Century.* Oxford: at the Clarendon Press, 1948.

Russell, Henry B. *International Monetary Conferences, Their Purposes, Character, and Results . . . .* New York: Harper and Brothers, 1898.

Saloutos, Theodore. *Farmer Movements in the South, 1865-1933.* Berkeley: University of California Press, 1960.

Savelle, Max. *Seeds of Liberty: The Genesis of the American Mind.* New York: Alfred Knopf, 1948.

Schlack, Adolf W., and Henning, D. C. (eds.). *History of Schuylkill County, Pennsylvania.* n.p., State Historical Association, 1907.

Shannon, Fred A. *The Farmer's Last Frontier: Agriculture, 1860-1897.* New York: Rinehart and Co., Inc., 1945.

Sharkey, Robert P. *Money, Class, and Party: An Economic Study*

of Civil War and Reconstruction. Baltimore: The Johns Hopkins Press, 1959.

Smith, Henry Nash. *Virgin Land: The American West as Symbol and Myth.* New York: Vintage Books, 1957.

Smith, Timothy L. *Revivalism and Social Reform in Mid-Nineteenth-Century America.* New York: Abingdon Press, 1962.

Smith, Walter Buckingham. *Economic Aspects of the Second Bank of the United States.* Cambridge: Harvard University Press, 1953.

Sparks, Earl Sylvester. *History and Theory of Agricultural Credit in the United States.* New York: Thomas Y. Crowell Company, 1932.

Spaulding, Elbridge Gerry. *History of the Legal Tender Paper Money Issued During the Great Rebellion. . . .* Buffalo: Express Printing Company, 1869.

Sprague, O. M. W. (ed.). *Economic Essays by Charles Francis Dunbar.* New York: The Macmillan Company, 1904.

——. *History of Crises Under the National Banking System.* Senate Miscellaneous Document No. 538, 61 Cong., 2 sess.

Sraffa, Piero (ed.). *The Works and Correspondence of David Ricardo.* Cambridge (England): The University Press, 1951.

Staff, Board of Governors of the Federal Reserve System. *Banking Studies.* n.p., 1941.

Stebbins, Homer A. *A Political History of the State of New York, 1865-1869.* New York, 1913.

Stedman, Murray S., Jr., and Stedman, Susan W. *Discontent at the Polls: A Study of Farmer and Labor Parties, 1827-1948.* New York: Columbia University Press, 1950.

Stover, John F. *The Railroads of the South, 1865-1900. A Study in Finance and Control.* Chapel Hill: University of North Carolina Press, 1955.

Strout, Cushing. *The Pragmatic Revolt in American History: Carl Becker and Charles A. Beard.* New Haven: Yale University Press, 1958.

Studenski, Paul, and Krooss, Herman E. *Financial History of the United States.* New York: McGraw Hill Book Company, Inc., 1952.

Swank, James M. *History of the Manufacture of Iron in All Ages* . . . . Philadelphia: American Iron and Steel Association, 1892.

Tarbell, Ida M. *The Tariff in Our Times.* New York: The Macmillan Co., 1911.

Taylor, Charles H. (ed.). *History of the Board of Trade of the City of Chicago.* Chicago: Robert O. Law Co., 1917.

Taylor, George Rogers. *The Transportation Revolution, 1815-1860.* New York: Rinehart and Company, 1951.

Thomas, Harrison Cook. *The Return of the Democratic Party to Power in 1884.* New York: Columbia University Press, 1919.

Usher, Ellis B. *The Greenback Movement of 1875-1884 and Wisconsin's Part in It.* Milwaukee, 1911.

Vickers, Douglas. *Studies in the Theory of Money, 1690-1776.* Philadelphia: Chilton Company, 1959.

Viner, Jacob. *Studies in the Theory of International Trade.* New York: Harper and Brothers, 1937.

Ware, Caroline F. *The Early New England Cotton Manufacture: A Study in Industrial Beginnings.* Boston: Houghton Mifflin Company, 1931.

Ware, Norman J. *The Labor Movement in the United States,*

1860-1895: A Study in Democracy. Gloucester, Mass.: Peter Smith, 1959.

Warren, Charles. *The Supreme Court in United States History.* Boston: Little, Brown, and Company, 1926.

Wells, David A. *Recent Economic Changes.* New York: D. Appleton and Co., 1895.

Wilhite, Virgil Glenn. *Founders of American Economic Thought and Policy.* New York: Bookman Associates, 1958.

Williamson, Harold Francis (ed.). *The Growth of the American Economy.* New York: Prentice-Hall, 1951.

Wish, Harvey. *The American Historian: A Social-Intellectual History of the Writing of the American Past.* New York: Oxford University Press, 1960.

Woodward, C. Vann. *Reunion and Reaction: The Compromise of 1877 and the End of Reconstruction.* Boston: Little, Brown and Company, 1951.

Wright, Ivan. *Bank Credit and Agriculture Under the National and Federal Reserve Banking Systems.* New York: McGraw-Hill Book Company, 1922.

Young, Edward. *Labor in Europe and America: A Special Report on the Rates of Wages, the Cost of Subsistence, and the Condition of the Working Classes in Great Britain, France, Belgium, Germany. . .also in the United States and British America.* Philadelphia: S. A. George and Co., 1875.

Zornow, William Frank. *Lincoln and the Party Divided.* Norman, Okla.: University of Oklahoma Press, 1954.

B. BOOKS: BIOGRAPHIES

Adams, Charles Francis, Jr. *Richard Henry Dana, A Biography.* Boston: Houghton Mifflin and Company, 1891.

Barnard, Harry. *Rutherford B. Hayes and His America.* Indianap-

olis: The Bobbs-Merrill Company, Inc., 1954.

Belden, Thomas Graham, and Belden, Marva Robins. *So Fell the Angels.* Boston: Little, Brown and Company, 1956.

Bloss, G. M. D. *Life and Speeches of George H. Pendleton.* Cincinnati, 1868.

Burton, Theodore E. *John Sherman.* Boston: Houghton Mifflin and Company, 1906.

Byars, William Vincent. *An American Commoner; The Life and Times of Richard Parks Bland.* Columbia, Mo.: E. W. Stephens, 1900.

Caldwell, Robert Granville. *James A. Garfield, Party Chieftain.* New York: Dodd, Mead and Company, 1931.

Cary, Edward. *George William Curtis.* Boston: Houghton Mifflin and Co., 1894.

Chandler, Alfred D. *Henry Varnum Poor: Business Editor, Analyst and Reformer.* Cambridge: Harvard University Press, 1956.

Current, Richard Nelson. *Old Thad Stevens: A Story of Ambition.* Madison: University of Wisconsin Press, 1942.

Eckenrode, Hamilton James. *Rutherford B. Hayes, Statesman of Reunion.* New York: Dodd, Mead and Company, 1930.

Elder, William. *A Memoir of Henry C. Carey.* Philadelphia: The American Iron and Steel Association, 1880.

Fairman, Charles. *Mr. Justice Miller and the Supreme Court, 1862-1890.* Cambridge: Harvard University Press, 1939.

Flick, Alexander C. *Samuel Jones Tilden: A Study in Political Sagacity.* New York: Dodd, Mead and Company, 1939.

Foulke, William Dudley. *Life of Oliver P. Morton.* Indianapolis: The Bowen-Merrill Company, 1899.

Freidel, Frank. *Francis Lieber, Nineteenth Century Liberal.* Baton Rouge: Louisiana State University Press, 1947.

Fuess, Claude M. *Carl Schurz, Reformer.* New York: Dodd, Mead and Co., 1932.

Green, Arnold W. *Henry Charles Carey, Nineteenth Century Sociologist.* Philadelphia: University of Pennsylvania Press, 1951.

Grodinsky, Julius. *Jay Gould: His Business Career, 1867-1892.* Philadelphia: University of Pennsylvania Press, 1957.

Grossman, Jonathan P. *William Sylvis, Pioneer of American Labor: A Study of the Labor Movement During the Era of the Civil War.* New York, 1945.

Hart, Albert Bushnell. *Salmon Portland Chase.* Boston: Houghton Mifflin and Company, 1899.

Hesseltine, William B. *Ulysses S. Grant, Politician.* New York: Dodd, Mead and Company, 1935.

Holzman, Robert S. *Stormy Ben Butler.* New York: The Macmillan Company, 1954.

Howe, M. A. De Wolfe. *Portrait of An Independent; Moorfield Storey, 1845-1929.* Boston: Houghton Mifflin Company, 1932.

Hutchinson, William T. *Cyrus Hall McCormick.* New York: The Century Co., 1930-1935.

Joyner, Fred Bunyan. *David Ames Wells, Champion of Free Trade.* Cedar Rapids, Iowa: The Torch Press, 1939.

Kaplan, Abraham D. *Henry Charles Carey: A Study in American Economic Thought.* Baltimore: The Johns Hopkins Press, 1931.

King, Willard L. *Lincoln's Manager, David Davis.* Cambridge: Harvard University Press, 1960.

Larson, Henrietta M. *Jay Cooke, Private Banker.* Cambridge: Harvard University Press, 1936.

Leonard, Lewis Alexander. *Life of Alphonso Taft.* New York: Hawke Publishing Company, 1920.

Lindsey, David. *"Sunset" Cox, Irrepressible Democrat.* Detroit: Wayne State University Press, 1959.

Lippincott, Joanna Wharton. *Biographical Memoranda Concerning Joseph Wharton, 1826-1909.* [Philadelphia]: Printed for Private Circulation by J. B. Lippincott Company, 1909.

Lowitt, Richard. *A Merchant Prince of the Nineteenth Century, Wil-*

liam E. Dodge. New York: Columbia University Press, 1954.

McCall, Samuel W. *Thaddeus Stevens*. Boston: Houghton Mifflin and Co., 1899.

McElroy, Robert. *Levi Parsons Morton, Banker, Diplomat, and Statesman*. New York: G. P. Putnam's Sons, 1930.

McGrane, Reginald Charles. *William Allen, A Study in Western Democracy*. Columbus: The Ohio State Archeological and Historical Society, 1925.

Mack, Edward C. *Peter Cooper, Citizen of New York*. New York: Duell, Sloan and Pearce, 1949.

Merriam, George S. *The Life and Times of Samuel Bowles*. New York: The Century Co., 1885.

Merrill, Horace Samuel. *William Freeman Vilas, Doctrinaire Democrat*. Madison: State Historical Society of Wisconsin, 1954.

Mitchell, Broadus. *Alexander Hamilton: The National Adventure, 1788-1804*. New York: The Macmillan Co., 1962.

Mitchell, Stewart. *Horatio Seymour of New York*. Cambridge: Harvard University Press, 1938.

Munroe, James P. *A Life of Francis Amasa Walker*. New York: Henry Holt and Company, 1923.

Nevins, Allan. *Abram S. Hewitt, With Some Account of Peter Cooper*. New York: Harper and Brothers, 1935.

———. *Hamilton Fish: The Inner History of the Grant Administration*. New York: Dodd, Mead and Co., 1936.

———. *Study in Power: John D. Rockefeller, Industrialist and Philanthropist*. New York: Charles Scribner's Sons, 1953.

Oberholtzer, Ellis Paxson. *Jay Cooke, Financier of the Civil War*. Philadelphia: George W. Jacob and Co., 1907.

Pearson, Henry Greenleaf. *An American Railroad Builder, John Murray Forbes*. Boston: Houghton Mifflin Company, 1911.

Richardson, Leon Burr. *William E. Chandler, Republican*. New York:

Dodd, Mead and Company, 1940.

Sage, Leland L. *William Boyd Allison, A Study in Practical Politics*. Iowa City: State Historical Society of Iowa, 1956.

Samuels, Ernest. *The Young Henry Adams*. Cambridge: Harvard University Press, 1948.

Sherman, Ellen Ewing. *Memorial of Thomas Ewing of Ohio*. New York: The Catholic Publication Society, 1873.

Sherwin, Oscar. *Prophet of Liberty: The Life and Times of Wendell Phillips*. New York: Bookman Associates, 1958.

Smith, Elbert B. *Magnificent Missourian: The Life and Times of Thomas Hart Benton*. Philadelphia: J. B. Lippincott Company, 1958.

Smith, George Winston. *Henry C. Carey and American Sectional Conflict*. Albuquerque: University of New Mexico Press, 1951.

Smith, Theodore Clarke. *The Life and Letters of James Abram Garfield*. New Haven: Yale University Press, 1925.

Starr, Harris E. *William Graham Sumner*. New York: Henry Holt and Company, 1925.

Storey, Moorfield, and Emerson, Edward D. *Ebenezer Rockwood Hoar, A Memoir*. Boston: Houghton Mifflin Company, 1911.

Stryker, Lloyd Paul. *Andrew Johnson: A Study in Courage*. New York: The Macmillan Co., 1929.

Sylvis, James C. *The Life, Speeches, Labors and Essays of William H. Sylvis, Late President of the Iron-Moulders International Union; and Also of the National Labor Union*. Philadelphia, 1872.

Tansill, Charles C. *The Congressional Career of Thomas Francis Bayard, 1868-1885*. Washington: Georgetown University Press, 1946.

Thompson, E. Bruce. *Matthew Hale Carpenter, Webster of the West*. Madison: State Historical Society of Wisconsin, 1954.

Thornton, Willis. *The Nine Lives*

of Citizen Train. New York: Greenberg, 1948.

Trefousse, Hans Louis. Ben Butler: The South Called Him BEAST! New York: Twayne Publishers, 1957.

Turnbull, Clive. Bonanza: The Story of George Francis Train. Melbourne, The Hawthorn Press, 1946.

Vanderbilt, Kermit. Charles Eliot Norton, Apostle of Culture in a Democracy. Cambridge: The Belknap Press, 1959.

Warden, Robert B. An Account of the Private Life and Public Services of Salmon Portland Chase. Cincinnati: Wilstach, Baldwin and Company, 1874.

Williams, Charles R. The Life of Rutherford Birchard Hayes, Nineteenth President of the United States. Columbus: The Ohio State Archeological and Historical Society, 1918.

Williamson, Harold Francis. Edward Atkinson, The Biography of An American Liberal, 1827-1905. Boston: Old Corner Book Store, 1934.

Woodburn, James Albert. The Life of Thaddeus Stevens. Indianapolis: The Bobbs-Merrill Company, 1913.

C. ARTICLES

Adams, Charles Francis, Jr. "The Currency Debate of 1873-74," North American Review, CXIX (July 1874).

———. "The Granger Movement," North American Review, CXX (April 1875).

Adams, Henry. "The Bank of England Restriction, 1797-1821," North American Review, CV (1867).

Ander, Fritiof O. "The Immigrant Church and the Patrons of Husbandry," Agricultural History, VIII (October 1934).

Anderson, George L. "The Proposed Resumption of Silver Payments in 1873," Pacific Historical Review, VIII (September 1939).

———. "The South and Post Civil War Finance," Journal of Southern History, IX (May 1943).

———. "Western Attitudes Toward National Banks, 1873-1874," Mississippi Valley Historical Review, XXIII (September 1936).

Anonymous. "Carey and Greeley," Social Economist (Gunton's Magazine), VII (September 1894).

Anonymous. "The Tory Economist," Social Economist, IX (November 1895).

Armstrong, William H. "Henry C. Lea, Scientific Historian," Pennsylvania Magazine of History and Biography, LXXX (October 1956).

Atkinson, Edward. "Veto of the Inflation Bill of 1874," Journal of Political Economy, I (December 1892).

Beale, Howard K. "The Tariff and Reconstruction," American Historical Review, XXXV (January 1930).

Black, John D. "Agriculture Now?" Journal of Farm Economics, IX (April 1927).

Carleton, William G. "The Money Question in Indiana Politics, 1865-1890," Indiana Magazine of History, XLII (June 1946).

———. "Why Was the Democratic Party in Indiana a Radical Party, 1865-1890?" Indiana Magazine of History, XLII (September 1946).

Carlton, Frank T. "Ephemeral Labor Movements, 1866-1889," Popular Science Monthly, LXXXV (November 1914).

Clonts, Forrest William. "The Political Campaign of 1875 in Ohio," Ohio Archeological and Historical Publications, XXXI (1922).

Degler, Carl N. "The Locofocos: Urban 'Agrarians,'" Journal of Economic History, XVI (September 1956).

Del Mar, Alexander. "Henry C. Carey's Round Table," Gunton's Magazine, XIII (August 1897).

Destler, Chester M. "Agricultural Readjustment and Agrarian Unrest—Illinois, 1880-1896," *Agricultural History*, xxi (April 1947).

De Witt, Brainerd T. "Are Legal-Tender Laws Ex Post Facto?" *Political Science Quarterly*, xv (March 1900).

Dunbar, Charles F. "Economic Science in America, 1776-1876," *North American Review*, ccl (January 1876).

———. "Safety of the Legal Tender Paper," *Quarterly Journal of Economics*, xi (April 1897).

Fairman, Charles. "Mr. Justice Bradley's Appointment to the Supreme Court and the Legal Tender Cases," *Harvard Law Review*, liv (April 1941 and May 1941).

Farmer, Hallie. "The Economic Background of Frontier Populism," *Mississippi Valley Historical Review*, x (March 1924).

Felix, David. "Profit Inflation and Industrial Growth," *Quarterly Journal of Economics*, lxx (August 1956).

Fels, Rendigs. "American Business Cycles, 1865-1879," *American Economic Review*, xli (June 1951).

Ferkiss, Victor. "Populist Influences on American Fascism," Sidney Fine and Gerald S. Brown (eds.). *The American Past: Conflicting Interpretations of the Great Issues*. New York: The Macmillan Co., 1961.

Freidel, Frank. "The Loyal Publication Society: A Pro-Union Propaganda Agency," *Mississippi Valley Historical Review*, xxvi (December 1939).

Gates, Paul Wallace. "The Role of the Land Speculator in Western Development," *The Pennsylvania Magazine of History and Biography*, lxvi (July 1942).

Geiser, Karl F. "New England and the Western Reserve," *Proceedings of the Mississippi Valley Historical Association for the Year 1912-1913*, Vol. vi.

Graham, Frank D. "International Trade Under Depreciated Paper: The United States, 1862-1879," *Quarterly Journal of Economics*, xxxvi (February 1922).

Grob, Gerald N. "Reform Unionism: The National Labor Union," *Journal of Economic History*, xiv (Spring 1954).

Hamilton, Earl J. "Prices as a Factor in Business Growth," *Journal of Economic History*, xii (Fall 1952).

Hammond, Bray. "Banking in the Early West: Monopoly, Prohibition and Laissez Faire," *Journal of Economic History*, viii (May 1948).

———. "Free Banks and Corporations: The New York Free Banking Act of 1838," *Journal of Political Economy*, xliv (April 1936).

———. "Jackson, Biddle, and the Bank of the United States," *Journal of Economic History*, vii (May 1947).

———. "The North's Empty Purse," *American Historical Review*, lxvii (October 1961).

Handlin, Oscar. "American Views of the Jew at the Opening of the Twentieth Century," *Publications of the American Jewish Historical Society*, xl (June 1951).

———. "Prejudice and Capitalist Exploitation: Does Economics Explain Racism?" *Commentary*, vi (July 1948).

Hesseltine, William B. "Four American Traditions," *The Journal of Southern History*, xxvii (February 1961).

Hicks, John D. "The Political Career of Ignatius Donnelly," *Mississippi Valley Historical Review*, viii (June-September 1921).

Higham, John. "Beyond Consensus: The Historian as Moral Critic," *American Historical Review*, lxvii (April 1962).

———. "The Cult of 'American Consensus,'" *Commentary*, xxvii (February 1959).

Hofstadter, Richard. "Parrington and the Jeffersonian Tradition," *Journal of The History of Ideas*, ii (October 1941).

————. "William Leggett, Spokesman of Jacksonian Democracy," *Political Science Quarterly*, LVIII (December 1943).

Hoogenboom, Ari A. "An Analysis of Civil Service Reformers," *The Historian*, XXIII (November 1960).

House, Albert V. "Men, Morals and Manipulation in the Pennsylvania Democracy of 1875," *Pennsylvania History*, XXIII (April 1956).

Jordan, Henry D. "Daniel Wolsey Voorhees," *Mississippi Valley Historical Review*, VI (March 1920).

Kirkland, Edward C. "Divide and Ruin," *Mississippi Valley Historical Review*, XLIII (June 1956).

Klement, Frank. " 'Brick' Pomeroy: Copperhead and Curmudgeon," *Wisconsin Magazine of History*, XXXV (Winter 1951).

————. "Middle Western Copperheadism and the Genesis of the Granger Movement," *Mississippi Valley Historical Review*, XXXVIII (March 1952).

Kohler, Max J. "The Board of Delegates of American Israelites, 1859-1878. . . ," *Publications of the American Jewish Historical Society*, No. 29, 1925.

Leach, J. A. "Public Opinion and the Inflation Movement in Missouri, 1875-1879," *The Missouri Historical Review*, XXIV (1929-30), XXV (1930-31).

Lerner, Eugene M. "Investment Uncertainty During the Civil War: A Note on the McCormick Brothers," *Journal of Economic History*, XVI (March 1956).

Lester, Richard A. "Inflation and the Farmer," *Journal of Farm Economics*, XVI (April 1924).

Libby, Orin G. "A Study of the Greenback Movement, 1876-1884," *Transactions of the Wisconsin Academy of Sciences, Arts and Letters*, Vol. XII, part II (1900).

McGrane, Reginald C. "Ohio and the Greenback Movement," *Mississippi Valley Historical Review*, XI (March 1925).

McKelvey, Blake. "The Jews of Rochester: A Contribution to Their History During the Nineteenth Century," *Publications of the American Jewish Historical Society*, XL (September 1950).

Martin, Roscoe C. "The Greenback Party in Texas," *The Southwest Historical Quarterly*, XXX (January 1927).

Miller, George H. "Origins of the Iowa Granger Law," *Mississippi Valley Historical Review*, XL (March 1954).

Miller, Raymond C. "The Background of Populism in Kansas," *Mississippi Valley Historical Review*, XI (March 1925).

Mittleman, Edward B. "Chicago Labor in Politics, 1877-1896," *The Journal of Political Economy*, XXVIII (May 1920).

Moore, Clifford H. "Ohio in National Politics, 1865-1896," *Ohio Archeological and Historical Publications*, XXXVII (1928).

Musson, A. E. "The Great Depression in Britain, 1873-1896: A Reappraisal," *The Journal of Economic History*, XIX (June 1959).

Nichols, Jeannette P. "Bryan's Benefactor: Coin Harvey and His World," *Ohio Historical Quarterly*, LXVII (October 1958).

————. "John Sherman and the Silver Drive of 1877-1878: The Origins of the Gigantic Subsidy," *Ohio State Archeological and History Quarterly*, XLVI (1937).

————. "John Sherman: A Study in Inflation," *Mississippi Valley Historical Review*, XXI (September 1934).

O'Leary, Paul M. "The Scene of the Crime of 1873 Revisited: A Note," *Journal of Political Economy*, LXVIII (August 1960), *passim*.

Pollack, Norman. "Hofstadter on Populism: A Critique of 'The Age of Reform,' " *Journal of Southern History*, XXVI (November 1960).

————. "The Myth of Populist Anti-Semitism," *American Historical Review*, LXVIII (October 1962).

Ratner, Sidney. "Was the Supreme Court Packed by President

Grant?" *Political Science Quarterly,* L (September 1935).

Redlich, Fritz. " 'Translating' Economic Policy into Business Policy: An Illustration from the Resumption of Specie Payments in 1879," *Bulletin of the Business Historical Society,* xx (December 1946).

Rezneck, Samuel. "Distress, Relief, and Discontent in the United States During the Depression of 1873-78," *The Journal of Political Economy,* LVIII (December 1950).

Richardson, Lyon H., and Garrison, Curtis W. (eds.). "George William Curtis, Rutherford B. Hayes and Civil Service Reform," *Mississippi Valley Historical Review,* XXXII (September 1945).

Ridge, Martin. "Ignatius Donnelly and the Greenback Movement," *Mid-America, An Historical Review,* XXXIX (July 1957).

Roach, Hannah Grace. "Sectionalism in Congress (1870-1890)," *American Political Science Review,* XIX (August 1925).

Ruggles, Clyde O. "The Economic Basis of the Greenback Movement in Iowa and Wisconsin," *Proceedings of the Mississippi Valley Historical Association for the Year 1912-1913,* Vol. VI.

Saloutos, Theodore. "The Agricultural Problem and Nineteenth Century Industrialism," in Joseph T. Lambie and Richard V. Clemence (eds.), *Economic Change in America: Readings in the Economic History of the United States.* Harrisburg: The Stackpole Company, 1954.

————. "The Spring-Wheat Farmer in a Maturing Economy, 1870-1920," *Journal of Economic History,* VI (November 1946).

Schell, Herbert S. "The Grange and the Credit Problem in Dakota Territory," *Agricultural History,* X (April 1935).

————. "Hugh McCulloch and the Treasury Department, 1865-1869," *Mississippi Valley Histori-*

cal Review, XVII (December 1930).

Sellers, Charles G., Jr. "Banking and Politics in Jackson's Tennessee, 1817-1827," *Mississippi Valley Historical Review,* XLI (June 1954).

————. "Jackson Men With Feet of Clay," *American Historical Review,* XLII (April 1957).

Shapiro, Samuel. "Aristocracy, Mud and Vituperation: The Butler-Dana Campaign in Essex County in 1868," *New England Quarterly,* XXXI (September 1958).

Shipley, Max L. "The Background and Legal Aspects of the Pendleton Plan," *Mississippi Valley Historical Review,* XXXIV (December 1937).

Taussig, Frank W. "The Iron Industry in the United States," *Quarterly Journal of Economics,* XIV (February 1900).

Unger, Irwin. "The Business Community and the Origins of the 1875 Resumption Act," *The Business History Review,* XXXV (Summer 1961).

————. "Business and Currency in the Ohio Gubernatorial Campaign of 1875," *Mid-America, An Historical Review,* XLI (January 1959).

————. "Business Men and Specie Resumption," *Political Science Quarterly,* LXXIV (March 1959).

————. "Money and Morality: The Northern Calvinist Churches and the Reconstruction Financial Quarterly, LXXIV (March 1959). History,* XL (March 1962).

Volwiler, A. T. "Tariff Strategy and Propaganda in the United States, 1887-1888," *American Historical Review,* XXXVI (January 1931).

Wells, O. V. "Depression of 1873-1879," *Agricultural History,* XI (July 1937).

White, Horace. "The Financial Crisis in America," *Fortnightly Review,* CXIII (May 1, 1876).

Wilcox, Benton H. "An Historical Definition of Northwestern Radicalism," *Mississippi Valley Historical Review,* xxvi (December 1939).

Woodward, C. Vann. "The Populist Heritage of the Intellectual," in Woodward, *The Burden of Southern History.* Baton Rouge: Louisiana State University Press, 1960.

D. UNPUBLISHED DOCTORAL DISSERTATIONS

Anderson, George LaVerne. "The National Banking System: A Sectional Institution." University of Illinois, 1933.

Grob, Gerald N. "Trade vs. Reform Unionism: The Emergence of the Modern American Labor Movement, 1865-1896." Northwestern University, 1958.

Gutman, Herbert G. "Social and Economic Structure and Depression: American Labor in 1873 and 1874." University of Wisconsin, 1959.

Hoogenboom, Ari A. "Outlawing the Spoils: A History of the Civil Service Reform Movement, 1865-1883." Columbia University, 1957.

James, Edward T. "American Labor and Political Action, 1865-1896: The Knights of Labor and Its Predecessors." Harvard University, 1954.

Kindahl, James K. "The Economics of Resumption: The United States, 1865-1879," University of Chicago, 1958.

Ricker, Ralph R. "The Greenback-Labor Movement in Pennsylvania." Pennsylvania State University, 1955.

Shipley, Max L. "The Greenback Issue in the Old Northwest, 1865-1880." University of Illinois, 1929.

Unger, Irwin. "Men, Money and Politics: The Specie Resumption Issue, 1865-1879." Columbia University, 1958.

E. MISCELLANEOUS SECONDARY

The American Annual Cyclopedia and Register of Important Events of the Year. . . . (Title varies.) New York: D. Appleton and Company, 1865ff.

Biographical Directory of the American Congress, 1774-1949. 81 Congress, 2 session, *House Document, No. 607.*

Burnham, W. Dean. *Presidential Ballots, 1836-1892.* Baltimore: The Johns Hopkins Press, 1955.

Dunbar, Charles F. *Laws of the United States Relating to Currency, Finance and Banking from* 1789 to 1896. Boston: Ginn and Company, 1897.

Johnson, Allen, and Malone, Dumas (eds.). *Dictionary of American Biography.* New York: Charles Scribner's Sons, 1928ff.

Larson, Henrietta M. *Guide to Business History. Materials for the Study of American Business History and Suggestions for Their Use.* Cambridge: Harvard University Press, 1948.

National Cyclopedia of American Biography. New York: James T. White and Company, 1892ff.

INDEX

Abbott, Lyman, 276, 399
abolitionists, 110
academic economists, finance in general, 126ff; and Bland Bill, 363. *See also* college professors, colleges, reformers, Social Science Association
Adams, Charles Francis, Jr., contempt for businessmen, 132; influenced by John Stuart Mill, 136; and Social Science Association, 138; and Boston Reform League, 139f; and Loyal Publication Society revival, 141; opposed to Inflation Bill, 240; and Ohio state campaign of 1875, 276
Adams, Charles Francis, Sr., hurt by inflation, 23; sees decline of New England, 135; sees tone of national life declining, 137n; sees little hope for resumption, 168; suspects Chase, 175n; and Inflation Bill, 240
Adams, Dudley W., 293n, 338
Adams, Henry, disillusioned with postwar America, 131f; takes refuge in academe, 133; edits *North American Review*, 134; and Boston Reform League, 140; mentioned, 168; and legal tender decision, 173, 177; assails Boutwell, 192; and anti-Semitism, 212; and Ohio state campaign of 1875, 283; becomes silverite in 1890's, 338n
Adams, John Quincy (1767-1848), 34
Adams, John Quincy (1833-1894), 240
Advance, The, 121n
Agassiz, Louis, 139n
Agrarian myth, 28f
Agrarianism, 28ff, 34f, 195ff, 407
Agrarians, 44
agricultural fundamentalism, 195
agricultural prices, 200f
agriculture, aid to, 378
Aiken, D. Wyatt, 305
Albany Regency, 85
Alison, Archibald, 51n
Allen, George, 388
Allen, William, elected Ohio Governor, 266ff; and Ohio state cam-

paign of 1875, 269; defeated for reelection, 280f; and 1876 Democratic Presidential nomination, 303; and Presidential campaign of 1876, 317
Alley, John, 41
Alley Resolution, 41f, 254
Allis, E. P., at Detroit Greenback convention, 300; at Indianapolis Independent convention of 1876, 305; candidate for Governor of Wisconsin, 346; defeated for Governor, 349; at Toledo National convention, 377
Allison, William B., mugwumps regard him as salvageable, 143; and anti-contraction campaign, 160; urged not to join inflationists, 236; and Resumption Act, 253; reports western business fears, 324; and Bland Bill, 361; Sherman tries to influence him, 361n; defends resumption, 364
American Alliance, 385n
American Bankers' Association, supports hard money, 161; fraudulent "confidential circular" of, 313f; endorses resumption, 325; endorses cooperation with Treasury, 396n
American Industrial League, 55. *See also* Industrial League
American Iron and Steel Association, *see* Iron and Steel Association
American Manufacturer, and free banking, 62, 223; warms to resumption, 326; and silver, 335
American School, 50ff, 56
American Social Science Association, *see* Social Science Association
Amory, William, 240
Anthony, Susan B., 110
Anti-Monopolist, attacks H. W. Beecher, 126; on the Civil War as the triumph of business, 210; Donnelly tries to sell it, 321
anti-monopoly, Jacksonian, 32; among farmers, 201, 202-203
Anti-Monopoly Association, 111
anti-Semitism, 210ff, 340. *See also* Jews
Arator, 407